EXPLORING SUSTAINABLE DEVELOPMENT

EXPLORING SUSTAINABLE DEVELOPMENT

Geographical Perspectives

Edited by

Martin Purvis and Alan Grainger

Earthscan Publications Limited
London • Sterling, VA

First published by Earthscan in the UK and USA in 2004

Reprinted 2006

ISBN: 1-85383-472-6 (paperback)
      1-84407-107-3 (hardback)

Typesetting by TW Typesetting, Plymouth, Devon
Printed and bound in the UK by CPI Bath
Cover design by Danny Gillespie

For a full list of publications please contact:

Earthscan
8–12 Camden High Street
London NW1 0JH, UK
Tel: +44 (0)20 7387 8558
Fax: +44 (0)20 7387 8998
Email: earthinfo@earthscan.co.uk
Web: **www.earthscan.co.uk**

22883 Quicksilver Drive, Sterling, VA 20166-2012, USA

Earthscan publishes in association with WWF-UK and the International Institute for
Environment and Development

A catalogue record for this book is available from the British Library

Library of Congress Cataloging-in-Publication Data

Exploring sustainable development: geographical perspectives/edited by Martin Purvis and
Alan Grainger
        p. cm.
    ISBN 1-84407-107-3 (hardback) – ISBN 1-85383-472-6 (pbk.)
        1. Sustainable development. 2. Economic geography. I. Purvis, Martin. II. Grainger, Alan.

  HC79.E5E985 2004
  338.9′001–dc22

                                                                          2003023957

Contents

List of Figures and Tables

Figures

Tables

List of Contributors

Ken Atkinson	Senior Lecturer, School of Geography, University of Leeds
Alan Grainger	Senior Lecturer, School of Geography, University of Leeds
Gordon Mitchell	Senior Research Fellow, School of Geography and Institute of Transport Studies, University of Leeds
Martin Purvis	Senior Lecturer, School of Geography, University of Leeds
Richard Smith	Honorary Research Fellow, School of Geography, University of Leeds
John Soussan	Professor, Stockholm Environment Institute, University of York
Rachael Unsworth	Lecturer, School of Geography, University of Leeds
Paul Waley	Senior Lecturer, School of Geography, University of Leeds

Preface

This book is the product of a collaborative effort amongst geographers who are past and present colleagues at the University of Leeds to counter the relative neglect of geographical perspectives in previous research into sustainable development, and to indicate some possible directions for future research. As editors we would particularly like to thank the colleagues who have contributed to this volume for their intellectual input to the project. Other members of the School of Geography have also played an important part in the development of the ideas represented here. In particular, we must single out Adrian MacDonald and David Preston for their valued contributions and advice at the outset of our discussions about sustainable development. It is also a pleasure to record our gratitude to the School of Geography for its financial support of the original research upon which some of the present chapters are based. Staff at Earthscan have been unfailingly patient and supportive since the inception of the project and in this context we extend particular thanks to Jonathan Sinclair Wilson.

Martin Purvis
Alan Grainger
Leeds, June 2004

List of Acronyms and Abbreviations

AEPS	Arctic Environmental Protection Strategy
AFL-CIO	American Federation of Labor – Congress of Industrial Organizations
ANCSA	Alaskan Native Claims Settlement Act
ASEAN	Association of Southeast Asian Nations
BEQUEST	Built Environment Quality Evaluation for Sustainability through Time
BKCMB	Beverly-Kaminuriak Caribou Management Board
BP	British Petroleum
BSE	bovine spongiform encephalopathy
CAP	Common Agricultural Policy
CBD	Convention on Biological Diversity
CBI	Confederation of British Industry
Cdn$	Canadian dollars
CFCs	chlorofluorocarbons
CITES	Convention on International Trade in Endangered Species of Wild Fauna and Flora
CO	carbon monoxide
CO_2	carbon dioxide
COP	Conference of the Parties to the Framework Convention on Climate Change
DEFRA	UK Department of the Environment, Farming and Rural Affairs
DETR	UK Department of the Environment, Transport and the Regions
DIY	do it yourself
DoE	UK Department of the Environment
DoT	UK Department of Transport
DTI	UK Department of Trade and Industry
EC	European Community
EEA	European Environment Agency
EMAS	eco-management and audit scheme
EMS	environmental management system
EQ	environmental quality
ESRC	Economic and Social Research Council

EU	European Union
EUFORES	European Forum for Renewable Energy Sources
EWEA	European Wind Energy Association
FAO	Food and Agriculture Organization of the United Nations
FCCC	Framework Convention on Climate Change
FoE	Friends of the Earth
FSC	Forest Stewardship Council
FUG	forest user group
G77	Group of 77 Developing Countries
GATT	General Agreement on Tariffs and Trade
GDP	gross domestic product
GIS	geographical information systems
GM	genetically modified
GMO	genetically modified organism
GNP	gross national product
GPS	global positioning system
GWh	gigawatt hours
HCFCs	hydrochlorofluorocarbons
HDI	Human Development Index
HFCs	hydrofluorocarbons
ICC	Inuit Circumpolar Conference
ICLEI	International Council for Local Environmental Initiatives
IEA	International Energy Agency
IFRC	International Federation of Red Cross and Red Crescent Societies
IIASA	International Institute for Applied Systems Analysis
ILO	International Labour Organization
INC	International Negotiating Committee on the Framework Convention on Climate Change
IMF	International Monetary Fund
IPCC	Intergovernmental Panel on Climate Change
IPM	integrated pest management
ISEW	Index of Sustainable Economic Welfare
ISO	International Standards Organization
IT	information technology
IUCN	International Union for the Conservation of Nature
LA21	Local Agenda 21
LASALA	Local Authorities Self-Assessment of Local Agenda 21
LETS	local exchange trading systems
LGMB	Local Government Management Board
MAFF	UK Ministry of Agriculture, Fisheries and Food
MITI	Japanese Ministry of International Trade and Industry
MoC	Japanese Ministry of Construction
MOSOP	Movement for the Survival of the Ogoni People
NAFTA	North American Free Trade Association
NEPA	National Environmental Protection Act
NFU	National Farmers' Union
NGO	non-governmental organization

NIAB	National Institute of Agricultural Botany
NO_x	nitrogen oxides
NPO	non-profit organization
NWMB	Nunavut Wildlife Management Board
OECD	Organisation for Economic Co-operation and Development
OPEC	Organization of Petroleum Exporting Countries
OPP	Orangi Pilot Project
PDE	population–development–environment
RC	resource capital
RCP	Royal College of Physicians
RDA	regional development agency
RS	Royal Society
RSD	regional sustainable development
RSE	Royal Society of Engineering
SATURN	Simulation and Assignment of Traffic to Urban Road Networks
SCP	United Nations Sustainable Cities Programme
SDI	sustainable development indicator
SERP	South-East Regional Planning Conference
SME	small- and medium-sized enterprise
SO_x	sulphur oxides
SPARTACUS	System for Planning and Research in Towns and Cities for Urban Sustainability
SWP	Social Welfare Programme (Sri Lanka)
TR Net	Tsurumigawa River Network
UK	United Kingdom
UN	United Nations
UNCED	United Nations Conference on Environment and Development
UNCHS	United Nations Centre for Human Settlements
UNCTAD	United Nations Conference on Trade and Development
UNDP	United Nations Development Programme
UNEAP	United Nations Environmental Assessment Programme
UNEP	United Nations Environment Programme
UNESCO	United Nations Educational, Scientific and Cultural Organization
UNGA	United Nations General Assembly
US	United States
VAT	value added tax
VOC	volatile organic compound
WBCSD	World Business Council for Sustainable Development
WCD	World Commission on Dams
WCED	World Commission on Environment and Development
WHO	World Health Organization
WMO	World Meteorological Organization
WSSD	World Summit on Sustainable Development
WTO	World Trade Organization
WWF	World Wide Fund for Nature

1

Introduction

Alan Grainger

Introduction

Sustainable development, which meets the needs of the present generation without undermining the ability of future generations to meet their own needs, was widely adopted as a policy goal in the 1990s by many international agencies, governments and non-governmental organizations (NGOs). It was also translated into a theoretical concept that has become a major focus for academic research. Yet the speed and breadth of its adoption were surprising to many people, who regarded it, at best, as nothing more than a vague concept and, at worst, as a means to perpetuate the exploitation of developing countries. What is the reason for such conflicting attitudes? The answer to this question holds the key to a better understanding of sustainable development, and of the geographical perspectives that are explored in this book.

Sustainable development was originally devised as a compromise between two contradictory aims: on the one hand, the pursuit of environmental conservation and, on the other, the pursuit of economic growth and the development that generally followed as a result. Unfortunately, however, sustainable development has assumed two contradictory meanings among different governments and NGOs around the world. Broadly, from the perspective of developed countries, sustainable development is primarily about conserving the environment; while, as viewed from the developing world, it means the continued pursuit of development with the aim of reducing poverty and attaining the status of modern societies.

A similar disparity of views is found among academics. In response to the apparent vagueness of early definitions, economists devised theories of sustainable development and conditions for achieving it. Viewed in this way sustainable development holds the key to understanding the historical development of human civilization and predicting its long-term prospects. However, the two leading economic theories differ in significant respects, and neither of them takes much account of the spatial dimension. For many other social scientists, who are more concerned with the politics of development, sustainable development has as little currency as the ideal of development that the poorer countries of the world have been persuaded to pursue since the end of World War II. Seen from the standpoint of existing political economy theories, sustainable development, like 'development' before it, can never benefit developing countries, but will only continue their long-standing exploitation by developed countries.

These disparate views are perpetuated because there is so little interaction between them. This breeds ever more confusion about the meaning and significance of sustainable development. The subject is discussed by the governments of developed and developing countries at major international conferences – such as the United Nations Conference on Environment and Development (UNCED), held in Rio de Janeiro in June 1992, and the recent follow-up conference, the World Summit on Sustainable Development (WSSD), held in Johannesburg in August 2002; but they usually talk past one another and there is seldom a meeting of minds. Academics also tend to stay within the realms of the particular type of theory that they favour, instead of exploring the merits of other theories.

It is in a situation like this that geographers have much to offer. Being concerned with the planet as a whole they are ideally suited to studying sustainable development, a field of truly global dimensions. They are also good at seeing the whole picture by combining its many disparate elements. Their skills of synthesis are needed as never before to grasp the full immensity of sustainable development from the many different viewpoints that currently exist. Another geographical skill is important in this particular context – namely, an ability to see the whole in its diversity, rather than feeling the need to enforce conformity upon different views and circumstances. As we shall see in this chapter, this is one of the greatest challenges facing those who study sustainable development. Geographers also apply this skill within their own discipline. As this book shows, different geographers look at sustainable development from different perspectives. Finally, geographers tend to look at a topic from a spatial point of view and cannot understand why other people do not do so too. As the spatial dimension of sustainable development has been relatively neglected, this is one important gap that they can help to fill.

This book is only a first step towards portraying geographical perspectives on sustainable development. It attempts to grapple with the diversity both of political views on the subject and theoretical approaches, and to show how thinking geographically can enhance our understanding of them. The variety of geographical perspectives presented is a microcosm of the range of approaches already taken by other geographers. We are not the first geographers to explore sustainable development, but we hope that this book will demonstrate to both geographers and non-geographers alike that there is more to the subject than they realize, and encourage them to pay greater attention to sustainable development in the future.

This chapter provides a conceptual foundation for the book as a whole by reviewing the current range of views on sustainable development, and by showing how they differ and what they have in common. It begins by introducing the political conflicts that are at the heart of sustainable development. The chapter then outlines some key theoretical concepts and reviews the two leading economic theories in this field. After suggesting how these various disparities might be reconciled, the chapter ends by identifying the key questions that are tackled in the remaining chapters in the book and outlining the principal themes that emerge from this discussion.

Conflicting Political Ideals

The environmentalist ideal: bridging the gap between conservation and economic growth

The idea of sustainable development was first specifically identified in 1980 in an attempt to overcome two fundamental conflicts that became increasingly apparent during the last half of the 20th century. The first of these is the seeming incompatibility between maintaining a healthy environment and the economic growth needed for development. The second is the continuing gap between the quality of life in developed countries (the global 'North') and developing countries (the 'South'). These concerns have given rise to the two conflicting ideals of sustainable development that continue to this day.

Mounting and widespread disquiet about the environmental impacts of unfettered human population growth and industrialization sparked off an 'environmental revolution' during the 1960s. What began as a critique of relatively localized pollution had, by the end of the decade, developed into a conviction among environmentalists that the entire planet was under severe threat from resource depletion and pollution driven by population growth and capitalist greed. During the 1970s these emergent concerns led to environmental protection being accepted as a minor, but significant, goal by the governments of the leading developed countries. However, they still tended to regard a healthy environment as rather a luxury and as something separate from economic activity. This attitude did not begin to change until the 1980s, when there was a realization that the environmental impacts of economic activity could rebound on the whole of humanity, through stratospheric ozone depletion and global climate change.

The rise of environmentalism as a political force was paralleled by increasing efforts on the part of conservationists to protect as many of the planet's remaining pristine natural ecosystems as possible. Yet they encountered major obstacles, particularly in developing countries in the tropics where a significant proportion of the Earth's surviving biological diversity is located. Setting aside large areas for conservation was incompatible with the demand by the peoples of these countries for more space to accommodate their rising populations and for the right to exploit their natural resources in order to achieve more development. National parks whose boundaries had been designated on maps to give maximum protection to a country's natural wealth therefore often remained mere 'paper parks', as it was not feasible to protect them against expanding human numbers. Poor people would not relinquish their hopes for development simply to safeguard the beauty of nature, primarily for the enjoyment of rich people in their own countries and abroad.

Hitherto, many conservationists had retained the idealistic, not to say naive, belief that something as important as conservation must automatically receive widespread popular support. They gave a lower priority to development and saw no reason why others should not do the same. Eventually, however, they realized that they could no longer ignore the reality and inevitability of development. If they were to achieve their goals of conservation, they would have to recognize that others, particularly in developing countries, held equally legitimate goals of development. This led to the launch of new integrated conservation and development projects, such as those in the United Nations Educational, Scientific and Cultural Organization (UNESCO) Man and Biosphere Programme, which combined the establishment of protected areas with initiatives to improve the lives of local people.

It was a short step from integrating conservation and development to conceiving the ideal of sustainable development. This first emerged, rather tentatively, in the *World Conservation Strategy* published in 1980 by the International Union for the Conservation of Nature (IUCN), now the World Conservation Union:

> Humanity's relationship with the biosphere ... will continue to deteriorate until a new international order is achieved, a new environmental ethic is adopted, human populations stabilized, and sustainable modes of development become the rule rather than the exception ... For development to be sustainable it must take account of social and ecological factors, as well as economic ones; of the living and non-living resource base; and of the long-term as well as short-term advantages and disadvantages of alternative actions.

Sustainable development was recommended, in particular, to developing countries as a development path that would not replicate the environmental degradation that had been incurred in the industrialized countries. However, at this stage it was expressed in rather general terms, and lacked both proper definition and any accompanying guidance as to how it might be achieved in practice (Adams, 2001).

The developmentalist ideal: a new beginning for development

Political leaders in developing countries, on the other hand, had a different agenda during the 1980s. The last major political ideal that the governments of the developed countries had persuaded them to adopt was the notion of 'development', by which they would replicate the success of developed countries. From the perspective of the developed countries, this was intended as a well-meaning attempt to reduce the gap that separated them from the poorer countries of the world and thereby increase intra-generational equity. The developed world also backed up its advice with financial aid. However, with a few notable exceptions such as South Korea and Taiwan, most developing countries failed to realize the development ideal. They still suffered from poverty, famine and ill health, and so were in no mood to adopt the new environmental goal that had become popular in developed countries or the supposedly more realistic ideal of sustainable development. Developed countries had become wealthy by despoiling their environments and those of developing countries too. So it was seen as hypocritical of the former now to ask developing countries to protect their environments and control population growth at the expense of the chance of economic development. Indeed, in some countries, such as Malaysia, governments saw population growth as vital if they were to achieve the kind of development that they wanted.

Development planners had already responded to slow rates of development by rethinking the strategies they employed. The initial 'top-down' modernization strategies of the 1950s and 1960s, which equated economic development with economic growth and relied on the centrally directed expansion of industry and commerce to generate more income for the whole country, had not been generally successful. Where they had succeeded, the benefits had often accrued disproportionately to foreign investors and already powerful and affluent indigenous elites. So during the 1970s new 'bottom-up' participatory strategies were introduced that addressed the requirements of the poorest people first, by attempting to meet the basic needs of specific local populations for water and sanitation, shelter, food, fuel, income and employment. However, the benefits of this new approach were not immediately visible to the rich elite and government leaders. The growth in income that stemmed from the increase in commodity prices in the 1970s had been short lived, and many developing countries now faced a debt crisis because they could not repay the massive development loans they had taken out in the 1970s.

The governments of developing countries, therefore, also wanted a new development ideal. But their priority was for a type of development that could be sustained over a long period of time, rather than brief periods of economic growth, as experienced in the 1970s, followed by periods of stagnation. This would allow them to rid their countries of the scourges of poverty, famine and ill health, and to replicate the modern societies they could see in developed countries.

Some of the more astute government leaders had been influenced by new political economy theories, such as that proposed by Frank (1969). These argued that developing countries were in an inevitable state of economic dependency on developed countries, since the very structure of the world economy put them at a severe disadvantage. A fundamental duality had been created between a politically powerful and economically wealthy Core – originally centred in Europe, but later extending to North America and East Asia – and a dependent Periphery. Within this Periphery local economic and social systems were vulnerable to disruption and destruction to meet the roles allotted to them within the global system, chiefly as suppliers of raw materials to the industrial Core. So changing from top-down to bottom-up strategies would have little impact on poverty because it would only treat the symptoms of uneven global development and not its causes.

The most strident critics even claimed that development was a 'cruel hoax' (Esteva, 1992) imposed on developing countries by their developed counterparts, whose sole aim was to extract their economic surplus and leave them in poverty. Any attempt by the poorer countries of the world to follow the path of economic modernization undertaken by developed countries, and to participate in the world trading system, could only, in their view, lead to further *under*development because the structure of the world economic system was biased against them. This would divert the bulk of any income they generated to the developed countries, making it unavailable to fund their own development. The ideal of 'development as progress' was therefore an illusion promoted by developed countries to perpetuate a pattern of exploitation that was only transformed, not replaced, when developing countries gained political independence from the industrialized countries that had colonized them.

If correct, such thinking would indicate that only a fundamental change in the economic and political relationships between North and South could ensure real and lasting improvement in the social and economic fortunes of the world's poor. This was the basic argument of the Brandt Commission (1980) report, *North-South: A Programme for Survival*. The report called for more development in developing countries, and for a new spirit of global togetherness to bridge the North–South divide, thus ensuring greater equity in world development, finance and trade. But these idealistic proposals came to nothing. In response, leading politicians in developing countries became more assertive. They believed that a necessary precondition for sustained future development was that developed countries should offer greater compensation for the exploitation suffered during the colonial era. This would require hard cash in the form of more official aid and the removal of trade barriers. The latter would allow them to supply manufactured goods to the markets of the industrialized world, thereby reducing their dependence on exporting primary commodities of low and variable value.

Sustainable Development as an Ambiguous Compromise

The Brundtland Report

In an attempt to reconcile these two different perceptions of development, the United Nations (UN) General Assembly established the World Commission on Environment and Development (WCED), chaired by Gro Harlem Brundtland, then Prime Minister of Norway. The solution proposed in the report of the 'Brundtland Commission' (WCED, 1987), as it became known, was to aim for sustainable development, which it defined as:

> [Development that] meets the needs of the present without compromising the ability of future generations to meet their own needs . . . It contains within it two key concepts: the concept of 'needs', in particular the essential needs of the world's poor, to which overriding priority should be given, and the idea of limitations imposed by the state of technology and social organization on the environment's ability to meet present and future needs.

This gave a new meaning to the term 'sustainable development' from that identified by IUCN seven years earlier. It recognized the need to ensure inter-generational equity by minimizing the harmful environmental impacts of human activities, in deference to the concerns of the developed countries. However, its primary aim was to meet the needs of the developing countries by reducing poverty. This should have happened already, of course, if these countries had become more economically developed. However, for the reasons given above, many of them had not, and in calling for poverty reduction, the Brundtland Commission added an important new intra-generational equity element to sustainable development. It argued that environmental degradation would continue unless poverty and inequality in developing countries were addressed urgently. Poor people who are desperate for food, fuel or income cannot always afford to have regard for the future environmental consequences of their actions. Consequently, economic growth must continue in order to alleviate poverty and maintain development. The Brundtland Commission did, however, state that this economic growth should be a 'new form' of growth that was less harmful to the environment and did not deplete the Earth's remaining stocks of natural resources.

The Brundtland Report, *Our Common Future* (WCED, 1987), was important for securing wide public exposure for sustainable development and establishing it on the international political agenda. Both developing countries and environmentalists and conservationists from developed countries could agree with what it said. However, it had two basic flaws. First, it did not say how continued economic growth could in practice be balanced against the need to conserve resources and natural environments. This effectively put human needs before those of the environment (Redclift, 1992a). Second, it was sufficiently ambiguous to enable each of the two main interest groups to interpret the meaning of sustainable development in a way that reflected their own agenda. So governments and campaigners in developed countries believed that sustainable development would mean better environmental protection. Their counterparts in developing countries, on the other hand, believed that it would bring them more development, and that is the ideal of sustainable development which *they* adopted.

The United Nations Conference on Environment and Development

A universal ideal

This ambiguous compromise, which effectively allowed the simultaneous existence of two interpretations of the sustainable development ideal, established sufficient common ground between developed and developing countries for them to agree to meet in the Brazilian city of Rio de Janeiro in June 1992 at the UN Conference on Environment and Development (UNCED) and the 'Earth Summit' of heads of state which followed it. Sustainable development was the core theme of the conference and permeated the texts of the agreements signed there, including the Framework Convention on Climate Change (FCCC), the Biodiversity Convention and Agenda 21.

UNCED made two special contributions to the evolution of sustainable development. First, it succeeded in translating the ideal proposed in the Brundtland Report into a *universal ideal* for all countries, whether developing or developed. This was an incredibly important achievement. For what had been previously just an ideal recommended to developing countries became an ideal to which every country in the world could now aspire. What this meant in practice in developed countries, however, was that the goal of increasing environmental protection that had been gaining momentum there for 40 years was simply given a new name.

Ultimately, UNCED was a failure because the conflicting goals of these two groups of countries could not be hidden once government representatives were in close proximity in a meeting hall. Indeed, UNCED was also notable for the emergence of a new collective assertiveness by developing countries, irritated at the neglect of their needs by the developed countries. This had a major influence on the wording of the agreements reached at UNCED, particularly the Biodiversity Convention, the Rio Declaration and Agenda 21. These were phrased with sufficient ambiguity to be compatible with the conflicting ideals of sustainable development held by the developed and developing countries.

Agenda 21, for instance, is often portrayed as a grand 470-page blueprint for sustainable development (UN, 1993). Yet its final consensus format was only reached by a clever use of language which, as in the Brundtland Report, was ambiguous enough to acknowledge both sets of goals, without attempting to resolve the contradictions between them. Agenda 21 must therefore be regarded as a political document, not a technical manual. Some key aspects of development – such as population growth and the associated policy debate – even had to be excluded altogether because of their political sensitivity.

The political process of sustainable development

UNCED's second contribution was to launch what may be called the *political process* of sustainable development through which many governments, international agencies, NGOs, firms and individuals have tried to realize the new universal ideal and take action to make our world a better place. The notion of sustainable development as a process was inherent in the text of Agenda 21, which never actually defined it but stated that it would 'integrate environmental and developmental decision-making processes', contrary to the prevailing custom which was 'to separate economic, social and environmental factors at the policy, planning and management levels'. Principle 4 of the Rio Declaration repeated part of the preamble of the UN General Assembly Resolution which launched the whole UNCED process, in stating that 'In order to achieve sustainable development, environmental protection shall constitute an integral part of the development process and cannot be considered in isolation from it'.

Since UNCED the political process has become particularly apparent in the increased momentum generated for improving environmental management, both internationally and at national and local levels. National and local Agenda 21 action plans have been devised and implemented in many countries. Governments are committed to reporting their progress to the Commission for Sustainable Development which the United Nations established. A Special Session of the UN General Assembly was held in New York in June 1997 to review progress in the five years since UNCED (Osborn and Bigg, 1998). In spite of all this enthusiasm, however, the basic contradiction remains between the two different interpretations of the political ideal of sustainable development. Developing countries want better development, while developed countries want a better environment, preferably without harming their own development prospects too much.

The World Summit on Sustainable Development

Ten years after UNCED, the two interpretations persisted at the World Summit on Sustainable Development (WSSD), held in Johannesburg, South Africa, from 26 August to 4 September 2002. However, the results of this huge gathering were very meagre indeed, consisting of: a short Political Declaration – the Johannesburg Declaration on Sustainable Development; a 67-page Plan of Implementation of the World Summit on Sustainable Development, which was as general, voluntary and devoid of specific targets as Agenda 21; and commitments to halve the proportion of the world's people who do not have access to basic sanitation by the year 2015 and to establish a representative network of marine-protected areas by 2012.

Developed countries were just as reluctant as in the past to give new financial and other commitments to promote development in developing countries, while the intransigence of the US government prevented further progress on the environmental side (see Chapter 12 in this volume).

A formal definition of sustainable development was again missing from the principal documents of the WSSD. However, the Johannesburg Declaration did further the understanding of the concept in the United Nations system by referring to 'the mutually reinforcing pillars of sustainable development – economic development, social development and environmental protection' (UN, 2002). The Plan of Implementation of the World Summit on Sustainable Development similarly noted the need for:

> ... the integration of the three components of sustainable development – economic development, social development and environmental protection – as interdependent and mutually reinforcing pillars. Poverty eradication, changing unsustainable patterns of production and consumption and protecting and managing the natural resource base of economic and social development are overarching objectives of, and essential requirements for, sustainable development (UN, 2002).

Nevertheless, the Plan of Implementation was just as reticent as Agenda 21 in explaining how to reconcile continued economic growth with environmental protection. It referred to 'our common pursuit of growth, poverty eradication and sustainable development' (Article 83), and asked states to 'cooperate to promote a supportive and open international economic system that would lead to economic growth and sustainable development in all countries to better address the problem of environmental degradation' (Article 101).

The need for greater clarity

What is so surprising about the political process of sustainable development is that so much has been, and still is being, attempted without a very exact description of what sustainable development should entail. It has been commonly assumed that, starting from only the vague definition in the Brundtland Report, the transition from unsustainable to sustainable development can be achieved by a process of pragmatic experimentation that will clarify the real meaning of sustainable development and how it can best be secured. A less charitable, but perhaps more realistic, view is that this approach is more likely to breed confusion than clarification, and that this will be counterproductive in the long term. The great risk is that the process of experimentation will degenerate into a virtual free-for-all, in which almost anything and everything can be presented as a contribution to greater sustainability.

It is for this reason that academic research has much to offer in clarifying the meaning of sustainable development and the conditions for actually achieving it in practice. We therefore now examine existing theories, prefacing this with a review of the evolution of thinking about development in general, in order to link sustainable development with earlier ideas.

From Economic Growth to Sustainable Development

Over the past ten years a considerable amount of academic effort has been invested into translating the political *ideal* of sustainable development into a more rigorous theoretical *concept*. To put the results of this work into proper perspective, it helps to regard sustainable development as just the latest stage in the evolution of our understanding of human development. It builds upon, and extends, two other key concepts – economic growth and economic development – both of which are still widely used. Just as the concept of economic development was devised to overcome the limitations of economic growth, so the emergence of sustainable development reflects a similar frustration with the conventional concept of economic development. We therefore begin our theoretical analysis by exploring the definitions and origins of these three concepts.

Economic growth

Economic growth refers to an increase in an economy's output of goods and services, and the overall amount of income that it generates. Measured by the gross domestic product (GDP) index, it is still given a high priority by governments all over the world. This is despite a long history of protests by environmentalists that economic growth destroys the environment and depletes stocks of natural resources because it prioritizes consumption to generate income. Maximizing consumption requires using up the planet's resources and the processes by which these are extracted and transformed into commercial products generate pollution and other forms of environmental degradation (Mishan, 1967). Politicians feel obliged to continue to proclaim the virtues of economic growth because of the almost universal attractions of higher income. Generally, the amount by which a society can advance is seen to depend upon how much extra income its economy can generate, and the rise in average income partly eases the political strains caused by inequalities of wealth and income.

Economic development

Growth in mean income alone does not, however, guarantee that the full range of human needs and aspirations will be satisfied – hence the need for another concept to describe this more all-embracing trend. Economic development can be defined as a rise in the well-being of society as a whole, as reflected in the expanded set of opportunities available to the present generation (Perrings, 1994; Simpson, 1987). It requires not just a rise in mean income, but that this income be distributed as equitably as possible among a population to increase the welfare of the whole of society – for example, by increasing access to food, clean water and housing, and improving standards of health and education. Economic development therefore leads to greater intra-generational equity, though no particular degree of equity is specified as a target that a country should meet in order to be called 'developed'.

The concept of economic development echoes humanity's historic struggle to improve its general standard of living. At the heart of this is the long-standing conflict in the industrialized countries between Labour and Capital over the distribution of income and wealth. But the concept was not specifically articulated until after the end of World War II (Potter et al, 1999), when it was used to refer to the process by which the world's poorer countries would replicate the economic and social achievements of the richer countries. As a result, economic development was initially equated with increasing mean income through the extension of industrialization and the economic growth resulting from this. It was assumed that the income generated by the 'modern' sector of the economy would automatically 'trickle down' to improve the fortunes of the traditional farming population, who still constituted the majority of the citizens of what was known then as 'the Third World' and later as the 'developing countries'. By the 1970s, however, it was clear that this was not generally the case. This led to the present definition of economic development, which equates it with 'rising well-being' instead of 'rising income'. Economic growth can lead to economic development, but only if a combination of market forces and societal institutions ensure that the extra income it generates is distributed relatively evenly throughout society.

Despite reservations about equating economic development with economic growth, the former is often still measured in broad income terms by the index of GDP per capita, which is estimated by the mean income received by each person in US dollars. 'Developed countries' are distinguished from 'developing countries' by their level of GDP per capita, and each group is divided into further sub-categories on the same basis. However, since average income is not a reliable guide to well-being, a number of alternative indices have been proposed. One of these indices merely corrects for the distortions introduced when the GDP per capita of all countries is measured in US dollars, by estimating income instead on the basis of 'purchasing power parity', in order to reflect more truly the goods and services that may be actually purchased by a unit of national currency in each country. A more radical alternative is the United Nations Human Development Index (HDI) (UNDP, 1991). This has become increasingly popular since the early 1990s because it takes account of distributional features, such as health and educational standards, which are crucial to economic development as it is now defined. The HDI has its limitations, but it is a valuable tool, building on attempts since the late 1960s to use multiple indicators to monitor social and economic improvement.

Economic development, as defined above, is an objective *concept* that can be used to describe both positive and negative economic and social changes. It often shares the opprobrium of critics of the original development *ideal* described earlier, but the two are not the same. The concept requires neither a preferred rate of economic development nor a high level of economic development – two alternative interpretations of the development ideal. On the contrary, if measured by a properly estimated index or set of indicators, the concept can be used to either prove or disprove the rival claims of those who promote or criticize the development ideal. Although current indices have their limitations, they can distinguish between countries that are developing in objective terms and those that are not, between countries that are developing rapidly and those that are developing slowly, and between countries that have reached a high level of development and those at a lower level.

Sustainable development

The concept of economic development, however, takes no account of the environmental impacts of the activities needed to generate the income upon which it depends. This is because its view of human welfare is restricted to social welfare alone. Sustainable development was initially proposed by IUCN (1980) as a compromise between development and conservation, two goals that were previously regarded as incompatible. It offered the hope that humanity could continue to advance socially and economically, while still conserving the life-support systems provided by the global environment that make an indispensable contribution to human welfare.

Unfortunately, as IUCN did not define exactly what it meant by sustainable development, it was left to the Brundtland Report to fill the gap. This it did, although only the first part of its definition – advocating development that 'meets the needs of the present without compromising the ability of future generations to meet their own needs' – subsequently became widely accepted. Without the important qualifying sentences about reducing poverty in developing countries this definition is entirely consistent with the original environmentalist ideal, which aimed to achieve greater inter-generational equity in access to natural resources and environmental services.

While the Brundtland definition was easy to understand, it was too vague to use as a basis for operational monitoring and theoretical study. So academic researchers have tried hard to devise better definitions. By the early 1990s no fewer than 70 attempts had been made to improve upon it (Holmberg and Sandbrook, 1992; Pearce et al, 1989). By the late 1990s this had allegedly risen 'into the thousands' (Pezzey, 1997). Some, like Pezzey, have concluded that trying to arrive at a 'perfect' definition is therefore a fruitless task. Yet there is much to be said for a simple definition proposed by environmental economists (Pearce, 1991; Solow, 1986) that sustainable development is that which 'leads to non-declining human welfare over time'. This is equivalent to the first sentence of the Brundtland definition but is more specific and offers greater scope for monitoring sustainable development because it identifies a quantity – human welfare – and a rule for how this should vary over time. Of course, a lot depends upon how human welfare is defined. In this context it is generally assumed to include not only the economic and social dimensions of welfare (the increase in which constitutes economic development) but environmental welfare, too.

What this means, in practice, is that a country, or any other territory, will develop sustainably provided that: (a) any rise in its income today (ie economic growth) is not obtained at the expense of its social welfare today or that of any future generation; and (b) any rise in its income and social welfare today (ie economic development) is not obtained at the expense of its environmental welfare today or that of any future generation. This can be applied to any territory, and even to the world as a whole, if some assumptions are made about the equity of distribution of the social element of human welfare.

Until now a lack of universal agreement over the definition of sustainable development has allowed different interpretations – both as a political ideal and a theoretical concept – to continue. With each passing year, more definitions and interpretations are proposed, and so the notion becomes even more diffuse. However, just as important as achieving a perfect definition is identifying the specific conditions which, linked to a particular definition, can be used to determine whether development is sustainable or not. Two important sets of conditions, derived from theories devised by ecological economists and environmental economists, are reviewed below. The terms 'sustainable development' and 'sustainability' are often used interchangeably. However, the latter also has a more restricted meaning, as the goal of constraining human impacts on the environment in order to protect life support systems (Bowers, 1997). It is therefore a necessary, but not sufficient, condition for sustainable development (Rao, 2000).

If we now look back at the *political ideal* of sustainable development from the viewpoint of the *theoretical concept* we can see that they are not the same. This is because the ideal as interpreted by developing countries – namely, a call for better access to world trade and a substantial transfer of resources from developed countries to reduce their poverty – is merely a *strategy* intended to enable them to achieve the earlier 'development' ideal. The strategy is a response to what they perceive to be an inherent bias in the structure of the world economic system that prevents their rate of economic development from being as rapid, and their overall level of economic development from rising as much, as they would like. However, there is no need for a new concept to describe this lack of progress. It can be described perfectly well by the concept of economic development.

The theoretical concept of sustainable development, on the other hand, is unique in that it adds to the economic and social dimensions and the notion of intra-generational equity included in the concept of economic development: (a) an environmental dimension; (b) an inter-generational equity element. The latter requires that the judgement of whether a country is or is not developing sustainably must be determined by the quality of its long-term *development path*, with a consistent rate of improvement rather than short spurts of economic growth.

Sustainable development and economic development also differ in another important respect. For a territory to have developed sustainably it must, in principle, have followed an ideal development path since it was first settled by human beings. Given the human propensity for uneven development and environmental degradation, this is practically impossible. Therefore, unlike the process of economic development, which can be achieved at widely differing rates in many countries, the process portrayed in the theoretical concept of sustainable development is a *theoretical ideal* that will probably never be achieved in practice. Attempts to realize either it or the political ideals of sustainable development will also face the same obstacles that currently hamper economic development in developing countries. Nevertheless, countries can still aim to move their actual development path closer to the ideal sustainable development path and thereby increase their *degree of sustainability of development*.

Capital: A Unifying Thread in Development Theories

To show the links between these three concepts of economic growth, economic development and sustainable development it helps to use the notion of 'Capital'. This has long played a major role in both economic and political economy theories of economic growth and development, and it now features prominently in economic theories of sustainable development.

Capital accumulation as the key to economic growth

'Capital', 'Labour' and 'Land' (or 'Environmental Resources') constitute the three scarce factors of production recognized by economists. Their allocation is the basic problem tackled by the discipline of economics. Adam Smith (1776), one of the leading classical economists, identified the accumulation of fixed, or reproducible, Capital (which is embodied in productive machinery) as one of the key factors leading to economic growth, the other being the specialization of Labour.

The concept of capital has, however, become more sophisticated over time as economic understanding has matured. The focus on fixed capital as a factor of production has been retained, although it is now common to regard fixed capital and the circulating – or financial – capital required to purchase it as interchangeable. Meanwhile, conventional fixed capital has been divided into:

- Productive Capital, which refers specifically to industrial machinery;
- Economic Overhead Capital, which is the public infrastructure, such as roads and railways, needed to support economic activity; and
- Social Overhead Capital, which is embodied in the schools, hospitals and other institutions that supply the public goods required for social advancement.

These different dimensions of fixed capital are now also collectively referred to as 'Man-Made Capital' in the sustainable development literature.

An important characteristic of capital is that at any time it has a particular spatial distribution over the surface of the world that is typically uneven, both on a global basis and within individual countries. This reflects preferences regarding the optimum location of capital accumulation, which geographers have used to explain the uneven spatial distribution of economic growth and economic development. Preferential concentrations of capital in some regions have been traditionally linked to innate economic advantages of location and resource endowment. However, the unequal terms on which inter-regional trade is conducted have enabled the most powerful economies to supplement their own indigenous capital by appropriating resources from elsewhere. At the global level this is reflected in the enduring differences between the capital-rich Core of developed countries and the capital-poor Periphery of developing countries, as portrayed in the political economy theories discussed above. In recent decades the magnitude and speed of capital flows around the world have risen to such an extent that the world economy is said to have become increasingly globalized (Dicken, 2003).

Human Capital and economic development

A further step in elaborating the concept of capital was taken in the late 1950s, when the notion of 'Human Capital' was proposed to describe the combination of knowledge, health and skills that contribute to personal productivity (Mincer, 1958; Schultz, 1961). Investing in the accumulation of Human Capital, it was argued, is central to economic development, just as investing in the expansion of fixed capital is the key to economic growth. The importance attached to Human Capital has since increased, not least as a result of the new endogenous growth theory advanced in the 1990s, in which technological innovation – another key factor contributing to modern economic growth – is linked to the accumulation of Human Capital (Romer, 1990).

While the idea of Human Capital was originally confined to the sum of attributes embodied in human individuals, it has since been extended in scope to include the wealth associated with productive social interaction and collaboration. The formal and informal structures through which individuals and groups in society cooperate for mutual benefit also accumulate during development and are essential for a sustained rise in welfare. These structures are referred to by some authors as Social Capital (Ostrom, 1990), although others assume them to be included in Human Capital.

The capitalization of nature

Economic theories of sustainable development have stressed their continuity with previous development theories by extending the concept of capital to include nature. Natural Capital has two main components: Resource Capital and Environmental Quality. Resource Capital comprises the stocks of all natural resources. It can be divided, in turn, into Renewable Resource Capital and Non-Renewable Resource Capital, which respectively refer to stocks of renewable resources, such as forests and fisheries, and non-renewable resources, such as minerals and oil. Environmental Quality, on the other hand, is related to the condition of the three main environmental sinks: the land; freshwater and marine environments; and the atmosphere. The present quality of these sinks depends upon the characteristics and functioning of the renewable resources in natural ecosystems. Human beings have extensively modified these by exploiting resource stocks and depositing waste into the sinks.

The term Critical Natural Capital was devised to refer to that part of Renewable Resource Capital and its associated environmental services which, through its contribution to the major global cycles, is essential for life support – for example, areas of tropical forest with high biodiversity and carbon stocks (Pearce, 1991). As discussed below, the reason for doing this was to make the environmental economics theory of sustainable development more realistic by recognizing that there are limits to the amount of substitution that is possible between Natural Capital and Man-Made Capital, and to how low stocks of Natural Capital can fall without threatening the functioning of the biosphere.

Portraying the natural environment in terms of Natural Capital was a major step in conceptualizing sustainable development, because it enabled changes in the natural world, such as the depletion of natural resource stocks and environmental pollution that result from human activities, to be directly compared with the changes in human society made possible by the income generated by these activities. This allows a more complete assessment of the net costs and benefits of economic development, something that is not possible with conventional economic models. Indeed, one reason for the widespread depletion of resource stocks and environmental degradation in the world is that there is no obligation to pay the full economic costs associated with such activities: many important environmental features and functions lack values in the market place. On the other hand, 'capitalizing nature' is controversial. Indeed, any attempt to assign economic values to environmental features, such as the maintenance of river flows from watersheds or the beauty of a particular landscape, can lead to claims that this demeans nature and promotes its destruction (Pearce, 1991).

Having reviewed these changing conceptions of capital, we now show how economists have used them to construct theoretical explanations of sustainable development.

Economic Theories of Sustainable Development

There are two significant challenges in theorizing about sustainable development. First, deciding how to integrate the economic, social and environmental dimensions of development. Second, ensuring that any theory has practical relevance. These tasks are complicated by the need to achieve internal consistency within a given theory and to treat development as a long-term phenomenon. The two leading theories of sustainable development, devised by ecological economists and environmental economists, use some of the same terms and regard development as a long-term path, but they take different approaches to integrating the three dimensions of development. This has given rise to a number of conditions for determining whether development in a particular territory is sustainable. As environmental economists also use one of the ecological economics conditions this does not promote clarity, but we try to minimize the potential for confusion by identifying the origins of each condition as clearly as possible.

Ecological economics theory

Ecological economics is a new interdisciplinary field of study that aims to remedy the traditional neglect of the environment in economics. To realize this aim it portrays the human economy as a subsystem of the global ecological system (see Figure 1.1). Rather than attempting to integrate environment and society by forcing the former into what some regard as an 'unnatural' economic framework, it views the flows of income and materials within an economy as part of the wider transfer of energy and materials within the biosphere. Thus, the long-term viability of human activities is deemed to depend upon how well they comply with the rules governing the biosphere.

The Ideal Condition for sustainable development
At the heart of the ecological economics approach to sustainable development is the relationship between the scale of the human economy and the scale of the biosphere, or 'natural economy'. If the scale of the human economy grows too large in relation to that of the biosphere, then it will threaten not only its own sustainability but that of the biosphere too. The Ideal Condition for sustainable development is therefore, that the scale of the human economy must not exceed the critical level – equivalent to the ultimate carrying capacity of the planet (Folke et al, 1994) – at which it threatens the sustainability of the biosphere (Daly, 1999). Any development path is compatible with this condition as long as it does not breach this upper limit.

Constant Natural Capital – the Strong Sustainability Condition
The Ideal Condition is, however, difficult to put into practice as there are no reliable estimates of ultimate carrying capacity. Consequently, a 'minimum safe condition' for sustainable development has been devised to substitute for it. Known as the Strong Sustainability Condition, it simply requires that there is no decline in Natural Capital. This equates the requirement for non-declining human welfare, advanced by Pearce (1991) in his definition of sustainable development, with one generation passing on to

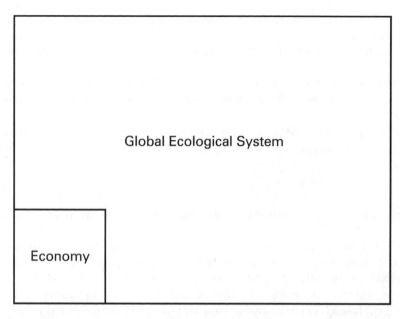

Figure 1.1   The Ecological Economics Model of the relationship between economy and environment

the next the same quantity of Natural Capital that it received from its predecessors. This does not mean that human beings cannot alter nature in any way. Stocks of non-renewable resources may, for example, decline, provided that renewable re-sources stocks rise to compensate for this. Since ecological economists regard Natural Capital and Human and Man-Made Capital as complements, rather than perfect substitutes, they think it wrong to assume that a fall in Natural Capital can be fully offset by a rise in Human and Man-Made Capital.

The Daly Principles

Daly (1990) proposed a set of operational principles for sustainable development (see Table 1.1). The first repeats the Ideal Condition, which sets an upper limit on the scale of human activity, while the remaining four are strategies for realizing the Strong Sustainability Condition. Daly originally combined the third and fourth principles, but they are separated here for convenience.

The Daly Principles are necessarily a prescriptive approach to sustainable develop-ment, outlining a desirable set of strategies. Implementing the last four principles perfectly would move the actual development path of any territory closer to its ideal sustainable path. The second principle points to the role of technological change in allowing the scale of human activity to grow without impacting unduly upon the environment. However, it is rather ambiguous in not stating whether technological innovations are likely to occur inevitably in response to market signals, or whether some form of state intervention is required. Adhering to the last four principles would preclude any further decline in Natural Capital by preventing the depletion of renewable resources and the degradation of environmental sinks, and by off-

Table 1.1   The Daly Principles

1	Limit the human scale to a level which, if not optimal, is at least within the carrying capacity and is, therefore, sustainable.
2	Achieve technological change that increases efficiency and durability while limiting throughput.
3	Preserve the harvesting rate of renewable resources at a level below the regenerative capacity of the environment.
4	Preserve waste emission rates at a level below the assimilative capacity of the environment.
5	Restrict non-renewable resource use to levels equalled by the creation or accessing of renewable substitutes.

setting any loss of non-renewable resources with a rise in renewable resource stocks.

The last four principles have been widely adopted as the basis for sustainable development strategies as they can easily be translated into practical actions. They have inspired many national and local initiatives, from increased recycling and renewable energy use to conserve natural resource stocks, to improvements in public transport to cut fossil fuel consumption and air pollution. Yet despite their practicality, the Daly Principles, and the ecological economics model upon which they are based, focus almost exclusively on the environmental aspect of development and neglect its social and economic dimensions and intra-generational equity. This has, ironically, helped to perpetuate sustainable development's isolation from mainstream economic planning. Consequently, the principles have nothing to say about the reduction in poverty and social inequality which is at the heart of economic development. Nor do they give any guidance about how to offset such socio-economic progress against the inevitable environmental impacts that it entails. It is the need to make such trade-offs that will make it difficult in practice to implement the principles perfectly.

Environmental economics theory

Environmental economics theory is more comprehensive than its ecological counter-part as it encompasses and differentiates between all three dimensions of development: the economic, the social and the environmental. It also provides a more descriptive framework for analysis, and uses terminology that is more consistent with the concepts of capital and welfare recognized in existing economic and political economy theories of economic growth and economic development. In contrast to ecological economics, it is based upon a modified neo-classical economic model in which the environment is integrated into the economic system (see Figure 1.2). Development is portrayed as an accumulation of Human and Man-Made Capital at the expense of a reduction in Natural Capital. Development is generally deemed sustainable when a balance is struck between these processes of gain and loss, so that capital stocks do not decline.

Three Constant Capital Conditions
Three principal conditions – the Strong, the Weak and the Very Weak – have been proposed to determine whether a development path is sustainable (see Table 1.2).

Figure 1.2   The Environmental Economics Model of the relationship between economy and environment

Table 1.2   The Constant Capital Conditions

1	Strong: there is no reduction in the total stock of Natural Capital.
2	Weak: there is no reduction in the stock of Critical Natural Capital.
3	Very Weak: the value of depleted Natural Capital does not exceed the value of the rise in Human and Man-Made Capital derived from it.

Essentially, the Very Weak and Strong conditions are alternatives to one another, while the Weak condition is used to qualify the Very Weak condition.

The Strong Condition equates sustainable development with inter-generational equity in access to Natural Capital alone. It simply restates the Strong Sustainability Condition of ecological economics and is therefore open to the same criticisms.

The Very Weak Condition, on the other hand, requires each generation to pass on at least as much Total Capital as it received from the preceding generation. Hence, the sustainable development path is portrayed by the trend in Total Capital, ie the sum of Natural, Human and Man-Made Capital, rather than just Natural Capital as in the Strong Condition. This is also referred to in some texts as 'weak sustainability'. The condition derives from the Hartwick-Solow Rule, which was originally devised by resource economists before the notion of sustainable development emerged. This was stated by Solow (1986) as:

> A society that invests in reproducible capital the competitive rents on its extraction of exhaustible resources will enjoy a constant consumption stream in time ... The accumulation of reproducible capital exactly offsets the inevitable and efficient decline in the flow of resource inputs ... This can be interpreted as saying that an appropriately defined stock of capital, including the initial endowment of resources, is maintained intact. Consumption can be interpreted as the interest on that [stock].

If Total Capital is not to decline, then logically any fall in Natural Capital in the course of development must be at least offset by a rise in Human and Man-Made Capital of equivalent value. This crucially assumes substitutability between the different forms of capital, and that it is justified – and practically feasible – to compare these two changes directly.

One of the weaknesses of the Very Weak Condition is that it does not impose absolute limits on the depletion of Natural Capital. Thus, it would be entirely possible to deplete Natural Capital totally and still achieve sustainable development, according to this condition, as long as the value of the Natural Capital lost was less than that of the Human and Man-Made Capital gained.

The Weak Condition was introduced by Pearce et al (1989) in response to this criticism, and in recognition of the limits to substitutability between Natural Capital and Human and Man-Made Capital. If the Very Weak and Weak Conditions are applied together, Natural Capital may still be drawn down, but only if it does not reduce the stock of Critical Natural Capital, whose maintenance is, as noted above, crucial to the life-support functions of the biosphere.

Other important limitations remain, however. Natural Capital and Human and Man-Made Capital are assumed to be good substitutes; but clearly there are limits to how far human technology can substitute for the workings of nature. It is not easy, either, to compare changes in Natural Capital and Human and Man-Made Capital directly, given the absence of good data on resource volumes and the difficulties of valuing changes in different forms of capital in equivalent units. Aggregating Human and Man-Made Capital as a single variable is also problematic. It gives no scope to balance change in the economic dimension of development against change in the social dimension. As a result, it ignores the equity of welfare distribution that is central to the concept of economic development.

Reconciling the Political and Theoretical Discourses

Confusion over the meaning of sustainable development is quite understandable. As this chapter has shown, sustainable development is the subject of both political and theoretical interpretations, or discourses. Moreover, each of these major sets of discourses, in turn, consists of a number of competing discourses; in the case of theory, for example, there are the ecological economics and environmental economics discourses. How can these differences be reconciled? We would make five observations.

First, in theoretical discourses sustainable development is essentially a matter of optimizing the balance between the economic, social and environmental dimensions of development. In practice, associated with each of these dimensions is a set of interest groups, broadly representing Capital, Labour and Environment. Each is apparent in different forms – for example, in the case of Capital, individual capitalist entrepreneurs, bankers, corporations or even states that pursue a predominantly capitalist agenda, such as the USA. Therefore, from the point of view of an economist, what should be just a simple mathematical optimization problem for planners becomes distorted in the real world by these political pressures, so that the actual optimum path reflects the balance of power between them. Consequently, none of the discourses of the competing interest groups – even that of the Environment – can ever be regarded as the 'correct' one. So a society that did develop sustainably would *never*, virtually by definition, fulfil all of the requirements of the environmentalist discourse, or of the other two competing discourses. This should give those who equate sustainable development with a 'green society' pause for thought.

Second, taking these political influences into account, the typical political ideal of sustainable development adopted by developed countries reflects the hypocritical way in which they regard the environment as important for developing countries, while at the same time separating it from the economic and social dimensions of their own development. If developing countries conserve their environments, this will conserve the global environment and maximize the environmental welfare of the developed countries. Meanwhile, the ideal held by developing countries also gives top priority to the economic and social dimensions of their own development, while calling upon the developed countries to pay the environmental costs which they have incurred over the centuries.

Third, within the set of theoretical discourses, ecological economists focus upon the environmental dimension because they consider that if the human economy is to be integrated into the natural economy then the former must obey the rules that govern the sustainability of the biosphere. Environmental economists, on the other hand, assume that the only way to achieve this integration is within the same framework by which human beings identify and satisfy all of their preferences – namely, the market system. This is best represented by modifying the standard neo-classical economic model, rather than replacing it.

Fourth, it is possible to encompass the goal of greater global intra-generational equity, held by the developing countries, within the environmental economics definition of sustainable development, quoted above. If the definition is assumed to have a global scope, then it can be interpreted to mean that any rise in the income, social welfare and environmental welfare of one territory or group of territories during one period should not be at the expense of the income, social welfare and environmental welfare of any other territory or group of territories in the same period. If this is extended to include inter-generational equity, any rise in the income, social welfare and environmental welfare of one territory or group of territories in one period should not be at the expense of the income, social welfare and environmental welfare of the same territory or any other territory or group of territories in the same period or in future periods.

Fifth, there is an interesting synergy between the competition between different political discourses and the ideal global path of sustainable development. If development at global level had been perfectly sustainable in the past, then – in line with the interpretation of the definition in the last paragraph – any welfare generated would have been equitably allocated between all countries and all generations. The developed countries would not have accumulated a large deficit of environmental costs by their historic pollution. Nor would they have exploited the resources of developing countries to favour their own development and leave developing countries in poverty and financial debt. If developing countries do make environmental concessions to the developed countries in return for additional financial resources and trade concessions to promote their own future development, these transfers could be seen as de facto compensation in lieu of (a) the past exploitation of developing countries, which limited their ability to develop; and (b) the accumulation of unpaid environmental costs which all countries in the world are now having to pay, not least through the impacts of global climate change or in programmes to mitigate it. Developed countries would lose some income and wealth and developing countries would become less poor than they are now. The compensation would never fully match the developmental and environmental advantages secured by the developed countries, and would merely allocate welfare more equitably between all countries over all generations. However, in line with the first point made above, we would not expect perfection: in the real world, equity is always *politically* determined.

This suggests that the political and theoretical discourses are actually just two sides of the same coin. Each needs the other as a reference point but, taken alone, each offers only a partial explanation of sustainable development.

Questions about Sustainable Development

Even if it is accepted that the great diversity in views about sustainable development can be reconciled as suggested above, many questions remain unanswered. Sustainable development is a young and rapidly growing field, and we still know comparatively little about it, in spite of the impressive body of theory that has been produced over the last 15 years and the various strategies that have been tried. This section highlights six key questions which formed the starting point for investigation in the remaining chapters of this book. Linked with each of these primary questions are a host of subsidiary queries.

Will current strategies lead to sustainable development?

Many of the strategies currently being implemented in the framework of the political process of sustainable development, launched at UNCED in 1992, and continued at the World Summit on Sustainable Development in 2002, are attempts to improve the quality of human life and the sustainability of resource and environmental management, placing particular emphasis on the use of a participatory approach and/or technological innovations. However, the overall focus of the political process is poorly defined. While its general aim is to realize the goals of Agenda 21, these goals are ambiguous and they are interpreted differently in different states. The process is also taking place in the absence of a proper framework for defining sustainable development and for identifying the conditions necessary to achieve it. At best, the political process is merely a well-intentioned attempt at pragmatic experimentation, in which communities try to learn more about sustainable development 'by doing'. How well do current strategies integrate the economic, social and environmental dimensions of development? Will they really shift the actual long-term development path closer to the ideal path that constitutes sustainable development? Or will they only lead to short-term incremental improvements?

What are the spatial characteristics of sustainable development?

The spatial characteristics of sustainable development have been rather neglected. It is commonly assumed that participation at local level holds the key to sustainable development. But is sustainable development really a meaningful concept at the local level and, indeed, at all other levels on the spatial scale? How is the sustainability of development of a particular territory affected by interactions with other territories on the same level of the spatial scale – for example, through trade and pollutant flows between countries? How is the sustainability of development at one level on the spatial scale affected by interactions with other levels – for example, through constraints imposed on national action by international agreements, and by the impact on national sustainability of uneven development within a country? Can local participation be effective without supportive measures at higher levels on the spatial scale? Can the sustainability of an urban area be judged independently of the region from which it draws its workers and raw materials, and to which it exports its pollution?

How is sustainable development affected by political influences?

Sustainable development is now firmly established on local, national and international political agendas. But how do political factors influence the sustainability of development and attempts to improve it? Do current political systems inherently favour the dominant influence of elites and preclude real progress toward more sustainable development? If so, how can such bias be detected and documented? Can a more balanced approach to development be achieved? Are environmentalists correct in believing that the increasing flows of goods, capital and information that constitute globalization harm not only national sovereignty but also the environment and sustainable development in general? If so, are tougher international regulations needed to protect all countries – particularly, developing ones – from such exploitation? Or would they only make matters worse?

Does achieving more sustainable development require or lead to societal change?

Can sustainable development be achieved by means of evolutionary changes to present societies? Or is it only possible if a radical shift is made to so-called 'ecocentric societies' (Jordan and O'Riordan, 2000) whose morality is based on ecological principles? If sustainable development is really incompatible with present societal structures in most countries, which are inherently linked with capitalism, are current technocentric and participatory strategies just a smokescreen, intended only to preserve the status quo and, hence, the power and wealth of capitalist interests?

How well do existing theories explain sustainable development?

Equity is at the heart of sustainable development, yet current economic theories focus only on inter-generational environmental equity, to the exclusion of intra-generational equity within countries and between countries. Could they be enhanced to correct for this? Intra-generational equity between developed and developing countries is central to political economy theories of development, and to the theory of political ecology derived from it; but both theories ignore inter-generational environmental equity. Could they be modified to correct for this? Or is the only practical solution to this dilemma to apply economic theories and political economy theories together? Is the neglect of the spatial dimension of sustainable development linked to inherent limitations in current theories, or is it possible to extend them? Would it be better, instead, to extend the scope of theories that already incorporate the spatial dimension to encompass sustainable development too? Or are new theories needed?

How can existing theories be made more practically relevant?

If sustainable development is to fulfil its potential as a new comprehensive planning framework then the environmental dimension must be integrated into current planning techniques. These tend to focus on the economic and social dimensions of development, and treat the environment as a constraint on economic and social change, rather than as integral to development. Since planners will be reluctant to throw out their proven existing methods, it would help if the new sustainable development methods were compatible with them. Yet one reason why policy-makers and planners have chosen to 'learn by doing' in selecting sustainable development strategies is that they are not convinced that current theories of sustainable development meet their practical needs. This is understandable, given that ecological economics theory makes no specific reference to the economic or social dimensions of development, and the Very Weak Condition of environmental economics aggregates the economic and social dimensions and therefore cannot account for trade-offs between these. Can existing theories be modified to remove these deficiencies? Or is a new condition, or even a new theory, needed?

Geographical Perspectives on Sustainable Development

In this book we look at sustainable development from both political and theoretical perspectives, and tackle the major questions highlighted in the previous section. We do not claim to provide a comprehensive geographical analysis of sustainable development; but the collection of different geographical perspectives covers key areas of interest to geographers and the most important theoretical and practical aspects of sustainable development. In this final section we highlight some of the main points made in each chapter.

We do not propose any new theories of sustainable development in this book. Instead, as befits a transitional text, we confine ourselves to exploring the potential for extending existing theories. This includes extending sustainable development theories to incorporate a spatial dimension and, in the process, assessing the limitations of these theories in this regard. It also includes extending geographical theories to encompass sustainable development. The range of geographical perspectives displayed by contributing authors is, we believe, a fair reflection of the current engagement of geographers with this subject, reviewed by Purvis in Chapter 2. Thus, while some authors make use of the concepts of the economic theories reviewed above, others frame their analysis more loosely within a combination of the ecological economics framework and the environmentalist political discourse adopted by developed countries. The authors also vary in the degree to which they draw on other existing theoretical structures, both geographical and deriving from political economy.

Purvis begins our analysis in Chapter 2 by offering a succinct picture of how geographers view the world. He argues that geography's distinctive preoccupation with place, space and synthesis adds a new dimension to the analysis and pursuit of sustainable development. Previous neglect of the spatial dimension of sustainable development has meant that some of the key spatial assumptions implicit in current strategies have received only limited critical scrutiny. Links between the sustainability of development and equity issues in relation to specific places and populations have also been largely ignored. Current political initiatives in the name of sustainable development could even reinforce existing exploitative relationships between places and territories. Although geographers' engagement with sustainable development has, so far, been limited, there is considerable potential to build on a broad range of established geographical work, which, until now, has not been directly linked with this field. For example, geographical expertise in linking human welfare to the spatial form of settlements could be used when planners allocate new developments between 'greenfield' and 'brownfield' sites. The quest for more sustainable development also confers added significance on geographical studies of the evolution of capitalism to its present globalized form. The unpredictability and frequency of shifts of capital, people and goods undermine the ability to plan the long-term sustainable development of territories. However, regulation theory may provide some cause for optimism, suggesting that new regulatory structures could secure more sustainable development, even in a globalized world economy.

One theme that recurs throughout the book is the importance of examining sustainable development at different levels on the spatial scale. In Chapter 3, Grainger outlines a basic framework for this discussion by looking at some of the key spatial characteristics of sustainable development. He considers whether sustainable development is a meaningful concept at all levels on the spatial scale, how interactions between different territories at each level affect the sustainability of development of each territory, and how the sustainability of development at one level is affected by interactions with other levels. The chapter is important in the context of the book as a whole for examining sustainable development at the national level, and for engaging with the two leading economic theories of sustainable development. Grainger attempts to remedy the neglect of these theories by geographers – and the simultaneous neglect by economic theories of the spatial dimension – by exploring the role of spatial scale and spatial interactions in sustainable development within the framework of environmental economics theory and, in particular, the Very Weak Condition. Surprisingly, this is one of the most extensive evaluations undertaken so far of the condition's potential applications and limitations. Although it does allow sustainable development to be discussed in terms of changes in the spatial distributions of Natural, Human and Man-Made Capital, in the context of economies which are open to trade and pollution flows, Grainger shows that the condition has its limitations. He looks at the role of intra-generational equity in world trade from both development and sustainable development perspectives and evaluates the merits of applying existing sustainability indicators to open economies. Grainger complements his economic analysis with a discussion of the transmission of political influences between territories and between different levels of the spatial scale. In the final section of his chapter he looks at the problems of planning for sustainable development and suggests that there is much to be said for combining participatory approaches with traditional top-down planning methods, which have the virtue of ensuring the spatial coherence that participation often lacks.

Broadly based popular participation is commonly assumed to be crucial for devising and implementing practical strategies for sustainable development. However, in Chapter 4 Soussan offers a political and institutional analysis which demonstrates the fallacy of such a simplistic assumption. Drawing on a range of practical case studies from Asia, he shows the importance of links between different levels on the spatial scale. This leads him to argue that local participation alone cannot overcome the obstacles to sustainable development that arise from ineffective state organizations and the exercise of political power at national level. In reality, local and national actions are not alternatives, and local action works best if it is facilitated by institutional arrangements at national level. Consequently, states that are serious about pursuing more sustainable development should think carefully about how they divide responsibility for implementing programmes between actors at different levels on the spatial scale.

In addressing urban sustainability, Mitchell, in Chapter 5, and Unsworth, in Chapter 6, focus on the level of the spatial scale that has been as popular as the national level in theoretical and empirical studies of sustainable development. Geographers have much to contribute here, given the proud heritage of urban geography. Cities are a mass of contradictions: on the one hand, their concentrations of Human and Man-Made Capital are the powerhouses that generate the income needed to achieve development; on the other hand, the resources that they metabolize and the waste that they produce have turned urban territories into concentrations of depleted and degraded Natural Capital. Both authors take up the theme of interactions between places and scales that runs through earlier chapters, arguing that urban sustainability cannot be considered in spatial isolation, since towns and cities are connected to wider systems of trade and exchange in commodities, goods, pollution, people and financial capital.

Mitchell highlights the value of harnessing existing geographical expertise in devising mathematical models of urban systems to understand the accumulation and depletion of capital that lies at the heart of theoretical models of sustainable development. After reviewing the history of urban geographical modelling, he critically evaluates urban sustainability models and indicators, which he finds to be heavily influenced by ecological economics theory. He argues that the difficulties of planning for sustainability could be reduced if policy-makers and planners made greater use of sustainability models for predicting the possible outcomes of policies and projects.

Unsworth offers a more human and social perspective on cities, and her prescriptive approach complements Mitchell's generally more descriptive approach. She reviews attempts to redefine the scale and spatial form of urban settlements in order to create places that are characterized not only by greater environmental and economic efficiency in the use of resources, but also by a better experience of urban living. The latter may be achieved by improving the aesthetics of urban landscapes, cleaner and safer residential environments, greater social diversity and higher standards of welfare overall. She questions the practicality of strategies intended to improve sustainability through the wholesale transformation of urban form. Such utopian ideas seem particularly inappropriate when contrasted with the reality of urban misman-agement in developing countries. Referring to case studies, she explores the potential for making amends for ineffective top-down planning by placing greater reliance on grassroots initiatives to make rapid and positive changes in the quality of urban environments, in line with the participatory approach in Agenda 21. Unsworth is more positive about participation than some other authors in this volume, arguing that the actions of the individual urban resident may be just as important as the city's physical fabric in achieving more sustainable development. But she, too, is cautious about opting exclusively for participatory strategies. Indeed, given the multiple levels on the spatial scale at which the impacts of urban metabolism are felt, the most logical strategy would encompass many levels, and not just one.

The next two chapters focus on key sectors of the economy that transcend spatial scale and are as important for understanding sustainability at global and supranational levels as they are at national and local levels. In his discussion of the business sector in Chapter 7, Purvis questions claims about the potential for achieving greater sustainability through techno-centric and managerial innovation, in view of the attractions of preserving the status quo. While economic growth can be partially decoupled from environmental degradation, he suggests that it would be wrong to assume that all environmental problems can be tackled in this way. The rhetoric of eco-efficiency, particularly as articulated within the business community, also does little to address the social dimension of sustainable development and concerns for intra-generational equity. This suggests that there is a valid case for at least considering the merits of proposals for adopting an alternative spatial scale of economic organization by placing greater emphasis on local trade and production. Although Purvis finds flaws in the argument for a 'return to the local', his analysis raises important questions about how to secure more equitable treatment for individual localities in a world characterized by economic globalization and high levels of capital mobility.

Agriculture is of fundamental importance for sustaining human life on Earth, but at the same time its environmental impacts have a crucial influence on overall sustainability. In their discussion of the agriculture sector in Chapter 8, Purvis and Smith highlight the vital contest about relationships between society and nature that underpins thinking about sustainable development. The contrasts and tensions between different conceptions of sustainable development are clearly apparent in agriculture. This chapter assesses the merits of the different types of agricultural strategies that have been proposed to promote more sustainable development. These range from reliance on farming systems that harness traditional knowledge and notions of harmony between humanity and nature, to increasing use of new developments in biotechnology by planting genetically modified (GM) crop varieties. The chapter also puts previous attention to on-farm change in its proper spatial context by showing how the practices of any individual farmer or farming community are shaped by more than local considerations of environment, knowledge and access to financial capital. Viewed in this way, attempts to foster more sustainable agriculture require attention to wider national and international contexts of trade, debt, the politics of state agricultural subsidies and priorities for investment in agricultural research.

Chapters 9 and 10 examine how perceptions of sustainable development vary in specific regional contexts. There is a great danger in viewing sustainable development solely from a Western, modernist, techno-centric viewpoint, for it can be perceived quite differently in other cultures. In Chapter 9, Waley and Purvis discuss, by reference to river management, the dialogue established between indigenous and imported ideas about environmental management and sustainable development in Japan. They follow earlier chapters in questioning the efficacy of over-reliance on participatory strategies, and provide support for Soussan's argument in Chapter 4 that success in achieving more sustainable development ultimately depends upon the willingness of national political and economic elites to countenance more than cosmetic changes in economic activities and institutional relationships. Waley and Purvis show how modern techno-centric management approaches have become deeply entrenched in powerful state institutions, making it difficult to achieve acceptance for alternative views. They also consider the erosive effects of the rise of modernism upon traditional social structures. As a consequence, any new attempt to encourage popular participation in river management faces the additional challenge of creating new structures to replace those that have been lost.

The importance of national political will is starkly apparent in Chapter 10 in Atkinson's analysis of recent trends in the Arctic territories of Canada, the USA and Russia, where traditional cultures still thrive. His discussion is highly relevant to proposals for securing more sustainable development through social and political change. It has long been assumed that traditional societies are best suited to managing renewable resources sustainably in environmentally marginal regions since the necessary mechanisms are embedded in their cultures. All too often, unfortunately, the potential for sustainability falls sharply as traditional cultures disintegrate under pressure from modernization. In all three territories the boom-and-bust exploitation of resources by outsiders has had major social and environmental consequences. There are encouraging signs that the situation could improve in northern Canada, following the recent transfer of significant political power from the national government to a new self-governing Inuit territory. If successful, this could provide a model for more sensitive and sustainable 'post-colonial' development strategies in other Arctic territories, particularly Russia. However, Atkinson raises important questions about the practicality of reviving or reinventing indigenous livelihoods based on the sustainable management of renewable resources, and whether this can be balanced against the continued extraction of oil and other non-renewable resources. The feasibility of such efforts is fundamental to complying with the Strong Sustainability Condition. The chapter considers whether political reforms can foster improved standards of environmental management and a more equitable distribution of revenues generated by the oil and gas industries. Potentially, devolution of authority to Arctic populations within existing state structures may prove sufficient to secure significant change. However, there are also calls for a grander vision – that of securing more sustainable development for the Arctic as a whole through greater cooperation between all of its inhabitants, transcending current state boundaries.

The book concludes by returning to the global level with which it began. In Chapter 11, Purvis explores two issues arising from the relationship between climate change and sustainability that, until now, have been characterized by lack of dialogue. First, whether climate change might pose a threat to sustainable development, and whether efforts to achieve more sustainable development through technical and managerial changes in the energy sector could help to counter climate change. Second, what is the nature of links between recent changes in the structure of the energy sector and attempts to frame policy at sub-national, national and international levels to secure effective and equitable action to curb climate change? These themes go to the heart of concerns for both inter-generational and intra-generational equity that feature so prominently in discussions of sustainable development. Purvis shows how the concept of equity itself, far from being a unifying focus for action, can actually become a matter of contest.

In Chapter 12, Grainger combines discourse analysis and international relations theory to tackle political influences on sustainable development at the national and international levels. Like Purvis, he examines the negotiations on climate change and other topics at the UN Conference on Environment and Development in 1992 and thereafter, but takes a different approach. Instead of assessing whether implementing the agreements resulting from these negotiations will lead to more sustainable development, he uses the negotiating stances of different states to draw inferences from their political discourses about the priority they accord sustainable development in national policies, and how they rank the economic, social and environmental dimensions of their development paths. This leads on to a detailed comparison of the discourses of developed and developing countries on sustainable development, elaborating on the brief discussion at the start of this introductory chapter. Grainger concludes that each group of countries ranks the environment the lowest of the three dimensions of development, and favours integrating the economic, social and environmental dimensions of development only when considering the record or prospect of the other group. While developed countries often seek to ignore the contemporary consequences of the unpaid environmental costs which they accumulated during their unsustainable development, developing countries are all too aware of them, probably as they are now being asked to contribute towards 'footing the bill'. The discourses of developed countries are dominated by a 'globalist' perspective that isolates the global environment from their own development, and from that of developing countries, which are expected to meet uniform global environmental and labour standards regardless of their state of development. This raises important issues about the links between the globalization of the world economy and current proposals to modify existing global institutions by adding such standards to world trade rules. Made with the intention of increasing inter-generational equity, such moves could undermine intra-generational equity. Grainger suggests an alternative 'gradualist' strategy, which developing countries should find more realistic and more equitable.

In the final chapter Purvis and Grainger reflect on the implications of the book as a whole, noting how its coverage of both the theoretical and political aspects of sustainable development has drawn attention to the links between them. They contrast the need to think of sustainable development in terms of progress along a long-term path with the common assumption that contemporary participation provides a panacea, and that uncertainty about the meaning of sustainable development can be countered by pragmatic experimentation. This raises questions about the link between spatial scale and the social organization of actions intended to promote more sustainable development. No amount of action at local level can substitute for action at national level, and local action may be ineffective without a facilitating national institutional framework. No government seems to have yet grasped that better technology alone cannot provide a total solution to our problems, and that trade-offs between the economic, social and environmental dimensions of development are inevitable if there is to be real movement toward a more sustainable development path. Indeed, placing emphasis on local participation and techno-centric strategies could be a device to avoid making unpleasant political decisions at national level. Such decisions will be difficult because three-way trade-offs between the economic, social and environmental dimensions of development will be much more complex than the two-way trade-offs customary at the moment. Clashes could also arise between inter-generational equity and intra-generational equity. Current theoretical analyses have also been shown to be inadequate: economic theories have focused on inter-generational equity to the detriment of intra-generational equity, while other theoretical treatments have focused on intra-generational equity to the detriment of inter-generational equity, ignoring the methods used by economists to describe the balance between the economic, social and environmental dimensions with rigour rather than generalities. Thinking geographically should help us to gain a better understanding of the complexity of sustainable development than has so far been possible.

Conclusion

Sustainable development has aroused much criticism for its vagueness and ambiguity. This opening chapter has attempted to provide a foundation for those that follow by showing how the different approaches have developed, and how they can be understood within a wider context. In our view, sustainable development is best understood as consisting of two different sets of discourses: political and theoretical. They are connected with one another in various ways; indeed, the theoretical discourses are a response to the alleged vagueness of the political discourses. However, both are still being perpetuated in parallel, and they continue to expand in scope.

Sustainable development was originally devised as a political ideal in an attempt by conservationists to persuade the governments of developing countries to undertake less environmentally damaging development paths than previously followed by the developed countries. The aim was for future generations to share the same natural riches that the present generation enjoyed – in other words, inter-generational equity. However, the governments of developing countries also sought a 'new' form of development, which consisted of the very development ideal that developed countries had undertaken, and which they felt the latter had promised them, but which they had so far failed to realize. They rejected the new environmental goals adopted by developed countries because they wanted to become richer themselves first in order to become closer to developed countries in their economic status. Thus, they sought greater intra-generational equity. In an attempt to bridge the gap between the two competing ideals, the Brundtland Report offered an alternative ideal of sustainable development. This said that it was possible both to conserve the environment and achieve economic growth to reduce poverty in developing countries, but it did not say how this could be done.

Sustainable development was the compromise notion that brought the developed and developing countries together at the UN Conference on Environment and

Development in 1992. Three particular outcomes of this conference are of importance here. First, it achieved agreement on two international conventions and other documents. Second, it transformed sustainable development into a universal political ideal for all countries, whether developed or developing. However, this did not prevent continuing differences in the interpretation placed on sustainable development by developed and developing countries. Third, it gave rise to a new political process of sustainable development, which is mainly an attempt to improve our quality of life and the sustainability of resource and environmental management, placing emphasis on wider participation in decision-making.

Theoretical discourses of sustainable development sprang mainly from an attempt to add more rigour to the popular one-sentence definition of inter-generational equity offered by the Brundtland Report. Consequently, their primary emphasis has been on defining a new theoretical concept of sustainable development that adds an environmental dimension to the economic and social dimensions of development already recognized in the theoretical concept of economic development. Sustainable development can therefore be pictured as an ideal development path that perfectly balances the economic, social and environmental dimensions of development. The ideal path may never be achieved in practice; but countries can still aim to move their actual development path closer to the ideal path, thereby increasing their degree of sustainability of development.

From this perspective, the ideal of sustainable development held by developing countries is merely equivalent to the accepted concept of economic development. Within the set of theoretical discourses, ecological economics theory focuses exclusively on the environmental dimension of development, while only the Very Weak Condition balances economic and social change against changes in natural resource stocks and environmental quality. Crucially, however, it does not disaggregate economic and social change, and so is not able to encompass economic development as conventionally understood.

For geographers, the present situation is just as perplexing as it is for the general public. They can recognize the existence of two parallel sets of discourses and link the political discourse to the long-running conflict between developed and developing countries concerning the right to free and unfettered development. They also recognize the validity of economic theories, but find them inadequate for dealing with this political dimension. Since many geographers working in this field regard the latter as pre-eminent, they have not closely engaged with economic theories so far. On the other hand, economists have neglected the role of space and failed even to exploit the potential spatial applications of their own theories.

In trying to extend the contribution of geographers to this field, we must begin from the state of the art as seen by ourselves and other geographers. We therefore analyse political discourses against the background of established geographical and political economy theories, while at the same time building on currently accepted economic theories and practical strategies, some of which have potential for expansion to encompass the spatial dimension of sustainable development. Yet we also consider it equally valid to assess the potential to start by re-examining existing geographical theory concerning major aspects of this field, such as urban form and functions. The various geographical perspectives presented in this book are, in our view, a fair cross-section of those currently taken by geographers generally. From whatever existing perspectives readers approach this book, we hope that by the end of it they will think about sustainable development in a different way, placing their current understanding within a larger and more holistic framework.

2

Geography and Sustainable Development

Martin Purvis

Introduction

The current state of the world has led many commentators to conclude that the unequal priority given to economic growth, social welfare and the health of the environment renders established development patterns unsustainable. The alternative ideal of sustainable development – that which 'meets the needs of the present without compromising the ability of future generations to meet their own needs' (WCED, 1987) – has, therefore attracted increasing support. But once we look beyond such broad definitions, much remains elusive and contested about sustainable development. As noted in Chapter 1, the scope of existing economic theory is limited, and few others have taken up the challenge of establishing a sound theoretical foundation for future action. It is, of course, also true that the label of sustainable development is applied to an increasing number of practical measures. However, the sheer number and diversity of such initiatives, and the mixture of motives that inspire them, only adds to the ambiguity which surrounds the concept. There is still, therefore, much work to be done if sustainable development is to be established as a credible blueprint for the 21st century.

The chapter begins by comparing geography's long-standing interest in both society and nature, and the links that unite them, with the new agenda of sustainable development. This is followed by a brief review of the attention given to sustainable development in the geographical literature, and to the themes of place and space in discussions of sustainable development. The chapter then moves on to consider the potential for applying geographical skills in planning for more sustainable develop-ment. Arguably more important, however, is a greater geographical contribution to critical reviews of current thinking about sustainable development, both in practice and in theory.

A Case for Geography

Sustainable development in disciplinary perspective

The concept of sustainable development is innovative and distinctive in pointing to the need for simultaneous attention to maintaining economic growth, meeting social needs and conserving environmental quality. This broad and challenging agenda requires that the exploration of sustainable development as theory and practice is grounded in a profound understanding of social, economic and environmental systems. It will necessarily draw upon the input and insights of a wide range of academics, and also of many others, including politicians, planners, development workers, business managers, farmers and consumers. The emphasis placed here on thinking geographically should not, therefore, be misinterpreted. What follows is not a claim of perfect knowledge or a bid for intellectual hegemony. Rather, our case is that geography can make a valuable and distinctive contribution to wider debates about sustainable development.

Although geography – like sustainable development – is often seen as resisting unambiguous definition, three themes may be taken to constitute its core. The first is the study of relationships between humanity and the environment. The second is the exploration of the distinct and differing characters of particular places. And, thirdly, geography is concerned with the documentation and analysis of the spatial patterning of phenomena across the surface of the Earth. The variety of studies embraced by these themes, and the potential for tension between different approaches, have sometimes been regarded as marks of disciplinary weakness. Taken together, however, the different facets of geographical study have the power to advance our understanding of the world in important and distinctive ways (see Massey, 2001). In part, this reflects geography's transcendence of the conventional intellectual divide between the social and natural sciences. An important element of geography's purpose is to explore the ways in which specific environmental contexts influence human society, and the impact of human actions on the form of the landscape, environmental quality and biodiversity. It follows that geography does not define itself as the exclusive study of a single category of phenomena, but as a discipline concerned with connections, associations and distributions. Thinking geographically can, therefore, encourage a breadth of vision and capacity for synthesis that seem particularly appropriate to the study of sustainable development (on the need for this holistic perspective see Belsky, 2002; Liverman, 1999; Redclift, 1998). More than this, however, there are clear echoes in the contemporary agenda of sustainable development of long-standing geographical concerns with documenting and improving the state of the world.

Development and environmental change

Until recently, mainstream economic theory has exhibited relatively little interest in the environment, or natural capital. By comparison, geographers have frequently – if not consistently – advanced perspectives more consistent with current thinking about sustainable development. Attention to the environmental impacts of human actions has led to an understanding of development as a process of transformation that is environmental as well as socio-economic (Simmons, 1996). More specifically, geographers have made a considerable contribution to documenting the environmental consequences of human population growth, the areal extension and intensification of agriculture, urbanization and industrial development (see, for example, two classic collections of essays from Thomas, 1956, and Turner et al, 1990). Environmental change can be a positive process, involving the 'taming' or 'improvement' of nature in order to yield greater rewards for humanity. Yet these studies also reveal the price invariably paid in terms such as air and water pollution, biodiversity loss, soil erosion and decline in landscape quality.

It is clear, moreover, that human impacts on environmental quality and the availability of resource capital may be on such a scale that they undermine not only current economic prosperity and social well-being, but also prospects for continued future development. Geographical research has thus presented important evidence pointing to the current unsustainability of human activity (Sneddon, 2000). In so doing, it has powerfully reinforced arguments for the necessity of a new balance between economic, social and environmental goals.

Place and space

Geographical synthesis is most distinctive when expressed as the study of place, aiming to describe and explain the unique character of specific portions of the Earth's surface (Agnew and Duncan, 1989; Hart, 1982). Often, too, geographers have been concerned with understanding the ways in which communities and individuals perceive the places in which they live, the importance attached to being 'in place' and the emotional and symbolic qualities attributed to particular sites (Gold and Burgess, 1982; Tuan, 1990). Such work has the potential to create a rich and insightful record of geographical difference. More than this, it encourages us to consider how such differences influence, and are influenced by, the course of human development.

The comparative study of place – or of specific attributes of particular places – also inspires an alternative construction of geographical research as the study of the spatial distribution of phenomena. At its most basic, this may be seen as an exercise in cataloguing the various dimensions of natural capital and in recording the accumulation of man-made capital, typically as embodied in the creation of urban and industrial regions, or as investment in the infrastructure of transportation, education and healthcare. The resultant evidence of difference has often been expressed through cartographic display (Dorling and Fairbairn, 1997; Kraak and Ormeling, 1996). This has proved to be a particularly effective way of communicating information about the state of the world, both to academic audiences and to publics, politicians and other decision-makers (see, for example, Dorling, 1995; Middleton and Thomas, 1997). Recent technological developments in remote sensing, geographical information systems (GIS) and computer mapping have further enhanced the potential of this visual medium (Wood, 1999). Together they give us a real and immediate – although not unproblematically 'truthful' (Wood, 1993) – sense of environmental, social and economic conditions at every scale from the local to the global, often reinforcing the case for a new and more sustainable form of development.

However, geography as a spatial science aims to go beyond description to offer an analytical understanding of the form and functioning of human and physical systems. Studies of spatial coincidence and correlation in the patterning of different phenomena have the potential to enhance our knowledge of the scale and causes of unsustainability. At its simplest, spatial association may provide an indication of causal links between particular human activities and unsustainable outcomes. In addition, previous studies have revealed the extent to which specific problems impact in multiple and mutually reinforcing ways upon particular places (Pacione, 1999b). Too often, economic insecurities caused by unsustainable livelihoods are associated with, and exacerbated by, low standards of social welfare and environmental quality. Such observed associations raise important questions not just about the incidence of unsustainability, but also about the underlying causes that link its different dimensions.

Spatial inequalities

Attention to geographical difference thus reflects an explicit concern about the uneven fashion in which capital is distributed and redistributed. It follows that interest in the intermeshing effects of economic, social and environmental changes is accompanied by attention to the ways in which they reshape or reinforce patterns of spatial inequality. Moreover, concerns about the negative consequences of economic activity are reinforced by evidence of the uneven spatial distribution of its social and environmental costs. Geographical studies have shown that there is often an underlying logic to this maldistribution that reflects the patterning of other characteristics – including income, class, gender and race – with the result that the greatest costs are borne disproportionately by the poorest and least powerful people and places (Knox and Pinch, 2000). These same communities may also be denied many of the benefits of economic growth, thus perpetuating their disadvantage and vulnerability. In such circumstances, documentation of inequality cannot be solely an end in itself. It is potentially the starting point for geographical work that seeks actively to promote a new ethos of social and environmental justice (Bunge, 1971; Harvey, 1973; Heiman, 1996; Smith, 1994).

Studies of spatial inequality have thus encouraged attempts to develop a more sophisticated understanding of the geographical form of social and economic systems, and of socio-economic processes as an influence upon the production and reproduction of space. Particular attention has been paid to the ordering of space under capitalism, leading to a recognition that spatial inequality – often characterized as uneven development – is an integral feature of capitalist development (Smith, 1990). Such attempts to understand the causes of social and spatial inequality highlight the extent to which local conditions are shaped by the wider interplay of economic and political forces at a national and international level. It follows that measures to secure positive change must often be directed towards points in time and space that are far removed from the most obvious symptoms of social injustice and environmental stress. Crucially, too, the argument that development in one region is necessarily predicated on underdevelopment elsewhere has profound implications for aspirations to secure greater intra-generational and inter-generational equity. It helps to explain why change is often so controversial and contested, which is a reality that is not always confronted in current economic theories of sustainable development.

Thinking geographically

Geography has a long record of studying both the environmental impacts and sustainability of human activity, and the equity with which the costs and benefits of development are distributed. In this sense, geographical attention to what is now termed sustainable development long predates discussions inspired by the 1987

Brundtland Report or the ensuing 1992 UN Conference on Environment and Development (UNCED) in Rio de Janeiro. Geography's record of applied work – in fields ranging from environmental management to access to welfare services – is also consistent with the desire to improve both the human condition and the health of the environment that motivates the study of sustainable development (for different perspectives on applied geography, see Burton and Kates, 1965; Pacione, 1999a; Peet, 1977; Stamp, 1963) Moreover, thinking geographically – which involves attention to the needs and circumstances of particular communities; to the spatial patterning of human activity; to the relationships that connect the human and environmental spheres; and to the links between individual localities and wider systems – has the potential to enhance and extend existing attempts to understand the theory and practice of sustainable development. In a context that demands a broad-based and integrative understanding, geography's intellectual diversity and capacity for synthesis constitute genuine strengths. Geography does not have answers for all of the questions posed by sustainable development; but, arguably, it has the right attitude to advance knowledge in this field. The chapter now turns, therefore, to consider the attempts already made to foster explicit engagement between geography and sustainable development.

Engaging with Sustainable Development

Putting sustainable development on the geographical agenda

Development – what it means, how it can best be achieved and what its consequences are – has always ranked high amongst geography's concerns (for recent overviews see Crush, 1995a; Dicken, 2003; Knox and Agnew, 1998; Potter et al, 1999; Power, 2003). The advent of the concept of sustainable development potentially marks a new phase in this record of engagement. Initial enthusiasm is evident in commentaries such as Wilbanks (1994), which argues that closer links between geography and sustainable development would be beneficial, both in increasing understanding of sustainability and in giving geography a renewed disciplinary coherence and sense of purpose. Indeed, there are echoes here of earlier calls for geography to champion a more explicit ethic of social and environmental justice (see, for example, Kates, 1987; Smith, 1977; Stoddard, 1987).

During the 1990s, sustainable development gained a place in geography's disciplinary lexicon (McManus, 2000). Its study is now part of the geography syllabus in UK schools (Grimwade et al, 2000) and the concept is explored in general textbooks aimed at an undergraduate audience (for example, Cloke et al, 1999; Daniels et al, 2001; Johnston et al, 2002). Geographers have also produced accessible accounts that review evolving ideas about sustainable development, often paying particular attention to its attempted translation into practice (Adams, 2001; Elliott, 1999; Middleton et al, 1993). These broad-ranging studies are complemented by treatments of sustainable development in particular geographical contexts, both generic and specific (Bowler et al, 2002; Haughton and Hunter, 1994; Jussila et al, 2001). In turn, debates about sustainable development and efforts to create composite indices of sustainability have begun to influence geographical studies of spatial differentiation (for example, Straussfogel,

1997). Such work is novel in attempting the integrated assessment of spatial variation in the state of the environment, individual welfare and the strength of social cohesion, alongside more conventional economic measures of development.

The growing geographical literature on sustainable development performs an important educational role: first, in raising awareness of the current unsustainability of economic and social systems worldwide and, second, in fostering debate about the need for change. If there is to be significant progress towards greater sustainability those currently in education – who will become tomorrow's consumers, workers, employers, voters and politicians – must make more informed decisions about the balance to be struck between aspirations for economic growth, social progress and environmental conservation. However, the potential also exists for geography to play a more explicit role in refining current understanding of the concept of sustainable development and its practical application. Indications that proposals for securing greater sustainability in practice often intersect with geography's defining interests in place, space and the spatial patterning and scale of activity provide some obvious points of departure.

Spatial form and scale

There are good reasons for thinking that the sustainability of development is, in part, related to its spatial form. It has long been evident, for example, that the concentration of population and economic activity in urban centres can create particular social and environmental stresses. Equally, it is hardly novel to argue that attention to the location and spatial design of development can reduce associated costs – both internal and external – and assist the delivery of intended benefits. It is unsurprising, therefore, that spatial form has been identified as a key to creating greater sustainability in a variety of contexts, including the urban. This is evident in calls for the development of compact cities, with a greater local diversity of population and land use than is currently the case (see Chapter 6). It is claimed that such changes allow urban economic functions to be maintained, while simultaneously promoting resource efficiency, social cohesion and improved access to essential facilities. Spatial planning is thus viewed as a tool to secure both intra-generational and inter-generational equity. The intent is to ensure that today's urban residents enjoy growing prosperity and a higher quality of life, while rural environments are protected from the destructive effects of urban sprawl. But more than this, economic growth, urban renewal and environmental conservation constitute a positive inheritance for subsequent generations (Murdoch, 2000).

Some commentators argue for change in the spatial form of development to be taken further, reshaping not just the internal plan and character of urban and regional systems, but also the relationships between them. At its most radical, this represents a call for the wholesale rescaling of human activity. Advocates of bio-regionalism, or for a 'turn to the local', argue that individual territories must develop a greater degree of self-sufficiency, basing their development primarily on the sustainable use of resources immediately available at a local or regional level (Mander and Goldsmith, 2001; Sale, 1985). Global sustainability would thus be achieved through a series of balances struck at the scale of individual states, regions and urban centres. A greater degree of dependency upon local resources would, it is claimed, encourage better long-term management of natural, human and man-made capital. Further environmental gains would follow from a reduction in the energy use and pollution currently associated with the international transportation of goods and raw materials. At the same time, greater political autonomy at a local or regional level is presented as an effective means of securing greater popular participation in decision-making, thus creating a guarantee of social justice.

Place and locality

The thinking behind calls for the rescaling of activity finds an echo in other arguments for the importance of the local arena to the pursuit of sustainable development. Local initiative has, for example, been widely identified as a key means to advance the vision outlined in the Agenda 21 document produced by the United Nations Conference on Environment and Development (UNCED) (see Chapter 6). The hope is that when individual communities take a leading role in planning for more sustainable development, this will result in greater stress on projects that meet local people's expressed needs, that are consistent with existing social and cultural mores, and that make effective and sustainable use of indigenous resources. Involving people themselves in securing positive change at the local level is also seen as a powerful means of overcoming the reluctance, or inability, of national governments and international agencies to take responsibility for promoting more wide-ranging reforms.

There are echoes here of broader dissatisfaction with the generic policies generated by conventional development planning, which have too often been applied with insufficient consideration for the needs and circumstances of particular people and places (Crush, 1995b). Faith in grand plans born of professional 'expertise' has thus given way to attempts to promote more locally appropriate development in a wide variety of different contexts (see, for example, Ferris et al, 2000; Ghai and Vivian, 1992; Wing et al, 1996). In principle, at least, greater attention in development planning is given to dialogue between a broad range of interested parties, including publics, businesses, planning professionals, governments and development agencies. Recent decades have, therefore, seen a growing emphasis on participation and the strengthening of local democracy as an essential starting point for better development. Often the hope is that mutual confidence gained in one sphere will encourage the extension of cooperation and participation to new activities. Equally, the creation of initial 'islands' of sustainability is presented as a means of inspiring equivalent actions elsewhere (Wallner et al, 1996).

The aspiration to foster development that is locally appropriate and sustainable in the long term highlights a need to know more about the economic, social and environmental circumstances of particular places and people. This is one of the chief tasks that geography has traditionally set itself, and an aspect of geographical study that merits renewed attention. Geographers themselves have much to learn from arguments about appropriate and sustainable development, with their injunctions to accord full respect to indigenous knowledges and to the accounts that local people offer of their own circumstances and aspirations. In turn, geography, as a discipline of synthesis, offers a model for the study of place that goes beyond the disaggregated documentation of specific local attributes. This is important: the pursuit of sustainable development creates a new demand for more holistic and integrated understanding of the character and circumstances of particular places. It requires that we appreciate the ways in which these are shaped and reshaped through the interaction of economic, social, cultural, political and environmental forces. No single aspect of the character of a place can be fully understood in isolation from this broader context.

Geography and the Pursuit of More Sustainable Development

On the one hand, these initial reflections on the importance of place and space in planning for sustainable development confirm the potential for greater application of geographical skills and understanding to the pursuit of progressive change. Yet adherence to the agenda of sustainable development as currently defined should not be unthinking. Geography also has a part to play in scrutinising existing ideas and proposals. Indeed, one of the most valuable services that a critical observer can perform is to highlight flaws and limitations in the diagnosis of a problem and the solutions offered in response. Ultimately, therefore, geography's most important role may be to help confirm the need for more sophisticated conceptions of sustainable development – in theory and in practice – and to begin to show how these might be achieved.

Applying geographical skills

Some of the ways in which geography could contribute to promoting more sustainable development in practice have already been alluded to above. Skills in spatial analysis might, for example, be applied to the search for greater resource efficiency. This would include attention to specific measures, such as the planning of new infrastructure for recycling, allowing facilities to be accessed with least financial cost and transport demand. More generally, such analysis could be refined and extended so that it helps to inform the design of geographies of development that are not simply efficient in narrowly economic terms, but which create an optimum balance across a broad range of economic, social and environmental costs and benefits (see Cowell and Owens, 1998; Owens and Cowell, 2001 for the discussion of particular cases). Geographical expertise in urban and regional modelling could also find new applications in the context of sustainable development (see Chapter 5). Modelling offers a means of gaining a more sophisticated understanding of the outcomes of economic and demographic growth, and the complex spatial transfers of costs and benefits between and within particular territories. The ability to predict future conditions not only allows an assessment of the sustainability – or otherwise – of development, but also enables an evaluation of the likely outcomes of a range of corrective policies. This should assist in identifying the most effective sustainability strategies.

The use of such techniques need not, moreover, perpetuate a model of decision-making driven entirely by external or governmental expertise. Work on information technology and, specifically, on the development and application of GIS now places growing stress on their use as a means of encouraging broadly based participation in decision-making about development (Craig et al, 2002). GIS allow the presentation and dissemination of information in a visual format that can be widely comprehended. This creates a new facility for individuals, community groups and other interested parties to assess the potential outcome of alternative development proposals, enabling them to take a more active and informed role in subsequent decision-making. Still more important are initiatives intended to put GIS and other information technologies in the hands of local populations themselves (for example, Jordan, 2002; Parker and Pascual, 2002). Such projects often aim to empower people who have hitherto been marginalized, enabling them not simply to respond to development policies created by others, but to set out their own agenda. This form of technology transfer may be of particular value if it enables local people to present a case in a format and with an implied authority that directly challenges the prescriptions of government, business, international non-governmental organizations (NGOs) and other outside interests.

A more questioning approach

The potential for refinement of existing techniques for planning more sustainable development should not, however, distract attention away from the need for critical scrutiny. Ideas about the re-scaling or re-siting of development cannot be regarded as a total solution to current unsustainability. It is vital, therefore, to question what is practical, what is effective and what is adequate as a prescription for more sustainable development.

Prime candidates for such interrogation are arguments that present the locality as an important arena for effective decision-making and action to foster more sustainable development. There is a risk that such arguments overstate the extent to which individual communities can improve their own situation. In part, this reflects profound inequalities in the spatial and socio-economic distribution of the various fractions of capital, which impose multiple deprivation upon the poorest communities. Moreover, the implication that local populations are characterized by shared values, and a willingness to work together equitably and cooperatively in pursuit of common goals, is not always borne out in reality. Geographical studies of place also confirm the extent to which the condition and character of specific localities reflect their interaction with external agencies and larger systems. These interconnections and the unequal relationships between places that they both create and embody are at the heart of the current experience of uneven development, and associated injustice in the distribution of the costs and benefits of economic activity. This recognition is vital for it clearly implies that the effective pursuit of more sustainable development by and for specific places will involve more than local reforms. Substantial progress will often require major changes in the constitution and distribution of power within national and international systems to redefine the terms upon which an individual locality participates in these larger entities. All of this reinforces the need to know more about the internal inequalities and power relations that characterize particular populations, and the local influence of generally operating economic and political forces (Mohan and Stokke, 2000).

Attempts to rethink planning policies so that specific developments are re-sited in the name of sustainable development also merit critical scrutiny. The notion of a locational fix is potentially dangerous if it encourages a presumption in favour of development. Spatial planning – which is often allied with the use of other techno-fixes such as pollution reduction and site landscaping – may give credence to the idea that there need be no curbs on development; that everything is possible provided that it is properly planned and correctly located. In practice, technical approaches invariably address only specific aspects of unsustainability. For example, the siting of additional industrial development in districts where natural capital is already degraded may appear justified as a means of minimizing damage to surviving areas of high environmental quality. Yet this apparent defence of inter-generational equity may exacerbate intra-generational inequality if it heaps further costs on places and populations whose existing levels of social and environmental welfare are low.

Arguments that financial compensation, social investment or environmental improvements can fully offset such differentials are also disingenuous. In practice, any deal is more likely to reflect the relative economic and political power of the interests involved rather than the full external costs of development. In truth, the latter are often beyond calculation and compensation. This points to a wider tension between abstract conceptions of capital as an input into the development process and other more complex interpretations of the value of environmental and social systems. The former viewpoint suggests the potential for maintaining the total value of capital through substitution, either between its different fractions or between capital located at different points in space. Yet place-based studies make clear that particular environments perform specific ecological functions that cannot be fully replicated through investment in the enhancement or environmental restoration of sites elsewhere. Equally, particular places are valued by their inhabitants in emotional and psychological terms that have no material equivalent and permit no substitute (Cowell, 1997; Robertson, 2000).

An emphasis on limited fixes is more generally a feature of readings of sustainable development advanced by business and other sympathetic interests – including many national governments – which equate the concept with eco-efficiency, thus marginalizing its social dimensions. The limitations of such approaches have already been highlighted in the geographical literature (see, for example, Bridge and McManus, 2000; Cloke et al, 1996; Eden, 1994; McAfee, 1999). In response we must remind ourselves that sustainable development represents a search for social equity as well as eco-efficiency; that intra-generational equity merits as much attention and concern as inter-generational equity; and that sustainable development requires change in both the developed and developing world. From this viewpoint we are again confronted by a sense of the breadth of perspective and understanding demanded by the pursuit of sustainable development. More specifically, we need to appreciate the extent and complexity of the connections that shape our terrestrial existence: between economic, social, political, cultural and environmental systems; between actions and events at particular times and places; and between activity and decision-making at different levels of the spatial hierarchy. By making these connections – something we have argued is inherent in a geographical approach – we can advance beyond a superficial concern with the symptoms of unsustainable development to engage with its causes.

Looking Deeper

Linkages and causes

The pursuit of sustainable development reinforces the importance of understanding the linkages between different dimensions of injustice and deprivation. There are powerful arguments that poverty and social injustice are products of a lack of access to all forms of capital, but also, in turn, causes of continuing environmental degradation. As a result of their economic insecurity, the most marginalized and exploited populations may be forced into a position of environmental exploitation. In a situation where there is no alternative, short-term survival comes to depend upon the unsustainable use of the local environment to extract an immediate surplus.

Such arguments, which engage with the causes as well as the symptoms of unsustainability, are particularly associated with work cast within a framework of political ecology (Bryant, 1992; 1998). This seeks a new dialogue between ecological studies of human society and (often Marxist-inspired) political economy. The potential of such analysis was well demonstrated in two seminal studies of land degradation in the developing world (Blaikie, 1985; Blaikie and Brookfield, 1987). These challenged accepted thinking, which attributed problems such as soil erosion to a combination of overpopulation and the ignorance, or indifference, of peasant farmers. Instead, erosion is argued to be a product of fundamental economic and political inequalities at the local, national and global levels, which concentrate land ownership in the hands of a small elite. This perspective confirms the limitations of technical solutions that, at best, treat the symptoms of unsustainability and injustice. Attention to sustainable agricultural development should, therefore, strengthen perceptions of the need for profound change, involving land reform at a domestic level and a critical review of the international trading system (see Chapter 8).

Thinking in this way about the larger causes of local unsustainability highlights wider concerns about the lack of compatibility between the constitution of the current world economy and the ideal of sustainability. Pursuit of more sustainable development may, therefore, confer added significance on studies that explore and explain the uneven and unstable geographical form of capitalism. As work on the political ecology of soil erosion demonstrates, it is not simply the case that current poverty and lack of potential for future development are the product of an absolute lack of capital (Yapa, 1996). Often they reflect socio-economic and political inequalities that enable some groups and individuals to claim access to resources at the expense of others. The wealth of particular people and places is, therefore, understood to be predicated on the deprivation of others (Frank, 1969; Smith, 1990). This presents a formidable barrier to both intra-generational and inter-generational equity.

The differential mobility of different fractions of capital raises further questions about the apparent tensions between the preservation of capitalism as an economic system and the wider agenda of sustainable development. In theory, at least, the growing mobility of financial capital in the contemporary world will exacerbate a tendency to produce economic activity that exploits and degrades particular environments and communities. This is because mobility confers the freedom to withdraw in search of new opportunities elsewhere, thus avoiding negative feedback that might choke off further economic growth, as well as responsibility for the long-term well-being of a population and its environment (see Chapter 7).

Such arguments, voiced particularly by the critics of multinational business, have echoes of attempts to produce a deeper theoretical understanding of the space economy, drawing on Marxist theories of growth under capitalism. The historical record of capitalist expansionism and the progressive penetration of new territories led Harvey (1975; 1982) to argue that the spatial switching of capital has been fundamental to the survival of an inherently unstable economic system. This 'spatial fix' is seen not so much as a device to evade external costs, but as a means to resolve crises caused by the inevitable over-accumulation of capital within established regional economies. The exploitation of new territories – as markets, as sources of labour and materials and as investment opportunities – is driven by the need to find profitable uses for otherwise surplus capital.

Harvey's analysis is not, of course, couched in the terminology of subsequent debates about sustainability. But his work indicates that the tensions inherent within capitalism have often been resolved in ways that are incompatible with sustainable development. The importance accorded to maintaining economic growth has led to a willingness to sacrifice both human welfare and environmental quality. More specifically, capitalism has shown itself ready to deal inequitably with particular places in an attempt to maintain the integrity of the system as a whole. This treatment is not confined to the expanding periphery of the capitalist world economy. Regions within the original core may be abandoned – sometimes regardless of the legacy of unemployment, social decay and environmental degradation – if they are no longer deemed capable of delivering a sufficiently profitable return on investment. Viewed in this way, the existing structures of capitalism seem likely to prevent any significant progress towards more sustainable development (compare with O'Connor, 1994).

The attempt to engage theoretically with the causes of unsustainability need not, however, lead to a wholly pessimistic conclusion. This is evident in the work of Drummond and Marsden (1999), who adopt a perspective informed by regulation theory. The latter – which has gained widespread currency in economic geography since the mid 1980s – focuses on the ability of capitalism to establish enduring regimes of accumulation despite its internal tensions and inherent tendency to crisis. Capitalism's stability is argued to be founded on the establishment of historically and geographically specific modes of regulation. These are evident as systems of conscious social management – embodied in the active creation of institutional forms, typically at the level of the state, but differentially affecting particular regions and economic sectors – which mediate contradictions in the behaviour of competing individuals, groups and social classes to maintain established accumulation regimes. Regulation is not, however, seen as a total solution to the instability of capitalism. Corrective regulatory mechanisms can themselves break down in the face of both internal and external crises. During the ensuing instability, new regulatory regimes are forged. But the consequences of regulatory failure are potentially dramatic, involving major changes in systems of production and consumption; in technologies and the organization of labour; in the use of natural capital; in cultural norms; and in geographies of economic activity.

Historically, the primary objective of regulation has been to preserve the value of financial investments, plant and machinery and institutional networks. Hence, crisis resolution has often involved the devaluation and increasing exploitation of human and natural capital. However, Drummond and Marsden (1999) argue – as does Gibbs (1996; 2002) – that regulatory regimes are not the inevitable enemy of sustainable development. Indeed, it is possible to envisage the construction of alternative regimes that maintain economic development without sacrificing human and natural capital. This requires that the existing economic objectives of regulation be qualified by more clearly stated social and environmental objectives.

Potentially, therefore, the barriers to sustainability evident in the contemporary world economy can be overcome; but this will require intervention at the deep level of regulation. At moments of crisis when capitalism is unusually malleable, there may be opportunities to reshape regulation to embrace defence of the environment; to reform labour rights; to reallocate access to natural capital; to rethink the logic of systems based on mass production and consumption; to change systems of pricing, taxation and subsidy; and to define new terms of trade. This is not, however, to claim that radical change in the prevailing orthodoxy of regulation will be uncontested. Drummond and Marsden (1999) themselves question whether any fundamental challenge to current neo-liberalism and related modes of social regulation can be mounted in practice. Their work is important, nevertheless, in influencing how we should think about the location, scale and potential of action to promote more sustainable development.

Scales of action

Clearly, the existence of powerful theoretical arguments for looking beyond the immediate local arena in any search for the causes of unsustainable development has important implications for the framing of corrective action. As yet, however, Drummond and Marsden (1999) remain unusual in outlining any means to secure fundamental change in practice. As with earlier work on the political ecology of environmental degradation, the task remains of going beyond initial diagnosis to show how economic and political barriers to any deep-laid transformation may be overcome. Peet and Watts (1996) argue that abuse of the environment might become a focus of popular mobilization, creating a 'liberation ecology' that would inspire the world's poor to claim economic and political rights hitherto denied them. The potential for more radical and assertive mass action could be increased by greater investment in education and international efforts to promote and protect effective and representative democratic institutions at every level of the political hierarchy. Perhaps, too, new information technologies, often seen as the means by which capitalist interests control increasingly far-flung operations, could become a means of coordinating resistance. Opportunities for building virtual communities of dissent may begin to erode the weakness, born of geographical separation, that has previously characterized many localized protests (Herod, 1998).

Such arguments about the importance of information and communications, and educational and political reform, have previously been highlighted in some of the more ambitious prescriptions for sustainable development (BBC, 2000). But the identification of these important enabling forces raises further questions about how, in practice, they can be promoted in ways that achieve more than localized or tokenistic change. The central question remains: why should existing powerful interests, which derive immediate advantage from current conditions of unsustainability and inequity, permit change that will imperil their own privileged position?

Such questions take us far beyond any specifically geographical perspective on sustainable development and point, once again, to the need for significant change in the constitution of contemporary economic, social and political systems at both national and international levels. They do, however, reinforce the case made earlier for the importance of geographical contributions to education, and to the dissemination of both information and information technologies. It is vital that initiatives in these fields look beyond immediate and local goals to consider how they may assist in generating a momentum for wider societal change in the longer term.

Thinking in this way about the potential for connections between initiatives at different levels of the social and spatial hierarchy suggests a more specific focus that could and should be accorded greater geographical attention. As has been noted, previous discussion of sustainable development frequently highlights projects at particular levels of action, often very localized. There is a danger that this becomes translated into a general prescription for the 'correct' level at which to promote more sustainable development, and encourages a tendency to focus on particular places and problems in isolation. This disaggregation could be countered by greater geographical attention to the role of spatial scale and spatial connections in conceptualizing and promoting sustainable development. Current debates about the wider rescaling of political life (Held and McGrew, 2000; Pierson, 1996), involving both the growing role of supranational authorities, such as the European Union, and the devolution of powers to sub-state territories, offer a starting point for a more sophisticated discussion of spatial frameworks for sustainability planning. Going beyond present assertions about the rescaling of activity, such work would explore the extent to which the distribution of authority and capacity between local, regional, national and international levels could and should be redefined to promote effective and coordinated support for more sustainable development.

It is also important to show that specific dimensions of sustainability must be addressed simultaneously within different arenas and at different levels of the spatial hierarchy. Measures to combat climate change, for example, require international coordination if they are to be efficient and equitable. But international agreement to the principle of action means little without initiative at other levels, including changes in national energy policies, planning reforms by local and regional governments, and acceptance of responsibility for managing energy consumption by individual households and businesses (see Chapter 11). It is vital to recognize these connections and the consequent potential for initiative at one level to be frustrated by inertia or ill-considered actions elsewhere. Attention to coordination, communication and the building of mutual confidence between actors and authorities in different places and at different levels of the spatial hierarchy must, therefore, be a key focus in planning for more sustainable development.

Theory, space and scale

Consideration of particular places and levels, and the relationships between them, is not only relevant to practical policy; it should also prompt us to review theoretical conceptions of sustainable development. Abstract economic formulations of sustainable development, as a balance between the accumulation and depletion of capital, are not grounded in place and make no reference to space or to spatial scale. As Grainger explores in Chapter 3, this omission is potentially very important. The ultimate aim of sustainable development may be to establish a balance between capital accumulation and depletion at the global level. At the same time, however, the goal of intra-generational equity requires that we consider the impact on particular people and places of measures intended to promote a global balance. The concept of sustainable development as the achievement of balance must, therefore, be qualified by the injunction to pursue this end in ways that challenge, rather than reinforce, existing exploitative relationships between places. This might be expressed as an extension of the well-known Brundtland formula: development is sustainable where it is conducted in a fashion that enables a population living within a particular territory to meet its immediate needs and secure the inheritance of future generations, without compromising the ability of other populations elsewhere to meet comparable present and future needs.

Such thinking has inspired the calls for greater self-sufficiency noted earlier. An alternative approach is to accept the value and necessity of interaction and exchange between places but to change its character. This would require, amongst other initiatives, moves to reform the terms of trade and the prices paid for the transfer of goods and resources in order to take full account of the social and environmental costs involved. Currently, the environmental services performed for one place by another, or, indeed, for the world as a whole, are often barely acknowledged. In future, it is important that they are properly valued and paid for. Such charges would not only be an incentive to pollution prevention and waste minimization; they would also be an important step towards a more equitable distribution of the costs and benefits of development. Such initiatives might, for example, change the ways in which conservation policies are viewed, turning them from a block on conventional development to an alternative means of generating income to invest in human and man-made capital.

Enthusiasm for such an outcome should, however, be qualified by attention to its practicality and desirability. It is far from clear how equity in allocating the costs and benefits of development could be defined and secured in practice. Any ideal of progress based on acknowledgement of shared responsibility for sustainable development also seems vulnerable to the desire of particular places and populations to pursue their own development path free from external considerations and constraints. Some measure of coordination is undoubtedly necessary to strike a balance between freedom and responsibility. State governments have usually discharged this role as a regulator and arbiter at a national level. In recent decades, however, a growing sense of the global scale of economic activity and environmental change has inspired efforts to strengthen institutional structures at an international level. However, such institutional arenas can become a focus of conflict, rather than of cooperation, as developed and developing countries attempt to advance contrasting readings of sustainable development (see Chapter 12). Indeed, the interpretation of fundamental concepts, not least equity itself, is potentially contentious (see Chapter 11). In a context where the distribution of economic and political power remains fundamentally uneven, we may continue to see constructions of the 'common good' that prioritize the interests of established elites.

Conclusion

This chapter has sought to demonstrate the affinities between the concerns of sustainable development and established geographical interests in the economy, social and environmental justice, and relationships between human society and the natural world. The consequent potential for dialogue will be explored further in subsequent chapters that revisit long-standing geographical concerns with themes such as environmental change, agriculture, urban form and function, and environmental management. In every case we show that it is logical and revealing to think holistically, linking environmental, economic, social and political considerations. An ability to challenge the conventional divide between the study of human and natural systems is vital, not least because contested readings of the relationship between society and nature are at the heart of debate concerning specific aspects of sustainable development. Nowhere is this more evident than in the very different conceptions of sustainable agriculture discussed in Chapter 8. For some, true sustainability can only be achieved through respect for the integrity of the natural world; others believe that an unprecedented human manipulation of nature through biotechnology is the best guarantor of future prosperity and security. The way in which such debate unfolds in the coming years seems likely to have profound implications, not just for sustainable development per se, but also for the wider characterization of the social and the natural.

This chapter has also made the case that geography's distinctive preoccupation with place and space adds a new dimension to the definition and pursuit of sustainable development. Existing theoretical treatments of sustainable development are limited by their lack of grounding in any sense of spatial context. Yet it is important to ask questions about the spatial scale at which any balance between the accumulation and degradation of capital is to be conceived. Moreover, we cannot ignore spatial inequalities in the distribution of capital, and in the power to appropriate and employ it, as important influences upon intra-generational and inter-generational equity.

We must also consider the implications of the division of continuous physical space into a series of discrete territorial units: particularly, but not only, at the level of the state. Each territory is differentiated not just by location, but often also by characteristic regimes of accumulation, regulatory structures, political institutions, cultural and social values, histories and environments. Such variation makes it inevitable that there will be debate between and within these territories about the theoretical conception and the practical execution of sustainable development. Potentially, space itself allows the accommodation of much of this need and desire for difference between places. Yet, in reality, no single territory functions in isolation. States, regions and localities are linked by flows of resources, goods, waste and pollution, capital, people, ideas and information. Ultimately, too, all share a common dependence upon the global resource of Critical Natural Capital (see p.15). It follows that any projects and proposals intended to deliver more sustainable development within a particular territory will affect, and be affected by, events and decisions elsewhere. Spatial disaggregation of the global space is accompanied by spatial interconnection, with the result that trade-offs required to secure more sustainable development will have a geographical, as well as a sectoral, dimension.

The implications of thinking geographically about sustainable development are so profound that it is surprising that the literature in this field is not more substantial. It is striking how reluctant geographers themselves have been to explore and extend existing economic theories of sustainable development to secure a more refined understanding of the implications of spatial scale and interconnections. But, as has already been suggested in Chapter 1, the holistic perspective that geographers espouse also highlights other absences in existing theory, especially a lack of attention to the social dimension of sustainable development.

This imbalance in the theoretical conception of sustainable development is echoed in another peculiarity of geography's attention to the concept. Although a broad range of geographical work, both physical and human, has added substantially to our understanding of the present condition of unsustainability, explicit attention to the alternative of sustainable development has been much more restricted. To date, discussion has been dominated by those whose primary interests are in environmental management, the environmental impacts of human activity and geographies of development. If geography is to fulfil its potential as a discipline capable of thinking in the round, the basis of this engagement must be extended to embrace the intellectual mainstream in economic, social and political geography, biogeography and studies of environmental change.

In particular, a broader geographical input into current debates might help to provide a more sophisticated understanding of the space economy, thus strengthening the existing theoretical treatment of sustainable development. Established economic theory does little to explain why the ideal of sustainable development is so difficult to attain in practice. Some of the answers are provided by theoretical characterizations of economic and social development under capitalism as not only inherently unstable, but also uneven in space and time. This presentation of development and underdevelopment as necessarily connected has particular implications for aspirations to intra-generational equity – a consideration which is itself often marginalized in popular definitions of sustainable development. Studies in the tradition of political ecology take the analysis a stage further in making important connections between socio-economic marginalization and environmental degradation. It is important to appreciate that poverty, as well as affluence, can place unsustainable strains upon the environment.

Such thinking gives greater rigour to criticism of orthodox strategies for achieving more sustainable development. It highlights the dangers of placing too great a faith in limited technical or managerial measures that only treat the immediate symptoms of environmental or social problems. The underlying causes, which often reflect much more deep-rooted inequalities in the distribution of economic and political power at every spatial scale from the local to the global, remain unchallenged and, perhaps, unheeded. It is important, therefore, to understand the condition of particular places not as discrete entities, but from a perspective that acknowledges their connections with wider human and environmental systems. Thinking in this way has very real implications for the local and participatory emphasis of many practical projects that are intended to promote more sustainable development. Promoting change from the bottom up can be effective in securing immediate improvements in livelihoods, social welfare and environmental conditions. But it is not always clear that the sponsors of such initiatives are willing or able to go beyond local change and rewrite the terms upon which particular localities participate in wider economic, social and political systems.

3

The Role of Spatial Scale and Spatial Interactions in Sustainable Development

Alan Grainger

Introduction

The spatial dimension of sustainable development has so far been rather neglected (Niu et al, 1993; Van den Bergh, 1996). For geographers, who have a particular interest in the analysis of spatial phenomena, this is both a crucial gap and an area in which they can make a significant contribution to improving our general understanding of sustainable development. It is beyond the scope of this chapter to cover all spatial aspects of sustainable development, so the focus here is on the role of spatial scale and spatial interactions. This seems highly appropriate, as much previous research has concentrated on studying sustainable development at a particular level of the spatial scale, such as the local or national, while ignoring interactions within and between these levels.

The chapter addresses sustainable development as a theoretical concept rather than a political ideal (see Chapter 1). However, it takes both a descriptive approach, by assessing the sustainability of development in the real world in relation to an ideal sustainable path, and a prescriptive approach, by examining the various strategies which are, or could be, used to make development more sustainable. A key broad underlying question is whether existing theories, largely conceived from an aspatial perspective, have limitations when applied spatially.

The development of a society is regarded here as sustainable if overall human welfare does not decline (Pearce, 1991), and this can occur if a society follows an ideal development path that optimizes the balance between economic, social and environmental change. In practice, actual development paths never coincide with the ideal, but the closer the two paths are, the greater the sustainability of development. Characterizing the ideal path is difficult, but various alternative conditions have been proposed (see Chapter 1). The primary analytical framework for this chapter is provided by the Very Weak Condition of environmental economics theory (see Table 3.1). This is the only condition that encompasses, and differentiates between, the economic, social and environmental dimensions of development, and it can be used to evaluate relationships between the spatial distributions of Natural Capital and Human and Man-Made Capital. The other Constant Capital Conditions are referred to, as appropriate, together with conditions proposed by ecological economists.

The chapter has four main parts, addressing key generic questions on the role of spatial scale identified by Gibson et al (1998). Part one compares the merits of different types of spatial scale and finds a socio-political scale to be most useful in this context. Part two examines whether sustainable development is a meaningful concept at all levels on that scale, from the global to the household. Part three assesses the extent to which the sustainability of development in a spatial unit at a particular level is determined by internal processes, and how much it is influenced by interactions with other units, for example, through trade and pollutant transfers. Part four looks at how the sustainability of development in a spatial unit at one level depends on patterns at other levels and interactions between them. This leads to a discussion of the role of uneven development and international conventions in sustainable development and the merits of participatory strategies.

Table 3.1   The Constant Capital Conditions for sustainable development

1	Very Weak: there is no reduction in the stock of Total Capital. The value of depleted Natural Capital does not exceed the value of the rise in Human and Man-Made Capital derived from it.
2	Weak: there is no reduction in the stock of Critical Natural Capital.
3	Strong: there is no reduction in the total stock of Natural Capital.

Structuring Global Space

Scales, levels and hierarchies

Sustainable development was devised with two global goals in mind: protecting the global environment by safeguarding the world's remaining pristine ecosystems; and increasing international equity by reducing inequalities within and between countries. To assess the overall effectiveness of actions intended to achieve these goals we need a scale to divide the planet into manageable segments. A *scale* was defined by Gibson et al (1998) as 'the dimension used to measure a phenomenon'. It encompasses the range of variation in a phenomenon and is usually divided for convenience into a hierarchy of discrete gradations, or *levels*.

Each level on a spatial scale provides an alternative picture of the world, dividing it into a large number of individual *spatial units*. At the national level, for example, these comprise some 190 countries. The lower the level on the scale, the greater the number of spatial units.

Geographical scale was defined by Delaney and Leitner (1997) as 'the nested hierarchy of bounded spaces of differing size'. In nested hierarchies the bounded spaces (or spatial units) at one level contain others at lower levels. If the hierarchies are constitutive, on the other hand, as is common in social hierarchies, then the properties of spatial units at one level help to determine the properties of units at higher levels (Mayr, 1982). Whether this is true for sustainable development is examined below.

Ecological scales

Of the various scales that could be used for this analysis, an ecological scale seems at first glance to have many attractions. It typically starts at the global level with the entire biosphere, and then proceeds through the levels of biome-type (a major type of global ecosystem), biome (a continental ecosystem type), landscape, ecosystem, community, population and organism (see Figure 3.1) (McTaggart, 1993).

The advantage of using such a scale is that it could help to identify critical limits to the depletion of biological wealth, from major biome-types, such as tropical rain forest, at the global level, down to the diversity of individual species, such as the teak tree, *Tectona grandis*. This would be particularly useful for monitoring trends in Critical Natural Capital, required to sustain the functioning of the biosphere (see Chapter 1). In the World Conservation Strategy (IUCN, 1980) the remaining distributions of the different biomes, landscapes and ecosystem types were mapped by rarity, richness and threat, forming the basis for a global network containing representative examples of each.

Monitoring the overall sustainability of development would be difficult, however, for three reasons:

1. Measuring change over time in a particular biome, such as tropical rain forest in Asia, would require the coordinated monitoring of trends in Natural Capital in many dispersed locations. Even with the help of sampling, this would be a huge undertaking.
2. Integrating development and environmental change would be hampered by data limitations. Global data on the potential and actual spatial distributions of ecosystems are limited in both quantity and accuracy. Moreover, environmental boundaries and societal boundaries do not necessarily coincide: for example, the huge natural region of the Amazon Basin is divided between eight countries. Ecological scales also tend to be structured around the distribution of renewable resources, whereas development patterns are also influenced by the distribution of non-renewable resources and the economics of their exploitation.
3. Even if all patches of a particular biome in each country could be identified and mapped, the socio-economic processes determining the sustainability of each patch would only partly originate inside its boundaries. So while, in principle, compliance with the Very Strong and Strong conditions could be monitored in a sophisticated way on an ecological scale, some of the key factors affecting compliance, such as the forces driving deforestation, would originate in other biomes. This would make integrated analysis of human–environment interactions difficult, if not impossible.

Social science scales

The main alternative is a social science scale. Scales used by geographers and political scientists, for instance, typically divide global space into a hierarchy of levels that starts with groupings of states (including both supranational regions and the international community) and moves down through the state, region, locality (city, town and village) to the household (see Figure 3.2) (Gibson et al, 1998). Although the

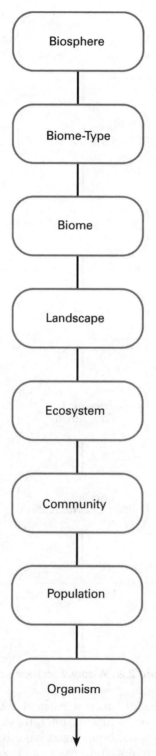

Figure 3.1   An ecological scale

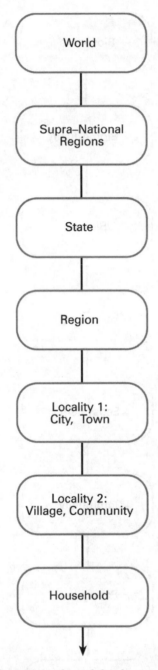

Figure 3.2   A social science scale

distributions of individual spatial units at each of these levels do not necessarily coincide with the distribution of Natural Capital, they are not totally divorced from it. Many national and sub-national boundaries have been chosen to follow natural features, such as mountains, rivers and coasts, and some even have an ecological significance. In Indonesia, for example, different types of rhinoceros are native to the islands of Java and Sumatra. An integrated analysis of human–environment relationships is helped by the cultural and legal homogeneity of individual spatial units, but the major advantage of using this type of scale is the abundance of social, economic and environmental data collected within the framework of political boundaries. This makes the comparison of changes in all these dimensions of development within a single territory far more practical than with an ecological scale. While a social science scale is by no means perfect, it seems the most pragmatic choice for present purposes.

Principal levels in a socio-political hierarchy

Spatial units at each level on a social science scale have their own distinctive characteristics and links with spatial units at other levels. These are now reviewed in order to decide which level provides the best reference point for analysis.

National level

States are sovereign territories with the freedom to order affairs inside their own borders. They are sometimes referred to as 'nation-states', though this strictly refers to countries populated by a single national group. The national level has many advantages for undertaking a generalized assessment of sustainable development. For while uneven development is common within states, national economic space is still relatively homogeneous, owing to the adoption of common currencies, laws and institutions (Radice, 1984). Governments have the authority to enforce this homogeneity, and a survey by the UK Environment Agency found that the need to comply with government regulations provided the main incentive for 80 per cent of British companies to raise their environmental performance (Gallagher, 1997).

National borders are, by definition, internationally recognized; compilations of international statistics on social characteristics, economic activity and environmental quality all use the state as the basic spatial unit; and international action on the environment requires voluntary cooperation between the governments of sovereign states. Claims that economic globalization has severely diminished the sovereignty of individual countries (see, for example, Ohmae, 1995) are widely contested (Dicken, 2003). Whatever the truth of this, social, economic and environmental characteristics still vary widely between states. This, and the need of governments to meet their international obligations to monitor sustainable development, provide a strong justification for using the state as the basic building block for analysis in this chapter. States can, in turn, be aggregated into supranational regions and divided into sub-national regions and smaller spatial units. Each is now discussed in turn.

Supranational level

There are three main types of supranational regions. The tightest groupings of states, such as the European Union (EU), are bound by treaty and pool some of their sovereignty so their economic, social and environmental standards can converge. Weaker groupings, for example, the North American Free Trade Agreement (NAFTA) and the Association of Southeast Asian Nations (ASEAN), are also bound by treaty, but their actions have less cohesion. They also tend to be committed to acting together in just one sphere, such as trade, or to voluntarily consult with one another or collaborate in a number of areas. This contrasts with more tightly regulated multifunctional groupings, such as the EU. In the third type, continental regions, states are grouped by virtue of contiguity alone, and regional social, economic and environmental trends are the simple sum of those in the states they comprise.

International level

States also join together in larger groupings, some of which are global in scale. The most inclusive global grouping is the United Nations Organization. Others, such as the Food and Agriculture Organization (FAO) and other specialized United Nations (UN) agencies are smaller, either because some states choose not to be members or because membership is restricted. Large numbers of states also join together to implement specific international environmental regimes, such as the Framework Convention on Climate Change (FCCC) (see Chapters 11 and 12).

Sub-national level

Below the national level, two main kinds of regional divisions may be found within countries: geographical regions and political/administrative regions. A geographical region, such as the Great Plains of North America, is 'any area with distinct and internally consistent patterns of physical features or human development which give it a meaningful unity and distinguish it from surrounding areas' (Goodall, 1987). Analysing human–environment relationships in these regions is facilitated by their relative environmental, cultural and/or economic homogeneity. Some regions span the broader catchment areas on which urban areas depend for labour and raw materials. Yet regional boundaries are often subjectively defined (Haggett, 2001) and may overlap with those of other regions, preventing the construction of a comprehensive nested spatial hierarchy.

States are often divided into political regions for statistical or administrative purposes. These have varying degrees of autonomy depending upon the administrative system of individual states. In federal states, such as the USA, regions are the next major level of administration below the national government. In unitary states, however, regions may have little or no power or autonomy. Thailand, for example, is divided into seven regions, but they have no administrative role. The distribution of power between the levels of a political hierarchy may, however, change over time. For example, in the late 1990s the British Government devolved a degree of administrative and legal authority to Scotland, Wales and Northern Ireland. As yet, however, there has been no equivalent process in England and the nine Regional Development Agencies established in 1999 have no significant authority.

Local level

The local level is the lowest level in the spatial hierarchy with well-defined boundaries. The spatial unit at this level is, for convenience, called a locality, even though it refers to a settlement that may range in size from a village to a metropolitan conurbation, and even small towns can be divided into multiple 'localities'. Almost half of the world's population live in cities, which are concentrations of Man-Made Capital, Human Capital, but regrettably also of low Environmental Quality. Given their global importance, they are a major focus of sustainable development research (Gibbs, 1994; May et al, 1996; see also Chapters 5 and 6 in this volume). The limited size and well-defined administrative boundaries of cities can be deceptive, since many of those who work within an urban core commute daily from other settlements within a wider 'contact zone'. The 'city region' which encompasses this zone is a well-established geographical concept (Haggett, 2001), though the actual urban footprint may be even larger when sources of natural resources supplies and the sinks where waste is deposited are also included (see Chapter 5).

Household level

Households have key roles as producers and consumers, and so are important units of analysis for assessing the sustainability of development at higher levels. They may be more meaningful units for assessing human pressures on the environment than the individual person, for even if population stabilizes, the number of households may continue to grow and with it demand for houses, cars etc. Indeed, 4.4 million new households are expected to be formed in the UK between 1991 and 2016 (DoE, 1995).

In developing countries, where labour is still predominantly agricultural, the household is an important spatial unit, because for a significant proportion of the farming population, it can be equated with the 'family farm', consisting of a homestead and a collection of fields. This general model is applicable even in short-rotation shifting cultivation in the tropics, characterized by a fixed homestead and a variety of plots farmed and fallowed in rotation (Grainger, 1993).

As countries become more developed the household is better described as a social unit than as a fixed spatial unit. At any point in time it occupies a particular territory, but the location of this territory can shift markedly, as household members change the location of their external activities to sustain their livelihoods. Since the overall territory associated with each household at any time can be divided into sub-territories at different locations, household territories are not mutually exclusive, as with spatial units higher up the spatial scale.

Firms

Firms do not constitute a specific level on the spatial scale, but they are included here as they are crucial actors in development and influence the spatial distribution of sustainable development. Many are still based in one location, and of these the largest have an impact on the environment equivalent to a large town. Where they locate their facilities influences the travel patterns of workers, and the networks by which raw materials and finished goods are transported. At the other extreme, transnational corporations have production facilities and sales outlets in multiple locations all over the world (Berry et al, 1999). Although, in principle, they are obliged to comply with the laws of the states within which they operate, such corporations extend managerial control across international boundaries and integrate national economies into their international operations (Gilpin, 1987).

Achieving Sustainable Development at Different Levels

Many researchers have tended to focus their studies of sustainable development on a single level of the spatial scale. National and city studies are particularly popular. In principle, each spatial unit at a particular level of the scale should have its own development path. But is it meaningful to talk about sustainable development at every level of the scale? In the context of the Constant Capital Conditions (see Table 3.1) this depends upon whether typical spatial units at each level contain all the types of capital, and the economic and environmental processes linking them, that are needed to satisfy a particular condition. This is not inevitable, since Human and Man-Made Capital, and the various components of Natural Capital, are distributed heterogeneously over the surface of the planet.

Supranational, national and regional levels

Most spatial units at supranational and national levels are large enough to contain sufficient stocks of Natural Capital and Human and Man-Made Capital to have the potential to comply with the Strong and Very Weak Constant Capital Conditions. However, the heterogeneous distribution of Natural Capital has left some countries and sub-national regions better endowed than others.

The situation is more complicated for Critical Natural Capital (see Chapter 1). The stipulation in the Weak Condition that this should not decline is less meaningful below the global level since some countries have little or no Critical Natural Capital within their territories, as strictly defined in global terms. In highly developed countries, in which little of the original cover of natural ecosystems remains unmodified, some types of ecosystems may be quite limited in extent. But when considered together with corresponding stocks in other countries the overall effect of this deficiency may not be significant at the global level. On the other hand, in those countries which do contain significant proportions of Critical Natural Capital, this may be concentrated in particular sub-national regions, such as Amazonia in the case of Brazil. Consequently, if an attempt were made to enforce the Very Weak and Weak Conditions together at global level then a relatively small number of countries would be obliged to conserve a large proportion of their territories, so that the whole of humanity could benefit from the continued operation of the biosphere.

Although most countries have sufficient Natural Capital to comply with the Strong Condition in principle, in practice compliance may not be feasible since this condition was not originally formulated in a spatial or developmental context. To meet the condition and prevent a decline in Natural Capital, any Non-Renewable Resource Capital that is lost in the course of development must be offset by a rise in Renewable Resource Capital, and existing Renewable Resource Capital must be managed in a perfectly sustainable way. Past experience, however, suggests that the general sustainability of renewable resource management only increases gradually as a country becomes more developed. Moreover, while countries are highly dependent upon renewable resources in the early phases of their development, they subsequently make increasing use of more energy-intensive non-renewable resources, and the contribution of renewable resources to overall energy consumption only becomes significant again at an advanced phase of development. Consequently, compliance with the Strong Condition should only be expected in countries that are still in an early phase of development or are highly developed. Compliance could, however, be achieved if the temporal scale were extended. For example, highly developed countries could establish new renewable resource stocks today in order to compensate for non-renewable resources stocks lost long ago. Compliance could also occur at a higher level on the spatial scale, since the total expansion of renewable resources in all countries could offset the total depletion of non-renewable resources in the same year.

Localities

The potential to satisfy conditions for sustainable development becomes more difficult to determine in localities and households, where spatial units lack the full range of capital stocks and processes. Most of the Resource Capital transformed in large cities comes from outside since local stocks are invariably non-existent or depleted. This alone would be sufficient to make an area unsustainable in some approaches to sustainable development – for example, the Environmental Space (Buitenkamp et al, 1992; Schmidt-Bleek, 1992) and Ecological Footprint methods (Wackernagel and Rees, 1996), discussed below. Both are based on the ideal carrying capacity condition of ecological economics in which the scale of the human economy must not exceed the planet's ultimate carrying capacity (Daly, 1999). In countries that have reached the post-industrial phase of their development, service industries account for a larger proportion of gross national product (GNP) and employment than manufacturing. In this context, the local absence of Resource Capital is less important and overall trends in Natural Capital in large cities will be dominated by the Environmental Quality component. The level of the latter will typically be quite low, reflecting pollutants emitted by manufacturing industry, vehicles, power stations and domestic waste disposal. It is probably unrealistic to think of cities ever satisfying the Strong Constant Capital Condition, yet they could satisfy the Very Weak Condition if the huge annual increment in Human and Man-Made Capital outweighs in value the reduction in Natural Capital caused by the environmental degradation associated with economic activity. Urban environmental problems are discussed in more detail in Chapters 5 and 6.

As the size of settlements declines, sustainable development, as understood within the framework of the Constant Capital Conditions, becomes progressively less meaningful. Not only are stocks of Resource Capital lacking, but so too are the processes that transform it into Human and Man-Made Capital. In well-established rural communities in developed countries, for example, stocks of Resource Capital, in the form of natural ecosystems, are relatively static; Environmental Quality declines as a result of agricultural pollution and the extension of settlements; the farming population gains its income from growing crops (assumed here to be a form of Man-Made Capital, although opinions differ on this); and many other livelihoods are based on employment in nearby towns and cities. However, these limits to the spatial resolution with which sustainable development may be assessed are more a reflection of the limitations of the Constant Capital Conditions than of the idea of sustainable development itself.

Households

The Constant Capital Conditions are also only partly relevant at the lowest level on the scale as many households lack stocks of Resource Capital. Nevertheless, Environmental Quality is of great importance to households. For example, the interior environments of many homes in developing countries are of poor quality because of smoke pollution from wood fires, a lack of piped drinking water and inadequate sanitation. This encourages the spread of disease and reduces the quality of life (McGranahan, 1993). As countries develop, more households are connected to water supply and sewerage networks. This raises the quality of life but also creates new problems, including groundwater depletion and river pollution.

At the household level, the primary concern is with the sustainability of livelihoods, rather than with the sustainability of development as a whole. Carney (1998) defines a livelihood as comprising 'the capabilities, assets (including both material and social resources) and activities required for a means of living'. To sustain their own livelihoods, households exploit material assets in various locations and substitute one asset or activity for another. According to Scoones (1998): 'Sustainable livelihoods are achieved through access to a range of resources (natural, economic, human and social capitals) which are combined in the pursuit of different livelihood strategies (agricultural intensification or extensification, livelihood diversification and migration)'. However, there is still no theoretical framework to explain how households choose their optimum combination of resources (Carney, 1999).

Implications for sustainable development strategies

Sustainable development, as understood in terms of compliance with the Constant Capital Conditions, is therefore a meaningful concept from the global level to the sub-national regional level, but is not universally applicable below this. Three implications follow from this. First, countries are not equal in their potential to satisfy the Constant Capital Conditions because of differences in their initial endowment of Natural Capital and their present phase of development. Second, even if cities, towns and households cannot develop sustainably themselves, they can still make an important contribution to strategies intended to increase the sustainability of development at higher spatial levels. Rees (1995) called cities 'nodes of pure consumption, the entropic black holes of industrial society', but argued that because of their high resource use and environmental impacts, improving how they function could significantly increase global sustainability. So while a 'sustainable city' may only ever be a highly efficient machine for metabolizing the various types of capital (see Chapter 5), it can provide a wide spectrum of benefits to higher spatial levels. Third, the limitations of the Very Weak Condition at lower levels on the spatial scale suggest that there may be scope for another method or condition that is more universally applicable.

Sustainable Development in Open Economies

The Constant Capital Conditions were originally devised to apply to the planet as a whole, and so implicitly assume that each spatial unit functions as a closed economy. But while Spaceship Earth is a closed system, individual spatial units at other spatial levels are not. Instead, they are best described as open economies, and trends in their Natural Capital and Total Capital are influenced by transfers to and from other spatial

COUNTRY 1

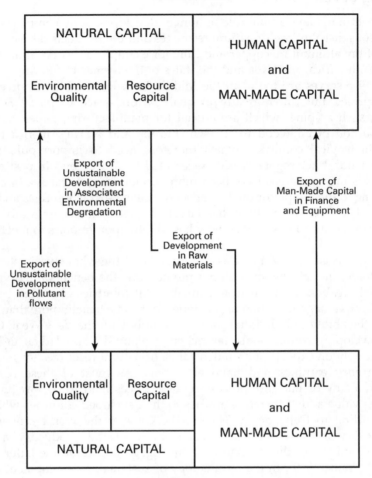

Figure 3.3   *Sustainable development of open economies*

units, through flows of goods, financial capital, pollutants and other environmental disbenefits (see Figure 3.3). This section examines, within the framework of the Very Weak Condition, how transfers between spatial units on the same level of the spatial scale influence the sustainability of their development. We look first at the effects of flows in natural resources, then at flows of the environmental quality associated with their exploitation, and finally at strategies to correct for inequities in these flows. This provides a test of the ability of the Very Weak Condition to explain actual patterns of development, and of its compatibility with political economy theories.

Exporting development

International trade plays a vital role in human development by compensating for the heterogeneous distributions of natural resources and the products derived from them. Reserves of tin, aluminium, copper and iron, for example, are concentrated in the US, Canada, South Africa, Australia and the states of the former USSR. More than half of all global oil reserves are found in the Middle East. Renewable resources are more highly dispersed but differ greatly in quality from place to place. For example, softwoods, such as pine, which are crucial for manufacturing paper, account for a large proportion of all wood reserves in Europe and North America but are not extensive in tropical countries, which therefore need to import pulp and paper. Patterns of natural heterogeneity are exacerbated by spatial bias in past exploitation since reserves in some areas have been more economically attractive to exploit than others, owing to their superior quality, species content, extraction costs and proximity to markets. The UK, for example, has largely depleted its economically extractable reserves of iron ore and coal and so now has to rely upon imports to meet most of its requirements.

According to classical and neo-classical trade laws, the whole world should benefit from free trade, though the laws do not predict how the benefits are divided (Berry et al, 1999). In reality, this is far from equitable. All countries gain from being able to specialize in advantageous economic activities, but some benefit more than others and this affects the ability of individual states to comply with the Very Weak Condition.

Many developing countries are far richer in Natural Capital than in Man-Made Capital, and rely on exports of a limited range of natural resources for much of their foreign currency earnings and national income. As most of these resources are exported in a raw or partially processed state, prices tend to be low and variable. Much of the value added therefore accrues to the developed countries which process them. According to Dependency Theory, the Core of the world economy (ie the industrialized world) extracts the surplus value of the productive activities of developing countries of the Periphery, so by engaging in trade the latter *export their development* (Frank, 1969). In the terminology of sustainable development this means that they export potential Human and Man-Made Capital. Consequently, the amount of Human and Man-Made Capital which accumulates in the country where Resource Capital is exploited is only a fraction of the total, undermining its ability to satisfy the Very Weak Condition.

Developed countries also benefit from low labour costs in developing countries, which keep raw material prices low. This is explained partly by the lower living costs in developing countries, and partly by the fact that workers do not have the same safeguards in terms of working conditions, social security and health services as are standard in developed countries. In this respect, exporting development also means exporting commodities and products that are produced at the expense of the social welfare of workers in developing countries. Continuing to rely upon the exports of primary commodities will perpetuate this, as insufficient capital is generated to invest in better working and living conditions.

Capital transfers within countries are often inequitable too, leading to a pattern of uneven economic development, discussed below. Commercial centres typically benefit from resource extraction at the expense of resource-producing regions, undermining the potential to satisfy the Very Weak Condition at regional level. For example, Nigeria's leading oil production area, the Delta Region, has historically received little of the wealth created by exploiting its resources and has also suffered substantial land and water pollution from leaking pipelines. This has led to unrest and violence. However, the situation could change following the Nigerian government's decision to include in its 2000 Budget a 'derivation principle', under which states will receive at least 13 per cent of revenues generated locally (Wallis, 1999).

Trade in sustainable development

Importing sustainable development

Inequity in trade is exacerbated by the impact which exploiting Natural Capital in developing countries has on local people and environments. Mining and logging, for example, often degrade the environment, and if the costs of this are not fully paid – as is often the case – then Environmental Quality is effectively transferred to those countries which ultimately consume the resource. Environmental laws are generally weaker and less well enforced in developing countries than in their developed counterparts. As a result, there is considerable variation in the sustainability of renewable resource management, and hence in the ability to comply with the third of the Daly Principles, which states that renewable resources should not be harvested at rates that exceed their regenerative capacity (see Chapter 1). Developed countries therefore buy resources and products more cheaply than would be the case if they were produced at home, in line with tougher domestic legislation (Satterthwaite, 1997).

So besides importing development by processing raw materials from overseas, developed countries also *import sustainable development* by not paying the full environmental costs of resource extraction. In the language of Dependency Theory, this adds an 'environmental surplus' to the economic surplus that the 'Core' expropriates from the 'Periphery'. Environmental degradation is also likely to occur if resources are processed in developing countries, again reflecting less stringent environmental regulations. According to Robins and Trisoglio (1995), shifting 'energy- and resource-intensive industries to the developing world . . . [has, in effect, displaced] . . . the environmental problems of production'.

Exporting unsustainable development

When one spatial unit exports pollution to another, thus reducing the latter's Environmental Quality, it effectively *exports unsustainable development*. Many countries release excessive levels of pollutants into the atmosphere, rivers and oceans, damaging the environment elsewhere. Emissions of sulphur and nitrogen oxides from coal-burning power stations in the UK, for example, have long been blamed for the acid deposition that damages forests and lakes in Scandinavia.

Transfers of Environmental Quality also occur within a country. The quality of urban environments in developed countries has greatly improved in recent decades; but much urban waste is deposited far outside city boundaries. Sewage is a leading source of river pollution in the UK (Environment Agency, 2001), and the impacts of urban air pollution are more widespread than previously thought, with high levels of hydrocarbons, nitrogen oxides and carbon monoxide being transported from urban to rural atmospheres (Weybourne Atmospheric Observatory, 1994). Each city's 'ecological footprint' (see p. 66) (Wackernagel and Rees, 1996) is therefore quite large and can even be regional in scale (Berry, 1990). Vancouver's footprint, for example, is estimated to be 20 times its legal area, and that of London 125 times (Jopling and Girardet, 1996; Wackernagel and Rees, 1996).

Monitoring sustainable development in open economies

Using the Very Weak Condition

As virtually all units at sub-global levels on the spatial scale are open economies, it is therefore vital to correct for these inflows and outflows if reliable estimates are to be made of the sustainability of development of a given area. To comply with the Very Weak Condition the value of the rise in Human and Man-Made Capital should be greater than, or equal to, the fall in Natural Capital from which it is derived, or:

$$\partial HMMC \geq \partial NC \tag{3.1}$$

where $\partial HMMC$ is the increment in Human and Man-Made Capital, and ∂NC the increment in Natural Capital, consisting of the sum of changes in Resource Capital (RC) and Environmental Quality (EQ). Transposing this equation, we arrive at an equivalent expression, which states that the difference between the two changes should be greater than zero:

$$\partial HMMC - \partial NC \geq 0 \tag{3.2}$$

Pearce and Atkinson (1993) devised the Genuine Savings Index to test for compliance with this rule. The net rise in Human and Man-Made Capital is calculated by deducting from each country's gross annual saving (S) – after adjustment for net foreign borrowing – the amount that must be invested to offset the depreciation of Human and Man-Made Capital (∂K_m). The Genuine Savings Index Z is then calculated as the difference between Net Saving and the depreciation of Natural Capital (∂K_n). Z is 'normalized' by dividing all terms by the country's annual income Y:

$$Z = [S/Y - (\partial K_m)/Y] - (\partial K_n)/Y \tag{3.3}$$

According to the Very Weak Condition, development is sustainable if Net Saving exceeds the depreciation of Natural Capital (ie if Z is greater than or equal to zero). Pearce and Atkinson (1993) found that countries as diverse as Japan ($Z=17$), Costa Rica ($Z=15$), The Netherlands ($Z=14$), Brazil ($Z=3$) and the USA ($Z=2$) were apparently developing sustainably during the 1980s. Other countries, such as Indonesia ($Z=-2$), Nigeria ($Z=-5$) and Mali ($Z=-14$), were not.

However, the above test assumes that each country is a closed economy. In open economies the decline in Natural Capital in each spatial unit should only be compared with the rise in Human and Man-Made Capital associated with exploiting Natural Capital within that unit. This means removing from the comparison any rise in Human and Man-Made Capital associated with processing imported Natural Capital.

The Environmental Quality associated with imported Natural Capital should also be deducted.

International trade statistics could be used to adjust for the value added by imports of Resource Capital at national level, though this would be complicated given the number of intermediate processing stages that can separate the raw material source from the destination of the finished product. Lack of data would make it more difficult to estimate the associated reduction in Environmental Quality. If corrections are only made for the effective transfer of Human and Man-Made Capital from importing country to processing country then this will only adjust for the import of development, *not* sustainable development. Transfers of Environmental Quality must also be incorporated to achieve the latter. Further corrections are needed for the unsustainable development exported by industrialized countries through their pollutant emissions.

Most developing countries will probably not satisfy the Very Weak Condition since much of the rise in Human and Man-Made Capital associated with the depletion of their Natural Capital accumulates in countries to which they export the latter. Equally, the apparent ability of many developed countries to satisfy the condition would be reduced if these transfers were fully accounted for, as a significant proportion of their annual rise in Human and Man-Made Capital would be excluded and the negative Environmental Quality exported as pollutants would be included. Making corrections for sub-national regions and localities would be more difficult because at these levels the flows are more complex and data are unavailable.

This form of adjustment has three limitations. First, correcting for flows of Resource Capital and Environmental Quality for all countries would remove a significant amount of the annual global increment of Human and Man-Made Capital from consideration. Second, to achieve perfect monitoring it would be necessary to follow each individual material export from source to market, which would be a massive undertaking. Third, compliance with the Very Weak Condition does not necessarily ensure the rise in social welfare that is fundamental to economic development because the condition is based on the sum of Human and Man-Made Capital, whereas economic development is concerned with the equity with which a country's total income is distributed. Human and Man-Made Capital would have to be disaggregated to monitor properly the export of development. Such difficulties associated with using the Very Weak Condition for monitoring sustainable development reflect its 'incremental comparison' approach, in which changes in Natural Capital are compared directly with changes in Human and Man-Made Capital. Monitoring would be made easier if a new method could be devised under which changes in the three dimensions of development could be monitored separately.

A first attempt to monitor the sustainability of development in open economies was made by Proops et al (1999), who adapted the Genuine Savings Index to allow for trade. They found that oil-exporting countries in the Middle East now appeared to be developing sustainably (ie $Z \geqslant 0$), while estimates made on the assumption that they were closed economies suggested they were unsustainable. In contrast, assessment of developed countries and African developing countries shifted from sustainable to unsustainable when modelled as open economies. Unfortunately, these estimates only gave approximate measures of the export of development, as defined above, not the export of sustainable development. This is because they only corrected the ∂K_n term in Equation 3.3 for trade in non-renewable resources, and ignored transfers of renewable resources and environmental quality. Furthermore, for ease of calculation, they compared the annual saving in a country only with the decline in Non-Renewable Resource Capital used in that country. So any exported Resource Capital was added to the balance sheet of the importing country and treated as though it had been extracted domestically. This is why the ∂K_n term fell in oil exporting countries (thereby raising Z) and rose in oil importing countries (reducing Z). This is a different method to that suggested above, and it raises questions not only about its partiality, but also about its reliability, because it does not truly reflect the decline in Resource Capital in the country where the stocks are held.

Using ecological economics conditions and indicators

The feasibility and relevance of using the ideal carrying capacity condition of ecological economics to monitor the sustainability of development at national and sub-national levels are even more questionable. This condition, under which humanity should not exceed its ultimate carrying capacity, is entirely reasonable at the global level, although even this upper limit is difficult to estimate given the rapid changes in demand for natural resources and in the technological sophistication with which this can be met. But the heterogeneous distributions of both natural resources and demand for them, and the complex patterns of trade which have developed to compensate for this, undermine its use at sub-global levels. Trade and technology combine to free many areas from the limitations imposed by their immediate physical environments.

Currently available indicators based on this ideal condition, such as the Environmental Space and Ecological Footprint methods, are too limited in scope to determine full compliance with it. The dependence of cities and developed countries upon importing large quantities of resources for processing, with all the consequences discussed above, is widely assumed to be encompassed by the Ecological Footprint method. Unfortunately, this fails to match the image conveyed by its name as it uses land area as a proxy for all Natural Capital. It may well illustrate external dependence, but this is not very relevant as an accounting practice, as it merely states that countries which demand more than the global mean area per capita to satisfy their resource needs are unsustainable (Wackernagel and Rees, 1996). The Environmental Space method is a modest improvement, regarding as unsustainable any country or spatial unit where resource use per capita exceeds the global mean (Buitenkamp et al, 1992; Schmidt-Bleek, 1992). But both methods are simplistic (Moffatt, 1996) and ignore how trade compensates for the heterogeneous global distribution of natural resources. Similar criticisms apply to the idea of the self-reliant 'bio-region' proposed by Register (1987). International trade has been a reality for most countries for hundreds of years and global interdependence continues to increase. Self-sufficiency is not essential to achieve sustainable development.

Strategies to compensate for trade in development and sustainable development

The inequities of trade and development are ameliorated partly by the actions of individuals and firms, and partly by government intervention to promote economic development and sustainable development. In practice, the two sets of strategies are linked in various ways.

Compensation by capitalists

Capital always has a tendency to search for and exploit profitable opportunities, so poorly developed or declining regions with high unemployment and low labour costs are potentially attractive to entrepreneurial capitalists. American and Japanese firms have, in recent decades, established manufacturing plants in developing Latin American and Asian states for this very reason. The same principle also applies to developed countries, where the injection of capital into depressed regions, such as north-east England, may partly offset the effects of previous capital withdrawals. In both types of countries, such capital investment may also be an attempt to gain access to new markets. On the other hand, in today's globalized economy all plants owned by transnational corporations, in particular, are vulnerable to closure as capital can be shifted elsewhere at short notice.

Financial assistance to depressed regions

The decisions of capitalists to locate new facilities in depressed regions in developed countries are often catalysed by state financial aid. Within the EU, the value of subsidies for expanding productive Man-Made Capital in depressed regions varies from country to country: for example, UK aid, under its Regional Selective Assistance scheme, is only one fifth of the EU average (Groom, 1998). Aid is limited by the European Commission to avoid anti-competitive practices, and in the late 1990s the Commission asked member states to focus regional assistance more closely on areas most in need of help and reduce the maximum proportion of the population which could receive it (Tucker, 1997). These restrictions may also be justified in view of the questionable long-term effectiveness of regional development schemes.

Aid is also given from three EU Structural Funds on condition that it is matched by funds from within the country. The European Regional Development Fund accounts for one third of the total EU budget and aims to secure 'balanced economic and social development' across member states. However, its focus on social and economic regeneration means that it is only used to fund environmental protection and regeneration if this can be directly linked to economic development (DoE, 1994).

Linking environment and development in overseas aid programmes

Over the last 50 years developed countries have also given financial aid to developing countries to facilitate their development and reduce the North–South gap. Increasingly, however, the terms of such assistance differ from those of internal aid programmes in linking environment and development by imposing conditions to curb the negative environmental impacts of development projects. Protests about the large-scale destruction of the Amazon rain forest resulting from highway construction partly funded by the World Bank were a major cause of this shift in policy. Some types of projects are now completely ineligible for aid from some countries: for example, the US government will not fund the construction of hydroelectric dams. This type of pressure does not curb a state's sovereign right to undertake any actions it chooses that may deplete resources or degrade environments, but it does limit its access to particular sources of overseas capital for this purpose.

This linkage could be further extended as part of international programmes to mitigate global climate change (see Chapter 11). For if developing countries were obliged to protect extensive wilderness areas as carbon stores this could ring-fence a significant proportion of their territories from settlement and resource extraction, thereby reducing their overall development potential. This could further widen the North–South gap, primarily for the benefit of developed countries whose prolonged greenhouse gas emissions have been the major cause of climate change. To prevent such inequity developed countries would be under an obligation to compensate developing countries for potential development income lost as a result of large-scale conservation (Grainger, 1997).

Migration as a compensation mechanism

In the absence of external assistance, households will make their own responses to uneven development to sustain their livelihoods. The simplest strategy is to migrate from declining or stagnant regions in search of better lifestyles in areas with growing economies. Thus, three of the UK's most depressed sub-regions, Merseyside, Tyne and Wear, and Clydeside, all experienced net out-migration in the 1990s (Groom, 1999d). Some migrants may remit part of their earnings to sustain family members who remain at home.

Rural–urban migration is common in the developing world, but it is not without its problems. If too many people leave rural areas then agricultural sustainability can decline, with the risk of adverse environmental impacts. Urban areas also experience 'migration overload' if insufficient new jobs are generated to meet demand from migrants. Some unemployed migrants may return to rural areas, clearing forests to grow food, thus causing environmental damage. In Indonesia and Brazil, the state has previously assisted large-scale migration from overcrowded areas to new settlements in under-populated rural districts, but such schemes have rarely been successful (Grainger, 1993).

In developed countries, technological advances now mean that people living in deprived peripheral regions may not have to resort to physical migration to compensate for locational disadvantages. For example, 13,000 information technology (IT) jobs have been created in recent years in the Highlands and Islands region of Scotland. Half of all new jobs in the region in 1999 were linked to either IT or telecommunications, although the North Sea oil industry is still a major source of employment. These two sectors, in particular, have contributed to a 20 per cent net rise in regional population between 1960 and the late 1990s, reversing the continuous depopulation suffered since the 1840s (Nicholson, 2000).

Transfers of political pressures between spatial units

People directly affected by what they perceive to be the socially or environmental harmful activities of transnational corporations often feel powerless to influence them, because the headquarters of these firms are so far away and national governments seem unwilling or unable to regulate their activities. But during the last ten years another type of compensatory mechanism has evolved in which non-governmental organizations (NGOs) from abroad help local people by reducing the constraints imposed by distance and international boundaries on transmitting pressures to major corporations.

Transferring protests between developing and developed countries

In one of these mechanisms, NGOs based in the headquarters country of a transnational corporation act as proxy pressure groups for NGOs from the developing country where the impacts occur. Transnational corporations are often alleged to apply lower environmental, labour and human rights standards to their operations in developing countries than they do in developed countries. For example, Royal Dutch Shell has extracted oil in Ogoniland, part of Nigeria's main oil-producing Delta Region, since the 1960s, but in doing so it has caused considerable environmental pollution. In 1990 an indigenous political group, the Movement for the Survival of the Ogoni People (MOSOP), began to campaign for self-determination and for compensation for lost earnings and the pollution created by oil extraction. Protests became so violent that Shell left the area in 1993, though it continued to operate elsewhere in the region. Ken Saro-Wiwa and nine other leading MOSOP members were put on trial for their role in these protests, and in November 1995 they were executed. Shell became the object of protests, both directly and via the media, from human rights groups and other NGOs in the UK and abroad for not demanding that the government halt the executions. Shell's reputation was badly damaged when organizations that had previously held it in high esteem, such as the Royal Geographical Society, disassociated themselves from its conduct in Nigeria. The board of Shell felt obliged to respond to these pressures by presenting a report on its environmental performance in Nigeria to its 1997 Annual General Meeting, and by rewriting its statement of general business principles to recognize its duty to support human rights, care for the environment and show commitment to sustainable development (Mortished, 1997). Shell is still rebuilding relations with the Ogoni people, and has funded community and environmental projects in the area. This expenditure, however, equates to only a fraction of the billions of US dollars in compensation and royalties that local people have demanded (Corzine, 2000).

Transferring protests between developed countries

NGOs may also use pressures in one developed country to force firms to take action in another. Greenpeace campaigned for ten years against MacMillan Bloedel (now part of Weyerhaeuser Corporation) for using the traditional clearfelling practice to manage its forests in the Canadian province of British Columbia. MacMillan Bloedel ignored the protests until in 1998 Greenpeace persuaded the UK do-it-yourself (DIY) stores B&Q and Do It All to boycott all timber from British Columbia. Only when the Canadian firm came under pressure from British consumers did it agree to switch to variable retention logging, which leaves 30–70 per cent of timber behind in the forest after harvest (Alden, 1998).

A different instance arose in February 1995 after Shell was given permission by the UK government to dispose of its disused Brent Spar oil platform, situated in the British sector of the North Sea oil field, by dumping it in deep water in the Atlantic Ocean. Greenpeace protested against this decision, twice occupying the rig, and launched a boycott of Shell petrol in Germany, Denmark and The Netherlands. Two petrol stations were firebombed and shots were fired at another. After ten days of this boycott, German Chancellor Helmut Kohl unsuccessfully requested that UK Prime Minister John Major withdraw authorization for the dumping. However, on 20 June

Shell's main board decided to abandon the plan. Significantly, Shell's policy shift was triggered not by protests within the UK, but by Shell Germany's concern about the damage to its reputation and profits: petrol sales had fallen by 10–20 per cent. Protests were greatest in Germany because its environmental movement was stronger than in the UK (*Wall Street Journal*, 1995). Not only did they influence a regulatory decision in another country; they also succeeded in overturning an environmental impact assessment made before the original proposal was submitted for government approval. John Cridland, Environment Director of the Confederation of British Industry, the leading employers' organization, complained that: 'We have latched the whole of our environmental policy on sound science and risk assessment leading to a balanced cost-benefit analysis. It is very worrying if it can be derailed by special interest groups' (Lascelles, 1995).

Imposing conditions on trade between developing and developed countries
NGOs have pressed for some time for environmental and social conditions to be imposed upon goods in world trade. Initially, in the 1980s the World Wide Fund for Nature (WWF) and other NGOs began to campaign for the governments of developed countries to ban imports of wood from tropical forests that were not managed sustainably. They did not win the necessary political support, but they were successful in establishing certification schemes that identify goods produced in environmentally sound ways. Some measure of cooperation has also secured from retailers, often reflecting consumer pressure. Hence, WWF and leading retailers such as DIY chain B&Q helped to establish the Forest Stewardship Council (FSC) in 1990. The FSC's accreditation identifies whether timber comes from sustainably managed forests. B&Q agreed that by 2000 it would buy timber only from FSC approved sources (B&Q, 1997). This initiative has led to the extension of certification to forests in developed countries. The Statement of Forest Principles agreed at the 1992 UN Conference on Environment and Development (UNCED), and the commitments made by temperate countries in the Second International Tropical Timber Agreement, have placed the sustainable management of all forests within a common international framework.

Policy implications

It appears from this discussion that the sustainability of development of an open economy can be evaluated within the framework of the Very Weak Condition in a way that is compatible with the key principles of Dependency Theory.

Developing countries will continue to export their development to developed countries until they become more industrialized. This requires that developed countries allow greater access to imports from their developing counterparts. As yet, few such concessions have been forthcoming. However, if developing states did secure greater market access then it might lead in the short- to medium-term to greater environmental degradation in these countries, since manufacturing processes would not initially be as environmentally friendly as in the global North. This would add to the existing import of sustainable development by developed countries, mainly through the environmental degradation caused by extracting primary commodities.

One way to reduce the present import of sustainable development by developed countries would be to impose uniform global standards on social welfare and environmental quality in all countries. If perfectly implemented, this would require developed countries to pay fair prices for goods purchased from developing countries, so the latter could ensure proper working standards and minimize environmental degradation when natural resources are extracted and processed. However, compliance with these standards would in practice be limited, since the 'globalist' approach is at odds with the apparent link, referred to earlier, between the level of economic development of developing countries, their living and working conditions, and the sustainability of their resource and environmental management. The approach would further strengthen the environmental component of globalization, which is ironic, as NGOs appear to be having more success than governments in combating the harmful effects of economic globalization by curbing the activities of transnational corporations.

An alternative 'gradualist' approach would not judge all countries by the same standard, but instead judge each country by reference to the standard expected at its particular level of development. This is consistent with the principle of differentiated obligations, currently employed in implementing international environmental regimes. Adopting this approach would mean that developed countries would continue to import sustainable development from developing countries for some time to come. On the other hand, the social and environmental performance of developing countries would be expected to improve in line with an agreed trajectory linked to their rate of development. If developed countries wished to achieve faster progress then they would need to provide sufficient funding to strengthen domestic monitoring and regulatory institutions in developing countries.

At the heart of the dispute between the globalist and gradualist approaches is a fundamental difference of opinion over the meaning of sustainable development. The globalist approach effectively ignores the changes that occur in the course of economic development, assumes that all countries have the same capabilities, and equates sustainable development with joint international action on a broad range of social and environmental issues. The gradualist approach, on the other hand, assumes that every country has its own unique development path. As it develops, the welfare and capabilities of its people increase and so too should its sustainability of development.

No strategy that flies in the face of reality is likely to succeed, however strong are the political pressures from the developed countries that promote it. Since the uniform standards that characterize a globalist approach are strongly opposed by developing countries they are unlikely to be put into practice. It would therefore seem pragmatic for developed countries to adopt a gradualist approach, accept that levels of social welfare and environmental management in developing countries will be lower than their own, and assist them to improve their performance at a rate commensurate with their pace of economic development. Developed countries should also pay greater attention to integrating the economic, social and environmental dimensions of their own development, in particular, by including environmental factors in the provision of financial aid to depressed regions.

Interaction between Different Spatial Levels

Assessments of the sustainability of development at discrete levels on the spatial scale are, of course, rather arbitrary, as environmental phenomena often overlap various levels. A large number of households emitting carbon dioxide from their cars, for example, can help to change global climate; and deforestation in the Asian regional tropical rain forest biome contributes to a decline in the global tropical rain forest biome-type. There is insufficient space here to discuss all of the interactions between different levels on the spatial scale which affect the sustainability of development, so this section focuses on just two main types. First, influences 'from above' in which, for example, agreements at supranational and global levels impose constraints on national development paths and promote convergence between groups of countries. Second, influences 'from below' in which the sustainability of national development is affected by development patterns and activities in regions and localities. This category also includes influences on national policy-makers from groups and individuals at lower spatial levels who engage in 'bottom-up' participatory consultation and decision-making in an attempt to counter the failure of 'top-down' planning. The Very Weak Condition again provides the basic framework for analysis but the main focus is on how state intervention conditions economic and environmental processes in response to pressures from a wide range of interest groups and policy actors.

Influences from above

Every state has its own unique development path, which is a response to economic, social, environmental and political conditions both within and outside its territory. However, the size of the spread between the paths of individual countries can be reduced when groups of countries agree to work together for common ends.

Promoting regional convergence in environmental performance
When countries belonging to supranational regional groupings agree to conform to common environmental standards, this imposes constraints on their economic activities that should cause their environmental performance gradually to converge over time. Generally, the tighter the grouping the faster the convergence should be. The cohesiveness of the EU is such that Ohmae (1993) termed it a 'region state'. In practice, however, most member states do not necessarily adhere strictly to directives from the European Commission and while the Commission can take action against defaulting states in the European Court of Justice, the latter had no power to enforce its verdicts until recently. This, together with continuing differences in policy between countries, means that EU member states still vary greatly in their environmental performance. The UK, for example, has one of the lowest rates of domestic waste reuse in Europe – 15 per cent compared with 70 per cent in The Netherlands (DTI, 1998) – though it is trying to raise this to conform with EU common minimum standards.

Such 'top-down' influences raise questions about the role of the democratic process in improving environmental performance. The interests of Capital and Labour have traditionally dominated formulation of government economic policies. Environmental policy tends gradually to expand in scope and effectiveness as: (a) public awareness of the environment increases; (b) environmental interest groups become relatively more powerful; and (c) levels of democracy and pluralism advance to enable such groups to increase their influence over policy-makers. The imposition of centralized directives from the European Commission on all EU countries is an admirable attempt to speed up this evolutionary process, but it could be counterproductive if its circumvention of the democratic process alienates domestic support for such measures.

Other groupings of states commit themselves to less stringent or more specific standards than the EU. For example, members of the UN Economic Commission for Europe, which includes Western Europe, Scandinavia and Eastern European countries, have since 1979 collaborated to cut gaseous emissions that cause transborder air pollution and acid deposition. The North American Free Trade Agreement (NAFTA) contains some environmental safeguards, but enforcement is poorer than in the EU and so convergence is slower. For example, considerable pollution is generated by the concentration of industries situated in the free trade zone on the Mexican side of the US border, attracted by the economic advantages of operating there. As the Mexican government gives highest priority to the contribution made by the zone to the national economy, it chooses not to enforce its own environmental laws strongly, and is not pressed by its partners to do any better. Mexico's level of economic development is greatly inferior to that of the USA and Canada, and clearly the members of NAFTA have decided that there are limits to the amount of mutual convergence that they can achieve in such conditions.

Weak regional regimes, which are not binding on those that sign them, have even less chance of success than groupings bound by treaty. For example, all of the states surrounding the Mediterranean, except Albania, committed themselves in the Mediterranean Action Plan of 1975 to 'take all appropriate steps to prevent, abate and combat pollution in the Mediterranean Sea area and protect and improve the marine environment in the area'. In 1985 they went further and agreed to realize a specific list of improvements within ten years. But both the original and revised plans were voluntary and the states did not realize either of them, giving a higher priority to economic development instead (F Pearce, 1995).

Promoting global convergence in environmental performance

States are also constrained by the global agreements which they sign, particularly the strong environmental regimes which are binding on signatories (see Chapter 12). Parties to the Framework Convention on Climate Change (FCCC), and its subsequent protocols, for example, have committed themselves to limiting their emissions of greenhouse gases, and this, in turn, will affect their national trends in Natural Capital and Human and Man-Made Capital. Developing countries are often allowed to proceed more slowly in complying with strong regimes, in line with the principle of differentiated obligations – which recognizes that they are less able to afford to improve their environmental performance than developed countries – and with the 'gradualist' approach mentioned above.

Since the mid 1990s, attempts have been made to extend international environmental commitments beyond the confines of purely environmental regimes such as the FCCC. Proposals have been made, for example, to limit the import of sustainable development by adding environmental conditions to international trade agreements under the auspices of the World Trade Organization (WTO). These conditions would reduce the environmental impacts associated with the extraction of raw materials or the manufacture of goods exported from developing countries (Costanza, 1994; Williams, 1999b). No agreement on this issue was reached in the abortive Seattle round of trade talks in 1999 or in the follow-up meetings in Doha in 2001 and Cancun in 2003, but the topic is likely to be raised again in future talks (see Chapter 12). However, such proposals, referred to earlier in this chapter as stemming from a globalist approach, seek to apply the same conditions to developing and developed countries. This completely ignores evidence that the sustainability of resource management and the level of environmental quality initially falls in the course of development and only improves when societies have become highly developed – a relationship portrayed in the Environmental Kuznets Curve (Cole et al, 1997). Achieving more sustainable development will depend upon a growing awareness that convergence is feasible but uniformity is impossible.

Influences from below: patterns of development at lower levels

Even though a particular spatial unit is undergoing economic development not all the smaller sub-units which it comprises may be developing equally rapidly. Some may be stagnating or even in recession, perpetuating the uneven pattern of development found in most countries in which levels of income, social welfare and Human and Man-Made Capital are preferentially concentrated in some regions. The sustainability of development is often uneven too, since environmental management is better in some spatial units than others. Is such unevenness inevitable, and to what extent does it constrain the performance of the entire state or other spatial units?

Uneven economic development
Inequitable transfers of capital between regions, of the kind mentioned above, contribute to uneven development within countries. To provide some structure to complex regional mosaics in developed countries, Williams (1987) distinguished between wealthy 'rapid accumulation' regions, which now account for the majority of economic activity, and poorer 'slow accumulation' regions, which include the 'rust-belt' areas found in most developed countries, such as South Yorkshire in the UK and Michigan in the USA. Many of the latter used to be economically thriving, often as centres of mining or manufacturing, but fell into decline as economic activity shifted to other regions. Man-Made Capital became obsolete, and thousands of households unable or unwilling to search for new jobs elsewhere were left in poverty, usually in an environment degraded by decades of resource extraction and waste dumping.

Marxist economic geographers, such as Harvey (1985), explain uneven development as an inevitable consequence of the accumulation of capital and the crises to which this is subject:

The process of accumulation must be understood as inherently spatial because it depends on labour power which, in the short term at least, is place bound ... Capitalist development has to negotiate a knife edge path between preserving the values of past capitalist investments . . . and destroying them in order to open up fresh geographical space for accumulation.

As a country becomes more developed it is normal for the government to intervene to ensure that the rise in overall economic activity is matched by greater equity in the distribution of national income. Yet development is still uneven in many developed countries today, and this raises two questions. First, how much unevenness is compatible with a highly developed society? Second, could a limited degree of unevenness be acceptable in principle and yet be politically and morally unacceptable in practice? There is still, for example, a vigorous debate about the reality of the so-called 'North–South divide' within England. According to Townshend and Gordon (1999), data from the 1991 National Census reveals that:

England remains a nation of immense social and economic differences . . . Problems of unemployment, poverty and ill health are concentrated in the major cities, the depressed industrial north, and in the forgotten corners of England. By contrast, areas of affluence and privilege are found in the extended suburban South-East. . . . Divisions of wealth between rich and poor seem to be getting more marked.

This is supported by another study of variation between English regions, which used a synthetic Competitiveness Index, based on indicators of average earnings, business density, unemployment, the number of knowledge-based businesses, economic activity and gross domestic product (GDP) per head (Huggins, 2000). This found that relative to a UK average of 100, the north-east was the least competitive region with a score of 89, while London was the most competitive, with a score of 116.

However, development in the UK as a whole is far more even than in other European countries. Compared with a 47 per cent difference between the GDP per capita of the UK's richest and poorest regions, expressed as a percentage of the EU mean, the difference for Italy is 93 per cent. Travers (1997) counters traditional concerns about the UK's North–South divide, claiming that it has the smallest inter-regional variation of any large European country: 'The myth of a UK with uniquely poor and rich regions is very powerful. The UK has, doubtless by accident, achieved a degree of regional equality of which it can be proud.' While inter-regional differences are important, they may be a distraction from even greater disparities within regions. In the English region of Yorkshire and Humberside, for example, the GDP per capita for North Yorkshire in 1994 was 99 per cent of the EU average, compared with 91 per cent for West Yorkshire and only 74 per cent for South Yorkshire (Eurostat, 1995).

Generalizing about the role of unevenness in development is difficult. It might be expected to decline as a country becomes more developed, but no straightforward pattern is evident. For example, regional differences in GDP per capita in the UK, as measured by the Coefficient of Variation, were declining until 1976, but then increased dramatically from 1976 to 1989 before falling again with the onset of the recession in 1990 (Dunford, 1997). There is also no consensus as to how wide a variation in regional development is consistent with a country being called 'developed'. A pragmatic limit of 75 per cent of the EU mean GDP per capita is currently used to identify regions that merit assistance through EU programmes, but a more rigorous assessment would be valuable, based on detailed research into the mechanisms of development.

Uneven sustainable development

The sustainability of development also often appears to be unevenly distributed among the regions of a country, within a region or even inside a city. Consider a typical country that has reached the middle to late phases of its development. Human and Man-Made Capital will tend to be concentrated in various core regions, and Natural Capital in poorer regions in the geographical and economic periphery. However, for such a country to comply with the Strong Condition or the Very Weak Condition in future, it would have to retain most if not all of its existing stocks of Natural Capital. So the regions in which Natural Capital is now concentrated could not be allowed to develop further, as this would inevitably reduce their Natural Capital. This might be politically unacceptable.

Contrary to the assumption underlying the Very Weak Condition, some areas have 'developed' but are now poor not only in Natural Capital but also in Human and Man-Made Capital. These include 'slow accumulation' regions, which used to be centres of industry but are now economically and socially depressed, and environmentally degraded. Similar conditions are found at the local level in inner cities and former mining communities. For example, mortality amongst infants aged less than one year is 7.3 deaths per 1000 live births in Inner London, but only 5.5 in suburban Outer London. According to Jacobsen (2001), Inner London is 'a southern European city in a northern European shell ... Areas of extreme poverty with poor health outlook exist cheek by jowl with great affluence.' Moreover, low-income groups in inner cities often live near areas of low environmental quality, such as industrial sites, refuse dumps and polluted canals (McGranahan et al, 1996). Current environmental economics theory takes no account of such spatial patterns, and there does not seem to be any way to modify it to encompass these cases within a sustainable development framework.

Planning for sustainable development

Interactions between different levels on the spatial scale pose two main challenges to planners. First, how to reduce the unevenness of development and sustainable development without undermining the sustainability of national development? Second, how to increase information flows between different levels to improve implementation of policies which, by common consent, are beneficial to the entire country? The failure of traditional 'top-down' planning methods has led to widespread adoption of 'bottom-up', participatory approaches to planning. Unfortunately, total reliance on such approaches can undermine the coherence of national policies, and it can also lead to problems as a result of the unequal distribution of political power in a country.

How unevenness complicates planning for sustainable development

The development of peripheral regions

Deciding whether or not to develop peripheral regions in developing countries may put planners imbued with the sustainable development paradigm into a quandary.

The inhabitants of such regions tend to be poorer on average than those in the metropolitan core, so there is a strong ethical case to improve their mean incomes. However, conventional development strategies tend to promote agricultural expansion or resource exploitation, which are likely to remove forest and other natural vegetation and generally degrade the environment. So while people might benefit economically and socially from such initiatives, the quality of their environment would probably decline. Even if the rise in Human and Man-Made Capital within the region did exceed the loss of Natural Capital, because peripheral regions usually contain a large proportion of a country's Natural Capital the loss could cause a significant reduction in the Resource Capital and Environmental Quality of the country as a whole, and so undermine its sustainability of development.

Critics argue that attempts to 'develop' peripheral regions are rarely undertaken with the improvement of local livelihoods as the main priority, and that most of the benefits from expanding logging, mining and plantations usually accrue to outsiders. As Atkinson shows in Chapter 10, resource-rich circumpolar regions have, in the past, received little of the Human and Man-Made Capital generated by exploiting their resources. The experience of Nigeria's Delta Region, referred to above, provides another potent example, showing how popular dissatisfaction with uneven sustainable development can lead to national political conflict.

Some governments openly state that they favour exploiting resources in peripheral regions for the sake of national economic development, rather than for the good of local people. In 2002, for example, US President George W Bush declared that the overall benefits of further oil exploration in Alaska exceeded the resulting environmental costs. In developing countries which depend heavily upon resource exploitation, the stakes can be far higher. For example, the Ok Tedi copper mine, located in a remote mountainous area of Papua New Guinea, accounts for 10 per cent of the country's GDP and 20 per cent of its exports. Yet its operations have caused serious damage to the local environment, and its owners have had to pay hundreds of millions of dollars to store mine waste and compensate villagers for damage to their water supplies, land and vegetation. The World Bank recommended closing the mine to end environmental degradation, but this created a dilemma for the government, which must balance the environmental benefits of closure against the repercussions for the national economy (World Bank, 1999). In September 2001 the government decided that the mine should stay open, but be run by a new publicly-controlled company operating under strict environmental safeguards.

Identifying sustainable strategies for urban development

A related problem concerns the role of cities in sustainable development. While the vigour of regional development often depends upon urban economic activity, cities must import resources and tend to be both spatial concentrations of pollution and the centres of regional networks of environmental degradation. Consequently, they may never attain sustainable development in their own right on the basis of the Constant Capital Conditions.

One solution to this dilemma is simply to try to keep cities as compact as possible. This has become a favoured model for urban sustainability (Haughton, 1999; see also Chapter 6 in this volume). If a large number of people live and work in a small area then transport and energy demand will be low, offsetting the pollution and social welfare problems associated with the high population density. Dispersed urban and suburban settlements might be socially and aesthetically more attractive places to live, but they are more dependent upon vehicular transport and less energy efficient (ICLEI, 1993).

Another approach is not to focus on the city, but to assess its sustainability in the context of the region on which it chiefly depends for resources and labour. For example, in 1997 planners in the Hertfordshire town of Stevenage estimated that 65,000 new homes were needed to sustain future local economic growth, but found that only 85 per cent of them could be accommodated within its boundaries. One option for locating the remaining houses was to disperse them throughout the surrounding countryside, which would be to the detriment of rural landscape quality. Another was to concentrate them along an existing major transport corridor, the A1 trunk road, with its associated rail and bus routes. The town council chose the second option because of its lesser landscape impact and the potential to minimize additional fuel use and associated traffic pollution. The UK Department of the Environment, Transport and the Regions (DETR) supported this decision to adopt an integrated regional view of the proposed development. It approved the removal of 2.5 square miles of land from the Green Belt along the A1 corridor, provided that in compensation five times as much land was added to the Green Belt elsewhere in the region.

Rethinking top-down planning

In top-down planning methods, state officials draw up plans at a national level which must be complied with at lower levels by regional and local governments. However, this approach often fails to ensure successful development because the policy is either poorly formulated or poorly implemented, or both. The more removed planners are on the spatial scale from the level at which activities are to be undertaken, the greater the likely differences in perception between planners and local inhabitants. A classic example of a divide between supranational planners and priorities at lower levels occurred in the late 1990s when the European Court of Auditors ordered all EU governments to restrict the width of hedgerows to under 2 metres because it believed that oversized hedgerows were being used to exaggerate field sizes to make fraudulent claims for farm subsidies. At the supranational level financial stringency was perceived to be more important than any associated biodiversity loss. In the face of protests from the Council for the Protection of Rural England and other NGOs, the UK Ministry of Agriculture responded that it was powerless to change the new measure, even though it was accused of applying EU rules too strictly.

By the 1970s, the top-down approach to promoting development in developing countries was recognized as inefficient and ineffective, reflecting numerous failures in many countries. Prominent amongst these was the scheme to build a highway through Brazilian Amazonia and resettle along it large numbers of poor people from overcrowded areas in drought-stricken north-east Brazil. Unfortunately, the route chosen for the Trans-Amazonian Highway by remote government planners was covered almost entirely by infertile soils. Consequently, few people joined the resettlement scheme and many of these eventually returned home when their crops failed (Grainger, 1993).

Reaction to the limitations of the top-down approach has led to growing use of an alternative 'bottom-up', participatory approach, in which people at the spatial level where development is to occur participate actively in its planning and implementation. In principle, this should ensure a better two-way flow of information between national and sub-national levels. This ought to improve policy formulation by balancing the national government's overview and coordinating role with local people's creativity and knowledge of specific conditions in the area concerned. It should also lead to better implementation of a policy or project because local people will be more enthused about something that they have helped to plan, introduce fewer obstacles in the way of its implementation by government agencies, and may assist in implementing it themselves. In the context of development projects funded from overseas, aid agencies can feel more confident that money devoted to bottom-up projects will improve the living standards of the very poorest, as it is transmitted directly to the specific communities where they are concentrated rather than being diverted to further enrich the elite. Aid will also be used to empower the poor to escape from the poverty trap in which they are confined by national and international power structures.

A bottom-up approach is also often assumed to be good for the environment on the assumption that everybody is keen to conserve their own immediate surroundings. This may be over-optimistic, but local people's knowledge of the natural and cultural environments in which they live is invariably superior to that of external 'experts'. Because of this, and the other reasons given above, Agenda 21, the blueprint for sustainable development agreed at the 1992 UN Conference on Environment and Development, advocated a participatory approach to sustainable development. This inspired the slogan 'Thinking globally, acting locally', and the idea of 'glocalization', in which local action can bypass constraints imposed from a higher level on the spatial scale (Beauregard, 1995).

There is much more to participation, however, than improving links between national and local levels. It is a more generalized philosophy with applications to all forms of planning involving different levels on the spatial scale. As such, it has given rise to strategies in which state planners do not just consult people at lower spatial levels, but also devolve management responsibility to them. The Philippines government, for example, has been taking such an approach to environmental management since the late 1980s.

Problems with participatory planning and management

Experience with these new forms of planning and management is still limited, but is sufficient to show that they do not provide an instant solution to all the problems that have long plagued planning. Nor can they guarantee sustainable development. This sub-section highlights some of the practical problems that have arisen so far. They are instructive in their own right, but also for the light that they shed on interactions between different levels on the spatial scale.

Conflicts between states and regions

In federal states, such as the USA and India, regional governments have legal authority to formulate and implement policies to suit regional needs. Although this is an excellent example of devolved decision-making, it can create obstacles when states attempt to make coherent improvements in the quality of life for the entire country. It is common in such circumstances for the balance of power between the state and the regions to be strongly contested. Regions that differ in political philosophy from the national government may therefore take a different line on a given topic merely to assert their autonomy, regardless of the social, economic or environmental merits of their actions. In India, for example, state governments are sufficiently powerful to ignore national environmental and social criteria for the construction of hydroelectric dams.

Conflicts can also arise over the sustainable rates of growth of different regions. For example, in 1999, the South-East Regional Planning Conference (SERP) – which represents local councils in the region – wanted to control development by building only 718,000 new homes between 1996 and 2016, believing that anything more would have significant negative environmental and social impacts. The UK Government's Department of the Environment, Transport and the Regions (DETR) thought that it had a better understanding of regional capabilities than local people and favoured a higher total of 860,000. SERP objected to this and the dispute continues (Groom, 1999a).

Limitations on the autonomy of regional authorities

In the UK, where experiments with devolution are still at an early stage, the national government is learning to accept that regional assemblies in Wales and Scotland have the right to adopt different policies. On the other hand, it has heavily restricted the powers of the Regional Development Agencies (RDAs) it has established in England. These are charged with making their regions more competitive by planning economic development and coordinating the regeneration of communities, land and buildings, but their efforts have been frustrated by inadequate powers and finance. So while they can identify the needs of their regions, they cannot meet them. Their joint claim in 2000 for additional funding to meet the unique needs that they had identified was rejected by government, which asserted that 'our strategy is not to set up one region against another' (Groom and Newman, 2000). As the RDAs were established to make their regions more competitive it is difficult to see what else they could be expected to do.

Each RDA presented a ten-year strategy document to the government in 1999, and these reports reveal interesting differences in regional perceptions of the most desirable goals for future development. The principal aim of the North-east RDA, representing one of England's poorest regions, was, not surprisingly, to develop more in a conventional sense by raising GDP per capita to the UK average from its present value of 80 per cent. The RDA for the richest region, the South-east, might have been expected to give higher priority to the social and environmental dimensions of development. Indeed, it recognized that 'we must release the potential of the region as a whole measured in sustainable economic prosperity, social inclusion and environmental quality'. Yet it still gave top priority to economic growth because it judged itself mainly on international criteria and wanted to move into the 'top ten' of the 77 European regions, as ranked by GDP per capita: it was then ranked 23rd. In contrast, the South-west RDA put more stress on the environment, arguing that it has the highest environmental quality of any region in the country and that 'the natural place for environmental industries is where the quality is good'. It aimed to create 24,000 jobs and £370 million of output in environmental industries, with 12,000 more jobs and £260 million of output in the renewable energy field (Groom, 1999b; 1999c).

Limitations on local autonomy

Local governments are invariably at a greater disadvantage than regional bodies in their relations with national government. This prescribes their freedom of action, making it difficult to implement the idea of 'glocalization'. Since UNCED, there has been considerable local action in the name of sustainable development, including the production of Local Agenda 21 plans, and this compares favourably with the limited action at national level (see Chapter 6). Yet while local councils are supposedly responsible for 'deciding the most sustainable way of meeting the needs of their communities' (Taylor and Parker, 1998), most are unable fully to realize their potential. An Audit Commission (1997) report considered the environmental performance of most UK local councils to be 'patchy'.

One reason for this is that local authorities lack sufficient autonomy to respond to local needs. On matters of housing policy, for instance, councils in the UK must work within national guidelines, and can only release rural land for housing after all other options for building on derelict land and converting offices and other buildings have been exhausted (DETR, 1999c). They are also expected to devise plans to integrate different modes of transport in their areas. Yet national government insists on retaining powers of final approval. While this is supposedly intended to ensure uniformity across the country (DETR, 1998a), in practice the result has often been to delay progress.

Problems with local participation

Participation does not always lead to a desirable outcome for local government. For example, a citizens' group in the American city of Seattle decided, in the spirit of Agenda 21, to devise a set of sustainable development indicators in a participatory manner. The 'Sustainable Seattle' group defined sustainability by a consensus process as a state of 'long-term cultural, economic and environmental health and vitality', and developed a set of 40 indicators to reflect these various different dimensions. It decided not to aggregate them into a single index, or to compare indicator values with benchmark values denoting sustainability levels. Instead, the direction of movement in each indicator was used to show progress towards sustainability (Atkisson, 1996). Unfortunately, the City Council rejected the set of indicators, as it felt obliged to monitor sustainability in terms of compliance with the critical goals in the 'Comprehensive Plan' that is obligatory for all municipalities in the State of Washington. The Sustainable Seattle indicators were not compatible with these regional goals and so council officers had to devise an entirely new set (Brugmann, 1997; City of Seattle, 1996).

Policy implications

States keen to achieve more sustainable development must give careful attention to interactions between different levels on the spatial scale. Promoting convergence between the social and environmental performances of groups of states is to be commended. It must not, however, overwhelm national democracy, or exceed either the capacities of the states involved or their willingness to accept common standards. If any of these conditions are breached, this may prevent effective action or produce results that are not sustainable in the long term. Attempts at regional convergence between states at a similar phase in their economic development are likely to be far more successful than trying to achieve global convergence by setting uniform standards. This is just one instance of how the uneven distribution of economic development at one spatial level can affect performance at higher levels.

The mechanisms used for implementing sustainable development programmes also need careful scrutiny. Devolved and participatory planning approaches are still in their infancy, and lessons continue to be learned. But if the experiences recounted here are in any way typical they are unlikely to provide a magic solution to planning problems. This is because tensions inevitably arise between politicians, civil servants, groups and individuals at different levels of the spatial scale as a result of differences in perceptions and the need to maintain or increase political power. Expectations in some quarters that they will automatically lead to sustainable development are just as illusory as alternative claims that the key lies solely in international collaboration.

Top-down and bottom-up approaches both have their merits. Top-down planning at national level can ensure overall coherence and a flow of information down the spatial scale, while a bottom-up approach can generate popular enthusiasm, improve relevance to specific problems and ensure a flow of information up the spatial scale. However, neither approach on its own holds the key to success. Without some controlling influences from higher levels on the spatial scale, bottom-up projects could degenerate into a 'free for all'.

Perhaps what is needed is a synthesis of the two approaches, a 'top-and-bottom' approach which combines the best features of both. There may be no need to impose this specifically, as it is likely to develop automatically in most situations where tensions arise between top-down and bottom-up methods. The solution arrived at in each case is unlikely to be theoretically ideal or satisfactory to all, and will be determined by the balance of power between the various groups involved in the issue. On the other hand, it will probably be more acceptable than any solution which might have been reached by using just one of the methods.

Another solution to the contradictions between the two planning approaches is to place more reliance on market mechanisms. In many countries national and local governments are adopting liberalization strategies to improve public services, relying less on public organizations and more on private commercial or non-governmental bodies. In the UK this has led to the privatization of housing estates originally built by local councils for rent to low-income groups. Initially, many houses were sold to their tenants in the 1980s. In the 1990s, faced with the estimated £40 billion cost of refurbishing their remaining housing stock, councils have gradually transferred ownership to housing associations or trusts that can raise the capital (Burns, 2000; Burns and Timmins, 2000). The Asian Development Bank (1997) has likewise suggested that city governments in developing countries should switch from being providers of services, such as water supply and public transport, to being facilitators of services provided by others on a profit-making basis. Some see in this a sign of government failure, but others view it as the next step in the expansion of economic democracy. If it does not reduce social welfare, and it frees public money for spending on other areas, such as environmental management and regeneration, then it could make a positive contribution to sustainable development.

Conclusion

Viewed from a spatial perspective, sustainable development is a far more complicated concept than is commonly assumed. Within the framework of the Very Weak Condition of environmental economics theory, it is not necessarily meaningful at all levels on the spatial scale used here, particularly at the local and household levels, owing to the absence of some capital stocks and the conversion processes which link them.

Examination of the sustainability of development in typical spatial units at different levels of the spatial scale has revealed the need to treat individual units as open economies, rather than in isolation, in order to match real world conditions. At the national level, the Very Weak Condition can be used as a criterion for sustainable development in open economies, provided that national trends in Natural Capital and Human and Man-Made Capital are corrected for inequities associated with the inward and outward flows of raw materials, pollution and other forms of environmental degradation. These result in countries or sub-national regions importing economic development, or importing or exporting sustainable development. This leads in turn to uneven patterns of economic development and sustainable development, both at the global level and within countries, though the effects of inequitable transfers may be ameliorated by various compensation mechanisms, such as migration and state intervention. Making corrections for such transfers at sub-national levels is far more difficult because of the complexity of flows and lack of data.

A new kind of international framework is needed to reduce the incidence of sustainability transfers. However, since development is so uneven at global level it would be inequitable to expect all countries to achieve the same degree of sustainability of development at the same time, as is required by 'globalist' proposals to impose uniform environmental and social standards on world trade. A 'gradualist' approach might be more appropriate. This would assess the sustainability of development, or environmental and social standards, relative to the norm expected for each country's current level of development. This is not yet another ambiguous compromise, like the portrayal of sustainable development in the Brundtland Report (WCED, 1987), but a genuine alternative that could be monitored just as rigorously, provided that acceptable relationships between the rate of increase in social and environmental performance and the level of economic development could be constructed on the basis of theoretical and empirical studies.

Two types of interactions between different levels on the spatial scale were examined here: influences from higher levels and influences from lower levels. Influences from above can lead to limited convergence in the development paths of countries at a similar phase of development. But taking a globalist approach and trying to impose uniform environmental and social standards on all countries, regardless of their level of development, is neither equitable nor advisable. A gradualist approach, typified in the principle of differentiated obligations often employed in international regimes, would be far more equitable to developing countries. No firm conclusions were reached about the relationships between levels of economic development and sustainable development and their spatial unevenness. More in-depth theoretical and empirical studies of these relationships are needed in view of their tremendous importance to international, regional and national planning.

Sustainable development is often mistakenly equated with either successful international collaboration to solve global environmental problems or participatory actions at the local level. The former approach is inadequate because global environmental problems are merely symptoms of unsustainable development at the national level. Consequently, the real solution to global climate change lies in improving the sustainability of development of every country. International agreements can provide an equitable framework for this, but that is all. Nor is participation a magic solution to unsustainable development. It is merely the most popular development strategy today. Experiments in recent years with participation, and devolution of management responsibility to lower levels on the spatial scale, suggest that while these have an important role to play in improving the sustainability of development, they too have their limitations. It was suggested that a combination of top-down and bottom-up approaches might be optimal for implementing programmes because it should achieve the best balance between coherence and enthusiasm, and promote better flows of information in both directions on the spatial scale.

The Very Weak Condition, suitably corrected as necessary, appears from this discussion to provide a reasonable framework for analysing the role of spatial scale and spatial interactions in sustainable development. Other conditions, from environmental economics and ecological economics theories, were not so appropriate. However, the Very Weak Condition did have its limitations, particularly relating to the aggregation of Human and Man-Made Capital and the requirement that changes in this be compared directly with changes in Natural Capital. To provide a more comprehensive and practical explanation of spatial aspects of sustainable development we need a better theoretical model which disaggregates the economic, social and environmental dimensions of development. This would be more flexible than the Very Weak Condition and more suited to monitoring transfers between different countries and other spatial units. It would also allow planners to be far more discriminating when making trade-offs between the three dimensions of development. It is all too easy at present to portray sustainable development as being 'anti-development' and concerned solely with the environment. A three dimensional model would dispel this misconception and reduce current constraints on realizing the potential of sustainable development.

4

Linking the Local to the Global: Can Sustainable Development Work in Practice?

John Soussan

Introduction

The idea of sustainable development is no longer new but still remains challenging. It is now more than 15 years since the report of the Brundtland Commission (WCED, 1987) gave it worldwide publicity. The United Nations (UN) General Assembly that reviewed progress since the UN Conference on Environment and Development (UNCED) in Rio de Janeiro in 1992 has come and gone with much rhetoric but little demonstrable impact (Dodds, 1997; Osborn and Bigg, 1998). The 2002 Johannesburg Summit on Sustainable Development did little to change this situation. The concept has many definitions and meanings, but has rarely transcended this rhetoric to become a basis for meaningful, effective action (Redclift, 1987; Reid, 1995). Why is this the case? Does it reflect inherent flaws in the basic concept, or is it, rather, that sustainable development is a good idea that people are unwilling or unable to put into practice?

The Agenda 21 document produced by UNCED advocated a balanced programme of action at all geographical levels from global to local (UNCED, 1992b). However, it particularly encouraged local initiatives; indeed, much of the action undertaken so far in the name of sustainable development has been at local level. This local emphasis reflects the participatory paradigm that has been in vogue for some time in development planning. But can local action really make development more sustainable and thus substitute for action at national and international levels?

This chapter assesses the effectiveness of the participatory approach, and of local action in general, and identifies the lessons that can be learned for implementing sustainable development at local level in all countries. It is not suggested here that actions at local level are unnecessary – rather, that they will not be effective unless and until there are concerted efforts to create a legal, policy and institutional context which provides adequate and secure rights and entitlements to the poor. In other words, the process of local-level change is contingent upon measures at national and international levels that create the conditions to enable grassroots initiative to succeed. This is fundamental to sustainable development, which is – or should be – about giving more choices and better options to the poor. Furthermore, the creation of any new legal and policy framework needs to be supported by the development of an institutional context through which potential choices can become reality. This institutional context must provide the poor with secure access to the resources – financial, technological, material, intellectual and others – through which choices can be realized.

Approaches to Development

Challenging established orthodoxies

In the 1950s, during the early years of modern development aid programmes, it was widely believed that any international aid given to developing countries would produce broadly based development through a trickle-down effect. The benefits of economic growth were thus expected to percolate down to the poorest of the poor, leading to the ultimate alleviation of poverty. However, it soon became evident that there was little basis for this expectation (Hall, 1983). As a result, many development agencies, including the UK Overseas Development Administration (now the Department for International Development), increasingly focused their aid directly upon the poorest sectors of society. This had long been the approach taken by non-governmental organizations (NGOs), whose success in facilitating development owed much to their network of contacts at the grassroots level.

Development planning was also formerly characterized by a top-down approach. Theorists saw development as the replacement of a traditional agriculture-based society by a modern industrial society, an approach that implied planning by an elite educated in the techniques of industrial modernity. The mass of the population, lacking knowledge of modern ways, were excluded on the assumption that they could contribute nothing to the process. All that was needed was to formulate the 'correct' national policies, and state institutions would implement them by passing instructions down their chains of command from headquarters to the grassroots.

However, the ineffectiveness of these institutional structures was eventually recognized. State-centred planning has been supplanted by a more bottom-up, participatory approach through which, in principle, everyone can contribute something and benefit from empowerment (Haverkort et al, 1991; Hiemstra et al, 1992; Nelson and Wright, 1995). This new thinking reflects a belief that local institutions can be more effective in implementing development projects than their national counterparts. Even the poorest peasants may possess vital knowledge of how to manage their local environments sustainably. The participatory approach, based on the work of authors such as Chambers (1983), Oakley (1991) and Conway (1985), has had many positive effects, not least the rejection of top-down technical fixes that were all too often damaging to both local societies and the environment.

Participation is fine in principle, but it has taken time to translate it into practice. What has not yet emerged is a coherent and consistent set of development approaches that are widely applied and can produce the type of tangible benefits anticipated. This chapter argues that this reflects the role of 'outsiders', especially those responsible for providing overseas aid, in engendering such a process. These efforts have largely been misdirected. Often, it seems, the need for local-level development has been taken far too literally. An over-concentration on the grassroots level has led to the exclusion of actions at the policy, legal and institutional level where development assistance is more likely to succeed and can have a greater impact. The whole debate has become polarized, with proponents and opponents of participation adopting dogmatic positions that mask the initial rationale for the approach. Elsewhere, local initiatives have regressed to some form of tokenism, where the appearance, but not the substance, of participation is created (see Chapter 9).

There are also constraints on those supposed to implement this approach. All too often, government officials in developing countries, even those committed in principle to 'participation', find it hard to escape from their old routine. They still regard participation as simply informing local people in advance about how a development project will be implemented, without inviting their comments and suggestions for improvements to the initial plan. Similarly, 'involvement' is often understood to mean mobilizing as many people as possible to work as labourers in projects or as passive recipients of schemes.

From local to national

At the heart of the participatory approach to development is the notion that individual communities can create their own development in a way that meets their specific needs. But the unstated assumption is that successful action can be achieved on a large scale, typically at national level, by cumulative action in hundreds and thousands of local communities, achieving results impossible with a top-down approach. While the importance of first establishing pilot projects in selected localities has been accepted as a prelude to national schemes, there are still questions about replication. Pilot projects are unlikely to be the starting point of a snow-ball effect that can spread nationwide unless the right conditions are in place at the outset for individual local projects to be self-sustaining once administrative, financial and technical inputs from external agencies have been withdrawn. As a similar philosophy is espoused in some sustainable development circles, it is worth at least identifying some of the drawbacks inherent in this assumption.

There are many examples of actions by NGOs and others that have been effective at the local level (Edwards and Hulme, 1992; Krishna et al, 1997; Ndione et al, 1995); but where these have taken full account of local diversity, they often depend upon such intensive levels of external inputs and personal commitment that they cannot be sustained once the project ends. These efforts are praiseworthy and provide exemplars of what can be done, but they are limited by the classic problem of scaling up: how to replicate effective but restricted local efforts to create change at a scale which impacts upon poverty and resource degradation at the national or regional level.

Sustainable development will really mean something when it works not in one village, but in the 100,000 villages of Bangladesh or the 1 million villages of India. It is inconceivable that this can be achieved through the intensive interaction between 'outsiders' and individual farmers, women or even communities that has become so fashionable. Perhaps we should reverse the old slogan and think locally, but act nationally or even globally. In other words, we understand and build upon local-level livelihoods, resource management systems and patterns of social relationships, but act upon a larger scale to develop a legal, policy and institutional framework that creates the conditions through which people can realize more and better choices, with greater security and less variability in the conditions that affect their livelihoods.

Sustainable livelihoods

If sustainable development is to advance the human condition it must be effective at the local level in the developing world, where there is least sustainability and evidence of development. It could even be argued that the touchstone for success should be its effect on the livelihoods of the poorest of the poor, who are often the most vulnerable of all to social, economic and environmental shocks.

According to Carney (1998):

A livelihood comprises the capabilities, assets (including both material and social resources) and activities required for a means of living. A livelihood is sustainable when it can cope with and recover from stresses and shocks and maintain or enhance its capabilities now and in the future, while not undermining the natural resource base.

This definition transcends the rather limited economic view of human welfare that has been dominant for so long, acknowledging that a good environment and access to resources are also vital components of human welfare.

But does bottom-up, participatory development really work? The ultimate test of any development paradigm is whether it actually makes individual livelihoods more sustainable. The remainder of the chapter looks at various examples that show the problems created by focusing solely upon action at the local level. Such drawbacks may be overcome by putting local action in the proper context. The analysis of individual case studies generates conclusions about how development practice could be changed for the better and how lessons from the development field can be applied in sustainable development planning.

Can Local Action Substitute for Ineffective State Institutions?

Bureaucratic state institutions are notoriously ineffective in delivering public services, and it is easy to become resigned to this, turning instead to local action to achieve more sustainable development. This is exactly the thinking that informed a project in Bangladesh, which was planned quite dogmatically from a participatory point of view. Managing water resources is fundamental to the functioning and viability of the country's livelihood systems and has been at the centre of national planning and donor investments. These have concentrated, however, on flood control to the exclusion of most other issues. This was particularly true following the major floods of 1987 and 1988, during which a large part of the country was inundated. As a response, a huge Systems Rehabilitation Project was launched in 1988, at a cost of US$110 million, with two main aims: first, to rehabilitate and develop a sustainable maintenance system for water control infrastructure, such as embankments, sluice gates and canals; and, second, to establish local water user organizations to control the rehabilitated structures.

However, the project failed in these goals, and the situation when the project ended in 1997 was no better than when it was first planned. Its approach to participatory development, involving the formation of water user groups of farmers, was a total disaster. Few, if any, active groups had been formed by the end of the project and there were no examples of water control structures being managed by local communities. This was despite the existence of a wide range of traditional systems where local people worked together to manage water resources with no outside help or resources.

The basic problem was that the project attempted to make progress within an existing framework of organizations and authorities. Yet it became evident that it could only succeed if there were also fundamental reforms to the structure of the whole sector. There was an urgent need to devolve authority away from a highly centralized and bureaucratic agency, the Bangladesh Water Development Board. However, the government shied away from transferring power from the board to local government and community-based organizations. A total move to the grassroots was not required since many aspects of water control cannot be addressed at the purely local level. Rather, the ideal for the future would be multi-agency subsidiarity, including many organizations, not just one. This would facilitate efforts to find the appropriate level, whether national, regional, district or local, at which different decisions should be made (Soussan and Datta, 1998). In the absence of such wholesale reform, action at the local level alone could not compensate for the failures of existing institutional structures.

This type of tokenism has characterized many development projects and is likely to persist in programmes intended to make development more sustainable. All too often the search for sustainable development has become confused with, and replaced by, efforts to create participation. This, in turn, is interpreted as creating social change through which excluded sections of the population – especially women, but also the poor – are empowered through a process of social organization (Nelson and Wright, 1995). This naive participation, captured in the classic slogan of the environmental movement 'Think globally, act locally', is based on an implicit, but rarely articulated, assumption that the barriers to sustainable development can most effectively be surmounted at the local level, and that such profound changes to local social relationships and power structures can be achieved by the efforts of outsiders.

The Political Limits of Local Action

Many so-called development failures are not failures at all because they were never intended to succeed in the first place. In many developing countries, and not a few developed countries too, governments enact legislation with fine-sounding goals, such as encouraging sustainable resource management. But these are rarely fulfilled because the policy as stated on paper does not correspond with the government's actual intentions. The government cannot articulate this hidden agenda (Rees, 1990) because it would risk upsetting powerful interest groups.

During the late 1980s, at the request of the government of Somalia, the UK government funded a project to develop more sustainable woodland management in the Bay Region of Somalia, 200 kilometres west of the capital Mogadishu. But all efforts at local management were undermined by large-scale clearance of woodlands to produce charcoal for the Mogadishu market. Efforts to control clearance and improve the efficiency of production proved fruitless, so the present author was commissioned to prepare an alternative energy strategy to try to reduce demand. The strategy proposed was obvious and straightforward in technical terms: allow the import of kerosene and kerosene stoves, which at full economic costs would be cheaper than charcoal and preferred by the city's residents.

However, the government refused to reduce the very high import tariffs or remove restrictive import and distribution regulations that, in effect, created a state monopoly. Publicly, it claimed that it was afraid of problems with foreign currency availability and the exchange rate. But the real reason was that the then President's family controlled the lucrative charcoal trade and so government actions could not contradict this vital interest, even if it meant creating the conditions in which the largest national forest was destroyed. No amount of local action could change this while the policy persisted. The key to the sustainability of forest management, and the communities that depended upon this, therefore lay with national-level policies and actions (Soussan, 1990).

National Constraints on Participation in Sri Lanka

National policy constraints also curbed local initiatives to improve plantation housing estates in Sri Lanka. There are few more fundamental requirements for a sustainable livelihood than healthy housing conditions. Yet in both developed and developing countries affordable public housing estates built to realize this goal have become increasingly difficult to manage. So the authorities have had to consider radical alternatives to improve the management of remaining housing estates, such as privatization or community management schemes.

A traditional approach to improving social welfare

Most of the workers on Sri Lanka's 500 tea and rubber plantations are the descendants of indentured labourers brought over from the Indian state of Tamil Nadu before World War II. They are Tamil Hindus in a country that is overwhelmingly Sinhalese Buddhist and bitter conflict between the two communities persists. The estate Tamils are somewhat detached from this conflict, but have nevertheless been affected by the growth of Sinhalese chauvinism over the last decade.

The Tamil workers and their families – some 800,000 people altogether – are closely tied to the plantations on which they live. The estate provides their main source of income and also supplies housing, healthcare, water and sanitation, and other social facilities. The work force is highly unionized and has been successful, in the past, in negotiating a central bargaining system that has improved their pay rates and working conditions.

Nationalization of the plantations in the early 1970s led to poor management and under-investment that, together with falling prices for tea and rubber, undermined their productivity and profitability. The living conditions of workers declined too. The 1980s saw a two-fold response. The World Bank granted a large loan to finance refurbishment of the productive side of the estates. At the same time, joint Dutch and Norwegian funding supported what was dubbed the Social Welfare Programme (SWP), intended to improve the health, living conditions and welfare of the plantation workers and their families. It launched a relatively successful primary healthcare programme; but a new piped water supply system, essential for preventing ill health, soon deteriorated.

Apart from a few token new houses the main initial approach to improving housing was simply to provide new corrugated iron roofs for the existing dwellings. The old houses were so small, however, that this did little to improve conditions. A detailed survey (Soussan, 1992) revealed endemic overcrowding and limited access to electricity and piped water. The houses were in a poor physical condition: 42 per cent needed major structural repairs and a further 34 per cent lesser repairs. In 33 per cent of all houses surveyed, residents had illegally built one or more extra rooms, either attached to, or situated close by, the main house, typically for use as kitchens or extra bedrooms.

Privatization and a new participatory approach

The need to move away from centralized state management was finally accepted in 1990 and a process of partial privatization was therefore initiated. Although there was no transfer of ownership, June 1992 saw the award of management contracts for 22 groups of plantations to private companies. This followed a long period of negotiation when the unions used their power to insist that, as part of the privatization deal, a solution to the intractable housing problems be found by handing over the houses to the workers – although exactly what this meant was never specified.

The new management teams were more concerned with employee welfare than their predecessors had been and were happy to consider innovative solutions to the housing problem. They were, however, reluctant to make major investments them-selves. A self-help approach was, in principle, acceptable to both sides. This reflected developments in the previous few years. In the period leading up to privatization, the SWP tried out new approaches to housing improvement which included model self-help schemes, typically 20 houses at a time, on some estates. Although well received, these were closely controlled by the management and were only a token gesture when measured against a problem involving close to 200,000 houses. But they did establish the principle of self-help, which was no mean achievement given that most managers – who were invariably Sinhalese – seemed to regard the workers as akin to backward children incapable of doing anything on their own initiative.

The SWP team therefore devised a new strategy to create conditions whereby the residents of estate housing could be transformed into communities of homeowners who would improve their houses to acceptable standards through self-help initiatives. This initiative was based on past experience of squatter housing improvements in urban areas of the developing world, which found that given secure rights to land, financial help and an organizational base, people were perfectly capable of finding their own solutions to their housing needs (Gugler, 1997; Roberts, 1995; Skinner and Rodell, 1983; Turner, 1976; see also Chapter 6 in this volume). The strategy required:

- giving residents title to a plot of land – preferably including their existing house or, alternatively, a plot for a new house – that included space for expansion;
- a mechanism for financing and administering loans for self-help improvements that was adaptable, efficient and reflected the realities of estate life;
- a community-based organization so that residents could manage their settlements.

Problems and responses

The new strategy quickly ran into two major problems. First, implementing the principles required initial action by national government to define people's rights – particularly individual eligibility for land – and then to create a framework for local negotiations between management and residents on specific details of the scheme, such as plot sizes and the award of credit. Second, it encountered opposition from several quarters. The unions were reluctant to see their control over residents diminished as they would now lose their ability to intervene between residents and management on housing issues. The management side, for its part, was attracted to many aspects of the approach, but often proved unwilling to provide enough land to make the schemes viable. Externally, some political and religious leaders used the scheme to inflame anti-Tamil sentiments among the general population. Typically, it was claimed that the scheme accelerated the transfer of the Singhalese 'homeland' to Tamils from India.

The government's initial response was to refocus the initiative at the estate level by sponsoring further pilot schemes. Inevitably, these had minimal impact. Meanwhile, the residents began to create their own solutions by a rapid expansion of self-built structures. Eventually the situation reached an impasse, with the government unwilling to upset powerful political lobbies by taking the policy steps needed, but having no alternative solution to offer.

Centralized state ownership in Sri Lanka failed the plantations and their workers. To date, the government has gone half way to addressing the poor management of the plantations by bringing in private management. Yet it did not go the whole distance and privatize them. Radical attempts to tackle the living conditions of workers, by empowering them, have also failed because local action was constrained by national political opposition. Although the real issues have become more transparent, this experience again shows that local action has its limits, and that without sufficient backing from a national policy and legal framework it may fail.

Institutional Change and Community Forestry in Nepal

If local people are to be empowered to manage local resources, then the experiences already described in this chapter show that they need effective institutions to organize this management, as well as a supportive framework of national policies and institutions. The history of community forestry in Nepal over the last 30 years presents a more positive picture, showing how progress can be made as new institutions evolve and tensions with existing institutions are resolved.

Deforestation and its causes

Deforestation in the hills of Nepal has received widespread publicity during recent decades and has led to concerns, both inside and outside the country, that continuation of existing trends will lead, inevitably, to environmental catastrophe and the collapse of rural livelihoods (Soussan et al, 1995). However, popular generalizations are misleading: annual deforestation rates were 2 per cent between 1964 and 1979 in the southern plains area, but only 0.2 per cent in the hills. Similarly, deforestation is jeopardizing the very survival of some sections of the community; but others remain unaffected and some may even benefit from the changes. Thus, the loss of forest resources has different impacts according to the gender, economic position and geographical location of the users. These dynamics can only be understood within the context of the localized and complex economy–environment relationships that characterize Nepal.

These issues have many parallels throughout the developing world (Bromley, 1991; Hobley, 1996; Leach and Mearns, 1996; Scoones, 1996). The development of community forestry as a positive management initiative in Nepal, therefore, is an important model that embodies the ethos of sustainable development. Its goal is to combine action to meet human needs with conservation of the resource base. This is realized through the devolution of control over resources to local level. However, a point of departure for understanding these issues is the realization that the immediate local manifestations of deforestation are not an adequate base for analysis. An understanding is also required of structural features of the local society and economy, including land tenure and unequal access to resources. This must be complemented by attention to external factors such as government policies and actions on forest management; migration and land colonization; subsidies; taxes and prices for agricultural and other products; and the development of infrastructure.

The deforestation debate in Nepal has often centred on the identification of population growth as the main 'cause' of forest loss and associated environmental degradation. In other words, the poor were often blamed for the destruction of Nepal's forests. However, Barraclough and Ghimire (1990) refute the widely held position that population growth and poverty are the main causes of deforestation. Their argument follows authors such as Ives and Messerli (1989) and Blaikie (1985) in seeking explanation for environmental degradation in the social relations of resource rights and management. It follows that sustainable management of resources will only be possible when these fundamental issues are addressed within an effective social, legal and organizational framework.

Changing approaches to forest management

In these circumstances, meeting human needs and conserving the resource base become complementary goals which can be achieved, in principle, by devolving control over resources to the local level. The present participatory approach to forest management in Nepal emerged in the late 1980s after the failure of previous attempts at state management (forests were nationalized in 1957) and technically based social forestry plantations. Its central tenet is that communities contain within them the means for self-regulation and the equitable distribution of the products of common forest resources. Past disruptions to communities by population growth and techno-logical changes are considered to be surmountable, either by revitalizing old resource management institutions or by building new ones. As Bromley (1991) noted: 'The real tragedy of the commons is the process by which indigenous property rights structures have been undermined and delegitimized.' Hence, new common property regimes were promoted as an institutional answer to forest management for reasons of efficiency, equity and welfare.

The recent history of forest management in Nepal has thus seen a fundamental restructuring of forest policies, the laws which define rights and responsibilities, and the mandate and functioning of the Forestry Department and other government agencies charged with responsibility for this sector. The idea that control over forest use is the prerogative of the state has a long history. Yet there is also a well-established tradition of informal local forest management, which has recently become recognized and enshrined in law, policy and practice. Therein lies the difference between this case and the previous example. Whereas the Sri Lankan state was unwilling to countenance sufficient policy reforms, in Nepal there have been fundamental shifts in the government's stance over the last two decades.

Earlier attempts to encourage community forestry failed because, rather than empowering the broad mass of local people, they concentrated control in elites linked to central power structures. The 1977 Forest Act, for example, established different forms of Panchayat Forestry, where influence rested with the traditional local elite of the Panchayat, or 'council of five'. The 1987 Decentralization Act was thus vital in introducing a legislative structure through which responsibility for planning and administration could be devolved more effectively. Crucially for community forestry, it introduced the concept of forest user groups for the local control and implementa-tion of policies.

The Master Plan for Forestry, prepared between 1986 and 1988, provided the policy context for community forestry, declaring that all accessible forests in the hills should be handed over to 'the community'. Therefore, by the late 1980s the concept of community forest management was enshrined in national policy and became the focus of a number of donor-funded projects intended to encourage it. However, the impact of these efforts was at best only locally significant. The vast bulk of the forest area nationalized in 1957 was still under the *de jure* control of the Forestry Department and the *de facto* control of informal local institutions in some places; in many others there was no control at all.

The role of national political changes

At the beginning of the 1990s, sweeping political changes ended the centralized and autocratic Panchayat system and laid the foundations for democratic decision-making. This fundamentally changed the political context within which forestry policies operated and removed one of the main barriers to the development of genuine community forestry. National policy-makers also displayed a new and real desire to devolve authority for most aspects of forest management to community groups formed from the forest users who live in the vicinity of state forests.

The accumulation of experience in community forestry gained from previous projects, combined with an invigorated political will to end the domination of policies by the old elites and to enact populist measures, gave fresh impetus to community forestry. This was embodied in the 1993 Forest Act, which further defined the rights and responsibilities of community forestry groups, and the Forest Rules of 1995, which clarified the powers and duties of forest user groups (FUGs). As a result, both the legislative framework and the policy environment in Nepal currently favour the development of sustainable community-based forest management, and the country provides an excellent example of the importance of getting the national framework right before effective and widespread change can occur at the grassroots level.

Koshi Hills case study

The growth of community forestry is well illustrated by trends in the four districts of the Koshi Hills in eastern Nepal, which have been the focus of UK government support to community forestry since 1986. The early phase of the project focused on community mobilization and the formation of FUGs. However, little, if any, post-formation support was provided and there was an emphasis – perhaps an overemphasis – on the knowledge base of local communities. Initial progress was slow; only 41 groups had been formed by the end of 1991. This reflected difficulties in scaling up an effective but over-long formation process, a lack of knowledge concerning community forestry at the local level, and problems with the legal and policy framework, which at that time only gave limited control to the local community.

However, the political changes at the start of the 1990s created an environment in which people were motivated to discover and assert their rights. This allowed a remarkable momentum to develop in the community forestry process. Whereas change was initially largely externally driven, in the new climate the Forestry Department had increasing difficulty in keeping pace with demand for group formation from all over the region. By the middle of 1997 there were 960 FUGs in the four districts, with a membership of 82,285 households and 72,583 hectares of forest lands under their management (Soussan et al, 1998). The general condition of forests in the Koshi Hills is improving and many of the more established FUGs are extending into other arenas of community activity (Branney and Yadav, 1998).

Institutional developments

Experience in the Koshi Hills parallels that in Nepal as a whole. Community forestry is now well-established and there is a self-sustaining process of group formation, which is chiefly limited by the capacity of the Forestry Department to meet its procedural obligations. The fact that this has happened reflects the development of a legal and policy framework which creates the rights and entitlements that enable community forestry to function, allied to the emergence of a political environment in which people are willing and able to seek out these rights. Moreover, the Forestry Department has itself undergone change. Much less emphasis is now placed on the department's technical role and control over resource management, which lay at the heart of its previous adversarial relationship with many local communities.

Changes to the legal context of community forestry in Nepal constitute an example of much wider significance. The process of changing laws that define rights and responsibilities is a notoriously difficult one and is typically beset by compromises and delays. This is particularly the case where, as with community forestry, change entails the state divesting itself of control over valuable resources that are a source of power and revenue both to the collective entity and to individual officers and officials. The willingness to change laws and policies has, to a significant degree, developed through a lively and constructive process of learning and interaction between policy-makers and political authorities at the national level and practitioners on the ground. This process itself has meant that community forestry has become engaged in the wider process of political change and development of civil society in Nepal.

There still remain challenges for the future. For example, there are concerns about the extent to which the benefits of community forestry are shared by all sections of the community and about the effectiveness of the management regimes that the FUGs are implementing. But Nepal's experience shows that continuing degradation of common property resources in the developing world is not inevitable. It can be stopped and even reversed in ways that continue to meet local needs – a sustainable pattern of development if ever there was one. This requires a clear and concerted willingness on the part of the state to create the context through which real and effective local-level control can take place. In this, the key is a combination of political will, good laws and policies and institutional change.

Conclusion

It is commonly assumed that action at the local level can achieve sustainable development by circumventing the constraints at national level which have impeded it until now. However, experience with projects in developing countries has shown that national policy and institutional constraints often prevent this from happening. Local action to promote more sustainable development only has a chance of being effective when it is freed from such obstructions. Better still is if there is a supportive policy, legal, institutional and political environment. This can only be achieved by confronting fundamental problems with the social and institutional structures that link the locality to the outside world and channel information, materials, credit and other resources to it.

In Bangladesh the political will was lacking to make fundamental changes to a state institution; consequently, participation was mere tokenism. In Sri Lanka local action was hampered by the lack of a supportive political and social environment. For a long period, national political and institutional limitations prevented Nepal's stated forest policies from being realized; but, ultimately, the situation changed after a sequence of radical political and policy reforms.

Where a supportive framework exists, the need for outsiders to intervene in local actions is limited and is only justified in response to the expressed needs of the local community – which, given the chance, can itself prove highly effective in building sustainable livelihoods (Guha, 1989; Hinchcliffe et al, 1999; Leach and Mearns, 1996; Whiteside, 1999). The key is to provide a range of choices to make this possible.

Several examples quoted in this chapter demonstrate that local people are adept at creating spontaneous, informal institutions to promote their development. But without a suitable framework they find it difficult to participate in formal decentralized institutions, making it hard to attain the participatory momentum needed to replicate local action throughout a country or region.

It is important to avoid the trap of writing new prescriptions, as well as new deterministic and normative models of how to build sustainable development. What needs to be done in any place will vary according to the specific characteristics of that place. What we can do here is set out some basic guiding principles that can provide a framework within which individual situations can be assessed.

The first is that good governance is a prerequisite for sustainable development. We have seen how good policies operating in a bad body politic ultimately fail. Sustainable development is fundamentally about the redistribution of power. This is not a plea for anarchy or revolution, but more a recognition that the lack of sustainable development more often than not reflects concentrated and distorted power structures. Good governance is itself based on two things. First is the structure of rights and entitlements, which are enshrined in laws, customs and policies. These should be egalitarian, appropriate and, above all legitimate – that is, understood and accepted by all (Davies, 1996; Sen, 1981). Second, the institutional processes through which governance operates should be representative, transparent, efficient and accountable.

Representation is far more important than participation, which became a sacred cow of development during the 1980s. The latter has too often been taken to mean that everyone must be involved in everything, which is both unworkable and undesirable. Representation is fair and effective when the interests of all are taken into account in making decisions. Such a situation can – and often does – occur where decision-makers appear to outsiders to be unrepresentative elites, for the nature of social pressure and conventions restricts their scope for abusing their authority. This, in turn, means that we should be wary of futile and often counterproductive efforts to change the fundamental nature of local social structures, since good representation is not contingent upon such changes. What it often does require is a diverse and durable civil society that provides a range of agencies through which communities can be involved in development activities.

Another important requirement is subsidiarity – that is, finding the most appropriate level for taking and implementing decisions, with a presupposition that the more devolved the better. This must include both the right to make decisions and the means to ensure that they are followed through. The means will be:

- material: the financial, technological and physical resources needed;
- legal: power based in law and enforceable through the legal process;
- informational: people must know about and understand the choices open to them; and
- social: the community as a whole must accept the decisions made and cooperate to implement them.

Community involvement in development activities acts as a countervailing force to over-dominance by the state, which has for so long characterized many developing countries.

If sustainable development is to have any relevance to the world's poor it must go beyond the present orthodoxy of participatory development, and combine action at local level with changes at national and international levels (Soussan et al, 1999). The fact that this is not happening yet does not entirely reflect an unwillingness to try, for most development projects now pay at least lip service to sustainable development and participation, and many major donors have substantially redirected their aid programmes towards sustainable development. However, many would claim that these changes, well-intentioned as they are, have not made any real difference, with sustainable development remaining as remote a goal today as it was in 1992. There are too many examples of 'old wine in new bottles', with conventional approaches dressed up in sustainable development rhetoric, for the simple reason that those who wield power today are unhappy about relinquishing some of it. Ultimately, such a redistribution of power is required if there are to be fundamental changes to policies and legal and institutional structures.

Taken together, these principles provide a first tentative framework through which genuine and effective sustainable development can be built for the world's poorest and most vulnerable. Although abstract, they reflect the real challenges we face in supporting and enhancing sustainable livelihoods. These challenges are more about the wider context, the external policy, and the legal and institutional framework in which local-level development occurs than about the actions necessary at the local level. As has been argued throughout this chapter, defining and creating this context is the basis upon which sustainable development should be built. Without it the prospects for creating the changes that will give the world's poorest people hope are very remote indeed.

5

Forecasting Urban Futures: A Systems Analytical Perspective on the Development of Sustainable Urban Regions

Gordon Mitchell

Introduction

Throughout history, urban settlements have displayed both the best and the worst of human achievement. Towns and cities have acted as major centres of economic activity, political decision-making and cultural creativity. But they have also been the seats of many of the most severe social and environmental problems generated by demographic and economic growth. The 20th century saw an unprecedented increase in the global scale of urbanization. As a result, around half of the world's 6 billion people are now urban residents and the concentration of population in individual cities has reached new heights. In 1950 only New York and London had a population of more than 8 million; by 1990 there were 28 such mega-cities, including many of the fastest growing urban centres of the developing world (UN, 1991). Such urbanization has economic, social and environmental impacts at every level up to the truly global (Berry, 1990; see also Chapter 6 in this volume). Thus, moves to improve the sustainability of towns and cities are not simply of interest to urban residents; they are vital for the sustainable development of the planet as a whole.

This chapter begins by describing the key sustainability problems faced by contemporary European cities. In this it adopts a metabolic approach, focusing upon the flows of materials and energy that underpin urban systems of production and consumption. The inefficiency of current urban metabolisms reflects many different factors, including city size, urban planning and design, the workings of the market economy, and the lifestyles and aspirations of individual consumers. Hence, as the chapter next discusses, there are complex issues to be addressed if cities are to be redirected along a more sustainable development path. Current understanding of urban processes is incomplete, attempts to delimit urban settlements are often arbitrary and inadequate, and the very ethos of sustainability is itself contested. Such problems reinforce the argument that a more systematic approach to sustainable urban development is required, especially as ad hoc policies may redefine or redistribute problems rather than ensuring effective solutions.

The chapter then turns to explore the major role that urban modelling can play in this new integrated approach as part of a range of sustainability assessment techniques. New initiatives in this field will build upon existing achievements in modelling and the definition of sustainable development indices and indicators. Hence, the chapter proceeds to a brief review of progress in these areas, revealing that few of the efforts made so far to produce sustainability models address urban systems. In part, this reflects the difficulty of creating a truly comprehensive model of urban functions on which to project more sustainable futures. However, given the urgency of the social and environmental problems associated with cities, a more pragmatic approach is urged here. As the ensuing discussion of the Quantifiable City Programme reveals, there is no need to wait for the creation of the perfect total urban model. This is because there is considerable potential for the production of models that can simultaneously address issues of economic efficiency, environmental impact and social equity within particular domains, or that can explore difficult problems relating to specific common property resources, such as air and water. It is stressed, however, that urban sustainability modelling must be seen as one amongst many methods for urban sustainability assessment. Such techniques should be developed and applied with sensitivity to the circumstances of specific towns and cities, reflecting the needs of local stakeholders and the capabilities of urban institutions.

Impacts of Urban Development

The study of urban metabolisms

For the cities of the developed North, which form the principal focus of this chapter, attempts to improve sustainability are often dominated by the so-called 'Green agenda'. In a context where the basic economic and social needs of the vast majority of the population are already met, sustainable development is characterized chiefly as a drive for greater environmental quality and efficiency. This is intended to reduce the environmental damage inflicted by human activity, ultimately to the point where a society comes to live within the limits of its environmental carrying capacity. It is acknowledged that such changes should be secured without unacceptable losses of the socio-economic benefits associated with environmental transformations; but less attention is focused explicitly on quality of life or social equity issues (see Chapter 6 for alternative perspectives on urban quality of life). In this, the Green agenda contrasts with the 'Brown agenda' of the developing world, under which the present necessity for economic growth to alleviate poverty, secure livelihoods and fund investment in health and welfare services may take priority over concerns for the future condition of the global environment (see Chapter 6). While the many different studies of urban sustainability in the developed world have adopted a variety of approaches – some holistic, others sectoral, or deriving from a particular disciplinary perspective – there is a common emphasis on physical sustainability (amongst holistic studies see Elkin et al, 1991; Tjallingi, 1995; sectoral and disciplinary approaches include Nijkamp and Perrels, 1994, on energy; Rees, 1993, on water; Blowers, 1993, on land-use planning; and Barton et al, 1995, on architecture and urban design).

The concentration of population in towns and cities creates demand for goods and services far in excess of what can be supplied from within urban boundaries. Thus cities have massive throughputs of natural and manufactured materials as resources are gathered from elsewhere to support urban production and consumption. Urban activity creates not only the goods and services valued by consumers, but also waste and pollution. Cities have habitually disposed of many of these unwanted by-products by exporting them beyond urban boundaries. The exploration of this flow of materials and energy that links the city to external economic and environmental systems is the basis of the study of urban metabolisms.

Every day a typical European city of 1 million inhabitants consumes 11,500 tonnes of fossil fuels, 320,000 tonnes of water and 2000 tonnes of food. The transformation of this material creates waste on a similarly substantial scale: 25,000 tonnes of carbon dioxide, 300,000 tonnes of waste water and 1600 tonnes of solid waste (EEA, 1998; Stanners and Bordeau, 1995). The sourcing of inputs is often determined by cost considerations that include little attention to social and environmental consequences beyond the urban boundary. Similarly, most cities dispose of their unwanted outputs wherever they can and few make a significant attempt to reuse or recycle their waste products. This perpetuates a linear metabolism in which the links between inputs and outputs are only partially acknowledged. Thus attention focuses on the economic efficiency of resource use within the city, rather than the wider process of resource procurement, conversion and disposal.

It is easy to see how linear urban metabolisms have developed. Urban consumption has always been reliant upon an external hinterland, where supplies of resources have effectively been considered limitless. Indeed, as transportation systems improved over time, urban consumers were able to draw upon supplies from a rapidly expanding territory. It became easier and cheaper to gather resources from this growing hinterland than to consider how needs could be met more locally. Today it is commonplace to obtain raw materials and even perishable foodstuffs from the other side of the world (Paxton, 1994). Thus the collapse of local resource productivity no longer signals a city's demise. Attention to urban health and waste disposal also encouraged a linear metabolism. Outbreaks of cholera and typhoid in the industrializing towns of 19th-century Europe and North America, for example, were eventually linked to the inadequacy of water supply and sanitation systems. Such problems were often dealt with by extending the city's zone of influence. Clean water was piped in from distant uplands and systems of sewers were constructed to flush waste water beyond the urban boundary. While the urban benefits were considerable, new problems were created elsewhere with the inundation of productive land by reservoirs and the downstream pollution of rivers and tidal estuaries. During the 20th century a similar story can be told about some of the measures adopted to tackle acute urban air pollution caused by fossil fuel use. Reductions in the urban incidence of respiratory disease have to be set against increased acid precipitation on ecosystems downwind (McCormick, 1997).

Recognition of the complexity of the economic, social and cultural systems underpinning urban metabolisms increases the challenge of effecting change. It does not, however, diminish the clarity of the central message that change in urban metabolisms, replacing linearity with a cyclical flow of materials through the city, is a vital element of progress towards sustainable development (Boyden et al, 1981; Di

Castri et al, 1984; Girardet, 1992; Wolman, 1965). The effects of new efficiencies in the procurement and consumption of resources, waste minimization and a greater emphasis on reuse and recycling of materials within urban systems should be apparent in improvements in the quality of the urban environment. But such changes will also reduce the external impacts of urban centres, contributing to the wider achievement of sustainable development. The scale of the task involved in transforming urban metabolisms is, however, formidable – a reflection not only of the institutional forces underpinning existing linear systems, but also of the sheer diversity and extent of the environmental impacts of urban settlements.

The environmental impacts of European cities

The impact of urbanization is particularly apparent in the transformation of local environments (Douglas, 1983). But urban systems also have regional and global effects (see Table 5.1) through their consumption of resources and production of wastes (Girardet, 1992; Haughton and Hunter, 1994). In turn, cities themselves may suffer the negative feedback caused by change in these wider environmental systems. The importance and severity of urban environmental change vary substantially; but many problems are common to cities throughout Europe. The following overview draws chiefly upon two major environmental studies produced under the auspices of the European Union (EU) (EEA, 1998; Stanners and Bordeau, 1995).

Within the boundaries of European cities, environmental concerns focus chiefly upon air quality, noise, water management, housing standards and the quality of the built environment. Damage to urban air quality is evident in the finding that between 70 and 80 per cent of EU cities with over 500,000 inhabitants experience breaches of World Health Organization (WHO) standards at least once a year. Thus, in the 115 largest cities, 25 million people are exposed to unhealthy levels of sulphur dioxide and particulates, and 37 million experience ozone levels above recommended limits. Emission controls and technical measures have reduced pollution in some cities; but, in general, air quality is expected to deteriorate further as increasing urban traffic raises concentrations of nitrogen oxides, carbon monoxide, volatile organic compounds and fine particulates.

As well as degrading air quality, road traffic is the major source of noise in urban areas. One quarter of EU cities have reported particularly serious problems in this respect. Some 450 million people – 65 per cent of the EU's population – are exposed to noise levels officially deemed 'high' (above equivalent sound pressure levels (Leq) 24h 55dB(A)), while 9.7 million suffer exposure to 'excessive' noise (above Leq 24h 75dB(A)). Moreover, while average vehicle speeds have declined by 10 per cent over the last 20 years, largely as a result of increasing congestion, road accidents still exact an annual toll of 1.7 million injuries and 55,000 deaths.

There are also serious problems with water management in cities. Urban development creates impermeable surfaces, causing the rapid runoff of precipitation. Sewers may overflow as a result, discharging untreated waste into local rivers and lakes. The sudden release of water can also create flood waves that scour riverbanks, reducing their value as habitat. Replenishment of groundwater is prevented, with the result that a valuable economic resource is lost and the foundations of some buildings are destabilized. Urban surface water bodies, too, have been degraded by draining or

Table 5.1   Environmental impacts and issues generated by urbanization

	Local	Regional	Global
Climate			
Solar radiation at ground surface reduced due to airborne particulates	•		
Air temperature higher due to energy use and heat storage in buildings	•		
Humidity lower as less transpiration and water-retaining surface soil	•		
Cloud and fog more frequent and intense; wind speeds lower	•		
Precipitation higher with more extreme rainfall events	•		
Water			
Permeable surfaces replaced by impermeable surfaces	•		
Evapotranspiration loss reduced and higher water yield potential	•		
Runoff response faster with higher peak discharge and flood risk	•		
Groundwater replenishment reduced; subsidence and saline intrusion risk	•		
Discharge reduced at times of low flow	•		
Land inundation for water supply and hydropower	•	•	
Land and resources			
Productive agricultural land lost through development; soil erosion	•	•	
Overbuilding of mineral reserves	•		
Deforestation	•	•	•
High dependence on non-renewable energy; depletion of fossil resources	•	•	•
Energy efficiency of distribution networks, buildings and production	•	•	•
Risks from nuclear energy, waste disposal and facility decommissioning	•	•	
Conservation of built heritage	•		
Waste and pollution			
Emission of ozone depleting gases (CFCs, HCFCs)			•
Emission of greenhouse gases (carbon dioxide, ammonia, CFCs, nitric oxide, HFCs)			•
Emission of acid gases (SO_x, NO_x)	•	•	
Emission of toxic gases (carbon monoxide, VOCs, ozone)	•	•	
Emission of toxic metals (lead, cadmium, mercury, argon and nickel)	•	•	
Noise	•		
Pollution of water by sewage, industrial effluent and non-point sources	•	•	•
Contamination of land otherwise suitable for food production	•	•	
Solid waste production exceeds capacity of available disposal sites	•	•	
Hazards			
Road traffic accidents	•		
Elevated flood risk, coastal inundation, water supply failure	•		
Land instability: subsidence, land slip and earthquake	•	•	
Residential proximity to industrial processes	•		
Non-conformity of buildings to construction standards	•		
Crime and civil unrest	•		
Health and welfare issues			
Vector-borne and communicable diseases	•	•	
Respiratory diseases	•		
Cancer, cardiovascular disease and long-term genetic effects of toxins	•		
Adequacy of basic services (water, sanitation, waste disposal)	•		
Access to adequate shelter	•	•	
Access to basic health, education and welfare services	•	•	
Access to green areas and open spaces	•		
Access to employment and income opportunities	•	•	
Access to work and service opportunities	•	•	
Ecological issues			
Reduction of habitat space	•	•	•
Toxicological effects on plants and animals	•	•	
Reduced species abundance and diversity (extinctions)	•	•	•
Biomass appropriation (reduced carbon fixation capacity)	•	•	•

culverting so that their benefits as a source of local climate regulation, ecological diversity and recreational amenity are lost (see Chapter 9). The environmental quality of many of the remaining urban lakes and rivers is poor, reflecting ineffective controls on water use and pollution. Most European cities have now extended mains drainage to at least 95 per cent of dwellings; but some sewage systems still discharge waste into natural watercourses without proper treatment. Although many Western European countries made progess during the latter half of the 20th century in curbing the worst instances of water pollution, it is still the case that water management is largely ignored in development planning (Mitchell, 1999a).

The fabric of the built environment, including both buildings and the spaces between them, is another significant dimension of urban environmental quality. Even in Western Europe, marginalized social groups have not shared fully in the general improvement in housing standards. The failure of urban management is still clearer in parts of Central and Eastern Europe, where up to 20 per cent of homes lack piped water, sewerage facilities and adequate heating. But modern urban development creates its own environmental problems. Indoor air quality, for example, is increasingly recognized as a significant public health concern and attention is only now focusing, somewhat belatedly, upon the implications of building design for efficiency in water and energy use. In its destruction of historic buildings and other elements of the built environmental heritage, redevelopment may also damage a city's image and identity. Inadequate attention to the layout of the urban plan imposes further penalties when development encroaches upon green and open spaces. The value of these spaces for recreation, conservation and as a means of connecting urban residents to the natural environment is increasingly being recognized (see Chapters 6 and 9). As a result, several European countries have revised their planning regulations to encourage the incorporation of ecological corridors and other green space within urban development. Nevertheless, there are still few systematic assessments of the scale of loss and degradation of urban green space.

Concerns about the condition of the urban environment have their counterparts in the wider impacts of urban systems upon environmental quality (see Table 5.1). Work on European cities has also explored the implications of inefficient urban metabolisms for regional and global sustainability, highlighting the need for improved management of energy, water and other material inputs to urban systems of production and consumption.

Solar power is the main energy source entering cities, but very little is captured or transformed for human use. Thus, urban activities are largely driven by imported fossil fuels or their derivatives. The procurement of these fuels may impose significant environmental and social costs in locations far removed from the city, and their consumption is a major source of the greenhouse gases that threaten destructive changes in global climate (see Chapters 10 and 11). Yet such considerations do not weigh heavily with most urban consumers. Although increasing attention is paid to energy-demand management, many opportunities for using energy more efficiently remain unexploited (see Chapter 11). Overall, the recent decline in the industrial use of energy – chiefly a product of economic restructuring during the 1980s and 1990s – is more than offset by increasing consumption in transportation and the domestic sector.

Urban water use may also create serious environmental problems beyond the city boundary. Daily per capita consumption of water in Europe currently averages between 100 and 400 litres. But rising demand, combined with inefficient distribution systems that commonly waste between 30 and 50 per cent of supplies, creates a constant search for new water resources. This inevitably affects the regional environment, degrading aquatic and wetland habitats, or requiring the inundation of rural land. Similarly, the problems created by sewage disposal and the pollution of waterways by industrial effluent may extend far downstream from individual urban centres.

Cities also import a wide range of other materials, although few data are available to allow the assessment of the external environmental burdens that this creates. One surrogate measure is the production of waste within urban economies. On average, EU cities produce an annual total of around 500 kilograms of waste per capita, a figure that is rising by about 3 per cent per year. Although some waste is composted and about 20 per cent is incinerated, most is buried in landfill sites. Although burial has important implications for the local and regional environment, it was long regarded as a cheap and easy means of waste disposal. However, rising transport costs, increasing concerns about pollution and public health, and a lack of suitable dumping sites have forced a re-evaluation of attitudes towards waste. Serious efforts are now being made to minimize waste production and recycle materials, thereby promoting a more efficient urban metabolism (see Chapter 7). But while many European cities have achieved significant reductions in the amount of waste generated by each unit of economic output, total waste production has continued to rise as a result of economic growth, and changing lifestyles and consumption habits.

The assessment of resource use reveals significant variation between European cities and regions. Despite a lack of good comparative data, it is evident that urban material flows are not a direct function of settlement size. Nor are metabolic efficiencies and environmental quality related simply to the health of an urban economy, as both growth and decline create problems. Rather, these measures reflect the complex interaction of factors relating to urban design, the density of development, consumption and mobility. Urban metabolisms have long had a deleterious effect on environmental quality, but the scale and severity of their current impacts are unprecedented. While it remains difficult to assess how close human activities have taken us to ecological limits, either within urban areas themselves, or nationally and globally, it is clear that cities have a major contribution to make in promoting sustainability at all levels.

The Complexity of Urban Sustainability

Cities are complex entities and have always presented major management challenges. However, progress towards sustainable development requires more comprehensive and holistic assessments of urban processes than ever before. Additional sources of complexity are thus revealed, including very tangible problems – such as the spatial delimitation of urban territories – and more subtle, but important, issues, including the accommodation of different perspectives on the definition of meaningful goals for sustainable development.

Defining urban boundaries

Contest and confusions over the definition of urban boundaries are hardly novel (Carter, 1983; Pacione, 2001). But the urban metabolism concept focuses renewed attention on the inadequacies of traditional markers used to trace urban limits. Established administrative boundaries vary widely in origin and may bear little relation to the current size, functions or influence of the city. Equally, attempts to define the city in terms of its built-up area ignore the much wider sphere of urban influence that is a vital component of any exploration of urban metabolisms. Such definitions of urban boundaries are of themselves problematic in that they often rest on essentially arbitrary and geographically inconsistent distinctions between different densities of population and development. Attributing urban functions to particular settlements can also be controversial. In the contemporary world, there are extensive built-up areas – including, for example, the self-proclaimed 'cities' that crowd the Los Angeles Bay area – that are almost exclusively residential, lacking most of the productive and market functions that have traditionally been regarded as urban hallmarks.

By implication cities are not sustainable within any of the boundaries common to conventional urban geographical analysis. In this sense the sustainable city is an impossible ideal. It is more realistic, therefore, to pursue the goal of creating sustainable urban regions, drawn on a sufficiently large scale to incorporate the full extent of urban metabolic systems and environmental impacts. Attention must be paid to the spatial distribution of population and economic activity within the urban region, as these are key determinants of resource use and pollution. Equally, an understanding of the region's physical characteristics is also important. Knowledge of the extent and spatial distribution of pollution assimilation capacities can be used to ensure that the over-exploitation of individual sinks does not reduce the total assimilative capacity of the region.

The definition of such urban regions is, however, as challenging a task as delimiting the city. One approach is to construct regional boundaries based on river basins and other prominent landforms that physically constrain the spatial extent of metabolic flows. However, the application of this bio-regional approach to urban centres, especially the largest cities, is questionable. Urban air pollution, for example, rarely respects topographic boundaries. Although processes of resource supply and waste disposal can be influenced by physical geography, the flows of materials, goods and capital that characterize contemporary economic systems transcend regional boundaries with increasing ease and speed. An approach that is too narrowly defined in regional terms cannot adequately attend to national and international influences upon urban development, including demographic growth, global economic forces and the actions of governments and multinational business.

Conceptual problems

Efforts to develop urban sustainability are also complicated at a more abstract level, as the concept is itself fuzzy. The goals of sustainable urban development are open to question as a reflection of different ideological perspectives. Pearce et al (1989) describe a 'sustainability spectrum' within which positions vary from Cornucopian, viewing nature as a resource to be exploited for human benefit, to that of Deep Ecology, which accords all natural systems, including the abiotic, intrinsic value and moral rights. These varied perspectives foster different types of economy – the former encouraging a totally free market, while the latter is likely to advocate a much greater degree of regulation of economic systems. Moreover, each promotes a distinctive management approach. From a Cornucopian standpoint new technology and market substitution appear appropriate solutions to resource scarcity, whereas Deep Ecology favours a reduction in population and economic activity as a means of restoring the balance between human demands and environmental capacity.

These different positions determine the relative importance attached to the key sustainability principles of inter-generational and intra-generational equity, and environmental protection. The Cornucopian perspective rationalizes the protection of environmental systems as a matter of enlightened self-interest and little attention is given to social equity. This is in stark contrast to Deep Ecology, which views natural rights and the collective interest as paramount. These contrary positions and the different forms of economic activity and management that they imply greatly complicate the task of establishing agreed sustainability objectives. However, some attempt to accommodate the different positions must be made if initiatives to promote sustainable development are to command widespread popular support.

Complexity of urban processes

These difficulties in defining basic terms and concepts compound the many problems that arise from an incomplete understanding of urban processes. Although some processes – particularly the physical ones – are well documented, there is no definitive theory that could provide a reliable and universally accepted framework for analysis. Understanding of the city is often still fragmented along disciplinary lines. Thus, demographers see urbanization as a product of variable rates of births, deaths and migration that produce a demographic cycle, each stage of which is associated with different occupational structures. Economists, however, regard urbanization as a series of growth phases that give rise to an increasing specialization of activity. Here economies and dis-economies of scale, labour and service availability, or external costs of pollution and congestion, are key factors influencing urban development. Sociologists, meanwhile, view urbanization in a cultural context, with the driving force being the change in the experience of individuals over time. The close kin links of a rural society disintegrate in an urban world dominated by mutual exploitation and competition. This urban context yields a new freedom for individuals to achieve a status based on merit, rather than a traditional role defined at birth. But the erosion of old ties also means that formal controls are required to maintain order in urban society. In practice, these different ways of understanding the nature of 'the urban' and viewing urban change are intimately linked and need to be understood as a totality if the problems arising from urbanization are to be tackled successfully. The creation of such a total understanding of urban development is, however, a formidable intellectual challenge. Moreover, the slow pace of academic advance contrasts sharply with the increasing sense of urgency that characterizes discussion of sustainable development.

A case for pragmatism

There is thus a powerful argument that if urban regions are to develop sustainably, change cannot be delayed until a complete understanding of urban processes becomes available. Rather, we must use the management tools at our disposal and hope that as our comprehension grows, we shall be able to apply them more effectively in order to minimize the problems and maximize the benefits that cities offer. Sustainability strategies currently proposed for Northern cities already address the urban metabolism concept to some degree by managing demand, increasing the efficiency of resource use and distribution, and closing material cycles through using waste materials as inputs to further productive processes. Actions directed at increasing the circularity of urban metabolisms include the use of telematics and land-use zoning to reduce traffic demand, waste minimization, water leakage reduction, energy recovery through waste incineration, and the use of sewage as an agricultural fertilizer. Other instruments – including congestion charging, traffic calming to reduce accidents, enforcing air and water quality standards, emission controls, green area planning, building codes and conservation standards – are primarily designed to improve environmental quality, but may also assist in the better management of urban flows of energy and materials.

There is thus an established 'kit-bag' of policy tools for urban management, with new and innovative solutions continually emerging to tackle sustainability problems. These tools can be divided into five groups: strategic planning; legislation; economic instruments; technology; and the provision of information and education. Within each group there are many specific instruments that can be applied to restructure urban activities and manage their impacts, as Table 5.2 exemplifies with respect to the promotion of energy efficiency. Some of these measures are explored by Unsworth in Chapter 6 and Purvis in Chapters 7 and 11. Barton et al (1995), Blowers (1993), European Commission (1990; 1994), Elkin et al (1991), Girardet (1992), Roseland (1998) and Stanners and Bordeau (1995) give further examples in other areas.

This is not, however, to argue for the unthinking application of existing policy tools. No single set of actions can be equally appropriate for all cities, as each is unique, with its own distinctive environmental, economic and demographic characteristics, cultural perspectives and urban institutions. Consideration must thus be given to the specific circumstances of individual urban centres, generating carefully tailored management approaches within a common framework of problem assessment and option evaluation. This process of assessment and evaluation must also aim to counter the ad hoc application of solutions that merely redistribute existing problems, or create new ones elsewhere. The introduction of land-use controls to create a more 'natural' water runoff regime, for example, could be counterproductive if it leads to a more rapid spread of contaminants into urban groundwater. In London such initiatives have also given rise to concerns about a heightened risk of flooding and instability problems for buildings constructed since groundwater levels have been lowered (compare with Chapter 9). The importance of attending simultaneously to several interconnected spheres is also evident in attempts to raise air quality by reducing pollution emissions. If these are to be effective they require not only emission controls, but also new initiatives in land use and transport planning. The need for an understanding of the relationships between different aspects of urban systems is thus a recurring theme in discussions of urban management and sustainability.

Table 5.2   Instruments for sustainable development

Policy Instrument	Example Applications in Energy Sector
Strategic planning is the coordination of key urban functions at local and regional levels. It often addresses land-use planning to manage competing economic, social and environmental needs. It also seeks to provide the appropriate infrastructure required to address identified needs and deliver key services. Infrastructure may include transport and utility networks, public buildings, housing, key services (eg schools and hospitals) and central functions such as waste disposal facilities.	• Land-use controls to locate energy sources near use points to reduce transmission losses (eg district heating schemes) • Land-use controls to reduce travel demand • Provision of facilities to recover energy from waste (digesters, landfill biogas collection, incinerators) • Development and exploitation of renewable energy sources • Public transport infrastructure provision
Technological solutions to development problems have often created new problems or shifted the costs of development elsewhere, frequently impacting on environments and populations that gain no direct benefit from the development. Nevertheless, there is a role for technical innovation in promoting sustainable development, particularly through clean technologies, and those that promote the efficient use of resources and exploitation of renewable energy.	• Efficiency in energy production • Design and construction of energy efficient buildings (eg insulation, passive energy use and heat exchangers) • Energy efficient processes (eg reuse of braking energy in vehicles and thermostatic controls) • Advances in renewable energy technologies: solar, biogas, wind and waves • Telematics to reduce travel demand
Economic instruments are increasingly seen as powerful tools with which to promote sustainable development. They may take several forms, including direct manipulation of price (eg pollution charges and resource-use taxes), indirect alteration of price or cost using subsidies and market creation (eg tradable permits).	• Subsidies for energy conservation measures • Demand management through price control • Internalization of environmental and social costs in charges • Public transport subsidies • Carbon taxes
Legislative controls involve the establishment and policing of minimum standards. Prevailing social, economic or cultural circumstances may mean that such standards are routinely ignored.	• Implementation and policing of emission standards • Implementation and policing of energy efficiency standards • Mandatory purchasing by power companies of energy derived from non-fossil fuel sources
Education and awareness raising are required so that individuals and organizations are better able to make informed decisions about their own activities that have sustainability implications.	• Energy efficiency advice • Driver advice for fuel economy • Encouragement of attitudinal change through education (eg information on costs/impacts of energy use)

A Systems Perspective: Urban Modelling and Sustainability Assessment

Promoting sustainable urban development in practice requires urban institutions to apply an appropriate mix of management instruments, tailored to changing local circumstances. The simplicity of this formulation belies the difficulty of the challenge. As noted above, the complexity of urban systems, the contest surrounding definitions of sustainable development and the diversity of potential management tools all conspire against the ready identification of effective sustainable development strategies. However, as with all complex phenomena, systems analysis can foster an understanding of the processes involved and accelerate the identification of effective management strategies. Systems analysis inevitably involves some degree of abstraction and generalization; but the correct identification of the most significant elements of the system and the structural and functional relationships between them creates a model that can be used to explore the workings of the whole. Crucially, such an approach allows an assessment of the wider effects of change in one part of the system. The understanding of interconnections within urban systems provided by modelling is thus of particular value in planning for sustainable development, which must acknowledge the role of many different interacting subsystems and multiple, potentially conflicting, development objectives.

A new direction for urban modelling

Interest in urban modelling can be traced back to early studies undertaken in North America during the 1950s. Subsequent work on large-scale urban modelling included important contributions from Lowry (1964), Harris (1968), Wilson (1974; 1984), Batty (1976), Echenique (1994) and Anas (1994). The models developed by this school focused on the city as a system in which interactions take place between people, land use and services. They also explored how and where these interactions are realized as social and economic subsystems within the city. Vital components of such urban models typically included population, employment and housing, residence and workplace location, and the provision and use of services and infrastructure.

Large-scale models were developed with the intention of advancing understanding of urban form, internal structure and process, with the ultimate goal of supporting the work of urban planners. However, in a keynote study, 'Requiem for Large-Scale Urban Models', Lee (1973) criticized modellers for failing to meet these objectives. Lee's conviction that urban modelling had little future reflected his identification of fundamental weaknesses in existing work. The construction of comprehensive models, attempting to replicate highly complex processes in a single step, was seen as self-defeating given the fundamental lack of understanding of urban structure and process. Invariably, also, models were constructed at levels of spatial resolution that were too coarse to represent processes in a way that would be useful to policy-makers. Furthermore, the models contained little theoretical structure, created data requirements that could not realistically be met and proved complicated, error prone and expensive.

Given these influential criticisms, and the perceived failure of the urban modelling efforts of the 1950s and 1960s, it might be assumed that modelling had disappeared from the urban research agenda. However, as Batty (1994) makes clear in his overview of the field since 'Requiem', urban modelling has continued to develop. This is particularly true in Europe where a scientific approach to urban management, including computer modelling, was taken increasingly seriously by planners, perhaps because planning systems are more centralized than in the USA (Klosterman, 1994a). Modelling theory has been extended in three main areas (Batty, 1994). First, existing models, particularly of land use and transport movements, have been further refined through innovations in defining optimal zone size, the disaggregation of models better to reflect available data and improvements in the estimation and calibration of parameters. Second, recent developments in mathematics – including theories of catastrophe, chaos, complexity and non-linear dynamics – have allowed models to represent time more effectively. The city need no longer be represented as a system in equilibrium, and urban processes once thought to be in a stable state have been shown to have a previously unseen dynamism. It is also now possible to explore the impacts of shock changes, such as a stock market crash. Third, locational optimization theory has been advanced using new economic theory, gravity models and network equilibrium models, allowing linkages to be made between disaggregated and aggregated entities, giving an improved representation of actual behaviour.

Vital technological advances have created computers that can process ever-larger data sets with increasing speed and that are capable of presenting data in graphical formats, ranging from computer-aided design to interactive multi-media visualization. The sophistication of geographical information systems (GIS) has developed rapidly, creating a new capacity to manipulate information through a combination of spatially referenced data and attributes characterizing the data. GIS have evolved separately from urban modelling, but are used widely within the field. To date, however, applications have largely been limited to mapping, with relatively few spatial decision-support systems integrating GIS and model functionality. Yet the potential for such a productive engagement is illustrated by the work of Geertman and Ritsema van Eck (1995). Their investigation of access to jobs and services in The Netherlands combines a GIS and a gravity model, with the aim of informing policies for allocating new land for residential building while minimizing travel demand. Technical developments have been paralleled by significant improvements in the availability of digital data, now collected in increasing quantities by local authorities, utilities, marketing companies and other commercial organizations.

These advances have done much to address previous criticism. Thus, Wegener (1994) identifies key opportunities for the practical application of urban modelling, involving greater linkage of models to expert systems and the use of microsimulation techniques to allow the functional potential of GIS to be realized. Lee (1994), however, still questions the reality of progress as few models have displayed proven utility when subject to performance evaluation. A continuing lack of transparency in modelling makes it difficult to interpret its results correctly and to communicate them to planning professionals and other decision-makers. Greater replicability is also required, enabling different groups of researchers to reproduce one another's results. Analysts should be able to change model assumptions and parameters to see how results differ, and this is particularly important if models are to be applied in different geographical or cultural settings. Lee (1994) believes that these standards can be met, but only through pragmatic testing to evaluate both the utility of individual models and the contribution of modelling, in general, to urban theory and planning practice. Klosterman (1994b) concurs that the greatest challenge facing urban modelling still lies in the development of practical applications that are accessible to planners.

At the same time, there is increasing recognition of the ways in which planners' needs are changing. Hitherto, urban modellers have concerned themselves with a very narrow set of planning problems and, while their models address key aspects of urban development, they ignore many of the critical issues raised by a growing interest in *sustainable* urban development. Resource use, pollution and other environmental effects of urban activity remain largely unexplored, and quality of life has been defined chiefly in relation to employment and income. Thus, Wegener (1994) calls for the techniques of urban modelling to be applied to new problems:

> . . . models should be made more sensitive to issues of equity and environmental sustainability. Only if the models prove that they are able to give meaningful answers to the urgent questions facing cities on these matters can they establish for themselves a firm position in the planning process of the future.

Quantitative assessment of sustainable development

If modelling is to be seen as a valid tool for investigating and promoting sustainable development, then a new set of output variables is required to assess development options and scenarios with respect to sustainable development objectives. However, identifying appropriate outputs in complex urban systems is a significant challenge in itself.

The Agenda 21 document produced at the 1992 Rio Earth Summit recommended that 'indicators of sustainable development need to be developed to provide solid bases for decision-making at all levels and to contribute to self-regulating sustainability of integrated environmental and development systems' (UNCED, 1992b). Yet the European Community's Fifth Environmental Action Plan recognized 'a serious lack of indicators and environmental assessment material' (European Commission, 1993). Subsequently, considerable effort has been invested in attempts to remedy this deficiency. The majority of measures have been designed to assess the current status of economic and environmental systems, and to monitor progress towards the goals of sustainability. At the same time they also force stakeholder groups to express their development objectives as unambiguously as possible, in this way helping to identify and resolve disagreements over appropriate development options. While few of these measures have been developed with modelling in mind, they can be employed as output variables for models of sustainable cities and urban regions.

Quantitative assessments take two principal forms: indices of sustainable development, which create a single composite measure of economic, social and environmental well-being, and suites of indicators, which address several specific issues separately.

Sustainable development indices
Sustainability indices have been developed from three main perspectives – ecological, economic and socio-economic – each with its own distinctive characteristics (Mitchell,

1996). Ecological indices commonly address sustainable development by attempting to quantify what proportion of a system's carrying capacity has been appropriated for human use. Thus, Vitousek et al (1986) estimate that 40 per cent of global net primary productivity – that is, the product of photosynthesis – is lost annually to consumptive activities, such as agriculture, and pre-emptive activities, including urban development. The 'ecological footprint' concept also quantifies carrying capacity use by expressing resource consumption relative to physical ecosystem limits (Rees, 1992). Thus, an ecological footprint analysis of the planet reveals that a land area several times that available would be required if the consumption patterns currently found in developed countries were to be extended worldwide (Wackernagel and Rees, 1996). Application of this technique to Scotland (Moffatt et al, 1994) produced an estimated per capita footprint of 1.9 hectares, demonstrating that a land area 20 per cent greater than the Scottish total was needed to support the current national population. Hence, Scotland was importing sustainability. Such approaches can also be used to identify resource reduction targets to curb this dependency and to move towards sustainable development. For example, from their application of the related 'Environmental Space' technique – a measure based on resource use per capita – Friends of the Earth Europe concluded that a tenfold reduction in resource use in Europe is necessary by 2060 to achieve sustainability (FoE, 1995; Spangenberg, 1994).

Economic indices of sustainability are measures of income. But unlike their conventional equivalents, such as gross domestic product (GDP), they acknowledge the full costs of economic activity. Such indices address the contradiction that 'a country can exhaust its minerals and forests, erode its soil, pollute its water, and hunt its wildlife to extinction, but the loss of these assets would not show up in current measures of income' (Repetto et al, 1989). An economy is considered sustainable, therefore, only if its savings equal or exceed the depreciation in human and environmental capital. Prominent indices include Green GDP (Repetto et al, 1989; Young, 1990), the Z value (Pearce and Warford, 1993), the approximate environmentally adjusted net national product (Hartwick, 1990) and the Index of Sustainable Economic Welfare (ISEW) (Daly and Cobb, 1989). The ISEW, for example, incorporates the externality costs of development, plus the value of household labour and new human capital, into conventional economic accounts. Its application to the USA (Daly and Cobb, 1989), Germany and the UK (Jackson and Marks, 1994) and Scotland (Moffatt and Wilson, 1994) showed a consistent pattern. Divergence between ISEW and GDP, particularly during the 1970s, reveals a move away from sustainable development, chiefly reflecting the depletion of key resources and rising social and environmental costs.

Socio-economic indices commonly take the form of a measure of quality of life employing multiple, subjectively weighted factors that address needs defined as basic (such as food, water and shelter), physical (for example, a clean environment, employment and access to services) and cultural (including social relations). Thus, the widely accepted Human Development Index is a composite of life expectancy, educational standards and income (UNDP, 1998). Such indices are commonly used by bodies such as the UN and the Organisation for Economic Co-operation and Development (OECD) to predict social needs and identify inequalities at a variety of spatial scales (Mitchell et al, 1995).

Indices of sustainable development represent valid alternatives to classical economic measures of welfare, recognizing the environmental and social costs of development. However, difficulties remain with attempts to perfect each of the three main approaches. Ecological indices are distinctive in explicitly recognizing the limits that the natural world places on development; but they are not currently supported by adequate techniques for assessing environmental assimilation capacities for all significant pollutants. Thus, while acidifying gases (such as sulphur dioxide and nitrogen oxide) can now be addressed, along with carbon dioxide, in a revised ecological footprint, other polluting substances cannot be accommodated in a similar fashion (Holmberg et al, 1999). This makes it difficult to gauge the true extent of the 'sustainability gap' between current and desired states. Further work is also necessary if ecological techniques are to be extended to incorporate attention to social equity, or to evaluate alternative policy options for reducing the environmental impacts of human activity.

By comparison, economic measures do not adequately address the value and function of environmental capital. Tools such as contingent valuation, developed to attribute monetary values to assets – including flora and fauna, clean air and water – which are not traded in the marketplace, remain controversial. Equally, the ultimate implication that all environmental capital can be lost, provided that it is replaced by an equivalent value of human capital, is unacceptable to most observers. The neglect of social equity issues in other approaches can be overcome by the use of socio-economic indices. However, their explicit treatment of quality of life, including the less tangible psycho-social elements, creates its own problems. There is no consensus as to which variables should be included within a quality of life index; there are difficulties with weighting components and in quantifying intangible components, such as mental health, that depend upon human perception; and little regard is given to ecological elements, particularly those without a direct resource value.

All indices also suffer from structural problems in that they are difficult to maintain consistently as definitions of sustainability are revised to take account of changing circumstances. In averaging data, indices may conceal potentially important aspects of specific problems. Indices also lack resonance, meaning that it is often difficult for users to understand how a particular index value has been constructed. So, while sustainability indices offer improvements over conventional measures of development, and are particularly effective at monitoring changes in the condition of the whole system, they have not yet gained the same attention in practice as single-issue indicators of sustainability.

Sustainable development indicators

Single-issue sustainable development indicators (SDIs) have been created and implemented at many levels (see Table 5.3). The UN Environmental Assessment Programme has coordinated work on defining indicators by a number of supranational bodies – including the UN, the OECD and the World Bank – aiming to harmonize approaches and encourage greater user involvement (UNEAP, 1995). At a national level, particular progress in identifying indicators has been made by signatories to the Agenda 21 agreement, who require indicators to assess the performance of their own strategies for sustainable development (see, for example, DoE, 1996a). Local government has also invested considerable effort in developing indicators, responding enthusiastically to the challenges of Local Agenda 21 (for example, Birmingham City Council, 1998; LGMB, 1994a; 1994b; 1995; Sustainable Seattle, 1993). More recently, attention has

Table 5.3   Example indicators of sustainable development proposed at European, national and city levels

European Environment Agency Urban Environment Indicators (Stanners and Bordeau, 1995)	UK-Proposed Headline Sustainability Indicators (DETR, 1999b)	City of Birmingham Sustainability Indicators (Birmingham City Council, 1998)
URBAN PATTERNS • Population/population density • Land cover (km² by type) • % derelict area • % urban renewal area • Urban mobility: number and length of trips per capita per day by mode; number of commuters in and out of city per day; flows as number of vehicles and vehicle kilometres **URBAN FLOWS** • Water consumption in litres per capita per day; % groundwater resources in total supply • % dwellings connected to sewer system; number and capacity of treatment plants by type • Electricity use in GWh per year; energy use by fuel type and sector; number and type of power and heating plants in conurbation • Transport of goods moved into and out of city (kilograms per capita per year) • Solid waste production (kilograms per capita per year); waste composition • % waste recycled; % incinerated; % to landfill **URBAN ENVIRONMENTAL QUALITY** • Quality of drinking water (days per year in breach of WHO standards); quality of surface water as milligrams oxygen per litre • Air quality as pollutant values and breach of standards • Exposure to noise above 65 decibels • Traffic accident fatalities • Housing quality (area per capita) • % population within 15-minute walk of urban green area • Urban wildlife quality as number of bird species	**ECONOMIC** • Total economic output (GDP, GDP per capita) • Investment in public assets: transport, schools, hospitals, etc • Employment: people of working age in work (male/female/total) **SOCIAL** • Health: expected years of healthy life (male/female) • Education and training: % of population with level 2 qualifications at age 19 • Housing quality: % homes judged unfit to live in (by type) **ENVIRONMENTAL** • Climate change: emission of greenhouse gases (million tonnes per year CO_2 equivalent) • Air pollution: days of air pollution (urban and rural sites) • Transport: road traffic (billion vehicle miles per year) • Water quality: % of total river length of good or fair quality • Wildlife: population of wild birds (index value on woodland/farmland/all land) • Land use: % of new homes built on previously developed land • Waste: waste production (million tonnes per year); % by disposal route See DoE (1996a) for full list of 122 national UK sustainability indicators.	**(No categories)** • Number of members of credit unions and local exchange trading systems • Unemployment rate • Access by wheelchair to public buildings and transport • % population within half a mile of local amenities • % population in fear of crime • % people voting in elections • Number of fatalities from heart disease • % of children under five in nursery or pre-school education • Suicide rate • Adult literacy rates • Quantity of land regenerated • % of businesses working to a recognized environmental standard • % of households with energy-efficient light bulbs • % of wildlife sites managed • Total area of wildlife habitat • Litter dropped as ratio to litter in bins • % domestic waste recycled • Number of homes well insulated • Air quality • Passenger miles by transport mode • Average number of miles selected food items (apples, lamb, potatoes) travel to reach a Birmingham plate

turned to developing indicators for specific users and applications, including, for example, corporate performance (ENDS, 1999e), land-based industries (Walker and Reuter, 1996) and climate change (DETR, 1999a).

By comparison with sustainability indices, SDIs have several major advantages. They enable specific attention to be directed at all issues of concern. No weightings are required and they are simple, reflecting data closely, thus ensuring resonance. Hence, the information they convey is less controversial and more likely to promote appropriate action. However, despite their potential for comprehensive coverage of issues, they place the burden of interpretation on the user and do not readily communicate a sense of the condition of the whole system. Moreover, many SDI programmes do not adequately address sustainable development principles. As a result, indicators are often very similar to existing environmental or socio-economic measures, and pay insufficient attention to ecological limits – that is, carrying or assimilative capacities – or the equity concerns that define sustainable development. Such problems can be addressed, however, by using an indicators methodology, within a roundtable (Delphi) environment. This forces a clear recognition of sustainability concerns, as a series of independent statements are advanced and debated until agreement is reached (Mitchell et al, 1995).

Despite the caveats noted above, it is apparent that existing sustainability measures can offer significant improvements over conventional performance measures of societal development. They constitute powerful tools for sustainable development, and are already widely used and taken seriously as assessment measures. These measures have been developed principally as instruments for assessing and monitoring current progress in reducing the social and environmental costs of economic activity. But they may also be usefully employed in a predictive context to strengthen decision-making about the goals of sustainable development.

Models of Sustainable and Urban Development

Models of sustainable development

Amongst the range of sustainable development models described in the current literature, none yet explores the use of the indices outlined above. Instead, output variables are defined with reference to single-issue indicators. Where complete systems are addressed, the ecological approach is favoured over its economic or socio-economic counterparts, and ecosystem limits are recognized through the application of thermodynamic laws. The law of energy conservation is used to balance the flows of energy and other materials in an economy, recognizing the inevitability of pollution and resource depletion. Thus, the development scenario under which the rate of entropy change is lowest is deemed most sustainable.

In some models, the thermodynamic laws are explicitly addressed, and all processes are expressed in units of energy, as in the Enhancement of Carrying Capacity Options model (Gilbert and Braat, 1991), applied at the national scale using 700 equations. Models that address greenhouse gas emission are also often of this type (see, for example, Edmonds et al, 1991). In other cases, for example the World3 model of

Meadows et al (1972; 1992), thermodynamic laws are obeyed; but the stocks and flows are described using units appropriate to the specific resources and pollutants. In both types of model, flows of energy through the economic–ecological system are estimated using either input–output analyses or dynamic simulations of material flows. The former are commonly employed when an entire economy is examined, and national statistics are used in an attempt to account for all energy required in the production, distribution and consumption of goods (Moffatt, 1997). In dynamic simulation models, relationships within the system must be described in more detail, particularly any feedback mechanisms connecting the major state variables.

In reviewing existing dynamic simulation models of sustainable development, the International Institute for Applied Systems Analysis (IIASA) has both highlighted the limitations of current work and identified a strategy for future progress (Sanderson, 1994). Many models were seen to have a weak conceptual structure, lacking, in particular, a clear expression of the relationships between variables. For example, World3 (Meadows et al, 1972; 1992) was considered unreliable, switching all too easily between growth and collapse, because the variables and linkages in the model were poorly specified and were too sensitive to parameter changes. These nebulous relationships between variables reflected, in part, a lack of geographical grounding. Most models have not been developed to represent specific places, preventing testing and refinement of qualitative and quantitative states and relationships.

The importance of developing place-specific models, allowing relationships to be expressed and tested with more confidence, is exemplified in the SOCIOMAD population–economy–environment model of the Sahel region of Niger and Chad (Sanderson, 1994). Although limited in focus, this model of a simple agricultural economy based on a common property resource that had no price and limited potential for substitutions proved reliable. Unfortunately, the lessons of the SOCIOMAD model are not directly translatable into other more complex economic contexts, where account must be taken of the role of resource pricing and substitution, and technological change in creating significant negative feedback loops. Sanderson (1994) recommends, therefore, that sustainability models should, in general, concentrate on the degradation and depletion of common property resources – air, land and water – as complex and fundamental problems.

Many of the models examined by IIASA could only test the effects of change in one specific policy dimension – for example, population (Aricia et al, 1991) – on the development process. They thus generated a limited range of solutions. As a reaction against this, Sanderson (1994) further recommends that models must be able to test a broad range and mix of policies, addressing different dimensions of development and sustainability (note the diversity of sustainability indicators in Table 5.3).

The approach advocated by Sanderson (1994) is found in Giaoutzi and Nijkamp's (1993) regional sustainable development (RSD) model and in IIASA's own population–development–environment (PDE) model (Lutz, 1994). The RSD model is a dynamic simulation of the Sporades islands in Greece. It explores common property concerns regarding freshwater and coastal resources by linking an economic input–output model with a water resource model and a dynamic ecological model addressing maximum sustainable fish yield. The PDE model has also been constructed by linking a series of separate modules. In this case an existing, well-specified population model is allied with an economic module using a mix of input–output and general equilibrium modelling. The economic module is linked, in turn, to other components describing change in biodiversity, air and water quality, land use and energy consumption. The model is notable in permitting feedback loops between its different modules, even when relationships are ambiguous. Relationships between human fertility and economic or environmental parameters, for example, are well studied, but remain poorly defined. Incorporation of feedback is achieved by allowing the user to define variation in the parameter of interest with socio-economic or environmental change, and it is this scenario-setting capability that gives the model particular relevance in exploring local policy and cultural processes. The model has been applied to Mauritius, where the most critical common resources are fresh water and the fringing coral reefs, which help to generate the tourist revenue that constitutes the main source of national income. PDE has proved useful in promoting sustainable development policies in this particular context, raising the hope that similar success can be achieved elsewhere.

Defining the scope for urban sustainability modelling

Given the evident interest in modelling as a tool to support sustainable development and the importance of cities as development centres, it is surprising how little progress has been made in producing models of sustainable urban development. In large part, such apparent lack of initiative is a reflection of the scale of the challenge. Attempts to construct such models must overcome all the problems encountered both in measuring sustainable development and in urban modelling. Sustainable development indices have been routinely applied at a national level, where data are readily available. By comparison, urban studies, including an attempt to apply the Index of Sustainable Economic Welfare to London, have been hampered by a lack of data not just at city district level, but also for the city as a whole (D McGillivray, pers comm). Data availability is less problematic when dealing with SDIs, as these are commonly developed specifically to monitor urban performance within the constraints imposed by existing data. However, modelling implies many more components of interest than are currently employed in most monitoring studies and the need to quantify driving and state variables creates significant additional demands for urban data.

Urban sustainability modelling throws up another, more intractable, problem. The attempt to model a complex multivariate sustainability index, or a suite of SDIs, effectively creates a requirement to produce a comprehensive model. As Lee (1973) pointed out, the results of attempts to create such models through a few simple steps are inevitably flawed. Indeed, urban sustainability models are even more demanding than conventional urban models as more components and weak or poorly understood interactions must be quantified. Thus, even if data problems were overcome, the limitations of current understanding of urban systems would preclude the development of a comprehensive urban sustainability model. Nor is there any guarantee that models developed to explore sustainability at larger spatial scales can be successfully adapted for use in urban studies. A team from the Stockholm Environmental Institute is attempting to translate POLESTAR (Raskin, 1992), an economic–ecological input–output model of the sustainability of continental regions, to the scale of the city. The logic of this exercise is, however, questionable as relationships developed for a regional model do not necessarily apply at the urban scale and may not adequately address urban sustainability concerns. While regional input–output models may be well suited to addressing regional sustainability issues, such as the urban metabolism, it is not clear whether they can be applied at the city scale where complex issues of environmental quality raise important additional sustainability issues.

Such difficulties do not imply that sustainable urban development modelling is a fruitless exercise. But modellers must address the criticisms of Lee (1973; 1994) and develop verifiable models that are theoretically sound, avoid nebulous relationships between variables and are well supported by data, including those at fine spatial and temporal scales. As comprehensive urban sustainability models cannot yet be produced to these specifications, immediate progress will necessarily be based on models that focus upon specific dimensions of the urban system. This work should give priority to 'difficult' problems, particularly those associated with common property resources (Sanderson, 1994).

Such an approach will draw upon the many existing simulation models that adequately represent parts of the urban system. In following this route, however, it is important to ensure that modelling develops in ways that properly address the new concerns of urban sustainability, rather than merely perpetuating the established agenda of urban modelling. The 'common property' criterion provides an initial guide to the relevance of particular models. However, as a more sophisticated definition, it is proposed that to qualify as a sustainability model, an urban subsystem model must either address environmental, social or economic concerns collectively – preferably with explicit recognition of inter-generational and intra-generational equity and environmental impact – or integrate several processes in sufficient detail so that a range of policy options can be investigated when addressing difficult common property problems. Ideally, sustainability models will meet both criteria. The Quantifiable City Programme, which is developing a decision-support capability for urban sustainability, initially for the English city of Leeds (May et al, 1996), exemplifies the first criterion in its water resources module and the second criterion in its air quality module.

The Quantifiable City Programme: Sustainable Urban Development Modelling in Practice

Water resource sustainability

Sustainability failures in water resource management have been characterized in the UK by the 'supply-fix' approach, as water utilities have sought to meet rising consumption through additional resource provision, rather than manage demand. This approach risks causing environmental damage – for example, through over-abstraction from rivers – as supply limits are approached. Despite the perception that water is plentiful in the UK, the national excess of supply over demand is small. There are few suitable sites for new reservoirs, and in the south-east, one of the country's driest regions, the first desalination plants are now operating. Thus, a demand management approach, combining demand reduction with water conservation, appears to offer a more sustainable alternative to expanding supplies and should meet the needs of both the consumer and the environment.

Domestic customers account for the largest share of growth in demand for water in the UK, so a key demand management strategy will be the introduction of metering of domestic water use. Currently, most households pay a flat rate for water, based on property value, rather than a volumetric tariff. Trials in the UK and experience elsewhere indicate that metering can significantly reduce domestic demand. However, there is public and political resistance to metering, reflecting fears that low-income households with high water needs – including large families and those individuals suffering from certain long-term illnesses – may be unable to pay for all the water that they require. So, although demand management may address economic and environmental needs, there is a risk, in the UK context at least, of a social sustainability failure (Mitchell, 1999b).

In the water resource module of the Quantifiable City model, water use indicators were identified to address the inter-generational equity (economic efficiency), social equity and environmental aspects of water resource use. The indicators were developed using the PICABUE methodology (Mitchell et al, 1995), an objective approach applied within a roundtable (Delphi) environment in which a series of independent estimates were advanced and debated. Inter-generational equity was represented by total annual regional water demand (from currently developed resources) as a percentage of the estimated resource stock in a drought year with a 50-year return period (about two generations); social equity by the percentage of households spending more than x per cent of household income on meeting basic water and sewerage needs; and environmental aspects by the number of days per annum on which the flow of abstraction rivers drops below the minimum level recommended for maintaining a healthy river ecosystem. This represents an advance over previous approaches, which have usually equated water sustainability simply with maintaining levels of water use per capita.

It was important to develop a capability to forecast water demand that would allow indicators to represent the level of the spatial hierarchy appropriate to water consumers, while at the same time enabling sufficient demand scenarios and policy options to be investigated. Domestic demand was modelled using a microsimulation approach, which uses chain-conditional probabilities to simulate household characteristics for small areas, typically comprising 10 to 20 houses (Clarke et al, 1996). Characteristics were selected that are relevant to water use, including household size, number of occupants, socio-economic group, and the presence of a washing machine or dishwasher. Once population and household characteristics had been simulated for an area, water-use coefficients specific to household types – derived from water utility surveys – were used to forecast demand both for small areas and the whole urban region. Long-term domestic demand at a regional and a small area scale was simulated at five-yearly intervals to 2025, using a regional demographic simulation based on a government model to constrain the population growth scenario (Williamson, 1998). Non-domestic demand was forecast using an econometric model, built from time-series data of metered demand, which can produce individual forecasts for nine economic activities defined according to the standard industrial classification. By making use of reliable forecasts from other sources (Barker, 1996), the model can be used to investigate the effects of changes in regional economic activity, water supply and effluent disposal charges, as well as regional climate, including drought. The potential impact of waste minimization on water demand can also be assessed (Mitchell, 1999c), although forecast certainty here remains low because insufficient data are available to calibrate this part of the model. Leakage is currently addressed using monitored data and water utility leakage targets.

The results of simulations of water resource sustainability using the model contrast with the findings of regional supply forecasts by the local water utility, which address climate change scenarios and rising demand under a 'business-as-usual' approach. The utility's scenarios indicate a decline in the surplus of supply over demand, implying that water resource management is currently on an unsustainable trajectory. The new model shows that demand management measures can offset forecast increases in non-domestic demand through a combination of economic instruments and waste minimization practices. However, these gains may be negated unless domestic demand is also constrained. This could be achieved through metering; but the likely impacts of this cannot be investigated properly within the microsimulation model without realistic price elasticity functions, which are currently unavailable for the UK.

Further refinements and extensions of the water resources module are planned. These include a preliminary study of the impact of metering on demand and the potential impacts on low-income families using the microsimulation model which, because of its fine treatment of scale, is well suited to the task. The impact of water resource management policies on the environmental indicator will also be explicitly addressed by entering the small area demand forecasts into a regional water network model – WRAPSIM (Likeman et al, 1995) – used to optimize efficiency in water distribution, given constraints of demand, minimum acceptable river flows or reservoir levels and costs.

Air quality, transportation and land use

Low air quality is a serious concern in many European cities and, as a common property problem that is difficult to manage, with complex causes and wide-ranging impacts, it is the kind of issue that sustainability modelling should seek to address. The air quality module of the Quantifiable City model achieves this through a series of integrated models of transport, land use, pollutant emission, pollutant dispersion and health impact. First, a tactical transport model, SATURN (Simulation and Assignment of Traffic to Urban Road Networks) (Van Vliet, 1982), was used to model vehicle flows, speeds and delays at each of several thousand junction and road links for the Leeds urban road network. A second module, ROADFAC (Namdeo and Colls, 1994), used SATURN output variables to estimate emissions of several key air pollutants using emission factors based on the work of EU expert groups. Emission estimates are commonly made for daily average or rush hour traffic. Estimates of emissions from buildings are also made using land-use and economic activity data, discharge consent applications, and observed data collected for consent compliance monitoring. These stationary and mobile emission estimates, produced for lines, points and areas, were combined within a GIS, using grid cells as a common data format. The combined emission estimates were then fed to a pollutant dispersion model (AirViro or ADMS urban), which, once initialized with appropriate topographic data, can calculate air quality in three dimensions given specified or typical meteorological conditions (Namdeo et al, 1999).

This combination of models has already been used to identify areas of particularly poor air quality in need of urgent remedial action. It can also be used to investigate the impact on air quality of modifications to the road network (for example, new road construction, reduced capacity or vehicle exclusions), the introduction of road pricing and changes in vehicle fleet characteristics (such as traffic volume, fuel type, engine size distribution and cold-start performance). Capacity to study further policy options and impacts will be increased by additions at both ends of the model chain. First, the incidence of respiratory disease will be estimated using modelled air quality data, employing the methods described and trialled by Mitchell et al (2000). This will permit investigation of the spatial pattern of respiratory disease burden in Leeds. The knowledge thus gained should assist in identifying transport policies to improve air quality and tackle the inequitable distribution of ill health linked to transport emissions. Second, extending the links between land use and transport to accommodate feedback mechanisms will permit a greater range of policy options to be tested. The SATURN transport model takes as its input a matrix that describes the demand for trip origins and destinations, and then assigns these trips to the network based on travel cost or time constraints. The matrix is derived from information about the current pattern of urban land use. In the short term, therefore, traffic patterns are assumed to be determined by land use. In the long term, however, land use may itself be modified as a function of changes in accessibility and environmental quality that relate to developments in transportation. By integrating a model (DELTA) that can predict land use from land availability, price, demand, accessibility and environmental quality (Still and Simmonds, 1998), it should be possible to mount a more comprehensive investigation of the land-use–transport system and its external impacts, including air quality, respiratory disease and noise.

Defining policy combinations

The key criteria for an urban sustainability model defined above are also met by the SPARTACUS (System for Planning and Research in Towns and Cities for Urban Sustainability) model (LT Consultants, 1999). This also uses a land-use–transport model (MEPLAN) to investigate urban land-use and transport policies, and associated effects. SPARTACUS models three main types of indicators:

1. environmental (gaseous emissions, fuel consumption, land coverage);
2. social (exposure to gaseous emissions, noise, accessibility, travel cost); and
3. economic, defined as the total net benefit per capita arising under alternative policies.

To allow comparison of model runs, variables of each main type are aggregated within an index, weighted according to the results of a roundtable exercise. Nearly 70 policy options and their combinations have been tested, representing different pricing, regulatory, land-use, transport and investment measures.

Combining policies allowed the negative side-effects of certain individual policies to be mitigated. It was discovered, for example, that pricing policies alone would tend to concentrate people and work opportunities within city centres, leaving the suburbs without services. This could be avoided, however, by a combination of pricing and teleworking policies. The model also proved a useful tool for investigating aspects of the debate about the merits of the compact city as against decentralized concentration (Breheny, 1992; European Commission, 1990; see also Chapter 6 in this volume). Applying the model to Helsinki, Bilbao and Naples gave rise to a number of policy recommendations for European cities. Crucially, this work also revealed situations in which the negative side-effects of particular initiatives pointed to the need for the revision of policy combinations and further testing.

The SPARTACUS study showed that environmental, social and economic city sustainability can be increased by adopting not just single policies, but innovative policy combinations. Typically, this involved a greater emphasis on a mix of pricing initiatives and a lesser reliance on regulatory controls. Amongst the latter, action to reduce traffic speeds was found to have the greatest social and environmental benefits; but as a policy option it was economically unacceptable. In all three cities studied, the pressure of urban sprawl was strong and individual measures such as teleworking or car pooling, designed to reduce travel demand, were shown to increase private car use in the long term. This was because reduced congestion allowed households to move to more peripheral areas without suffering the penalty of greatly increased journey times. An alternative course – adopting a combination of policies that would increase private travel costs, promote investment in public transport and teleworking, and tighten controls on land use – could halt the rise in mobility and improve urban sustainability. This could only be achieved, however, by strict adherence to the total policy package – otherwise, the negative side-effects of individual elements would not be mitigated.

These studies demonstrate the value of modelling as a tool for coping with the inherent complexity of urban sustainability. It allows the exploration of alternative development paths, identifying the most promising options without recourse to costly or mistaken trials. Modelling can help to map out combinations of policies that, cumulatively, have a positive effect which would not otherwise be identified. It is also vital in detecting unforeseen, deleterious and even irreversible effects of sustainability initiatives that are not easy to recognize intuitively. Modelling emphasizes the importance of long-term strategic planning over short-term problem management and can address a series of processes operating simultaneously, so that optimal solutions for potentially competing economic, social and environmental objectives can be identified. The process of modelling also helps to operationalize the sustainable development concept. It encourages creative thinking about societal goals, and about the expression of these goals as sustainability indicators and their relation to the root cause of societal problems. Thus, while modelling is certainly not a precondition for sound policy formulation, it can be a powerful tool for policy-makers.

Problems and Prospects for Urban Sustainability Modelling

Urban sustainability models such as SPARTACUS and the Quantifiable City represent a real advance on previous urban models. While older models operated largely within a 'human economy' subsystem, the agenda of sustainable development has stimulated increased attention to the other key areas of quality of life, environmental conditions and urban metabolisms. However, the new urban models are still far from comprehensive and give only a partial view of reality. No model has yet been created that can represent all key processes and interactions within and between economic, social and environmental subsystems. This partial treatment is inevitable given the complexity of urban systems, and it is acceptable if critical subsystems are captured and models are validated by checking performance against reality.

Inevitably, place-specific differences mean that models developed within one context may not be applicable in another. Critical systems and key causal chains may be specific to particular urban centres as a reflection, for example, of differences in development goals, or the degree to which urbanization and industrialization are linked. Thus, for example, McGee's (1994) study of Asian mega-cities views Singapore and Kuala Lumpur as embodying a Western model of urbanization, under which a functional and ideological differentiation between 'urban' and 'rural' is echoed in a clear spatial divide. In contrast, the growth of Bangkok, Taipei-Kaohsuing, Shanghai and Beijing-Tianjin as urban regions incorporating two or more cores linked by fast transportation routes has created extensive zones of mixed rural–urban land use. These different patterns of land use have marked sustainability implications, not least in their effects on the scale and efficiency of urban material flows.

A sustainability model should not, therefore, be applied without demonstrating that its underlying theoretical structure is locally applicable. Where no such case can be made, it may be appropriate to restructure the model. But this is not necessarily an easy option, given the current limitations of knowledge in many areas impinging upon urban sustainability. For example, a UN conference concluded that because of their dominant role in national economies, mega-cities required unique solutions to sustainability problems, and that it was inappropriate to scale up work based on smaller cities. However, the identification of such solutions is constrained by the limited availability of basic data for mega-cities, particularly on areal sub-units, and a lack of fundamental, systematic and policy-relevant research focused on understanding mega-cities (Fuchs et al, 1994).

Other common problems discussed above include those of adequately representing processes without oversimplification, drawing boundaries without treating key processes as exogenous to the model, treating scale appropriately and tackling uncertainty – for example, over the treatment of poorly understood assimilative capacities. Modelling is also a lengthy, resource-intensive process, especially if work is to be properly validated. Integrating existing operational models within a common framework – an approach adopted in the Quantifiable City project – can provide a short cut to the development of a more extensive model, but only if practical problems caused by the use of different computer languages and platforms, varied ownership of constituent models and diverse working practices in different disciplines can be overcome. Once developed, there will be a trade-off between the cost of model application and the derivation of recommended policy, validated for specific cities.

Modelling must be seen as only one of many tools available for analysing urban issues. Jowsey and Kellet (1996), for example, detail the use of other quantitative techniques for assessing urban management alternatives, including environmental impact assessment, strategic environmental assessment, project-level impact assessment, environmental auditing, and a range of pricing techniques for socio-economic and environmental appraisal. Identifying the best technique, or mix of techniques, to apply to promote urban sustainability in a particular case is a problem in itself. This is being addressed through the EU BEQUEST (Built Environment Quality Evaluation for Sustainability through Time) network and associated advances in decision-support tools (Curwell et al, 1998; Mitchell and Vreeker, 1999). Most of the alternative quantitative techniques are applicable to all cities, and pragmatism dictates that many are more appropriate than modelling when addressing the problems of mega- or Southern cities. However, models can provide much more powerful insights into the interactions involved in urban systems. They have the potential to address economic, social and environmental concerns simultaneously, with explicit consideration of intra- and inter-generational equity issues. There are, thus, good reasons to continue to invest effort in the development of urban sustainability models, for they have much to offer in terms of understanding complex systems and enabling long-term strategic management.

Batty (1994) looked forward to a modest renaissance of urban modelling, reflecting a belief that models cannot reclaim the centrality they once possessed within urban studies. In practice, the limitations of urban modelling are now widely acknowledged and urban sustainability modelling is likely to develop gradually. The immediate future will see the production of improved subsystem models that address difficult common property problems. These will be integrated into a wider modelling framework to represent the city as a whole, allowing causal chains to be followed. Within the Quantifiable City programme, for example, separate models are currently being developed to address greenhouse gas emissions, respiratory disease associated with poor air quality and non-point source water pollution. These models draw upon the common population–land-use–transport model core; but links may also be required to other downstream model processes. Water demand, for example, has implications for the energy used to pump water around the network, while atmospheric deposition associated with poor air quality is a significant source of urban non-point surface water pollution.

Experience to date suggests that urban sustainability modelling should progress on two broad fronts. First, dynamic simulation models are required that can address the city as a unit, focusing on key environmental quality problems with sustainable development indicators (SDIs) as the principal outputs. Second, city metabolism problems should be addressed at the urban regional scale, using economic input–output models, or simulation models where data resolution allows. The latter can use SDIs to tackle specific problems. But to enable a comprehensive assessment of urban sustainability, sustainable development indices should also be quantified, preferably developing ecological indices that recognize the metabolism concept and ecosystem limits. Further understanding should be gained by integrating these two complementary approaches wherever possible. Increasingly, also, models will be applied in a backcasting mode, where model output values are set to represent targets for sustainable development and models are run to identify system conditions and policy options that will enable the target to be met.

These developments will require advances in theory, methods and data. Currently, for example, there is an understandable lack of confidence in sustainability indices. This reflects a lack of replicability of results so that their repeated use for the same place and time period yields radically different sustainability trajectories (Moffatt et al, 1994), and the current lack of knowledge of critical thresholds associated with sustainability indicators. Feedback mechanisms and non-linearities are also often poorly represented. Thus, for example, both SPARTACUS and the Quantifiable City model seek a better understanding of land-use–transport interaction flows, and particularly the interactions between land use and environmental quality. Similarly, advances in microsimulation and better use of GIS will allow improved representation of processes in space and time. Simulation models must also be developed to act as components of more flexible decision-support systems, comprising a mix of GIS, expert systems embedded within local knowledge and dynamic models in which neural networks or fuzzy logic are used to describe relationships that defied description in earlier models. Such advances offer the prospect of greater insights into urban processes and, hence, enhanced opportunities for identifying policies for sustainable urban development. Besides overcoming the technical problems, modellers will have to pay far more attention to developing practical tools that are designed from the outset to recognize the needs and capabilities of end users.

Conclusion

All cities experience sustainability failures. In Northern cities where population growth rates are low, the principal concerns often focus on environmental quality and efficiency, particularly the promotion of the circular urban metabolism within socially and economically acceptable constraints. In Southern cities the picture is very different, and the chief concerns are those relating to poverty, health and basic needs, although development strategies must still recognize ecological constraints. To meet these challenges, new and creative policy solutions are constantly being devised and tested. But because of the complexity of urban systems and the nature of the sustainability paradigm itself, it is difficult to assess their success. A systematic approach to urban sustainability is therefore required to enable the assessment of the long-term effectiveness of remedial strategies; to compare and contrast alternative strategies; to gauge the transferability of strategies between different locations; and to identify previously unseen strategies. Measures of sustainable development tailored to cities will provide the focus for this systems approach. But they must be married to an understanding of urban form, function and process, and it is here that geographers and urban modellers can make significant contributions.

Urban geography has always been concerned with spatial pattern and process. As the earliest empirical studies of urban location and land-use segregation gave way to a search for universal laws, urban modelling was adopted as a vehicle for testing laws and formalizing knowledge about urban systems. The initial foray into modelling during the early post-war decades met with limited success and dwindled to become a minority interest within urban geography. However, some 25 years after its apparent demise, there is renewed optimism that modelling can provide useful urban management tools. If this faith is to be justified, a much greater degree of integration between the urban modelling and sustainable development assessment communities will be required, allowing the potential of both approaches to be realized. Cities and urban regions should become a focus for sustainable development modelling, exploiting the existing experience of the urban modelling school so that past mistakes are not repeated and ensuring the fastest possible development of useful operational assessment tools. Equally, urban modelling needs to widen its scope to address environmental quality issues and to improve its treatment of social equity, an area in which there has already been considerable urban geographic research (see, for example, Pacione, 1999b; Smallman-Raynor and Phillips, 1999). Modelling must also explore the distribution of social and environmental costs and benefits accruing from consumption, as well as influences upon the efficiency of use of physical resources. There are increasing signs that the urban modelling school is beginning to recognize both the desirability and necessity of addressing sustainable development issues. Indeed, there can be few objections to such a change in emphasis. The established objective of understanding urban processes as a foundation for the more efficient planning of urban functions is fundamentally consistent with the aims of sustainable development.

In the past, urban management was perhaps too rationalist and reductionist, and demonstrably inadequate in its ability to cope with uncertainty. Urban institutions were too preoccupied with technical solutions to their own narrowly defined problems, neglecting cross-sectoral issues as a result. A more adaptive form of management is now required, where functional experts working in compartmentalized areas give way to an organizational framework supportive of collaborative work by multi-functional teams, including empowered stakeholder groups. This new structure requires an ability and commitment to provide multi-disciplinary information to decision-makers, educators, the public and those researchers seeking to develop appropriate tools and analyses to support decision-making.

Undoubtedly, perceptions of the role of modelling in shaping the future of cities will be coloured by attitudes towards the past failures of rational comprehensive planning. However, rationality should be seen simply for what it is: the ability to distinguish between good and bad actions made on the basis of logic, empirical data and analysis. In this light, a rational systems approach and modelling, which is one expression of that approach, have much to offer as tools for identifying appropriate solutions to urban sustainability problems.

6

Making Cities More Sustainable: People, Plans and Participation

Rachael Unsworth

Introduction

The study of urban settlements has rightly assumed a central importance within the wider discussions of sustainability. This is not just a reflection of the size and number of towns and cities in the contemporary world, but also because such urban centres embody many of the tensions and contradictions of development. The concentration of population in urban centres often reveals with particular clarity the extent to which economic activity creates both costs and benefits. Worldwide, the burgeoning urban population is responsible for more than half of the global production of goods and services; but they also account for a much larger proportion of all waste and pollution. Inevitably, activity on this scale has much wider consequences, not least because many resources are imported, and many wastes are exported, far beyond urban boundaries. At the same time, the juxtaposition of wealth and poverty within urban centres itself reminds us that the rewards of development are rarely distributed equally or equitably. It is against this background that practical initiatives are increasingly being taken – internationally, nationally and at the scale of individual municipalities and neighbourhoods – to create more sustainable cities. One dimension of this effort is to increase the efficiency with which resources are consumed, thus minimizing the output of waste. However, a more rounded conception of sustainable development must embrace efforts to foster social equity and to make urban life more tolerable, healthy and rewarding.

After a brief review of the problems characterizing urban centres in both developed and developing countries, this chapter explores the ways in which thinking about sustainable development has changed key aspects of urban management. Attention is paid, first, to debate concerning the role of large-scale land-use planning in raising the quality of urban environments and creating more resource-efficient settlements. In particular, the perceived need to promote energy efficiency and counter problems created by increasing dependency upon motor vehicles has led to advocacy of alternative urban forms. The logic of strategic planning for sustainable development must, however, be set against the need to involve the broad mass of urban residents in defining development priorities that are seen to be equitable and legitimate. Participation is thus the theme of the second half of the chapter. Residents themselves are potentially key agents in the execution of more sustainable development, both through the everyday decisions that they make about consumption and in their willingness to take an active role in projects for urban improvement. Individual and communal initiative in raising urban quality of life and improving environmental conditions is arguably particularly important in the developing world where the formal institutional structures of urban government are often weak. Grassroots change can make a real and positive difference to the lives of urban dwellers. But this approach embodies its own challenge of extending the benefits of local best practice to a global population in need.

The reorientation of urban forms and functions, so that they contribute positively to the search for more sustainable development, is thus an immense and daunting undertaking, dogged by uncertainty at every step from the conceptualization of aims through to the monitoring of results. This chapter will argue, however, that despite the many barriers to progress, the quality of urban life is improving in ways that will benefit the majority of current and future urban residents. In attending to problems within their own boundaries, the people of the world's cities are also making a significant contribution to the solution of global problems of environmental change, social inequality and economic marginalization.

Continuity and Change in Urban Problems

The environment is a relatively recent addition to urban geographers' concerns with the form and functions of towns and cities, perhaps reflecting initial perceptions of urban centres as the antithesis of a 'natural' environment (Hall, 1995). However, as Mitchell (see Chapter 5) details in the context of European cities, urban inhabitants exert a profound influence upon ecological systems through the consumption of resources in the construction, maintenance and use of the built environment. Urban activity also generates a particular concentration of waste and pollution. Moreover, the effects of urban production, exchange and consumption upon air and water quality, land use and biodiversity are not confined to the immediate locality (Douglas, 1983). The resources consumed within urban systems are drawn from hinterlands that have long been international, and much of the waste that accompanies urban consumption returns to the wider world. The demands of British consumers, for example, play a part in encouraging the over-exploitation of tropical forests; in creating the pollution that causes acid rain in continental Europe; and in perpetuating systems of agricultural land use that displace and marginalize indigenous peoples in parts of the developing world (see Chapter 8). In an era of economic globalization, it is more obvious than ever before that not only are patterns of resource use in urban centres 'inherently unsustainable', but that the scale of urbanism 'is now a major threat to *global* sustainability' (Elkin et al, 1991, emphasis added).

The environmental impacts of towns and cities located in the global North are not simply a product of the scale of urban development. They also reflect the demands on material resources made by a population that has attained an unprecedented level of affluence. Yet the benefits of contemporary consumer society are questionable. Such doubts reflect both the evidence of increasing environmental strain and a growing realization that the happiness promised by consumerism is often fleeting (LaTouche,

1993). Furthermore, rising levels of material affluence throw into sharp relief the continuing social inequality experienced throughout the developed world (Low et al, 2000). Indeed, it is in urban centres that the extremes of wealth and poverty are often most closely juxtaposed and, hence, most evident. It is not simply the case that poorer households are denied many of the benefits of consumer society; they also endure lower standards in healthcare, education and other essential services. Frequently, too, poorer communities bear a disproportionate share of the environmental costs generated by urban traffic, industrial pollution and waste disposal. This evident social inequity must be addressed in any attempt to promote more sustainable urban development. But we must also ask what can be done to create more humane cities that will combat pathologies such as crime and social isolation, which diminish the real quality of life for the broad mass of urban residents.

Problems generated by social inequality are, of course, also evident in the cities of the global South. However, urban life in the developing world is characterized by its own distinctive concerns. In part, these reflect the sheer scale and pace of urban expansion. In most Southern states, population growth remains strong, reinforcing the necessity for rapid economic development if the majority are to meet even their most basic needs, including food, shelter and security of income. Demographic and economic growth seem certain to be increasingly concentrated in urban areas. The urban proportion of the population in most developing countries is, as yet, much lower than the 80 to 90 per cent that is common in the developed world. But, while the latter has seen some movement of population and economic activity away from the largest urban centres, the urban population of developing countries is growing at a rate of 150,000 per day, or 55 million per year. The pace of urbanization is beginning to slow in Latin America; but these changes have no parallel in much of Africa and Asia (UN, 1995). By the end of the 21st century, therefore, 'more people will be packed into the urban areas of the developing world than are currently alive on the planet today' (UNCHS, 1996).

Comparison with previous European experience of urban growth reinforces perceptions of the sheer scale of the challenge presented by urbanization in the developing world. Leeds, for example, was not unusual amongst UK cities in tripling its population during the first half of the 19th century (Burt and Grady, 1994). This, however, produced a total population of only 180,000 by 1850, a far cry from the millions of new inhabitants now crowding into Southern mega-cities such as Bombay, Manila and Sao Paulo (see Table 6.1). Many other cities experienced at least a tenfold

Table 6.1   Urban population growth in selected Southern cities, circa 1950–2000

City	Post-war population, circa 1950	Estimated population, 2000	Percentage growth, circa 1950–2000
Bangkok, Thailand	1.4 million	7.3 million	520
Bombay (Mumbai), India	2.9 million	18.1 million	620
Karachi, Pakistan	<0.5 million	12.0 million	circa 2400
Manila, the Philippines	1.5 million	10.8 million	720
Mexico City, Mexico	3.1 million	16.4 million	530
Sao Paulo, Brazil	2.4 million	17.8 million	740

Source: Fuchs et al (1994); Lari (1996); UNCHS (1996)

population increase between 1950 and 1990, including Abidjan, Dar-es-Salaam, Khartoum, Kinshasa, Lagos, Nouakchott and Nairobi in Africa, Amman in the Middle East and the Asian centre of Seoul (Hardoy et al, 1992).

Rapid population growth will only exacerbate the existing problems of urban poverty throughout the developing world. In many African, Asian and Latin American states, more than half of the urban population lives below the poverty line (UNCHS, 1996). The consequent lack of individual and collective resources to invest in urban infrastructure and services is reflected in clear North–South differentials in many key determinants of quality of life (see Table 6.2). Provision of medical care, education, housing, water supply and sanitation is frequently inadequate in Southern cities, with consequences for both human health and welfare, as well as environmental quality. Such problems are compounded by a limited capacity for technological and managerial innovation (Pugh, 2000). Levels of car ownership, for example, are much lower in Southern cities than in the developed North. However, many vehicles are old and poorly maintained, emissions legislation is frequently weak or unenforceable, and road networks are inadequate and congested. As a result, pollution is often intensely concentrated and damaging, and death rates from traffic accidents are high (Hardoy et al, 1992; World Resources Institute, 1996). It is more generally true that efficiency in resource and energy use is low in developing countries, so that the environmental impact of each unit of economic output can be markedly greater than in the developed world. Moreover, in the absence of effective land-use planning, polluting industry is still found in inner urban areas, often in close proximity to densely populated residential districts. Residents and workers are thus exposed to environmental dangers and health hazards that have largely been eliminated in the more regulated context of the North.

It is evident, therefore, that fundamental reforms are necessary to lay the foundations for long-term improvements in urban conditions in the developing world. It is vital not just to tackle the immediate problems caused by a lack of infrastructure, but also to address the deeper roots of poverty and injustice. In total the task is formidable, for it requires an end to political instability and mismanagement at a national level and a new equity in international economic systems. However, important advances may also be secured at a more local level through the creation of a new institutional capacity to promote and manage urban improvement. The weakness of urban governance in many parts of the developing world is profound. Again, comparisons with the experience of the developed North are instructive. The urban and industrial transformation of Europe and North America during the 19th and early 20th centuries may initially have been largely unplanned. However, effective urban management systems were instituted long before the scale of urban development reached anything approaching that of contemporary Southern mega-cities. But this is not to argue that aspirations to improve urban form, functions and quality of life must inevitably lead to the global extension of Northern models of urban politics and formal development planning. Within the developed world itself, critics of established modes of urban government have questioned their ability to deliver development that is socially equitable and environmentally sustainable. Top-heavy governmental structures seem at odds with the participatory ethos of sustainable development. Hence, a more appropriate and, ultimately, more effective way forward may be the creation of alternative organizational structures to tap the considerable potential of human capital represented by urban inhabitants themselves.

Table 6.2   Urban

Region	Population growth (percentage per annum)	Net density (persons per hectare)	Household size	City product (US$ per person)	Poor households as percentage of total	Child mortality[1]	Access to clean water (percentage)
Africa	5.1	152.1	6.1	701	39	11.3	68.4
Arab states	4.5	202.3	5.1	2114	29	8.2	87.0
Asia Pacific	3.2	236.7	5.0	1059	20	5.6	89.0
Industrialized	0.6	68.6	2.5	21,434	13	0.6	99.6
Less advanced countries	2.4	156.1	4.2	2655	39	5.4	86.9
Transitional	0.0	102.3	3.0	3204	24	2.5	99.1
All developing	3.5	168.3	5.0	1546	31	7.3	81.4
All developed	3.1	154.3	4.6	4411	30	6.7	84.2
Development level, as identified in UNDP Human Development Index							
Very low	5.1	134.9	6.3	151	38	12.3	66.4
Low	5.0	231.3	5.6	376	33	7.4	75.8
Medium	1.9	170.2	4.2	914	36	6.7	89.5
Higher	1.5	132.5	3.5	2968	22	3.1	97.0
Developed	0.7	66.8	2.6	17,716	12	2.3	99.4

Note: 1 Probability of dying aged five or under.
Source: compiled from data in Flood (1997).

Outlining Sustainable Urban Development

The ideal of the sustainable city

The failures of the present make it all the more urgent to explore alternative futures, looking forward to the creation of urban forms and processes that are both more environmentally benign and better able to deliver improvements in quality of life to the majority of their inhabitants. There can be no single blueprint for a 'sustainable city' (Campbell, 1996). Indeed, both the goals of urban sustainability and the means of their achievement continue to be disputed. Some theoreticians and practitioners claim that only a radical reworking of relationships between economy, society and environment will create a truly sustainable urban society. Others, meanwhile, champion more pragmatic and incremental approaches (Baker et al, 1997). But it is possible to sketch out the broad ideals of sustainable urban development, considering the overall form of urban settlement; the changing character of the urban economy; the planning and provision of infrastructure; and measures to raise standards in welfare, education and cultural provision.

The model sustainable city will minimize resource inputs and waste output without destroying employment locally or further afield. This requires the transformation of the structure and workings of the local economy so that they are less resource intensive and deliver a higher quality of life, rather than just a higher material standard of living. Such an economy will cause a minimum of air, water and land pollution. But more than this, a sustainable city will invest resources in cleaning up

and housing indicators

Waste water treated (percentage)	Households having waste collected (percentage)	Road expenditure (US$ per person per annum)	Revenue (US$ per persons per annum)	Capital expenditure (US$ per persons per annum)	Persons per hospital bed	Children per primary classroom	Permanent dwellings (percentage of total)
15.7	35.9	6	15	10	1000	63	61
49.5	61.4	33	47	31	495	42	84
24.5	66.4	3	253	241	566	40	73
86.8	99.4	127	2763	1109	132	23	98
18.1	85.3	15	242	193	277	34	80
64.0	91.8	20	258	79	80	32	98
28.8	63.5	11	108	54	590	47	73
37.8	68.7	29	551	221	518	44	76
8.9	33.5	5	7	3	1080	70	47
22.7	50.6	4	22	14	754	47	78
33.7	73.5	6	129	63	337	36	79
51.6	93.8	27	249	83	230	35	92
78.6	98.6	107	2417	958	135	24	96

water bodies and land areas previously contaminated, and in ensuring that biodiversity is maintained and enhanced. Inputs for the urban economy will be derived from renewable and sustainable sources whenever possible and reliance upon local sources of supply will increase.

The shape and function of the urban environment will be transformed, producing multipurpose public spaces that are both green and safe. Buildings will be well designed, both with respect to their form and function, and to ensure high standards of ecological performance. This will create economies in the consumption of energy, water and other resources. A sustainable city will be less dominated by planning for the motor vehicle. Policy will be directed towards reducing car dependency and making travel less necessary by improving alternative means of access to urban facilities.

Information is vital to the creation of urban sustainability. Urban governments must collect, analyse and effectively disseminate information about the state of the environment and progress towards meeting tough environmental and social targets. Information and communications technology must also be used creatively and effectively to deliver services, and to involve citizens in designing change and providing information.

A sustainable city is also politically transformed. It will reform its local democratic processes and structures so that all citizens can be involved in decision-making about their area and its wider linkages. Residents are also motivated to change their own behaviour to complement the overall goals of sustainable development. A reformed system of governance will be dedicated to the promotion of social equity, making explicit links between action on health, housing, education, social services and crime prevention so that the poorest urban dwellers have their life chances significantly improved.

All the different aspects of urban planning, development and management will be incorporated within policy documents that must be endorsed by the population at large if they are to be successfully implemented. Beyond its own boundaries, the sustainable city will have effective links with other urban centres to share knowledge and best practice regarding the continuing pursuit of sustainability. Compared with cities that have not embraced the sustainability agenda, the new urban model is a more coherent centre physically and socially, creating a more enjoyable place in which to live. Holistic, inclusive thinking and action will become the norm. People of all kinds will become more aware of their relationship with the environment and their role in delivering sustainability.

In its most perfect form, the sustainable city is thus a very different place from any existing urban centre. To expect the sudden transformation of urban form and functions is clearly unrealistic. However, progress towards more sustainable urban development is both practical and necessary. Past experience, not only in the developed world, has shown that it is possible to raise housing standards, to curb air and water pollution, to conserve urban green space and plan land use to minimize the conflict between incompatible neighbours. Business may see its own commercial logic in promoting resource efficiency and waste minimization (see Chapter 7), and the technological transformation of patterns of travel, communications and access to goods, services and information is already an established fact. The pursuit of urban sustainability, coordinating all of these changes and many others, will not be easy or uncontested; but it is not an impossible dream. As the following sections show, many different initiatives are already being explored to translate the vision of sustainable urban development into reality. This involves actions that are relevant at a broad range of spatial scales, from the global to the local.

Urban sustainability in context: the city and the world

Sustainable development will rest on sure foundations if it is based on actions and initiatives at the local level. Decisions taken by individuals within households, businesses and other organizations ultimately determine the use made of resources and the extent to which production and consumption creates waste and pollution. Without grassroots support, any grand plans for more sustainable development are vulnerable to subversion. But acting locally is not of itself sufficient (see Table 6.3). Within the city there must be collective organization to support and coordinate neighbourhood initiatives. Other functions are best discharged at a citywide level, often building upon established municipal responsibilities in planning land use, transportation and economic development. Urban governance, in turn, works most effectively when it is supported by the national state. Ultimately, the sustainability of individual urban centres has to be set within overarching national and international frameworks designed to promote a common commitment to combating global environmental damage, socio-economic injustice and political oppression.

It follows that one of the greatest challenges in delivering sustainable urban development is to ensure that actions at each level of the spatial and administrative hierarchy are strong enough to support initiatives taken elsewhere, and that the different elements in the hierarchy are linked effectively. For instance, it is hard for individuals to reduce the problems caused by the disposal of household waste if urban

Table 6.3   *Urban sustainability and spatial scale*

Level of action	Example of action
International	• Setting overall targets for greenhouse gas emissions • Securing fairer trade relations so that national incomes increase, generating more resources for investment in urban sustainability
National	• Maintaining democratic structures, including the appropriate devolution of power • Framing laws and taxes to guide actions and alter decision-making – including provision for sanctions against non-compliance • Co-ordinating resource allocation and infrastructure networks • Gathering national data on social, economic and environmental matters; defining sustainability indicators
City	• Co-ordinating a citywide public transport network, water and drainage systems, waste collection and disposal • Integrated transport and land-use planning to reduce the need for travel, minimize resource use and improve environmental quality • Co-ordinating economic development • Gathering data about the city, its policy impacts and the views of its citizens
Neighbourhood	• Initiatives to provide infrastructure, waste management and employment in low-income residential districts • Initiatives to involve citizens in improving their own immediate surroundings and their income-earning prospects

governments do not support the infrastructure necessary for efficient waste management, recycling and reuse. In turn, urban authorities will struggle to implement waste minimization programmes if national planning for sustainable development sets inappropriate targets, or state governments do not devolve the necessary financial resources and legal powers to enable effective local action. These interconnections mean that not only are moves towards more sustainable development inevitably complicated and multi-stranded, there is also considerable potential for conflict and dislocation (see Chapter 4). When connections fail, initiatives at one level may be obstructed elsewhere. Local innovations may be frustrated by an overbearing national authority; but it is equally likely that national plans are undermined by a lack of local legitimacy. At each hierarchical level effort may be wasted and actors become disillusioned, so that they maintain less sustainable behaviour, if they perceive that neighbouring households, companies, districts or countries can act irresponsibly with relative impunity. Nor is the construction of an effective and interconnected hierarchy of initiatives and actors a once-and-for-all operation. The system requires effective leadership underpinned by a continuing process of information gathering, analysis and dissemination, education and awareness raising, and regular revision of the targets and standards that define sustainable development.

It is beyond the scope of this chapter to review the growing body of national and international initiatives designed to foster more sustainable development that impact upon urban areas (see Chapters 3 and 11). The importance of this wider context should, however, be borne in mind throughout the following discussion of changing approaches to urban sustainability. In turning first to plans for the management of urban systems, rather than specific towns and cities, this chapter sketches in some aspects of thinking about sustainable urban development as a national project. However, as is subsequently discussed, recent debates about planning for sustainable urban development have focused chiefly upon measures to change the form and character of individual urban centres.

Planning for Urban Sustainability

Managing urban systems: can the tide of urbanization be turned?

The evident problems of environmental damage, social dislocation and economic unsustainability caused by rapid and extensive urban growth might suggest that the key to greater sustainability lies in setting limits to urbanization. The essence of such ideas can be found in contemporary discussion of the failings of industrial cities in 19th-century Europe (Sutcliffe, 1993). However, it was during the decades after World War II that the most active efforts were made to manage national urban systems in the name of economic efficiency and social welfare. During the 1960s, it was widely asserted by planners and academics that there was an optimum size for settlements at each level of the urban hierarchy. It followed that where this ideal was significantly exceeded, inefficiencies would start to overcome the benefits of urban agglomeration (Berry, 1967; Berry and Horton, 1970; Spengler, 1967). Although it proved difficult to specify these threshold sizes, some commentators suggested that urban populations in excess of 2 million created 'dysfunctional' cities (Bairoch, 1975). These ideas gave rise to planning regimes that attempted to limit or divert urban growth to keep individual centres to a 'manageable' size. The overall form of some national urban systems was subject to review and a process of 'smoothing out' of the urban hierarchy was proposed. This commonly involved efforts to limit the expansion of the largest primary settlements and to accommodate growth elsewhere through the enlargement of existing centres deemed too small, or by the establishment of new towns. Such thinking was evident in post-war Britain, where new towns were championed as the antidote to the problems associated with the concentration of population in the major conurbations (Hall, 1996). Some developing countries – including India, China, Indonesia and South Korea – struggling to cope with the accelerating pace of urbanization also attempted to divert growth away from the largest centres towards the lower rungs of the urban hierarchy (Misra, 1972; Yeung, 1989).

This preoccupation with setting limits to urban expansion has echoes of wider arguments about the need to restrain economic and demographic growth so that it remains within the carrying capacity of supporting ecosystems (see, for example, Meadows et al, 1972). However, just as the logic and practicality of limiting the totality of growth was increasingly questioned during the 1980s and 1990s (Simon, 1981), so there has been a reaction against efforts to curb urban expansion. It is now widely accepted that attempts to stem or divert urban growth have been, at best, only partially successful. At worst, they have wasted scarce resources and have had a negligible effect on urbanization rates and the problems of urban living (Gugler, 1988; Richardson, 1993; Yeung, 1989).

The concept of sustainable development popularized since the 1987 Brundtland Report refers not to limiting growth, but to changing its character. An emphasis on the more efficient and equitable use of resources should mean that short-term economic benefits can be achieved with less damage to the environment, social justice and the welfare of future generations (von Weizsäcker et al, 1997; WCED, 1987). This shift in thinking has clear implications for the future of urban centres. If there is a continuing need for economic growth to improve quality of life and generate funding for environmental improvements, then much of the success of sustainable development will rest upon the creation of dynamic and efficient urban economies. Cities are crucial concentrations not just of complex problems, but also of the infrastructure, initiative and enterprise that will allow sustainable development to be delivered (Haughton and Hunter, 1994).

Reshaping the city: in search of a new quality of urban growth

The sheer scale of development is no longer viewed as the key determinant of urban environmental quality and the balance struck between socio-economic benefits and disbenefits. Rather, these characteristics are seen to depend more upon the ways in which cities are planned and managed internally. Thus, 'land use, the transport system and the spatial layout of a city . . . are critical factors for urban environmental quality' (Nijkamp and Perrels, 1994), and the adequacy of institutions of urban governance assumes a central importance in shaping sustainability. Problems derive not so much from rapid population growth, but from the failure of urban authorities to ensure that their citizens have access to the individual and institutional resources necessary to meet basic needs for income and employment, housing, sanitation, healthcare and education (Hardoy et al, 1992). As increasing numbers of people lead urban lives, it becomes ever more difficult to meet these needs in ways that do not add excessively to the environmental burden of urban consumption. Addressing this challenge requires more than increased investment in housing and infrastructure, the creation of resource-efficient employment and enhanced welfare provision. The spatial character of urban centres must also be reviewed, giving new thought to the siting of different functions: commercial, residential, recreational and environmental. The relative location of these various facets of urban activity can have important implications for the efficiency of resource use, transport demand, access to services, air and water quality, social coherence and community.

Priorities in research and policy development have thus moved away from the manipulation of urban systems as a whole to focus upon improving the functioning of individual centres. Criteria for success have also changed. Attention is no longer paid only to economic efficiency and material living standards; broader improvement in the quality of urban life must include attention to social, cultural, aesthetic and environmental considerations. In pursuing these ends land-use planning has assumed a new importance, not just in minimizing the most obvious and immediate problems caused by urban pollution or congestion, but in laying the foundations for greater long-term sustainability in urban form and function (Blowers, 1993; Campbell, 1996; Rees and Roseland, 1998).

Land-use planning

Urban land-use planning has its origins in 19th-century concerns about public health and social order (Hall, 1996). Initial activity in both Europe and North America attempted chiefly to eliminate the worst symptoms of urban decay and social deprivation through slum clearance. Only gradually did planners and municipal authorities evolve a more positive role in directing investments to improve sanitation and housing provision. During the 20th century, attention to the quality of the urban physical fabric was increasingly complemented by efforts to create a new rationality in spatial form. An increasing segregation of different land uses has been pursued in the cause of economic efficiency and social welfare. Access and the accommodation of the motor vehicle within urban centres have also assumed a growing importance in planning during recent decades.

Planners' attempts to improve urban environments have, however, met with only limited success. Many of the priorities of 20th-century planning now seem in need of radical review. The emphasis on modernization and redevelopment that particularly characterized the first three post-war decades produced townscapes throughout the developed world that are now regarded as ugly, soulless and a contributory factor in social decay and exclusion. The dominant presence of the motor vehicle within many city centres is increasingly questioned, as is the near total reliance upon private transport for access to services such as retailing and entertainment that have abandoned their established central locations for out-of-town sites. A consistent thread through much of this criticism is the recognition that past planning paid insufficient attention to the environmental characteristics of the new urban world that was being created. Although post-war Britain saw important legislation to improve urban air quality and curb other obvious sources of pollution, little note was taken of the resource efficiency of urban systems, the environmental health of urban landscapes or the ever-increasing ecological footprint generated by urban consumption.

During the 1990s, the ethos of urban planning has thus been subjected to increasing critical scrutiny. Working in tandem with other actors – including architects, developers and the owners of commercial and residential property – planners are attempting to encourage conservation and restoration of valued elements of the built environment. In particular, there is a new emphasis on revitalizing established town centres as commercial and residential areas, rather than surrendering land to development at the urban margins. In this and other ways, the role of the motor vehicle, particularly the private car, is being re-evaluated, with the aim of reducing traffic and congestion. Improving alternative means of access to key urban services is thus an important planning objective. This can be achieved both by the relocation of services to bring them closer to their consumers, and by better provision of public transport, cycle routes and pedestrian walkways. Development proposals are increasingly subject to evaluation of their wider environmental and social implications using techniques such as environmental impact assessment. At the same time there is also a new stress on the environmental performance of individual buildings, with the aim of encouraging efficiency in such areas as water consumption and energy use in heating and lighting (Vale and Vale, 1993).

Changes in planning aims are being actively encouraged by central government in many developed countries. In the UK, for example, the national Planning Policy Guidance Notes which shape the formulation of local plans have been overhauled to reflect the new priorities. The Labour government, first elected in 1997, has also instituted a more wide-ranging modernization of local government and planning, with sustainable development goals being woven more explicitly into the process of local administration (DETR, 1998b). Such ideals were encapsulated in a strategy for sustainable development published in 1999 (DETR, 1999e), accompanied by a revised series of sustainability indicators (DETR, 1999f). Subsequent progress has been charted in a series of annual reports (DEFRA, 2004a). A further phase of activity was launched in 2004 with the production of an updated series of indicators (DEFRA, 2004b) and a fresh round of public consultation regarding UK strategy for sustainable development. Other governmental priorities complement this explicit attention to sustainability, promoting a more integrated approach to urban problems. The Social Exclusion Unit, for example, is intended to improve 'joined-up thinking' in all policy areas relevant to the multi-faceted problems of deprived communities. Hence, its remit includes not just unemployment, poverty and social dislocation, but also the quality of the urban environment and the lack of access to key facilities. Many of the emergent changes in thinking were consolidated in the 1999 Urban White Paper (DETR, 1999d), based on the report *Towards an Urban Renaissance*, produced by the government's Urban Task Force (DETR, 1999b). These twin initiatives reflect an attempt to establish a new vision for urban regeneration founded on principles of design excellence, social well-being and environmental responsibility, within a viable economic and legislative framework. A key move to give concrete form to such thinking is the Sustainable Communities Plan, launched in 2003, with a budget of £22 billion (DEFRA, 2004a). Changes both at the national and local level are thus gradually fostering a new style of urban planning based on a holistic policy encompassing sustainable land use, economic development and social provision.

Resource efficiency and the compact city

In common with other analyses of urban problems, the Urban Task Force prioritizes a reduced dependence upon motor vehicles. In many of the world's major urban centres, planners are considering the role that change in urban form can have in curbing the economic and environmental penalties associated with car use. One option is to create more compact urban centres where facilities are easily accessible by non-car transport modes. In practice, however, the barriers to change are formidable. The increasing dominance of the car has literally been built into the existing urban fabric through land-use planning systems that segregate industrial, commercial, retail and residential functions. Few of the suburban housing estates that mushroomed in the post-war decades have adequate retail provision, and employment is concentrated either in urban centres or in business parks located alongside major arterial routes at the urban fringe.

Incremental decisions by millions of planners, businesses and consumers have moved most developed countries into increased car dependency. Any rapid and substantial reversal of this trend cannot, however, be achieved by individual piecemeal initiatives (Levett, 1998). Rather, there must be a coordinated effort to redirect urban planning and management towards reducing travel demand (Breheny, 1992; 1995; Owens, 1986). Amongst others, both the European Union (EU) and Friends of the Earth (FoE) have proposed more compact and higher density urban development as a means of combining enhanced quality of life with reduced dependency upon the car (Elkin et al, 1991; European Commission, 1990; European Conference on Sustainable Cities and Towns, 1994). Such thinking is evident in the Aalborg Charter of 1994, a declaration of intent regarding sustainable urban development agreed by towns and cities throughout the EU. In acknowledging the strategic importance of local government planning of land use and development, the charter specifically identifies:

> ... the scope for providing efficient public transport and energy which higher densities [of urban development] offer, while maintaining the human scale of development. In both undertaking renewal programmes in inner urban areas and in planning new suburbs we seek a mix of functions so as to reduce the need for mobility (European Conference on Sustainable Cities and Towns, 1994).

If the compact city model is to be successful in reducing transport demand, planners must establish accessible nodes for the delivery of essential services, creating a pattern of 'decentralised concentration' (Owens, 1986). There must also be a well-planned transport infrastructure. But rather than being orientated around the private car, transport planning will aim to increase the number of journeys made by foot, bicycle and public transport.

The energy efficiency achieved by reducing transport demand may be complemented by a reduced need for space heating in higher density developments. Areas of mixed land use are also particularly suitable locations for other innovative means of securing resource efficiencies, such as district heating and combined heat and power generation. Raising the density of development should reduce urban sprawl, thus preserving rural land for agriculture, recreation and wildlife habitat. Potential benefits are increased where planners and developers clean up and reuse brownfield sites in derelict or declining inner urban areas. High-density urban living, often in waterfront locations, has become newly fashionable in many UK cities, especially amongst the young and childless who happily trade suburban space for greater access to the facilities of the urban core. There is thus no necessary conflict between what is desirable and what is sustainable, although extension of the advantages of the city centre living currently enjoyed by an affluent minority to the wider urban population is a formidable challenge.

The potential environmental and social benefits of the compact city are recognized in the advice on planning policy given by UK central government to urban authorities. Guidance Note 13, issued in 1995, specifically identifies local authorities' responsibilities to reduce car use through better planning for other transport modes and a greater spatial mix of land uses. It also allows for limits to be placed on developments that could undermine traffic reduction. This includes restrictions on out-of-town developments that will detract from the viability and vitality of existing local service centres, and on additional parking provision in locations where effective alternative transport modes are available (DoE and DoT, 1995). Since the Transport Act 2000 passed into law, UK local authorities have acquired more powers to enable them to tackle congestion and pollution in their own areas. Arguably, however, this may also reflect the desire of central government to escape direct association with measures such as congestion charging. Despite the apparent success of the London scheme introduced in 2003 and plans for its emulation elsewhere in Europe and North America, congestion charging continues to attract criticism from some motorists and sections of the business community (Jowit, 2004).

Debating the shape of the city

The ideal of the compact city remains, however, controversial, both in the UK and in the USA, where the 'smart growth' or 'new urbanist' movement has gained momentum during recent years (*New Urban News*, 2002). It is far from certain that raising development density will reduce transport demand, energy consumption and pollution emissions (see Chapter 5). There are also wider doubts about its desirability and practicality. Advocates of the compact city draw a clear distinction between their vision of a more sustainable urban form and previous problematic high-density development. Although density of development can be associated with housing stress, it is overcrowding – evident in excessive rates of occupancy per room, rather than large numbers of dwellings per hectare – that creates the most serious social problems (Gove et al, 1979). High-density development does not have to involve high-rise construction, the absence of open space and greenery, and poor environmental quality. The creation of mixed-use and traffic-free urban spaces may reduce social segregation (Burton, 2000) and give greater scope for community cohesion, countering the anonymity of urban existence. Thus, the provision of high-density, but high-quality, housing in a landscaped environment with good access to urban facilities can provide a better quality of life than decanting people to the suburbs. Moreover, as the architect Richard Rogers – a proponent of lively mixed cities – observes, many of the environmental penalties of inner urban living have diminished. The industrial pollution and coal smoke that drove affluent residents of 19th-century cities into the suburbs are largely a thing of the past (Rogers, 1997).

Such arguments do not, however, command universal support. In the UK, for example, the Town and Country Planning Association has expressed concerns that the creation of more compact urban centres will lead to 'town cramming' (Breheny and Rookwood, 1993). Rather than guaranteeing a new quality of urban development, the compact city may involve an inequitable sacrifice of urban interests to preserve the quality of rural life and landscapes. High-density living without adequate attention to transport planning and provision may actually increase congestion and pollution (Burton, 2000). At the same time, there are claims that established trends for the decentralization of population and employment – to smaller towns and villages, as well as the suburban fringe – may already be reducing the length of commuting for some individuals (Gordon and Richardson, 1989). Moreover, the decentralization of urban population and activity may prove unstoppable (Breheny, 1995). Stress on urban containment as part of post-war planning regimes has not prevented suburban development. Even cities that have exemplary core areas also have suburbs that cannot now be reconfigured to any significant extent. Nor do critics share the enthusiasm for inner urban life that is inherent in the compact city model. Many still regard major urban cores as 'dysfunctional curiosities to enjoy as visitors and theatres for civic life, but barely suitable as home or place of work' (Lock, 1999).

A dose of reality

Overall, experience 'casts serious doubt on the ability of central or local government to resist, still less reverse, counter-urbanization trends as a device to reduce urban energy consumption' (Breheny, 1995). In addition, the scale of capital now sunk into peripheral housing and business developments is substantial. As the Urban Task Force report acknowledges, 90 per cent of the buildings and infrastructure that make up today's towns and cities will still be present in 30 years' time (K Williams, 1999). Thus, the built environment can only be altered gradually and mean densities of development are unlikely to be substantially altered by physical planning measures. Whatever blueprint is advanced for urban planning, people will still make leisure, business and other trips to specialist locations that cannot be brought within easy reach of everyone (Breheny, 1995). As a result, short-term progress in reducing transport emissions may be limited.

If critics reject the grand vision of reshaping urban form, their thinking often echoes the socio-economic and environmental goals of the compact city model. Several, indeed, offer their own prescriptions for reducing traffic, energy use and pollution. Immediate progress in improving energy efficiency could, for example, be made by investing in improved insulation, heating systems and ventilation for existing buildings (Lenssen and Roodman, 1995; Vale and Vale, 1993; see also Chapter 11 in this volume). A more effective strategy to reduce vehicle use and emissions may combine fiscal elements – road pricing, increased duty on fuel and higher taxation of less fuel-efficient cars – with increased investment in effective and integrated public transport to serve the existing urban layout (Gordon and Richardson, 1989; see also Chapter 5 in this volume).

Rather than attempting to meet growing housing needs by squeezing development onto inner-urban brownfield sites, it may be more practical to create new settlements. Planners and developers will thus have a freer hand to design sustainability in from the beginning by adopting urban forms and technologies that minimize resource input and waste output (Breheny and Rookwood, 1993; Hall, 1996). Curitiba in Brazil is a frequently quoted example of successful planning to integrate public transport within the fabric of a city as it develops. It is also a place where many other sustainability elements have been integrated into urban structure and functions (Rabinovitch and Leitman, 1996). Curitiba remains, however, an isolated success story. Significantly, moreover, its planners have not tried to cut vehicle use by increasing urban densities. Instead, adequate space has been set aside for major public transport arteries. A coherently functioning public transport system, combined with careful planning of the relative location of employment and residential development during a phase of rapid urbanization, has been the key to containing congestion and pollution from private car use.

Alternative technologies may further reduce the environmental impacts of transportation. The development of a less-polluting replacement for the internal combustion engine is one trajectory of innovation; but encouraging teleworking may also reduce commuter traffic. Increasingly cheap and powerful computer systems and telecommunications links make it more feasible for service-sector employees and contractors to work from home or from satellite offices, rather than having to congregate physically in a central location (Castells, 1996). However, the effects of new employment conditions remain unclear, for despite its increasing incidence, teleworking still only involves a minority of the work force. Any reduction in commuting may be offset by an increase in non-work trips, resulting in the temporal and spatial dispersion of vehicle pollution, rather than a net decrease (BT Environment Unit, 1997). Information and communication technologies will not, therefore, automatically deliver urban sustainability objectives; but, properly managed, they could be a powerful tool for sustainable development policy (Borja and Castells, 1997; Bristow, 1997). Many urban authorities are encouraging intensification of information technology (IT) networks to ensure that their central areas are strengthened as nodal points in the networks of information exchange that underpin business and commerce (Graham, 1992). Better access to information could not only reduce conventional travel demand, but also help to achieve economic development goals. IT is creating new communities of professionals, suppliers and markets that are geographically dispersed, but highly connected to existing urban nodes (Short and Kim, 1999). The potential for improvement in educational opportunities, as well as community participation and coherence, further underlines the social importance of access to information (van den Berg and van Winden, 2002). However, such changes set new challenges to counter the emerging differentiation between individuals and communities who are part of the new network society and those who are excluded from the opportunities created by the information revolution (UNDP, 1999).

People as Planners: Participation in the Search for Sustainable Urban Development

Local Agenda 21

It is, in part, to counter such concerns about inequality that most approaches to sustainable development acknowledge that any grand vision or strategic overview must be complemented by the active participation of the mass of the population. This will involve individuals and households in defining their own needs and in establishing shared priorities for development that is more socially equitable, as well as environmentally sustainable. Moreover, the solution to global environmental problems depends, ultimately, upon the will and ability of individuals and communities to change their own behaviour. This perspective, prominent at the 1992 Rio Earth Summit, is encapsulated in the slogan 'Think globally, act locally'. Thus, Agenda 21, the summit's global blueprint for action to promote more sustainable development (UNCED, 1992a), was envisaged as inspiring a multiplicity of local plans (Selman, 1998). The Local Agenda 21 (LA21) process is designed to foster a participatory approach to sustainable development, involving citizens both in setting priorities and in taking action to secure them. Existing structures of local government often provide a territorial framework for consultation exercises, with each area producing its own plan, addressing the balance to be struck between environmental conservation and socio-economic development. The creation of such local plans typically involves an initial report on the current state of the environment, providing the information necessary for participatory planning of more sustainable futures. Also vital is the establishment of a strategy for implementing and monitoring change, as well as a series of sustainability indicators, against which progress can be gauged.

In practice, however, the development of LA21 plans has been relatively slow. Most UK local authorities claimed a commitment to the principle by 1996, the initial target date for the implementation of the LA21 process (Tuxworth, 1996). One third of authorities had completed or updated state of the environment reports and a slightly higher proportion were working on sustainability indicators (Table 5.3 outlines the indicators developed by Birmingham City Council). Yet, as the wider European perspective summarized in Table 6.4 confirms, progress in specific sectors is accompanied by continuing difficulties both in countering deep-seated urban problems and in integrating sustainability provisions within all areas of council activity (see also Gibbs et al, 1998). Many UK authorities have recorded progress in environmental management and land-use planning; but few have made significant headway in promoting new standards in health, welfare and social equity (Selman, 1998). Moreover, the existence of a LA21 document does not, of itself, guarantee that the process of its production and the future action suggested are entirely sound, or will secure more sustainable development.

The LA21 process reveals the problems of attempting extensive public consultation and participation (see Chapter 9). There are inherent contradictions in such a process being led by government, even at the lowest level of the administrative hierarchy, which might be expected to be closest to its citizens. It takes special skills on the part of local authority officers to draw people into the process in such a way that they feel actively involved in decision-making, rather than having a top-down approach imposed upon them (Burgess et al, 1998). Without genuine grassroots motivation, sustainability in its most thorough sense cannot be achieved and the participatory approach risks being hijacked by Green activists and other special interest groups, rather than reflecting a broad base of popular opinion (Selman, 1996).

But so often, it is local authorities that have picked up the sustainable development baton. Self-assessment by nearly 150 local authorities in 27 different European countries, coordinated by the International Council for Local Environmental Initiat-

Table 6.4   *Sustainable development across Europe: summary of Local Authorities' Self-Assessment of Local Agenda 21 (LASALA) results*

Instances of progress	Continuing problems
• Policies for utilizing renewable energy (led by Germany and Scandinavia)	• Increases in car use and other forms of energy demand
• Policies to improve air, water and soil quality	• Continued urban decline
• Introduction of sustainability principles into land-use plans	• Limited regeneration of brownfield sites and continuing pressure to build on greenfield sites
• New and innovative approaches to city planning	• Low level of integration of sustainability principles across all policies and practices – LA21 is still too marginal
• Encouragement of walking and cycling	• Limited progress on overall monitoring of LA21
• Some adoption of EMAS, precautionary principle and polluter pays principle by business	• Insufficient stakeholder involvement in LA21 process
• Adoption of sustainability indicators	• Inadequate support from central government

Source: ICLEI (2001)

ives, showed that LA21 can be a strong force for stimulating action in moving towards sustainability. This can only occur, however, where there is a highly integrated approach, high levels of public awareness and active participation. A well-developed partnership between council and community thus provides a basis for the production of an action plan and a context for its implementation (ICLEI, 2001).

Experience in developing LA21 plans in major UK cities, including Bradford and London, suggests that popular interest in community-based projects is best secured by concentrating on tangible issues of immediate local concern, rather than engaging with more abstract concepts of sustainability (Saunders, 1997; Wagland, 1997). Selman (1996) has reviewed the conditions that have promoted greatest progress towards more effective planning for sustainable development. He concludes that the design and implementation of LA21 plans must be based upon a common understanding of the key issues amongst a broad range of participants and a commitment to communication, prioritizing transparency and accountability. Only in this way will appropriate and comprehensible goals be formulated, linked to existing structures and processes. Planning for more sustainable development requires flexibility and conflict resolution skills to ensure that a genuine consensus emerges. The definition of goals should provide clear evidence of the added value to be created through specific projects, rather than simply outlining a vague wish list. The planning process must be supported by adequate financial and administrative resources; but it is important that the community as a whole is actively involved in both design and execution. Clarity of direction is vitally important; but experts should be on tap, rather than on top. Progress towards sustainable development is not defined simply by the achievement of specific end points in terms of environmental restoration or employment creation. Rather, it involves an active process of change that builds new skills and institutional capacity within the home community, rather than relying heavily on outside expertise.

Paradoxically, in the UK, the LA21 process has been somewhat eclipsed since the implementation of the Local Government Act of 2000, which required councils to prepare community strategies to focus and coordinate their activities in promoting the well-being of their local communities. Some of those working on LA21 have expressed concerns that community planning, while encouraging fine-grained attention to local areas, often lacks the sense of thinking within a global context.

The ability to harness the power of people to help themselves often relies initially on the inspirational example of individual leadership. In Sweden the LA21 process is most advanced where high-profile local politicians, backed by key bureaucrats in strategic positions, have actively advanced issues of sustainability within their own community (Eckerberg and Forsberg, 1998; see also Chapter 9 in this volume). Academics have taken the lead in some instances – for example, in suburban Lima (Hordijk, 1999) and in Manizales, Colombia (Velásquez, 1999). The Orangi Pilot Project detailed below owes much to the vision of the founder, Dr Akhtar Hameed Khan, and the innovative working methods adopted by his organization. In the Peruvian coastal city of Ilo, successive mayors have brought a positive and creative vision to bear upon the planning process. The Spanish term *concertacion* is used to encapsulate an ideal of community interaction based on flexibility, tolerance and unity. *Concertacion* is more than just consultation or coordination; it implies not only the involvement of all stakeholders in discussions, but also the achievement of agreed positions acceptable to all stakeholders. On this basis, Ilo has made substantial progress in integrating economic, social and environmental goals and in raising the quality of life of the majority of its citizens (Lopez Follegatti, 1999). Ilo is thus a reminder of the value of human resources, especially when applied collectively to the solution of urban problems. In the context of the developing world, where other resources are often scarce, the mobilization of a collective will for urban improvement may represent the best hope for positive change.

Urban Challenges in the Developing World

Meeting basic needs

However pressing concerns about socio-economic inequality appear within developed countries, differences in urban opportunities are still starker at a global scale. The vast majority of the 280 million urban dwellers without access to safe drinking water and the 590 million who lack sanitation infrastructure live in the global South (UNCHS, 1996). Thus, the concerns of urban planning and management in the developing world are frequently very basic. At the same time, the institutions of urban governance are often poorly developed, while financial resources are severely constrained. As a result, 'the new urban agendas – the Global Strategy for Shelter and the new post-Rio UNCED environmentalism – are extremely difficult to convert into effective delivery systems and impossible in some countries where economies and states are collapsing' (Pugh, 1997). In such circumstances it is impractical and ineffective to try to achieve sustainability goals through ambitious urban master plans, based on models of planning and management imported from the Organisation for Economic Co-operation and Development (OECD) countries (Eigen, 1998; McAuslan, 1985; Nagpaul, 1988). Nor is it realistic to attempt to bring all aspects of urban structure and functions up to the standards expected in Northern cities (Anzorena et al, 1998; WRI, 1996). Instead, 'low-tech', lower-cost solutions are often the most effective means to promote sustainability. Moreover, heavy-handed control of the private sector rarely provides the answer to urban problems; as in the developed world, incentives to positive action are as important as regulation. Thus, it is increasingly recognized that the task of urban planners and managers is to support investment in people, infrastructure and economic activities, while preventing businesses, households and other organizations from passing on their own costs to others (Hardoy et al, 1992). This new equity and efficiency in urban management, however, creates its own demands for the radical restructuring of systems of governance in many Southern cities (Gilbert et al, 1996; Hordijk, 1999). The creation of greater urban democracy and new administrative competence is thus a crucial first step towards more sustainable development.

Even if this institutional foundation can be achieved, the scale and intensity of urban problems in the developing world highlight the difficulties of applying the Brundtland formulation of sustainable development. It seems hollow to talk of restricting current consumption to safeguard the interests of future generations when 'those who are presently in abject poverty . . . will not have had their present needs met by tomorrow' (Chapman and Thompson, 1995). Attempts to meet current demand for the basics of life imply greater immediate resource consumption, potentially prejudicing the quality of life for future generations. Yet social justice can tolerate no delay in making cities into places that allow their inhabitants greater security of income and quality of life (Stephens, 2000). Urban management priorities in the developing world are thus defined by the so-called 'Brown agenda': improving basic infrastructure to widen the delivery of water, energy, sanitation and waste collection in ways that are cost effective and resource efficient (Wyn Williams, 1997). If investments to reduce the environmental problems and health hazards that restrict the life chances of the urban poor are not made, there is little prospect that other sustainability goals – including environmental restoration and protection of biodiversity – can be met (Harpham and Werna, 1996).

Economic development to reduce current poverty is thus an essential aim in Southern cities. But the need to change the character of economic growth is as great here as anywhere else. The pursuit of growth will not be sustainable if it does not make efficient use of resources, whether financial, environmental or human. Moreover, attacking poverty without also challenging the increasingly pervasive culture of consumerism will not help to achieve sustainability. The urban poor currently contribute to environmental problems when, in the absence of effective sanitation systems, their waste pollutes urban watercourses, or they are forced to rely on elderly and polluting vehicles for transportation. But solutions can become problems if increased wealth leads to greater consumption and more waste (Wyn Williams, 1997; World Bank, 1992). The benefits of economic growth and investment in urban infrastructure must also be more equitably distributed than has hitherto been common. Such changes in the quality and outcome of economic growth reinforce claims that an inclusive, participatory approach is needed. Hence, the central challenge of planning for urban sustainable development arguably reflects the need to promote workable ways of involving as many people as possible in the active pursuit of social and environmental improvement as a foundation for secure and sustainable livelihoods.

Redefining appropriate action: the potential of community development

Viewed as a totality, the urban problems of the developing world may appear enormous and intractable. However, at the most local level – at a scale below that of entire towns and cities – there are positive signs of change. Progress is not universal, continuous or consistent, but it is being made. It may not be defined through comprehensive land-use planning or fully developed LA21 plans, but the quality of life for millions of urban dwellers is being improved in novel, integrated ways.

Where urban populations are growing rapidly, land for all uses is in short supply. Shortages are exacerbated by speculators, who buy up and hoard land, hoping for large profits on later resale. Consequently, individuals who cannot afford to buy or rent housing or land are often forced into illegal occupation (UNCHS, 1996). Millions live in low-quality dwellings on land to which they have no official right. Their problems are exacerbated by a lack of infrastructure, including sanitation, energy supplies, roads and other transport provision, often reflecting the unplanned nature of these settlements.

The effective coordination of development and the implementation of land-use planning is thus a key underlying factor in the achievement of a healthier population and economy. As McAuslan (1985) observes: 'Land – its abuse, control and ownership – is the central problem of the city.' This is not, however, to advocate large-scale redevelopment to remove illegal settlements, or to promote public and international investment in huge new road schemes and other infrastructure. Instead, it is an argument for finding ways of advancing development that is appropriate, in that it improves the quality of life for most ordinary people, and sustainable, in that it makes provision for the long term as well as the immediate future.

Until the 1970s, the main policy tools used to combat housing shortage and the illegal occupation of land were slum clearance and government provision of serviced plots or supposedly low-cost housing (UNCHS, 1996). But housing programmes could never keep pace with demand and the units provided were too costly for many of the poorest people. Moreover, planned residential developments were often located in urban districts far from employment opportunities. Subsequent diagnosis of continuing urban problems has concluded that such initiatives were flawed on two counts; first, because government institutions were incapable of managing rapid change, but, second and crucially, because they did not 'tap the knowledge, resources and capacities among the population within each city' (UNCHS, 1996). There is mounting evidence that greater success can be achieved by helping people to help themselves. This involves working with individuals, communities and businesses to establish basic rights over the land they occupy (Pugh, 1997) and helping to establish priorities for improving their quality of life; finding ways of enabling the people themselves to contribute towards upgrading the local area, the built environment and housing provision; and involving them in improving access to jobs, health, education and other essential services (Baharoglu, 1996; Harris, 1992; Hordijk, 1999; World Bank, 1991). The aim is thus to maximize local self-sufficiency. The poorest and most deprived urban residents must not, of course, be thrown entirely on their own reserves of finance, creativity and motivation. But intervention by national and local government should be limited, strategic and appropriate, rather than overbearing and unaffordable (Devas and Rakodi, 1993).

As part of this changing approach to the Brown agenda, attention has turned to land adjustment policies. These attempt to regularize squatter settlement and transfer title to the land, reflecting a recognition that people have nowhere else to go. Enabling strategies, often involving non-governmental organizations (NGOs) as well as government agencies, are designed to give urban residents access to the finance, building materials and know-how that will enable them to improve their own neighbourhoods. Such initiatives have many potential advantages. People who possess their own property are much more likely to invest time, money and effort, not just in improving individual dwellings, but also in upgrading infrastructure and services for the wider area. This should benefit the community as a whole, improving health, quality of life, social stability and life chances for children. Advances secured through community initiatives may also enhance a sense of self-worth and foster the mutual confidence necessary to undertake increasingly ambitious improvements. Communities can thus become more self-sustaining if a sufficiently enlightened and holistic approach is adopted. The gains, both tangible and intangible, are much greater than could be achieved through direct local authority provision of housing and infrastructure. The role of the municipal authority may also be redefined. The available funds and institutional capacity can be put to better use if local governments concentrate their efforts on establishing the highest level of infrastructure, including provision of sewage treatment plants, main roads, specialist hospitals and high schools, as well as securing land rights (Pugh, 1997).

Towards community development in practice: changing urban priorities in Karachi

The positive potential of a community-centred approach to urban improvement is evident from the success of specific projects where local residents have transformed their environment and quality of life. One of the best known of such examples is located in the Pakistani capital of Karachi. There are over 700 squatter settlements, or *katchi abadis*, in the city, together housing more than 50 per cent of the city's 12 million people (Hasan, 2002). *Katchi abadi* residents are crowded into houses that are structurally unsafe, vulnerable to the effects of pollution and natural disasters, and lacking in basic amenities (Fernandes, 1994). Consequently, levels of ill health are high and living conditions are dismal and insanitary. The haphazard pattern of development and construction creates further obstacles to improvements in amenity provision (Kamal, 1993).

Until the 1980s, the most common governmental response was to attempt to destroy the *katchi abadis*. Bulldozing of slum areas was common and the land recovered was redeveloped for commercial profit. Little attention was devoted to the welfare of displaced populations and the newly homeless received no adequate compensation. Some alternative housing plots were provided; but these were, invariably, poorly serviced and far removed from the existing social networks and sources of livelihood of *katchi abadi* residents. Moreover, the number of new dwellings was grossly inadequate. The government initially planned to provide 300,000 housing units; but as a result of financial constraints only 10,000 were actually built. Even these were beyond the financial reach of the poorest of the poor.

The first signs of policy reform date from 1978, with the passage of a law regularizing the status of most existing *katchi abadis* as developed urban areas. Slums in locations deemed environmentally hazardous were, however, excluded, and clearance and evictions continued. The resultant protests led to the enactment of a revised law in 1983, extending the scope of regularization to all major settled areas. In 1987 the Sindh Katchi Abadi Authority was established to coordinate community improvements. Its first tasks included mapping the existing developments, establishing ownership rights to property for residents and upgrading infrastructure provision. The authority provides a focus through which input from government agencies and NGOs can be channelled into basic environmental improvement, such as upgrading lanes and providing water, electricity and sanitation. At the same time, regularization was extended to cover any existing settlement on public land encompassing 40 or more households, excepting only those sites designated amenity land, liable to health hazards or transected by high-tension electricity cables. Subsequent progress has been slow; but the rate of evictions has fallen significantly. Some 101 squatter settlements were provided with basic amenities by 1995, funded jointly by the Pakistani government, the World Bank and the Asian Development Bank (Ministry of Environment, Urban Affairs, Forestry and Wildlife, 1996).

Although an improvement on previous slum clearance policies, experience in Karachi confirms the shortcomings of continuing reliance on government for service provision. The costs of officially planned infrastructure development are often prohibitive and experience has shown that even concerted lobbying by community groups cannot stimulate effective municipal responses. This reinforces arguments that community-built alternatives offer a better solution. Although many slum dwellers live below the poverty line, others can afford to contribute towards the costs of improving their environment. Moreover, while the sheer scale of the challenge will inevitably defeat any single, centralized attempt at improvement, important incremental progress can be made by the local provision of urban basic services. More can be achieved with the same limited financial resources if they are invested in community action, involving local people and providing them with technical expertise and organizational skills. Residents are thus enabled to construct a coherent overview of their own needs and the ways in which they can be involved in meeting them.

The Orangi Pilot Project

This participatory ethos is the guiding principle of a project located in Orangi, a squatter settlement on the north-west side of Karachi. Established in 1965, Orangi is home to 1.2 million people. Few residents are employed in the formal sector and most work for small family enterprises. The Orangi Pilot Project (OPP) was initiated during the early 1980s as a means of forging links between planning professionals, the informal sector and the wider community. The OPP considers itself to be a research institution, established to analyse Orangi's major problems and, then, through prolonged action research and extension education, to discover viable solutions (Hasan, 1992).

Orangi residents themselves identified sanitation as the top priority for investment. Although some external funding was available for infrastructure improvements, it was recognized at the outset that resources were insufficient to pay for an officially executed sanitation scheme. However, costs could be drastically reduced if the local community were to become actively involved in providing the labour for construction. This effort was coordinated by the OPP, which organized fundraising and advised on the most cost-effective materials and methods. But it is noteworthy that the work proceeded without a master plan.

Community organizations were created based on the lanes within Orangi, which each contain 20 to 30 households. These formed the basic units for the coordination of collective labour, supported by extension work which has, for example, shown people how to mix concrete and communicated basic skills in sewage engineering. As a result, the majority of the investment and work has been put in by the residents. Lanes now organize themselves, maintaining the newly installed sewage system with the support of advisors from the OPP. The project's leaders can thus claim success in demonstrating:

> ... that the dilemma of modernizing sanitation in *katchi abadis* can be solved by mobilizing managerial and financial resources of the house owners themselves by providing them with social and technical assistance (Hasan, 1992).

Families have been enabled to construct their own modern sanitation systems, with connections to main sewers. But even more important is the extension of the momentum of neighbourhood organization to secure other objectives. Residents have established a low-cost housing programme that aims to improve construction standards. They have also made provision for basic healthcare and family planning. This includes an element of preventative care, including immunization against disease and efforts to improve diet by growing vegetables within the community. The need to increase security of household incomes has been addressed through the establishment of a supervised credit programme. This is designed to fund increased production and employment, while inculcating managerial skills and business integrity. Attempts to redress the particular vulnerability of female labour are evident in women's work centres, which organize seamstresses and other garment workers into co-operatives that can deal directly with wholesalers and exporters. Importance is also attached to education provision: Orangi contains nearly 600 private schools and the OPP is involved in upgrading buildings, equipment and teaching standards (Hasan, 1992).

Such a broad-based approach covers many key elements of sustainable development. Effort is focused on improving the quality of the immediate environment; but the indirect effects of the OPP contribute to the reduction of environmental damage, and water and air pollution, far beyond the confines of the individual locality. The community's own resources are mobilized, reducing the waste of human resources and creating a new sense of individual and collective self-reliance that provides a foundation for future initiatives. There is also a conscious attempt to strike a balance between immediate gains in the quality of life and investment in improving future conditions. In attending to employment creation, education, healthcare and disease prevention, the community and the OPP are making long-term plans. If Orangi shows what can be done in a particular locality, the challenge remains of replicating such initiatives throughout the numberless urban neighbourhoods of the developing world. Orangi is far from being an isolated success story; other bottom-up projects of urban renewal and community development can be quoted (Asian Coalition for Housing Rights, 2001; Dutta, 2000; Gaye and Diallo, 1997; Gaye et al, 2001; Moctezuma, 2001). But substantial progress towards more sustainable development will only be secured if the advances enjoyed in Orangi come to be shared by the majority of urban residents.

Communicating Good Practice

Translating the initiative displayed within the most innovative and organized urban communities into a general experience will be no easy task; but already substantial effort is being invested in developing national and international networks for communicating best practice. Support for such initiatives is evident at the highest levels of global diplomacy with the creation of the UN Sustainable Cities Programme (SCP) (Eigen, 1998) and the International Council for Local Environmental Initiatives (ICLEI, 1995). The ideal of common endeavour fostered by LA21 has also encouraged cities themselves to establish new networks and partnerships, including links, such as those between projects in Canada and Brazil, that connect the developed and developing worlds (Ontario Institute for Studies in Education, 2002). The EU provides an important forum for international discussion (Expert Group on the Urban Environment, 1996) and within the UK the Local Government Management Board (now the Improvement and Development Agency) has taken a leading role in encouraging an active commitment to sustainable development amongst local authorities (Percy, 1998).

Exchanges, meetings and conferences help to promote productive discussion of the means of achieving more sustainable development. Since 1989 the journal *Environment and Urbanization* has gathered together and disseminated many inspiring case studies and overviews from around the world. The creation of an international community of interests is also increasingly facilitated by new information technologies. The late 1990s saw an explosion of websites crowded with information about innovative ideas and projects. The UN Centre for Human Settlements has also produced an important synthesis of current understanding of urban development in a major volume, *An Urbanizing World*, published to coincide with the Habitat conference on human settlements, held in Istanbul in 1996 (UNCHS, 1996). This is not only a masterly presentation of the complexities of urban conditions and trends across the globe, but also a demonstration of the ways in which human settlements can be made more sustainable. It cites many instances where international organizations, governments, NGOs and community groups have successfully tackled urban problems in holistic ways and delivered sustainable improvements in quality of life. A further volume (UNCHS, 2001) updates the analysis of problems, policies and their outcomes.

Equally important are the multiplicity of handbooks outlining initiatives to make cities more environmentally sound and socially secure places in which to live (see, for example, Carley et al, 2001; Elkin et al, 1991; Gilbert et al, 1996; Girardet, 1992). Increasing effort is also being invested in the projection of future urban scenarios that clarify the scale and direction of change necessary to secure more sustainable development. The potential role of urban modelling in this attempt to introduce a new precision into the assessment of best practice is detailed by Mitchell in Chapter 5. Elsewhere, Ravetz (2000) outlines the results of a huge and impressive analysis of the Manchester city-region, highlighting the differences between the 'business as usual' and sustainability scenarios. A novel feature of this work is the adoption of a 20-year horizon, rather than the 5 or 10 years typically employed in local and regional planning. The work is now being expanded to consider possible, probable and desirable outcomes up to 2050 (University of Manchester, 2002). Arguably, this kind of thinking will have to be adopted by planners and citizens if effective, holistic policies are to be put in place (Saunders, 2001).

Making the Local Universal: A Concluding Reflection

The attempts to locate local initiatives within a wider context serve as a reminder of the universalistic aims of sustainable development. Improvement in quality of life for some people should not result in the problems of others being ignored or exacerbated. All urban neighbourhoods and citizens must share in the progress towards sustainable development. But more than this, 'the environmental performance of cities has to improve not only in terms of improved environmental quality within their boundaries, but also in terms of reducing the transfer of environmental costs to other people, other ecosystems and to the future' (Satterthwaite, 1997).

This acknowledgement of the world beyond the boundaries of the urban is important, not least because it raises questions about the whole conception of urban sustainability. Urban centres seem inherently parasitic, bound to consume resources from a wide area and produce waste and pollution that cannot be contained within their own boundaries. As those involved in producing 'Green accounts' have found, it is impossible to assess the environmental impacts of individual cities precisely because so many of their activities draw upon, and have repercussions for, areas far beyond the immediate administrative region (see Chapter 5). This is not simply a reflection of the concentration of consumption by a city's own permanent residents; many urban functions fulfil the demands of a wider regional population. It might be questioned, for example, whether a city should be held responsible for all of the environmental costs of an international airport located within its administrative area.

Even with the most organized and committed of approaches to environmental goals, the ecological footprint of a city cannot be contained within its own boundaries. In this sense the individual city can never be sustainable. Thus, a more fruitful approach may be to accept that improved environmental performance 'is not achieved by focusing on sustainable cities, but on how city consumers, enterprises and governments can contribute more to sustainable development' (Satterthwaite, 1997). Efforts to reduce waste and pollution, to increase the efficiency of energy consumption and resource use, and to change the quality of economic development and the equity with which its rewards are distributed cannot simply be seen as discrete urban projects. Their importance is in the contribution that they make to wider sustainability at every scale, including the global. In practice, the transition to more sustainable development cannot be realized through the creation of individual 'islands' of self-sustaining perfection. The extent to which sustainability is imported and exported can, and should, be reduced; but both the physical and the economic reality of an interconnected world dictate that North and South, states and their neighbours, urban and rural are bound together in any journey towards sustainability. As Wilbanks (1994) has observed, it is impossible for anywhere to be truly sustainable until this ideal is achieved everywhere.

Such an argument does not, however, preclude continuing attention to a distinctively urban agenda. The form and functions of towns and cities must be reassessed not just in relation to the resource efficiencies demanded by the wider project of sustainable development, but also with the objective of making urban centres better places in which to live (Elkin et al, 1991). The ideal of the 'liveable city' is thus more than a manifestation in the built environment of the need to cut resource use and pollution production; it is a place in which people feel at home and enjoy living. This requires attention to standards of urban design, starting with the basics of shelter, sanitation and safety, but embracing considerations of social community and environmental quality. Buildings must be designed to be efficient and attractive spaces for living and working. The urban plan should also incorporate green areas for recreation and relaxation, as well as making a contribution to the preservation of biodiversity.

As this chapter has argued, however, a liveable city is as much about people as it is about physical fabric. Given sufficient financial resources and the political space within which to realize their full potential, residents themselves are not simply the beneficiaries of urban improvement, but the collective agents of its definition and achievement. This is the message embodied both in the specific example of the Orangi project and in the wider participatory ideal of LA21. In his 1995 BBC Reith Lectures, the architect Richard Rogers also emphasized that cities can be reinvigorated and made attractive as places in which to live and work by an emphasis on contact and community, rather than on separation and selfishness. The city should be 'open minded', rather than 'single minded', replacing the pursuit of individual property owners' objectives with active encouragement for the involvement of citizens in determining and achieving priorities for urban improvement (Rogers, 1997). Ultimately, urban form and the encouragement of this spirit of community may be linked. Rogers is a supporter of the notion of the compact city, extending its principles to the design of individual buildings, public spaces and whole neighbourhoods. His approach has social and political dimensions that go beyond any narrowly defined concentration on design for spatial efficiency. Rogers advocates creating residential layouts that are not simply energy efficient in their incorporation of safe and easy access for cyclists and pedestrians, but also form the foundations for a high environmental and social quality of life. This accords with the design principles set out by Punter and Carmona (1997), who argue that layouts should 'maximise the level of local autonomy' and include a linked series of safe and usable public spaces that 'respect the natural qualities of the site and create a clear sense of place'.

Rogers concluded his series of lectures by advancing the aim of achieving:

> . . . a new and dynamic equilibrium between society, cities and nature. Participation, education and innovation are the driving forces of the sustainable society . . .
> With vigilance and popular determination the concept of sustainability will grow in importance until it becomes the dominant philosophy of our age (Rogers, 1997).

Such declamatory statements raise many questions about the reality of the potential for change. As other authors (see Chapters 4 and 9) in this volume show, it is not always easy to mobilize 'popular determination' in support of sustainable development. Nor are existing political authorities necessarily willing or able to play a constructive part in the search for more sustainable development, either by supporting individual communities in their efforts to create a better quality of life, or by advancing a strategic overview of sustainability targets. It is clear that there can be no complete break with the past, either in terms of the distribution of political and economic power within urban areas, or in the inheritance of urban forms and functions. There is a long way to go before sustainable development criteria are instinctively incorporated into daily decision-making.

Yet Rogers's optimism is not entirely misplaced. Change, albeit piecemeal, is gradually altering mindsets, the structure and functioning of institutions, and individual and corporate behaviour. Rather than expecting sudden and total transformation, it is now understood that a more pragmatic approach will yield better results. Rather than attempting to sweep away urban systems or to contain urban growth, it should be possible to target sustainability initiatives in time and space on the points at which they will do most good. Sustainable development itself may still be a weak agent of urban change, but it is possible to work within the existing dynamic of urban growth and renewal to create a more sustainable environment. Thus, as cities are extended and redeveloped to accommodate new demands, they are increasingly being planned, built and managed in ways that curb growth in the consumption of energy and other resources, check waste output and improve quality of life. Such changes reflect an emergent regulatory and fiscal context in which social and environmental standards become more exacting and greater efforts are made to define the true costs of economic activity. The role of technology is also changing from a narrow focus on the promotion of economic growth to the achievement of a new form of development that seeks a better balance between costs and benefits. At the same time, there are signs that urban institutions are being recast as the ideal of sustainable development becomes integrated within policy-making. Businesses, community groups and individual residents are being encouraged to take an active role in setting priorities for economic, social and environmental policy. They must also come to understand how small-scale changes in behaviour, resource use and urban design are the ultimate building blocks for achieving a total global project of sustainable development.

7

Business, Capital and Sustainable Economic Development

Martin Purvis

Introduction

Historically, economic performance has been a crucial measure of a region's success and state of development. Societies and individuals have sought to maximize economic growth, industrial production, employment and material living standards. Few have questioned this construction of progress and development. Yet there are, invariably, social and environmental costs to be set against the benefits of economic development. During the 1960s and 1970s, attention to these costs led environmentalists to argue for the necessity of setting limits to economic growth. The agenda of sustainable development, however, makes a rather different case, not for curbing growth, but for a fundamental change in its nature. Such ideas have been endorsed as the basis for future economic development by many national governments and the European Union (EU). The reframing of development has also inspired a revision of attitudes to business. Optimistic analysts now proclaim that business innovation can contribute positively to more sustainable development. Hence, Agenda 21 seeks to encourage business stewardship of the environment and resources, as well as an increasing commercial involvement in the design and implementation of sustainable development policies.

The chapter begins by reviewing the environmental impacts of modern industrial economies and the role of business in both the creation and solution of environmental challenges. It then explores arguments that it is in companies' own commercial interests to adopt environmentally responsible behaviour and claims made that business efficiencies can deliver a change in the quality of economic growth that will make it environmentally sustainable. The win–win argument that simultaneous commercial and environmental gains are possible must, however, be subject to critical scrutiny. Thus, the chapter proceeds to question the claims made for business initiative and to consider how well the ideals of sustainable development accord with existing commercial priorities. The complexities of sustainable development are further revealed by the final section, which refocuses attention away from individual businesses to examine aspects of the broader character of economic growth under capitalism. The supposed incompatibility of global capitalism with sustainable development has led some to argue for alternative, localized geographies of economic activity. Such visions may appear impractical; but they help to identify the need for active political engagement in the process of making economic activity more sustainable.

Business and the Environment

Industrial modernity and the environment

Economic activity creates valued outputs of goods and services and, over the long term, has immeasurably increased the sum of human and man-made capital. Yet production is socially and environmentally disruptive, affecting both environmental quality and stocks of natural capital. Industry changes land use, eroding biodiversity and habitat. Manufacturing, in particular, consumes raw materials and energy, thus depleting the resource base. From these resources are produced not just the goods demanded by consumers, but also wastes and emissions to land, air and water. Bringing goods to market requires transport, again depleting resources and producing waste and emissions. Once in the hands of consumers, some goods and services require continuing inputs of energy and other resources to discharge their functions. Ultimately, nearly everything that we acquire is disposed of as waste (El-Fadel et al, 1997).

Concerns about environmental quality and resource depletion are not peculiar to the modern era; but they became more serious with the onset of large-scale industrialization (Brimblecombe, 1987; Sheail, 2002; Simmons, 1996). Since the late 18th century, the scale of industrial activity has increased markedly, not only through new growths, but also with the transformation of key sectors of the pre-modern economy, including agriculture (Bairoch, 1982; Grigg, 1992; Landes, 1969; see also Chapter 8 in this volume). Industrial development has spread internationally, but within this expansion the urbanization of production and population has concentrated the effects of environmental change in particular localities (Berry, 1990; Gugler, 1996; Knox and Agnew, 1998; see also Chapters 5 and 6 in this volume). The economy's relationship with the resource base of natural capital has also been transformed. In the pre-modern era, industry drew chiefly upon renewable resources for its raw materials and energy. Over the past two centuries, however, its dependence upon non-renewable minerals and fossil fuels has increased strikingly (Humphrey and Stanislaw, 1979; Wrigley, 1988). Moreover, systems of production and consumption have become less localized (Chisholm, 1990). Cotton, a mainstay of industrial revolution during the 18th and 19th centuries, was the first major European industry to rely exclusively upon an imported raw material (Chapman, 1987). Subsequently, both materials and finished goods have become traded in greater quantities over longer distances. Thus, by 1991 the energy used globally in freight movement by shipping equated to the total consumption of the economies of Brazil and Turkey combined. Freight movement seems set to increase further in the 21st century, with air freight, its most energy-intensive form, growing particularly fast (Goldsmith, 1999; Menotti and Sobhani, 1999).

Current environmental concerns reflect mounting evidence that the damage caused by economic activity extends beyond localized pollution or resource depletion, to global problems of biodiversity decline and climate change (see Chapter 11). This is an aspect of a wider societal re-evaluation of modern industry's engagement with science and technology. Once seen as the very foundation of progress, science and the businesses that employ it are argued to have forfeited public trust and become associated with threat and risk (Beck, 1992). Yet there has been no simple link between increasing environmental damage and the economic growth of the past two centuries. New industrial technologies have contributed to rising public perceptions of risk and environmental change. But at the same time, industry's own commercially inspired search for cost savings has increased the efficiency of resource use by established sectors. In trades such as steel, making each unit of output currently demands only a fraction of the input of materials required a century ago and production creates less waste. Technological innovation has also extended the resource base, relieving economic and environmental concerns about over-exploitation and exhaustion of traditional raw materials. In the process, profitable new industries, such as petrochemicals, have been created, based on reserves with a previously unsuspected economic potential. Innovative products and technologies have also weakened the links between product value and the physical consumption of materials. The industrial achievement of the mid 20th century was embodied in the motor car, in which materials accounted for 40 per cent of product value. By contrast, the microchip, as the foundation of a new era of information technology, derives only 0.3 per cent of its worth from its material basis (Myers, 1997).

The challenge of future growth

Although some encouragement can be derived from the increasing efficiency of resource use and curbs on pollution in the developed world, both economists and environmentalists identify the next half century as a particularly challenging period. Their concerns about the potential environmental effects of economic activity reflect the prospect that any efficiency gains will be swamped by the growth of production and consumption. A five to tenfold increase in economic activity could be required by the mid 21st century to provide basic amenities for a global population twice the current total (Hart, 1995). As more of the world's peoples aspire to the heights of material consumption now found in North America, Western Europe and Japan, demand will increase still more sharply (Stern et al, 1997). Yet substantial economic expansion using existing technologies and production methods will not be ecologically sustainable.

Change without growth is, of course, possible. Existing levels of economic output might be redistributed so that the needs of all the world's people are met (see Myers, 1997). The message of sustainable development promoted in the Brundtland Report, however, is that such limits to growth are unnecessary and unhelpful (WCED, 1987). Economic growth is to be encouraged in both developed and developing countries as the best means of meeting basic and universal needs for food, clean water, fuel and shelter; to fund social investment in education, health and welfare; and to pay for initiatives to enhance environmental quality. However, the character of economic activity must be transformed. Existing efforts to promote resource efficiency and pollution prevention must be redoubled to decouple growth from increasing demands on the environment. In addition, the ideal of sustainable development requires greater equity in the social and geographical distribution of economic growth and wealth, giving priority to improving the life chances of the world's poor.

Sustainable Economic Development as Eco-efficiency

A role for business

Environmentalists have traditionally been hostile towards business, an antipathy often reciprocated. Much environmental argument has been characterized as anti-growth, anti-business and anti-profit (Elkington, 1994). Responses to environmental concerns have often been portrayed as imposing a brake upon development and innovation: increasing business costs and undermining competitiveness, jobs and living standards. By comparison, the notion of sustainable development seems much more likely to resonate with business. Indeed, some commentators have allotted business a crucial leadership role in promoting sustainable development, arguing that major corporations are the only institutions with the financial resources, technical knowledge and institutional capacity to facilitate the necessary change (Hart, 1995; Holliday et al, 2002; Marcil, 1992; Shrivastava, 1995). These claims echo wider changes in the framing of the functions of business and its relationship with government. The past quarter century has seen a retreat from direct economic management by the state. Greater emphasis is now placed on innovative business behaviour in response to market stimuli as an important means of promoting environmental and social welfare, as well as economic progress.

Hence, definitions that characterize business as functioning primarily to generate profits for the owners of capital, are being challenged by formulations that highlight relationships with broader constituencies of stakeholders (Blair, 1998; T Clarke, 1998; Wheeler and Sillanpää, 1997; for an alternative perspective see Vallance, 1993). The links between a business and its stakeholders – including customers and suppliers, employees and their families, and the local community – need not be directly financial. But just as stakeholders are affected by a company's operations, so they themselves influence business performance. Cooperation, rather than confrontation, between business and stakeholders may thus prove mutually beneficial. Environmental issues may forge business–stakeholder links; but the natural environment can be constructed as a stakeholder in its own right (Starik, 1995; for a counter-argument see Phillips and Reichart, 2000). Either way, a positive reading of this redefinition of business functions is that it should encourage the 'greening' of business, as companies pay greater attention to their own environmental impacts and construct more positive relationships with environmental campaigners (Enmarch-Williams, 1996).

Benefits to business

Advocates of business greening indicate that their reforms will protect the environment by mitigating resource scarcity, reducing energy consumption and curbing demand for waste disposal (Craighill and Powell, 1996; Howes et al, 1997). But equally important are claims of enhanced business profitability and growth (Elkington, 1999).

Eco-efficiencies and improved resource management systems can reduce production costs, protect the supply of essential inputs and curb pollution damage to economically valuable assets. Environmentally irresponsible behaviour is thus presented as being against the self-interest of business. The risk that individual companies will evade this collective responsibility is reduced by legislation setting out common minimum standards of environmental practice and penalties for non-compliance. Prosecution for breaching legislative standards imposes direct costs upon business in the form of fines and liability for environmental restoration. Still more damaging to a company's performance may be a loss of confidence by customers, investors and insurers if it becomes known as an environmental 'criminal'.

At the very least, therefore, compliance with environmental legislation seems to make commercial sense. However, enthusiasts for business greening argue that companies benefit from voluntary efforts to raise standards still further (Elkington, 1994; Howes et al, 1997; Roome, 1992). In part, this reflects a tactical calculation that business initiative allows it to define progress in its own terms, reducing pressure for further environmental regulation (Beder, 2002). A more positive argument, however, is that companies which take environmental initiatives can reduce costs and increase their competitive advantage and market share (Azzone and Bertelè, 1994). New business opportunities may be created as consumers and investors increasingly favour Green products and companies (Elkington, 1999; Hill et al, 1994; see also Chapter 11 for a discussion of 'climate-friendly' business).

Champions of eco-efficiency assert that over 90 per cent of materials bought and consumed within modern economic systems do not become part of saleable products and 80 per cent of products are discarded after a single use. If we accept these figures, the calculation that the wealth extracted from each unit of natural resources could be quadrupled seems credible (von Weizsäcker et al, 1997). Such arguments relate to wider visions of ecological modernization (Murphy and Gouldson, 2000; Simonis, 1989; Spaargaren and Mol, 1991; for a critical perspective see Hajer, 1995; 1996). These proclaim that current deficiencies in the environmental performance of industrial systems will stimulate new economic development and technical innovation. Commercial success will be built upon the adoption of effective environmental management strategies. The search for Green technologies and products is thus presented as a key motor of economic growth. Moreover, in an era of globalization, the opportunities for capturing emerging Green markets may extend worldwide. Environmental policy and the innovation it is deemed to inspire are thus argued to be a key influence upon the competitiveness of national economies (Porter, 1990; 1991).

Case studies of manufacturing and service industries allegedly attest to the technical and commercial potential of eco-efficiency in reducing costs and legislative liability, improving employees' health and safety and promoting a positive company image (Dowie et al, 1998; Petek and Glavić, 1996; WBCSD, 2003). Dow Chemicals, for example, reports a 60 per cent return on pollution prevention investments (Hart, 1995). Such claims also feature in a growing literature aimed at business itself, which uses studies of existing initiatives to encourage other companies to follow their example (see, for example, DoE, undated; DoE, 1996b). Moreover, clean systems and technologies are themselves marketable commodities (Rompel, 1996). Environmental business is a growing sector, including companies specializing in pollution control, waste management, land de-contamination, recycling and production of renewable energy and raw materials. The European Commission estimated that there were over 1 million jobs in eco-industries within the EU in 1994 and that future output and employment growth will outstrip the rest of the economy (European Commission, 1997a). Globally, markets for environmental technologies and services were valued at US$335 billion in 2000 and are forecast to reach US$640 billion by 2010 (DTI, 2000).

Creating the sustainable corporation

The literature on business greening stresses the importance of integrated management, looking beyond the specifics of particular production processes for ways to cut waste and costs at source. This may involve the extension of tools and systems developed to improve products themselves, through total quality management to a new engagement with the environment (Hillary, 1997). Audits can be used to identify and monitor the full range of a company's environmental impacts. Armed with this information, businesses may be able to develop more effective management systems for environmentally sensitive processes. Moves by individual businesses to establish environmental management systems (EMS) are supported by external agencies. The British Standards Institution (BS7750), the International Standards Organization (ISO14000 series) and the EU (Eco-Management and Audit Scheme or EMAS) all sponsor EMS (Hillary, 2000; Welford, 1995). In theory, at least, this ensures their effectiveness and legitimates claims made for a firm's environmental performance.

Improvement in environmental management, however, is rarely a once-and-for-all change. As a base level of performance, companies must comply with legislation covering pollution control and the treatment and safe disposal of waste. Often this involves investment in 'end-of-pipe' technologies that trap, treat and dispose of emissions. Increasingly, however, more positive strategies of pollution prevention and waste minimization are being implemented. These may be consistent with existing technologies and products, requiring little more than good housekeeping, improved staff training and attention to plant maintenance to reduce waste and pollution. However, audits can reveal potential efficiencies requiring significant investment and changes in industrial practice. These might include waste sorting to recover elements for reuse, material substitution favouring non-toxic, recycled or renewable inputs, and adoption of clean technologies that conserve energy, water and other inputs throughout the production process (Hillary, 1997; Petek and Glavić, 1996).

To be effective, EMS must cover all aspects of a company's operations, not just the most obvious core functions. Hence, new information technologies may be adopted, not just as tools to enhance business efficiency, but also as a means of reducing waste and pollution. Computer-based systems of communication and data storage raise the prospect of a paperless office and, together with innovations such as video conferencing, may reduce transport demand (von Weizsäcker et al, 1997). Purchasing and accounting departments can play an important internal role in promoting efficiencies in resource use (McComas, 1995).

For the longer term, research and development capacity should be applied to enhancing the environmental, as well as economic, potential of industrial systems. Some products can be redesigned to increase their eco-efficiency; others must be replaced with environmentally sound alternatives. In both cases, environmental considerations should be integrated into the design process, alongside issues such as quality, safety and ease of manufacture and maintenance. Design for environment stresses not only resource efficiency and clean production technologies, but also increased durability of the product in use and enhanced potential for repair, reuse or recycling at the end of its lifespan (Charter and Tischner, 2001; Fiksel, 1996). Ultimately, the basis of a company's operations may be transformed as old products and functions give way to greener alternatives. Thus, mining companies are using their own experience in land reclamation and restoration to market environmental services and oil companies are reinventing themselves as energy providers, with interests in renewable resources and clean technologies (see Chapter 11; Rompel, 1996; Shell, 2000).

The new demands placed on product development reflect moves to calculate the total environmental impact of industrial products and processes. Every stage of the product life cycle must be considered, from extraction and processing of raw materials, product manufacture, distribution to consumers, product use, potential for reuse and recycling, through to final disposal. Life-cycle analyses are applied to both conventional industrial products and other sectors, including housing and recycling schemes (Craighill and Powell, 1996; Smith et al, 1997). Their use raises significant methodological difficulties in identifying and evaluating all environmental impacts. In setting this challenge, however, life-cycle analysis helps to explore the spread of economic activity's environmental impacts across time and space.

The web of business

In the context of the product life cycle, the importance of a single company as the creator of that product may appear to be diminished. Different and geographically dispersed businesses may be responsible for producing raw materials and components that make up a finished product, and for transport and distribution functions. Subsequently, it is often the consumer who makes decisions about reuse, recycling and disposal. The complexity of production and consumption systems should not, however, absolve business of environmental responsibility. Rather, it sets new challenges to reach out beyond the workplace.

A key objective of design for the environment is to encourage the consumer to behave responsibly – for example, by creating a product that is long lasting, easy to use efficiently and can be recycled on disposal. Customers themselves, both domestic and corporate, may be active partners, keen to buy Green products and efficient technologies. This relationship can be consolidated through product stewardship programmes, where a company retains a lifetime interest in its products. It may offer advice and support, ensuring that health or environmental problems associated with use and disposal are minimized, perhaps including final recovery and recycling facilities. This approach has been pioneered by the chemicals sector, chiefly to address concerns about toxic materials. But producers of other goods, including motor vehicles and consumer durables, could complement design for recycling and reuse with direct involvement in product recovery for disassembly.

Product stewardship schemes may increase business involvement in encouraging sustainable consumption (Flaherty, 1996; see also Stern et al, 1997). The advertising and promotional power of business is also being directed to the sale of environmentally sound products and energy efficiency. However, more substantial challenges to the ethos of mass consumerism could prove difficult to accommodate within the business agenda. Suggestions that consumers, particularly the more affluent, should use products more efficiently and, ultimately, consume less are both controversial and at odds with established business aims of market expansion (Myers, 1997; Shrivastava, 1995; Vincent and Panayotou, 1997).

Businesses not only contract external relations through product sales, most are also buyers of components and raw materials. The scale of commercial purchasing has led to its identification as an important mechanism to promote business innovation. By setting quality standards for inputs and production systems, purchasing organizations may encourage diffusion of environmentally informed business practices and technologies (Green et al, 1996; Hill, 1997; New et al, 2000). Initiatives include moves to reduce packaging and transportation, and to increase the use of materials derived from environmentally sustainable sources. However, more ambitious schemes involving a coordinated assessment of opportunities and problems throughout the entire purchasing chain could yield greater dividends. Novel partnerships might also be forged as companies find new uses for the waste generated by other businesses. Where this extends beyond recycling of materials to projects such as reuse of waste heat and water, it is likely that economic integration will require spatial proximity. Hence, an ecological, as well as a commercial, logic may underlie the geography of economic development.

Such principles are embodied in the creation of eco-industrial parks in Europe and North America, bringing together complementary activities on a single site (Potts Carr, 1998). At Kalundborg in Denmark, for example, an oil refinery has become the focus of an industrial community. The refinery shares its coolant water with other companies, reducing consumption by 25 per cent, and provides waste gas to fuel a power plant. By-products from the power plant are used in the production of cement, road fill and gypsum wallboard. The excess steam produced during power generation is harnessed to heat local homes and businesses, including a fish farm (Ehrenfeld and Gertler, 1997). Combined heat and power schemes, sometimes fuelled by domestic waste, are also a potential tool for improving environmental efficiency in existing urban developments.

Indeed, Welford (1995) advocates extension of EMS to develop integrated local or regional policies. Ecological integration and other means to minimize environmental damage would become key elements of regional economic development policy, complemented by a coordinated programme of environmental rehabilitation. In principle, such a regional EMS could become a new basis for the construction of comparative economic advantage, as inward investment would be attracted to an area by its reputation for innovative and efficient management and high environmental quality. In practice, however, the necessary cooperation between businesses, local government and the wider community may be hard to achieve. Even within individual local authorities there is still more evidence of tension than of synergy between departments prioritizing conventional economic development targets and those concerned to protect local environments (Gibbs et al, 1998). Other attempts to incorporate the principles of sustainable development within regional planning for south-east England confirm the importance, but also the practical difficulties, of securing meaningful participation from a wide range of stakeholders (Doak et al, 1998).

Forging international links

Any regional focus must not, however, become inward looking if it is to address the larger challenge of sustainable development. The search for the accommodation between economy and environment claimed for eco-efficiency has universal potential. Some of the greatest challenges are found in developing countries and the transitional economies of the former Soviet bloc. Transfer of management systems and technologies to these states is often difficult, not least because communities who would most benefit from environmental initiatives lack the means to pay for them. International agencies, national governments and the EU have funded technology transfers. However, business also has an important role. Some analysts see this as reinforcing arguments for free trade and capital mobility (Shaw and Hanson, 1996). Multinational corporations are portrayed as powerful agencies for the transfer of technology and EMS, thus promoting compliance with international environmental regulation. Pursuit of their own internal efficiency gains may also lead to the extension of practices on health, safety and the environment, derived from the developed world, as common standards for all of a company's plants (Poduska et al, 1992; Susskind, 1992). Countervailing suspicions persist that inappropriate technologies may be transferred and mobile international capital is drawn to states least able to enforce effective social and environmental legislation. However, empirical evidence suggests that those developing and transitional economies most open to international investment and trade have seen the greatest recent improvement in environmental standards (French, 1997; 1998; Rompel, 1996).

Other partnerships claim to invest international capital in promoting economic and social development, while protecting environmental integrity. Initiatives include eco-tourism and bio-prospecting schemes that treat nature itself as a valued and marketable commodity. For example, a deal with Merck, a US supplier of healthcare products, has led to Costa Rica's National Institute for Biodiversity assuming responsibility for one quarter of the country's rainforests. Conservation and management is partly funded by Merck, in return for exclusive exploration rights to the territory's bio-resources. If new commercial drugs are subsequently developed, the institute will receive royalty payments (Blum, 1993). Such schemes claim to make conservation profitable, and Shrivastava (1995) suggests that technology transfer could be supported in the same way. Major chemical producers, such as ICI and DuPont, might see commercial advantage in acquiring rights to genetic resources from tropical forests. In return, they would trade environmental technologies, such as the means to produce alternatives to the ozone-depleting chemicals demanded in rapidly growing applications such as refrigeration and electronics.

Changing the business context: pricing, tax and subsidies

Moves to price and sell nature conservation form part of wider changes that may be necessary if business is to champion the environment. Rather than attempt to change the commercial logic of business, it is argued that nature can be protected by incorporating it within the monetary sphere of value. Where financial advantage can be derived from environmentally sound behaviour, the established practices of the market may prove to be powerful agents of environmental protection. To harness this potential, companies and markets must adopt full-cost accounting.

Currently, prices of goods and services reflect only part of the true cost of production. Other costs, including damage to the physical environment and human health, have been externalized. Society at large pays, often through taxation, for environmental restoration, healthcare and other services. Some costs are not so much shared as exported. As the means of transferring capital, materials and goods across space have increased, it has become easier to distance those who profit from, or consume, particular industrial products from the social and environmental damage incurred as a result of production. Similarly, costs are transferred across time to subsequent generations, when they inherit degraded environments, depleted resource bases and distorted social structures. If the market is to promote more sustainable development, this evasion and transfer of cost must end. Product prices must reflect all environmental and social costs created throughout their entire life cycle from first design to final disposal.

Such moves cannot be implemented effectively by individual businesses. Change must be comprehensive, avoiding the market distortions that would arise if some goods carried a full cost price, while competing products established an apparent price advantage through continuing to externalize costs. Implementation of full-cost accounting thus requires a legislative foundation much as other elements of the market system are enshrined in law. Some limited moves have been made in this direction through the 'polluter pays' principle embodied in legislation that imposes liability for environmental damage and associated clean-up costs (OECD, 1975). But further action is necessary, not only to promote the full-cost principle, but also to remove existing market distortions.

Past efforts to secure traditional economic objectives of growth, full employment and protection of strategically important sectors such as agriculture and energy have created systems of subsidy and price support. These have had unwelcome consequences in sponsoring environmental damage and encouraging the misuse of resources (Anderson, 1995; Steenblik and Coroyannakis, 1995; see also Chapter 8 in this volume). Champions of the free market may take this as an argument for curbing state intervention. However, reform of subsidies and other financial instruments, including taxation, to promote environmental and social objectives will yield greater benefits. Increased taxation should be placed on pollution, waste, energy consumption and exploitation of virgin materials. By contrast, clean technologies, recycled materials and public transport might benefit from tax credits and subsidies (Fullerton and Wu, 1998). The UK has moved in this direction – for example, introducing differentials in excise duty for leaded and unleaded petrol. In 1996, this was followed by taxation of landfill disposal, which together with EU packaging regulations has increased attention to waste minimization. The policy also attempts to encourage employment, offsetting taxation on waste with a cut in the 'jobs tax' embodied in the employer's National Insurance contribution (Turner et al, 1998). A similar switch in the target of taxation was made with the introduction of a climate change levy on business use of energy in 2001 (see Chapter 11). Together, such initiatives might promote an increasing substitution of labour for polluting processes and consumption of non-renewable resources (Bossier and Bréchet, 1995).

Too Good To Be True: Are Win–Win Arguments Sustainable?

The limitations of change in practice

So far the argument has not challenged the positive message on the environment promoted by Green business and its champions. But there are questionable aspects to eco-efficiency, ecological modernization and business endorsement of sustainable development. Nor are repeated arguments that business *must* become more environmentally responsible always properly supported by sophisticated accounts of *how* and *why* this will come about (Newton and Harte, 1997). It cannot simply be assumed that a realization of the supposed coincidence of commercial and environmental interests will engender change. Empirical studies reveal the complexity of business greening.

This is not to suggest that business managers are necessarily unsympathetic to environmental concerns. Surveys of business attitudes in Western Europe and North America regularly reveal majority support for environmental goals as a key element of corporate management strategy. Similarly, interviews in the UK, Germany and France, conducted for a study focusing on small- and medium-sized enterprises (SMEs), found echoes of wider public concerns about environmental damage, pollution and the state of the world to be inherited by interviewees' children. The principle of reducing costs through efficiencies and waste minimization also resonated well with managers. But only a minority actively endorsed the Green message. Many found it difficult to reconcile attention to environmental concerns with their specific managerial responsibilities (Purvis et al, 1998; 2000).

In part, this reflected perceptions that environmental initiatives conflict with established commercial priorities on cost and competitiveness. Even the potential for cost savings as a result of environmentally beneficial initiatives is no guarantee of action by business. This sometimes reflects problems of time scale; investment that could generate long-term economic and environmental benefits is at odds with the perceived need to minimize immediate costs. Moreover, other means of saving, such as shedding labour, often appear quicker and easier (Purvis et al, 1998). Increasingly competitive UK energy markets have enabled businesses to lower their costs by switching suppliers or renegotiating tariffs, rather than by investing in energy efficiency. Overall, businesses are more likely to address specific pollution problems in a reactive manner than they are to embark upon strategic greening with the aim of improving competitiveness. Managers often see themselves as lacking the resources of capital, time and knowledge to invest in the larger goals of life-cycle analysis, or to make the significant changes to management systems, products and processes potentially required by design for the environment. Formal EMS remain rare amongst smaller European companies and many managers appear sceptical about official environmental management standards. The development of other motors for change, including supply-chain pressures and fiscal instruments, is partial and uneven. Individuals also perceive themselves as lacking the power necessary to effect significant change, either within their own company or impacting upon the wider world. Smaller businesses, in particular, often see their own actions as insignificant when set against the global scale of environmental damage (Hill, 1997; Merritt, 1998; Purvis et al, 1998; 2000).

Moreover, the empirical basis of the win–win argument is weak. Much rests upon highly selective case studies. There is no comprehensive evidence to substantiate arguments that superior environmental performance confers market advantage on either national economies or individual businesses. Industries characterized by high rates of investment may be able to take advantage of cost-reducing clean technologies; but Gray and Shadbegian's (1995) study of US producers of pulp and paper, oil and steel concluded that the costs of improved environmental performance outweighed productivity benefits. Attempts to relate economic and environmental performance often prove inconclusive (Repetto, 1995), perhaps because many factors other than the environment influence patterns of international trade and investment, and the costs and profitability of individual companies.

Walley and Whitehead (1994) thus rightly argue that 'It's not easy being green', and the potential for financial returns from environmental investment is limited. Consequently, the goal for business may be more realistically constructed as minimizing loss of shareholder value caused by environmental costs, rather than the creation of value through environmental initiatives. For all the rhetoric about business greening and efficiency, concern for the environment still conflicts, in practice, with immediate economic goals of maximization of growth and profitability.

Eco-efficiency or environmental quality: differing definitions of sustainable development

The need to temper win–win arguments with a dose of reality is not the only reason to conclude that the broad programme of sustainable development demands more than most businesses are willing or able to give. Gladwin et al (1995) distinguish between the business greening already evident and more substantial changes required for sustainable development. While the best elements of greening have extended business responsibilities throughout the product life cycle, the emphasis remains on instrumental or process objectives such as pollution reduction. There is little attention to sustainable development per se, involving deeper exploration of the effects of business practices on the health and integrity of ecological and social systems.

Business greening and eco-efficiency echo the more limited interpretations of sustainable development in devoting greater attention than hitherto to environmental concerns. But the focus remains on the performance of individual components of the economy and regulatory compliance, rather than upon the overall condition of the environment. No specific environmental quality targets are set and the impact of eco-efficiency initiatives upon the environment often remains untested and uncertain (Jacobs and Stott, 1992). Indeed, if output grows faster than eco-efficiency gains, the condition of the environment will deteriorate. Where this involves the erosion of Critical Natural Capital – such as the ozone layer and the global climate system – that underpins planetary life-support functions, the consequences could be particularly serious (see Chapter 11).

The case is thus made for a more rigorous interpretation of sustainable development that focuses upon the overall condition of the environment and sets specific performance goals for business, designed to ensure that environmental quality does not decline below a minimum level necessary to maintain social and economic well-being. The imposition of such targets and timetables for the achievement of specific environmental goals is already a feature of national and international regulatory frameworks. Examples include targets for the reduction of emissions of greenhouse gases and other pollutants, and legislation that prescribes performance in areas such as recycling and waste minimization. This approach builds upon the search for eco-efficiency; but in prioritizing the defence of the environment it creates new potential for contest.

The translation of the need to preserve environmental quality into specific performance targets and timetables is itself often difficult and disputed. Hence, for example, environmentalists have claimed from the outset that the measures enshrined in the Kyoto Protocol were inadequate to achieve the desired result of preventing significant climate change (Parry et al, 1998). Yet setting more stringent targets would have been politically impossible, not least because of opposition from influential business interests to any significant curbs on greenhouse gas emissions (see Chapter 11). In creating environmental targets, a stronger construction of sustainable development raises the prospect of constraints upon economic growth, business profitability and consumer behaviour.

Whether the defence of the environment necessarily imposes restrictions upon economic growth is a matter of debate. Jacobs and Stott (1992) are optimistic in arguing that preservation of environmental integrity is not incompatible with existing economic planning aims of fostering enterprise that is high skill, high wage and technologically innovative. Government and regulatory authorities that define environmental targets might also provide incentives to support this economic transformation through provision of information, grants, research support and direct investment. Ekins (1993), however, regards the scale of technological change required to enable improvement in environmental quality and continued economic growth as too great to be realistic. Moreover, as social and economic justice and the relief of global poverty require substantial economic growth in developing countries, the simultaneous task of meeting the environmental challenge could set particularly severe constraints upon business in the developed world.

Even if the overall effects of prioritizing environmental quality could be shown to be economically neutral or positive, individual companies and sectors would still contest the imposition of particular costs and constraints upon their operations. Environmental sustainability may allow overall growth of output, employment and profitability; but it does require economic change. Pollution- and energy-intensive industries, at a disadvantage in this process of transformation, will contest its necessity. Action against climate change as a specific instance of such contest is noted in Chapter 11. In this context, potential business losers from environmentally driven change include energy providers, motor vehicle producers and the freight transport industry. These are powerful vested interests, unwilling to sacrifice economic performance and profitability. Their ability to shape public debate and political process to meet their own sectional interests is strikingly at odds with the equitable ethos of sustainable development. Key sectors of American business, in particular, have formed the backbone of domestic political resistance to US ratification of the Kyoto Protocol. Without US participation, the effectiveness of the protocol will be severely diminished. Hence, American business has been allowed an effective veto over this important aspect of global environmental policy and vital foundation for sustainable development (see also Chapter 12).

The complexity of environmental challenges

If we argue that the agenda should be defined by the need to preserve environmental quality, rather than by the availability of opportunities for eco-efficiency, then we must also acknowledge that business does not always have the means to play a positive role. Advocates of ecological modernization assume that companies have the expert knowledge and technical capacity to transform an environmental challenge into a commercial opportunity. In practice, however, business may face confusions and uncertainties. In part, this reflects contradictory advice regarding, for example, the relative environmental merits of diesel- and petrol-fuelled vehicles, or the credentials of recycling schemes. But the complexity of environmental systems may create dilemmas that are impossible for science and society, as a whole – let alone individual businesses – to resolve unambiguously.

Damage to the stratospheric ozone layer, for example, prompted international regulatory initiatives to phase out production of ozone-depleting substances. But action was also required by business to develop alternative ways of delivering services, such as refrigeration, previously reliant upon the proscribed chemicals. This has been complicated by debate regarding the operational and environmental criteria defining a successful refrigeration technology. Different parties prioritize particular environmental considerations: not just ozone depletion, but concerns about the potential of refrigerants as greenhouse gases and the energy consumption of systems in operation. All are legitimate issues, as are cost, system performance, and the health and safety implications of using toxic or flammable refrigerants. Suppliers have actively promoted a diversity of refrigerants and systems, especially in relation to equipment for commercial and retail users. But no single currently available technology fully satisfies all of the performance criteria. In this context the managers of companies producing and servicing refrigeration equipment are ill equipped to make rational trade-offs between, for example, technologies claimed to eliminate damage to the ozone layer against those which supposedly minimize global warming impacts (Purvis et al, 2001). According priority to particular aspects of environmental change is a judgement beyond the capabilities of current science, while recourse to legislation or the market only gives the illusion of logical environmental decision-making in the absence of full understanding of costs and benefits.

What price equity?

Although notions of corporate social responsibility are increasingly urged upon companies (see, for example, European Commission, 2002), attention to the environment in the business discourse of sustainable development has tended to obscure the social dimensions of the concept. There is relatively little in the existing literature on business sustainability that engages directly with the aims articulated in the Brundtland Report of reducing poverty and social inequality, and improving quality of life for the world's poor (WCED, 1987). In so far as they address wealth distribution and social equity, business champions often only repeat discredited assumptions about the trickle-down of wealth through the socio-economic hierarchy, within and between states. Thus groups such as the World Business Council for Sustainable Development relate their arguments about reconciling economic and environmental goals to support for international free trade (Schmidheiny, 1992). Global economic integration and free movement of capital and commodities are deemed to promote eco-efficiency, while fostering economic progress and wealth creation. Developing countries are claimed to derive particular benefit from access to global markets for the specific commodities in which they have a comparative advantage. Such trade is argued to generate income sufficient to pay for other goods, including environmental services, contributing to a virtuous circle of socio-economic and environmental gain.

Environmentalists and social campaigners, however, advance a very different view of free trade as reflecting the self-interest of international business. The influence of multinational capital within an increasingly global economy and the strengthening regulatory authority of the World Trade Organization (WTO) are claimed to have created freedom without responsibility for international business in pursuing market expansion and economic growth. Under regimes for trade, investment and intellectual property being established by the WTO, mobile capital is freer to search out short-term opportunities to benefit from the unsustainable exploitation of human and natural resources, especially in developing countries (Friends of the Earth, 1999; Shrybman, 1999).

Business, and particularly the largest international corporations, thus stands accused of hijacking the rhetoric of sustainable development, recasting it as a tool for business efficiency and gain, and evading difficult questions about the impacts of economic growth upon social welfare (Eden, 1994). It is, of course, unrealistic to expect that business will find a new purpose as the champion of social equity; but it is important to challenge the application of the label of sustainable development to initiatives that are manifestly inequitable, even neo-colonial (Middleton et al, 1993). The charge that the social and environmental welfare and economic potential of developing countries is being sacrificed to maintain Northern affluence can be applied even to the new wave of more imaginative partnerships between multinational corporations and Southern states.

Developing countries have long been resource reservoirs for the industrialized world, a trade in sustainability that has contributed to the social and environmental burdens facing many Southern states. Arguably, this inequality is perpetuated in a new guise – rather than being transformed – by initiatives such as eco-tourism and bio-prospecting. International investors claim to contribute to the economic and social development of the host area, while protecting its ecological integrity. However, these projects also represent a new manifestation of Northern claims to the greatest share of global resources and wealth, inspiring accusations of 'bio-piracy' and disregard for environmental justice (McAfee, 1999; Shiva, 1999). Through such schemes governments sell decision-making powers about the development of their own land and resources. There is no guarantee that the payments received are equitable, or that they are used to address the needs of communities inhabiting the designated land. Southern governments may themselves be active partners in schemes that ignore the aspirations of local people for development and deny their rights of access to land and natural resources. When governments, international capital and even international non-governmental organizations (NGOs) which sponsor conservation projects cannot be held accountable, local communities' powers of resistance are limited (however, Neumann, 1995 sees some potential for positive change).

A Space for Sustainable Development?

Capitalism, crisis and sustainable development

Theoretical constructions of sustainable development deriving from economics present a goal of balance between resource creation and destruction in abstract and aspatial terms (Turner, 1993). Distributional effects over time, between the generations, often appear to be prioritized over attention to intra-generational equity. Acknowledgement of the need to create new opportunities for the world's poorest people is not always accompanied by detailed discussion of the mechanisms through which this is to be achieved. Despite a tradition of geographical work that reveals injustice in the distribution of the environmental, as well as social, costs and benefits of economic growth (see, for example, Heiman, 1996; Mitchell et al, 1999), relatively little attention has been given to the spatial construction of sustainable development. If particular communities bear the costs of economic activity, or forego economic development to preserve natural capital, equity demands that they share in the consequent benefits. Communities are unlikely to accept arguments that they have contributed to a total national or global project of sustainable development if rewards accrue chiefly to other people and places. However often the injunction to think globally is repeated, it cannot displace the tendency to prioritize our own space and time.

Thinking in this way also requires that the ideal of sustainable development be related to the reality of socio-economic and environmental change in particular communities. Development under capitalism is inherently uneven over space and time (Smith, 1990). Hence, the experience of many individual communities has been the antithesis of sustainable development, even as global wealth and welfare have apparently increased. Periods of growth have been punctuated by dramatic collapse as capitalism restructures itself through crisis (Drummond and Marsden, 1999; Harvey, 1982). Some communities have been exploited for their resources, material and human, and have then been abandoned by mobile capital in search of better returns elsewhere. The ability of business to externalize costs has generated a legacy of pollution, scarred landscapes and abandoned factories and mines. The work force and the wider community dependent upon them may also be rejected as jobs are lost and skills become redundant. From this perspective residents of decaying industrial communities in Europe and North America may feel themselves just as much victims of 'unsustainable' development as are populations in developing countries. While financial capital has the potential for geographical mobility and redeployment in new ventures, the human capital embodied in particular individuals and communities is often relatively immobile and inflexible. Human skills are not necessarily transferable and social ties to particular locations cannot be easily broken to take up employment elsewhere.

There is not the space here to engage properly with arguments surrounding the reality, novelty and consequences of the apparently accelerating trend to globalization over recent decades (see Held and McGrew, 2000, for an excellent overview). But the expansion, integration and deregulation of global markets have widened differentials between the mobility of capital and labour, and arguably sapped the regulatory influence of individual states over multinational business. A shift in manufacturing to the developing world has been apparent for at least four decades as declining profitability forced businesses to adopt a dual strategy of enlarging markets and reducing production costs (Coffey, 1996; Dicken, 2003). Such changes have led to charges of the exploitation of low-cost labour and evasion of responsibility for social and environmental costs that are at odds with sustainable and equitable development (Beder, 2002; Klein, 2000). In recent years, however, the global economy has arguably entered a new phase of extreme capital mobility in which financial flows represent short-term speculative opportunities in currency and commodity trading, rather than investment in specific industrial ventures (Martin, 1994; Swyngedouw, 1996; Warf, 1999). This disengagement of financial and industrial geographies may redefine, rather than remove, the potential for social and environmental damage.

When episodes of economic growth built upon speculative investment break down, as happened throughout much of East Asia during the late 1990s, this can trigger a dramatic rise in unemployment rates (Wade, 1998). In the Asian context, this caused not just social dislocation, but also increased pressures on the environment (Dauvergne, 1999). In the absence of effective state welfare systems, many of the new urban unemployed in countries such as Thailand returned to their original rural communities. The sudden increase in the farming population prevented social collapse, but potentially at the cost of long-term damage to rural ecosystems (Crispin, 1998; Deen, 1998; Oxfam, 1998). At the national level, the immediate need to generate additional income through trade may also have created environmental damage that cannot easily be remedied. In particular, it is suggested that increased timber exports may pose a renewed threat to the sustainability of forestry in countries such as the Philippines (Howard, 1998).

Turning towards the local: an alternative economic geography

The spatial dynamic of capitalism is thus potentially at odds with the local experience of security and progressive continuity that is necessary if individuals and communities are to feel that sustainable development has achieved its ultimate objective of maintaining and improving their life chances. Such arguments have led some commentators to redouble their attacks against globalization and argue for 'a turn toward the local' (Mander and Goldsmith, 2001). In this they assert that economic security, social welfare and ecological integrity demand that capital be more strongly rooted within particular communities. Only a long-term commitment to a place and its people guarantees economic practices that are environmentally and socially sustainable. Otherwise there will always be the temptation for external capital to maximize short-term returns and move on.

Such arguments call for radical changes in the conduct and geography of economic enterprise so that local people determine their own social and economic circumstances, rather than being dictated to by national and transnational organizations. Greater emphasis would be placed upon production to meet consumer needs, rather than to maximize profit. Decentralization of economic activity would mean that more of these needs were met from local sources, giving employment to local people. This form of development from within would harness and enhance the resource of human capital represented by the individual's skills, knowledge, motivation and creativity, and by the institutional organization of collective endeavour.

In theory, business and, by extension, Capital would develop a stronger sense of place. Localized systems of production and trade would curb the influence of impersonal market forces and bureaucracies, providing insulation from the disruptive boom and bust of capitalist economic cycles. Local purchasing also promotes the circulation and multiplication of local wealth, potentially an advantage for poorer communities. A reduced reliance upon mass transportation would yield environmental benefits, as well as cost savings. Moreover, if there were lesser recourse to trade as a means of importing sustainability, greater care would be required in the husbanding of a region's own resources. Complementary economic activities would develop, feeding off each other's by-products, encouraging recycling and other forms of waste minimization. The reintegration of production within a regionally bounded context might encourage all inhabitants to pay new attention to protecting their environment, reducing modern society's dangerous alienation from nature (Dickens, 1996). Ultimately, this bio-regional ideal envisages development being shaped by the maintenance of balance between human aspirations and the health of ecological resources within a particular regional territory (Sale, 1985; 1996; Welford, 1995). This is not intended to set limits to growth, but to increase the likelihood of its sustainability.

Bio-regionalism has echoes of other calls, often informed by anarchist and socialist ideals, for greater local economic self-sufficiency, political democracy and harmony between humanity and nature (see, for example, Bookchin, 1980). Attempts at applying these ideas have a poor track record. However, Welford (1995) claims that, far from being impractical, bio-regionalism is 'fully consistent with new modes of industrial organisation' that are the hallmark of an emergent post-Fordist economy. Contemporary economic activity is argued to be already characterized by a shift from production based on the intensive use of materials and energy to a greater emphasis on creating value through the application of knowledge. Thus, adoption of clean technologies will be encouraged by a pervasive perception that, in a climate of economic uncertainty created by globalization and deregulation, constant innovation and the reinvention of products, processes and managerial culture are necessary to maintain competitive advantage (see the wider argument advanced in Cooke, 1996). Moreover, the adoption of information-based technologies, allowing increasing control over production processes, is argued to be changing the whole framework of economic activity as the rigidities of mass production are replaced by new flexibilities permitting diversified low-volume production (Dicken, 2003). Output is thus tailored to the needs of individual consumers and local markets and may be produced by smaller organizational units. Such changes are seen by many commentators to be creating a distinctive geography of economic activity (Cooke, 1996; Storper, 1997). Large firms are becoming disarticulated into separate divisions, international production is increasingly likely to be organized through the subcontracting of work to independent local suppliers rather than by direct foreign investment, and so-called 'new industrial districts' have been defined, with a potential for growth based on a localized network of small innovative firms (Piore and Sabel, 1984).

The extent, coherence and economic significance of trends towards post-Fordism are still disputed; but any claims that a new era of flexible specialization will necessarily create the potential for more sustainable development are questionable (Gibbs, 1996; 2002). The appearance of more dispersed and self-contained local and regional economies belies the reality of the continuing centralization of power within multinational companies and their networks of dependent suppliers and subcontractors. If local control is a key to better environmental management, it will not automatically be delivered by post-Fordist economic restructuring. This is not to argue that there is no potential for positive change; but localization is not a total nor an automatic solution to the challenge of sustainable development. Greater sustainability requires conscious planning and even the creation of economies in which production, trade and control were more localized would not obviate the need for other technical, managerial and attitudinal changes. It is important to recall the patchy environmental track record of the existing small business community.

Progress towards sustainable local economic development

If it is hard to envisage the total creation of a new bio-regional geography of decentralized economic activity, there are ways in which local people and institutions can cooperate to promote their own economic and social interests, while defending the health of their environment. Commentators such as Ekins and Newby (1998) have identified existing initiatives that exemplify aspects of their agenda for sustainable local economic development. Often the intention is not to overturn dominant tendencies to globalization, but to explore an alternative development path that may be especially relevant in restoring the economic, social and environmental fortunes of areas marginalized within global markets.

The purpose of existing systems of regional and local development planning could be redefined to give priority not simply to economic growth, but to the creation of employment that is environmentally sound, socially fulfilling and dedicated to creating goods and services that meet the needs of local consumers. To pursue such a development path, existing agencies providing advice and support for business would pay increasing attention to environmental concerns, the transfer of clean technologies and skills development within the workforce (Gibbs, 1998; 2002). Investment in education and training must assume a wider importance as a foundation of a contemporary economy in which knowledge is the most strategic resource (see the wider argument advanced in Morgan, 1997). New information technologies and the potential of e-commerce should also be harnessed to create newly extensive markets for small businesses and distinctive local produce, trading the promotion of employment and enterprise against strict adherence to minimization of transport and distribution.

Such innovations confirm that it is unrealistic to expect that all local needs be met from local resources. However, there is potential to revive localized exchange, especially in sectors such as timber, energy and food (Ekins and Newby, 1998). Food producers, in particular, could benefit from growing resistance on the part of consumers to mass production and associated concerns about product quality and safety, and the restriction of choice that results from the concentration of production and distribution in the hands of a few major companies (Imhoff, 1996; see Chapter 8 in this volume; for a wider discussion of economic and cultural change in relation to food see Ritzer, 1993). Locally distinctive produce, with claims to environmentally sound production, might thus increase its market share.

Other less conventional forms of economic initiative may have a role to play in increasing community enterprise and sustainable local development. At the local level, mutuality retains its potency as a critique of capitalism. Credit unions – which provide low-cost capital by pooling the resources of small savers – and Local Exchange Trading Systems (LETS) – which employ socially useful resources otherwise superfluous to the mainstream economy – can improve individual welfare and enliven local economies (Bowring, 1998; Lee, 1996; McCarthy et al, 2001; Meeker-Lowry, 1996; Williams, 1996). Neither guarantees development that is environmentally and economically sustainable. But LETS, in particular, promote increased local self-sufficiency and self-worth by harnessing labour rather than material resources and encourage the sharing, repair and recycling of industrially produced goods. Moreover, where capital is derived from a local source such as a credit union, it cannot be easily exported. The effective underwriting of an individual investment by the broader community makes it more likely that respect is accorded to common environmental resources.

Embedding mobile money

Local sustainable economic development cannot, however, rely totally upon internal resources of capital and entrepreneurship. External capital is a potentially beneficial catalyst for change within a regional economy, introducing environmentally innovative products and technologies and providing jobs for local workers and markets for local suppliers (Gibbs, 2002). Therefore, rather than attempting to exclude external investment and influence, development planners should explore ways of developing partnerships with exogenous capital that will bind it into a more lasting and positive relationship with a particular community. Conventional local sourcing schemes by major business purchasers could be refined in ways that echo the environmental logic of eco-industrial parks. Purchasing links could also form the basis of mutually beneficial initiatives to promote learning, skills development and capacity for innovation within the local economy (Gibbs, 1998). Individual multinational businesses, such as Bosch, with an established reputation for attention to the environmental and social dimensions of production have already embraced the partnership vision. The company's Welsh branch plants have become a focus for networks of innovation that draw in training and educational institutions, as well as local SMEs (Morgan, 1997). Such initiatives are still relatively rare; but they form a model for the more active promotion of sustainable local development that could be replicated elsewhere.

The potential for withdrawal of external capital will always raise questions about the long-term health of a local economy. However, as Markusen (1996) points out, many of the most enduringly successful industrial districts have multinational investment, rather than localized networks of small companies, at their core. Through conscious long-term planning, communities can both maximize the benefits of inward investment and develop a degree of insurance against any adverse effects created by the departure of a major investor. The ideal of flexibility constitutes a key element of this blueprint. If, as described above, effort is consistently invested by business – both large and small – local government, educational and training institutions and other local partners in learning, skills development and industrial innovation, the foundation will be created for long-term economic success. If equal emphasis is placed on the maintenance of environmental quality, a community will be doubly attractive as a home for economic enterprise and inward investment. Such a vision has echoes of Welford's (1995) ideal of the application of the principles of EMS at a regional level. But if such moves are to be effective in promoting more sustainable development, they may have to be reinforced by regulatory provisions. One potential way forward is to adapt and extend previous thinking about the reform of taxation.

Local sustainable development might be supported by a greater degree of local hypothecation of business taxation. Only a proportion of revenue would be allocated in this way, as funding generated by taxing business must continue to support the wider delivery of state services. Equally, local revenue cannot come exclusively from local sources without exacerbating existing differences between richer and poorer localities. However, those communities who live with a particular business have an especial claim to a share in the profit it generates, a principle once enshrined in the system of property rates used to fund local government, but now long since debased. The restoration of a direct fiscal link between business and the community would have only a marginal impact upon the total system of taxation and government finance; but it could ensure that a proportion of the wealth generated within a community is retained for investment in the collective creation of a more sustainable future. Such a system could be doubly advantageous if the basis of taxation were redefined.

The reform of company taxation to embrace Green principles could benefit many local communities in encouraging job creation at the expense of polluting and environmentally destructive activities. Particular transitional assistance would, of course, have to be given to communities currently dependent upon energy- and material-intensive industries to enable them to build an alternative, cleaner economy. But the situation of such communities in many ways simply reinforces the importance of specifying the use made of funding raised through Green taxation. Often it is simply absorbed into general government revenue. Some very limited attempts at hypothecation have been made – for example, directing a proportion of the funds raised by vehicle fuel duty towards transport investment. An alternative approach would be to target revenue in ways that are geographical, rather than sectoral, and defined more by communal need than government diktat.

Simply expressed, the aim would be to promote positive investment in the host community while a business remains in operation, and to provide environmental and social insurance against its removal or failure. Revenue from Green taxation would be identified for local expenditure on environmental improvement, including the reuse and rehabilitation of industrial sites on business closure. The social obligations that some businesses already express towards their host communities through sponsorship and other involvement in local projects would be extended. Taxation revenue would thus be locally directed for investment in infrastructure and educational provision to develop capabilities and flexibilities that would retain their value, even if mobile capital were withdrawn.

It is equally important that business be rewarded for investments that are locally beneficial, and socially and environmentally sound. Tax incentives and subsidies could, for example, be offered for the reuse of existing premises, or for recycling of equipment and building materials. Existing grants and incentives to incoming business should be redesigned to encourage initial attention to flexibility for reuse and recycling in the design of buildings, plant and production processes (compare with Cragg, 1998; Gibbs, 2002; Shrivastava, 1995). The overall aim would be to foster both a sense of local consciousness and a long-term commitment to enhancing environmental quality and human capital.

For such a framework for business operations to be viable, there would have to be a strong degree of public and political commitment. The proposal is quite different in spirit from the assumption of inevitable progress towards sustainable development under ecological modernization. Rather than sustainability being regarded as essentially a technical and managerial programme for business, it becomes a political project that must be supported by an effective and democratic infrastructure of governance (Gibbs, 1996). The proposal also places particular emphasis on local democracy and partnership to ensure that revenue is spent effectively and that financial, human and natural resources are employed in ways that genuinely reflect the full range of a community's long-term needs. This would require the creation of more energetic and representative institutions of local governance – increasingly widely acknowledged as a foundation for, and facet of, more sustainable development (see Chapters 4 and 6). But, as is stressed by other contributors to this volume, local democracy must be embedded within an efficient and equitable national system of taxation and regulation, creating common conditions for business operations. In an era of global capital, the role of political authority constituted at still larger scales is increasing (Prakash and Hart, 2000; Schaberg, 1999). Strong political jurisdictions created through new institutional frameworks such as the EU, or embodied in specific multilateral agreements to defend common social and environmental standards, are thus an integral part of making business more sustainable. Only in this way can mobile capital be prevented from evading the full range of its economic, social and environmental responsibilities. And only in this way can the experience of sustainable development be made to seem more real to communities across the world. Hence, it may be necessary to act globally while thinking locally.

Conclusion

The central argument of this chapter rests on the need to look beyond conventional recipes for business sustainability. Eco-efficiency and management systems can reduce the environmental impacts of business; but to equate this with sustainable development is patently misleading. Nor is the greening of business an easy or inevitable process. If sustainable development requires a broadly based defence of environmental quality, rather than a partial reduction in the pace of environmental decay, it will demand more than most businesses are currently able or willing to give, whether in terms of technical innovation or sacrifice of economic gain. Thinking about the sustainability of economic activity also requires engagement with social and geographical issues of equity and an acknowledgement of the fundamental instability of economies under capitalism. It is this recognition that makes sustainable economic development necessarily a political project – a refinement of the state's long-standing role in the regulation of the economy and the management of regimes of accumulation (see Drummond and Marsden, 1999, for an extended treatment of this theme). If sustainable development is genuinely to become the foundation for future economic development, it must be the focus of active planning, regulation and taxation reform.

This requires a clearer vision of what constitutes sustainable development that places at its centre the coordinated defence of environmental and social integrity, rather than eco-efficiency for the individual business. Strong sustainable economic development may be unattainable; but it is nevertheless a potentially powerful critique of existing constructions of relationships between economy, society and environment. It is also absolutely necessary to retain this vision of strong sustainability against the complacency of the win–win arguments about the greening of business, which present a weak and debased version of sustainable development under which it is too easy to discount continuing environmental and social damage.

8

Sustainable Agriculture for the 21st Century

Martin Purvis and Richard Smith

Introduction

In providing food and other raw materials, agriculture meets some of humanity's most fundamental needs. Adequate nutrition is essential if individuals are to be healthy and economically productive (Conway, 1997; WCED, 1987). Worldwide, agriculture underpins the livelihoods of billions of people, ranging from peasant farmers to employees of the chemical, life science and food companies that are so influential in modern farming. Through agriculture, humanity transforms the environment, changing landscape, land use and biodiversity. These different dimensions of agriculture – its importance in life support and socio-economic development, and its influence upon environmental quality – make it an essential component of any discussion of sustainable development.

This chapter begins by assessing the achievements of modern farming, before exploring concerns about the social and environmental price paid for agricultural change. Alternative interpretations of sustainable agricultural development are then reviewed, ranging from advocacy of the organic restoration of balance between human and environmental systems, to the emergent science of biotechnology. Particular constructions of sustainable agriculture call for the redistribution of resources, including the natural foundations of land and water, state funding for agriculture and investment in research and development. This is a reminder that the adoption of various agricultural forms depends not so much upon their demonstrable superiority in meeting particular economic or environmental criteria, but upon the wider politics of agricultural change.

Modern Agriculture: Reviewing the Account

Prioritizing production

Modern intensive agriculture is a result of the increasing application of energy and other off-farm inputs to production. It rests upon a series of generic technologies: large-scale mechanization, extension of irrigation, application of chemical fertilizers and pesticides, and selective breeding of crop and livestock species. Adoption of new technologies has been encouraged by rising demand for agricultural produce and by state programmes of agricultural extension and subsidy. As a result, output of staple commodities has increased markedly. World grain production, for example, more than doubled between the 1950s and 1990s (L Brown, 1996).

In the global North, a combination of rising domestic agricultural efficiency and increasing international trade has supplied consumers with an unprecedented range and quantity of goods (Goodman and Watts, 1997). Agriculture has also released resources of labour and capital to expanding industrial and service sectors. As a global average, each agricultural worker currently produces sufficient food for five people. However, each US farm worker – as the embodiment of agricultural modernity – feeds 60 individuals (Crone, 1989). The American farming population declined from 32 million – around one third of the national total – in 1910 to 4.6 million – under 2 per cent of the total – by 1991 (Berry, 1999). Hence, agricultural change has not simply fed more people, but has also contributed resources to the larger process of development and wealth creation.

Such wealth is still lacking in the global South; but here, too, agricultural extension has played an important part in socio-economic change. Intensive agricultural technologies have been applied to increase food supplies in a context where one fifth of the global population still experience daily hunger (Gardner, 1996). Foundations for a Green revolution that promised to transform agriculture in the developing world were laid with the creation of new strains of wheat and rice during the 1950s and 1960s. When used with fertilizers, pesticides and irrigation water, the new cereals yielded heavily and rapid growth enabled the double cropping of land in a single year. The Green revolution spread quickly during the 1970s and 1980s, at least to favoured agricultural areas. Hence, cereal production in the developing world increased by 90 per cent between 1965 and 1989, with especially rapid growth in the southern and eastern quarters of Asia. The Green revolution bred a vision of increased security and wealth for the multitudinous rural poor. Not only would farming communities be able to feed themselves, sales of surplus production to urban consumers would generate new income. Extension of agricultural trade would increase the efficiency of production, creating opportunities for economic diversification. Rather than following Northern trends to urbanization and large-scale industrialization, many commentators envisaged a rural model of Southern development, producing wealth through industry based on agricultural raw materials.

A failing system?

Yet, worldwide, farmers and farming face many problems. In developed countries initiatives to ensure food security through state subsidies for domestic production have led to excess rather than sufficiency. The Common Agricultural Policy (CAP), for example, enacted by the European Community (EC) from 1962, established guaranteed prices for key commodities. Increasing output meant that the EC exceeded self-sufficiency in temperate products by the early 1970s (Potter, 1998). Yet production still rose annually by 2 per cent between 1973 and 1988, while consumption increased by only 0.5 per cent (EU, 1999a). The resultant costs of subsidizing production, as well as storage and export of surpluses, accounted for 70 per cent of the entire EC budget by the late 1980s (Potter, 1998). Despite subsequent reforms, agricultural spending remains an excessive burden on European Union (EU) finances (Fennell, 1997). The system alienated consumers by pushing food prices above global market levels and the CAP's impact upon the farming industry has long been questioned. Subsidies intended to guarantee the incomes of small producers have disproportionately benefited the larger farmers most responsible for overproduction. By contrast, small family farms and producers in upland areas remain commercially marginal. The CAP has failed to maintain a living countryside in which agriculture contributes positively to social and environmental well-being.

Perpetual subsidy of production has blocked structural reform of European agriculture and allowed farming costs to rise. Moreover, inefficiency has accompanied overproduction. Energy inputs have reached unprecedented levels and agro-chemicals are applied routinely, rather than to achieve specific benefits. At the same time, traditional resources including animal manure are increasingly regarded as waste. The chief beneficiaries of this farming policy have been the producers of agro-chemicals and other inputs, whose markets have expanded significantly with state-sponsored agricultural intensification.

The transformation of farming into a quasi-industrial system has also raised concerns about the end product. At its most extreme, this reflects evidence that some production methods threaten human health. In the UK, recent public and political anxiety has focused on a series of specific issues, including pesticide residues on fruit and vegetables, salmonella in intensively reared poultry and BSE amongst cattle raised on contaminated feed. But food quality and nutritional value, and the treatment of livestock, have prompted wider concerns (Body, 1991; Johnson, 1991; Lacey, 1998). There are fears that such problems will grow as big business strengthens its hold over agricultural production (Goodman and Watts, 1997). Farmers are already dependent upon inputs from agro-chemical and machinery suppliers. They are also increasingly contractually tied to major buyers, including food processors, distributors and retailers. It is these powerful players who set agricultural prices and determine the conditions of production. If commercial pressures for the mass production of cheap food increase, they may conflict with both the long-term interests of consumers and the sustainability of farming livelihoods. A continued search for scale economies will affect small farmers, in particular, eroding the agricultural population and depleting a reservoir of human capital that has traditionally made a positive contribution to environmental management.

Globalization of production means that Southern farmers, too, are increasingly enmeshed within commercial networks, in circumstances where production for export can work against domestic food security (Raynolds, 1997; Thrupp et al, 1995). Other external forces have further increased pressures for export-led production. Countries accumulating significant international debts during the 1970s were forced into structural readjustment programmes, often under conditions determined by the World Bank. Land and water were employed in producing export crops, including cotton and groundnuts, in an attempt to increase foreign exchange earnings, while cultivation of some staple foods declined. At the same time, efforts to reduce state expenditure adversely affected rural development planning, including agricultural extension schemes, credit services and research (Gibbon et al, 1993; Hussain, 1991; Simon et al, 1995).

Such problems have been severe in sub-Saharan Africa, an area that benefited little from the Green revolution (Simon et al, 1995). Traditional farming systems have become overextended and much of Africa has experienced declining per capita food production over the past three decades. South Asia will also be a focus of global hunger in the early 21st century and projections by the United Nations Food and Agriculture Organization (FAO) suggest declining food security in North Africa and West Asia (FAO, 1997; 2002). In part, this reflects demographic growth. The global South will bear the brunt of the projected increase in global population from the current 6 billion to approximately 8 billion by 2020 (Gardner, 1996). More food will be needed; the FAO estimates that annual world demand will total 10.6×10^{12} kilocalories by 2025, more than twice the global supply in 1995 (P Clarke, 1998; Nuffield Council on Bioethics, 1999). Yet it is unclear whether this increase can be delivered. African agriculture is stagnant and, particularly in the south of the continent, the tragedy of AIDS is compounded by its depletion of the rural labour force (FAO, 2002). Elsewhere, the Green revolution is stalling. Throughout much of Asia, including India and China, growth in yields of food staples during the 1990s was only around half the levels achieved during the 1960s and early 1970s (Nuffield Council on Bioethics, 1999).

It is questionable, moreover, whether increased agricultural output and productivity have delivered the socio-economic benefits originally envisaged for the developing world (Glaeser, 1987; Lipton, 1989; Pearse, 1980). Many inputs in the Green revolution package of seeds, agro-chemicals and irrigation have had to be imported. Southern states have suffered increased dependency as government attempts to balance international trading accounts have failed. This has increased the emphasis on production for export at the expense of domestic food security. At the same time, the Green revolution's impacts on rural livelihoods have been inequitable. Throughout South Asia, existing inequalities in the distribution of land and other means of production have resulted in the advantages of agricultural innovation accruing disproportionately to richer farmers (Patnaik, 1995). Even initiatives to assist the poorer majority through provision of cheap credit and co-operatives distributing seed, fertilizer and water have been captured by rural elites. While the largest farmers' yields have grown significantly, smaller producers working with limited resources of capital, inputs and information have rarely enjoyed comparable success (*New Agriculturalist*, 1998c). Spending on inputs has increased the indebtedness of many poor households and resources, including land, have flowed from smaller to larger farmers. For many, 'development' has increased their dependency upon wage labour. Where alternative rural employment opportunities are limited, migration may appear the only option. Many move to urban centres, fuelling problems caused by rapid and unplanned growth (see Chapter 6).

Too high a price: environments under strain

Critical scrutiny of contemporary agriculture's record in delivering increased production and food security has reinforced concerns about the associated environmental penalties (Ruttan, 1991). Humanity has long engineered environmental change to increase agricultural yields (Simmons, 1996). So successful has this been that the extent to which landscapes and ecosystems are man-made – through woodland clearance, drainage and irrigation, enclosure and management, selective breeding, and diffusion of crops and livestock – is often underestimated. It is important to acknowledge a tradition of agricultural stewardship that has created and maintained valued rural environments. But long-term imbalance between the accumulation and depletion of natural, human and man-made capital will render agriculture unsustainable, undermining its productivity and guardianship of resources for future generations. Basic resources, including human health and environmental knowledge rooted in the experience of farming in a particular locality, as well as soil, water and biodiversity, are now exhibiting increasing signs of strain. Growing dependence upon external inputs also means that intensive production of renewable organic resources is depleting non-renewable mineral reserves. Agricultural regimes are, thus, increasingly destructive of the resource base and environmental quality, the two main dimensions of natural capital.

Evidence of declining environmental quality is clearly apparent in intensively farmed regions in the developed world (Conway and Pretty, 1991). Increased use of chemical pesticides and fertilizers has made arable farming the greatest non-public source of water pollution within the EU. Symptoms include the explosive growth of aquatic vegetation, such as algal blooms, caused by over-enrichment of surface water with nitrogen and phosphates leached from fertilizers. This destroys the natural capacity of a water body to produce oxygen, undermining its ability to support other life. Intensive livestock farming can prompt similar effects if large quantities of slurry or silage are released into watercourses. Use of chemicals to support continuous cropping of cultivated land also damages soil quality. Fertilizers cannot mask long-term decline in organic content and breakdown of soil structure. Chemical treatment of land reduces the diversity of micro-organisms, many of which maintain soil health and assist in biological control of pests and diseases.

Overuse and displacement of chemical inputs extends the geographical range of impacts, affecting natural, human and man-made capital deployed in other economic sectors. Farmers themselves are exposed to pesticides at the time of application. In the UK, particular concerns have been expressed about the links between organophosphates used in a variety of applications, including sheep dip, and the incidence of nervous disorders (NFU, 1995; RCP, 1998). Globally, estimated cases of occupational pesticide poisoning number between 3 and 25 million (Gardner, 1996). But pesticides enter the food chain and freshwater systems, affecting extensive populations of human consumers, animals and plant life. Human health problems, including concerns about fertility and childhood cancer, are linked to ingestion of pesticide residues (ENDS, 1999c; White, 1998). Other costs are widely borne; the UK water industry, for example, spends around £120 million annually on treatment to remove pesticides, a bill paid, ultimately, by all customers (Pretty, 1998).

Equally important is the depletion of natural resources, both renewable and non-renewable. Loss of agricultural land is a particular concern, which the FAO estimates will involve forgoing annual production equivalent to 1.25×10^{12} kilocalories by 2025 (P Clarke, 1998). In part, this reflects encroachment by urban and industrial development or the preservation of land as wilderness. But land is also devalued through agricultural mismanagement and overuse. The natural process of soil erosion has long been accelerated by human activity; but modern farming systems have caused unprecedented damage (Simmons, 1996). Attempts to cultivate the High Plains of the USA during the 1920s and 1930s created the classic Dust Bowl. Government incentives to maximize agricultural exports threatened a return to these conditions during the 1970s. American farmers increased their planting of a monoculture of row crops, including cotton, soyabean and corn, while soil conservation measures were often abandoned. The result, by the late 1970s, was an annual soil loss of nearly 2.7 billion tonnes (Potter, 1998).

Soil erosion and degradation are not confined to intensively farmed prairie land in developed countries. The proportion of cropland affected in the global South could be as high as 80 per cent. Soil degradation and loss is severe in regions inhabited by some of the world's poorest people, including uplands in Asia and Latin America, semi-arid areas of sub-Saharan Africa and saline and waterlogged soils in South Asia (Conway, 1997). Some damage is attributable to over-extension of traditional forms of cultivation and herding. Poverty and the inequitable distribution of land rights compound the pressures of population growth, leading to overuse of existing land and the spread of farming into environments too fragile to permit continuous or intensive use (Brookfield and Blaikie, 1987). Clearance and cultivation of marginal land often leads to rapid collapse of both yields and farming livelihoods. The associated damage to the soil is, however, only very slowly reversible. Biodiversity loss also imposes penalties, including the depletion of economically important resources of timber and tree crops. During the past 150 years more than 4 million square kilometres of forest cover have been cleared worldwide, and in recent decades rates of loss have been particularly high in the humid tropics (Williams, 1990a). Some land that proves unsuitable for cultivation can be used as pasture; but other areas become totally unproductive. Overgrazing itself has a degrading effect, as denudation of the vegetative cover exposes the soil to accelerated erosion.

Biodiversity loss is also a facet of resource depletion in developed countries. In North America there is an established distinction between agricultural land, where the range of plant and animal life is limited, and areas conserved for their landscape and habitat value. By contrast, in parts of Europe, including the UK, farmland has itself been an important reservoir of biodiversity; a role threatened by agricultural intensification and monoculture. The decline of mixed farming has been hastened by pursuit of scale economies. Moreover, extension of arable cultivation encouraged by agricultural subsidies has depleted woodland, heath, semi-natural grassland and wetland. Removal of hedgerows and woods has also reflected the reshaping of landscapes to accommodate larger farm machinery. In pastoral areas, overgrazing of moors and upland grasslands has reduced the diversity of plant species (Potter, 1998; Pretty, 1998). The consequent loss of habitat and food sources, together with the direct effects of agro-chemicals, has reduced the size and diversity of farmland wildlife populations (Baldock, 1990; Krebs et al, 1999; Pain and Pienkowski, 1997). Such changes can rebound on agricultural productivity. Modern agriculture creates biological imbalances that increase crop vulnerability to pests, while simultaneously undermining populations of birds and other biological agents of pest control. The result is often greater reliance on chemical pesticides, creating additional costs for farmers and a heightened threat to environmental quality.

Water and wetlands constitute another important aspect of the intersection between farming and the environment. The long-established process of wetland drainage to extend the area available for agriculture and other uses has accelerated sharply in recent decades (Williams, 1990b). Any resultant economic gain must, however, be set against potentially significant losses. Wetland habitats not only support a rich variety of life, but have also traditionally yielded valued resources, including pasture, peat, fish and wildfowl. At least as important is their central role in the delivery of a series of environmental services, including flood control, the protection of coastal lands from erosion and storm damage and the maintenance of water quality (Goss-Custard et al, 1997; Maltby, 1986; Ruddle, 1987; see also Chapter 9 in this volume). Amidst growing concern about climate change, the potential of wetlands as carbon sinks is also receiving increasing attention (Maltby et al, 1992; see Chapter 11 in this volume).

Land reclamation is not the only threat to wetland systems; they also face destruction as a result of the increasing human appropriation of water for other uses (Hill, 1992). Again agriculture is a major driving force for change. Irrigation has contributed greatly to increased agricultural production. Worldwide, over one third of crop yields now come from the one sixth of arable land that is irrigated (*New Agriculturalist*, 1998a). Water use, however, is often unsustainable. Overuse of water, combined with poor drainage, has led to waterlogging and salinization on 10 to 15 per cent of irrigated land. More problematic still is groundwater extraction at rates faster than recharge of source aquifers, already a concern in countries including the USA, China, India, Pakistan, Iran and Libya (Conway, 1997; Gardner, 1996). The exhaustion of groundwater reserves, together with micronutrient depletion and build-up of pest predation, is held responsible for reduction in yield growth in Asia during the last two decades (Nuffield Council on Bioethics, 1999). Water scarcity caused by unsustainable consumption is increasingly regarded not only as a constraint upon development, but also as a potential source of international conflict (Ohlsson, 1995).

Modern agriculture is an increasing consumer of energy and non-renewable minerals. Energy consumption on-farm has itself risen dramatically and human and animal power have given way to imported fossil fuels. On an early 19th-century English farm, the latter accounted for 2 per cent of total energy consumption; by the late 20th century, the proportion had risen to 99 per cent (Simmons, 1996). Overall, some commentators claim, the increased productivity of modern agriculture is illusory, achieved only by the growing application of resources in ways that are not immediately comprehended (Brown, 1998). Particularly significant is agriculture's increasing reliance on off-farm inputs and activities. Upstream, resources are invested both in producing existing inputs of machinery and agro-chemicals, and in research and development to refine and extend the range of inputs. Downstream, agriculture is increasingly tied to complex and resource-demanding systems of food processing and distribution.

There is also evidence that the use of external inputs does not always deliver the intended results. Chemical pest control, for example, is not the permanent solution once anticipated. Global insecticide applications increased tenfold between 1945 and 1989; yet the proportion of crops lost to insects grew from 7 to 13 per cent. The number of diseases, insects and weeds resistant to common forms of chemical control increased from around 180 in 1965 to over 900 by the mid 1990s (Gardner, 1996). For some small farmers in India whose livelihoods depend upon the production of cotton as a cash crop, the falling yields that result from the decreasing effectiveness of pesticides have initiated a cycle of decline that leads to indebtedness, the loss of land rights and, at worst, suicide (Simms, 1999a). The failure of pest control poses wider threats to human health as well as agricultural production as the malarial mosquito is amongst the species developing pesticide resistance. Growing use of antibiotics on livestock has also prompted fears that effective treatment of human and animal disease will be undermined. Official investigations in both the UK and the USA have, consequently, recommended that routine use of antibiotics on livestock be curbed (Whitworth, 1999; Young, 1999).

Sustainable Farming: Different Places, Different Solutions

The environmental penalties of current agricultural practice are readily apparent and the insecurity of many rural livelihoods, throughout the world, is testimony to the economic and social ambiguities of 'progress'. Therefore, agriculture must rediscover its role of environmental stewardship or risk destroying the very basis of its own existence. At the very least, the environmental impacts of agriculture must be reduced. Moves have already been made to define more specific targets for water chemistry, habitat protection and other aspects of environmental quality. Such measures are consistent with a new ethos of efficiency in the use of inputs. Renewable inputs, especially those generated on-farm, should be prioritized over the use of imported inputs and non-renewables. Potentially, agriculture can both reform its own productive practices and supply renewable resources to increase the sustainability of other activities. The socio-economic goals of production must be modified. Increased output and the pursuit of commercial profit are not valid aims if short-term gain is bought at the cost of long-term environmental damage and socio-economic inequity. By contrast, the central purpose of sustainable agricultural development is increasing security, both in food supply for consumers and livelihoods for rural producers. The challenge of providing for a growing global population is formidable and obligations to the future must be matched by responsibilities to promote the welfare of the poorest amongst the world's current inhabitants.

Given the breadth of this ambition and the variety of local circumstances to be addressed, there can be no single recipe for sustainable agricultural development. Policies and practice must acknowledge such existing sources of diversity as socio-economic structures, farming traditions, ecological regimes, resource endowment and management capabilities, and population growth. Attention to the appropriateness of development is an advance upon previous models that imposed order upon the countryside through universal application of the 'superior' knowledge of formally trained external 'experts' (Crush, 1995b). It does not follow, however, that there is any consensus about the means of achieving greater sustainability. In some quarters, sustainable agricultural development is envisaged as the creation of modern science. Others, however, claim that only the pursuit of the natural principles informing organic farming can achieve truly sustainable agriculture.

Ultimately, a more pragmatic approach may necessarily prevail, combining the most desirable elements of these two alternatives. Sustainable development is often presented as involving active partnership between external agents of agricultural improvement and local communities (Alders et al, 1993). Scientists and agricultural extension workers have increasingly recognized the importance of harnessing local environmental knowledge and building upon traditional forms of agriculture, soil conservation and water management (Chambers, 1983; Hecht, 1989; Moock and Rhoades, 1992). If such initiatives are to realize their full potential, however, they will require engagement with larger economic and political questions about the ownership and allocation of resources, which necessitate action at national and international levels.

Viewed in this light, sustainable agricultural development involves much more than enhanced techniques of crop and livestock husbandry, or improved practice in resource management. Agricultural sustainability will require a new commitment to rural development by the governments of many Southern states, including reforms to correct the maldistribution of access rights and ownership of land and water. The momentum for change within the developing world must be supported by external political and financial initiatives, including moves to cancel or reschedule international debt. In the North, the ideal of sustainability has heightened existing controversy over agricultural subsidies. Nor can agricultural change be divorced from debate about the future of a wider economic sector that includes agro-chemical producers and the food industry. The resources devoted worldwide to agricultural research must be redeployed, although the direction of any such change is inevitably contested as a reflection of wider debate about the best foundation for agricultural futures. However, for individual farming communities, especially in the global South, more sustainable development may, ultimately, rest upon reform of systems of finance and credit, the creation of equitable markets for produce, investment in education and the construction of effective and democratic local institutions.

The following sections outline the main elements of a complex debate regarding different visions of sustainable agricultural development. They begin with an exploration of divergent and sometimes contested approaches to reducing farming's environmental impacts and the creation of more secure livelihoods. This is followed by consideration of the need to redistribute key resources, including natural capital, finance and knowledge, which takes the discussion deep into political territory.

Greater Resource Efficiency

Common ends and contested means

A central element of sustainable development is the decoupling of economic growth from environmental disruption and resource depletion. One way of achieving this is to build upon existing initiatives to reduce agricultural dependence on external inputs (Reijntjes et al, 1992). Hence, the UK government – initially through the Ministry of Agriculture (MAFF), and, since 2001, under the auspices of the new Department of the Environment, Food and Rural Affairs (DEFRA) – is one amongst many to have sponsored research on lower intensity and integrated farming. Non-governmental organizations (NGOs) and global agencies, including the World Bank and the FAO, are supporting parallel initiatives in the global South. Low-input agriculture is also commercially endorsed by some food companies and encouraged through increasingly stringent terms regarding pesticide and fertilizer use in their contracts with farmers.

Such changes are promoted in the name of food safety and environmental responsibility; but they also make economic sense for food producers and retailers in enhancing the marketability of their products.

Simple measures, such as avoidance of minor farmyard spills of pesticides, can yield environmental dividends without constraining farmers or imposing economic burdens (ENDS, 1999b). However, questioning the very need for chemical inputs can result in greater environmental benefits. Some farmers are abandoning total pest control for systems of integrated pest management (IPM), a more considered approach to the costs and benefits of pesticides. If pests are controlled only when they threaten economic injury to the producer, pesticide use can be reduced by 20 to 30 per cent (van Emden and Peakall, 1996). Greater accuracy in the timing and placement of chemical inputs further increases their efficiency; up to 75 per cent reduction in fungicide use has been claimed from field trials (Gardner, 1996). Lower-input farming can also make economic sense. Savings on inputs benefit farmers, potentially improving livelihoods, whether for the rural poor in developing countries or for European farmers facing increasing exposure to global markets.

Resource efficiency and environmentally sound management need not conflict with efforts to strengthen rural economies and livelihoods (Francis et al, 1990; Pretty, 1995; 1998; Stanhill, 1990; Trenbath, 1976). Indeed, concerns for resource efficiency and environmental quality are inherent in some of the most productive forms of traditional agriculture in the developing world. The Chinese dike-pond system, for example, achieves high rates of productivity by recycling renewable resources through an integrated operation involving fish farming as well as crop and livestock production (Korn, 1996; Ruddle and Zhong, 1988). Although this system is a product of particular social and environmental circumstances, its combination of mixed farming and reliance on renewable on-farm inputs could be more widely integrated within small-scale and organic farming throughout much of the developing world (Smith, 2001). Collective action within rural communities may also offer a route to economic and environmental benefits. Indian sugar growers, for example, have formed co-operatives for primary processing of sugar from cane and to employ wastes in producing animal feed, industrial alcohol and biofuels. This has reduced dependence upon non-renewable inputs while generating income and rural employment. Some communities use money raised through economic diversification to fund health and education provision (Kinnon, 1997). Hence, resource efficiency supports the less tangible tools that are essential for rural progress: the development of individual, communal and institutional capabilities that enhance people's ability to help themselves.

Environmentally sound farming practices also reduce long-term external costs, including health damage to human and animal populations, biodiversity loss and environmental degradation. Estimation of such costs raises difficult economic and moral questions. The sums involved are likely to be substantial – two studies of pesticide use in US agriculture placed external costs at between US$1.3 and US$8 billion per year – with a correspondingly large scope for savings (Pretty, 1998). However, recognition of the potential scale of gain only heightens discussion about how more resource-efficient and sustainable farming is to be achieved. One pole in the debate is represented by major businesses in sectors including agro-chemicals and food processing, backed by elements of the scientific and political establishment. Such interests advocate technocentric means to ensure that continuing use of off-farm inputs of energy and chemicals is characterized by increasing efficiency. By contrast, campaigners interested in maintaining both the environmental and the social fabric of the countryside, and the growing number of consumers concerned about food quality, dispute the need for such inputs. Instead, they argue for a more 'natural', or organic, agriculture based upon the twin resources of human environmental knowledge and the biosphere itself.

Efficiency through working with nature

Integrated pest management and low-input farming

In practice, farming that aims to work with natural systems need not depart totally from modern agricultural methods. There are, thus, some affinities between elements of the ecocentric and technocentric models of agriculture. A case in point is integrated pest management (IPM), which aims to reduce the use of chemical inputs by complementing more efficient application of pesticides with an enhancement of biological agents (Unwin, 1990; van Emden and Peakall, 1996). Preservation and enhancement of habitat for predator species encourages pest control by birds, insects and bacteria. Methods of cultivation and culture are modified, with tillage and compaction both being used to reduce the levels of insect pests living or pupating in the soil. Other measures, such as removal of crop residues after harvest, can prevent carry-over of pest populations to subsequent years. IPM also harnesses the resource of human observation and decision-making in implementing planned, rather than routinized, pest control. Efficiency in continued pesticide use is determined by the precision of its application. However, the necessary information about the precise distribution of crop predation may increasingly come from sophisticated information technology. In this form, IPM should perhaps be regarded as a facet of the technology-dependent precision farming discussed in a later section (see p. 193).

Refocusing on cropping systems

Alternatively, IPM may be associated with more far-reaching changes in agricultural regimes. The reintroduction of rotation, alternating host and non-host crops can reduce pest and disease predation. Improvements in pest management are also claimed for mixed cropping systems, including inter-cropping and agroforestry. As work in locations including Nigeria and the Philippines shows, the dividend of pest and weed control may be reinforced by beneficial reductions in wind damage, soil moisture loss and soil erosion (Okoji and Moses, 1998; Pattanayak and Mercer, 1998). At the same time, soil and light resources are more fully exploited by a range of species. Soil fertility and health are maintained, and can be directly enhanced by initiatives such as the inclusion of nitrogen-fixing crops in a polyculture (Chandler et al, 1998; King, 1990; Power, 1990). Synergies between the individual elements of mixed cropping systems can lead to significantly higher levels of total productivity than under monoculture, with evidence of particular gains on poorer, acid soils of the tropics (Trenbath, 1976). Moreover, the diversity of products, potentially yielding food, fibre, animal fodder, fuelwood and tree crops, may better sustain farming livelihoods (New Agriculturalist, 1998b; Padoch and de Jong, 1989). These advantages help to explain the prevalence of mixed cropping within indigenous farming systems in the tropics, where diversity of individual cultivars is common, as well as the growth of crops in polyculture. Farmers in temperate zones may, in theory, obtain similar dividends (Francis et al, 1990; Pretty, 1995). However, greater application of mixed cropping will require investment in research and development to define the most advantageous crop combinations.

One possibility already being explored in Europe is mixed cropping involving cultivation of energy and industrial crops. Strips of poplar and willow for coppicing to produce bioenergy could, if planted around conventional crops, yield additional benefits in bio-control and wildlife habitat. Such initiatives also extend production of renewable resources for the wider economy and commercial interest in bioenergy is increasing, albeit fitfully, as a means of mitigating emissions of greenhouse gases (Scholes, 1998; Venendaal et al, 1997; see also Chapter 11 in this volume). Around 5 per cent of EU land area is currently devoted to industrial crops, including inputs for biotextiles, paints and pharmaceuticals. This scale of production looks set to increase, not least because of poor financial returns on conventional crops (Blake, 1998; DEFRA, 2002a; MAFF, 1998).

Going organic

Advocates of organic farming, however, argue that low-input methods and polyculture cannot ensure true environmental sustainability, or provide the quality of food necessary to promote human health and welfare. As originally conceived in the mid 20th century, modern organic agriculture marked a radical break with intensive farming, eschewing agro-chemicals in favour of a greater reliance on the farm's own resources (Blake, 1990; Lampkin, 1992; Smith, 2001). Organic farmers work with biological processes to build the soil and the farm as a single living entity. Such farms commonly raise both stock and crops. There is little concept of waste as by-products from one part of the system are used as raw materials elsewhere. Soil fertility is promoted through application of compost and animal manure, and the adoption of rotational systems – including leguminous 'green manure' crops – designed to balance plants' nutrient requirements and maintain a beneficial diversity of soil micro-organisms (Aubert, 1985). Rotation is also central to the non-chemical management of weeds, pests and diseases. Equivalent principles are applied to livestock husbandry, where emphasis is placed on preventive healthcare and use of homeopathic remedies, rather than conventional treatment of disease.

Reassessment of relations between economic and biological systems may yield more than an immediate reduction in environmental pollution. Organic agriculture can be highly productive, thus contributing to food security. However, given efforts to curb overproduction in developed countries, it may be beneficial that organic farming in temperate regions generally results in yields and stocking rates lower than those of conventional agriculture (Halberg et al, 1994; Lampkin, 1992). The security of farming livelihoods should be maintained by a combination of benefits, including reduced input costs and lesser vulnerability to fluctuations in demand for single commodities. State funding under initiatives such as the UK's Organic Farming Scheme – although hardly generous by comparison with total expenditure on agricultural support – may also facilitate transition to organic farming. Some UK water companies are experimenting with payments to farmers who adopt low-input or organic agriculture, as a cost-effective way of curbing water pollution (Wessex Water, 2002). However, the viability of an expanding organic sector rests chiefly upon a growing consumer appetite for its output. UK demand for organic produce increased by 400 per cent between 1990 and 1998 (Craig, 1998; Freeman, 1999). The value of annual sales of organic food and drink topped £1 billion for the first time in the year ending March 2003 and further growth to around £3 billion is projected by 2005 (Day, 2001; Soil Association, 2003). Significant growth has also been experienced in some European markets – particularly Denmark, Austria and Switzerland – and in North America (Hamm et al, 2002; Henley et al, 2001). Here, too, these moves have been encouraged by concerns about the safety and quality of food produced by intensive agriculture. Against this background, organic goods have attracted both premium prices and the support of major food distributors and retailers (Clover, 1999; *Guardian*, 2001; Solman, 2000).

Organic farmers are also in the vanguard of efforts to boost agricultural incomes and rural employment by on-farm processing, including butchery and the manufacture of dairy products such as cheese and yoghurt. Returns are increased where food is marketed locally, either through conventional channels or popular new initiatives such as co-operatives, farmers' markets and box schemes that distribute goods directly to customers (Herbert, 1999; Nuttall, 1999b; Pretty, 1998). Such moves towards more localized trade and greater balance between production and ecological capacity may yield further dividends (see Welford, 1995 for discussion of new models of regional development). Consumers benefit from improvements in food quality and freshness, and resources used in food packaging and extensive distribution systems are saved (Norberg-Hodge, 1998). At the same time, the very foundations of rural life may be reinforced (Flora, 1990; Pretty, 1998). New enterprises associated with organic agriculture can contribute directly to increased employment opportunities and enhancement of managerial capabilities in rural areas. In tandem with other forms of rural economic diversification, including tourism and commercial activity enabled by new information technologies, they also maintain a critical mass of population and income. This is vital to support services, including shops, schools and public transport, which underpin the social sustainability of rural communities.

A green light for a better future?
The agro-ecological approaches outlined above possess considerable potential to promote sustainable productivity through small-scale agriculture. Such initiatives can form an effective platform for rural development, combining long-term environmental protection with greater immediate security of livelihood and food supply. This does not, however, guarantee the widespread adoption of such systems. Particularly in the global South, many of the rural people who would benefit most from greater security or self-sufficiency are landless, not least as a result of previous attempts to modernize agriculture. Even those still farming may be frustrated by powerful vested interests. A study of Thai cotton producers, for example, reveals barriers to the introduction of IPM, despite widespread awareness of its economic and environmental advantages. Farmers find it difficult to change production methods without the support of their customers or the government. They also face hostility from producers and distributors of agricultural inputs, unwilling to surrender lucrative markets for their goods (Castella et al, 1999).

Moreover, the contribution of agro-ecological ideas to the larger project of sustainable development continues to be fiercely disputed. It is clear that reduced reliance on chemical inputs will diminish the environmental impact of agricultural production. More specific claims for the environmental benefits of organic farming are supported by studies documenting improvements in soil quality and biodiversity, including the restoration of bird and wildlife populations on agricultural land (Armstrong-Brown et al, 2000; Azeez, 2000; Lytton-Hitchins et al, 1994; Reganold et al, 1993). Environmental gains may be complemented by higher rates of profitability for organic farming (Cobb et al, 1999). Indeed, evidence that differentials between organic and conventional regimes are most marked in the driest years seems increasingly persuasive in a context of climate change (Lockeretz et al, 1984). However, even organic agriculture may satisfy only the weaker criteria for sustainable development in diminishing the pace of environmental decline, rather than necessarily delivering an overall improvement in environmental quality or social welfare.

Such doubts are reinforced by the manner of organic agriculture's recent growth. While some champions of agri-business continue to attack organic farming, questioning claims made for the superiority of its products (Avery, 2000; Norton, 2000), others see new commercial opportunities in growing consumer demand. The consequent creation of an industrial organic sector is particularly evident in North America; in California, for example, five giant farms control half of the US$400 million organic produce market (Pollan, 2001). This results in a style of farming that avoids chemical inputs, but otherwise replicates many of the failings of modern food production. Crops are grown in monoculture, sometimes to provide the ingredients for processed foods that are produced and sold many kilometres away from the farm gate. Moreover, the advent of mass production is eroding the organic premium. This may extend organic markets; but it also threatens the livelihoods of many smaller producers. The growth of an international trade in organic produce is also evident in Europe, particularly in the UK, where imports currently account for 75 per cent of the organic food market (Left, 2002). More generally, demand from the affluent West is the driving force behind the increasing certification of farms in Eastern Europe, particularly Poland and Hungary, for organic agriculture (Connolly, 2001). Such moves may help to secure a future for farmers struggling to survive the transition to a market economy; but they are hardly consistent with the ideal of the local sourcing of food. This, together with concerns about the profitability of domestic organic production, led the UK government to launch an action plan for organic food and farming in 2002, which aims to ensure that domestic producers meet 70 per cent of UK organic demand by 2010 (DEFRA, 2002b). However, the extent to which a truly localized trade could be established in the UK is questionable, given the current concentration of the population in urban centres – especially in south-east England – away from major regions of agricultural production.

On a global scale, critics question whether organic systems are sufficiently productive to guarantee total food security, especially given the projected growth and urbanization of populations in developing countries (DeGregori, 1996; see Woodward, 1998, for a counter-argument). Agro-environmental approaches have also been criticized as inconsistent with developing countries' aspirations for economic modernization. Labour-intensive agriculture may be advantageous in providing immediate employment for the rural population. In the longer term, however, it could hamper the release of labour for more productive industrial employment, which some commentators see as an essential foundation for development (Pinstrup-Andersen et al, 1999). Resolving such claims is by no means easy. Indeed, the very premise of some challenges is open to debate. Rather than allowing the functioning of agriculture to be dictated by demographic growth, for example, greater emphasis should arguably be placed on curbing population increase as an important step towards more sustainable development.

Greater reliance on agro-environmental approaches would create uncertainties, potentially involving both costs and benefits (Madden, 1990). Organic farming currently accounts for only a small proportion of agricultural production in most developed countries (Foster and Lampkin, 2000). Estimates for 2001 indicate that 3.3 per cent of the EU agricultural area was in conversion to organic cultivation or already in production; in the UK the proportion was slightly higher at just under 4 per cent (Organic Centre Wales, 2002). Substantial extension of this sector might alter the shape of both domestic and international agricultural markets. Models of the impact of significant conversion to organic production in the UK and Germany confirm that domestic food security and farming livelihoods would be preserved. However, a reduction in the numbers of grazing livestock would be accompanied by increased production of forage crops. This would reduce demand for animal feed imported from sources as distant as Brazil. It is difficult to determine whether the effects would be harmful for Brazil, reflecting the loss of foreign earnings, or beneficial in releasing resources to meet domestic needs, including land for redistribution to the rural poor (Midmore and Lampkin, 1994).

Pinstrup-Andersen et al (1999) question the extent to which agro-ecological systems alone can combat the low and declining soil fertility experienced in many developing countries. Techniques such as the cultivation of leguminous crops to produce green manure are considered inappropriate where rainfall is inadequate and land is scarce. They argue, therefore, that agro-ecological approaches must be employed in tandem with the selective application of chemical fertilizers and improved seeds if declines in yields and soil fertility are to be reversed. This makes a pragmatic case that agricultural futures lie not with total adherence to agro-ecological ideas, but in a balanced package that retains access to modern agricultural inputs. This may fall short of the ideal of raising environmental quality; but it arguably represents the most effective and immediate means to combine improvements in food security and rural incomes with reduced environmental damage.

Efficiency through technology

Precision farming
For some farmers in North America and Western Europe the answer to commercial and environmental pressures for greater resource efficiency lies not in engagement with agricultural traditions, but in a very different approach to knowledge. Precision farming involves initial capital investment in information technology in the expectation of long-term gains through greater effectiveness of agro-chemical use. Sensors mounted on tractors, harvesters and other agricultural equipment are employed together with remote sensing platforms to generate site-specific data, covering such variables as soil nutrient and moisture content, crop development and disease status

(Clark and Lee, 1998; Lu et al, 1997; Weiss, 1996). Using this information, the application of inputs can be more finely judged, costs reduced and the quality of the end product improved. Mapping of insect distribution within individual fields, for example, allows control measures to be applied only where necessary, cutting insecticide use by up to 60 per cent (Abel, 1998b).

Precision farming based on the use of capital-intensive equipment on large farms has little relevance for most Southern producers (compare with Wolf and Buttel, 1996). But some analysts look forward to its extension, calling for greater efforts to broaden access to the new technologies of geographical information systems (GIS), global positioning systems (GPS) and remote sensing. The development of inexpensive equipment for use by small farmers and in developing countries would help to provide the information necessary to improve production efficiency and yields (Pinstrup-Andersen et al, 1999). In the short term, however, devoting resources to research in this area seems a dubious priority as many of the poorest farmers in developing countries are hard pressed to afford any agro-chemical inputs.

Biotechnology

Genetic modification is another innovative application of technology to agriculture, which its promoters claim provides 'one piece in the puzzle of sustainable development' (Monsanto, 1998). Biotechnology companies present their work as a safe and beneficial extension of conventional initiatives in the selective breeding of crops and livestock. Indeed, the new science appears to convey added benefits in ensuring quick and easy identification of desirable traits and a more controlled introduction of the genes that determine these traits into plant and animal species (Persley and Doyle, 1999). Biotechnology research began during the early 1980s; but as recently as 1994/1995, no genetically modified (GM) crops were grown commercially. Subsequent development has been rapid but geographically uneven, with early adoption being concentrated in North America. In the USA, GM seeds accounted for one third of the area under corn and half that devoted to soybeans and cotton in 1999 (Abel, 1999). By 2001, 44 million hectares were under GM crops worldwide, chiefly in the USA, Canada, Argentina and China. Ten other countries grew small amounts; but in the EU a moratorium on commercial GM cultivation restricted planting to small-scale trials (Vidal, 2001b).

Taken at face value, arguments for biotechnology appear strong. Genetic modification is being used to increase crop yields and improve the storage and handling characteristics of foodstuffs. Crop varieties are also being created that exhibit enhanced resistance to pests and diseases, and tolerance of drought and salt. Farmers are thus provided with greater security against risk of crop failure. Genetic modification to reduce water consumption by crops is especially significant, given concerns about the sustainability of irrigation and increasing aridity as a result of climate change (Rozenzweig and Hillel, 1998). Consumption of other inputs should also be reduced. For example, Monsanto claimed that their GM potatoes would require 40 per cent less chemical insecticide than existing varieties and similar characteristics have been introduced into maize, cotton and oil-seed rape (Abel, 1998a; Monsanto, 1998). This should reduce both farmers' costs and environmental pollution.

Although greater productivity is a dubious priority for developed countries already awash with surplus food, in the global South current hunger and poverty arguably create an imperative for the adoption of biotechnology (Conway, 1999; Nuffield Council on Bioethics, 1999). GM crops promise increased production without total reliance on conventional chemical and mechanical inputs, and their attendant environmental and financial costs. In theory, therefore, improved nutrition and food security should be combined with rising farm incomes, erosion of rural poverty and defence of environmental quality (Macilwain, 1999). Biotechnology, which is claimed to deliver as much as a threefold increase in the productivity of farmland, could also be an important guardian of biodiversity and fragile environments if it curbs current trends to extend the cultivated area beyond ecologically sustainable limits.

A second generation of GM species may further enhance biotechnology's potential to contribute to more sustainable development, especially in the South. Innovations include crops that facilitate plant nutrition, such as cereals capable of fixing nitrogen from the air and extracting phosphorus from acid soils. Equally important is the development of 'functional foods'. Potatoes and bananas, for example, are being developed to carry edible vaccines against disease. Efforts are also being made to improve the nutritional characteristics of staple foods, including enhancement of protein content. Work to produce vitamin A-enriched rice will overcome a dietary deficiency that causes eye damage currently affecting 14 million children in the developing world (Nuffield Council on Bioethics, 1999; Nuttall, 1999a; Wambugu, 1999). In addition, research on large animal transgenics aims to enhance the nutritional value of products such as milk (Whitelaw, 1999).

Curse or cure?

Biotechnology is, however, highly controversial. Opponents see it not as fostering more sustainable development, but as its very antithesis – a dangerous experiment that could undermine human health, environmental quality, economic self-sufficiency and social welfare (Charles, 2001; Ho, 1999; Lappé and Bailey, 1998). Concerns about biotechnology, expressed by some scientists and environmentalists since the late 1980s, have become a focus for public debate and political uncertainty (Goldsmith, 1999; Wheale and McNally, 1990). The organic movement, in the UK embodied particularly in the Soil Association, and environmental groups such as Greenpeace have made opposition to GM crops a major campaigning issue (see for example, Soil Association, 2002). Furthermore, in the wake of previous concerns about food safety and quality, many consumers distrust the reassurances about biotechnology offered by government and big business.

Public reaction against GM material in foods has been clearly voiced in Europe since the late 1990s. The UK, perhaps because of the strength of its domestic biotechnology industry, has also had particular experience of direct action by environmental protesters to destroy field-scale trials of GM crops (Vidal, 2001a). Consequently, key food manufacturers and retailers have fought shy of supporting GM agriculture (ENDS, 1999d; Riley, 1998). In turn, EU governments have discussed curbing GM trials and concerns about the adequacy of GM licensing laws led to the *de facto* suspension of EU approval for new crops in 1998. The US government responded by invoking the principle of free trade; it has protested unofficially to the World Trade Organization (WTO) about discrimination against GM foods and threatened trans-Atlantic sanctions to force the entry of GM seeds produced by US multinationals into European markets (Brown, 2002; Murray, 1999). New EU licensing laws introduced in 2002 potentially signalled an end to the European moratorium on new crop approvals, although continued disagreement amongst the member states prevented any immediate positive decisions to this effect. In the UK, a first step, involving approval for the commercial cultivation of a specific variety of GM maize, was taken in 2004. However, Bayer, the German biotechnology company concerned, subsequently withdrew its application, claiming that regulatory constraints made the venture uneconomic. The stringent standards set within the EU for risk assessment and associated rules concerning the labelling and traceability of GM content in all foodstuffs also seem likely to attract continued American hostility (Osborn, 2002a; Vidal, 2004).

US exports of agricultural commodities have already been affected by concerns about GM foods and the introduction of strict labelling regimes in overseas markets, not just in Europe, but elsewhere, including Japan, Taiwan and South Korea. Consequently, a new ambiguity is evident in North American farmers' attitudes to GM agriculture. Acreages continue to rise; but a survey of members of the American Corn Growers' Association revealed that 78 per cent would consider abandoning GM crops to recover lost export markets (BBC, 2002; Vidal, 2001b). US consumers, too, seem to be reconsidering their previous passive acceptance of biotechnology, leading to increasing calls for the labelling of GM foods (*The Campaign*, 2003). An initial attempt in 2002 to make such labelling mandatory in the state of Oregon, although unsuccessful, attracted considerable publicity (Oregon Concerned Citizens for Safe Foods, 2002). The GM sector is not, therefore, growing with the speed previously anticipated. This is reflected in falling investment in biotechnology research by leading pharmaceutical companies, static profits and depressed stock market valuations. A desire for consolidation and cost-cutting has encouraged several high-profile agri-business mergers, involving Monsanto and Pharmacia in the USA, and Novartis and AstraZeneca in Europe (Vidal, 2001b).

As yet, the developing world remains largely marginalized in much of this international debate. Some states, including China, Argentina and Cuba, have embraced biotechnology (Saywell, 1998). The UN Development Programme has also endorsed GM crops. However, even in the face of the drought and famine experienced in 2002, concerns about potential impacts on health, the environment and trade led Zambia to refuse food aid in the form of GM maize (Carroll, 2002). Domestic controversy also reigns in many developing countries. In India, opinion amongst scientists, politicians and farmers is sharply divided and such tensions may be expected to increase still further in the wake of government approval for the first commercial GM crop – a type of cotton – in 2002. India's change of heart has also increased the pressure on other major Southern states, such as Brazil, to embrace GM agriculture (Branford, 2002; Jayaraman, 1999; Kingsnorth, 1999; Neto, 1999a; 1999b).

Public concerns about biotechnology frequently reflect perceived threats to human health and the environment (ESRC Global Environmental Change Programme, 1999). Although government regulatory agencies concur that, in principle, GM material poses no greater risk to health than novel food produced by conventional means, the long-term effects remain largely unexplored (Butler and Reichhardt, 1999a). The environmental impacts of biotechnology are equally uncertain. Research sponsored by DEFRA in the UK seems to have reinforced some earlier concerns about the risks of genetic pollution and the transfer of characteristics such as herbicide resistance to non-crop species through cross-fertilization (Chamberlain and Stewart, 1999; Connor,

1999; Crawley, 1999; NIAB, 2002). Increasing use of GM technology could also accelerate the genetic erosion caused by failure to conserve traditional plant species (ENDS, 1999a). Overall, however, the message from UK government advisers remains that the long-term implications of GM crops for biodiversity are unclear (Butler and Reichhardt, 1999b). Against this background, opposition to testing and commercial cultivation of GM crops rests more on the precautionary principle than any specific risk (Ho, 1999).

Hostility towards biotechnology is also a function of concern about increasing corporate influence over food production and farming livelihoods, and the prospect of commercial ownership of the very building blocks of life. The embedding of modern agriculture within wider business structures has already caused a significant shift of power from the farm to the corporate headquarters of agro-chemical companies, commodity brokers and food processors. The advent of biotechnology, a sector dominated by only five or six major companies, threatens new extremes of dependency. Indeed, it may prevent farmers themselves from making further contributions to agricultural innovation. This clearly runs counter to designs for more sustainable development that aim to increase rural communities' own independent capabilities as a foundation for greater economic, social and environmental security. Already biotechnology companies provide packages of seeds and herbicides that must be used together, supplied under contract terms that curb farmers' rights over the use and disposal of these inputs (Lappé and Bailey, 1998). GM technology also makes it possible to ensure that farmers purchase fresh seed each year, rather than retaining a portion of the harvest for replanting. Although biotechnology companies have renounced the use of a 'terminator' gene that renders seed infertile after a single harvest, the potential threat remains.

Corporate influence could be further strengthened as systems of intellectual property protection and patenting now include the natural world. Biotechnology companies are thus able to claim legal ownership of the genes that they isolate and the novel plant varieties created. Such rights are arguably necessary to encourage private-sector investment in biotechnology research. However, they may create a stranglehold over the supply of seeds and research to develop new crop varieties, including those based on conventional selective breeding. The actions of biotechnology companies in exploring and appropriating the genetic resources of the global South have given rise to charges of 'bio-piracy' (Shiva, 1999). In theory, the 1992 Convention on Biological Diversity enables national governments to assert their ownership of native biodiversity and to control exports of genetic material. The FAO-sponsored International Treaty on Plant Genetic Resources for Food and Agriculture, set to enter into force in 2004, should also establish a legal framework for the equitable distribution of benefits deriving from the use of such material. It remains to be seen, however, whether such initiatives can prevent effective control of important bio-resources from passing into the hands of multinational business (Barton, 1999; Shrybman, 1999).

Although some developing countries see positive potential in the science of genetic modification, many governments are mistrustful of Northern-based biotechnology companies. African states, in particular, have successfully argued for an international Bio-Safety Protocol that will allow governments to refuse entry to imported genetically modified organisms (GMOs) where they feel that associated environmental risks or socio-economic impacts are unacceptable (McCarthy, 2000; Masood, 1999). Such moves also reflect the suspicion, shared by some in the developed world, that biotechnology companies are being disingenuous in arguing that their products are necessary to prevent global hunger and poverty (Jury, 1998; Kimbrell, 1998). Even crops specifically created to combat the effects of malnutrition in the developing world may not be immediately beneficial. GM rice, for example, cannot of itself end the vitamin deficiencies that cause blindness and other illnesses: in the absence of a balanced diet containing sufficient quantities of fats and oils, the body is unable to absorb the additional vitamin A (Schnapp and Schiermeier, 2001). Moreover, inadequate farming incomes in the global South are not simply a result of low productivity. They also reflect a legacy of debt and inequitable terms of trade, including the distortion of Southern markets by subsidized imports from Europe and North America. As the first thrust of biotechnology is directed towards increasing the productivity of Northern agriculture, its most immediate effects on the developing world could be to exacerbate the problems caused by the dumping of cheap imported food.

Biotechnology is far from the only answer to food security problems. As noted above, agri-environmental approaches are generally advanced as more sustainable routes to greater productivity and improved livelihoods. But initiatives in areas other than production will be equally important. These should address, for example, failings in food storage and the infrastructure of distribution that cause 10 to 15 per cent of the harvest to go to waste in parts of Africa, Asia and Latin America (FAO, 1998a). A broader social and political agenda must also underpin efforts to improve access and entitlement to food (Bush, 1996; Dréze and Sen, 1990; Fine, 1997; Macrae and Zwi, 1994). Poverty, the maldistribution of land and other resources, social dislocation and discrimination, and war are greater obstacles to universal food security than any agricultural deficiencies.

Contested solutions

The different, and often mutually exclusive, systems discussed above do more than confirm the lack of unanimity about what constitutes sustainable agricultural development. They reflect fundamentally different attitudes towards the relationship between science and nature, towards the social and environmental dimensions of sustainability and regarding the geographical scales at which the foundations of a more sustainable agriculture should be laid. Furthermore, the discussion reveals the importance of setting farms and farming communities within a wider context. Progress towards sustainable development does not only rest on the efficiency with which the individual farmer deploys resources. Account must also be taken of the enmeshing of modern farming within commercial networks that extend upstream to the producers of agricultural inputs and downstream to food processors and retailers. It is within this wider context that many of the most important decisions about the commitment of resources to particular types of agriculture will continue to be taken, so long as systems of world trade remain as constituted today. However, farming is also subject to more overtly political determinants of the resources available to individual producers. Systems of state subsidy and regulation are perhaps the most obvious political influence upon agriculture. Farming futures are also bound up in the outcome of intergovernmental negotiations regarding the creation of global trading regimes. At a national level, moreover, the maldistribution of such basic resources as land and water within the farming population is a reflection of the equally distorted distribution of political power in many Southern states. Issues of ownership, access and distribution of resources are thus a vital part of any discussion of sustainable agricultural development.

Redistributing Resources

Key dimensions of change

The resources employed in farming are diverse, ranging from traditional ecological knowledge to modern applications of information technology and bioscience. Here the discussion will focus on the potential for creating greater sustainability through the redeployment of resources in three critical contexts. First, it is important to explore the distribution of the most basic agricultural resources of land and water. Current inequalities in access to such resources in much of the developing world suggest that land reform is an essential foundation for greater security and sustainability. The potential political ramifications of such an argument are profound. The second theme, state subsidies for agricultural producers, is also marked by a high degree of political sensitivity. Here, the geographical focus of the discussion shifts to Europe and the continuing debate about reform of the CAP. While there is little dispute that agricultural systems encouraged by the CAP are failing, it is by no means clear that the political will exists to redeploy state funding to create a more sustainable countryside. Third, it is logical to explore the resources of research and development that are being deployed to map out agricultural futures. Recent developments in biotechnology have heightened fears that these vital resources are being disproportionately directed towards projects that will create the largest commercial profits, rather than those that will safeguard rural environments, livelihoods and food supply for the global majority.

Access to basic resources: land reform in the developing world

Maldistribution of access to, and ownership of, land is profound throughout much of the global South. In Peru, El Salvador, Brazil, the Philippines and many other countries, the richest 10 per cent of the population own at least 70 per cent of all land. Worldwide, the FAO estimates that 168 million rural households possess little or no land. Most of these people are rooted to the bottom of the socio-economic hierarchy and suffer the greatest insecurity of livelihood and food supply. If there is to be any significant erosion of current social inequity, sustainable development must address the marginalization of this substantial rural population. The redistribution of land rights is arguably an essential foundation for such social progress. Moreover, land reform is also consistent with the environmental principles that inform sustainable development.

Many of the landless rural poor survive through a combination of wage labour and cultivation of marginal land, which they occupy either as squatters or as tenants. In neither case do most households have the security of tenure to encourage ecologically sustainable farming. Instead, effort is necessarily concentrated on production to meet immediate need for food, fuel and income. Continuous cultivation may also be prompted by farmers' fears that others will take possession of any land left fallow. Landlords, especially absentees whose agricultural and environmental knowledge is limited, often increase the pressure on farmers to maximize short-term returns at the expense of sustainability. This general problem is exacerbated by the fragility of much of the land involved, which compounds the environmental penalties caused by overuse. Continued clearance of marginal land has important implications for deforestation and loss of biodiversity, and for climate and hydrological regimes. Resources of timber, wild food plants and game are lost and the cleared land remains fertile for only a few seasons.

Land reform could remove the injustice that perpetuates poverty and environmental damage. The redistribution of good-quality agricultural land, combined with a greater security of tenure, would help to ensure that households possess the means of providing for themselves and the incentive to plan for the long-term. Secure tenure might also improve small farmers' access to credit and the other inputs required for more productive farming. Although universal success cannot be guaranteed, experience suggests that where small farmers are more equitably treated, they use land sustainably and productively (Feder et al, 1988). Indeed, land reform is an important foundation for the spread of polyculture, agroforestry and other agro-environmental initiatives described above, which all require security of tenure to underpin the commitment to investment in long-term sustainability of production.

The arguments favouring land redistribution as an effective step towards more sustainable agricultural development in much of the South are strong. Yet the attempted execution of reform, in practice, is often flawed. In Zimbabwe, for example, the potential welfare benefits of a state-led programme of land reform and resettlement pursued since independence in 1980 have been increasingly undermined by violence, corruption and political controversy (Kinsey, 1999; Meldrum, 2002; Moyo, 2000; Winter, 2000). Elsewhere, pressures for change are often resisted by powerful political and economic elites (Diskin, 1991). Experience in various parts of Asia and Latin America has shown that even when governments pledge to implement land reform, they can be defeated by vested interests, corruption and even the exercise of military power (Brockett, 1990; Putzel, 1992). Where inequity in landownership is a function of wider political and economic inequality, the prospects for land redistribution remain poor. Established elites also block moves to redistribute resources to favour the small farmer in other ways (Thiesenhusen, 1995). For land reform to be effective it must be accompanied by a reorientation of agricultural research, extension schemes and credit provision to meet the needs of small farmers and previously marginalized sections of the community, especially women. Increased resources must also be devoted to providing rural infrastructure, including education, training and energy services (Conway, 1997; Dudley et al, 1992; FAO, 1998b; *New Agriculturalist*, 1998c).

The statement of the ideal of sustainable development, itself, does nothing to alter the essential political reality in many Southern states. Attention to land reform, however, confirms the character of sustainable development as a project that rests on political commitment to change. The creation of a political will for land reform cannot be separated from wider efforts to extend democracy. Some of the necessary impetus for reform could be provided externally if international aid donors were to link their assistance more explicitly to progress in land redistribution. However, reliance upon such neo-colonial pressures sits awkwardly with a commitment to greater autonomy for local communities in defining their own needs and the best means of achieving them. Pressures for reform ultimately have greater power where they involve the mobilization of the rural poor themselves through the formation of groups such as the Brazilian Landless Rural Labour Movement (de David, 1992). Encouragement of effective local democratic institutions figures explicitly in the programme of sustainable development advanced by the FAO (FAO, 1998b). Such sponsorship is important; but, in practice, the barriers to popular democracy and agricultural reform remain formidable.

Funding production: state agricultural subsidies in the developed world

Although the context is very different, reform of state support for agriculture within the EU is as dogged by political controversy as the land reform discussed above. The need to curb the growth of agricultural expenditure, first highlighted in the 1980s, resurfaced during the 1990s in the light of planned EU enlargement into Central and Eastern Europe, which will greatly increase its agricultural capacity (European Commission, 1997b; 1998). European policy has also been subject to growing criticism from the USA, Australia, New Zealand and other major agricultural exporters. The argument that the CAP constitutes an obstacle to free trade and must therefore be dismantled, and, particularly, the invocation of the powers of the WTO against agricultural subsidies and protectionism, have reinforced the pressures for reform (Potter, 1998). A series of changes to the CAP have thus been made since the mid 1980s. Initially, these selectively reduced support prices, introduced production quotas and provided financial incentives to set arable land aside from production. Only in 2003, and after prolonged wrangling, was an apparently more decisive move secured, which should change the basis on which most subsidies are paid after 2005. This breaks the link between payments and production levels and should remove the incentive to produce ever-greater food surpluses (EU, 2003).

The latest reforms offer some hope that the EU can move beyond initiatives designed simply to curb growth in output and, instead, begin to address the larger task of creating more sustainable agriculture. This will involve positive support for environmental stewardship and the production of environmental goods, rather than simply a reduction in the incentive for destructive agricultural intensification. The essential basis of farming operations must also be re-examined in order to create a system in which the security of farming livelihoods rests on the production of good quality food, in quantities that reflect consumer demand. A greater share of funding must also be devoted to rural economic diversification, so that income from farming is complemented by new opportunities in tourism, light industry and information-based services (see, for example, Ibery et al, 1998). The existing agri-environmental strand of the CAP, introduced in 1992, offers one model of what is possible. Its provisions have been used by national governments to offer financial support for schemes with aims including reduced water pollution, promotion of low-input and organic farming, and arable conversion to grassland and wetland (MAFF, 2000; Potter, 1998). Such changes remain marginal, however, and in their first four years of operation agri-environmental initiatives accounted for only 3.6 per cent of total EU farm support (Potter, 1998). A much more radical shift in expenditure patterns will be necessary in future.

Ironically, it may be the current parlous state of agriculture and the countryside in many EU states that advances the strongest case for further change. Political calls for reform have grown as perceptions of crisis have been sharpened by specific events, including the spread of BSE and the outbreak of foot-and-mouth disease that affected Britain particularly badly in 2001. Responses in the UK itself have included the creation of a new government ministry (DEFRA) which brings together for the first time responsibility for the environment, farming and rural policy. Even before this, research commissioned by the former Ministry of Agriculture endorsed the view that expenditure should be shifted away from production subsidies towards support for less intensive farming, higher standards of animal husbandry and environmental stewardship (Wintour, 2001a). These conclusions are reinforced by DEFRA's publication of a *Strategy for Sustainable Food and Farming* (2002c) with provisions including additional funding for agri-environmental schemes, greater attention to maintaining farming livelihoods, and initiatives in food quality assurance and regional branding. It may be, as Drummond and Marsden (1999) have argued in other contexts, that a crisis created by the obvious failure of existing systems creates not only the need for change, but also an opportunity to put in place a new regulatory regime that will promote more sustainable development.

Much, however, remains uncertain. Critics continue to worry that the CAP will have disastrous environmental impacts in the new EU member states of central and eastern Europe (BirdLife International, 2004; RSPB, 2004). This reflects concerns that existing low-input systems and many small farms will be swept away amidst the economic realities of an enlarged common market for agricultural produce. It is significant, also, that current CAP reform proposals do not envisage that change in the basis on which subsidies are allocated will be accompanied by a significant reduction in expenditure. The domestic political power of the farming lobby in France and several other member states has habitually blocked any moves in the latter direction.

A case can be made that dramatic cuts in agricultural subsidies would prove counter-productive. If funding were withdrawn, farming incomes and profits would fall sharply, at least in the short term, prompting decline in the value of land and other assets, and accelerating the demise of small and marginal farms. This loss of individual livelihoods would remove many of the farmers who most embody agricultural traditions of stewardship, and whose manpower and knowledge are essential for the maintenance of the environmental and cultural fabric of the countryside. Biodiversity and landscape quality could decline in some areas if grassland were abandoned to scrub or commercial forestry. Mediterranean Europe would also suffer increased soil erosion if terracing and other conservation measures were allowed to decay. None of this, however, justifies the planned continuation of expenditure at the current level of £30 billion per year, most of which will still go to a small minority of large farmers.

The CAP reforms of 2003 will, moreover, do little to curb the distorting effects of subsidies and protectionist policies on world trade and development. Agricultural producers in developing countries will still be denied access to European markets for much of their output, while continuing to face competition at home from subsidised EU exports. Nor is the EU alone in maintaining substantial funding for its farmers. Together, the EU, the USA, Japan and other developed countries spend over US$300 billion per year on agricultural support. The unwillingness of an increasingly assertive group of developing states to accept such unfair conditions for international trade was one key reason why the 2003 WTO summit in Cancun ended in failure (Watkins, 2003).

Future capacity: research and development

Agricultural futures rest on more than land and money; investment in research and development is also crucial. Such activity has an important role in determining what is deemed practical as a foundation for agricultural progress. It is a long-standing concern of critics of modern intensive agriculture that the substantial investment in research made by major producers of agro-chemicals and other industrial inputs have few equivalents in the organic sphere. In the absence of this commercial involvement, research into the refinement of organic farming and other agri-environmental initiatives has often been hampered by a lack of resources. Such biases increase the organic sector's difficulties in overturning its image as old-fashioned and impractical, and establishing itself as a mainstream alternative to conventional modern farming. State research spending has often followed the same pattern. During the late 1990s, UK government expenditure on research and development for organic farming was the equivalent of only 1.2 per cent of the total MAFF research budget (Craig, 1998; Marsh, 1998). Much more could and should be done by European governments, under the provisions of the EU's agri-environmental policy, to support research on organic farming methods and improvements in crop varieties and productivity. Some limited progress in this respect is evident in the DEFRA action plan on organic farming, which identifies the organic sector as 'a high priority for research spending', supported by the commitment of £5 million over five years, starting in the financial year 2003/4 (DEFRA, 2002b).

The advent of genetic modification has caused fresh controversy about the direction of research. Its critics deplore the huge investments made in biotechnology, often arguing that an equivalent commitment of research funding to the improvement of polycultural systems, low-input farming and organic agriculture would better meet the goal of environmentally sustainable and socially equitable development. Even some commentators who accept the desirability of biotechnology argue that if it is to be effective in countering hunger and poverty in the developing world, resources for research must be redirected. To date, priority has been given to crops such as soya that are the staples of modern intensive agriculture. In attempting to capture these most lucrative markets, biotechnology companies have sidelined the interests of farmers and consumers in the global South. Commercial imperatives for change are weak. Alternative institutional capacities must therefore be constructed that will redirect research towards improving staple crops for developing countries. Comparisons with the Green revolution, when many important innovations were a product of publicly funded research, suggest the need for a renewed commitment to public funding for agricultural research.

Some such moves are already evident. The Rockefeller Foundation, previously an active promoter of the Green revolution, is now funding biotechnology research. Some developing countries, including Kenya and Cuba, are strengthening their national research programmes, while India spent US$15 million on transgenic plant research during the 1990s (Jayaraman, 1999). However, as India lacks a domestic source for genes that confer properties including insect resistance and herbicide tolerance, it has encountered commercial and scientific obstacles to progress. Biotechnology companies have hitherto used intellectual property protection to deny access to such genes, which they regard as their patented property. If the results of existing commercial research are not shared, it is doubtful whether developing countries will be able to make short-term progress in creating crop strains that meet their own needs (Macilwain, 1999).

Securing access to research will not, however, be easy. India has attempted to bargain with Monsanto, trading market access for the company's existing products for a partnership agreement regarding new research on rice and sugar cane (Jayaraman, 1999). In theory, developing countries could also use international property rights regulations as a negotiating weapon. Access to genetic resources by multinational biotechnology corporations could be made conditional either on arrangements to share any resultant benefits, or on support for research programmes that address developing countries' needs (Barton, 1999). Ironically, the hostility of Northern consumers to GMOs could also have a part to play. Not all future projections are equally optimistic; but controversy elsewhere could rebound to the advantage of the developing world. Biotechnology companies may, in future, take greater care to accommodate criticism and concern. This may allow an opening for negotiations about access to the results of existing biotechnology research for developing countries (Macilwain, 1999).

Conclusion: Sustainable Futures

The goal of more sustainable agricultural development focuses attention upon the need for systemic political and commercial change to support technical and managerial innovation by individual farmers. However, the theoretical statement of the ideals of sustainable development does not guarantee change in practice, especially given the contested understanding of agricultural sustainability. Moreover, the challenge of sustainable agricultural development is vast. It means more than an attempt to ensure that agricultural productivity is achieved in ways that are environmentally sensitive. True development requires a redistribution of resources to reduce rural poverty, linking agricultural change to economic diversification and a new security of livelihoods. Hence, the suspicion remains that although many governments and international agencies have publicly committed themselves to sustainable development, their adherence may be superficial.

Projections of agricultural futures are arguably as complicated and contested as they have ever been. This reflects, on the one hand, a growing sense of the unsustainability of current practice, and, on the other, unease about the pace and direction of change. For many observers, this uncertainty is embodied in the debate about biotechnology.

But even if concerns about the health and environmental implications of GMOs were to be answered, the effects of their widespread adoption on European agriculture would still be controversial. Trends towards the quasi-industrial mass production of food would be accelerated, squeezing smaller farmers out of the commercial mainstream. European rural landscapes might become more akin to those of North America: less populated and more divided between extensive tracts devoted to agricultural monoculture and areas set aside for habitat and biodiversity conservation. Such departure from European tradition might deliver the goals of sustainable development; but that would not guarantee its cultural or political acceptability.

The decline of European agriculture outside the most productive core regions is not, however, inevitable. A more secure future can be built through the development of new forms of agricultural enterprise. As consumers react against mass-produced food, smaller farmers and producers in upland areas could find a new demand for their distinctive produce and reap greater financial rewards through direct involvement in its processing and marketing. An increasing emphasis on organic and low-input systems throughout the whole of European farming should also be consistent with reform of agricultural subsidies to promote the production of environmental goods. Such changes will protect farming incomes and interests, but will also create new alliances with consumers and environmentalists in defence of rural economies, societies and landscapes. The diversification, both of farming livelihoods, and the wider rural economy could thus support a more populated, self-sufficient and ecologically diverse countryside. Such moves would not require the rejection of scientific advances, or aim to eliminate external business interests. But they would involve a conscious effort to redress the imbalances of power within farming, giving producers and consumers greater influence over the adoption of agricultural innovations.

Farming futures are no less uncertain in the global South. The potential of biotechnology to improve the income, food supply and nutrition of rural populations is enormous. But such promises have been made – and broken – before, particularly during the era of the Green revolution. Optimism must also be tempered with a proper awareness of the environmental and health risks that could be associated with genetic modification. Equally important are the terms of access to biotechnology for developing countries and their people. If developing countries are to embrace biotechnology, they must become stakeholders in the industry, creating their own research capacity and trading biological resources for enhanced food security. The alternative is increasing and damaging dependence upon the major multinationals currently promoting GM crops.

Likely differentials in access to biotechnology within developing countries also pose potential problems. In India and Brazil, small farmers and landless peasants have participated in legal and direct action against GM crops, reflecting fears about the implications of biotechnology for the rural poor. More efficient food production will tend to reduce agricultural employment. Properly managed, this will release labour for application to other forms of development, including rural economic diversification. But it could also lead to increasing rural poverty and out-migration that exacerbates the problems of urban growth. In areas that are distant from major centres of active industrial and urban development, where alternative employment is limited, labour-intensive agriculture remains a better guarantor of livelihood security. This will involve more than the greater use of traditional forms such as polyculture. The productivity and environmental benefits of existing systems must be enhanced through new initiatives in agricultural research and extension. The creation of secure livelihoods for small farmers will also require market reforms to promote fair trade in agricultural produce.

Viewed in this way, agricultural futures are not about the dogmatic promotion of particular technologies and management systems, whether based on organic, chemical or biotechnological inputs. Instead, there should be a more pragmatic search for locally appropriate ways of meeting the economic, social and environmental goals embodied in sustainable development. This reinforces the case for partnership between local communities and external agencies of development. But to be effective, such partnerships must have a measure of equality, built upon respect for a diversity of local knowledges, different economic and environmental values, and divergent constructions of social welfare and progress. The cultural and political protection of this human diversity against homogenizing and destructive forces is arguably as important to sustainable agricultural development as are any initiatives to check environmental degradation.

It is vital that we consider the full implications of the different versions of sustainable development that are presented to us. Farming futures should be the active concern of all, not simply a matter for producers themselves, or the anonymous forces of the state and international capital. Sustainable development must be socially, as well as economically, appropriate for particular places and people. Moreover, true sustainability within a particular locale cannot be achieved at the expense of negative impacts elsewhere. These are fundamental, and inherently geographical, truths that must be explored if we are to put flesh on the skeleton of economic theory that underpins the ideal of sustainable development. The goal of sustainable agricultural development involves more than adopting particular technologies and management systems. It cannot be separated from cultural and political judgements about the types of rural society and landscape that we aim to encourage. Pursued in different ways, sustainable development could be associated with very different geographies of land use and biodiversity, urban and rural settlement, production and consumption, and national and international trade. The choices we make, and the choices made for us, about agriculture today and tomorrow are of huge importance to all of the world's people.

9

Sustaining the Flow: Japanese Waterways and New Paradigms of Development

Paul Waley and Martin Purvis

Introduction

The potential for conflict between ecological and non-ecological objectives is widely apparent in the comprehensive programme of river restoration projects that has been initiated in Japan over the past two decades.[1] Yet, despite the potential importance of these initiatives and the intense domestic scrutiny that they have provoked, little has been written in English that reviews river restoration in Japan (Gippel and Fukutome, 1998; Waley, 2000b). Hence, the aim here is to place the Japanese experience of river restoration and integrated river management – or comprehensive river planning, as it is called in Japan – within the context of wider attention to sustainable development.

The chapter begins by reviewing Japanese attitudes to economic growth and environmental sustainability. River management is identified as an important dimension of the construction-led development evident in the decades immediately following World War II, and of more recent moves to create a better balance between economic and environmental interests. The tensions inherent in this new thinking are highlighted in two case studies, which focus on efforts to foster public interest in both large-scale catchment management and smaller-scale river restoration work. The case studies raise wider questions about the reality of change and, in particular, the problems of defining meaningful environmental goals, and of fostering genuine public participation in the planning process.

21st-Century Japan: Poised for Sustainable Development?

On the face of it, Japan enters the 21st century displaying a genuine and growing commitment to sustainable development. A high ranking in international indices that claim to gauge the progress of individual states towards sustainable development suggests a degree of success in reducing the social and environmental costs of economic growth (Broadbent, 1998). Japanese industry has a strong reputation for the pursuit of energy and resource efficiency through technical innovation, and Japanese firms have become world leaders in the production of pollution-control equipment (OECD, 1977; 1994). Other sectors of an emergent Green economy are also well developed. Japan has, for example, an effective network for the distribution of organic food (Lam, 1999).

The Japanese government displays an increasing commitment to national and international initiatives to protect the environment. For example, Japan hosted the third Conference of the Parties to the international Framework Convention on Climate Change (FCCC) at Kyoto in 1997 and played a significant role in brokering the resultant protocol on the reduction of greenhouse gas emissions (see Chapter 11). While the term 'sustainable development' itself is little used in popular discourse, the principles it embodies have slipped smoothly into the lexicon of official thinking and policy drafting amongst the Japanese elite. Thus, in framing their own national policies, Japanese governments have adopted the rhetoric of sustainable development and compliance with the precepts of the 1992 Rio Earth Summit. In addition to a 1994 Basic Environmental Plan, predicated on a 1993 Basic Environmental Law, Japan now has a governmental Council for Sustainable Development, established in 1996. The language of sustainable development is also widely used within the Environment Ministry, as it was by its precursor, the Environment Agency. This is evident, for example, in the framing of the annual *White Paper on the Environment (Kankyō hakusho)* for 1996, which examined Japanese policy in relation to the resolutions of the Rio Earth Summit (Kankyōchō, 1996).

Past Imperfect

This engagement with sustainable development might be viewed as a necessary corrective to the previous course of economic and social change in post-war Japan. Indeed, the policy shifts of the 1990s could be seen as marking the culmination of an effective response to doubts, first raised publicly in the 1960s, about the sustainability of extensive industrialization and urbanization. Nevertheless, reliance on growth through construction continues to cast a long shadow over both the Japanese economy and the Japanese landscape. It is still vital to subject policy pronouncements on issues relating to the environment to critical scrutiny (McCormack, 2001).

Post-war priorities: planning for economic growth

In the decades following World War II, Japanese governments planned for a rapid recovery from the economic weakness associated with military defeat. Their priorities included greater self-sufficiency in agricultural production and increased security in energy supply. But, above all, the ruling elite aimed to establish Japan as a global economic power through comprehensive industrial modernization (Hein, 1993). Initial emphasis was placed on heavy industrial development – especially steel, shipbuilding and chemicals – and the acquisition of strategic technologies in leading sectors, including petrochemicals, machine tools, electronics and motor vehicles. Economic transformation was orchestrated by successive governments through a series of five- and six-year plans from the mid 1950s onwards. Government ministries, especially those responsible for Finance, for International Trade and Industry (MITI) and for Construction (MoC), became powerful agencies dictating targets for economic growth and directing investment to particular industrial sectors and regions.

The pattern of economic growth directed by government was led by substantial construction projects. Industrial development was concentrated in major complexes, sometimes on coastal land reclaimed from the sea (Broadbent, 1998). These centres also became the foci of a new wave of urbanization, transforming the character of extensive areas along the Pacific coastal plain (McCormack, 1996). Moreover, the progressive appropriation of land for urban and industrial use was associated with increasingly technical regimes of river management. Weirs and barrages were strung across river mouths. Lower reaches were re-engineered in the name of flood control, while upstream, many rivers were dammed, often several times, to provide water supplies and hydroelectric power. Initially, urban and industrial growth was concentrated particularly in the region around Tokyo Bay; but the New National Development Plan of 1969 signalled a growing emphasis on economic decentralization and the creation of heavy industrial capacity throughout Japan. Such thinking was evident in the 1972 programme Building a New Japan: the Remodelling of the Japanese Archipelago, put forward by Prime Minister Tanaka Kakuei. This outlined grandiose regional development plans, involving the creation of new industrial growth poles and investment in transport infrastructure, including tunnels and bridges linking the main islands.

Judged on its own terms, Japanese government policy appeared largely successful during the third quarter of the 20th century. Although the country remained heavily dependent upon external sources for food and energy supplies, its industrial economy was transformed. Output and productivity grew rapidly and, with equally impressive advances in quality control, Japanese industry gained a major share in international markets. While the immediate post-war years saw an emphasis on industrial growth at the expense of investment in social welfare, material living standards were rising rapidly by the 1960s as Japan saw the creation of a society based on mass consumption.

Environmental penalties

In planning for economic growth, successive Japanese governments paid little attention to the state of the environment. Yet the costs of environmental damage were increasingly obvious. The loss of rural land to urban and industrial uses transformed the Japanese landscape, with serious implications for the functioning of environmental systems and the erosion of habitat and biodiversity. The effects of urban construction on hydrological regimes were reinforced by the concretization of river channels and banks as flood control measures, creating new areas of ecological desert. Uplands, too, were transformed as attempts to counter landslides led to hills and mountains being reshaped and encased in concrete. The promotion of forestry resulted in many of the remaining slopes being carpeted with densely packed conifers, causing aesthetic blight and ecological damage through the loss of biodiversity and water retention capacity (Knight, 1998). But the most intense environmental problems were associated with the pollution spawned by urban industrialism. In the early post-war decades factories were built in and around the major cities with little thought for pollution control. As a result, the quality of river and coastal waters declined dramatically. Extremes of local pollution, such as the mercury poisoning caused by waste discharged from an aluminium plant into Minamata Bay during the 1950s, were linked to ill health, birth defects and death. Air quality in many major urban centres, where industrial pollution combined with traffic exhaust to create photochemical smog, was also an increasingly serious health hazard.

By the late 1960s, Japan was arguably amongst the most polluted countries in the world (Huddle and Reich, 1991; Ui, 1992). Initial efforts to counter growing environmental problems were largely ineffectual. The Basic Law for Environmental Pollution Control enacted in 1967 failed to enforce effective pollution prevention, either by government or industry. Similarly, the call in the New National Development Plan of 1969 for 'balance between nature and human life' made little practical difference to the construction-led agenda of economic growth. But the late 1960s did see the growth of anti-pollution citizens' movements and a series of lawsuits that resulted in ultimately successful claims against polluting businesses (McKean, 1980). Slowly, the environmental damage that had once been seen by many as a necessary price to pay for economic modernization became a matter of public concern. A previously quiescent media started to penetrate the habitual secrecy surrounding the operation of Japanese businesses. Increasing publicity for major pollution cases and the associated incidence of death and disease threatened to turn the electorate against the established political elite. This sense of the failure of government was reinforced during the 1970s as the Liberal Democrats, the perpetual ruling party, were shaken by allegations of corruption involving major cash donations from business in return for contracts and favours.

Crisis and planning for efficiency

The foundations of a more effective national environmental policy were laid in 1970 when the government set specific quality standards for air, water, soil and noise pollution. But the effects of the first oil crisis of 1973 to 1974 overtook such moves. Japan's dependency on imports for almost all of its energy needs meant that the economy was particularly badly affected. A combination of cuts in oil supplies and soaring costs precipitated recession, unemployment and increasing public hostility towards big business. The oil crisis also provided an immediate spur to a new efficiency in the use of energy and other resources. The government launched an energy-saving programme in November 1973 and postponed the large-scale construction projects promised by the Building a New Japan programme. In the longer term, the events of the early 1970s encouraged the restructuring of the Japanese economy; over the following ten years, Japan's gross national product (GNP) increased by 30 per cent, while energy consumption grew only slightly. The focus of growth moved away from chemicals and other heavy industries that were both energy intensive and polluting. At the same time, the production of energy-efficient technologies and pollution-control equipment developed into important new industrial sectors (Broadbent, 1998). MITI, which had previously spearheaded the rush to economic growth, was granted new powers to direct industrial investment towards energy conservation. The ministry, acting through its Natural Resources Agency, also led the development of new energy sources, including hydroelectric power, solar energy and, more controversially, the expansion of Japan's nuclear capacity. The success of these various initiatives was reflected in the rapid recovery of the Japanese economy during the later 1970s. But a combination of environmental crisis, internal political scandal and external economic shocks had begun to expose the inherent unsustainability of the rush to industrial modernity.

The reality of change

There are, however, reasons to question the depth of change in Japan during the 1970s and 1980s. Indeed, such doubts have persisted despite the more recent adoption of the rhetoric of sustainable development. The 1970s did not see the loss of governmental faith in construction-led development. Elements of the Building a New Japan programme were reinstated as early as 1975. Only amidst the renewed economic recession of the 1990s was the traditional reliance of central government on public works projects to boost the economy again widely questioned. Other marks of economic and environmental failure remain all too obvious. Throughout the 1990s, for example, Japanese agriculture was mired in a crisis that echoed difficulties facing farmers elsewhere in the developed world, reflecting a policy of subsidy and protectionism that has led to intensification, overproduction and environmental damage (McCormack, 1996; see also Chapter 8 in this volume).

It is also the case that Japan's apparent transition to more sustainable development as measured in international indices has been achieved, in part, at the expense of her neighbours. Domestic business may be a model of energy efficiency and pollution prevention; but Japanese capital now underpins industrial development throughout much of the Asia–Pacific region. Japanese transnational companies have exported much of their heavy industrial capacity, and its attendant pollution, to South-East Asia and China. They have done so, moreover, in a way and at a speed that contributed significantly to the Asian financial crisis of 1997 and 1998. Such a balance sheet, where domestic progress is offset by wider failings, calls into question the commitment of Japanese political and business leaders to implementing an effective, equitable and truly sustainable development policy.

River Management: The Context

Changing environments and attitudes

The remainder of this chapter will search for the substance beneath the Japanese government's rhetoric of sustainable development through exploration of the specific case of river management. Water has traditionally been accorded a particular cultural, aesthetic and economic significance in Japan as a source of life, beauty and agricultural prosperity (Waley, 2000b). Yet rivers and their valleys, as well as floodplains, have been amongst the environments most transformed by post-war economic growth. Japan is a densely populated country and the alluvial floodplains that characterize the lower reaches of most of its rivers have been intensively settled, urbanized and concretized. The impacts of water extraction, pollution and changes in land use upon water quality and hydrological regimes have been significant and frequently deleterious. The natural propensity to flood exhibited by Japanese rivers – a reflection of topography, heavy seasonal flow following summer rains and high sedimentation loads – has been exacerbated by the loss of traditional agents of water retention and absorption, as paddy fields have given way to urban development and broadleafed woodland has been cleared or replaced with conifers (Ichikawa et al, 1980; Knight, 1998; Takahashi, 1995). At the same time, the urbanization of low-lying land has increased the size of the population and the value of the property exposed to flood hazards. The need to combat this growing flood problem was central to perceptions of the importance of river management. Thus, rivers have been subjected to extensive re-engineering. Their banks were routinely raised to defend surrounding land and property. In many cases, river channels were also deepened and straightened, and their beds and banks encased in concrete – work intended to flush water quickly out to sea. Artificial outlets were dug at the mouths of major rivers and – in an effort to reduce flooding associated with typhoons and high tides – their lower reaches were contained within high concrete barriers. This attention to flood control, together with an enthusiasm for damming rivers as a source of power and water, led to river management being identified as an important element in the Japanese government's construction-led development policies of the early post-war decades.

Since the 1970s, however, the established orthodoxy of river engineering has been subject to a growing challenge, both from within government and outside. New thinking about the cultural value of water and rivers and active campaigning against dam construction have formed part of the context for the adoption of less intrusive and environmentally damaging approaches to river management. The 1980s saw both a renewed emphasis on the traditional aesthetics of Japanese cultural landscapes and a growing awareness of overseas initiatives to redevelop urban waterfronts. As a result, a greater emphasis was placed on the positive creation of 'greener' environments that are aesthetically pleasing, and socially and educationally useful. An explicitly ecological dimension to river management gained ground during the 1990s. This decade also saw important legal changes, including revisions to river law and the enactment of a new law defining the status of non-profit-making organizations, many of which are active in environmental debate and planning. Reform of river management policy thus has two dimensions, echoing the need under sustainable development to balance economic gain against both environmental integrity and social equity.

New perspectives on river management: techniques and tensions

Environmental objectives require a change both in the way that river systems are understood and in the methods applied in their management (Nienhuis et al, 1998). Rather than viewing rivers principally in economic terms – whether as a resource or as a threat – reformed management practice starts from a more holistic understanding of rivers as integrated ecological systems. Attention is therefore paid to the impact of human activity upon water quality, and the condition and diversity of flora and fauna, acknowledging that the effects of human intervention at a particular location may be transmitted widely throughout a river system. Such integrated river basin management is complemented by a positive programme of river restoration, capitalizing on the 'innate ability of freshwater biotic systems to recover from damage' (Newsom,

1997). River restoration to recreate ecological, holistic and integrated systems has become a central pillar in the sustainable management of river basins not only in Japan, but also in much of Europe and North America. New management programmes have reintroduced meanders to previously straightened rivers, recreated other landscape features along river banks and reactivated water retention and retarding features (Brookes and Shields, 1996). Such work, in tandem with initiatives to improve water quality, aims to re-establish rivers as corridors for plant and animal life in urban areas and other potentially hostile environments (Mori, 1995).

The definition of techniques for river restoration does not, however, ensure rapid or uncontested progress towards more sustainable development. There are practical limitations on what river restoration programmes can achieve. River basins, especially in their lower reaches, are often severely degraded landscapes. There is thus little immediate possibility of the dramatic reversal of existing processes of technological river engineering and urban development. In practice, river restoration projects are often confined to short stretches. Although these may be intensively researched and carefully executed pilot projects, there is a danger of a descent into tokenism if the means are not forthcoming to effect a more comprehensive change in the condition of river systems.

The slow pace of change may represent more than inertia. Where river basins are heavily populated – as is the case in Japan – the ecological objectives of large-scale river restoration projects will almost inevitably 'conflict severely with non-ecology functions of rivers, such as flood control, sediment transport and urban and agricultural use and land ownership' (Nienhuis et al, 1998). To the extent that river basin restoration appears to compromise human safety and provoke damage to property, planners, politicians and publics are often less than enthusiastic. River management thus encapsulates the difficulties of balancing different needs and objectives, which are ever present in planning for sustainable development. The tyranny of the economy over the environment cannot be overturned only to be replaced by an ecological challenge to economic prosperity or social justice. Such a change would not only be against the spirit of sustainable development; it would also be counterproductive in eroding the popular legitimacy of river restoration projects.

Participation and consultation

A common response to the challenge of setting out a development path that is not only sustainable but also widely supported is to encourage public consultation and participation in defining development priorities. This is the thinking behind the promotion of Agenda 21 and Local Agenda 21 (LA21) as key elements of a common global programme of sustainable development (see Chapter 6). A series of participatory mechanisms have thus been incorporated into the reform of river management practice in Japan. Their presence reflects a desire to win over popular support for river restoration. But participation also attempts to ensure that river management projects meet the expressed needs of particular local communities, and that their effects promote social equity, as well as a new accommodation between economic and environmental objectives.

Participation is a touchstone of sustainable development; yet it can be highly contentious. When participation involves consultation, it engenders problems if participants simply defer to those considered to hold authority or expertise (Goodwin, 1998). The history of the genesis, formulation and representation of sustainable development makes it self-evidently an elite-driven project. But in its search for legitimacy it frequently strives to portray itself as a popular crusade, directed from the bottom up. There is a risk that tokenistic participation and consultation is adopted merely as a device to achieve this sleight of hand. Even where participatory efforts are more sincerely motivated, they may chiefly attract those with property and leisure, whose vision of their environment is steeped in conservative values. This 'urban middle-class army of rural workers', as Adams (1997) calls them, are invariably inclined to support the status quo and interpret issues of social justice and the environment in terms of conservation and liberal free market values.

The case of river management in Japan provides a vehicle for engaging with wider debates regarding LA21 and the value of social and participatory elements in sustainable development. LA21 is widely promoted as an effective medium for involving individual neighbourhoods in the larger project of sustainable development, underpinning not only successful local initiatives, but also the creation of more equitable global links between communities in the developed and developing world (Buckingham-Hatfield and Percy, 1999). Yet many commentators are sceptical. They worry that projects launched under the rubric of LA21 are concerned chiefly with the management of existing inequalities, rather than any more fundamental redistribution of access to land and other resources (Middleton et al, 1993). Initiatives led by local government may lack the budgetary and political means to effect real change (Gibbs et al, 1998; see also Chapter 4 in this volume). Ultimately, the emphasis on local participation and community projects is seen by some critics as part of a more general retreat of government before the forces of globalizing capital – a retreat from the collective disguised through a rhetoric of faith in civil society and new social movements (Doyle, 1998).

Testing the waters

Comprehensive river planning in Japan is now linked to a growing environmental discourse centred on river basins and public participation in planning systems. As such, it represents one of the most tangible expressions of ideas about more sustainable development in the Japanese context. Some of the new thinking borrows from ideas and practices developed in Switzerland, Germany, Britain and the USA (Larsen, 1996; Seki, 1994). But the intensity with which interest is focused on rivers in Japan and the proliferation of river-based environmental campaign groups far outweigh the limited, if growing, attention to river restoration in Europe and North America (Newson, 1997; de Waal et al, 1998). The extent to which the new planning programme has been successful in translating individual enthusiasm and government rhetoric into real change on the ground – in both environmental form and popular attitudes – is thus a valuable measure of progress towards sustainability in Japan. More than this, exploration of the Japanese experience provides a new perspective on the wider difficulties of securing substantive progress towards sustainable development. The potential techniques for sustainable river management have been defined with increasing clarity over the past two decades. Yet there is no diminution in the contest surrounding the balance to be struck in their execution between economic, social and environmental goals. In searching for this balance, planners and publics often appear at odds with each other. Nor is the encouragement of community consultation and participation necessarily a remedy for such tensions. The challenge of securing effective participation in the design and execution of sustainable development initiatives may itself be formidable.

Technocentric River Planning and the Ministry of Construction

The rise of river engineering

Viewed from the economic perspective of the early post-war years, Japan's river basins were valued chiefly as territory for industrial and urban development. Hasty and large-scale construction increased both the likelihood of flooding and the scale of the resultant damage and loss of life. Rather than question the overall thrust of development policy, a growing reliance was placed on engineering-based flood control measures. At the same time, rivers themselves were also increasingly harnessed as a source of water and hydroelectric power, and as a means of waste disposal. By contrast, little value was placed on the aesthetic presence of waterways within urban landscapes. Crucially, also, no account was taken of the ecological impacts of technocratic river management regimes, either directly upon rivers themselves, or as part of a wider programme of economic growth that was erosive of environmental quality and often profligate with resources.

Although concrete and steel had first been used for water control and river bank reinforcement during the late 1920s, the early post-war decades saw an unparalleled reliance on these materials in river management. The channels of smaller rivers were routinely encased in concrete, their beds dug ever deeper within sheer, concrete banks. Rivers too broad to be treated in this way were hemmed in by sheaths of concrete-clad steel known as 'razor-blade embankments'. The choice of construction material itself embodied the priority accorded to economic over environmental considerations in river management. Concrete is not only an alien material that transforms hydrological regimes and turns river courses into ecological deserts; its use and production epitomize the turn to unsustainability represented by modern industrialism. Locally appropriate, natural and renewable resources were abandoned as construction materials in favour of the apparent convenience of concrete, which is the product of a resource- and energy-intensive industrial complex.

As urban development spread, it also prompted significant changes to the form of many small waterways, including irrigation channels, which had previously played an important agricultural role. Thousands of kilometres of waterway quickly fell into decay and were officially reclassified as 'useless rivers' (Miyamura, 1989). Slow-flowing or stagnant water became polluted by household and industrial effluent. The waterways were also a breeding ground for mosquitoes, reinforcing their characterization as a health hazard. On receiving the inevitable complaints and petitions from the residents of newly urbanized areas, local governments were inclined to take the easiest option and culvert the waterways. This further accelerated the effective removal of rivers and waterways from Japan's urban landscapes and ecosystems.

State direction and planning

The programme of essentially technocratic and engineering-based river policy was coordinated and managed by the Ministry of Construction (more recently recast as the National Land and Transport Ministry). During the early post-war years, when many of Japan's embankments and flood defences lay in a serious state of disrepair, the River Bureau was considered the most important and powerful of the ministry's several internal departments (Woodall, 1996). Moreover, Japan's national planning system accords a leading role to the MoC's nine regional offices, each of which includes a department supervising riverine work. Japan's river basins are divided into categories according to their importance (Kiya et al, 1992). Responsibility for the management of the most significant, or class-one, river systems rests with the MoC and its regional offices; but work is normally delegated to prefectural governments. Class-two rivers and their banks are maintained and repaired at the municipal level. Irrigation channels are normally the joint responsibility of associations of farmers and the local municipal government. Coordination of these different agencies of management – vital in view of the number of rivers that cross administrative boundaries – is effected through the drafting of river basin plans that relate to targets set in the national five-year plans.

Another important area of control and supervision for the MoC is the construction and maintenance of most of the country's dams. Japan's programme of dam-building accelerated during the immediate post-war years, inspired by the example of the Tennessee Valley Authority, which had impressed government planners on their visits to the USA (Ōkuma, 1988). As a result, Japan had built 2678 dams over 15 metres in height by March 1999 (Nihon Damu Kyōkai, undated). Although the construction work involved has often been substantial, the constraints of the terrain are such that many of the resultant reservoirs are relatively small fingers of water confined within narrow valleys. Almost a quarter of the country's dams are multipurpose, providing water for industry and irrigation as well as for power generation, and most of these include a flood-prevention function. Despite inherent technical difficulties in using multipurpose dams for flood control, their role in this respect has assumed increasing importance as restrictions on downstream flood prevention measures have grown.

Agriculture, however, is still by far the largest user of water resources in Japan, accounting for about two-thirds of the national total. With nearly all of the country's rivers dammed at least once, new channels for irrigation, again constructed in concrete, have had to be installed to ensure regularity of flow. Hence, the vestiges of customary rights to water use have disappeared. Their place has been taken by a range of interest groups and ministries, including those overseeing agriculture, industry and public health, as well as those with responsibility for construction, transport, local government, and the environment. These ministries have statutory rights in the formulation of policy and therefore form an important part of the intricate web of forces that control water use in Japan. In this way, water has become an ever-more deeply entrenched element within the complex of state control of natural resources –

a process dubbed the 'étatization' or 'enclosure' of water by the Japanese geographer Takeuchi Keiichi (1996).

Reassessing the Role of Rivers

Policy evolution

Since the mid 1970s there has been a slow and partial realization of the fundamental unsustainability of Japan's approach to river engineering and water management. This has formed part of an unmistakable reassessment of a whole range of policies that were once seen as encapsulating the Japanese model of construction-led economic growth. A growing understanding that engineering works were an ineffective means of flood control initially propelled the shift in river policy. A renewed spate of flooding during the 1970s provoked a series of court rulings in which the MoC was held responsible for damage resulting from inadequate flood defences (Ōkuma, 1988). Further flooding in subsequent years has strengthened the argument for an end to purely technocratic answers to flood control. As events revealed the deficiencies of existing policy, even when judged in terms of economic and engineering efficiency, a new space, albeit small, was created for the environment in Japanese river management.

While citizens' groups and environmental activists have been increasingly vocal in opposing dam construction, much of the impetus for other changes in river management policy has come from within the MoC itself. During the 1970s and 1980s, the ministry launched initiatives in comprehensive river planning that were the precursors of the integrated river management that has become a hallmark of European policy during the 1990s. As a result, comprehensive river plans have been drafted for each of Japan's 109 river basins. In practice, however, the shift in policy emphasis has been gradual. During the 1970s, attention was focused on the redefinition of flood control policy following the agenda set by a report published in 1976 by the MoC's advisory council on rivers. Rather than attempt to eliminate floods through ecologically intrusive engineering work, efforts were redirected towards reducing the damage caused by flooding (Ōkuma, 1988). Future flood protection measures were to be designed to counter only extreme events (Gippel and Fukutome, 1998). The report advocated a series of 'soft' measures, including re-landscaping of embankments, and reactivation of retention ponds, retarding basins and flood meadows as alternatives to established technological and engineering solutions. The 1980s saw a new emphasis on combining measures to limit flood damage with the recovery of riverside land as a public amenity. An MoC report of 1987 recommended replacing the concrete walls constructed to contain urban rivers with 'super embankments' (sūpā teibō) (Ōkuma, 1988). These broad earthen levées could also provide an important space for recreational activities within the crowded and cluttered urban growth that had colonized Japan's alluvial floodplains. Official recognition of this value restored the status of rivers as a cultural amenity: a 'natural' space that reflected celebrated scenery.

Finally, river restoration with an explicit ecological dimension became an inescapable part of river planning and water management during the 1990s. River restoration was first established as an important focus of government policy through changes to MoC planning systems introduced in 1990. These ushered in a new approach known as *tashizen-gata kawa-zukuri* – literally, multi-nature-style river planning – but, in practice, simply ecological engineering. Ecological restoration was viewed both as an end in itself and as consistent with earlier moves to revise flood control policies by working with the landscape. This form of comprehensive river planning aims to preserve or create environments that are aesthetically pleasing and provide habitat for a diversity of flora and fauna (Seki, 1994). It follows that human intervention in the re-landscaping of rivers should be kept to a minimum. Where such work is necessary, natural materials should be used whenever possible. It was not envisaged, however, that the use of concrete in the engineering of river channels and banks would be outlawed; rather, it would be covered with local stone or topsoil to reduce its visual impact and encourage the re-establishment of habitat (Ribāfuronto Seibi Sentā, 1996). This new approach to river planning was endorsed in the national five-year plan for 1997 to 2002, which stipulated that half of all repair work on river banks and beds should involve materials other than concrete (Asahi Shinbun, 1996). The revised River Law of 1997 also identified the protection of nature as a central aim of all riparian work.

Championing and contesting change

The drive to change the technocratic ethos prevalent within the MoC was directed by a handful of officials in the River Bureau. One individual in particular, Seki Masakazu, played a leading role until his premature death in 1995, both in the dissemination of new ideas about river management and in enforcing their adoption. Seki was initially inspired by river rehabilitation projects near Zurich, which he first visited in 1988. Swiss and German ideas of *Naturnaher Wasserbau* (natural water engineering) were reflected in an MoC administrative guidance paper on multi-nature-style river planning written by Seki in 1990. This stressed the importance of broadening river channels, maintaining the variety of riverine environments and designing projects appropriate to Japan's climate and topography. These approaches were developed further – and the links with indigenous traditions of pre-modern river management strengthened – in Seki's subsequent book, which proved an influential exploration of the potential for river restoration in Japan (Seki, 1994). Equally important, however, was Seki's administrative position within the MoC. In 1990 he assumed control over budget submissions to the Ministry of Finance. Seki determined the allocation of funding for all plans for riparian work submitted by the MoC's regional offices and by local governments. From this influential position he was able to introduce the requirement that requests for central government funding for riparian work should include an element of multi-nature-style river planning. Those offices which did not share Seki's enthusiasm were threatened with a reduction in their budgets (Seki, 1994).

These strong-arm tactics were necessary in a context in which there was considerable opposition to the new idiom of river planning. Multi-nature-style river planning can impose direct financial costs that are twice those of orthodox construction-based schemes (Ishikawa, 1999). Moreover, engineers and officials within the MoC and elsewhere in central and local government remain deeply immersed in a tradition of technological engineering. Their commitment to the socio-economic goal of the protection of people and property from flood hazard is allied to an ideology that equates safety with construction in concrete. Indeed, the MoC retains various models for river planning, several of which contradict the main thrust of both multi-nature-style river planning and the broader agenda of sustainable development. Opposition within the MoC is reinforced by an external network of vested interest. Engineering orthodoxy is deeply embedded in Japanese institutional life. It is maintained through elite establishments for education and research, amongst which the Engineering Faculty of Tokyo University is pre-eminent. The powerful construction industry, which has grown rich on decades of construction-led development, is equally resistant to change in established and lucrative methods of river management. Where budgets or methods have been called into question, old arguments about maximizing protection from flood hazards have often prevailed. Long-standing procedures and deeply entrenched habits of thought have produced an unthinking attachment to a growth dynamic.

The transformation of river management is essentially a 'top-down' project, conceived and orchestrated by members of Japan's bureaucratic and academic elites. However, to be successful it must acquire popular legitimacy; here, too, a mixture of active opposition and inertia may obstruct change. Many citizens fear that the replacement of established engineering practice with less interventionist management strategies will increase the threat of flooding and create new health hazards through the summertime proliferation of weeds and mosquitoes. Thus, they remain wedded to the previous reliance on concrete channels and banks despite the argument that these represent a short-term palliative rather than a true guarantor of flood security. Others who favour change advance alternative models that are not always easy to reconcile with multi-nature-style river planning. These include calls for river-bank land to be developed as recreational space, or for a more elaborate landscaping of rivers in order to recreate traditional cultural landscapes. Thus, multi-nature-style river planning can be divisive, creating tensions between a new – and disproportionately middle-class – stratum of environmentally aware citizens and other more traditional sections of the community.

Education and participation

Against this background, moves to promote multi-nature-style river planning necessarily involved a conscious effort to win converts to its new ecologically informed ethos. Two MoC-affiliated foundations were established to disburse funds for research programmes, to sponsor publications and to promote an interest in new techniques of river landscaping that avoided the use of concrete. Visits to river restoration projects in Germany and Switzerland were instrumental in enthusing and educating a core of planners and government officials. Pilot projects have been set up, best-practice manuals published and workshops and seminars organized. River Bureau officials have tutored and cajoled local government engineers and designers into paying greater attention to ecological restoration in river management.

Equally important, however, is the stipulation introduced in the revised River Law of 1997 that local residents be consulted in the drafting of comprehensive river plans. Public involvement in the planning process is consistent with the participatory principles that are increasingly identified as an important element of sustainable development. This suggests a new emphasis on managing rivers in ways that accord with a balanced range of local needs, rather than the dominant economic objectives of a rigid national planning system. However, the policy also represents an attempt to engender an awareness of the value and significance of river basins amongst their residents. This is an educational project to recruit support for the MoC's policy shifts. As long as local inhabitants see rivers chiefly as a potential source of flooding, their attitudes towards river management are unlikely to change. Attempts to redress the balance between environment and economy – or, more precisely, between environmental quality and the defence of property – in river management must, therefore, reach out beyond the confines of government to encourage a broader political debate.

The picture on the ground – on the beds and banks of Japan's waterways and in their catchment areas – is a highly varied one. At one level, little has changed, and flooding remains a constant threat in the rainy months of summer. Comprehensive river planning, involving whole catchment areas, has failed to make substantial advances. It is now the case that all catchment areas must have river management plans, the drafting of which must involve some input from local residents. However, the success of the process depends very much upon the particular social and political dynamics of individual localities. As a result, attention and interest are still directed towards a small number of pilot projects, including the Tsurumigawa River Network discussed below. In the words of an MoC official interviewed in August 2000: 'Comprehensive river planning needs more thought, more development; it is not working.'

Yet, change the focus of enquiry and the picture revealed is somewhat different. A host of smaller-scale river restoration projects have been undertaken, based on the principles of multi-nature-style river planning, and the whole subject of eco-friendly river restoration is increasingly widely discussed (Waley, 2000b). In this sense, Japan has moved a long way since the early 1990s, when the first projects – including the small-scale experiment in river restoration at Hino that forms the second case study – were launched. Looking forward into the 21st century, the question is no longer one of the number of local projects, but of the quality of the restoration work they promote. When interviewed for this research in August 2000, both officials of the MoC and leading members of community groups raised concerns that many projects incorporate eco-friendly river restoration techniques only in a formulaic way. Moreover, limited practical understanding of such techniques means that, too often, their application on the ground is either clumsy or perfunctory. This reflects, in part, the personal and improvisational nature of the genesis and development of multi-nature-style river planning in Japan. It was accepted at the outset that progress would be made through trial and error and that, as a result, the content of the early projects would be highly variable. Catalogues of approved methods and techniques only began to appear during the mid 1990s and they have yet to have a widespread impact upon local practice.

From Words to Deeds

The two case studies that follow allow a more detailed examination of both the environmental and social dimensions of river planning. The first is a large-scale project, part of a pioneering attempt at comprehensive river management for the

Tsurumi River basin, initiated by the MoC through its regional office. In an area where recent urbanization has created both environmental damage and social alienation, particular attention has been paid to developing and funding initiatives that will encourage interest in the river. The second study is a project with a much more local focus: the creation of an 'ecologically friendly' water channel in Hino, a municipality in the western suburbs of Tokyo. Here, immense care and enthusiasm have been directed towards the rehabilitation of a disused irrigation channel to create a model environment for aquatic and other animal life.

Tsurumi basin: raising public awareness in recently urbanized areas

Reshaping the physical context

The main stream of the Tsurumi River (Tsurumigawa in Japanese) is 42.5 kilometres long, with a further 2 kilometres flowing through landfill at its mouth. The river rises in the loam-rich diluvial uplands of the Tama hills in the Tokyo Metropolis, then flows through suburban Kawasaki and reaches the sea in a heavily industrialized district of Yokohama. The river basin has a population of 1.7 million spread over an area of 235 square kilometres. Upstream, the hillsides are scarred with continuing urbanization. The middle reaches of the river flow through a confusing patchwork of recent urban developments before entering the mature industrial districts of its lower course and mouth. During recent decades of rapid urbanization the area's population has grown substantially. Most of these new arrivals commute to work in Tokyo or Yokohama, a daily exit from their home territory that reinforces their detachment from the natural environment of the Tsurumi basin. Few local residents have a strong sense of place or a well-developed consciousness of the river as a key element in the landscape. Nor have many of them directly experienced its capacity to overflow its banks. The Tsurumigawa last flooded in 1982; but the basin has a history of such events. Following particularly severe floods in 1958 and 1966, the MoC re-designated the river as class-one, and thus assumed responsibility for its management (Uchida, 1994).

The Tsurumi was the first river basin in which comprehensive river planning was attempted. This involved the exploration of new ways to meet the continuing and fundamental aim of flood control. In practice, physical changes to the river have been limited. Widening its course is no longer feasible because of the difficulties involved in purchasing the necessary land. Hence, much of the effort of physical transformation has been concentrated on recovering and maintaining floodplain reservoirs. This is also consistent with the new approach to river planning that seeks more natural means of achieving the economically and socially desirable ends of protection of life and property. Yet this shift of emphasis in planning has not precluded some potentially controversial new development, including the construction of a football stadium to stage the finals of the 2002 World Cup on the banks of the Tsurumi River. The claim that attention to the absorption of flood water in the stadium's design means that it does not detract from moves to restore the storage capacity of the floodplain has still to be seriously tested.

Frameworks for participation

A second main thrust of the project is to promote public interest in the river as a source of environmental benefits and to foster local involvement in improving its landscape and ecology. The aim is not only to bring local residents into the planning process and secure their endorsement for a more eco-friendly approach to river restoration and flood control, but also to help implant a feeling of local belonging in a population largely composed of recent in-migrants.

At the centre of participatory activities in the basin is the Tsurumigawa River Network, known as TR Net. This organization was launched in 1990 at the instigation of the Yokohama city government, with seed-corn funding from the regional office of the MoC. Initially, it was an umbrella body for 13 local river-oriented environmental groups. It now includes nearly 50 such groups, with a range of activities including 'nature watching', 'river walking', games for the children, clean-up campaigns and seminars on local history and geography. Activities are advertised in periodic publications packed with drawings and quizzes for children. TR Net receives occasional subsidies both from the regional office of the MoC and the Yokohama city government; but these are normally given for specific projects. In 1997 a non-profit foundation was established to manage project coordination. The work of TR Net is followed with interest by river-related environmental campaigners throughout Japan and it is now regarded as a model for similar initiatives elsewhere.

The groups and activities in the Tsurumi basin are most likely to involve older people, women and the young. The under-representation of household heads reflects their patterns of work, which commit them to spending most of their time in Tokyo or Yokohama. Despite the diffusion of the two-day weekend, many such individuals remain reluctant to participate in activities within their residential neighbourhoods. Creating a participatory spirit that matches the planning rhetoric is thus difficult, and such problems are often exacerbated by tensions within and between the residents of particular communities. As in many areas where population is growing, relations between incomers and long-established residents are often poor. The latter tend to be more hostile towards the new forms of community action and unwelcoming of local government attempts to engage with officials of neighbourhood associations (Robertson, 1991). Tensions and animosities have also materialized between upstream and downstream inhabitants. Finally, while the river flows through some heavily industrialized areas, business participation in the activities of TR Net has been restricted to the occasional cosmetic exercise. The absence of business interest exacerbates the distortions of partial public participation, although a more active engagement with business would run its own risks of appropriation by powerful vested interests.

TR Net thus exemplifies a certain type of environmental campaigning, the most prominent example of a growing move towards consensus-based environmental action focused on river basins (Ōsawa, 1999). It shares points in common with other umbrella organizations around the country and incorporates some of the language and ethos of Japanese-style community planning, with its emphasis on cultivating grassroots opinion. TR Net's coordinators are involved in the work of enlightening, proselytizing, mediating and facilitating. But in concentrating on 'soft pursuits' – local history and culture, walking and nature-related activities – the Net avoids controversial campaigning issues. Thus, despite its prominence as a model project, it represents only the weakest of moves towards sustainable development. A new value is placed upon the natural world and the local focus of the river itself; but the goals of any environmental initiatives are ill defined and there is no coordinated effort to foster

comprehensive improvements in environmental quality. The lack of business participation is particularly significant, for it deprives TR Net of any potential as a
foundation for a new partnership between local economic and environmental
interests.

Hino: ecological river restoration in disused irrigation channels

Hino is located in the outer commuter belt of west Tokyo, a 40-minute ride to the
centre of the city by express train. Situated at the confluence of the Tama River and
one of its larger tributaries, the Asagawa, Hino lies between the uplands at the far
west of the Tokyo metropolis and the more densely urbanized satellites that ring the
Japanese capital. Urbanization has proceeded in a piecemeal fashion since the 1960s
and continued apace throughout the 1990s. Manufacturing industry – notably, Hino
trucks – has long since replaced agriculture both as the principal source of
employment and the main use of land. Yet, this now predominantly urban territory
still contained 180 kilometres of irrigation channels in 1995. The municipal government considered this network too extensive to be maintained and many channels have
now been filled in. Of those that were retained, particular attention has been focused
on a single 400-metre long section identified for rehabilitation in 1993 and 1994, using
what were then pioneering techniques in the Japanese context. The project cost about
200 million yen (about UK£1 million at the exchange rate of the time), with central
government and the Tokyo metropolitan government supplying three-quarters of this
sum. The annual budget for upkeep in its first few years was around 400,000 yen
(UK£2000).

The initial objective of the Hino project was to recreate an environment for wildlife
(Waley, 2000a). The successful promotion of biological diversity is evident in the
presence of ten species of fish now living and breeding in the waterway, despite the
predatory presence of carp released into nearby rivers. They share their habitat with
kingfishers, fireflies and dragonflies, and in summer the waterway itself is almost
concealed by the surrounding greenery. Elements of the Japanese cultural landscape
have also been reconstructed. Traditional stone-facing techniques, which allow for
water permeability, have been used on the banks of the waterway, and at one end a
watermill has been built using local techniques and materials. The other end of the
waterway opens out into a pond, one side of which lies within the grounds of the local
junior school, where it is used as a teaching resource. There is no protective fencing
between the pond and the schoolyard, and children are encouraged to come to the
water's edge. Access for the wider community has been facilitated by the construction
of bankside walkways on land purchased for the purpose by the city government.

The initiative described above was instigated by a single local government
official; but other river restoration projects have since been undertaken in Hino.
Some involve the construction of features, such as ox-bow formations and pools
and shoals, to enhance existing waterways as a habitat for fish. Others focus
on the protection of the smallest irrigation channels to ensure that they are
not cast into concrete. Schools and schoolchildren are involved where possible.
Thus, in Hino the rehabilitation of waterways has become the springboard for
a range of environmental activities sponsored by the municipal government. Again,
however, the emphasis is on a limited agenda of environmental improvement

designed to yield social and educational benefits. Deeper and potentially controversial engagement with the environmental consequences of the city's industrial economy is generally avoided. The result is a spatially variegated territory in which investment in green 'islands' of environmental quality is offered as a counterbalance to the continuing assault on the environment elsewhere. There are, thus, echoes of other limited projects favoured for European and North American cities which treat a modest 'greening' of the urban environment as a surrogate for more substantial, but also more controversial, progress towards more sustainable development.

Problems Behind the Projects: Environmental Quality and Participation

The case studies raise questions about the ambiguity of moves to improve environmental quality, both as an end in itself and as a goal that is potentially at odds with other economic and social considerations. Japanese river restoration projects remind us that concerns about environmental quality are not adequately captured in essentially arbitrary sets of indicators of pollution, land use or biodiversity. Nor can such indicators define an ideal landscape as the end point for restoration work. A more broadly expressed aim of recreating 'natural' river environments may be appealing in principle; yet, in practice, it is both impossible and illogical. Rivers cannot be returned to some 'original' state. There is no precise record of past flows or channel patterns and, as dynamic systems, rivers will never retain the same form over time, even in the absence of human intervention. At a smaller scale, the environment created in Hino, while appearing natural, is cleverly manipulated and is, in its own way, just as much a human creation as any instance of concretization. Ultimately, therefore, the new environments created are engineered, albeit designed with an emphasis on ecological sustainability rather economic growth. The solution is still technologically based, even if it is no longer technocentric. Thus, there is no clearly defined or undisputed standard against which to work; the goals of river restoration are determined by subjective – and thus contested – judgements.

The planners and ecologists promoting the new ethos of river management in Japan – as in Europe and North America – face a series of challenges. At one level, these reflect initial uncertainty over the identification of appropriate techniques for river restoration. But there are also value judgements to be made, first, about the extent to which restoration of environmental quality is defined in terms of creating visual beauty, ecological diversity and locally appropriate conditions, and, second, about the meaning of these terms when applied to particular projects. Ecological river restoration represents a new language of landscaping. As yet, best practice is undefined; there is no primer of techniques or systematic training for engineers. Decisions have to be taken about when to use natural materials and when their artificial substitutes are to be preferred. Although concrete must be concealed in new river management work, it has not been expunged entirely from the range of building materials (Ribāfuronto Seibi Sentā, 1996). The most recent phase of river restoration work has seen a greater emphasis on the use of traditional regional or local techniques, prioritizing the preservation of diversity and distinctiveness alongside the broader ecological aims of landscape restoration. Yet the general preference for the creation of locally appropriate landscapes may be over-ridden when exogenous materials or plants are necessary to meet particular constructional needs. Indeed, the definition of a 'native' flora is potentially controversial; it is not always clear what is 'natural' and locally appropriate. The balance to be struck between spontaneous growth of vegetation and landscaped planting may also prove problematic in both aesthetic and ecological terms. During hot Japanese summers, when humidity is maintained by high rainfall, plant life grows luxuriantly. Some human involvement in maintaining 'natural' environments is thus desirable, if not inevitable. Similar debate surrounds efforts to incorporate elements of the traditional cultural landscape within river restoration work. For some planners and environmentalists, the incorporation of elements such as the Hino watermill runs counter to their ecological priorities for river restoration.

Evidence of debate and uncertainty about the objectives of river restoration amongst its supporters increases the scope for opposition amongst the many groups and individuals who continue to prioritize established economic and social goals over a new environmental sensibility. Although future economic opportunities for the construction industry and the engineering establishment may be linked to a continuing reliance on technocentric management, wider public concerns about river restoration focus more on the threat posed to the existing accumulation of human and man-made capital. Personal safety and the defence of property continue to be important issues for many floodplain residents. Such concerns have been a cause of tension regarding the Tsurumi basin project and there is ample evidence of similar disputes elsewhere. For example, an MoC project to build a riverside park in Fukushima City, in north-eastern Japan, was opposed by local residents on safety grounds. The Hino project, too, was undertaken as a pilot scheme in the face of opposition from both residents and some local government officials. Protests in this instance reflected concerns that the restored waterway would create a public nuisance and health risk by becoming a breeding ground for mosquitoes.

The limitations of participation

The Japanese experience also reveals the limited success of consultation and participation schemes intended to broker common agreement about a new accommo- dation between socio-economic and environmental goals in river management. The Tsurumi River project attempts to involve a substantial number of local residents and other stakeholders in promoting a more sustainable environmental agenda. In practice, however, it probably has no impact on more than a minority of people and interests. Moreover, the work of the TR Net is largely educational and it eschews active involvement in debate concerning competing priorities in river management. The encouragement of effective and representative citizen participation in environ- mental projects and initiatives promoted under the aegis of Local Agenda 21 has proved difficult in the UK and many other countries. In Japan, however, despite an emergent tradition of social action and environmental campaigning – which has focused upon opposition to specific construction projects, including dams, airports and roads – the cultural barriers to widespread public participation are particularly strong. Patterns of work allow many adults little leisure time and Japanese society has still not entirely abandoned its attitudes of deference to the political and economic elite. Equally, it might be questioned whether the Japanese state truly believes its own rhetoric of consultation and participation to the extent of compromising its traditionally close control over civil society.

This combination of circumstances creates problems regarding decision-making about who, how and when to consult. Older systems of community involvement through flood prevention committees are long since dead and have no obvious successors. The principle of community participation has been elevated as an important part of local government consensus-building. Yet despite the inclusion of consultation with local people as a mandatory element of the drafting process for river basin plans, the government has still to define a way of involving a representative cross-section of residents in the planning process. Nor have moves to increase the role played by non-governmental organizations (NGOs) – known in Japan as non-profit organizations, or NPOs – been uncontested. The 1998 NPO Law stakes out a new place in Japanese society for these bodies; but the gestation of the legislation took over three years, as politicians and officials sought to defend the domain of the state in public affairs (Yamamoto, 1999).

The ambiguity of attitudes manifest within national government has created a situation in which the rhetoric of consultation and participation can be disregarded at the local level, sometimes with results that generate active public hostility towards river planning. The failure of Tokyo metropolitan government officials, for example, to implement proper consultation procedures regarding river restoration work on a tributary of the Tamagawa led to prolonged conflict (Ishikawa, 1999). Local residents claimed that the planned re-landscaping did nothing to improve animal habitat or human access. Resorting to law, however, did little to promote a new accommodation between residents and planners. While the discussions dragged on inconclusively, the planned river management work was completed.

Such confrontations may be relatively rare, but government difficulties with the process of consultation more often lead to a recourse to co-option. Some commentators, at least, regard this as continuing evidence of government reluctance to relinquish authority. Officials recruit the support of established local leaders who may be seen more as conduits for the communication of established policy than agents who can facilitate genuine dialogue between government and the local community. Thus, in Fukushima City local opposition to the MoC's planned riverside park prompted ministry officials to form a Watari Riverside Society with the aim not of consultation, but of changing public opinion. Leading local figures were persuaded to lend their names to the society and its arguments that residents should adopt a more mature approach to flood safety and cease to regard it as a problem to be tackled solely through state-directed engineering work (Yoshida, 1999). In other cases the approach adopted has been even more at odds with the rhetoric of consultation. Governments have planted their own off-duty officials within activist groups to act as local-level mediators (Yamamoto, 1999).

Co-option of the leaders of neighbourhood associations and other local opinion formers often sits alongside the more overt involvement of officials, experts and academics as the originators and prime movers behind environmental campaigns. A substantial body of activity has been generated – societies formed, meetings held, seminars organized and books published – around issues relating to rivers and water, with the names of a handful of leading campaigners regularly recurring. These individuals, drawn mostly from universities and government organizations, are effectively directing an elite project. They are international in outlook, but keen to foster a sense of locality and community. Most are aware of the contradictions of a situation in which they are trying to engender local-level interest without appearing to act in a top-down, dirigiste fashion. Equally, they are generally conscious of the limits of their actions and the strength of opposition within other elite structures. Acting in a lay capacity enables motivated officials to promote their ideas amongst colleagues and the general public. It also facilitates an exchange of ideas and opinions, and creates an important space for the mediation of potential contests. At the same time, however, the potential clearly exists for conflicts of interest and for the appropriation of local activism by government bodies. Elite environmentalism remains at some remove from the common search for a new accommodation between economy, environment and social welfare envisaged in the more democratic constructions of sustainable development.

Conclusion: Points of Ideological Cleavage

Not all environmental action in Japan is oriented towards compromise and engagement with government. An alternative, more confrontational, approach to government has been evident in campaigning against major construction projects, such as the barrier across the lower reaches of the Nagara River and the dyke shutting off the tidal flats of Isahaya Bay (Amano, 2001). The cleavage between different types of environmental action is, however, of less significance than the broader clash of ideologies. The ideological conflict embodied in the Japanese debate concerning river management exists at a number of different levels and finds expression in several related arenas, of which the environment is one of the most prominent. On one side of the divide lie those who subscribe to the modernist tradition of faith in engineering technology as a guarantor of human safety and prosperity against dangerous and unpredictable natural forces. Their opponents form a smaller, but growing, band who support an approach to natural elements, including water and rivers, that attempts to harmonize human activity and ecological systems. Between these two positions stand a diversity of individuals, both within and outside the elite of government and the specialized professions, who are looking for points of compromise between the secure and tested way and a more morally audacious and intellectually speculative path.

Rivers are excellent yardsticks against which to test the sustainability of development. There is no escaping the consequences of ill-conceived activity, evident in erosion upstream, neglect of farmland in midstream valleys, pollution and concretization in downstream areas. At present, few would deny that engineering orthodoxy still prevails in Japan. River restoration projects, such as that at Hino, while painstakingly researched and executed, are necessarily limited in their impact because of their small scale. The Hino example may prove a valuable educational resource and a focus for the mobilization of local environmental awareness; but given its costs, the initiative is hard to replicate on other local sites. Larger-scale river restoration work, too, is constrained by funding, but also by the tensions between ecological and socio-economic objectives, especially as perceived by residents of the densely settled floodplains of Japan's major rivers. Elsewhere the implementation of novel forms of river planning may be constrained by the nature of the terrain. Steep, narrow valleys are unsuitable for the new techniques because of the difficulties of access and the danger of erosion.

Acceptance is, however, growing amongst the technocentric elite of the need to seek compromises to meet at least some of the objections and ideas of their critics. The Tsurumi basin and the Hino project are part of a broader programme to introduce a more environmentally benign regime of river landscaping without increasing the threat to people and property from flooding or other hazards. In recent years, the MoC has abandoned a number of plans to construct new dams and scaled back other proposals. A revised river law specifies the duties of authorities to protect the environment in their riparian projects. The intention is clearly to create waterways that are more sustainable. The techniques used involve fewer interventions in the landscape, less manipulation of terrain and river channels, and thus reduce the introduction of alien construction materials. The careful husbandry of resources, the concern for the vitality of ecosystems, and the observance and use of natural contours and materials all speak of an adherence to techniques that are inherently sustainable. Despite popular concerns, social and economic considerations need not be compromised as a reduction in intrusive hydrological engineering, combined with more careful maintenance of floodplains, should actually lessen damage from inundation. The programme can also deliver long-term financial savings as the heavy initial costs of small-scale pilot projects will be more than offset by reduced expenditure on engineering work.

As yet, however, the potential of the new ethos of river management as an exercise in sustainable development is not matched by widespread popular faith in its efficacy. Despite governmental adherence to the rhetoric of sustainable development and a growing strand of environmental activism in Japan, the foundations of engineering orthodoxy remain largely secure. Vested interests within government and business are unlikely to surrender their attachment to construction-led development without a struggle. Legislation and financial penalties have been used to force change in the attitudes of planners and engineers; but it is questionable whether such tactics can secure popular legitimacy for significant changes in river management policy. Education to change public perceptions of the economic, cultural and environmental role of rivers is important. But current Japanese initiatives often fail to go beyond this to engage in genuine dialogue between government, environmentalists and local residents. Only if this can be secured will river management become more inclusive, more responsive to public concerns and more tailored to meeting local needs. Legitimacy is an important foundation for sustainable development, both practically and morally. Without popular support, progress towards more sustainable development remains vulnerable to subversion and reversal. But more than this, truly sustainable development seeks the equitable resolution of tensions between competing economic, social and environmental goals, rather than the continued imposition of expert plans and outside opinion, however 'enlightened'.

An examination of changing ideas about river planning confirms that the environmental and social strands to sustainable development need more than individual enthusiasm and spirit if they are to become an effective element of the Japanese planning process. A project of ideological reprocessing is also required. It would be difficult to overstate the ultimate scale of this challenge. Tensions over river planning reform are a reflection of a much broader ideological conflict affecting the whole range of development policies. This, in turn, is driven by the continued hold exercised by construction-based economic policies, as well as by wider events stemming from change in the global capitalist system (McCormack, 2001). Until these underlying ideological conflicts are resolved, there is little prospect of the new regime of river planning being much more than an exercise in re-aestheticization. After all, there is a fundamental contradiction in gently swaddling the middle reaches of a river in willow shoots while damming it several times over further upstream.

For some, sustainable development carries the aura of a quasi-spiritual quest; for others, it takes the form of a model with properties that can be measured and calculated, calibrated and compensated, and eventually traded. But sustainable development is a concept that cannot exist outside the parameters of dominant modes of thought. So long as Japan's ruling elite – its politicians, bureaucrats, bankers and business bosses – continues to seek to buy its way out of the country's economic woes through new and ever-more unnecessary construction projects, it seems hard to envisage anything more than a tokenistic application of sustainable development in Japan.

Note

1 The field-work upon which this chapter is based was conducted during visits to Japan in 1995, 1996 and 2000, funded by grants from the Japan Foundation Endowment Committee and the School of Geography at the University of Leeds. In 1995 and 1996, Paul Waley was affiliated to Tokyo Metropolitan University and would like to thank Professor Sugiura Yoshio for his help in making this possible. Paul Waley would also particularly like to thank Sasaki Nobuhiko and Ōsawa Kōichi for providing a wealth of detail on the Hino and Tsurumigawa projects. The following people gave precious background information and material: Wanami Kazuo, Mori Seiwa, Inuyama Kiyoshi, Takahashi Katsuhiko, Kaneko Hiroshi, Yamamichi Shōzō, Adachi Toshiyuki, Takehara Kazuo, Yasuda Minoru and Kishi Yūji.

All names of Japanese are given in the usual Japanese order, that is to say, family name before personal name.

10

Sustainable Futures for the Arctic North

Ken Atkinson

Introduction

During the 1980s and 1990s, interest in sustainable development in the lands of the Arctic North increased markedly. In part, this reflected an external identification of indigenous Northern populations as environmentally sensitive and caring communities and, hence, potential role models in the search for some ideal practice of sustainability (Martin, 1978; Mulvihill and Jacobs, 1991; Usher, 1987). However, the slogan 'Think global, act local', as a popular expression of the ethos of sustainable development, has become an internal rallying call for Arctic peoples themselves in their search for economic well-being, political recognition and a feeling of self-worth.

As an ideal, sustainable development offers a powerful alternative to the erosion of environmental quality and social cohesion that came to be associated with the accelerating pace of economic development in the Arctic North during the 20th century. But the principles of sustainable development must be translated into an achievable blueprint for local communities facing the twin challenges of rapid demographic growth and exposure to external sources of change and dislocation associated with the increasing globalization of economy, society and culture. The key to enhancing well-being for expanding Arctic populations lies in the promotion of community health, in the broadest sense, and in the creation of employment that is sustainable, both economically and environmentally. Thus, moves towards more sustainable development will involve local policies designed to strengthen community development and popular involvement in decision-making, and employment provision, especially the promotion of small-scale industry that is ecologically sound and labour intensive (Kassi, 1987; Pell and Wismer, 1987; Weeden, 1985). But such initiatives must be underpinned by the broader redefinition of the economic and political rights of Arctic communities and indigenous peoples. Moves at national and international levels to restore aboriginal land rights and promote regional reinvestment of revenue generated by the exploitation of non-renewable mineral resources are important preconditions for progress, creating a new framework of self-determination for Northern lands (Duerden, 1992; Robinson and Pretes, 1988).

In entering the debate concerning Arctic futures, this chapter will first place sustainable development within a typology of models of development. Subsequent discussion focuses upon the North American and Russian Arctic in reviewing the past record of exploitation and management of resources, both renewable and non-renewable. Discussion of current understanding of the principles of sustainable development in the specific circumstances of the Arctic leads to an evaluation of their translation into practice. This reveals the need for coordinated action at different spatial and political scales, from the local to the circumpolar.

Varieties of Development

Development that is sustainable, in that it balances environmental, economic and social objectives, is not a wholly new goal. Firey (1966), for example, writing two decades before the term 'sustainable development' entered the academic and political vocabulary, declared that the aim of development is to achieve a state of systems equilibrium based upon environmental soundness, economic feasibility and social acceptability. However, such ideals find only muted echoes in the past experience of the Arctic North, which is better understood as a manifestation of what Colby (1990) dubs a system of *frontier economics* – the most unsustainable form in a fivefold typology of development. Powerful external interests view such frontier territories as a source of near-limitless supplies of natural resources to be exploited for maximum immediate profit. Dominant political and commercial interests in the states that surround and control Arctic territory have traditionally treated the far North as just such a reservoir of resources. However, as this chapter documents, recent decades have seen signs of positive change. During the 1970s, practice in many Arctic lands moved towards *resource management*, Colby's second model of development. This implies increasing concern for environmental degradation and a growing recognition of the need for conservation and efficiency in the extraction and use of natural resources.

Colby's remaining models place increasing emphasis on environmental quality. Indeed, both *selective environmentalism* – which involves a voluntary adoption of environmentally friendly options, such as recycling and pollution prevention – and *deep environmentalism* – whereby ecological integrity is identified as the foundation for all human activity – prioritize the environment above economic growth. However, of all of Colby's models, it is *sustainable development*, with its aspirations for balance between the preservation, creation and consumption of natural and human capital, which has the greatest potential to change development policy for the better in circumpolar regions.

Given the relative poverty of the indigenous population and the still considerable potential of untapped Arctic resources, any approach to sustainability that sets stringent limits upon economic growth is unlikely to appeal to the people and governments of the North (compare with IUCN et al, 1991). Rather, the project of sustainable development as expressed by the Canadian federal Department of the Environment (1991) is embodied in policies that offer 'genuine hope of economic development without environmental decline'. If resources are managed for the long term and revenue is reinvested in Arctic communities, it is not impossible that aspirations for greater security of income and employment, and higher material living standards can be reconciled with preservation of environmental quality and biodiversity. The foundations of sustainable development are thus likely to include both traditional and modern forms of agricultural and industrial production, investment in education, healthcare and social welfare, as well as advances in pollution prevention and the technologies of habitat renovation and reclamation.

During the 1990s, the goal of social equity also came to the fore in public and political debate over Arctic futures. Thus, a definition of sustainable development advanced by the Standing Committee of the Canadian Parliament in 1997 refers to a search for 'human well-being through an equitable and democratic utilization of society's resources, while preserving cultural distinctiveness and the natural environment for future generations' (House of Commons, 1997). The explicit reference to democratic decision-making and the preservation of traditional culture is of major significance for circumpolar regions. Sustainable development in this context marks a departure not simply from a colonial frontier model of resource exploitation, but from the accompanying marginalization of indigenous peoples. It is not only in the conventional 'Third World' of Africa or Asia that the promotion of sustainable development has an especial importance as a means of empowering local communities; of redressing existing inequity; of meeting needs that people define for themselves in accord with their own values; and of enhancing the positive virtues of social and geographical difference. These hopes for the future must, however, be set against the reality of the past exploitation of Arctic environments and entrenched attitudes about the primacy of economic growth.

Unsustainable Development: Past Practice and Conflict over Renewable and Non-renewable Resources

Wildlife as a renewable resource

Although many of the indigenous peoples of the Eurasian Arctic derive their livelihoods from reindeer herding, the most ubiquitous renewable resource of the circumpolar North is its wildlife. The Arctic is a hunting ground where the quarry includes fish and marine mammals, such as whales, walrus and seals, and the major land mammals, including musk ox, caribou, Arctic fox and polar bear. The exploitation of these populations has historically been carried out by two distinct sets of harvesters with very different attitudes towards resource stocks: first, the indigenous peoples of the Arctic and, second, hunters or fishers from external industrial societies.

Hunting, trapping and fishing as practised by indigenous peoples yield food and raw materials for household use, as well as providing some cash income through the sale of meat, hides, furs, ivory and bone (Fondahl, 1998). Native peoples have logically had an interest in the long-term survival of wildlife populations as the basis of their own future livelihoods. However, there is no scholarly consensus regarding the extent to which past indigenous populations actively managed wildlife stocks. Biologists such as Thomas and Schaefer (1991) have argued against the existence of any conscious aboriginal systems of wildlife management. Rather, they suggest that the past impacts of hunting and fishing were kept in check simply by the small scale and limited technological sophistication of human populations. Anthropologists and sociologists, on the other hand, see an effective means of wildlife management in traditional knowledge (Berkes et al, 1991; Usher, 1987). They argue, moreover, that the social structure of pre-contact aboriginal societies discouraged individualism and promoted communal systems of property sharing. In a situation that was the antithesis of Hardin's (1968) 'Tragedy of the Commons', the exploitation of wildlife was governed by an effective system of customary law (Brody, 1998). The strength of these unwritten rules related to the cultural, as well as economic, significance of wildlife. Animals were not just key economic and dietary resources; they were also imbued with spiritual value and, hence, accorded considerable respect (Wenzel, 1991).

What both these perspectives on aboriginal practice have in common, however, is an acceptance of the past sustainability of indigenous hunting and fishing. Whether or not they were actively managed, wildlife populations were viewed as a resource that should be used to benefit the whole community, both present and future. By contrast, the hunters and fishers who exported Arctic resources to meet the demands of external industrial societies displayed no such commitment to sustainability or concern for indigenous livelihoods. The effects of a pattern of hunting driven largely by a desire for maximum short-term yields and immediate profit were apparent from the 18th century onwards in the decline of important Arctic species, including whales, walrus, seals, musk ox and Arctic fox. Indeed, commercial boom was often followed by bust as wildlife populations were decimated and even locally exterminated.

The severity of these human impacts on such animal populations is also a reflection of the difficulties of achieving ecological sustainability in hostile Arctic environments. Arctic ecosystems are typically extremely fragile, displaying limited diversity, low productivity and slow growth rates (Atkinson, 1988). They also possess a low buffering capacity, lacking the resilience to recover quickly from any disturbance, whether natural or man-made. Thus, regional studies, including work on Lancaster Sound in eastern Canada, have emphasized three defining characteristics of Arctic ecosystems (Welch et al, 1992). First, they are simple; therefore, a disproportionately large percentage of energy flows through specific species within the food web. In Lancaster Sound, the Arctic cod plays a major role, both as a consumer of organisms at lower trophic levels and as an agent concentrating these small particles of energy into units large enough to be eaten efficiently by seals, whales, polar bears and birds at higher trophic levels. Second, these ecosystems have a low resistance to impacts. Consumption of the annual production of cod by the main marine mammal, in Lancaster Sound the ringed seal, is close to the maximum possible. This leaves little leeway for any increased harvest of cod or seals by polar bears and human hunters. Third, Arctic ecosystems exhibit bio-amplification, reflecting the length of the food chain supporting the higher vertebrates. Human impacts – including over-harvesting, pollution and environmental change – on the plankton, shrimps and smaller fish that make up the lowest trophic levels of the marine food chain may thus precipitate the collapse of populations of larger mammals such as seals and polar bear.

External influences and the exploitation of non-renewables

Over-harvesting of wildlife has been one important source of stress undermining Arctic ecosystems and the sustainability of indigenous livelihoods. However, government and commercial policies related to other forms of development, particularly the exploitation of non-renewable resources, have also led to enforced and destructive change. Native peoples have not only suffered the effects of environmental damage, but also the denial of legitimacy to traditional lifestyles based on hunting and herding. Their initial powerlessness to resist such disruption was a reflection of their status as colonial peoples, even within a single contiguous political territory. Canada's native peoples have been governed from Ottawa by the federal Department of Indian Affairs and Northern Development. In the former USSR, state socialism produced an even more undemocratic form of administration under which governors appointed by the central power in Moscow ruled Arctic territories. By contrast, Alaska has enjoyed a much greater degree of autonomy within the federal structure of the USA. However, incoming populations and commercial interests have allowed native peoples little role within state government in Alaska, and the indigenous population has become a minority within its own lands. Even at the time of the American purchase of the territory from Russia in 1867, native peoples accounted for only 50 per cent of the Alaskan population. By the late 20th century, the proportion had fallen to 10 per cent. Thus, a common denominator in these three very different political systems has been the political and geographical marginalization of their native peoples. As a result, indigenous populations have suffered the denial of both political self-determination and traditional rights of ownership and inheritance of land.

The intensity of exploitation of the non-renewable mineral and energy resources of the Arctic has historically varied between different countries. For over 200 years, Russia has exploited the non-renewable resources of its northern territories for export to support economic growth elsewhere. This characterization of the Russian Arctic as an enormous repository of resources was particularly apparent during the Soviet era. Hence, Stalin observed in 1936 that 'The Arctic and our northern regions have colossal wealth. We must create a Soviet organization which can in the shortest period include this wealth in the general resources of our socialist structure' (Armstrong, 1952). By contrast, apart from the Yukon goldfield boom of the 1890s, both the USA and Canada virtually ignored their northern regions and peoples for much of this period. Only during and after World War II, in a climate of heightened concern about national security and the future availability of key raw materials, did they give serious consideration to exploiting Arctic mineral and energy reserves. Metal mining boomed in the North American Arctic from the 1940s until the 1970s. During the 1960s, both Canada and the USA also launched large-scale Arctic energy development programmes. Both national governments offered generous financial incentives to stimulate private-sector exploration for oil and gas, and for the development of hydroelectric power capacity.

The increasing intensity of industrial development in the North American and Russian Arctic during the 20th century has had a growing and destructive impact upon local environmental and social systems. The new metal mines developed in post-war North America were often individually short lived. Typically, a metalliferous vein might be mined for an economic life of ten years and then abandoned as capital, equipment and the work force of imported skilled labour were transferred to the next deposit. In the initial absence of anti-pollution legislation, there was little preliminary planning of new mines or consultation with local governments. Although North American developers took care to design plant and infrastructure to minimize permafrost thawing and consequent subsidence, they did not undertake wider assessments of impacts on the environment, wildlife and the livelihoods of indigenous hunters. Upon mine closure, no attempts were made to clean up the site beyond recovering equipment that had some market value for future reuse. In the absence of planning regulations, mine operators were not required to remove or revegetate mine tailings, or to clean up areas affected by acid mine drainage. As a result, 'islands' of environmental damage have been left in Alaska and Canada. Some of these are quite extensive, for pollution is not restricted to the land directly affected by mining. In an environment of impermeable permafrost, rates of overland flow of meltwater and precipitation in spring and summer are high, with the result that even small sites can contaminate substantial land areas and significant watercourses.

Economic development in northern Canada during the 1950s and 1960s was also accompanied by enforced social change as native peoples were moved into permanent settlements by a combination of government incentives and duress. This further undermined the livelihoods and cultures associated with traditional trapping and hunting. However, little thought was given at the time to the importance of sustaining indigenous modes of life. It was assumed that alternative employment would be found in the expanding minerals and energy sectors, and in the development of commercial processing of renewable resources. In practice, these new jobs have been slow to appear. Much of the labour employed in mining and hydrocarbon exploration has been brought in from southern Canada. Moreover, individually short-lived mining and energy developments provided little basis for long-term security of employment for the indigenous Northern population. Jobs – particularly for those without specific technical skills – have disappeared, with little prospect of replacement as operations are closed down and capital is relocated. Consequently, unemployment has reinforced the identification of the native settlements with various social pathologies, including high rates of suicide, crime and violence, and endemic drug and alcohol dependency.

It is, however, the Russian Arctic that has experienced the most extreme examples of environmental and social damage inflicted in the name of economic progress. Soviet pressures for absorption of native populations into an industrializing economy were always intense. Greater and more consistent coercion was exercised than in other circumpolar countries, both in the state appropriation of land and mineral resources, and in the enforcement of permanent settlement upon native populations. State control over the deployment of labour also led to the in-migration of southern workers on a much greater scale than elsewhere. This was not only socially disruptive; it also increased still further the political marginalization of native peoples. They were, in many instances, effectively excluded from any local government or commercial decision-making about their own homelands (Espiritu, 1997).

Environmental pollution from industrialization in the Russian Arctic was also on a greater scale than in Western Europe or North America (Peterson, 1993). The most substantial instances of pollution anywhere in the circumpolar North all lie in Russian territory, on the industrialized Kola peninsula, in the White Sea region and the Yamal peninsula of north-west Siberia. The mining of heavy metals in the first two of these regions has inflicted particular damage on marine and terrestrial ecosystems. There is also an added threat from nuclear power generation and military nuclear installations in the Murmansk region. In north-west Siberia, significant damage to the environment has followed the extraction of oil and gas since the 1960s (Stewart, 1995).

Twentieth-century developments have increased the extent to which traditional and industrial economies are thrown into competition for the use of the same land. The Yamal peninsula, for example, is home to reindeer herding Nenets nomads who have latterly worked within a framework of state planning that divided the peninsula into four large state farms, or *sovkhozy*. However, one third of the proven gas reserves of the former Soviet Union also lie within this territory. The central government of the USSR, and now Russia, allowed free use of land and water resources by state industrial corporations, with little account being taken of the true environmental and social costs of their activities. It was inevitable, therefore, that the essentially traditional, pastoral economy of the Nenets would be subject to increasing disruption and the loss of land through industrial development. One estimate suggests that 6 million hectares of pasture have been destroyed in the Yamal-Nenets region (Vitebski, 1990).

Damage to land and water reflects, in part, the direct pollution caused by the Russian oil and gas industry, which has been slow to adopt environmentally sound technologies (Sagers, 1994). This has been compounded, however, by the indirect damage caused by melting of the permafrost, where disturbance erodes the insulating properties of vegetation and the soil surface. Experience in Alaska and northern Canada has shown that judicious planning can overcome the engineering and ecological problems presented by permafrost (Williams, 1989; Worsley, 1988). In the former Soviet Union, however, the excellence of pure scientific research on permafrost was not translated into industrial good practice and appropriate construction methods. The severe disruption of terrain in north-west Siberia, with thaw lakes and extensive thermokarst, thus demonstrates the scale of ecosystem degradation that can result from oil and gas development.

Sustainable Development in Principle

The problems described above are fundamentally a product of the unbalanced nature of the relationships between Arctic peoples and environments, and the dominant southern populations of the states making up the circumpolar North. External interests have been attracted to Arctic regions solely to exploit renewable and non-renewable resources for export to metropolitan industrial economies. In every case – with whales no less than oil and gas – the economic goal was to maximize immediate exploitation. This generated short-term profit, most of which was also exported, rather than being invested in Arctic development. When resources were depleted, discoveries disappointing or world commodity prices depressed, bust inevitably followed boom. The chief victims of this opportunistic economic activity were not the entrepreneurs themselves, much of whose capital was sufficiently mobile to allow its reinvestment elsewhere. Rather, the social and environmental costs of unbalanced and exploitative economic growth have been borne disproportionately by Arctic communities. All of this is a reflection of the past economic and political powerlessness of indigenous populations. Their interests in the long-term mainten-ance of environmental capital as the basis of traditional livelihood systems have often been disregarded.

A transition to sustainable development in the Arctic North demands attention to the long term. It requires that economic growth and diversification be accompanied by environmental protection. Central to this is a renewed emphasis on the managed exploitation of renewable resources, involving both the reassertion of the legitimacy of traditional aboriginal practice and a new imagination in exploiting sustainable opportunities for commercial gain in novel fields such as tourism. Such strategies do not preclude the continued exploitation and export of non-renewable resources. However, the costs and benefits of such activity must be distributed more equitably. This will involve a real commitment to curbing the social and environmental damage caused by the presence of extractive industries in Arctic regions. But more than this, a proportion of the profits generated from non-renewable resources must be retained locally. This should not only be directed to short-term improvements in environmental conditions and social welfare. Money must also be invested in the enhancement of renewable resources and the creation of new human capital through education and training. For such socio-economic and environmental changes to take place, there must be a redefinition of the geometry of political power. Arctic communities, so long marginalized, must take a bigger role in decision-making about their own futures. They, above all, can legitimately claim to have the permanent interests of the circumpolar North at heart.

The importance of increased self-reliance, both on the part of individuals and communities within the Arctic, is thus a central feature of Mulvihill and Jacob's (1991) analysis of future Canadian development strategies. Self-reliance, they stress, is an intangible trait that can rarely be achieved through negotiation or imposed from outside. However, it is possible to identify foundational changes that create the conditions in which a new spirit of confidence and independence can be fostered. First and foremost is the promotion of greater regional self-determination, allowing a population greater power to shape its own cultural, political, economic and environmental futures. Central to such change will be a conscious process of de-colonization – a rejection not simply of metropolitan economic and political control, but also of an alien consumer culture that has grown in potency as the recent spread of satellite television increases Northern exposure to the global mass media. If the predominance of external authority is to be challenged, Arctic communities must establish their own local political systems. These should be able to give democratic expression to local needs and possess the power to influence events, rather than deferring on important matters to distant governments in Moscow, Ottawa or Washington.

Local democracy requires appropriate institutional structures, both formal and informal, equitably representing the broad constituency of interests within the community. This might build on established traditions of the band councils, the most local institution of government amongst native American peoples, which have hitherto played an important role in negotiating consensus regarding the local management of the collective resource of wildlife. But the voice of indigenous peoples will only be effectively strengthened if greater local democracy is set within a larger framework of political change. This will require not just a redistribution of power within individual states, but also the creation of international forums for circumpolar cooperation and consultation. The 1990s saw the emergence both of links between Arctic peoples themselves – through unofficial groups such as the Inuit Circumpolar Conference (ICC), with representatives from Alaska, Canada, Greenland and Russia – and more formal political dialogue between governments, particularly in the new forum of the Arctic Council. Involvement in such bodies is important not simply as a means of advancing specific initiatives, but also for the wider assertion of the legitimacy of the rights and identity of Arctic peoples.

The importance of self-determination and political reform is echoed in Young's (1996) blueprint for Arctic development. In seeking to balance the need for the strategic coordination of more sustainable development with a greater emphasis on local knowledge, participation and decision-making, Young invokes the principle of subsidiarity. This allows for growing international cooperation in areas where it is appropriate, but also promotes the ideal that within any administrative hierarchy, policy is always made at the lowest level with the necessary powers and competence. Thus, it is hoped, political decision-making can be made more responsive to the diversity of needs and aspirations expressed within an extensive population. Young also highlights other economic, cultural and environmental dimensions of sustainable development in his prescription for Arctic futures. In addition to subsidiarity, he advances six further principles:

1. subsistence preference: subsistence users get preference in rights concerning resources over commercial and recreational interests;
2. co-management: all users have a voice in decision-making about resource management and exploitation;
3. prioritizing the long-term perspective: ensuring decision-making about resources that takes account of regeneration rates of renewables and discovery rates of non-renewables, in relating present consumption to the needs of future generations;
4. the precautionary principle: development only proceeds on the basis of sound scientific and traditional knowledge;
5. true cost accounting: incorporating all direct and indirect costs and benefits;
6. the adoption of environmentally appropriate practices and technologies.

Such principles, however, provide framework guidelines for policy creation, rather than constituting policy in themselves. Although governments amongst the circumpolar states, as elsewhere, have expressed their support for policies of sustainable development, there is still a long way to go before grand rhetoric is translated into practical and effective action. There are also clear differences between the North American and Russian experience. In Canada and the USA, social and economic policies have been developed since the 1970s that are more in sympathy with Northern cultures and environments. Renewed recognition is being given to the cultural and social value accorded by indigenous peoples to working on the land, to hunting and craft skills, and to the communal sharing of the results of the hunt. Both governments and private capital have been increasingly involved in policy approaches that stress that development can be very modern, and yet still based on traditional resources and skills. Some of the foundations for more sustainable development are thus relatively well grounded in the North American context. By contrast, Soviet Russia could not countenance moves towards greater local democracy or an economic and cultural pluralism that would embrace respect for Arctic peoples and environments. Yet, paradoxically, the collapse of Soviet rule has created few prospects for positive change. If anything, the problems and needs of Arctic regions have been marginalized still further as Russia struggles to adapt to changing economic and political realities. The desperate need for foreign capital means that oil, gas and minerals, the main foreign exchange earners, will inevitably be exploited as rapidly as is possible, whether by foreign corporations or by a new and powerful elite of Russian entrepreneurs.

Moves Towards More Sustainable Development: The North American Experience

Environmental management

Of Young's (1996) seven principles for Arctic development, it is those relating to environmental management and pollution prevention that have been established the longest in regulation and practice. The impact of national legislation to curb pollution and enforce environmental standards passed during the early 1970s was felt in both Alaska and the Canadian Arctic. In introducing new protection for terrestrial and marine environments, the regulation established the need to take account of environmental standards in the planning and operation of developments in the minerals and energy sectors. Pressures have thus increased for the adoption of cleaner technologies and more environmentally sensitive management practices, including the rehabilitation of industrial sites at the end of their economically productive life. The National Environmental Protection Act (NEPA) introduced in the USA in 1970, largely in response to the imminent prospect of oil extraction in northern Alaska, started a trend for pre-project environmental impact assessment that is now well established. This has gone some way towards implementing the precautionary principle and forcing developers to acknowledge the full costs, both direct and indirect, of their activities.

Self-reliance, subsidiarity and land rights

Moves that will lay the foundations for important changes in the structures of political decision-making have also been initiated over the past 30 years. In the Arctic context, subsidiarity has an especial potency as a reassertion of the voice, culture and rights of indigenous peoples. It is thus a central plank in the construction of the greater regional self-reliance that Mulvihill and Jacobs (1991) prioritize. More specifically, the creation of new and effective institutions of local government with powers over resource management, and especially land rights, forms an effective base from which to pursue several of Young's (1996) principles. These include subsistence preference, co-management and attention to the long-term social and environmental health of Arctic regions.

During the 1970s, the federal governments of both Canada and the USA began to pursue an active policy to resolve disputed claims to the title of Arctic lands. In 1971 the Alaska Native Claims Settlement Act (ANCSA) granted the title to about 12 per cent of the Alaskan land area – a total of 18 million hectares – to native-owned corporations. Similarly, in 1975, the Canadian government acknowledged the control of aboriginal peoples over 14,000 square kilometres in northern Ontario, with exclusive hunting, fishing and trapping rights in a further 152,100 square kilometres. In 1984 the Inuvialuit (Inuit) of the western Canadian Arctic gained title to 91,000 square kilometres of land in the Mackenzie delta region. Most significantly, an agreement contracted in 1993 transferred title to 354,000 square kilometres of land in eastern Arctic Canada to the Inuit people, guaranteeing rights for traditional forms of hunting and fishing over this extensive area. The settlement also led to the creation in 1999 of the new territory of Nunavut as an area where the majority Inuit population would enjoy a new degree of local self-government (Ministry of Indian Affairs and Northern Development and the Tungavik, 1993).

The willingness of the American and Canadian governments to settle the claims of indigenous peoples to rights over vast territories that they had traditionally occupied initially owed much to the desire to establish an undisputed legal foundation for the exploitation of mineral and energy resources. A process of claims-settlement ensued through which aboriginal groups received land, money and limited self-government in exchange for relinquishing all other claims over territory. However, this transformation of property rights has been accompanied by a wider redefinition of the political rights of indigenous Arctic populations. As a result, native peoples have gained considerable influence in decisions regarding natural resource development. In Nunavut, the Inuit have effective control over three important institutional agencies set up to manage wildlife, water and the environmental impacts of development. By extension, they also have a new influence over the exploitation of non-renewable resources as future developers will have to negotiate impact and benefit agreements with the Inuit authorities before major development projects may proceed (Ministry of Indian Affairs and Northern Development and the Tungavik, 1993).

Indigenous peoples have thus been able to redefine their relationships with southern industrial corporations seeking to exploit mineral and energy resources. The granting of property and political rights to native communities has provided a foundation from which they can bargain with developers for environmental protection, employment, training and the provision of community services. These changing circumstances have not, as was sometimes feared, established new obstacles to development. Rather, there seem to be fewer protracted conflicts, more cooperation with industry and a shared wish to make projects more sustainable, and less damaging to the environment and the local economy. This is exemplified in the sinking of a diamond mine at Lac de Gras in the Canadian Northwest Territories by the Broken Hill Proprietary Ltd, begun in the late 1990s. Approval for the project followed a process of environmental impact assessment, involving extensive public hearings in the affected areas and the consequent imposition of environmental and socio-economic conditions to be met by the mining company. Development is subject to stringent environmental regulations, and aboriginal people will participate with the company and the government in the establishment and revision of environmental management plans. Initial negotiations have addressed the need to protect the traditional hunting and fishing rights of local communities. Compensation for damage to fish habitats and caribou pasture caused by the mining operations has been agreed. Employment provision is also guaranteed with the requirement that 60 per cent of both construction workers and permanent employees should be Northerners, of whom

40 per cent should be drawn from aboriginal populations (Canadian Environmental Assessment Agency, 1996).

Debating 'environmentally appropriate' development

Such projects must, however, be viewed within a context of continuing debate in North America about the optimum balance to be struck between exploitation of renewable and non-renewable resources in future development strategies for Arctic lands. If there is increasing support for the principle of environmentally appropriate management and technologies, there is no consensus about the meaning of these terms in practice (Young 1996). Indeed, continuing differences have been thrown into sharp relief by changes in US energy policy announced in 2001 which have become the focus of much subsequent political debate. Planned measures intended to foster energy security by boosting domestic energy production envisage increased oil exploration in Alaska. This would involve drilling in the Arctic National Wildlife Refuge, which currently provides essential summer habitat for caribou, polar bears and hundreds of bird species. While the plan's supporters argue that environmental disruption will be minimal, opponents – including environmentalists and representatives of indigenous peoples – fear that the damage to wildlife, livelihoods and cultural identities will be profound (Campbell, 2003; Kettle, 2001).

More generally, influential voices, including economists in central government and economic development officers working in Arctic communities, continue to advocate a primary reliance on large-scale developments in the mining and energy sector as the only source of income and employment realistically capable of meeting the needs of expanding indigenous populations (Stabler, 1987). Such a perspective emphasizes the need for economic growth in the face of the continuing poverty and dependency of native communities. In recent decades unemployment has risen, as the creation of new jobs has not kept pace with the growth of Arctic populations. In Canada's Northwest Territories, for example, unemployment ranges from 20 to 50 per cent in small communities (Myers, 1996). Many households are dependent upon the state, either for employment in local and national government services, or for social assistance and unemployment benefits.

Yet these problems suggest that any development strategy which is overly reliant upon the exploitation of minerals and energy resources for sale in international markets is likely to be flawed. What job opportunities had been created for native peoples, particularly in Canada, in the expanding energy sector of the 1970s and early 1980s were quickly extinguished when the oil boom ended in the mid 1980s. The subsequent decline in world oil and gas prices led to a scaling down of investment and exploration by the major multinational energy companies. Although the Arctic oil sector may be set for a renewed phase of expansion, this past experience throws into question government adherence to an industrial model for Arctic development. The costs and benefits associated with extractive industries can be distributed more equitably to meet the interests of native peoples. However, such development will inevitably perpetuate Northern dependence upon external demand and the prices set in international markets. This maintains an economic trajectory of boom and bust that is difficult to reconcile with the immediate security of individual livelihoods and a longer-term aspiration for economically and environmentally sustainable development.

While mining and energy industries will continue to be an important sector in the economy of the Arctic North, their benefits for indigenous peoples and remote communities should not be exaggerated. There is thus an economic argument that supports the view taken by many environmentalists and sociologists working amongst Arctic communities that only the renewable resources of land and sea can provide truly sustainable employment for native peoples. This was one of the conclusions reached by the influential Berger report into the proposed Mackenzie Valley gas pipeline in north-west Canada (Berger, 1977), and the economic experience of the ensuing quarter century has maintained interest in the employment potential of industries exploiting renewable resources.

A utopian vision of a return to pre-contact self-sufficiency amongst Arctic populations is, of course, unrealistic. Northern communities will continue to require cash income in order to pay for the services and imported goods – including housing, utilities, ammunition and petrol – to which they have become accustomed. Hence, a future based on renewable resources cannot be built solely on traditional forms of hunting and fishing. A broader range of activities – including forestry in the southern sub-Arctic, tourism, provision of hunting and fishing facilities for paying sportsmen and the production of country foods and crafts – are being explored as a foundation for the secure and sustainable generation of income.

Myers's (1996) study of the Northwest Territories of Canada reveals that the traditional economy continues to form an important part of household incomes and lifestyles, particularly amongst the older age groups. Surveys during the late 1980s showed that 80 per cent of households in the Territories contained at least one hunter, with an average annual income equivalent to Cdn$10,000 to Cdn$15,000 in food, materials and fuel. However, her work also confirms the existence of an impressive number of other enterprises exploiting renewable resources. Growth is especially apparent in businesses supplying country food, fish and timber to local markets as substitutes for expensive imports. Such activity, unlike the tourism and export of food, fur and native artwork that are also growing, is largely unaffected by the vagaries of external market forces and changing tastes. Enterprises based upon the sustainable use of renewable resources are invariably small scale and locally based; but they are also flexible and are prized for their cultural value in Arctic communities. Moreover, this form of development is often labour intensive, a real bonus in a region with such high unemployment rates. Through tapping into the region's underexploited human capital, small-scale industries promise social as well as economic dividends, addressing Mulvihill and Jacobs's (1991) call for personal as well as communal self-reliance.

If such individual enterprises are to succeed, however, they must be located within a wider context of effective management of renewable resources. Thus, sustainable development for individual communities also depends upon strengthening the institutional framework for environmental regulation and management at the national and international levels.

Co-management

Nationally, the restatement of political and property rights for native people in Canada and the USA has provided the basis for negotiating new strategies of co-management of renewable resources, combining the best elements of traditional practice with knowledge gained from modern wildlife science. A co-management regime is any institutional arrangement covering a defined area in which government agencies with jurisdiction over renewable resources enter into an agreement with traditional indigenous hunters. Such agreements usually have three main elements: first, a clearly defined set of rights and obligations for those harvesting the resource; second, a collection of rules that parties to the agreement are expected to follow; and third, a set of procedures for making collective decisions affecting government agencies, user organizations and individual users. Berkes et al (1991) describe the various possibilities for co-management as the rungs of a ladder. The lowest levels represent the mere solicitation of local approval and advice by governmental authorities, while the top rungs represent increasing levels of power-sharing and the devolution of management responsibility to local native communities. The existence of such a pathway does not, however, make change inevitable or easy.

Past experience points to the potential for conflict between government departments and native groups over the right to exercise ultimate decision-making authority. Some observers see in this a manifestation of a deeper tension between two distinct forms of wildlife management, born of very different world views (Thomas and Schaefer, 1991). Traditional attitudes to the use of wildlife as a communal resource, shaped by spiritual belief and customary law, may be at odds with the more technical and intrusive elements of state-sponsored management systems. Initiatives, such as the collaring of caribou for satellite telemetry tracking, are thus opposed as disrespectful to the animals concerned. Conflict also occurs when the state attempts to impose its superior jurisdictional will upon aboriginal peoples, as in the imposition of quotas on the hunting of bowhead and beluga whales, or a ban on wildfowl hunting and egg collection. Laws and regulations that appear unnecessary or mistaken to indigenous peoples are liable to be ignored.

Huntington's (1992) study of co-management regimes in Alaska – covering the harvesting of caribou, beluga whale and wildfowl – concludes that to be effective such regimes require both governmental and aboriginal partners to understand and respect the other's perspective. There must, therefore, be clear lines of communication spanning any cultural divide between indigenous peoples and administrators. Success depends upon the grassroots support of native communities and the active involvement of all users – including native peoples, sport hunters and conservationists – at all levels in order to generate a shared sense of ownership of resources. Ultimately, cooperative initiatives must also be supported by adequate financial resources to enable effective management.

An example of the positive outcome of more informed dialogue between government and native communities is the Beverly-Kaminuriak Caribou Management Board (BKCMB) of the Canadian Northwest Territories. This was a product of an initial dispute during the 1980s about the state of caribou herds in the Territories. Basing their conclusions on official census figures, government managers believed caribou populations to be in decline because of over-harvesting by native hunters. The latter disputed this conclusion and their campaign against controls on hunting was later vindicated. An outcome was the establishment of the BKCMB in 1986 to act as a 'clearing house' for all information concerning the herds. The new board has no executive powers and effective management of caribou as a renewable resource is still vested in government. However, it represents an important acknowledgement of the need for cooperation between government and native communities, with both sides recognizing the futility of attempts to enforce management decisions on which there is no consensus.

The BKCMB thus represents a first step towards co-management and a model for initiatives elsewhere. Subsequent developments have signalled the potential for more radical change, shifting the balance of power in wildlife management decisively in favour of native peoples. With the creation of the new Canadian territory of Nunavut in April 1999 as a native-dominated state within a state, Inuit peoples were granted 'free and unrestricted right of access for the purpose of harvesting to all lands, water and marine areas within the Nunavut Settlement Area' (Ministry of Indian Affairs and Northern Development and the Tungavik, 1993). They will also be actively involved in wildlife management throughout the territory with the creation of the Nunavut Wildlife Management Board (NWMB). The board has nine members, the majority of whom are Inuit. This takes co-management a quantum leap beyond bodies such as the BKCMB. The Nunavut board has a mandate that focuses on the totality of an ecosystem, rather than upon a single species. Moreover, it overturns the established political and ideological dominance of the federal government in resource management. In this it follows the general statement regarding wildlife management set out in the Nunavut Land Claims Agreement, which reflects Inuit traditions of sustainable use of collective resources. The goals that will guide the NWMB are thus:

> ... first, the maintenance of the natural balance of ecological systems; secondly, the protection of wildlife habitat; thirdly, the maintenance of vital, healthy populations capable of sustaining harvesting needs; and, fourthly, the restoration and revitalization of depleted populations of wildlife and wildlife habitat (Ministry of Indian Affairs and Northern Development and the Tungavik, 1993).

NWMB also marks an important step in the devolution of real managerial authority. While government agencies are still important as a source of advice, decision-making powers are now vested in the NWMB. Decisions will be made on the basis of majority voting, rather than requiring total consensus, thus reinforcing the growing political influence of the Inuit representatives.

As yet, the NWMB is still in its infancy and the task that confronts its nine members in securing the multiple goals set out in the land claim is formidable. But the board is also an embodiment of many of the principles of sustainable development set out by Young (1996) and may prove an important testing ground of their practical relevance in securing a better future for the Arctic's environment and people.

Lessons for the Russian Arctic

In stark contrast to the beginnings of change in North America from the 1970s, the Soviet system allowed no prospect of reform. Even in the post-Soviet era, many questions remain regarding the future of the land and peoples of the Russian Arctic. In a state beset by wide-ranging problems of economic, social and political restructuring, the needs of peripheral Arctic regions have, if anything, sunk further down the order of governmental priorities. Little has been done to check the pollution caused by the energy sector in Siberia. Major accidental oil spills, such as those at Komi in 1994 and on the River Ob in 1998, have attracted particular publicity. More worrying, however, is the estimate by the US Arctic Research Commission that in the normal course of industrial operations oil is leaking into Russian soil at a daily rate equivalent to the spillage caused by the foundering of the supertanker *Exxon Valdez* (House of Commons, 1997).

The economic dislocation suffered by post-Soviet Russia has led to new gas exploitation, originally planned for the 1990s, being postponed until the 21st century (Vitebsky, 1990). However, these same economic troubles explain Russian efforts to maximize production from existing oil and gas facilities. As petrocarbons are Russia's largest source of foreign currency earnings, there is little prospect of any check to the pace of exploitation to allow the adoption of environmentally sound technologies. In the Russian context, the balance of political and economic power also remains firmly weighted to the advantage of metropolitan industrialism. Although the principle of representation for Northern peoples has been conceded with the formation of the Association of the Indigenous Minorities of the Russian Federation, this new body has no substantive political authority. Moreover, North American moves to acknowledge native rights of land ownership and inheritance find no echo in Russia (Fondahl, 1995). In the absence of effective initiatives to increase native peoples' powers of self-determination, there can be little prospect that the oil and gas industry will be forced to pay the true environmental and social costs of its activity. It would be foolish to imply that changes in property and political rights could alone guarantee the creation of sustainable lifestyles for the indigenous peoples of the Russian Arctic. But it is difficult to see how improved socio-economic or environmental conditions can be achieved without significant political reform (Bradshaw, 1995).

Arguably, the collapse of the Soviet system has created new problems, with few compensating advantages. The reindeer-herding economy of the Nenets people, for example, has been severely affected by the transition to a market economy in Russia. The Nenets' worsening circumstances reflect a combination of factors, including the non-payment of compensation from the oil companies to aboriginal nations for the use of their land, the loss of existing markets for reindeer products and the limited opportunities available for diversification of economy and lifestyle. The uncertainties of economic and environmental futures in the Russian Arctic are compounded by sharp cuts in the previously substantial state budgets for development. Although the effects of previous government spending have been decidedly ambiguous, its sudden with-drawal has caused even greater problems. There are no obvious alternative sources for the investment that is still required to improve the basic infrastructure for transport, distribution and marketing, and to maintain education, health and skills-training programmes. The withdrawal of central government support seems likely to delay any transition towards the creation of a modern sustainable economy and may even push traditional societies into re-adoption of their pre-contact self-sufficient livelihoods. Such moves may have some environmental, and even cultural, advantages; but they can do little to address the problems caused by poverty and social deprivation.

There are, however, some grounds for optimism in the opening up of Russia to more normal relations with other states and overseas institutions. The international transfer of ideas and expertise in methodologies of sustainable development may prove vital to the future of the Russian Arctic (Piers Vitebsky, pers comm). The potential wealth embodied in the resources of the Russian North is substantial. But if these reserves are to be tapped in a way that does not compromise the environmental and cultural integrity of the region, there will have to be significant modification of established economic practices. This will involve technical and managerial change, adopting the techniques of environmental impact assessment, best practice in the use of clean technologies and acceptance of responsibility for environmental restoration by mining companies and other commercial operations. More than this, long-term relationships must be built between Northern people and politicians and metropolitan government, institutions and companies, based on cooperation and mutual respect. In short, Russia must travel the first stages of the path towards more sustainable development that has already been mapped out in North America. Its journey may be made easier by the transfer of technology and human skills, effected either through international political cooperation, or direct foreign investment in the sustainable harvesting of the resources of the Russian Arctic.

International Initiatives to Promote More Sustainable Development

Circumpolar cooperation is a long-standing topic of debate, but has proved to be a somewhat elusive goal. For over four decades after 1945, the Cold War stand-off between the major regional powers undoubtedly limited the potential for constructive political dialogue. Circumpolar states participated in the new environmental diplomacy that emerged at the global level from the 1970s onwards, including anti-pollution agreements and moves to protect habitat and biodiversity, that were relevant to the defence of Northern environments. However, there were no parallel moves to promote dialogue concerning the particular challenges of Arctic development or environmental management.

Since 1989 the climate for international cooperation has improved. Finland, in particular, took an early lead in attempts to establish a basis for collective management of transboundary environmental problems, the promotion of scientific research and the dissemination of good economic and environmental practice. This gave rise to the declaration of an Arctic Environmental Protection Strategy (AEPS) in 1991 and laid the foundations for the creation of the Arctic Council in 1996. The establishment of the AEPS, based on voluntary cooperation between eight member states – Canada, the USA, Russia, Finland, Sweden, Norway, Iceland and Greenland – marked a potentially significant step forward in the management of Arctic environments. It identified a series of priorities for environmental action, including combating pollution from organic sources, oil, heavy metals, radioactivity, acidification and noise. As has often been the case elsewhere, joint scientific study of environmental challenges and the options available to meet them has been promoted as the first stage of international cooperation. Four working groups have thus been established to focus attention on the specific areas of conservation of flora and fauna, the protection of the marine environment, preventive and restorative action to cope with environmental emergencies such as major oil leaks, and monitoring and assessment of the condition of the Arctic environment.

The AEPS, however, represents only part of what is necessary to lay the foundations for an integrated sustainable development strategy. Initial concerns about its limitations focused on two main areas. First, as an intergovernmental initiative, the AEPS established no clearly defined status or role for indigenous Arctic peoples. Second, its concentration on environmental conservation appeared to be at odds with other equally legitimate aspirations for economic and social development. Subsequent discussion has attempted to address these issues. The role of indigenous peoples in environmental management was formally recognized by the Nuuk Declaration, agreed by the second ministerial meeting of parties to the AEPS in 1993. In 1996 the third meeting of the parties adopted the Inuvik Declaration, a statement of the importance of sustainable development to Arctic futures.

The creation of the Arctic Council in 1996 represents an effort to give an institutional form to these declarations. The new forum took over the environmental functions of the AEPS, but also signalled moves to extend international cooperation into economic, social and cultural spheres. Potentially, this creates a body that could play a leading role in promoting the principles of sustainable development, in encouraging the international dissemination of good practice and in strengthening pan-Arctic educational links (House of Commons, 1997). However, the establishment of the council has also sparked concerns about the politicization of the debate regarding Arctic futures and the balance to be struck between environment and development (Scrivener, 1999). The Nordic countries, in particular, are fearful that the strong environmental impetus generated by the AEPS will become diluted within the broader structure of the new institution. The council's effectiveness may also be limited by financial and political constraints. Opinion in the USA remains divided about the value of the council and Russia, too, is proving to be a less than whole-hearted member. Such scepticism underpins reluctance to commit funding to the council.

The establishment of the council also marked an attempt to extend the basis of representation in international cooperation. In addition to the eight states that were parties to the AEPS, participant status on the council has been granted to three major associations of indigenous peoples: the Inuit Circumpolar Conference, the Saami Council – which represents the native population of the Scandinavian Arctic – and the Association of the Indigenous Minorities of the Russian Federation. It is still the case, however, that as chairmanship of the council rotates every two years amongst the Arctic states, it will find its institutional home in successive state capitals. Suspicion thus remains that the council will become yet another 'southern-based' body that fails to acknowledge the full range of economic, social and environmental concerns expressed by Arctic inhabitants themselves. Such doubts have been voiced not only by the indigenous peoples, but also by non-governmental groups and academics. Young (1996), for example, asks whether 'this Arctic Council process will be so dominated by foreign ministries with poor connections or relatively little experience in dealing with grassroots people, that ... [Northern populations] will end up somewhat disenfranchised'.

Dialogue between the governments of the circumpolar states could simply perpetuate the marginalization of Arctic communities within metropolitan structures of power. Moreover, Arctic cooperation has still to go beyond the stages of consultation and voluntarism. There is little immediate prospect of any significant or binding commitment to promote environmental improvement and sustainable development. But it is possible to envisage a very different future in which the peoples of the Arctic themselves take the lead in circumpolar cooperation, gaining, in the process, a strong collective voice and a new ability to assert distinctive regional interests. It is perhaps too early to tell whether the Arctic Council will help or hinder this move towards self-reliance and sustainability. Indeed, there are echoes here of much wider debates about the future form of political geographies and the authority of the existing pattern of states as we enter the 21st century.

Conclusion

For most of the 20th century, the Arctic was treated as a resource-rich hinterland, potentially exploitable, but destined to stay on the periphery of the world economy. While its renewable resources have always been important to Northern inhabitants, external interests have directed investment into mining, oil and natural gas, and hydroelectric 'mega-projects', with associated drilling sites, dams, pipelines and shipping facilities. Since the 1970s, however, there have been signs of positive change: a new attention to the environmental consequences of the exploitation of Arctic resources; an increased respect for the social and cultural identity of the indigenous peoples of the Arctic; and greater efforts to secure more equitable distribution of rights of ownership of Arctic resources and the rewards of economic development. These trends represent important advances towards more sustainable development. Yet echoes of earlier neo-colonial attitudes remain. These are evident not only in Russia, where progress to date has been slow, but also in the enthusiasm of the US government for renewed exploitation of the Arctic to meet the energy demands of metropolitan America.

The ideal of sustainable development echoes thinking that is well rooted in the culture of the indigenous population of the Arctic. The desire to pass on the natural environment from one generation to the next in an unimpaired state, together with a society of cultural diversity, remains strong amongst aboriginal peoples. The goal of accommodating economic development within the carrying capacity of both environment and culture is a central part of their worldview. However, a strategy for sustainable development is easier to announce than to execute. There remain many familiar difficulties that reflect the fragility of Arctic ecosystems, the expense of environmental restoration and the future use of clean technologies, the high costs of developing infrastructure for small and scattered populations, and disputes over resource ownership and revenue sharing. Even within an emergent framework of consensus regarding the necessity for sustainable development, the nature and pace of change will continue to be disputed.

It is important, therefore, that moves towards sustainable development are underpinned by new political structures that will promote both local democracy and a strengthening and coherent identity for the Arctic region, as a whole. The moves that have already been made in the Canadian context to devolve authority to the indigenous peoples of the Arctic are important. They promise a greater degree of Northern control over the form and pace of development and a more equitable distribution of costs and benefits. This restoration of powers of resource management and wider political and cultural legitimacy to native peoples does not guarantee sustainable development; but it is a necessary precondition for progress. At the same time, there is an important role for international cooperation in defining a more sustainable future for the circumpolar North. International investment and the transfer of expertise and good practice will be vital to the extension of sustainable development. But forums such as the Arctic Council could also develop a clearer political role in the international assertion of Northern interests. New international institutions with real political influence are a vital counterpart to greater local democracy, strengthening the collective identity of Arctic populations and redressing long-established imbalances between the power of Northern societies and their metropolitan industrial counterparts. Whether the Arctic suffers further environmental and social degradation in the future, or develops in a way that is balanced and sustainable, will therefore be determined in large part by the ability of Arctic communities to cooperate and coordinate their activities.

11

Climate Change, Energy and Sustainable Development

Martin Purvis

Introduction

The optimistic assumptions of development currently appear increasingly vulnerable to the destabilizing effects of large-scale environmental change. Climate change, in particular, could derail economic growth and exacerbate existing concerns about matters such as food supplies, livelihoods and vulnerability to natural hazards. The potential costs of damage to socio-economic and environmental systems are huge and seem set to be borne disproportionately by the poor. Concern about climate change thus reflects our continuing inability to foster environmentally sustainable development, and the consequences of this failure for aspirations of greater socio-economic equity.

It is no coincidence, therefore, that the language of the 1992 United Nations Framework Convention on Climate Change (FCCC), which commits signatory states to the principle of restoring climatic equilibrium, echoes definitions of sustainable development. The convention effectively identifies the climate system as Critical Natural Capital, to be protected 'for the benefit of present and future generations of humankind, on the basis of equity and in accordance with their common capabilities but differentiated responsibilities and respective capacities' (UN, 1992). The need for action is widely perceived to extend beyond measures to reduce preventable future climate change. Existing changes to the chemistry of the atmosphere caused by human activity appear to make some degree of climate change inevitable. The policy response must, therefore, also include measures to mitigate the effects of climate change which, many would argue, is already evident.

The case for action to combat climate change is reinforced by claims of its wider benefits. Arguably, relatively modest initiatives today could yield substantial returns. First, because they will prevent major environmental costs accumulating in the future and reduce the threat that climate change represents to the long-term continuity of development. Second, because many individual elements of climate policy can contribute positively to the wider pursuit of more sustainable development, delivering economic and social dividends, as well as environmental security, to current and future generations.

The positive thinking embodied in such arguments is not, however, universally shared. Some commentators doubt whether an effective institutional framework can be constructed to coordinate policy that will necessarily involve initiatives at every level, from the global to the individual household. Progress to date has also been slowed by growing dispute about the relative merits of specific means proposed to combat climate change. Moreover, there are still vocal interests who assert that action is premature and ill conceived. This chiefly reflects concerns that measures to reduce greenhouse gas emissions will impose significant economic costs, especially in the short term. This position is particularly associated with commercial interests who fear for their own future profitability. But there is potentially a wider argument that unnecessary or ill-targeted action against climate change could slow the growth of prosperity and social well-being in the global North, and hamper efforts to provide decent living standards for populations in the global South. Persistent scientific uncertainty regarding the precise causes and consequences of climate change provide a degree of legitimacy for such arguments. While the precautionary principle – immediate action is justified to combat a threat that is serious but uncertain – is widely accepted in this context, the counter-argument remains: the only justified response is further research to reduce the scientific uncertainty.

Viewed in this way is it clear that action to combat climate change is not only a potentially important facet of any practical programme to promote more sustainable development, but also embodies much of the controversy that surrounds the latter. It is surprising, therefore, that previous accounts have noted only a limited engagement between studies of sustainable development and climate change (Cohen et al, 1998; Markandya and Halsnaes, 2002). This chapter begins by reviewing mainstream projections of the likely scale and consequences of climate change. It follows this with an exploration of practical responses, focusing particularly on the potential for reforming energy regimes. In assessing these options, account is taken of their wider potential to advance more sustainable development. Attention to what is technically possible must be complemented by consideration of the context within which any measures will be implemented. The chapter turns, therefore, to the need to establish and coordinate responses to climate change at all levels of the social and spatial hierarchy. In so doing, it highlights the contest surrounding many specific initiatives, and the social, economic and political barriers to change in energy regimes. Ironically, it also shows that the pursuit of equity can itself become a focus of conflict as different parties advance their own interpretations of its meaning.

Climate Change: A Threat to Sustainable Development?

Projected changes in climate and environmental systems

The science of climate change remains disputed (Philander, 1998). Some authorities maintain that observed increases in global temperature reflect natural variation rather than human activity, or that warming, even if anthropogenic, will trigger mechanisms that restore climatic equilibrium (see, for example, Lindzen, 1997; Michaels, 1998). Doubts about the ability of climate modellers to project the scale and consequences of climate change add further uncertainty. There is not the space here fully to explore scientific arguments about climate change, nor claims that the threat it presents has been exaggerated by academics, environmentalists and others (on climate change science, see Drake, 2000, and Harvey, 2000; on climate 'conspiracy', see Boehmer-Christiansen, 1997). What follows reflects the views of the scientific majority, particularly the Intergovernmental Panel on Climate Change (IPCC), established in 1988 as an international forum for the study of climate change.

Successive IPCC reports confirm that human activity is central to current climate change. Economic and demographic growth over the past two centuries has increased the atmospheric presence of so-called greenhouse gases, which trap outgoing terrestrial radiation, thus enhancing natural warming of the planetary surface (IPCC, 2001a). Fossil fuel consumption, and changes in land use and agricultural regimes are largely responsible for rising greenhouse gas emissions, particularly carbon dioxide, methane and nitrous oxide. Some man-made chemicals, such as the chlorofluorocarbons (CFCs) formerly used in products including aerosols and refrigerators, also have global warming potential. Continuing expansion of population, industrial activity, and demand for food and energy thus raises the prospect of further climate change (O'Neill et al, 2001; Tilman et al, 2001).

Global average surface temperature has increased by 0.6° Celsius over the past century and the IPCC projects a further rise of between 1.4° and 5.8° Celsius by 2100 (IPCC, 2001a). Environmental changes that are already apparent could thus be the harbingers of greater transformation. This need not be an entirely negative process. For example, a warmer climate and longer growing season could enhance the agricultural potential of land at mid to high latitudes in the Northern Hemisphere (IPCC, 2001b). However, majority scientific opinion holds that any gains from climate change will be overshadowed by environmental and socio-economic costs. Rising temperatures are likely to be accompanied by greater climatic instability and increasingly severe storm events. Changes in the temporal and spatial pattern of precipitation could lead to new extremes of drought and flood. Thermal expansion of the oceans and the release of meltwater as snow and ice cover retreats are projected to raise average sea levels by up to 0.88 metres over the coming century, threatening to inundate extensive coastal zones (IPCC, 2001a). Such changes raise the prospect of growing damage to all the dimensions of capital underpinning sustainable development (Martens et al, 1997).

The erosion of capital

Natural capital is vulnerable to climate change because of its limited adaptive capacity. Poleward and altitudinal shifts in plant and animal ranges could precipitate the destabilization and fragmentation of ecosystems, many of which are already stressed as a result of demographic and economic growth. Distinctive assemblages particularly at risk include polar and alpine ecosystems, native grasslands and boreal forests (IPCC, 2001b). Warming may affect the habitat, food supply and breeding patterns of wildlife populations, changes that could exacerbate existing biodiversity decline (Petchey et al, 1999; Sala et al, 2000; Thomas et al, 2001; Wuethrich, 2000). More frequent droughts, fires, storms and floods also threaten to destroy habitat and accelerate soil erosion, as well as impose a direct toll on plant and animal populations. Damage to agricultural land, woodland, wetland, coastal fishing grounds and other valued environments could seriously affect human livelihoods and future development prospects (IPCC, 2001b).

Millions of people currently live in coastal zones and other flood-prone areas. Climate change seems certain to increase the threat to their lives and livelihoods (IPCC, 1997). Existing subsidence problems will be exacerbated by a combination of rising sea levels, storm surges, intense or prolonged rainfall and changes in river regimes. Extensive low-lying areas are likely to be lost for settlement and agriculture through inundation, and other land and groundwater resources will suffer saltwater incursion. Accelerating coastal erosion and loss of wetlands will further increase vulnerability to storm impacts (IPCC, 2001b). Major flooding, as experienced in southern Africa during 2000, is seen by some concerned analysts as a warning of the destructive potential of climate change (FoE, 2000). Even temporary inundation can have lasting effects. Death and disease amongst human populations, the loss of livestock and crops, damage to homes, schools, transport infrastructure, and water supply and sanitation systems can seriously undermine a region's long-term development prospects (Abramovitz, 2001; IFRC, 2001).

Paradoxically, water shortages are also likely to cause problems. At high and mid latitudes in the Northern Hemisphere, shifting seasonal precipitation patterns may produce drier and warmer summers (IPCC, 2001a). Such changes are already being linked to the increasing incidence of forest fires in Southern Europe and the USA (Gonçalves, 2000). Lower summer rainfall totals will also affect levels of river runoff, with adverse consequences for riparian ecosystems and the quantity and quality of water available for human use. Still greater problems seem likely in the global South. Less frequent and reliable rainfall over subtropical areas of the Northern Hemisphere could create new extremes of drought in existing arid regions. Pressure on water supplies, often already severe as a result of demographic and economic growth, is set to increase (*Nature*, 1999; Vörösmarty et al, 2001). Resultant disruption to marginal agricultural regimes and acceleration of decline in biodiversity and soil quality would further undermine the fragile livelihoods of many of the world's poor (IPCC, 2001b; Rosenzweig and Hillel, 1998).

Damage to livelihood systems is likely to trigger rising levels of disease and death (Martens and Martens, 1998). However, climate change could work in other ways to curb the gains in life expectancy that are a key product of development. Deaths caused directly by natural disasters seem set to increase (IPCC, 2001b). Water shortages have further implications for health and sanitation, including a growing risk from diseases, such as cholera, associated with contaminated water supplies (Kovats et al, 2000). Environmental migrants fleeing hazardous events and the breakdown of livelihood systems are already beginning to outnumber those displaced by war (IFRC, 1999). Increasing population movement in the face of growing climatic instability is likely to exacerbate the spread of infectious disease (McMichael, 2001). Such migration may also intensify the health problems associated with overcrowding, pollution and inadequate infrastructure in many Southern cities (see Chapter 6). However, understanding of the health implications of climate change remains incomplete. Opinions differ, for example, on the extent to which warming would extend the territory of vector-borne infectious diseases, such as malaria and dengue fever, currently confined to lower latitudes (Martens and Martens, 1998; Martens et al, 1999; Rogers and Randolph, 2000). At high to mid latitudes, excess mortality and morbidity are also likely to be fuelled by more frequent and severe heatwaves (Kovats et al, 2000). Yet this may be offset by a decline in cold-related winter deaths (IPCC, 2001b; MacDonald, 2001).

It is clear, however, that climate change has the potential to impose a direct tithe on human capital. Indirect effects are also possible as a result of enforced reduction of investment in preventative healthcare, education and social development. Such sectors could suffer if climate change curbs income growth, or if funds are diverted to counter damage to property and infrastructure. Such expenditure reflects the potentially serious threat to man-made capital, which extends far beyond the destruction of specific property. The foundations of important economic systems could themselves be undermined.

The full implications of climate change for economic growth remain uncertain. Short-term variations associated with El Niño in 1997/1998, for example, reveal potential contradictions. In the USA, property damage and losses in such sectors as agriculture and tourism were outweighed by savings, including reduced heating costs, and growth in consumer spending and construction activity (Changnon, 2000). In Latin America and South-East Asia, however, the balance was less favourable as El Niño caused crop failures, political unrest and economic losses totalling US$14 billion (Buckingham, 1999). Sustained climate change would have serious consequences for activities such as agriculture and fisheries that depend directly upon environmental conditions (IPCC, 2001b; Rosenzweig and Hillel, 1998; Wood and McDonald, 1997). Yet other economic sectors are also vulnerable to its effects. Settlement, manufacturing industry and tourism are concentrated in coastal areas vulnerable to inundation. Reduction in river flow could prove economically damaging if shipping were disrupted or hydroelectric power generation diminished (IPCC, 2001b). Where tensions already exist between water users, the consequences could be still more serious, even exacerbating interstate tensions in regions such as the Middle East (Ohlsson, 1995).

A more unequal world

The effects of climate change on human and natural systems seem certain to be geographically and socially uneven. This partly reflects regional differentials in the alteration of temperature and precipitation patterns. Environments also vary in their vulnerability to climate change. Low-lying coastal territories such as Bangladesh are particularly threatened by rising sea levels. Equally, increased temperatures could prove especially disruptive in Arctic regions where permafrost thaw would cause extensive changes to landscapes and drainage patterns, and increased slumping threatens to damage buildings and infrastructure. Indications that the effects of climate change will be greatest where human and natural systems are already marginal are confirmed by studies of subtropical regions. Rising temperatures and reduced rainfall could have a dramatic effect in areas currently experiencing water stress and where plants and animals – including crops and livestock – are at the limits of their maximum temperature tolerance (IPCC, 1997, 2001b).

Variation in vulnerability also reflects socio-economic circumstances. The sensitivity of agriculture, forestry and fisheries to climate change will create particular problems for populations most reliant upon these primary industries. Potential victims include indigenous peoples in the Arctic north, whose aspirations for sustainability based on traditional livelihood systems would be undermined (see Chapter 10). Such problems are echoed throughout the developing world. Climate change is predicted to cause overall decline in crop yields in parts of Latin America, much of Asia and the Middle

East. Africa, however, faces the greatest difficulties. In part, these reflect existing environmental degradation and the marginality of much African farming. The continent is over-reliant on rain-fed agriculture and would thus suffer particularly if precipitation became less reliable. These troubles would be compounded by the loss of fertile land, including the northern Nile delta, through flooding and saltwater incursion (IPCC, 1997).

Africa's vulnerability is also economic. This is, in part, a function of its dependence for subsistence and income upon agriculture, which accounts for at least 20 to 30 per cent of gross domestic product (GDP) in the majority of sub-Saharan countries (World Bank, 2002). Climate change could affect other economic sectors, including hydropower and tourism. This threatens to perpetuate existing poverty. But, as is common throughout the global South, Africa's poverty is itself a factor in its exposure to external shocks such as climate change. Moreover, there are pronounced inequalities in the social distribution of insecurity within developing countries. Southern elites can buy some protection against climate change, a reassurance unobtainable by the poor majority. When local food sources fail, the latter lack the financial means to purchase surpluses from elsewhere. More fundamental is the absence of effective market mechanisms that would allow this trade to take place. Equally, technical and managerial capacities to adapt to climate change through, for example, better water conservation, are poorly developed in much of the South. Overall, the socio-economic impacts of climate change seem likely to increase disparities between rich and poor, at both national and global scales (IPCC, 1997, 2001b).

Contesting the need for action

The remainder of this chapter explores what could and should be done to counter climate change per se, and its implications for economic growth and social welfare. It is important to acknowledge, however, that the issue of climate change inspires a range of different responses. The case for immediate precautionary action to reduce its likely scale and consequences is strong. Initiatives taken now may secure a substantial reduction in the long-term costs of environmental damage and socio-economic dislocation (Metz et al, 2001; D W Pearce, 1995). But in the absence of scientific certainty about the cause and extent of climate change, such arguments do not command universal support. Key commercial and political interests argue that present climate change policy risks imposing punitive and unnecessary costs upon the current generation of producers and consumers (see, for example, Morris, 1997). The existence of such contest greatly complicates decision-making about how to respond to climate change.

Adaptation to Current and Future Climate Regimes

The least controversial aspects of climate policy focus upon improving the ways in which human societies respond to environmental conditions and constraints. Existing problems – including the abuse of marginal and hazardous environments, and the toll on life and property imposed by natural hazards – suggest that human activity is imperfectly attuned to today's climatic conditions. Given that alterations already made to the chemistry of the atmosphere render some degree of climate change inevitable, such problems seem likely to increase. Adaptation can thus be presented as a 'no-regrets' option that should yield both short- and long-term benefits. Broadly based efforts to improve the sustainability of development could play a key role in combating current and future climatic stress. Measures that improve environmental management, encourage responsible resource use, promote economic diversification and raise welfare and education standards for the world's poorest peoples will all reduce vulnerability to climate change. The context for enhancement of adaptive capacity is thus shaped by national and international development initiatives. Also potentially crucial is the correction of market failures and distortions that subsidize overuse of key resources and disguise the environmental costs of economic activity (IPCC, 1997, 2001b).

Within this general framework the range of specific adaptive measures proposed is huge. Options for agriculture include changes in crop and livestock varieties, planting schedules and tillage practices (IPCC, 1997). The development of crops and livestock better able to resist drought or saline soils may assume increasing importance in agricultural research. Irrigation to maintain agricultural productivity will rank highly amongst infrastructure investments prompted by climate change. This, in turn, will require improvements in water supply and demand management. Water management also has implications for human health. Other environmental measures, including attention to air quality, hygiene and food safety, and building design, can reduce the health effects of projected climate change. The already pressing need in most developing countries for additional investment in medical care must also be addressed. This should reduce current suffering as well as curbing any increase in climate-related disease and disaster (IPCC, 2001; McMichael, 2001).

To a degree, at least, land, buildings and lives can be protected against storm and inundation by raising construction standards and strengthening physical defences. However, adaptation strategies based on hard protection structures, such as sea walls, are giving way to other means of defence, including restoration of coastal dunes and wetlands (IPCC, 2001b; see Chapter 9 in this volume). A further strand of defence is financial; damage to livelihoods and economic systems can be offset by increased use of insurance as a form of risk-sharing. The sheer scale of the potential costs, however, may make extensive areas uninsurable (Brown, 2001a). This reinforces arguments that adaptation will require significant changes in land use, including the relocation of settlement away from risk-prone areas (IPCC, 1997, 2001b).

Adaptation is sometimes regarded as a sufficient response capable of defusing any immediate climatic threat without constraining economic development. However, such coping strategies concentrate on protecting human welfare, potentially at the expense of environmental quality, habitat and biodiversity. Irrigation, for example, may impose unsustainable demands on water resources and threaten supplies to other users, including wetland flora and fauna (see Chapter 8). Moreover, adaptation does not necessarily guarantee long-term security and can, ultimately, prove counter-productive. Over-reliance on insurance, for example, may encourage continued development of vulnerable sites (IPCC, 1997).

Approaches to adaptation also mirror wider social inequalities, as richer communi-ties and individuals are better able to command the financial and managerial resources necessary to defend their interests. This compounds the disadvantage of the poor, who are also frequently most exposed to the negative effects of climate change. Dutch expenditure on additional protection against rising sea levels, although substantial in absolute terms, will probably cost less than 0.5 per cent of GDP per annum (Whyte, 1995). The balance between expenditure and available financial resources will be very different in vulnerable small island states such as the Maldives, where adaptive and defensive measures could account for one third of current GDP (FoE, 2000; IPCC, 1997). Southern communities often lack the sophisticated warning systems that allow time to prepare for natural disasters. They are also frequently dependent upon external donors for rescue and relief measures when disaster strikes. The vulnerability of individuals is further compounded by the absence of insurance systems that provide some financial – if not emotional – defence against loss for property owners in developed countries.

Climate change thus highlights enduring North–South differences in economic development and social welfare, reinforcing calls for the promotion of greater equity as well as environmental sustainability. The prospect that many communities will suffer as a result of climate change emphasizes the need for investment to build adaptive capacity in developing countries. This process should be supported by international assistance from the industrialized Northern states chiefly responsible for increased greenhouse gas emissions. But it seems increasingly clear that such measures must be accompanied by the mitigation of climate change itself through moves to curb rising atmospheric levels of greenhouse gases.

Mitigating Climate Change

Acceptance of the need to reverse change in the chemistry of the atmosphere has not, however, inspired consensus about how this is to be achieved. Environmentalists, in particular, see emission reductions as the key to mitigation (FoE, 2000; Sachs et al, 1998). Hence, they point to the need for strict management of energy demand and greater investment in the development of emission-free sources of renewable energy. Yet other commentators claim that this will create unacceptable economic costs, and that equivalent results can be achieved by enhancing the capacity of forests, soils and oceanic waters as carbon sinks. The balance to be struck between different forms of technical and behavioural change is thus disputed, and both regulatory and market-led solutions have their champions. Moreover, action to curb climate change, as an exercise in advancing greater inter-generational equity, must also be judged in terms of its intra-generational impacts. Climate policy should not become a justification for abandoning existing aspirations to reduce current poverty and injustice.

The discussion that follows reflects the biases of the wider debate about climate change policy in focusing particularly upon the options advanced to reduce carbon dioxide emissions by innovations in energy demand management and supply. Attention is also paid, however, to measures that may curb emissions of other greenhouse gases and increase the capacity for carbon storage in the biosphere. These latter initiatives are variously presented by protagonists in the climate policy debate either as alternatives to radical change in the current carbon-based economy, or as measures to ease the transition to new energy regimes.

Energy conservation and efficiency

High levels of per capita energy use throughout the developed world have led to claims that there is significant scope for savings without loss of economic momentum (von Weizsäcker et al, 1997). Technical and managerial advances in the two centuries since the Industrial Revolution have already established a downward trend in energy consumption per unit of GDP. This is likely to continue, especially as knowledge-based sectors are assuming an increasing importance in the economies of the developed world. However, current progress, evident in a global annual average decrease of 1.1 per cent since 1971, could be accelerated by more explicit attention to energy conservation and energy efficiency (IEA, 2000). The former approach seeks to curb energy consumption by eliminating unrewarding uses; the latter aims to find better ways to deliver valued functions.

In theory, at least, energy consumption can be reduced by careful use of existing technologies. Electrical equipment can simply be switched off when not required. Similarly, improved management of building heating and ventilation systems can curb energy demand without affecting standards of comfort. Such changes rely largely upon altering consumer behaviour. However, technical means abound to secure greater energy efficiency. Power generation and transmission can be improved. Existing coal-fired power stations convert 35 to 40 per cent of fuel input into useful output. The new generation of gas-fired power stations in the UK achieves an efficiency in electricity generation of nearer 50 per cent. Combined heat and power systems, which capture heat released during generation for space and water heating, raise total efficiency levels to over 80 per cent (Alexander, 1996). Heat recovery can also be applied to increase the energy efficiency of other industrial processes. At the same time, energy savings on lighting and air conditioning, as well as space heating, can be secured through greater attention in building design and maintenance to ventilation, insulation and the capture of passive solar energy (Levermore, 1992; Meckler, 1994; Tuluca, 1997).

Further options include changes to industrial processes designed to cut energy consumption and careful use of materials, especially those such as aluminium that have an energy-intensive production process (Gottschalk, 1996; Linhoff et al, 1994). Specific technical innovations have also increased the energy efficiency of many functions. Some new heating boilers, for example, have efficiencies of over 80 per cent, a level twice that of many older models still in use (Alexander, 1996). Similar benefits flow from the use of fluorescent lighting. Energy efficiency is thus a factor in the development and marketing of a wide range of industrial, commercial and domestic equipment.

As transport is the only component of energy use still growing strongly in the developed world, particular importance must be attached to efforts to design more energy-efficient vehicles. However, a broader strategy of transport management offers potential for further gains. A reduction in traffic congestion should cut energy use, as will training in fuel-efficient driving techniques. Greater use of less energy-intensive transport modes, including the transfer of freight from road to rail or water, and the substitution of walking, cycling and public transport for private car journeys, could further curb energy use. At a systemic level, proposals to rethink the spatial form of cities and to encourage more localized patterns of economic exchange, as part of the wider promotion of more sustainable development, are also intended to reduce transport demand (see Chapters 6 and 7).

With climate change as a spur, it does seem technically possible that energy efficiency could be doubled in the developed world during the first quarter of the 21st century. Many of the technical and managerial measures responsible could also be adopted in the developing world. However, the World Energy Council predicts that global electricity consumption will rise by at least 50 per cent by 2020, as per unit efficiency gains are overtaken by the effects of continuing economic and demographic growth (Brierley, 1997). Much of this increased demand will reflect the efforts of the developing world to secure economic progress and rising living standards. It would be deeply inequitable, therefore, and at odds with the aim of poverty reduction if undue constraints were placed on this extension of energy use. It follows that improved energy management must be accompanied by increasing worldwide use of non-fossil fuels if greenhouse gas emissions are to be curbed.

Alternative energy sources

One immediate alternative to coal and oil as primary energy sources is natural gas, which has captured a growing share of UK energy markets since the late 1960s. The rapid expansion in the use of gas for electricity generation during the 1990s was originally prompted by the low cost and ready availability of supplies from the North Sea. However, its environmental benefits are also increasingly appreciated. Gas-fired power stations emit as little as half the amount of carbon dioxide per unit of electricity generated as do their coal-fired counterparts. In addition, climate change may revive the fortunes of nuclear power as an energy source free from greenhouse gas emissions. Cost and safety concerns have restricted the extension of nuclear capacity since the late 1980s. However, the sector's supporters in both the developed and developing worlds now argue that renewed nuclear programmes are necessary to ensure that climate change policy does not create a shortfall in energy supplies (Dong and Hong, 2000; RS/RSE, 1999; Sailor et al, 2000).

At the same time, there are calls to look beyond the finite resource of gas and the tarnished record of nuclear power to sustainable development based on emission-free and renewable energy sources (Dincer, 2000; Elliott, 2000). These draw ultimately upon the power of the sun, gravity and the Earth's rotation. Some renewables are already well established in a modern form. Hydroelectric power accounts for 19 per cent of global electricity generation and meets 40 per cent of the developing world's electricity demand (IEA, 2000; Ramage, 1996). Geothermal power, deriving from the heat of the Earth's core, is of more localized importance. Around 20 countries, including the USA, Iceland, Japan and the Philippines, use geothermal steam to produce electricity. Geothermal resources are also applied directly to space and water heating (G Brown, 1996).

Other traditional energy sources seem set for revival. Both wind and water have long been harnessed as sources of mechanical energy. In parts of the developing world such use will probably continue. However, the last 30 years have seen major advances in the turbine technology necessary to harness wind power for electricity generation (Taylor, 1996). Equivalent attempts to capture the energy of the oceans remain more tentative. Only a handful of barrages harnessing tidal power have, so far, been built in locations including the Rance Estuary in France (Elliott, 1996). Experimental attempts have also been made to generate electricity from wave power, using both on-shore and offshore devices (Duckers, 1996; Ross, 1995).

Solar power, too, has assumed a new importance. Attention to the orientation and glazing of buildings to maximize the potential of passive solar energy in heating and lighting can be complemented by the use of special panels designed to absorb and concentrate solar radiation. Indeed, if radiation is plentiful and sufficiently concentrated it can power electricity generation, employing conventional steam turbines (Everett, 1996). However, photovoltaics, which uses solid-state silicon cells to convert solar radiation into electricity, offers greater potential. Photovoltaic power stations connected to utility grids are operational in the USA, Germany, Italy, Switzerland and Japan. Photovoltaics can also create autonomous energy sources for individual communities, buildings and vehicles (Boyle, 1996).

In addition, solar energy is harnessed indirectly through power generation from biomass. The underlying principles are hardly novel. The burning of wood, straw and animal dung currently provides 40 per cent of the developing world's energy needs. Increasing fuel supplies could be derived from greater use of agricultural and forestry waste, including brushwood, straw, sugarcane fibre, and manure as a potential source of biogas. Additional agricultural resources are also being applied to the deliberate cultivation of energy crops (Klass, 1998). Many parts of Europe have seen experiments in planting fast-growing tree species such as hazel and willow, intended as fuel both for space heating and new wood-burning power stations. Although combustion releases carbon dioxide, biomass energy is carbon neutral as emissions are balanced against the gas absorbed by new crop growth.

Other energy crops yield vegetable oils as substitutes for diesel fuel. Brazil, meanwhile, has pioneered the use of ethanol fermented from sugar cane for use in road vehicles (Ramage and Scurlock, 1996). The ultimate Green motive power for transportation may, however, prove to be fuel cells that produce electricity from hydrogen and oxygen, leaving only water as an exhaust product (Cummings, 2002). Biomass energy is sometimes also taken to include power generation from the incineration of domestic waste, much of which is of biological origin. In addition, usable quantities of methane gas can be recovered from waste decaying in landfill sites, or through a more controlled processing of the organic fraction in specially constructed digesters (Ramage and Scurlock, 1996).

Curbing emissions of other greenhouse gases

The initiatives outlined above largely aim to curb carbon dioxide emissions. However, other greenhouse gases are more potent agents of climate change. Specific targets for phase-out include the hydrofluorocarbons (HFCs) used as coolants in the refrigeration industry. These could be replaced by systems using hydrocarbons or ammonia, which have no appreciable global warming potential (Purvis et al, 2001). The capture of methane from mines and landfill sites not only yields usable energy, it also lowers the atmospheric concentration of this important greenhouse gas. Alternatively, methane emissions can be cut by reducing the material going to landfill. Such policies may yield additional financial dividends. Hayhoe et al (1999) calculate that by reducing both methane and carbon dioxide emissions, rather than concentrating on the latter, the USA could cut the costs of meeting environmental targets by around 25 per cent. Yet attention to methane emissions from agricultural sources in the developing world, including paddy rice cultivation and grazing animals, is controversial. Some commentators regard it as a ploy to divert attention away from the emissions generated by industrial economies (Sachs et al, 1998). Reform of intensive agriculture to reduce chemical fertilizer use – a key tenet of sustainable agriculture – could, however, cut the chief anthropogenic source of nitrous oxide (see Chapter 8 in this volume and Robertson et al, 2000).

Enhancing carbon sinks

In addition to curbing emissions, it is also possible to reduce the atmospheric concentration of carbon dioxide by increasing its retention in the biosphere and oceanic waters. Current initiatives largely focus on preserving existing carbon sinks by reducing deforestation and other changes in land use. The clearance of growing trees removes a particularly effective biotic carbon store and the damage is compounded if the wood is burned, releasing carbon dioxide and methane (Houghton, 1994). The elimination of deep ploughing would also help to restore levels of carbon storage in soils. In addition, more active measures could increase sink capacity. Proponents of afforestation claim that land is available, particularly in the tropics, to allow the extensive planting necessary to make an appreciable impact on climate (Houghton, 1993; Stuart and Costa, 1998). However, such initiatives must be carefully managed to ensure the sustainable harvesting and constant replacement of timber, as only actively growing young trees make a net contribution to carbon storage. Other more speculative proposals include suggestions that oceanic waters should be seeded with iron to stimulate phytoplankton growth, or that carbon dioxide could be stored by injecting it into deep oceanic waters, geological formations and disused oil wells (Chisholm, 2000; Dalton, 1999).

The Wider Context of Sustainable Development

Gains all round?

An optimistic reading of the measures outlined above suggests that the means exist to respond effectively to climate change. Moreover, such initiatives may make a wider contribution to increasing the sustainability of development (Markandya and Halsnaes, 2002). Their central purpose is, of course, to minimize climate change itself, preventing damage that could undermine any emergent equilibrium between socio-economic development and environmental sustainability. Climate change policies also encourage efficient and responsible resource use. But it is widely recognized that energy reforms must enable continuing economic and social advances so that current problems are not solved at the expense of inter-generational and intra-generational equity. Indeed, specific initiatives may yield gains in social welfare, health and commercial profitability.

Access to reliable and affordable energy is a vital foundation for socio-economic progress in the global South (WCED, 1987; World Bank, 2000). Worldwide, however, 2 billion people still live beyond the limits of electricity transmission lines. In many instances, the costs of linking them to conventional systems employing centralized generation plant and fixed transmission lines would be prohibitive. The accelerated development of renewable energy as a result of climate change policy could therefore prove particularly beneficial. Localized systems, harnessing biofuels, wind, hydro and solar power to meet the needs of specific communities, frequently constitute the most efficient and cost-effective means of extending energy services (Byrne et al, 1998).

For countries without fossil fuel resources, renewable energy promises greater fuel security, savings on import costs and reduced exposure to volatile international energy markets. In addition, the uptake of renewables should curb the pollution and damage to landscape and habitat associated not only with coal and oil production, but also the unsustainable harvesting of fuelwood (Arimah and Ebohon, 2000; see also Chapter 4 in this volume). The potential value of forests as carbon sinks further reinforces arguments for their careful management.

Technical and managerial changes that increase energy efficiency allow individual consumers to combine environmental responsibility with cost savings on energy and other inputs. Equally, the development and marketing of the systems and technologies that are essential for a low-carbon economy can be commercially rewarding (McEvoy et al, 2000a). It is certainly the case that commercial investment in developing renewable energy has grown considerably over recent years (Farrow, 2000; Macalister, 2001a). Alongside new businesses created specifically to develop novel resources, renewables are attracting the attention of established multinational companies. The oil and gas giant British Petroleum (BP), for example, claims to be the world's largest producer of solar technology, with a turnover target of US$1 billion by 2007 (BP, 2002).

At a national level, a forecast for the USA predicts that innovations in energy production and consumption, together with an associated reduction in oil imports, will yield a net gain of 800,000 jobs and economic benefits averaging US$19 billion per year to 2010 (Bernau and Duckworth, 1998). Growth in the European Union (EU) renewables sector could generate 900,000 jobs by 2020, including opportunities in engineering and construction, and new uses for underemployed agricultural labour and land in the production of biomass and wind energy (EUFORES, 2000; Renner, 2001). Renewable energy might also create economic opportunities in the developing world. Millions of hectares of degraded land in Africa and Latin America could be devoted to biomass energy production with the potential to generate major fuel exports (Ramage and Scurlock, 1996). Still more significant, however, will be the indirect effects of new energy sources as a stimulus to broader economic growth.

Change in energy use could yield additional, and often immediate, welfare benefits. For example, the substitution of efficient stoves for the open fires still widely used in the developing world for cooking would create a cleaner and healthier domestic environment. Equally, improvements in building design in developed countries frequently raise both energy-efficiency and comfort levels. On a larger scale, energy-efficiency initiatives may significantly reduce urban air pollution, thus cutting associated ill health and premature deaths (Cifuentes et al, 2001). Strategies for tempering energy demand through urban design, changes in land-use planning and traffic reduction overlap with blueprints for more sustainable cities. These are envisaged not only as places where energy consumption is low, but also as communities enjoying standards of health, safety, social welfare and environmental quality superior to the contemporary urban experience (Capello et al, 1999; see Chapter 6 in this volume).

But is it that simple? The contradictions of reformed energy systems

We cannot, however, assume gain without pain. A more balanced review of climate change policy reveals potential tensions with sustainable development. Restructuring of energy production and consumption may entail social and environmental costs, especially given the scale of investment necessary to secure significant cuts in fossil fuel use. At the same time, there is far from universal agreement that climate change policy is consistent with continuing economic development. In truth, transition to a low-carbon economy will create both losers and winners, raising questions not just about the overall balance between costs and benefits, but also about the equity with which they are distributed. At a global level, some commentators argue that energy shortages and rising costs caused by enforced reductions in greenhouse gas emissions will undermine the international competitiveness of Northern industrial economies. Yet many in the developing world are equally worried that concerns about climate change will reinforce existing North–South inequalities. This does not simply reflect fears that the need for climatic stability may be invoked as an argument for limiting the South's economic development. Existing Southern dependency upon external sources of technical expertise may also be perpetuated in a future low-carbon economy, as Northern-based multinationals seek to dominate global markets for renewable energy technologies.

At the same time, climate policies raise a multitude of specific concerns. For example, some energy technologies are controversial. Renewed investment in nuclear power raises particular questions about public health and safety, and environmental impacts. Even apparently less risky options are not immune from criticism. Community groups and environmental organizations have raised concerns that windfarms are visually intrusive in rural landscapes, create excessive noise and adversely affect wildlife (Niesewand, 2000; Russell, 2001). On-shore installations harvesting wave power face similar criticisms. Extensive areas of solar panels or biomass crops could, if insensitively designed and located, also prove visually and environmentally disruptive.

The potential contradictions in renewable energy production are particularly evident in the hydropower sector. There is a growing recognition that large-scale dams are flawed as tools for water management and energy production. Many projects have not fulfilled their initial targets for water and electricity supply, while creating unacceptable and unnecessary social and environmental costs (WCD, 2000). Despite investment in environmental technologies and compensation for populations adversely affected, the distribution of costs and benefits associated with dam construction often remains inequitable (March and Fisher, 1999). Worldwide, 40 to 80 million people have lost their homes and livelihoods to projects that have dramatically changed river regimes and aquatic environments. Extensive areas, including land valued for its agricultural potential, environmental quality and cultural significance, have been flooded. Such costs still accrue disproportionately to groups – chiefly rural dwellers, and particularly subsistence farmers, women, indigenous peoples and ethnic minorities – who lack the political and economic influence to defend their own interests. Other costs are simply deferred to be borne by future generations. By contrast, the immediate gains of water and energy supply are frequently channelled away from local riparian communities to external beneficiaries at a regional or national level (WCD, 2000).

The development of renewable energy may demand a substantial commitment of capital and natural resources. Hence, some critics question whether the underlying process of production is environmentally sustainable. The manufacture, transportation and installation of plant to capture renewables will necessarily involve consumption of non-renewable resources, often including energy derived from fossil fuels. Biomass production may also rely on energy inputs in the form of chemical fertilizers and fuel consumed in harvesting and processing (Ramage and Scurlock, 1996). Charges have even been laid that some renewables consume more energy than they produce, perhaps reflecting the initial energy-intensive manufacturing process for photovoltaic cells (Boyle, 1996). Overall, however, emissions of greenhouse gases and other pollutants associated with renewable energy production can be shown to be less than for equivalent conventional facilities (Everett and Boyle, 1996).

Less clear cut are the economics of renewable energy development. Technical advances have generally reduced cost differentials between renewable and conventional energy. European wind energy prices, for example, fell by half between the mid 1980s and the mid 1990s as a result of improvements in the design, manufacturing quality and scale of generating units (EWEA, 1997). Further efficiency gains are necessary, however, if renewables are to secure a major stake in energy markets. Moreover, the initial capital costs remain a potential brake on the development of hydro, solar and wind power. The attempt to establish biomass as a fuel for significant electricity generation in the UK has encountered similar problems, evident in the fate of the ARBRE gassification plant in Yorkshire, declared insolvent in 2002 after only eight days in operation (ENDS, 2002c). This experience can only undermine the confidence of farmers in the potential market for biomass crops. It also highlights the wider difficulties of initiating change in energy markets. Without consumer demand for clean energy, supply will remain limited and costs high; but it is precisely these supply-side problems that inhibit the growth of consumer demand. More generally, the low cost of fossil fuels has restricted the growth of the renewables sector, thus reinforcing calls for political initiatives to redefine the commercial environment. Potential measures include the introduction of carbon taxation and other charges that reflect the full environmental costs of conventional energy production. Equally, subsidies and tax incentives could be redirected to promote the development of renewables. Long-term electricity supply contracts would further encourage investment in renewable energy. Ultimately, growth in the sector might become self-reinforcing if economies of scale reduced plant production and installation costs.

Even enthusiastic proponents of renewable energy agree, however, that its expansion will require careful management. Specific renewables are not equally viable in all circumstances. The economics of solar power, for example, are more favourable in the Mediterranean or California than in the UK. Britain, however, has plentiful wind resources. At a finer geographical scale, questions remain about the location of renewable resources and their ability to deliver consistent energy supplies. Wind is a variable resource and is frequently most powerful in areas distant from major centres of urban and industrial energy demand. Hence, plans announced in 2001 to build Europe's largest windfarm on the Hebridean island of Lewis would require the construction of a sub-sea cable system along Britain's west coast to bring electricity ashore (Harrison, 2001c). Even with government financial backing, critics claim that this infrastructure will be prohibitively expensive.

An inadequate response?

Whatever the economics of reforming energy regimes, it is also vital to consider whether the initiatives proposed can deliver significant reductions in greenhouse gas levels. Recent trends are not encouraging; emissions rose by around 10 per cent during the 1990s in Japan, the USA and Australia. The EU stabilized emissions over the decade; but this included largely fortuitous cuts resulting from investment in gas-fired power stations in the UK and economic slowdown in Germany following political unification (Meacher, 2000). By comparison, the future task is daunting. The UK's Royal Commission on Environmental Pollution has called for a 60 per cent cut in carbon dioxide emissions by 2050, an ambition endorsed in the 2003 Energy White Paper (Carrell, 2000; Gow, 2003). Environmentalists go further, arguing that energy-intensive developed economies must cut emissions by up to 90 per cent to restore climatic stability (FoE, 2000) Such projections heighten concerns about the adequacy of an essentially technocentric response to climate change. Doubts about the ability of proven technologies to deliver the necessary scale of change are compounded by claims that some proposed methods of reducing greenhouse gas levels are fundamentally flawed.

Particular questions have been raised, for example, about sinks as a means of storing carbon dioxide. Critics claim that attempts to use oceanic waters will damage marine ecosystems, without ensuring long-term carbon sequestration (Chisholm, 2000; Dalton, 1999). Afforestation and changes in farming are likely to produce significant, but finite, increases in carbon storage. Managed land sinks could meet 25 per cent of the global reduction in atmospheric carbon dioxide levels thought necessary by 2050; but thereafter the potential for expansion is limited (Adam, 2001). The value of afforestation could itself be undermined by environmental change. Under warmer and drier conditions trees could die back, and in a carbon dioxide-rich atmosphere they will mature more quickly and at a smaller size, thus reducing their carbon storage capacity (LaDeau and Clark, 2001). This prospect also highlights concerns about the inadequacy of current techniques for estimating the scale of sequestration (Schiermeier, 2001b). Over-reliance on carbon sinks might create the illusion, but not deliver the reality, of control over atmospheric carbon dioxide levels. This would be doubly dangerous if it slowed the implementation of emission cuts.

By comparison, the technologies of renewable and emission-free energy production are largely proven. Yet doubts remain about the practicality of change on a sufficiently large scale. Environmentalists and commercial sponsors of renewable energy are predictably positive. The European Wind Energy Association, for example, claims that recoverable wind power alone could generate sufficient electricity to meet world demand at 1997 levels four times over (EWEA, 1997). But developments, to date, are geographically uneven. Within Europe, Germany, Denmark and Spain lead other countries, including the UK, in the use of wind, wave and solar power. Denmark derives over 13 per cent of its electricity from the wind; yet in the UK, which has the continent's richest wind resources, the proportion is only around 0.3 per cent (Jeffery, 2001; Wintour, 2001b). Moreover, many energy companies have maintained their core spending on fossil fuel production even while investing in renewables (Macalister, 2001b). There is a danger of tokenism, with powerful businesses viewing a stake in emission-free energy as an insurance policy against long-term loss of markets, while vigorously defending their existing interests in fossil fuels.

Against such a background of commercial uncertainty it is hardly surprising that the International Energy Agency (IEA) sounds a note of caution. While expecting renewables to be the fastest growing sector of primary energy supply to 2020, the agency highlights the small scale of current capacity. Only hydropower is well established. Wind power, for example, met just 0.15 per cent of world energy demand in the late 1990s. Thus, the IEA's central reference scenario for future energy production shows increasing energy demand largely offsetting growth in renewables. Consequently, their contribution to the global primary energy mix is projected to rise from 2 per cent in 1997 to only 3 per in 2020. The scenario also assumes that safety concerns prompt the phase-out of nuclear power. Reliance on fossil fuels would therefore increase (IEA, 2000).

Such projections do not, of course, constitute a conclusive case that radical changes in energy systems are impractical or undesirable. The IEA acknowledges that increasing dependency on fossil fuels could be avoided and that greater use of renewables offers a potential means to secure this. However, the questions raised about non-fossil fuels emphasize the need for careful planning of new energy regimes. They also highlight concerns about the effectiveness of the agencies and mechanisms available to establish a climate-friendly energy sector.

Some of the apparent drawbacks of renewables can be addressed by parallel efforts to rethink the organization of energy supply systems. For example, offshore installations for wind and wave power might placate groups concerned about landscape quality. At the same time, the role of large, centralized power generation facilities may diminish in future. The development of renewables through small-scale installations, generating power for individual communities at the point of consumption, could reduce both environmental penalties and infrastructure costs. Moreover, devolution of responsibility for creating and managing electricity supply systems accords with the emphasis in many readings of sustainable development on meeting local needs from local resources (Vargas, 2000).

Logically, also, greater use of renewables may require rethinking of the geography of energy demand. In the long term, it may prove viable to relocate energy-intensive activity nearer to the best-developed renewable energy resources. This will require careful planning if it is not to raise further concerns about environmental impacts. However, such changes could become an element in the wider reform of economic activity in pursuit of more sustainable development.

Scales of Change: Theory and Practice

As noted above, business has a potentially crucial role to play in securing curbs on greenhouse gas emissions, not only through investment in developments such as renewable energy, but also by increasing its own energy efficiency, and in producing and marketing energy-efficient products for commercial and domestic use. However, moves towards a low-carbon economy cannot simply be understood as a business-driven process of technological innovation. The creation of new energy regimes and the wider execution of climate policy also have social and political dimensions. Other actors and agencies will play key roles in the continuing debate about energy and climate.

This recognition highlights the need to ensure that complementary initiatives are taken at different levels of the social and spatial hierarchy. Action against climate change demands a positive response from individual businesses and consumers; it is their decisions about energy use, transportation and the purchase of goods that effectively determine levels of greenhouse gas emissions. But the scope for individual action may be limited in the absence of more systemic change in energy regimes. Local and national governments must, therefore, identify and coordinate effective climate policy. Ultimately, however, global environmental change demands that all states accept a shared responsibility for protecting climate systems as Critical Natural Capital.

This chapter's final section considers the different levels of initiative that must mesh together to create an effective response to climate change. In the short term we might reasonably expect the greatest responsibility for reform to rest with the developed world, where existing levels of greenhouse gas emissions are highest. Such thinking is reflected in the geographical focus of the following discussion. The evidence also confirms the extent to which the theoretical potential for transition to a low-carbon economy is compromised in practice.

Changing consumer behaviour

Action by consumers, both domestic and commercial, is vital in combating climate change (Redclift, 1992b). This reflects not only energy use by individual households and firms, but also the influence that end-consumers have on the quantity and quality of goods and services brought to market, and thus on energy use throughout the chain of production and distribution. More particularly, consumers influence greenhouse gas emission levels through their willingness and ability to adopt energy conservation initiatives, to opt for energy-efficient alternatives when purchasing household goods and capital equipment, and to buy energy from renewable sources. It is a moot point, however, whether incentives for change outweigh the perceived disadvantages.

In theory, at least, behavioural change is an effective and painless way to curb energy use. For example, reductions in space heating levels, or greater use of energy-efficient transport modes, could cut total energy demand without perceptible impacts on business performance or social welfare. Energy conservation rarely necessitates major capital investment and offers the incentive of lower energy bills. Such win–win arguments are not entirely spurious (Edwards, 1998). Some businesses, in particular, place a growing emphasis on energy conservation, often within wider waste minimization programmes. High-profile companies appreciate the image benefits of being seen to be Green; but the ultimate justification is usually financial (Macalister, 2001a). The mechanism is therefore weakened when there is no clear cost saving. For smaller businesses, with modest energy bills, the scale of potential savings merits little attention. Even in relatively energy-intensive industries, cost reduction in other areas, such as labour, may appear quicker and easier (Purvis et al, 2001). The condition of energy markets is also an important consideration. Currently, the real price of electricity is low in many developed countries. Moreover, in the UK competition in privatized energy markets allows consumers to cut costs by renegotiating supply contracts, rather than by managing demand (Hammond, 2000). Expectations of immediate behavioural change are thus likely to be disappointed.

Indeed, consumers are often culturally conditioned to maintain their existing behaviour. Heating, for example, is set not at levels necessary to avoid discomfort, but at higher temperatures that reflect culturally determined expectations about the availability of warmth (Shove, 2000). Consumption is rarely a simple utilitarian matter. Businesses and households attach a range of meanings – often involving notions of identity and prestige – to the possession and use of goods. Promoting change in consumption is correspondingly more difficult when it seems to threaten the intangibles of status and full participation in consumer society. Perceived imbalances in the distribution of costs and benefits also hamper moves to reduce energy demand. Some behavioural changes, such as reduced private car use, may appear to require individual sacrifice without direct benefits. Since many individuals find it difficult to envisage a causal link between their own consumption and global environmental problems, they have little sense that behavioural change can secure a solution (Hinchliffe, 1996; 1997). Even if consumers acknowledge the cumulative impact of individual action, many believe that, in practice, their efforts to curb energy demand will be negated by a lack of commitment from others (Purvis et al, 2000).

Many of the same limitations apply to initiatives to foster consumer demand for energy-efficient and low-emission technologies. Incentives for change, both economic and environmental, are relatively weak. Moreover, consumers are often locked into existing technologies and patterns of energy use. This inertia is partly a product of the capital costs involved in replacing or upgrading buildings, industrial equipment and consumer durables. The disincentive to change is increased when energy-efficient products carry a price premium, even if this can be offset against lower running costs. Such difficulties are compounded when different costs accrue to different actors. Builders and landlords may fit space heating systems that minimize their capital costs, regardless of energy efficiency, knowing that fuel bills will be paid by the building's occupiers (Guy, 1994; Guy and Shove, 2000). Equally, the scope for incremental change is limited if the upgrading of one component of an energy-using system requires alterations to the whole. Not only does this increase likely costs, but premature replacement of plant and equipment may also waste the resources involved in producing such man-made capital.

The results of energy conservation and efficiency initiatives directed at business and domestic consumers have so far been limited and uneven. We may have to accept that the pace of adoption of energy-efficient technologies will be set by existing timetables for building and equipment renewal. It is, thus, vital to encourage consumers to take up energy-efficient options when purchasing and investment opportunities arise. If this is to happen, suppliers, salespeople and installation contractors must also be a target of energy-efficiency campaigns, as these intermediaries often influence consumer choice. Consumer attitudes and behaviour might also be affected by changes in energy cost structures. To date, subsidies from the government-backed Energy Saving Trust to promote energy-efficient boilers and refrigerators have secured only a modest increase in demand in the UK (ENDS, 2000b). Alternatively, carbon taxation, or other increases in energy prices, might encourage more conscious demand management and a switch to renewable energy. But it is by no means certain that the political and commercial commitment exists to pursue such reforms, or that consumers will respond predictably to changes in energy prices. Any increase in energy costs would also have to be carefully managed to avoid penalizing the poorest consumers. Climate policy is not consistent with sustainable development if it exacerbates fuel poverty amongst the old, the sick and low-income households.

Discussion of the role of consumers thus confirms the need to set their actions within a wider framework, to provide coordination and also to create incentives for change. As already noted, business has a role in supplying and promoting climate-friendly energy systems and technologies. But we must also look to the state, both local and national, to set and enforce emission reduction targets, and to encourage change in the culture and technology of energy production and consumption.

Local government and community action

Given the current vogue for participatory initiatives, it is not surprising that they are often invoked as a means of securing change in energy regimes, often as part of a Local Agenda 21 strategy (for example, Leeds City Council, 2000). A shared commitment to energy conservation and efficiency from the local level upwards is undoubtedly necessary if individual initiatives are to have any cumulative effect. In practice, however, it is local government, rather than the wider community, that is the most significant driver for change at this level (Burgess et al, 1998).

Urban authorities, in particular, are increasingly aware of links between local and global environmental conditions. Energy and climate initiatives are justified not only because local activity contributes to global climate change, but also because of the immediate improvements that they promise in urban air quality, health and well-being. As a significant energy consumer, local government shares in the general responsibility to promote conservation and efficiency throughout its own operations. By changing their purchasing policies local authorities could also help to create market demand for energy from renewable sources, thus encouraging investment in its production (McEvoy et al, 2000b).

Local authorities also have a potential role in facilitating climate-friendly behaviour by the wider community. In part, this reflects established functions such as property maintenance, waste management and the planning of land use, urban form and transport infrastructure. Attention to insulation and heating efficiency in council housing, for example, can both curb domestic energy demand and combat fuel poverty (Salman, 2001). More generally, the dependency of households on private cars for access to key facilities reflects planning policy, both regarding the siting of housing, employment, retailing and other facilities, and public transport provision (see

Chapter 6). Local planning can also help to mitigate the effects of climate change – for example, through discouraging construction on floodplains.

In addition, some urban authorities have launched specific initiatives to encourage and coordinate action on climate change. Often, these include educational measures to raise public awareness of the causes and consequences of climate change, allied with efforts to monitor and reduce local greenhouse gas emissions. One such example is PlanetYork, a year-long project which ended in September 2002, intended to make the UK city of York a model for sustainable energy use (PlanetYork, 2002). In cooperation with householders and businesses, York City Council promoted higher standards of building insulation and increased use of energy-efficient technologies, solar power and 'greener' transport. The hope is that this specific initiative will have a long-term impact on consumer behaviour and increase market demand for energy-efficient products and renewables. It remains to be seen whether such an approach can secure significant changes in local emission levels. Meanwhile, McEvoy et al (2000b) see few immediate signs that more ambitious proposals to promote sustainable energy supply systems at a city-regional scale will be realized. A cautious note is also struck by studies of other council-led initiatives, which suggest that the concept of sustainability may be devalued in the public mind by association with local governments perceived to be struggling to discharge other functions (Macnaghten and Jacobs, 1997)

Even if successful, initiatives such as PlanetYork would have to be repeated many times over to secure an appreciable reduction in global greenhouse gas emissions. Yet a survey of UK local authorities in 2001 indicated that while most appreciated the importance of developing a sustainable energy and transport policy, many felt that they lacked the understanding necessary to address the issue, and fewer than one third had a formal climate change strategy in place (Salman, 2001). This highlights the importance of over-arching initiatives to promote and support local efforts.

In the UK this function is partly discharged by the Energy Saving Trust, established in 1992 with joint government and business funding. As part of its remit to encourage best practice in energy conservation and efficiency, the trust works with partners including local authorities, as at York. A more specific, and global, effort to coordinate urban action is the Cities for Climate Protection Campaign launched by the International Council for Local Environmental Initiative (ICLEI) in 1993. This aims to create a worldwide network of cities committed to curbing greenhouse gas emissions. Targets are set for individual urban centres that reflect their economic and demographic circumstances. ICLEI's role is to encourage local initiatives, but also to offer practical advice and disseminate good practice (ICLEI, 2002).

The campaign claims success in helping cities to identify and realize significant opportunities for environmental improvements. Portland, Oregon, for example, is credited with securing a 3 per cent reduction in per capita greenhouse gas emissions below 1990 levels by 1997 (ICLEI, 2002). For the longer term, Portland and other cities have identified measures that promise emission cuts of over 20 per cent. By 2002 the campaign involved 561 municipal authorities, chiefly in North America and Europe, but also in Asia and the Pacific, Africa and Latin America. Together these urban centres account for around 8 per cent of global greenhouse gas emissions (ICLEI, 2002). A significant change in their emissions might therefore make some impression at the global level. Urban initiatives can also counter the reluctance of some national governments, not least the USA, to adopt effective climate policies. Ultimately, however, ICLEI has no means of enforcing participation by the many urban centres that do not subscribe to its cities campaign and no power of sanction against member cities that fail to meet their emission targets.

The national arena

Although it is possible to conceive of purely voluntary and market-driven reforms, much of the foregoing discussion has assumed a complementary role for national government in advancing climate change policy through a range of educational, regulatory and fiscal measures. National government thus plays an important role in encouraging and coordinating voluntary action by consumers. Equally, the stimulus to technical innovation by business often derives, ultimately, from political efforts to raise environmental standards. It is national government, too, that sets rates of taxation and subsidy for energy and energy-using products. Indeed, the broader decisions taken by government about economic development, housing, energy and transport policy can have a significant impact on greenhouse gas emissions.

State-sponsored educational initiatives to raise consumer awareness of climate change and the part that households and companies can play in combating it are now commonplace throughout the developed world. Typically, information campaigns directed at domestic consumers promote simple energy conservation measures and attention to energy efficiency when purchasing household goods. Within the EU this has been reinforced since the mid 1990s by a requirement for energy-efficiency labelling on key consumer durables at the point of sale. In 1995 the UK government also placed a statutory duty on local authorities to raise the energy efficiency of the existing housing stock, both private and council-owned, by providing advice to householders. Information for business is often more specific, including detailed examples of best practice and subsidized access to energy management consultants (O'Riordan and Rowbotham, 1996). In most instances, the aim is to encourage, rather than to force, change. The hope is that adoption of climate-friendly products and practices will follow from growing awareness of their advantages, both financial and environmental. In theory, growing demand will, in turn, encourage business to offer more and better climate-friendly products.

The foundations of many information-based initiatives are, however, enshrined in regulation and there are instances of recourse to more prescriptive measures. Energy labelling of goods, for example, has been reinforced by moves to raise energy-efficiency standards for a range of consumer durables and to withdraw the least efficient products from EU markets. In addition, the UK government has revised construction standards for new buildings to enforce improvements in insulation and the efficiency of heating systems (ENDS, 2000c). Since the mid 1990s government pressure has also been applied to energy suppliers to change the structure of the market. The Renewables Obligation, which came into force in 2001, aims to guarantee demand for alternative forms of energy by requiring that 10 per cent of electricity derives from renewable sources by 2010 (ENDS, 2000a).

Governments also employ financial measures to support regulatory and market-driven change. One option is to increase energy prices as an incentive to conservation and efficiency. Despite the lead set by Austria and the Netherlands in levying carbon energy taxes, UK moves have been halting (Haigh, 1996). Value added tax (VAT) was imposed on domestic energy from 1994 and for a period duty on vehicle fuel was raised at above the rate of inflation (O'Riordan and Rowbotham, 1996). Business energy use has been targeted through the Climate Change Levy introduced in 2001. Further measures are in prospect, including reducing transport demand by direct charging for road use.

Taxation and subsidy can also be used to alter price differentials between specific energy sources. This may involve the phase-out of existing subsidies that confer artificial price advantages on energy sources, such as coal, that are increasingly regarded as environmentally damaging. EU agricultural reforms have, rather fortuitously, supported biomass production as energy crops can be grown on land eligible for set-aside payments (Ramage and Scurlock, 1996; see also Chapter 8 in this volume). Equally, assistance can be directed towards encouraging energy efficiency and the expansion of renewables. The UK's 2003 Energy White Paper proposed raising existing support for research and capital investment in these fields to £1 billion per year by 2010. This is still, however, substantially less than the £7 billion given in 2003 to support the UK's nuclear industry (Gow, 2003).

Yet this array of political tools does not guarantee effective action to reform energy markets and combat climate change. In the UK, the Energy Saving Trust's work to promote and subsidize consumer investment in energy efficiency has been hampered by lack of funding (O'Riordan and Rowbotham, 1996). Bold words about reducing car use and the creation of an integrated transport policy have had little practical effect (Schoon, 1997). Equally, the 10 per cent target for the sourcing of electricity from renewables seems unlikely to be met by 2010 (ENDS, 2002b). The use of taxation to raise energy prices is controversial, and since the late 1990s governments have bowed to public pressure to reverse previous increases in VAT and fuel duty. Further controversy has surrounded the Climate Change Levy, which has been persistently criticized by groups such as the Confederation of British Industry and the Engineering Employers' Federation as threatening business survival while doing little to promote energy efficiency (CBI, 2002; Harrison, 2001a; 2001b). In part, such tensions reflect flaws in the design of specific taxes. VAT and the Climate Change Levy are raised on all forms of power, offering no incentive to switch to renewable energy. Such taxes are also widely perceived as opportunistic, reflecting government's desire to secure additional revenue, rather than a real environmental commitment. Moreover, successive governments have resisted any substantial moves towards the targeted application of money raised by energy taxes to directly relevant areas, such as investment in public transport.

With greater political will and finesse more could, undoubtedly, be achieved at the national level. In the UK, calls for more decisive action have been heard within parliament as well as from the environmental lobby. Yet the 2003 Energy White Paper advanced only an 'aspiration' to secure 20 per cent of electricity supplies from renewable sources by 2020, rather than the firm commitment advocated by the Cabinet Office Energy Review of 2002 (ENDS, 2002a; Gow, 2003). This lack of a clear target may prove significant if it discourages commercial investment. Specific energy and climate change policy must also be supported by a wider-ranging review of government thinking. The Energy White Paper promised swifter planning consents for renewable energy projects. Yet previous opponents of windfarm development have included the Ministry of Defence, which has claimed that wind turbines constitute a potential danger to low-flying military aircraft (Brown, 2001b). Equally, the government's plans for a major expansion in civil aviation traffic and airport capacity raise serious questions about the UK's willingness and ability to secure substantial cuts in greenhouse gas emissions (ENDS, 2002d).

A determined implementation of higher energy-efficiency standards, change in energy pricing and subsidies for development of renewables could not, however, immediately transform energy use. Much remains in the hands of individual consumers. Even supposing that the mass of householders and businesses want to 'do the right thing' – and evidence about public attitudes and the success of environmental education is ambiguous (Hinchliffe, 1996; 1997; Kasemir et al, 2000) – the constraints imposed by existing technological infrastructures, land-use patterns and cultural expectations cannot be suddenly overthrown. Governments are, perhaps, better able to direct change in the right direction than they are to accelerate its pace dramatically.

An exclusively national approach to energy and climate policy raises further questions about its environmental adequacy. It is difficult to be confident that specific initiatives are contributing in any meaningful way to the global reduction of atmospheric greenhouse gas levels. The economic implications of national policy are also debatable. A positive reading suggests that proactive climate policy will enable leading states to benefit from the early establishment of a low-carbon economy as a basis for long-term development. Yet reform can also be seen as a self-imposed penalty that undermines international competitiveness and short-term economic growth. Such uncertainties reinforce arguments that an international framework is vital for the effective and equitable coordination of action against climate change.

A wider context for national action

Reference has already been made to EU policy in areas such as energy labelling of consumer goods. The EU also supports work within member states to promote energy efficiency and greater use of clean energy sources, funding, for example, studies of improvements in urban transportation. The attention given to climate change in the EU's Sixth Environmental Action Plan of 2001 has inspired other initiatives that aim to foster coordinated action at an international level. Predictably, this includes support for research and technology transfers in the fields of energy efficiency and renewables. Greater cooperation in the planning of European energy and transport infrastructure may also help to curb greenhouse gas emissions – for example, by reducing congestion and revitalizing rail and water links. A programme of emissions trading between companies operating in EU member states planned to begin in 2005 may also help to implement the common commitment to cut emissions by reducing the associated economic costs (IEA, 2002a).

Initiatives at the supranational level of the EU must, in turn, be located within a wider international context. In part, this reflects evidence that the greatest penalties associated with climate change will be exacted in the global South. As a result, concerns about climate have begun to be reflected in established international aid and development programmes. Poverty and underdevelopment are major causes of Southern vulnerability to climate change. It follows that moves to promote economic diversification, social welfare and enhanced institutional capabilities should better enable countries and communities to adapt to climate change, and to contribute to its mitigation. Specific initiatives to foster innovation in energy production and management are also evident. The World Bank, amongst others, is rethinking its energy policy to increase support for renewables (World Bank, 1996). But the same caveats apply as in the earlier discussion of commercial investment. The World Bank still directs much greater funding to fossil fuel exploitation, and attempts to present itself as championing action against climate change can appear hypocritical (Tellam, 2000).

In parallel with development policy reforms, climate change has also prompted UN-led moves intended to reverse global warming trends. Indeed, most national policies are designed to support this international effort. The 1992 Framework Convention on Climate Change (FCCC) committed signatory states, numbering over 180 by 2003, to the principle of returning atmospheric concentrations of greenhouse gases to levels that will defuse the threat of anthropogenic climate change (O'Riordan et al, 1998; UN, 2003). It was envisaged that this process would be initiated by the most industrialized states, reflecting their historical responsibility for climate change. The FCCC imposed no binding targets for emission reduction. Rather, its purpose was to foster solidarity between signatory states as a foundation for effective international action (see Chapter 12).

Subsequent meetings of FCCC signatories led to the 1997 Kyoto Protocol, which outlined a regulatory regime to reduce emissions of six main greenhouse gases (Grubb et al, 1999). During an initial phase until 2008–2012, the protocol proposed that 38 developed states would cut their emissions by an average of 5.2 per cent below 1990 levels. Targets for specific states, reflecting their particular circumstances, were distributed about this average. However, these targets were not necessarily to be met by direct curbs on the individual state's own emissions. Measures to allow flexible compliance included granting credit for enhancement of carbon sinks. States could also discharge their responsibilities by funding measures to promote renewables and energy efficiency in developing countries (Wohlgemuth and Missfelt, 2000). These Joint Implementation provisions were, in part, a device intended to reduce the cost of emission reductions and thus overcome the objections of leading developed states – especially the USA – to the Kyoto targets. But they also reflected the hope that developing countries could be assisted to break the link between economic development and escalating greenhouse gas emissions (Forsyth, 1999; Jackson et al, 2001). Further financial support was promised through the establishment of a Clean Development Mechanism, thus increasing the resources available to the Global Environmental Facility jointly administered by the World Bank and the United Nations Development Programme (UNDP). As well as yielding immediate benefits, these measures were intended to prepare the ground for the future extension of emission targets to major developing economies, including India and China (Grubb et al, 1999).

Kyoto also endorsed the principle of international emissions trading. If emissions targets are regarded as effectively granting permission to release greenhouse gases up to a certain level, they may become tradable commodities (Grubb et al, 1999). Countries including the USA and Japan have championed trading as a cost-effective means of meeting emissions targets. Critics, however, see this as a cynical ploy. If the richest countries can set their continuing excess emissions against notional 'spare capacity', created initially by economic collapse in post-Soviet Russia and the Ukraine, this will delay real change in both energy systems and greenhouse gas emissions (Agarwal, 2002).

Although intended to reinforce international solidarity, the Kyoto Protocol has been bedevilled by political controversy reflecting the preoccupation of many of its parties with narrowly national interests (see Chapter 12). Emissions targets were set at levels deemed politically acceptable by negotiating governments, rather than reflecting the changes necessary to secure climatic stability. But they have still fallen foul of domestic opposition, especially in the USA, which alone accounts for 25 per cent of global carbon dioxide emissions.

Moreover, while the principle of flexible implementation enabled an apparently successful outcome at Kyoto, failure to define the practical details of such measures, has prevented the protocol's implementation. Predictably, Northern and Southern states have disagreed over the scale and administration of aid to promote clean technologies and adaptation to climate change in developing countries. Clear differences of opinion have also been evident within the developed world, with the EU urging greater emphasis on the direct reduction of domestic emissions by individual states than other countries – particularly the USA, Japan and Australia – were prepared to concede. The USA and Australia were first to withdraw from the Kyoto process. This put a particular stamp on subsequent meetings of the Kyoto parties during 2001. The EU states redoubled their efforts to implement the protocol. But they were forced to relax their emphasis on domestic emission cuts in an effort to secure the support of other industrialized countries, particularly Japan, Russia and Canada (Giles, 2001; Nordhaus, 2001). This tactic has not, however, yielded immediate success. Russia, in particular, has sought to derive further political advantage from any moves towards ratification (Paton Walsh, 2004).

Any change in the entrenched position of the USA is unlikely in the short-term. Important sections of American public and political opinion have been influenced by claims – also heard in other industrialized countries – that the adoption of emission targets by developed states alone would create domestic economic penalties and unfairly undermine their competitiveness in world markets. Such arguments, while largely founded in self-interest, are sometimes justified by a particular construction of equity that effectively discounts notions of historical liability (see Thompson and Rayner, 1998, and Tóth, 1999, for a more detailed treatment of equity in this context). The current generation of producers and consumers in the developed world, it is argued, cannot be held responsible for past emissions which they could not have prevented. By implication, at least, this also casts doubt over notions of responsibility to future generations. In part, this is addressed through the optimistic assumption that continuing and unrestricted economic growth will yield the financial and technical means to enable any environmental problems to be successfully addressed. However, the emphasis on intra-generational equity is redoubled by the assertion that an immediate effect of the Kyoto provisions would be to raise energy prices and trigger job losses, impacting most harshly upon the poorest in US society. Thus, it is argued, current environmental burdens must be shared more widely across the international community. More specifically, the USA has led calls for the imposition of emissions targets on developing countries such as China. The rapid development of the Chinese economy – viewed as a threat by many US businesses – will undoubtedly involve a dramatic rise in energy use and greenhouse gas emissions. The IEA suggests that

China could account for as much as a quarter of the global increase in energy-related carbon dioxide emissions between 2000 and 2030. But projected per capita emissions of 4.5 tonnes for China in 2030 would still fall far below the expected average of 13 tonnes for Organisation for Economic Co-operation and Development (OECD) countries (IEA, 2002b). The equity of imposing constraints upon China's growth while this inequality persists is highly questionable.

The fact that US arguments against the Kyoto process have often been disingenuous does not deprive them of their potency. Indeed, they serve the interests of key sections of US business, which are also major sponsors of the political elite. Such arguments ignore the likely costs of climate change and the direct vulnerability of areas such as Florida to flooding and storm damage (De Leo et al, 2001). Nor do they acknowledge alternative projections that even if specific sectors contract, curbs on greenhouse gases might be good for the US economy as a whole, prompting technical innovation, cost savings on energy and a net gain in jobs (Bernau and Duckworth, 1998). Concerns about social equity can be addressed by a modest redistribution of wealth to offset the effects of any rise in energy prices upon the least affluent in US society. But if intra-generational equity is truly an issue, the impact of climate change policy upon the USA must be set in a wider context. It is hard to accept the equity of arguments that profess to protect the American poor if the end result is to damage, still further, development prospects for populations in the global South whose poverty is so much more extreme.

In the short term, few commentators are optimistic that the international diplomatic process will lead to any significant action against climate change. EU states retain a political commitment to meeting their Kyoto targets for emission reduction, but it is questionable whether these can be achieved in practice. The USA, scheduled under the protocol to cut its greenhouse gas emissions to 7 per cent below 1990 levels by 2012, is now projected to generate a 34 per cent rise in emissions over this period (Connor, 2001). Russia's aim of doubling its GDP within the same timeframe seems incompatible with the freeze on emission levels envisaged at Kyoto (Paton Walsh, 2004). At best, therefore, the reduction in greenhouse gas emissions from the leading industrial states seems likely to be less than 2 per cent by 2012, rather than the original – and very modest – target of 5.2 per cent (Giles, 2001; Nordhaus, 2001). But this does not necessarily mean that the Kyoto process has been worthless; even some long-standing critics have viewed it as a potentially valuable experiment in the creation of a international environmental accord (Nordhaus, 2001). But Kyoto also issues a clear warning that securing further and more effective international cooperation will be no easy matter.

Conclusion

There is, clearly, considerable potential for a closer relationship between action to combat the causes and consequences of climate change and the broader aim of promoting more sustainable development. Defence of Critical Natural Capital, as manifest in the climate system, represents one of the surest ways in which current generations can protect the inheritance of their successors. Initiatives designed to reduce atmospheric levels of greenhouse gases also overlap in obvious ways with the agenda of sustainable development; both reflect a common interest in the protection of biodiversity, the promotion of resource efficiency, the greater use of renewables and curbs upon pollution. The potential welfare benefits of climate change policy are also wide-ranging, including higher standards of health, domestic comfort and access to the sustainable energy sources needed for economic advance in the global South. Equally, measures intended to secure more environmentally sustainable and socially equitable development should provide some measure of protection against the worst impacts of climate change for the poorest of the world's inhabitants.

Yet climate change policy also embodies many of the challenges and contradictions of wider efforts to promote more sustainable development. What is possible in theory is all too often unlikely in practice. Technical and cultural barriers to change in consumer behaviour are not easily overcome, nor are the difficulties of inspiring public confidence in the cumulative efficacy of individual action. Equally, the availability of technologies capable of delivering energy efficiency and emission-free renewable power is no guarantee of their adoption while the economic climate remains unfavourable. The need to coordinate actors and agencies at every level of the socio-economic hierarchy, from the local to the global, adds further complications, not least because it is evident that, in the short term, climate change policy will create losers as well as winners.

Moves to protect climate systems may lead to new penalties being inflicted upon other dimensions of natural capital. It is far from clear how the resultant trade-offs are to be made if we aim to ensure that development becomes more sustainable overall. In some instances we still lack sufficient scientific understanding to be able to predict the full consequences of alteration in particular environmental systems. Policy calculations are also complicated by the reflection that general benefits – whether cast in terms of global climate stability or the continued extension of energy supply – often result from specific costs being imposed upon the places that become, for example, the location of new windfarms, hydropower schemes or nuclear power stations. Equally, arguments that moves towards a low-carbon economy are consistent with continued development must recognize the likely impacts on the economic and social fortunes of industries and communities most wedded to an older pattern of intensive consumption of fossil fuels. The uncertainties involved in any transition to cleaner energy systems also raise fears amongst a wider constituency, especially in the global South, that their aspirations for future development and prosperity are to be sacrificed in the name of environmental protection.

The message that any such short-term costs will be more than offset by longer-term gains is not an easy one to sell. It is a calculation of advantage that is not consistent with the existing time frames for political and commercial decision-making. As Sandalow and Bowles (2001) observe, despite a rate of global warming unprecedented in the last 10,000 years 'the average temperature increase during the term of a US President would likely be less than 0.1°C. Political systems are not well designed to address problems that proceed at this pace.'

The empirical evidence of contest over action against climate change also makes clear that these dilemmas cannot simply be resolved by invoking the principle of equity. This does not lead, in practice, to the unambiguous definition of a 'correct' way forward. The different interests involved in the climate debate, particularly the major political and commercial players at an international level, have all advanced their own specific – and largely self-interested – interpretation of what is equitable. These are then set in opposition to each other, with the risk that when 'equity' prevails, it does so in a way that reflects the interests of the rich and powerful.

12

Sustainable Development and International Relations

Alan Grainger

Introduction

Sustainable development was originally, like the dominant 20th-century ideal of development, a creation of international relations, being offered by the developed countries to the developing countries as a 'guide to best practice'. But whereas developing countries can see working examples in developed countries of the ideal of development for which they are aiming, they cannot do this in the case of sustainable development. For if they did comply with the sustainable development ideal, as proposed in the World Conservation Strategy (IUCN, 1980), they would be avoiding the past development paths of the developed countries, with all the environmental degradation these caused, and not replicating them.

Development and sustainable development also differ in another important respect: there is no shared ideal of sustainable development. The developing countries have their own ideal, which is more in line with that of the World Commission on Environment and Development (WCED, 1987). This involves striving for a more equitable development path which improves their quality of life and narrows the gap between them and the developed countries. They might like to minimize the associated environmental damage if possible; but this is not their top priority. As explained in Chapter 1 of this volume, they still yearn for the development ideal which the developed countries promoted over 50 years ago, and which is still unrealized. If they have to use a different name for the same ideal, and meet additional conditions in order to continue to get support from developed countries, so be it. One aim of this chapter is to contrast these two different approaches, or discourses.

International relations must be central to the pursuit of sustainable development because some degree of international cooperation is needed to achieve its global goals, whether these be framed in terms of saving the planetary environment, or creating greater equity amongst its human inhabitants. However, some commentators, such as Rao (2000), go further. They appear to equate sustainable development with international action to protect the global environment, involving, for example, conventions to combat climate change and conserve biological diversity. But this is to confuse sustainable development as an optimum long-term development path with international strategies to tackle some of the key symptoms of unsustainable development. Others, including the present author, regard international collaboration as merely one of a set of strategies needed to achieve more sustainable development, which must address the totality of development at all levels on the spatial scale. So while this chapter examines international negotiations on how to mitigate global climate change and conserve biodiversity, these are only the means to an end, not the end itself. To create a sound international framework for more sustainable development by individual states it is vital to resolve the differences between the discourses of developed and developing countries on sustainable development, and that requires gaining a better understanding of these differences. That is another aim of this chapter.

Studying international negotiations also helps us to gain a better understanding of sustainable development as a theoretical concept, and how it might be applied in practice. As explained in Chapter 1, achieving sustainable development entails reaching an optimum balance between the economic, social and environmental dimensions of development. Exactly how this is done depends upon which of the various conditions for sustainable development is chosen as the optimal criterion. For example, complying with the ideal condition of ecological economics would require keeping the scale of human activity below the maximum carrying capacity of the planet. By contrast, to meet the Very Weak Condition of environmental economics the increase in Human and Man-Made Capital should be at least as great as the consequent fall in Natural Capital. So far, every state has charted a development path in which the balance between the three dimensions of development matches its particular needs, aspirations, culture and conditions. This national optimum, in turn, influences the position that a state adopts in international negotiations. So by observing the latter we should be able to learn how the state ranks the economic, social and environmental dimensions of development and whether they are integrated for planning purposes. This current optimum can then be compared with that required for sustainable development. Accordingly, this chapter is concerned less with examining the role of sustainable development in international relations, important though that is, than with seeing what we can learn about sustainable development by observing international relations.

The chapter has four main parts. The first provides a framework for the discussion by reviewing some key concepts and theories of international relations. Parts two and three use evidence from the negotiations before, during and after the UN Conference on Environment and Development (UNCED) in 1992 to draw inferences about the relative priorities given by different groups of states to the economic, social and environmental dimensions of development, and the extent to which they are willing to integrate them in practice. Part two focuses on the negotiations concerning the Framework Convention on Climate Change (FCCC), where the discourses of the developed and developing countries did not come into direct conflict. Part three looks at other negotiations concerning the Convention on Biological Diversity, the Statement of Forest Principles, the Rio Declaration and Agenda 21, where they did.

While the UNCED negotiations provide insights into how states rank the three dimensions of development, they only tell us a limited amount about how these dimensions are integrated. Because of how the negotiations were structured, states could, if they wished, treat them as merely 'environmental negotiations' and not bother to link measures to improve environmental management with the economic and social dimensions of development. However, during the 1990s some developed countries proposed that uniform social and environmental conditions be incorporated into the rules of three existing international institutions: the International Labour Organization (ILO), the General Agreement on Tariffs and Trade (GATT) and its successor, the World Trade Organization (WTO). These were deliberate attempts to achieve more integration between the three dimensions of development, so the fourth part of the chapter compares the discourses of the member states of these institutions in order to assess their attitudes to such changes.

The ILO and WTO debates are also important in that proposals to introduce uniform social and environmental conditions into world trade epitomize a 'globalist' discourse of sustainable development, which regards all countries as equivalent. This has generated fierce opposition from developing countries because it would effectively extend globalization, hitherto seen as confined to economic matters, into the social and environmental arenas. However, such globalist initiatives are not the only possible way to counter the inequities associated with importing sustainable development (see Chapter 3). The chapter ends by advancing an alternative 'gradualist' approach, which is more in harmony with the discourse of developing countries.

The World as Viewed by International Relations Theories

The study of international relations is an important area of academic research and so we begin by outlining some of its most relevant theories and concepts.

Conflict or cooperation?

The academic field of international relations has been defined as 'the study of all social phenomena not confined within a single state, such as the relations of states with one another, the operations of non-state actors, such as international organizations, multinational corporations and religious movements, and so on' (Ogley, 1994). Theories that seek to explain relationships between these actors may be divided into three groups.

Rationalist theories
The first group consists of the rationalist theories that have traditionally dominated this field, and which regard states as the primary actors in international relations. In Neo-Realist Theory, states are isolated, politically autarkic entities preoccupied with their own security. In recent years our understanding of security has been extended from the purely military aspects embraced by the earlier Realist Theory to include political and economic security in the broadest sense (Dunne, 1997). International affairs are deemed to be characterized by conflict and anarchy, and stability and justice occur only in exceptional circumstances. When states negotiate with one another, each is concerned only with how much it can gain relative to its counterparts. Neo-Liberal Theory, on the other hand, argues that international institutions provide a framework for cooperation between states, which can reduce anarchy and conflict. Moreover, states are deemed to enter into negotiations in order to achieve absolute gains for all parties and not just to serve their own ends (Baldwin, 1993).

Reflexive theories

Another diverse group, called reflexive theories by Smith (1997), attempts to broaden the narrow scope of rationalist theory. Most reject the dominant role of the state. Consequently, they give more prominence than rationalist theories to the roles of non-state actors, such as firms and non-governmental organizations (NGOs). One theoretical strand which is of particular relevance to the present topic is Post-Modernism, which rejects any single explanation of reality and studies how some particular ways of understanding the world, or discourses, come to achieve dominance (Walker, 1993). So while rationalist theories attempt to explain the tactics employed by states, a post-modern approach can give insights into their motivations.

Political economy theories

Political economy theories add an economic dimension to the study of international relations. As Gilpin (1987) notes: 'For the state, territorial boundaries are a necessary basis of national autonomy and political unity. For the market, the elimination of all political and other obstacles to the operation of the price mechanism is imperative.' In the modern global economy all states struggle to achieve development amid the rationalizing forces of the marketplace. Political economy theories use highly simplified models to explain the agglomeration of the diverse range of actors and territories under the influence of these forces. Some theories are akin to the rationalist perspectives outlined above. In Hegemonic Stability Theory, for example, which is Neo-Realist in outlook, an open world economy requires a single dominant (or hegemonic) power that is able to maintain long-term global security through the force of arms (Keohane, 1984). However, Strange (1998) has argued that this obsession with hegemony has caused neglect of other aspects of international power. Other theories, such as Dependency Theory (Frank, 1969) and Modern World System Theory (Wallerstein, 1974), referred to collectively as *structuralist* theories, divide the world into two zones. The first is a powerful Core, composed of the industrialized states, which exploits a weaker Periphery of less developed, or underdeveloped, countries.

While this chapter focuses primarily on examining the discourses of states in international relations, it does refer to the activities of non-governmental organizations (NGOs) and other non-state actors. It draws, as appropriate, on the perspectives of the above theories, but is most influenced by the post-modernist approach. So while it makes use of rationalist theories to explain the tactics of states in international negotiations, and political economy theories to explain the power relations between states, it rejects the notion of sustainable development as a monolithic ideal that is accepted by all countries. Instead, following the general post-modernist approach, we find that different states can have radically different understandings of 'sustainable development'. These, and not a utopian prescriptive approach, therefore constitute international reality and, by extension, national reality.

Institutions and regimes

When states decide to cooperate on a long-term basis they may establish a formal *institution*, which can be defined as 'a set of agreed principles, norms, rules, common understandings, organizations and consultation processes' (Greene, 1997). The members of each institution generally have a shared understanding of what they want to achieve, a structure of communication and a set of rules governing their behaviour (O'Riordan et al, 1998).

An agreement which establishes cooperation between states is called a *regime*, defined as 'a social institution with . . . agreed principles, norms, rules, procedures and programmes that govern the activities and shape the expectations of actors in a specific issue area' (Greene, 1997). There are two main kinds of regimes:

1. *Strong regimes*, such as the 1983 Vienna Convention on the Ozone Layer, as elaborated by the 1987 Montreal Protocol, are binding agreements that commit all signatories to specific actions. Often the regime begins with an interim non-binding framework convention, but for convenience the whole set of agreements is assumed here to be a strong regime.
2. *Weak regimes*, on the other hand, such as the 1977 UN Plan of Action to protect the Ozone Layer, are voluntary. They do not commit the signatories to any specific action, merely providing an international framework for discretionary national action.

Models of regime formation

In the Structural Model of regime formation, the main factor which determines the outcome of negotiations is the relative strength of states. One or more hegemonic states are assumed to put pressure on their weaker counterparts to join regimes (Keohane and Nye, 1977). In the Utilitarian Model, states behave as rational actors, but negotiating becomes harder as more states enter the negotiations and each party's bargaining position is increasingly unclear to the others. However, even the efforts of a small group of states to reach agreement can be obstructed by the veto power of a single state (Hampson, 1989). Neither model, nor any of the others that have been proposed, offers a comprehensive explanation of regime formation, but each highlights some of the key factors involved.

Discourses and dialogues

Each party in a negotiation will have its own view or *discourse*. Discourse is a central plank of post-modernist theory and was defined by Scott (1988) as 'a historically, socially and institutionally specific structure of statements, terms, categories and beliefs'. Geopolitical discourses may be inferred from the documents, statements and practices of foreign and economic policies (Agnew and Corbridge, 1995). Of particular interest here are the boundaries between different discourses. It is assumed that these can be inferred from studying the set of statements, terms, categories and beliefs that constitute each discourse, and the points of conflict which arise during negotiations.

World diplomacy consists of a multiplicity of self-contained *dialogues*, in which actors engage in communication or negotiation. By agreement, practice or tradition, some statements, terms and categories are regarded as relevant to each dialogue, while others are not. Those which are employed derive from the discourses of all the actors involved, but the boundaries of dialogues generally reflect the relative powers of these actors.

Negotiating stances and outcomes

Every state enters into international negotiations with certain aims, desires and beliefs. Inferences about its general discourse are made in the following discussion by trying to identify three aspects of a state's negotiating stance: (a) its *dominant paradigm*, which defines its general attitude to the subject under discussion; (b) its *primary goal*, which is what it most wants to gain from the negotiation, and to achieve which it may make concessions on other topics; and (c) its *minimum acceptable compromise*, which is its 'bottom line' and the ultimate limit on its freedom to negotiate.

Climate Change: The Predominance of an Isolated Globalist Discourse

All approaches to sustainable development agree that to achieve it requires a closer integration of the environment into development planning. However, so far economic growth and the interests of Capital have been given highest priority, and it took a long time for social needs to be accorded the recognition they deserve. The environment has habitually been treated separately from the economic and social dimensions of development and is ranked as less important than either. In practical planning situations it is generally regarded as more of a constraint on development than integral to it. So the economic and social goals of an initiative are evaluated first, and only then is a check made to see whether its environmental impacts exceed acceptable limits. This attitude has been perpetuated in negotiations on international environmental regimes, which are often seen as self-contained and restricted to 'environmental matters'. But when dialogues, and the discourses of the actors involved in them, are dominated by environmental statements, terms, categories and beliefs, it can be difficult to reach agreement on strategies to achieve the changes in economic practice on which improved environmental performance depends.

To explore the implications of this argument, the next two parts of the chapter contrast discourses advanced by developed and developing countries in the negotiations leading up to, and following, the 12-day UN Conference on Environment and Development (UNCED) in Rio de Janeiro in June 1992. This was attended by delegations from 176 states and representatives of some 1500 NGOs, and ended in an 'Earth Summit' of 103 world leaders. The discussion draws upon published recollections by individual delegates and reports in the printed media. It is, however, important to recognize that the latter tend to be biased towards reporting the actions of developed countries, and this may distort interpretations of the stances of different states (Dalby, 1996).

This part of the chapter examines negotiations on global climate change, while the next part examines other negotiations at UNCED. The aim is not to duplicate previous detailed descriptions of the negotiations (eg Bodansky, 1994; O'Riordan et al, 1998), but to develop a new analysis. This follows Borione and Ripert (1994) and Dasgupta (1994) in characterizing the negotiations as essentially triangular. The three principal groups of actors are the USA; other developed states (and fellow members of the

Organization for Economic Cooperation and Development (OECD)), and the developing countries, which form the so-called Group of 77 (G77), though it actually has over 120 members.

Negotiations on the Framework Convention on Climate Change (FCCC) took place over a 17-month period before UNCED at five sessions of the International Negotiating Committee (INC) established by the UN General Assembly (UNGA) on 21 December 1990. The UNGA itself claimed direct oversight of the INC, rather than devolving responsibility to the World Meteorological Organization (WMO) or the UN Environment Programme (UNEP), even though the latter had been preparing for the negotiations since 1989. This reflected the perception of the majority of UN members that global climate change was as much a development issue as an environmental concern and that the UNGA alone had the power to coordinate the involvement of all UN agencies with environment and development interests. This arrangement also meant that all UN member states, and not just UNEP or WMO members, could participate in the negotiations (Borione and Ripert, 1994).

The US position: postponing the day of reckoning

The US government was effectively able to control the composition of the dialogue and the formation of the FCCC by exercising its hegemonic power and veto role. The latter specifically reflects the fact that US carbon dioxide emissions account for one fifth of the global total. This reading of events is in accordance with the principles of Neo-Realist theory and both the Structural and Utilitarian models of regime formation. The US discourse was communicated forcibly and was allowed to achieve predominance because it did not have to accommodate other discourses.

FCCC negotiations began in February 1991, but little progress was made until the last session, divided between two meetings in New York in February and May 1992. States spent the first four sessions communicating and reiterating their positions, rather than negotiating to narrow their differences (Bodansky, 1994). This enabled the USA to maintain its discourse and avoid direct conflict with that of the developing countries until it had reached agreement with the other OECD countries. This occurred just before the start of the final meeting. According to Dasgupta (1994): 'Both the EC and the USA preferred to continue postponing substantive negotiations with the South, deferring it until they succeeded in arriving at a common OECD position.' For their part, neither the other developed countries nor the developing countries were keen to sign an agreement unless the USA was a party to it (Nitze, 1994). The compromise text essentially became the final text of the FCCC agreed at UNCED despite opposition by developing countries, which had played little effective part in the negotiations. It is highly ambiguous, committing states only to *communicating information* on policies and measures they take 'with the aim of returning individually or jointly to their 1990 levels of their anthropogenic emissions of carbon dioxide and other greenhouse gases' (Dasgupta, 1994). The rest of this section looks at the US discourse on climate change and the reasons for it.

The US discourse is best described as 'isolationist', in that it was restricted to environmental statements, terms, categories and beliefs that were not integrated with economic and social considerations. Its dominant paradigm reflected a 'globalist' view of the world environment (Adams, 2001) and was sceptical about the threat imposed by the greenhouse effect. The globalist view is planetary in scale; it regards safeguarding the world environment as an ethical concern for all states, rather than a social or economic necessity; it requires all countries to be judged by the same standards; and it is external to, and divorced from, the development of national economies. The perspective stems from the 'Spaceship Earth' paradigm that dominated the UN Conference on the Human Environment in Stockholm in 1972. This paradigm was advocated by a self-nominated elite dedicated to 'saving the planet' from disaster at the hands of the rest of humanity, regardless of the aspirations of developing countries. Indeed, the Stockholm conference was originally intended to discuss both environment and development, and improving the balance between the two was one of four main themes. Ultimately, however, this was overshadowed by discussions of the other themes: improving human settlements, slowing natural resource depletion and reducing pollution (Caldwell, 1990).

The sceptical attitude shown by the US Government, and its calls for more research to clarify the nature of the threat posed by climate change, reflected the uncertainty expressed in the full scientific assessment prepared before the start of negotiations by the Intergovernmental Panel on Climate Change (IPCC) (Houghton et al, 1990), as opposed to the summary document that was culled from it but phrased differently. But scepticism could just have been a convenient excuse for remaining within the bounds of a purely environmental discourse. The primary US goal throughout the climate negotiations was to delay action for as long as possible, in order to limit the negative impacts on its economy and optimize its present, as opposed to long-term, welfare. The USA seemed unwilling to make any precautionary trade-offs between the economic, social and environmental dimensions of its development. Its minimum acceptable compromise position in the negotiations was to ensure that the FCCC imposed no legally binding commitments on states to take remedial action (Nitze, 1994). This contrasted with the approaches of other OECD countries, which wanted the FCCC to commit all signatories to stabilize greenhouse gas emissions at 1990 levels by the year 2000.

The US government's determination to minimize the costs to its economy of mitigating global climate change, thereby ranking the environment a poor third behind the other dimensions of development, reflected the balance of pressures on it from internal interest groups. The influence of US environmental NGOs is the strongest of any country, but it is still outweighed by that of interest groups representing Capital and Labour, whose ideological opposition to what they saw as the 'anti-growth agenda' of environmentalists enjoyed strong support amongst senior officials in the administration of President George Bush (Nitze, 1994). Major US-based transnational corporations such as Exxon – as it then was – were prominent members of the Global Climate Coalition, which pressed the governments of the USA and other developed countries to avoid precipitate action to curb global climate change, claiming that it would be economically damaging. As late as 1997 Lee Raymond, the Chief Executive of Exxon, was still arguing that:

It does not make sense to cripple the economy by making changes in the environment that may prove unnecessary, premature, or don't stand the test of rigorous cost-benefit analysis (Pearce, 1997b).

Opposition was also voiced by the AFL-CIO, the main US trade union confederation, one of whose officials claimed that emissions reductions targeted only at rich states would 'export jobs, capital and pollution' (Pearce, 1997a).

The relative power of the two main political parties also had an important influence on US policy. The blatantly anti-environment attitude of the Republican Bush administration was only slightly moderated when the Democrat, Bill Clinton, assumed the presidency in January 1993. Clinton was more publicly supportive of action to curb global climate change. On 21 April 1993 he promised to return US greenhouse gas emissions to 1990 levels by 2000 and that October launched a US Climate Action Plan to show how this would be done (Sebenius, 1994). His freedom of action was, however, constrained by opposition from the Republican-dominated US Senate, which must ratify all international treaties.

There was a general perception in the Senate that 'external forces' were eroding US sovereignty and welfare by effectively extending economic globalization to embrace environmental considerations. Trent Lott, the Republican majority leader, argued that the Kyoto Protocol could 'empower international bureaucrats to impose financial obligations on the USA and failed to address the concerns of US business and labour organizations' (Clark and Hutton, 1997). A member of the US delegation at UNCED put such concerns more starkly: 'Environmental protection has replaced communism as the great threat to capitalism' (Lascelles and Lamb, 1992b). Whether or not this is true is beside the point: in politics, perceptions matter most of all.

The dominant US paradigm and primary goal remained unchanged in later negotiations, held at regular Conferences of the Parties (COPs) to the FCCC that culminated in an important benchmark statement, the 1997 Kyoto Protocol. To delay any consequent impacts on the US economy, its negotiators initially tried to push back the date for stabilizing greenhouse gas emissions at 1990 levels from 2000 – cited as a 'guideline' in the FCCC – to 2012. They also argued that any further reductions could not be demanded before 2017 (Pearce, 1997b). Even the first of these proposals was conditional on general agreement to the USA's minimum acceptable position, imposed by a US Senate resolution before the Kyoto meeting, that the protocol must include commitments to action by developing countries (Boulton, 1997a). This contradicted the earlier consensus, expressed in Article 3(1) of the FCCC, that the 'Developed country parties should take the lead in combating climate change'. The US condition is interesting because it is based not on the historical greenhouse gas emissions of developing countries, but on the expectation that their emissions will rise rapidly in future.

The USA also favoured the use of *flexibility mechanisms*. These include: (a) accounting for emissions of greenhouse gases other than carbon dioxide, such as methane and nitrous oxide; and (b) allowing countries to meet their individual targets by supplementing domestic emission cuts with the purchase of excess pollution permits from other countries and by funding actions to cut emissions elsewhere (Pearce, 1997a; see also Chapter 11 in this volume). This would reduce the cost to US firms and avoid steep cuts in US emissions, particularly if, as the US government argued, 'trading could account for up to 99 per cent of all action and still be considered supplemental' (Pearce, 1998). If this view had prevailed then developed countries would have been able to avoid paying some of the environmental costs that they had accumulated over the previous two centuries.

Discourses of other developed countries

Of the other developed countries, only Australia adopted a similarly extreme discourse. In contrast, European countries were enthusiastic about taking action. Although Sweden, Denmark, The Netherlands, France and Germany called for cuts in emissions, and other states, including the UK, favoured less radical moves to achieve stabilization, all of the European Union (EU) countries shared a dominant paradigm that reflected the Precautionary Principle (Goldemberg, 1994). So they treated uncertainty as a reason to take precautions against a possible threat, rather than an excuse to avoid or postpone action. While they also ranked the environmental dimension lowest of all, they appreciated its interconnection with other dimensions of development and the potential for building on these links to achieve net benefits. European countries were much more open than the USA to arguments that improving technology to increase energy efficiency can yield economic savings as well as environmental benefits (Nitze, 1994). The EU countries were also keen to achieve 'real' cuts in emissions by limiting the use of flexibility mechanisms, such as emissions trading, so that at least half of each state's target would be met by internal cuts in emissions. A third group of countries, including Canada, Japan and Russia, were more hesitant. They wanted to secure the best deal for themselves, taking maximum advantage of flexibility mechanisms in order to limit the impact on their economic competitiveness of implementing the protocol. But whereas the USA and Australia adopted a similar stance as a calculated preliminary to complete rejection of the protocol, the countries of the third group were willing to negotiate in earnest about its implementation.

Compromise and conflict

The negotiated compromise between these different positions led in November 1997 to the interim Kyoto Protocol, under which the EU, USA and Japan would cut their greenhouse gas emissions by 8 per cent, 7 per cent and 6 per cent, respectively, from 1990 levels by 2012. US negotiators succeeded in meeting many of their aims – for example, by ensuring that the protocol included all principal greenhouse gases and acknowledged the need for emissions trading. In spite of this, President Clinton reiterated that his country could not ratify the protocol unless it were modified to reflect the USA's minimum acceptable compromise position of 'meaningful participation by key developing countries' (Clark and Hutton, 1997). Since this did not happen in subsequent meetings of the Parties to the Convention, this further delayed the beginning of US emissions cuts. Indeed, US emissions actually grew by 11 per cent between 1990 and 1997 (Boulton, 1997b). As another bargaining chip, the US government threatened to withhold its contribution to the Global Environment Facility, which funds projects intended to mitigate global change.

Negotiations on refining the Kyoto Protocol eventually broke down at the Sixth Conference of the Parties in The Hague in November 2000. This meeting, which was intended to finalize the Protocol, ended without agreement when both the USA and the EU stuck to their established positions. When talks resumed in Bonn in July 2001, the newly installed US President, George W Bush – son of the former President – announced the USA's withdrawal from the entire negotiations. The remaining countries only reached a consensus when, ironically, the EU states backed down and allowed both unrestricted trading in carbon emission permits and limited offsets of emissions by carbon sinks. After some outstanding details were dealt with, the final version of the Kyoto Protocol was agreed at the Seventh Conference of the Parties, held in Marrakesh between 29 October and 10 November 2001.

By April 2004, the Protocol had been ratified by 121 states, together accounting for 44.2 per cent of global carbon dioxide emissions. For it to come into force, the cumulative share of emissions of participating states must exceed 55 per cent. Australia decided in 2002 not to ratify the Protocol, even though it was allowed to increase its emissions by 8 per cent. Its excuse was that without the participation of the USA and the developing countries the agreement would not be comprehensive and effective, so participation would undermine Australia's economic competitiveness for no good reason (Kemp and Downer, 2002). Ratification by Russia would still be sufficient to exceed the 55 per cent threshold. At the start of December 2003 the Russian government stated that it would not ratify the Protocol 'in its present form', on the grounds that this would harm the national economy, but in May 2004 President Putin announced that 'we will accelerate our movement towards ratifying this protocol' (Paton Walsh, 2004). This closely followed the EU's decision not to oppose Russia's application to join the World Trade Organisation!

The US government, meanwhile, announced its own climate change strategy in February 2002. Staying true to its discourse, this involved a voluntary scheme that aimed to cut greenhouse gas intensity – the rate of greenhouse gas emissions per unit of gross domestic product (GDP) – by 18 per cent over the next ten years (Dunne, 2002). However, this is likely to result in a substantial increase in emissions. Since greenhouse gas intensity had already fallen by a mean of 18 per cent per decade in the 1980s and 1990s, the new strategy effectively corresponded to a 'business-as-usual' scenario.

Stretching the boundaries: the view from the South

The discourses of developing countries in the climate change negotiations contrasted sharply with that of the USA. They did not take a uniform view, but scepticism about global climate change was not part of their dominant paradigm. Indeed, by April 2004 79 developing countries had ratified the Kyoto Protocol. The only group which consistently questioned the reality of the threat were members of the Organization of Petroleum Exporting Countries (OPEC), who regarded the FCCC as biased against their principal natural resource (Corzine, 1997).

The Group of 77 developing countries encompasses various networks of states, each with their own set of common interests, so its cohesiveness fluctuated during the negotiations (Djoghlaf, 1994). Most in favour of urgent action were the Alliance of Small Island States, which perceive themselves to be under direct and immediate threat from rising sea levels, and states in sub-Saharan Africa concerned about the increasing frequency of drought. In contrast, the Kuala Lumpur Group of 42 forested countries regarded the FCCC as an attempt by developed countries to restrict their national sovereignty over forest management (Borione and Ripert, 1994). China, although not a formal member of the G77, attended their meetings and often backed their position in negotiations.

The dominant paradigm of developing countries clearly linked the economic and environmental dimensions of development, but only with respect to the developed world. It stressed that the latter should bear most of the burden of curbing and mitigating global climate change because over the past two centuries it has been responsible for emitting a large proportion – perhaps two-thirds in the case of carbon dioxide – of the greenhouse gases that have caused the problem. Even today, per capita emissions of greenhouse gases in developed countries vastly exceed those in developing countries, and this gives rise to an important equity issue (Dasgupta, 1994; see also Chapter 11 in this volume).

The developing countries stated their paradigm in the Kuala Lumpur Declaration issued in April 1992, prior to UNCED. To paraphrase the words of Dr Mahathir Mohamad, the former Prime Minister of Malaysia, the developed countries have caused most of the pollution and destroyed their own environmental heritage, so they should clean up their own mess instead of laying claim to the resources of the developing world (Mallet, 1992). Developing countries succeeded in getting their paradigm recognized in Principle 7 of the Rio Declaration, agreed by all countries at UNCED:

> The developed countries acknowledge the responsibility that they bear in the international pursuit of sustainable development in view of the pressures their societies place on the global environment and of the technologies and financial resources they command.

Seen from another perspective, historical emissions of greenhouse gases have also led to the accumulation of environmental costs that the whole world is now being forced to pay. A disproportionate share of this burden will have to be borne by the poorest countries, which are least responsible for causing the problem and least able to pay to mitigate it (see Chapter 11). Andrew Simms, an official of Christian Aid (Simms, 1999b), has even equated the huge environmental debt accumulated by centuries of economic growth in the developed countries with the financial debt crisis of developing countries:

> New ways of accounting for the huge environmental debt that industrialized countries owe for global warming, far outweighing those owed by poor countries, are also turning the balance of power between rich and poor upside down . . . Poor countries could now justifiably demand repayments for eco-debt, greater redistribution, more technology transfer, and a fair system to minimize damage from global warming before even considering agreeing to a global deal.

However justified this argument may be in principle, in practice the developed countries can withstand such claims by virtue of their greater political power. The USA, in particular, has steadfastly refused to acknowledge that it has any such *historical* responsibilities, stating only that the participation of states in the climate change regime should be based on *current* conditions, or, more specifically, 'in accordance with the means at their disposal and their capabilities' (Dasgupta, 1994).

The primary goal of the G77 states when negotiating the FCCC, consistent with their dominant paradigm, was to gain firm commitments for action by developed countries.

When these were not forthcoming they called the FCCC 'fundamentally flawed' (Pearce, 1992a). Their minimum acceptable compromise position had five main components, reflecting a discourse that saw the environment as just one part of the broader development picture:

1. Common but differentiated responsibility: developed countries should bear the main cost of action, in line with their historical responsibility for causing the problem, and there should be special conditions to allow developing countries to participate. This actually led to a new interpretation of sustainable development in the Kuala Lumpur Declaration, in the shape of an argument that the onus should be on developed countries to adjust their current patterns of consumption and production to ensure more environmentally sound development (Vatikiotis, 1992).
2. Additionality: developed states should transfer 'new and additional' funds to developing countries to pay for any actions that they took to combat climate change, and not simply reallocate existing aid budgets.
3. No further loss of sovereignty that would perpetuate their exploitation by developed countries. Mahathir Mohamad has claimed that the environmental policies promoted by developed countries are extending imperialism and the dependency relationships that led to the export of so much of the past economic surplus generated in the developing world (Vatikiotis, 1992). This also explains the developing countries' opposition to notions of 'conditionality', under which any new funding received from developed states could only be used for environmental protection. They also wanted this money to come from a special fund, rather than the Global Environmental Facility, which they saw as being controlled by the World Bank and hence by the USA (Nitze, 1994).
4. The right to continue their social and economic development, asserted in the Kuala Lumpur Declaration (Corzine, 1997). From this perspective, it was totally hypocritical of the developed countries to ask their poorer counterparts to curb their development to mitigate an environmental problem caused by the past unsustainable development of the global North.
5. The right to prioritize action to tackle their own immediate environmental problems – such as poor air and water quality – before long-term problems like global warming. As Anwar Saifullah, Pakistan's Environment Minister at the time of UNCED, noted: '80 per cent of our water is untreated. That's our biggest problem. When I have to worry about the basic provisions of life, it's a luxury to talk of the [global] environment' (Lascelles and Lamb, 1992b).

So developing country discourses share the developed countries' short-term view. When they do take a long-term perspective it is concerned with the past, not the future. They also rank the economic and social dimensions of development far above the environment. Except for countries that are under the most imminent threat from climate change, they also give priority to local environmental problems that have a direct impact on the welfare of their people.

The key positions of the G77 were incorporated into Section 3 of the FCCC, which covers Principles. Yet inevitably compromises had to be made with the positions of developed countries, and this left much ambiguity (Minzer and Leonard, 1994). Thus,

Article 3(4) of the FCCC, which states that 'Parties have a right to, and should, promote sustainable development', can be read as acknowledging both the right of developing countries to develop *and* the view of the developed countries that development should be curbed to minimize environmental impacts. Article 3(5), which states that 'Parties should cooperate to promote ... sustainable economic growth and development in all Parties, particularly developing country Parties', is also ambiguous because it does not clarify how economic growth can be made sustainable. Section 4, on Commitments, recognizes the developing countries' position by requiring developed states to provide new and additional funds to cover the full costs incurred by developing countries in reporting information to the Conference of the Parties. But it also satisfies developed countries by requiring that these funds need only cover the incremental costs of implementing measures to combat global climate change. Despite these concessions to developed countries, however, it does make action by developing countries contingent upon the former fulfilling their own commitments.

Lessons from the climate change negotiations

States were the principal actors in the climate change negotiations, responding mainly to pressures from the interests of domestic Capital and Labour, with NGOs playing only a minor role. The contrast between the US and Group of 77 discourses was stark:

- The USA ranked the environment far below the economic and social dimensions of its development. It showed no interest in integrating the environment into economic planning. Instead, it adopted a globalist and isolationist approach which regarded conserving the global environment as of great importance, but did not link this in any way to the operation of its domestic economy, either past or present. Indeed, its stance required that any response it made to global climate change should not harm its economic interests. Most other developed countries took less extreme positions, even noting the synergies between the economic and environmental dimensions of development, which the USA ignored.
- The G77 states also gave top priority to their own economic and social advancement, but from a more justifiable position that identified climate change as the historical responsibility of developed countries. In this they took a long-term view and firmly integrated the economic and environmental dimensions of development, but only in respect of the developed world. They also linked the social and environmental dimensions, in giving top priority to solving local environmental problems that most directly affected the health of their people.

The USA was able to confine and stall these negotiations by virtue of its hegemonic power. When negotiating the Kyoto Protocol, it had the audacity to breach the UNCED consensus on differentiated obligations, stating that it would not reduce its greenhouse gas emissions unless developing countries followed suit. This deliberate ploy to stall the negotiations was only defeated when much of the rest of the world decided to proceed without the USA.

Discourses in Conflict at the United Nations Conference on Environment and Development

While the discourses of the USA and the developing countries did not come into direct conflict in the climate change negotiations, they did clash more overtly in other UNCED negotiations on biodiversity, forests, the Rio Declaration and Agenda 21, and it is to these that we now turn.

The Convention on Biological Diversity: the predominance of an integrated discourse

When the US government entered into negotiations regarding the other convention agreed at UNCED, concerning biodiversity, the boundaries of its discourse were apparently determined by the belief, already evident with respect to climate change, that it was engaging in a tightly bounded environmental dialogue. Its chief negotiator, William Reilly, stated that he thought that the Convention on Biological Diversity (CBD) would be merely concerned with 'protecting flora and fauna' (Lascelles and Lamb, 1992a). This explains why the US discourse was entirely environmental in content, with a dominant paradigm consistent with a 'globalist' view of the environment.

But the USA received a rude awakening from developing countries. Based on an acute sense of their previous economic exploitation, portrayed in the structuralist theories outlined above, their discourse was cast not just in environmental terms, but also engaged with social and economic perspectives. In this context, when the current exploitation of their natural resources was at stake, developing countries did not see the environment in isolation. Their dominant paradigm was that any action they took to conserve their environment must be consistent with preserving their economic sovereignty and the right to develop as they wanted. These were two of their primary goals in the climate change negotiations. With respect to biodiversity, their primary goal and minimum acceptable compromise position were identical: to establish the right to charge for access by other countries to their natural resources. They achieved this by gaining agreement to insert clauses into the convention which ensured that if their natural resources were exploited for biotechnology they could patent the genetic material contained in these resources, charge royalties for its use and claim preferential access to any resulting products. Marcos Azambuja, Brazil's chief negotiator, described the issue in this way: 'If the bark of a tree in Piaui state is found to have certain valuable properties, is that a Brazilian asset? Do we allow others to share it and can we charge royalties if someone synthesizes it?' (Lascelles and Lamb, 1992a).

The introduction of economic terms into the CBD made it incompatible with the US government's discourse. It also contradicted its minimum acceptable compromise position that the regime should not stray beyond the boundaries of a purely environmental dialogue, or have any negative impacts on the US economy. Consequently, the US government declined to sign the convention, alleging that it would: (a) undermine patents and licences over products and processes; (b) weaken its negotiating position on intellectual property rights in the Uruguay Round of GATT trade talks then in progress; (c) disadvantage US firms by imposing safety rules for the export of genetically engineered products; and (d) prevent the US government from influencing the destination of funds which it gave to implement the convention.

As with climate change, the US position reflected the dominant influence of its industry lobby. President Bush stated that: 'I will not sign a treaty that in my view throws too many Americans out of work.' Dick Godwin, President of the Industrial Biotechnology Association, was still more emphatic: 'It seems to us highway robbery that a Third World country should have the right to a protected invention on concessionary terms simply because it supplied a bug, or a plant or an animal in the first place' (Coghlan, 1992).

Crucially, however, in the case of biodiversity, the US government had less scope than with climate change to influence the content of the Convention by using its hegemonic power to impose its discourse on the dialogue. Nor did it have the potential to impose a veto. Instead, this power now lay with developing states, such as Brazil, Indonesia and Malaysia, whose territories contained a major share of global biodiversity. In the end, they were not obliged to use this veto. The developing country discourse was allowed to dominate the dialogue, and the economic connection between biodiversity and biotechnology was formally recognized.

Although President Clinton later signed the Convention, the contradiction between the discourses of the developed and developing countries remained. Consequently, little progress has since been made towards reaching agreement on protocols needed to implement the convention. The sole exception has been the Bio-Safety Protocol, agreed in 2000, which aims to ensure the safe use of genetically modified organisms. Not surprisingly, this chiefly serves the commercial interest of developed countries.

The defeat of globalism: the Forest Convention negotiations

Developing countries fought hard before UNCED to prevent agreement on a Forest Convention, which was publicly stated to be the USA's primary goal in Rio (Pearce, 1992b). This was to be expected, given its restricted globalist environmental discourse. US environmental groups, like their counterparts in Europe, had been pressing for a Forest Convention for some time. Given the high quality of forest management in the USA, implementing it would not incur high domestic social and economic costs or exceed the bounds of the US discourse. 'If one had been agreed', said Fred Pearce (1992b), 'these governments could have claimed they were tackling the number one concern of environmentalists at home.' However, the globalist environment discourse adopted by many NGOs from developed countries failed to address the everyday social and economic problems of developing countries (Rahman and Roncerel, 1994).

Developing countries strongly opposed a Forest Convention because they thought it would undermine their sovereign right to choose how they balanced the economic, social and environmental dimensions of development. As Mahathir Mohamad observed: 'A convention would only be fair if we could also tell the North that they could not have this or that factory' (New Scientist, 1992a). Another cause for concern was the cost of upgrading the quality of forest management. The Kuala Lumpur group of forested countries also thought that developed countries were using the convention as 'an attempt to spread the blame for the greenhouse problem' because of the carbon dioxide emitted by tropical deforestation (Goldemberg, 1994).

If a Forest Convention had been agreed at UNCED it would have been an important step towards extending globalization into the environmental arena by imposing uniform, instead of differentiated, global standards. However, owing to the strength of opposition only a bland, voluntary Statement of Forest Principles was approved. The wording of the final text sheds interesting light on the discourses of the various parties involved in these negotiations:

- The G77 removed all references to a future Forest Convention from the preamble, which refers only to 'appropriate internationally agreed arrangements to promote international cooperation'.
- Sensitivity over sovereignty aroused resistance to attempts to refer to the 'global' importance of forests, and the pre-eminence of national policies, so that the final version spoke of forests being 'essential to the economy as a whole'. According to Kamal Nath, then Indian environment minister: 'We do not talk about the globalization of oil. Yet oil has a greater impact than forests on the global environment' (*New Scientist*, 1992a). The G77 also ensured that the statement referred to unilateral boycotts on 'unsustainable' forest products as unlawful (Lamb, 1992).
- Developing countries wanted to include a phrase affirming the 'right to develop': one of their general minimum acceptable compromise positions. But US insistence on an environmental qualification resulted in a final version that spoke of the 'right to socio-economic development on a sustainable basis' (Pearce, 1992b). The USA was evidently willing to impose environmental constraints on development in developing countries, but not on its *own* development.

The G77 was a very influential negotiating group at UNCED, with India, Malaysia and Pakistan being among its most vociferous members. Its leaders knew that developed countries required their cooperation to realize the aim of a better global environment and so attempted to use this advantage to gain concessions on trade and aid. 'Fear by the North of environmental degradation', argued Mahathir Mohamad (*New Scientist*, 1992a), 'provides the South with the leverage that did not exist before.' However, developed countries did not promise more aid and freer trade as incentives to secure environmental agreements. They did offer a Convention on Desertification, a priority for African states, if the latter would support the Forest Convention. But the G77 proved sufficiently powerful to gain agreement on a Convention on Desertification – negotiated after UNCED – without any of its members having to sacrifice their principles by agreeing to a Forest Convention.

Agenda 21 and the Rio Declaration: the phraseology of compromise

Similar clashes occurred over two other UNCED documents, the Rio Declaration and Agenda 21; but these were not abandoned. Instead, they were simply rephrased to prevent their rejection by key parties.

Thus, the third of the 27 principles of the Rio Declaration (see Table 12.1) (UN, 1993) states that 'The right to development must be fulfilled so as to equitably meet the developmental and environmental needs of present and future generations'. This repeats the compromise phrase used in the Statement of Forest Principles that had

Table 12.1   Summary of the Rio Declaration

1   Human beings are at the centre of concerns for sustainable development. They are entitled to a healthy and productive life in harmony with nature.

2   States have, in accordance with the Charter of the United Nations and the principles of international law, the sovereign right to exploit their own resources pursuant to their own environmental and developmental policies, and the responsibility to ensure that activities within their jurisdiction or control do not cause damage to the environment of other states or of areas beyond the limits of national jurisdiction.

3   The right to development must be fulfilled in order to equitably meet the developmental and environmental needs of present and future generations.

4   In order to achieve sustainable development, environmental protection shall constitute an integral part of the development process and cannot be considered in isolation from it.

5   All states and all peoples shall cooperate in the essential task of eradicating poverty as an indispensable requirement for sustainable development in order to decrease the disparities in standards of living and better meet the needs of the majority of the people of the world.

6   The special situation and needs of developing countries, particularly the least developed and those most environmentally vulnerable, shall be given special priority. International actions in the field of environment and development should also address the interests and needs of all countries.

7   States shall cooperate in a spirit of global partnership to conserve, protect and restore the health and integrity of the Earth's ecosystem. In view of the different contributions to global environmental degradation, states have common but differentiated responsibilities. The developed countries acknowledge the responsibility that they bear in the international pursuit of sustainable development in view of the pressures their societies place on the global environment and of the technologies and financial resources they command.

8   To achieve sustainable development and a higher quality of life for all people, states should reduce and eliminate unsustainable patterns of production and consumption and promote appropriate demographic policies.

9   States should cooperate to strengthen endogenous capacity-building for sustainable development by improving scientific understanding through exchanges of scientific and technological knowledge, and by enhancing the development, adaptation, diffusion and transfer of technologies, including new and innovative technologies.

10 Environmental issues are best handled with the participation of all concerned citizens at the relevant level. At the national level, each individual shall have appropriate access to information concerning the environment that is held by public authorities, including information on hazardous materials and activities in their communities, and the opportunity to participate in decision-making processes. States shall facilitate and encourage public awareness and participation by making information widely available. Effective access to judicial and administrative proceedings, including redress and remedy, shall be provided.

11 States shall enact effective environmental legislation. Environmental standards, management objectives and priorities should reflect the environmental and developmental context to which they apply. Standards applied by some countries may be inappropriate and of unwarranted economic and social cost to other countries, particularly developing countries.

12 States should cooperate to promote a supportive and open international economic system that would lead to economic growth and sustainable development in all countries, to better address the problems of environmental degradation. Trade policy measures for all purposes should not constitute a means of arbitrary or unjustifiable discrimination or a disguised restriction on international trade. Unilateral actions to deal with environmental challenges outside the jurisdiction of the importing country should be avoided. Environmental measures addressing transboundary or global environmental problems should, as far as possible, be based on an international consensus.

Table 12.1 *Continued*

13   States shall develop national law regarding liability and compensation for the victims of pollution and other environmental damage. States shall also cooperate in an expeditious and more determined manner to develop further international law regarding liability and compensation for adverse effects of environmental damage caused by activities within their jurisdiction or control to areas beyond their jurisdiction.

14   States should effectively cooperate to discourage or prevent the relocation and transfer to other states of any activities and substances that cause severe environmental degradation or are found to be harmful to human health.

15   In order to protect the environment, the precautionary approach shall be widely applied by states according to their capabilities. Where there are threats of serious or irreversible damage, lack of full scientific certainty shall not be used as a reason for postponing cost-effective measures to prevent environmental degradation.

16   National authorities should endeavour to promote the internalization of environmental costs and the use of economic instruments, taking into account the approach that the polluter should, in principle, bear the cost of pollution, with due regard to the public interest and without distorting international trade and investment.

17   Environmental impact assessment, as a national instrument, shall be undertaken for proposed activities that are likely to have a significant adverse impact upon the environment and are subject to a decision of a competent national authority.

18   States shall immediately notify other states of any natural disasters or other emergences that are likely to produce sudden harmful effects on the environment of those states. Every effort shall be made by the international community to help states so afflicted.

19   States shall provide prior and timely notification and relevant information to potentially affected states on activities that may have a significant adverse transboundary environmental effect and shall consult with those states at an early stage and in good faith.

20   Women have a vital role in environmental management and development. Their full participation is therefore essential to achieve sustainable development.

21   The creativity, ideals and courage of the youth of the world should be mobilized to forge a global partnership in order to achieve sustainable development and ensure a better future for all.

22   Indigenous people and their communities and other local communities have a vital role in environmental management and development because of their knowledge and traditional practices. States should recognize and duly support their identity, culture and interests and enable their effective participation in the achievement of sustainable development.

23   The environment and natural resources of people under oppression, domination and occupation shall be protected.

24   Warfare is inherently destructive of sustainable development. States shall therefore respect international law providing protection for the environment in times of armed conflict and cooperate in its further development, as necessary.

25   Peace, development and environmental protection are interdependent and indivisible.

26   States shall resolve all of their environmental disputes peacefully and by appropriate means in accordance with the Charter of the United Nations.

27   States and people shall cooperate in good faith and in a spirit of partnership in the fulfilment of the principles embodied in this Declaration and in the further development of international law in the field of sustainable development.

Source: UN (1993)

proved acceptable to both developing countries and the USA. The second principle defends the notion of sovereignty by asserting that 'countries have the right to exploit their own natural resources', a position vital for the developing countries. But it also notes that countries 'have an equal obligation to ensure that activities within their jurisdiction or control do not cause damage to the environments of other states', which reflects the USA's globalist discourse. Similar qualifications of the basic discourse of developing countries can also be found in Principles 4, 5 and 7. The discourse emerges intact in Principle 11, which implicitly opposes the imposition of uniform environmental standards. The developed countries' discourse of an open world economy is prominent in Principle 12, though this also conforms to the developing countries' discourse in advising against trade barriers. Even though the USA agreed to the Rio Declaration, it still insisted on issuing a press release to explain how it interpreted key phrases – for example, stressing that 'Development is not a right. It is a goal we all hold' (Pearce 1992b).

Agenda 21, which extends to over 400 pages and 40 chapters, is often treated deferentially as a comprehensive programme of action for sustainable development. However, it is more a political document than a technical manual (UN, 1993). When it was formulated some issues were excluded at the insistence of lobby groups and national delegations, while in other instances the language was blurred to avoid offence. For example, OPEC, led by Saudi Arabia, opposed any mention of fuel efficiency, alternative sources of energy and curbs on car use in the chapter on the atmosphere (*New Scientist*, 1992b). The Vatican opposed any reference to the control of population, and industry lobby groups ensured that transnational corporations were only mentioned in a favourable light. The final document was condemned in a *Times* leader on 15 June 1992 as:

> A ragbag which conflates the marginally desirable with the vital, a document so heavily politicized that it barely nods to the obstacle rapid population growth presents to protecting the environment in some of the poorest countries (*The Times*, 1992).

Even the Secretary General of UNCED, Maurice Strong, stressed the absence of key topics in both Agenda 21 and the Rio Declaration by deliberately mentioning them in his opening speech to the conference. As he recognized, diplomatic compromise may maintain friendly relations between states, but rarely leads to feasible policies.

In spite of the two conventions which emerged from UNCED, overall it must be regarded as a failure. This is because it could not reconcile the conflicting discourses of the parties involved, merely finding a form of words to recognize both simultaneously. It was not just that different states had different goals. In many cases, they seemed incapable of understanding views different from their own.

Assessing the balance between competing discourses

These negotiations show that there is still some truth in the principles of rationalist theories. States were the principal actors and both the USA and developing countries tried to limit their relative economic losses when formulating the Biodiversity and Climate Conventions, in line with Neo-Realist theory. The discourses of developing countries were also heavily influenced by the desire to prevent the extension of the exploitative relations portrayed in structuralist theories. On the other hand, the governments of developed countries rarely behaved as unitary actors. They often negotiated at two levels at the same time: both externally, with other governments, and internally, with groups whose support they required in order to stay in power.

The US government intended to satisfy its powerful business and labour lobbies with the Climate Change Convention (FCCC), and the environmental lobby with the Biodiversity Convention (CBD) and Forest Convention. Unfortunately, the Biodiversity Convention was not restricted to flora and fauna, as it had expected, and the Forest Convention was blocked by developing countries which feared that it would infringe their sovereignty.

Overall, however, the USA played a clever game. By insisting that it would not participate in the Kyoto Protocol unless developing countries followed suit, it gambled that this would ensure that it would never have to ratify the Protocol. At the same time, it was able to dominate formation of the regime because its discourse did not come into direct conflict with that of the developing countries. But by deliberately trying to draw the latter into the dialogue in this way, it risked initiating this conflict. When this happened in other dialogues the more comprehensive developing country discourse proved to be surprisingly resilient. So there is a strong chance that this might have happened with climate change too, and then the USA could not have maintained the restricted boundaries of its environmental discourse. Ultimately, the USA chose to withdraw from the entire dialogue because its discourse was incompatible with those of virtually all of the other parties, both developed and developing. The Republican administration of George W Bush was not afraid to take an isolationist position in the world community. Indeed, it blocked attempts to include any targets for increasing renewable energy use at the expense of fossil fuels in the Plan of Implementation drawn up at the 2002 World Summit on Sustainable Development, held in Johannesburg in 2002, and even insisted on excluding climate change from the list of high-priority environmental issues included in the associated Johannesburg Declaration.

Sustainable development: optimum development path or unresolved compromise?

Sustainable development is mentioned not only in the Rio Declaration and Agenda 21, but also in the Climate Change and Biodiversity Conventions. Yet the analysis in this chapter raises doubts about the use of the term in UNCED documents. Did it refer to an optimum development path that was an intentional balance between the economic, social and environmental dimensions of development? Or was it was simply an unresolved compromise between two different discourses: that of the developing countries, which regarded *development* as a right, and that of the developed countries, which regarded 'sustainable development' as a codeword for development subject to certain constraints to protect the *environment*?

Hyder (1994), a prominent representative of the G77, was in no doubt that:

The entire UNCED process can be seen as a struggle between the developing and developed countries to define sustainable development in a way that fits their own agendas. The developed countries put the environment first. By contrast the developing countries put development first.

He believed that the developed countries rejected the link between environment and development because they were afraid that the developing countries would try to use it as a lever to gain more financial resources from them. Their globalist view of the environment suggests that they either could not conceive of integrating the economic, social and environmental dimensions of development, or they regarded it as politically impossible.

Hyder also pointed to another difference between the two discourses. While the developed countries tried to distinguish between global and local problems, developing countries saw them as linked, and even tried to put them on an equal footing to emphasize the relationship between environment and poverty.

The preamble of UN General Assembly Resolution 44/228, passed on 22 December 1989, which launched the whole UNCED process, stated that 'Environmental protection in developing countries must . . . be viewed as an integral part of the development process and cannot be considered in isolation from it'. This clearly identifies the necessity of integrating the environment with the other dimensions of development so that trade-offs can be made between them. Yet from Hyder's (1994) perspective, and that of the developing countries generally, it seemed that:

> As the global environmental negotiations unfolded . . . it became obvious that the developed countries, having acquiesced to Resolution 44/228, no longer felt bound by its language or its intent. In every negotiating forum they sought to give primacy to environmental protection at the cost of the universal right to development.

If this is correct – and, of course, developed countries might argue that developing states were equally focused on development as their main priority – then it means that 'sustainable development' was not used in the UNCED documents to refer to an optimum development path. It was simply a device to reconcile the aspiration of developing countries to develop and the developed world's desire to curb this development in order to protect the global environment. So the internal contradiction within the Brundtland Report (see Chapter 1) was left unresolved by UNCED.

Since UNCED many have looked to Agenda 21 as though it offered a master plan for sustainable development. O'Riordan et al (1998) went even further, stating that: 'Although not legally binding on national governments, the intense negotiations surrounding many sections accentuate Agenda 21's possible influence as a soft law instrument.' It might be wiser, however, to be more cautious about its potential contribution because in order to ensure a final consensus text, at least as many compromises had to be made as for the Brundtland Report.

A cynic might argue that the unresolved ambiguity in the Brundtland Report, and even the conflicts at UNCED over the meaning of 'sustainable development', were of no consequence. This is because sustainable development has only ever been, in the minds of states, a codeword for bargaining. The developed countries want a better global environment, while the developing countries want more development, and the groups of states will trade off one against the other in the course of extended negotiations. This means that sustainable development at global level remains a compromise, but a different and less attractive one from that which most idealists would like.

Modifying Existing International Institutions

While states may be able to remain within the strict boundaries of their environmental discourses in dialogues confined to environmental topics, it is more difficult to do this when attempts are made to incorporate an environmental dimension into dialogues that are predominantly concerned with economic or social topics. In order to gain additional insights into the attitudes of states regarding integration of the three dimensions of development, this final part of the chapter examines the debates that ensued when proposals were made to modify three international institutions – the International Labour Organization (ILO), the World Trade Organization (WTO) and its forerunner, the General Agreement on Tariffs and Trade (GATT) – to take account of human rights and environmental concerns.

Trade and development

Developing countries have struggled for decades to win better access for their exports to markets in the developed countries, hoping that this will enable them to generate more capital and thus accelerate their development. But such efforts have often been frustrated by trade barriers erected by developed countries, which, by default, give preference to imports of raw materials – characterized by low and fluctuating prices – over manufactured goods. Thus, of the 28 poorest countries in the world, 26 depend upon primary commodities for over 70 per cent of their export revenues (Barbier, 1994). This dependency, which has increased in the post-colonial era, makes it difficult for Southern states to implement long-term development strategies, inhibits their industrialization and development, and restricts their ability to secure more sustainable development. Indeed, when developing countries export raw materials for processing elsewhere, they are effectively exporting their development (see Chapter 3) since the value added to these natural resources by processing accrues to the importing countries, instead of being used to fund their own development.

During the 20th century, states formed a series of international institutions to advance their mutual interests. The General Agreement on Tariffs and Trade (GATT), established in 1948 following the Bretton Woods Conference, succeeded in reducing trade barriers between developed countries; but developing countries always felt that it neglected their needs. Even after 1964, which saw the start of regular meetings of the UN Conference on Trade and Development (UNCTAD) to consider the issue, barriers between developed and developing countries declined more slowly. Developing countries still feel like second-class members of the World Trade Organization (WTO), which superseded GATT in 1995. This perception was confirmed by their exclusion from key discussions at the start of the abortive round of WTO talks in Seattle in November 1999. They expressed their irritation in a declaration issued after an UNCTAD meeting in Bangkok in February 2000, which reminded developed countries of the need to take account of 'the development dimension' in trade (Barnes, 2000). Continuing restrictions on the exports of developing countries sit uncomfortably with pressures from the World Bank and the International Monetary Fund (IMF) to remove their own barriers to imports from developed countries so that they can allegedly reap the full benefits of liberalization.

In the 1990s, the prospect of another type of trade barrier emerged. While the boundaries of trade dialogues between developed and developing countries have long been biased against the latter, at least they were limited to trade. So when some developed countries suggested extending the boundaries to include labour and environmental standards, developing countries reacted strongly, believing this would further restrict their access to overseas markets. The proposals were a response to pressures from NGOs and other interest groups, which believed that when developed countries import resources and products from the developing world they are, effectively, importing development – in the form of low social welfare – and sustainable development – in the form of low environmental quality. Prices are lower than those for equivalent goods in developed countries because suppliers do not have to pay the costs of complying with the tougher social and environmental laws that prevail in the latter (see Chapter 3). At first glance, expanding international trade regulations to ensure a level playing field should reduce such inequities. But what if this severely constrains development, and appears to developing countries as a deliberate attempt by the developed countries to do this? Little has changed since Redclift (1987) stated that 'The problem in achieving sustainable development [is] related to the over-riding structures of the international economic system'.

Proposals to include labour standards in world trade rules

The International Labour Organization (ILO) is one of the oldest UN specialized agencies, originally founded in 1919 as part of the League of Nations. It has traditionally set voluntary standards for working conditions and helped countries to move closer to them, but it differs from GATT and WTO in that developing countries are strongly represented within it. When President Chirac of France proposed linking labour standards to trade at the ILO's annual meeting in 1995, his discourse was very much at odds with the traditional boundaries of ILO dialogue. He claimed that trade liberalization, the development of employment and respect for fundamental labour rights were 'inseparable'. As a result, he noted, 'We must seek a way to link respect for the social dimension ... and the liberalization of international trade' (Williams, 1995).

The idea that the production of all goods traded in international markets should conform to minimum uniform social standards, effectively corresponding to those currently accepted by developed countries, was a response to pressures on some ILO member states from two main sources. First, from trade unions and businesses, which feared 'unfair' competition from goods produced under poor working conditions, including forced and child labour. Second, from consumers' groups and other NGOs, which had moral objections to what they saw as labour exploitation. So, while states may have tabled the formal proposal at the ILO, the initiative originated with non-state actors, something which the traditional rationalist theories of international relations do not encompass.

In the discourse of those developed countries which supported this proposal it would have helped to enhance the social welfare dimension of development in developing countries, although it would not necessarily have redistributed income and wealth. Yet while it might appear that the developed countries were integrating the economic and social dimensions of development, they were only doing so in relation to their developing counterparts, and were motivated largely by a desire to protect their own economic interests.

If this proposal had been accepted it would have led to a major change in the ILO's rules. Common sets of rules help the ILO and other international institutions to minimize conflicts between members but this proposal aimed to turn a set of *voluntary* standards into *binding* rules for an entirely different purpose. In doing so it would have effectively expanded globalization into the social arena.

The proposal put the ILO in a dilemma. Accepting it might antagonize its developing country members by infringing their sovereignty while rejection might lead to some developed countries erecting their own trade barriers, thereby increasing disorder in the world trading system and labour markets. Its dilemma increased when, in 1996, the WTO refused a request by the US government to link labour standards to trade, suggesting that this fell under the ILO's jurisdiction.

Consequently, in 1997, the ILO secretariat drafted a Declaration of Core Labour Standards and asked member states to give the ILO a 'specific mandate' to ensure 'the protection and promotion on a universal basis of the fundamental rights of workers'. These rights would include freedom of association and collective bargaining, suppression of all forms of forced or compulsory labour, abolition of child labour, and equality of opportunity. A new global system of social labelling was proposed to guarantee that internationally traded goods were produced under humane working conditions. ILO staff would make regular inspections in member states to ensure compliance (Taylor, 1997a).

That year's ILO conference supported a Declaration of Universal Labour Standards, regarding it as entirely consistent with the ILO's traditional dialogue and *voluntary* approach. However, the G77 countries opposed going further, by linking these standards to trade, effectively in the form of a strong regime, since extending the boundaries of the ILO dialogue in this way threatened their national sovereignty. Their discourse on this linkage is well expressed in the following paraphrase of a statement by the Colombian government:

'It introduces an untenable link between labour standards and trade which we do not accept. The ILO has no role with regard to the multilateral trading system nor is it mandated to promote or impede globalization'. Developing countries should only have to conform to those internationally recognized labour standards which are 'voluntarily ratified' by states. The ILO should regard labour standards as 'benchmarks in the process of development' and assist in gradually attaining them by setting standards, promoting technical cooperation, and analysing labour trends, having regard to the stage of social and economic development in each country. An annual ILO report on social progress in each country is 'unacceptable'. 'The implication is the ILO would determine what is the "acceptable" level of comparative advantage and which countries are converting the benefits of liberalization into social progress'. A voluntary system of 'social labelling' is also unacceptable. 'There is no empirical evidence to support the view that there is a link between trade liberalization and labour standards' (Taylor, 1997b).

The developing country discourse was therefore dominated, as expected, by an insistence on sovereignty, and the limitation of international standards to 'benchmarks' that states can use at their discretion to assess their progress in economic development. There was no apparent desire to integrate closely the economic and social dimensions of development in the way that the developed countries wanted. The conference therefore gave the ILO secretariat a mandate to continue working on the declaration and monitoring mechanisms, but left undecided how any social conditions might be added to world trade rules in the future.

Proposals to include environmental conditions in world trade rules

Proposals and pressures

Proposals have also been made to add environmental conditions to world trade rules in order to prevent countries from exporting goods whose production incurs unacceptably high environmental impacts. The context is somewhat different from that discussed above, as GATT, and subsequently the WTO, have an established role in setting *mandatory* trade rules, as distinct from advisory standards. It would just be necessary to modify these to incorporate environmental provisions, though again it would breach the boundaries of the existing dialogue. Although developing countries lack power in the WTO, its existing rules are consistent with key terms in their discourse, not least the emphasis on national sovereignty.

As discussed in Chapter 3, lower environmental standards in developing states allow them to 'export sustainable development' in the goods they supply to developed countries. Importers obtain such goods relatively cheaply because they do not have to pay the environmental costs imposed in their own countries. Daly and Goodland (1994) defended the imposition of environmental conditions on trade from an ecological economics perspective, arguing that free trade converts local carrying capacity constraints into global constraints. So a problem that would, in their eyes, be manageable at a local level becomes unmanageable at the global level. Without international regulations, non-market environmental costs are not paid. They noted that 'many environmental problems cannot be resolved equitably, efficiently or sustainably by unregulated markets, and ... there is no alternative to public intervention in certain situations'.

As with proposals to change ILO rules, non-state actors took the lead in proposing environmental conditionality in world trade. The idea emerged in the 1980s when the Worldwide Fund for Nature (WWF) and other environmentalist NGOs proposed that developed countries ban the import of timber extracted from tropical rain forests that were not sustainably managed (Grainger, 1993). The Brundtland Report later argued that GATT should 'reflect concern for the impacts of trading patterns on the environment and the need for more effective instruments to integrate environment and development concerns into international trading arrangements' (WCED, 1987).

NGOs continued to press their case, receiving growing support from the governments of developed countries. Both share a globalist environmental discourse that gives a high priority to the needs of the planet, though there are important differences between them. For governments the globalist discourse is a convenient way to promote the cause of the environment overseas without having to impose too heavy a burden on their own economies. Although it would be unfair to deny that such a stance does have a moral dimension, intended to appeal to 'Green' opinion within the electorate, limiting artificially cheap imports from developing countries helps to defend jobs at home, something that is of even greater concern to the electorate.

The NGO discourse, on the other hand, is politically naive: for the sake of the planet developing countries cannot be allowed to repeat the mistakes made by the developed countries. If they will not curb their environmental degradation voluntarily, they must be forced to do so by trade sanctions. Environmental NGOs also equate free trade – of the kind promoted by the WTO – with the globalization of the world economy and all of its allegedly negative effects, including the erosion of national economic and environmental sovereignty. So they believe that uniform international environmental standards are necessary to protect developing countries against these forces. But what they are actually doing, albeit unconsciously, is helping to extend globalization from the economic into the environmental arena. Far from reducing the exploitation of developing countries, this will reinforce it.

Unsurprisingly, environmental conditionality is opposed by the governments of most developing countries. They are all too aware of the perils of economic globalization and are in no doubt that environmental conditionality is a deliberate attempt to extend it further, and thereby erode their sovereignty and ability to develop. They are not very enthusiastic about integrating the economic and environmental dimensions of development.

Other opponents are found amongst economists (for example, Bhagwati, 1999) and within the WTO itself, where officials believe that environmental conditionality could trigger a new round of domestic protectionism. GATT actually commissioned a study of the links between trade and the environment. This concluded that free trade alone does not cause environmental degradation; a country's environmental policy must also be inadequate. The study endorsed the sovereign right of each state to formulate an environmental policy that reflects its own values and priorities. It also noted that environmental protection usually improves in the course of development, but this might be hindered by imposing trade barriers that obstruct development (GATT, 1992).

Incorporating environmental conditions into world trade rules would strengthen existing non-tariff barriers. The latter are already present in the form of state subsidies for fishing (estimated at US$50 billion), energy (US$300 billion) and farming (US$350 billion) that the governments of Australia, New Zealand, Iceland, the Philippines and the USA claim distort world trade. These states have called for subsidies to be cut to make their own exports more competitive in world markets (Williams, 1999a). Ironically, environmentalist groups also oppose these subsidies, on the grounds that they lead to environmental damage through overfishing, inefficient energy use and the overuse of chemical inputs to produce food surpluses.

Current trade rules and the environment
Present trade rules, which WTO inherited from GATT, are consistent with the typical developing country discourse that it is an unfair restriction on trade for one country to restrict imports from other countries that do not share its environmental laws. These

rules were tested when the US government tried to integrate the economic and environmental dimensions of development by banning imports of Mexican tuna, because the tuna boats also caught dolphins, which are a protected species in the USA. GATT ruled in 1991, however, that the USA could not extend its own environmental laws beyond its borders in this way (Esty, 1994). The key point of disagreement in this case is the difference between product and process. GATT rules did not allow discrimination between imports on the basis of the *process* by which a particular *product* was made. It was the environmentally damaging process by which the Mexican tuna were caught that was objectionable to the US government, not the product itself, and GATT ruled that this was an illegal restriction on trade.

GATT was aware that its rules could conflict with attempts by individual countries to improve their own environmental performance and with proposals to enforce the eco-labelling of imported products. It also identified the potential for conflict with the principles of international environmental regimes, including the Montreal Protocol, the Convention on International Trade in Endangered Species (CITES) and the Basle Convention on Trade in Hazardous Wastes. When WTO replaced GATT in 1995 it established a committee to look into these issues. So far, however, the committee has not been able to agree on a set of recommendations.

Because GATT and WTO member states could not agree to modify trade rules in the way that environmentalist groups wanted, they have been criticized for being anti-environment. Greenpeace called GATT an organization 'subservient to multinational corporations' (Dunne, 1992). In the environmentalist discourse, these corporations are the primary beneficiaries of the globalization of the world economy, and free trade promotes environmental degradation as it ignores the non-market values of environmental services. The only way to prevent this is by imposing common global standards. The Worldwide Fund for Nature (WWF) opposed the creation of WTO, even calling it incompatible with the goal of sustainable development. It argued that any new body should not just recognize 'the need to set limits on trade in order to adequately protect the environment', it should also adopt environmental protection and poverty eradication as explicit objectives. WWF also called for NGOs to be consulted as of right and allowed to make submissions to trade disputes investigations, and for WTO to establish a trade and sustainable development council (Williams, 1993).

A tendency to secrecy, a trait that always arouses suspicion amongst NGOs, made GATT its own worst enemy. In 1994, for example, the US government suggested that environmentalists should be invited to a meeting of the GATT Governing Council called to discuss a panel report on the USA–Mexico tuna dispute. Other members, however, disagreed: the EU feared that it would set a precedent for other interest groups, while Brazil dismissed the proposal as inappropriate, impractical and unreasonable (Williams, 1994). Environmental groups did attend a GATT conference on trade and environment in 1994 and similar WTO conferences in 1995 and 1999. But despite WTO's desire to promote greater openness, it still attracts criticism from NGOs (Williams, 1999b).

The Seattle meeting and its repercussions
The battle to integrate labour and environmental standards into world trade rules continued at the WTO meeting in Seattle in November 1999 that was due to launch a

new round of trade liberalization talks. However, the inability of WTO member states to reach a decision on these proposals was more a consequence of the general failure of the meeting than of any specific problems with these proposals. The meeting ended in acrimony, proving an excellent example, if any more were needed, of the international anarchy and ineffectiveness of institutions as portrayed by Neo-Realist theory. It is customary for the agendas of international conferences to be agreed beforehand. But this did not happen in Seattle, making it impossible to structure the dialogue to move towards consensus. In the circumstances a chaotic end was probably inevitable.

The absence of an agreed agenda largely reflected the sheer diversity of expectations expressed by participating states. They had divided themselves into a variety of groups, each with its own aims and discourse. The USA and the Cairns Group of agricultural exporters wanted freer farm trade and cuts in European and Japanese agricultural subsidies. The EU, in turn, wanted to discuss 'anything but agriculture', including environmental standards and customs reform. The top priority of the developing countries was general trade liberalization to improve access for their goods in global markets but this was not shared by the other participants. On the whole, therefore, far greater stress was still placed on economic issues, rather than on social or environmental ones. Meanwhile, outside the conference hall, thousands of demonstrators protested against globalization and the 'evils' of capitalism, which they saw as embodied in WTO. When President Clinton opened the meeting he unexpectedly offered support for the introduction of labour and environmental standards, which only added to the confusion.

The developing countries emerged stronger from Seattle than they had been before, despite being sidelined by the developed countries, as in GATT conferences in the past. Indeed, it was generally acknowledged that one reason for the failure of Seattle was the exclusion of the developing country discourse from the overall dialogue. Dealing with this problem was therefore a precondition for the future success of WTO as a whole. Michael Meacher, then UK Minister of State for the Environment, argued that negotiations on a new round of trade talks, that would 'address contentious issues such as trade and envrionment in a balanced way', should not begin until the developed countries had built bridges with developing ones to explain the benefits of linking trade and environmental policies. 'Many developing countries were very angry that their demands had been ignored', he claimed. The EU, in particular, would find it hard to convince them that its proposals to add environmental conditions to WTO rules were not 'eco-protectionism' while it continued to subsidize agriculture and fishing so heavily (De Jonquières, 2000).

Because the developing countries now have a higher profile at the WTO, it is unlikely that a decision to incorporate social and environmental conditions into world trade rules will be reached in the near future. After almost two years of discussions, a new round of WTO trade negotiations was finally launched at a ministerial meeting held in Doha, in Qatar, in November 2001. At the EU's request, the subject of environmental conditions was included on the negotiating agenda; but it was not accorded a very high priority at the meeting. Instead, the concluding Doha Declaration merely 'took note' of 'the efforts by members to conduct national environmental assessments of trade policies on a voluntary basis'. It also asked the WTO's Trade and Environment Committee to undertake negotiations on 'the relationship between existing WTO rules and specific trade obligations set out in multilateral environmental agreements', principally to identify any potential points of conflict and to determine whether clarification of WTO rules was required.

The round of talks launched at Doha was portrayed as having been designed to meet the concerns of developing countries by freeing farm trade. Yet when the next WTO meeting took place, in Cancun, Mexico in September 2003, the developing countries discovered that the EU and the USA were offering only limited concessions on farm subsidies, while demanding in return that developing countries agree to a significant extension of WTO rules to include such areas as investment and government procurement, but not initially the environment. By this time the self-confidence and solidarity of the developing countries, now led by a smaller coalition, the Group of 21, was sufficient to withstand these pressures, and yet another meeting collapsed in acrimony.

The ongoing debates at WTO and ILO differ from those at UNCED in one important respect. They are primarily concerned with modifying existing institutions, while those at UNCED were concerned with creating new institutions. Existing institutions always contain considerable inertia to change, but the failure of a proposal at one meeting does not have the same degree of finality as when a proposal for a convention fails even to be discussed at a specially convened conference, such as UNCED. Proposals to impose environmental conditions on trade are likely to return to the WTO's negotiating agenda in the future, and the relationship between the obligations of states that are members of both the WTO and environmental institutions, such as the Convention on Biological Diversity, will continue to be debated. Attempts were made at the World Summit on Sustainable Development in 2002, for example, to include a clause in the Johannesburg Declaration that would give WTO rules primacy over all matters concerned with trade–environment links. This was defeated, however, by an alliance of developing countries and EU member states.

Alternative discourses of globalization and sustainable development

These dialogues at meetings of the ILO, WTO and GATT exhibit a similar kind of conflict between the discourses of developed and developing countries to those discussed earlier in the chapter. However, now the developed countries are trying to integrate the three dimensions of development, while the developing countries oppose this. At the heart of the developing countries' discourse is an assertion of the right to develop as they wish, according to the existing rules, while the developed countries want to change the rules in line with their own revised perceptions of how development should proceed. Developing countries also object to proposals to add social and environmental conditions to world trade rules as these contradict another basic element of their discourse: that their inferior economic position is a direct result of bias against their interests embodied in the very structure of the world economic system. The proposals would, in their view, consolidate and extend this inequity, and further the interests of the developed countries, rather than enhancing their own pattern of development.

Whereas the inability to integrate the economic, social and environmental dimensions of development in the UNCED negotiations could be explained by the low ranking given to the environment by different groups of states, the conflicts that have arisen in the ILO, WTO and GATT dialogues show that *the act of integration is itself politically divisive.* This is highly significant, though not unexpected, in view of the long conflict between Capital and Labour over integrating economic activity and social welfare. Developed countries are promoting integration in the context of trade because they will benefit economically from a reduction in low-cost imports from developing countries. Developing countries oppose integration because they regard it as both economically damaging and inequitable. They are also aware that the developed countries, and particularly the USA, are reluctant to integrate the three dimensions of development within other dialogues, including climate change, where it damages their own economic interests.

Disagreements over attempts to add social and environmental conditions to major international institutions also reflect alternative discourses on globalization. In one approach, the process of homogenizing global markets is seen to be gradually eroding national sovereignty, while in the other, sovereignty appears to be threatened more by political imbalances between different groups of states. *Conditionalists* adopt the first discourse. Thus, the governments of developed countries believe that their citizens need protection from weak developing states that cannot introduce and enforce sufficiently strong social and environmental standards. NGOs, on the other hand, believe that externally imposed conditions are essential to protect weak developing states from the voraciousness of hegemonic states and transnational corporations in the global market. Opposing them are *anti-conditionalists*, primarily the governments of developing countries, which believe that they are withstanding the erosion of their economic sovereignty but want to prevent any new 'fronts' from opening up on this global battleground.

This pair of discourses corresponds, in turn, to two alternative discourses of sustainable development. In the *globalist* discourse, development in all countries is measured against the same ideal balance between the three dimensions of development, whatever their level of development, and hence against the same uniform social and environmental standards. The *gradualist* discourse rejects uniformity and allows each country's labour and environmental standards to evolve in step with its economic development, just as it did in developed countries in the past. If sustainable development is represented by the globalist discourse, it could indeed be criticized as 'eco-imperialism' on the part of developed countries and their NGOs.

A common factor in these various conflicts is disagreement on how the global environment should be perceived in development. Sustainable development was originally conceived in the World Conservation Strategy as a way of adding economic and social dimensions to the pure globalist environmental discourse which had clearly failed to match the reality of development as perceived in the developing world. Unfortunately, this globalist approach to the environment has been retained in the sustainable development discourses of developed countries and environmentalist NGOs. In this approach the global environment is regarded as separate from the economic and social dimensions of development, and not integrated with them. This explains the blinkered attitude of the US government in the UNCED negotiations, and the almost evangelical zeal with which NGOs promote the addition of environmental conditions to world trade rules. An international consensus on sustainable development will not be possible until the environment is removed from its isolation and integrated with the other dimensions of development. This will allow the developed countries to appreciate the merits of the gradualist discourse on sustainable development, which is the only one compatible with the developing country discourse.

Lest the gradualist discourse appear too lenient in its attitude towards the environment and social welfare, it should be remembered that sustainable development has only ever been regarded as a compromise between the needs of development and those of the environment. This was true both of the original World Conservation Strategy proposal, which gave the environment greater priority than in the subsequent Brundtland formulation, which placed more stress on continuing economic growth to reduce poverty in developing countries. Ever since the publication of the Brundtland Report, in which the discourses of the developed and developed countries were both recognized but not reconciled, the two groups of countries have maintained their separate discourses on sustainable development. The consequences of this have been apparent throughout this chapter. The gradualist discourse is an advance on the Brundtland Report because it provides a concrete framework for achieving a meaningful compromise between environment and development.

Conclusion

The negotiating positions adopted by different states and groups of states in international negotiations give valuable insights into their discourses on the role of the environment in development, the extent to which they wish to integrate it with the economic and social dimensions of development to promote more sustainable development, and the relative importance they assign to each dimension, which determines their perceived optimum development path at a given time.

The contrast between the discourses of the developed countries, particularly the USA, and the developing countries in negotiations before, during and after UNCED supports the argument of Chapter 1 that the two groups of countries perceive sustainable development in very different ways. The Brundtland Report presented sustainable development as a compromise between the environmentalist priorities of the developed countries and the developmentalist priorities of the developing countries. But it did not show how to reconcile them in practice, and only succeeded in establishing common ground through ambiguity. When the two groups of countries met face to face at UNCED their differences could not be obscured.

At UNCED the USA presented a perfect example of a one-dimensional environmental discourse that was globalist in perspective and isolated from the economic and social dimensions of development. In other words, saving the planet is wonderful as long as it does not limit further economic and social advancement. The developing country discourse was differentiated, rather than globalist, placing greatest emphasis on the right to develop and the need to preserve sovereignty over domestic resources. Like the US discourse, it also ranked the environment lowest of the three dimensions but for different reasons. The developing countries also argued that it was important for developed countries to recognize that global climate change is a direct result of the historic environmental costs which they have accumulated during their unsustainable development paths, and which it is now their duty to pay. Neither approach gave much hope that either group of countries yet has the will consciously to integrate the three dimensions of development, or is even aware of the need for this. Discourses are usually slow to change, and a similar stand-off between the US discourse and the developing country discourse occurred at the World Summit on Sustainable Development, ten years after UNCED.

This chapter began by claiming that sustainable development is a creation of international relations. The subsequent discussion has demonstrated that international relations are, ultimately, about the exercise of power and its moderation by diplomacy. The exercise of power by the world's leading states over the developing countries, in particular, portrayed vividly by political economy theories, was certainly evident in the hegemonic approach taken by the USA to the climate change negotiations. The disparity between its discourse and the typical developing country discourse was all too evident, even though the two did not come into direct confrontation. When they did confront one another in negotiations on the Convention on Biological Diversity and the abortive Forest Convention, it was startling to see the developing country discourse emerge predominant. Rather more predictable, however, has been the lack of progress in these two areas since UNCED.

It was all too easy in the UNCED negotiations for the developed countries to adopt a purely environmental discourse and for the developing countries to advance a developmentalist one. It was more difficult to maintain this polarity when discussing proposals to incorporate uniform environmental and social standards into the rules of the WTO and ILO, respectively, since the proposals actually promote integration. However, such moves have been resisted by developing countries, reflecting concerns about erosion of sovereignty and the loss of competitiveness that would result from being forced to pay the full social and environmental costs of production. Developing countries also view this form of integration as a ruse by their developed counterparts to extend globalization into the environmental and social arenas, so as to exploit them further and limit their development.

Any economic policy debate today must pay careful attention to how a particular issue will affect the pace of globalization. Developing countries certainly have good grounds for concern about proposals to impose uniform social and economic conditions on international trade. But this globalist discourse is not the only possible route to integration. The alternative gradualist discourse would allow every country to develop at its own pace, with its labour and environmental standards evolving in parallel with its economic development. This is more politically feasible, and just as compatible with the principles of sustainable development. It could also help to resolve the current deadlock between developed and developing countries over what constitutes sustainable development.

If developed and developing countries wish to achieve a common approach they will each have to make concessions to the other's discourse. Developing countries will have to recognize that they may not be able to develop as rapidly as ideally they would like, while developed countries will have to relinquish their globalist environmental position, adopt a more realistic view about the ability of developing countries to moderate their environmental impacts, and take a more integrated approach to their own development. This will involve acknowledging the environmental costs which they have accumulated over the last few hundred years. Whether either group of countries will follow this advice is difficult to predict. But what should be clear from the discussion in this chapter is that each of the two sets of discourses contains the pieces of the jigsaw needed to assemble a picture that will be mutually recognizable by both groups of countries. Watching the complete picture being gradually assembled over the coming decades should be a fascinating occupation for students of international relations, although it will be an agonizing experience for those who want sustainable development to be achieved sooner rather than later.

13

Future Perspectives: Developing Sustainable Development

Martin Purvis and Alan Grainger

Introduction

Sustainable development is a multifaceted phenomenon of global proportions. Too often, however, it appears amorphous, confusing and inconsistent. One of the aims of this book has been to analyse it from a variety of geographical perspectives in order to reveal its many facets, while at the same time showing how they form part of a coherent whole. Many other studies have emphasized particular aspects of sustainable development; we have tried to bring together these various dimensions to show the 'big picture'. Sustainable development thus gives us new reasons to value geography's role in studying human and natural systems as an interconnected whole. At the same time, it presents new challenges to geographers to extend and communicate their understanding of the complex and evolving web of interconnections which underpin human society and its relationships with the planet that sustains it.

In this closing chapter we consider the answers that have emerged in the course of our book to the key questions about sustainable development which were posed at the outset. We begin with a critical review of some of the most commonly accepted strategies for securing more sustainable development. A recognition of their limitations leads us to consider the reality of contest that will characterize any significant moves towards greater sustainability. A reading of sustainable development that is, in consequence, more politicized requires that we consider a broader agenda of societal change. Defining the course of such change is, however, beyond the scope of the present volume. We end, therefore, with some more pragmatic thoughts about the potential for advancing understanding of sustainable development, both in theory and, more particularly, in practice.

Reflecting upon Existing Strategies

The concept of sustainable development is largely the creation of an international elite of politicians, academics, planners and environmentalists. It has found wider favour, in part, because of the leeway that initial formulations gave for particular interests to interpret sustainable development in ways suited their own established agendas. As a result, considerable effort has been invested in the design and implementation of a wide range of strategies and individual projects, all of which are claimed to promote more sustainable development. Yet such moves have not been matched by equal progress in the creation of an overarching conceptual framework. This is due in no small measure to the failure to resolve the conflict – discussed by Grainger in Chapters 1 and 12 – between the two leading political discourses on the sustainable development ideal: one regarding it as primarily environmental in focus, and the other prioritizing its developmental aspect. It follows that most sustainable development strategies are limited in scope, reflecting the biases of one or the other of these political discourses. Moves to foster more sustainable development are thus best characterized as a form of pragmatic experimentation. Yet this process has been at least as important as theoretical study in defining how sustainable development is generally understood. It is logical, therefore, to begin by considering the potential of the main strategies so far adopted. If judged on their own terms, many practical initiatives can claim a degree of success and in this sense the current book contains numerous examples which show that progress towards a greater degree of sustainability is possible. Any such optimism should, however, be tempered by the reflection that truly sustainable development requires simultaneous attention to economy, society and environment. Many existing strategies address only one or two of these dimensions of development and often tackle the symptoms of unsustainability, rather than its underlying causes.

We will first briefly review the claims made for sustainability strategies before proceeding to a more detailed, and critical, reflection on their merits and potential.

Technical and managerial 'solutions'

From some quarters we are told that a combination of regulatory incentives, limited market reforms and technological innovation holds the key to sustainable development. The technocentric riposte to the environmental doomsayers has been a powerful presence ever since debate on the future of the global environment began in earnest during the 1960s. Today – as Purvis shows in Chapter 7 – governments and businesses continue to stress technical innovation and win–win solutions to environmental problems. Increasingly, the emphasis in environmental legislation is less on punishing defaulting businesses, or on prescribing particular solutions to environmental problems, and more on encouraging progressive companies to seek innovative ways of improving their performance. The demands of environmentally conscious Green consumers and change in market pricing structures to incorporate more of the environmental and social costs of production are also identified as important drivers for change. In response, it is argued, companies' efforts to champion new products, technologies and management systems will increasingly be directed towards the twin goals of protecting environmental quality and fostering new efficiencies in natural resource use. Individual case studies confirm the potential of practical measures to reduce pollution and waste, to curb the use of unnecessary inputs and to promote the reuse and recycling of materials. More important still is the evidence that such moves can yield economic as well as environmental gains. Environmental good practice may therefore be consistent with business self-interest if the new efficiencies lead to reduced costs, increased profit margins or more sustainable livelihoods for smaller producers, both industrial and agricultural (see Chapters 7 and 8). If consumers, in turn, are provided with cheaper and better-quality products, they may reinforce the commercial logic of change by rewarding the most progressive companies with an increasing market share. Arguably, technocentric innovations do not only represent a means of reforming existing industrial economies. The transfer of Green technologies, enabling, for example, the efficient production of clean and renewable energy, is widely seen as a mechanism for promoting more sustainable economic development throughout the global South.

Indigenous knowledge systems and participation

Enthusiasm for a technical and managerial approach to sustainable development is not, however, universal. An alternative argument is that greater stress should be placed on harnessing and enhancing traditional technologies and knowledge systems, particularly – but not only – as a means of securing more appropriate, and thus more sustainable, forms of development in the global South. Traditional knowledge systems are increasingly valued as a guide to restoring balance between human and environmental systems, countering the alienation of humanity from nature that is one of the most damaging consequences of modern urbanization and industrialization. Most traditional knowledge is also rooted in the circumstances of particular places. Arguably, therefore, the promotion of dialogue between professional development planners and lay knowledge-holders is more likely to produce programmes and methods that are more appropriate because they are attuned to local environmental conditions, they respect the cultural values of particular communities and they help to meet the fundamental needs which people define for themselves. The success of specific projects does, indeed, seem to suggest that indigenous knowledge and values can play a positive role in creating more sustainable livelihoods for both urban and rural communities (see Chapters 6 and 10).

The emphasis placed on local expertise as a resource is also consistent with a more generally expressed interest in encouraging active public participation in creating and executing strategies to promote sustainable development. Indeed, participation has become a central plank of the political process approach to sustainable development and is frequently identified as a means of securing the goals of Agenda 21 at a local level. Broadly based participation, it is argued, helps to define development objectives that meet the needs of the community as a whole, facilitates greater openness in decision-making – perhaps compensating for deficiencies in existing structures of local governance – and encourages greater shared commitment to the achievement of project goals. Moreover, the collective will may generate the resources necessary for project execution, overcoming the constraints imposed by the limitations of external support, both material and organizational. As Unsworth shows (see Chapter 6) in an urban context, the combined investment of individually limited funds, material inputs, labour and skills deriving from within a community itself can help to create the resource base necessary to secure significant improvements in economic security and quality of life. Such schemes yield equally important – if less tangible – dividends when they foster a new sense of social cohesion and self-worth within marginalized communities. Experience also shows that successful participation in an initial project may create the mutual confidence, and perhaps the more formal institutional structures, that will enable communities to tackle other, more ambitious, goals.

Rescaling activity

Enthusiasm for more appropriate development and participatory approaches has helped to foster a greater emphasis on local initiative and decision-making. For some commentators, however, the rescaling of human activity assumes a central importance as a means of securing more sustainable development. The idea that individual communities should play an active part in defining the course of their own progress towards sustainability echoes a geographical interest in the celebration and perpetuation of difference between places. Certainly, the case for alternative thinking about development is strengthened if it can be presented as an antidote to the rigidity and insensitivity of the top-down planning that was widely attempted during the third quarter of the 20th century. The latter has rightly been criticized for, all too often, applying standard formulae in an effort to promote development, irrespective of local circumstances, values and needs. Moreover, a revitalized sense of place could foster a greater sense of social well-being, countering some of the insecurities that many associate with globalization. The protection of a positive sense of difference between places and cultures – a 'geo-diversity' – might legitimately be identified as a facet of sustainable development alongside biodiversity.

Frequently, however, the emphasis in local planning for more sustainable development is upon securing a greater degree of economic growth and self-sufficiency. In some ways, such initiatives are unremarkable in their aspirations to create new jobs and livelihoods. But many are also marked by a belief that this can best be achieved by drawing primarily upon a community's own assets. This has the potential to harness resources – not least human labour and skills – that would otherwise remain underutilized. Hence, many such projects represent a conscious attempt to overcome the social marginalization and alienation that afflict communities where long-term levels of unemployment or underemployment are high. As Atkinson (see Chapter 10) notes in the context of Arctic Canada, efforts to create a stronger and more independent economic base may also be driven by a desire to secure a degree of protection for particular localities against economic collapse triggered by the volatility of external markets.

In some instances, however, arguments for greater local economic integration also have a distinctive environmental dimension. In part, this reflects the hope that a greater reliance on local environmental resources will encourage their more sustainable management in the long-term interests of the community as a whole. Production may therefore come to focus more on meeting the needs of consumers, rather than encouraging new demand for an ever-increasing list of desires. In some individual instances, change in the focus of production is already a reality to the potential benefit of both producers and consumers. In the UK, for example, there are signs of a modest growth in the sourcing of foodstuffs from known local suppliers, encouraged by consumers' concerns about food safety and quality and the environmental impacts of modern agriculture, and by farmers' attempts to protect increasingly precarious livelihoods (see Chapter 8). If such initiatives prompt a wider questioning of the logic of long-distance trade, there may be further potential to curb the growth of pollution and energy use caused by the current spiralling demand for freight transport.

However, a new emphasis on the local in both economic organization and political decision-making is not the only possible driver for change in the geographical scale of human activity. A case can also be made that some of the responsibilities and powers that have traditionally been the prerogative of the state should be pooled, or transferred, to larger organizations constituted at an international level. In part, this represents a call for greater attention to social and environmental concerns by existing economic agencies, such as the World Trade Organization (WTO). But there is also a growing realization that local, and indeed national, efforts to plan for more sustainable development may be nullified by damage to Critical Natural Capital, which forms the Earth's life-support system. While greater self-sufficiency may promise a degree of protection from external economic shocks, the same argument does not hold for environmental change, the effects of which cannot be confined within particular territorial boundaries. Recent decades have seen mounting scientific evidence of the scale of damage inflicted upon the global environment by human activity, prompting, in turn, the recognition that demands for remedial management exceed the capacity of individual states acting alone. One important consequence has been the addition of environmental concerns to the established agenda of international diplomacy, evident in measures designed to curb damage to the stratospheric ozone layer and to regulate trade in particular sectors, including hazardous waste and endangered species. Although the authority of these initial regulatory structures remains open to challenge and subversion, they arguably represent a tangible step towards the greater international cooperation that will be a necessary precondition for any significant progress towards sustainable development.

A Necessary Critique

It is important, however, to be cautious when judging the apparent success of both strategies and individual projects. Frequent reliance on local initiatives raises doubts as to whether they can ever be sufficiently numerous to produce a general improvement in both environmental conditions and the socio-economic circumstances of the world's poorest people. Nor can more general signs of positive change be taken to imply that the achievement of perfectly sustainable development is imminent, or even practically possible. Specific gains in social welfare and curbs on the pace of environmental degradation will be offset by negative changes as substantial investments continue to be made in unsustainable development. Considerable emphasis is still placed by politicians, business leaders and most ordinary people on achieving the traditional goal of economic growth: whether to conquer poverty or to meet the continually rising material expectations of a more affluent minority. By comparison, regard for the associated environmental and social consequences remains limited. Crucially, too, individuals, communities and countries strive to enrich themselves with little thought for how this may impact upon other places and future generations.

Moreover, the claims made for the success of specific initiatives by governments, businesses and non-governmental organizations (NGOs) should be viewed with a degree of scepticism. Too often, it seems, the enthusiasm of such sponsors for particular measures which they assert will promote more sustainable development reflects a concern to defend their own self-interests, rather than a genuine desire to secure the general good. For example, technocentric options are particularly favoured by businesses, which see in this approach both a means to deflect any threat to existing economic interests, and an opportunity to establish their own legitimacy as a source of solutions to environmental problems. However, if we expose not just the technocentric case, but the entire range of strategies outlined above, to more critical scrutiny it becomes obvious that in every instance there are valid questions about their capacity to promote truly sustainable development.

Limits to technocentrism

In some respects, doubts about the viability of technocentric strategies are essentially practical. As others have noted before, it may only be in a minority of contexts that it is sensible to think in terms of the classic win–win formula, involving commercially rewarding investment in promoting resource efficiency and curbs on environmental damage. But much larger concerns have also been raised about the inherent bias of technocentric approaches. Often the emphasis in technological and managerial innovation is on making present patterns of economic development less environmentally damaging. Paradoxically, this may serve to weaken existing constraints on overconsumption by the most affluent of the world's inhabitants. Without equivalent attention to a more socially equitable redistribution of the rewards of economic activity, technocentric strategies risk perpetuating fundamental and damaging inequalities between rich and poor at every level from the local to the global. The international transfer of environmentally efficient technologies may, of course, provide a basis for more sustainable development to combat Southern poverty. In practice, however, the efforts of many Northern companies and governments to create global markets that will be dominated by their own Green products threaten developing countries with a new phase of economic and technological dependency.

Many critics also find it difficult to accept that business, which has frequently been identified as a major cause of environmental problems, could now take a leading role in developing effective remedial measures. Indeed, perceptions of the technocentric option are coloured by a growing sense that modern industrial systems are inherently risky. Moreover, the apparent threat that they present to the environment and human health arises not only from the incidence of accidents and malfunctions, but also as an outcome of routine operations. Such concerns do not simply focus on particularly controversial technologies, such as nuclear power, but extend to a wide range of industrial plant and products, from chemical pesticides to mobile phones. During the last decade, fundamental questions about the future development of plant and animal life have also been raised by the advent of biotechnology. Identified by its supporters as a crucial weapon in the global battle against hunger and disease, biotechnology also raises fears of damaging change that could further destabilize the already precarious relationship between society and nature (see Chapter 8).

Limitations of indigenous knowledge

Concerns about the destructive potential of technology help to explain the revival of interest in alternative and more traditional knowledge systems. We might, however, question whether established ways of thinking, rooted in the experience of a past in which human numbers were relatively small, can meet the demands of a rapidly growing global population. Projects that use indigenous resources – both intellectual and material – to secure basic needs may not fully match the progressive intent of sustainable development. This reflects concerns that a focus on the achievement of sustainable livelihoods may, ultimately, act as a constraint upon larger ambitions for social change and the extension of educational opportunities and political rights. Traditional societies do not always place a premium on social equity, or on equality of access to resources and opportunities. There are, thus, potential tensions, not least over issues such as the rights and status of women, between some established value systems and the thinking embodied in international declarations on sustainable development.

Limitations of participation and local initiatives

Concerns about the reality of progress towards social engagement and social equity also apply more generally to participatory projects. It can be difficult to secure full and open participation in sustainability initiatives. Official and academic enthusiasm may not be sufficient to overcome practical constraints upon participation. Broadly based popular commitment is unlikely if sections of a local population do not feel some pre-existing sense of community; if they lack belief in the potential of participation; or if they feel deterred from involvement as a result of social norms and expectations of deference towards established elites. As a result, it is all too easy for supposedly community-wide initiatives to become dominated by specific groups, who sometimes attempt to steer projects in a direction that chiefly serves their own self-interest. Some of these concerns are echoed by Waley and Purvis (see Chapter 9) in their study of Japanese river management, where the rhetoric of participation has done little to reduce conflict between sectional interests, or the prominent role played in promoting sustainability initiatives by planning professionals and academics. There is, thus, a risk that participation provides an illusion of political change and local democracy, while in reality perpetuating existing inequalities in the distribution of political and economic power.

The local focus of most participatory projects also raises questions about the validity of prioritizing initiative at this lowest level of the spatial hierarchy. Positive arguments about participatory and appropriate development cannot wholly disguise the reality that enthusiasm for localized projects also reflects concern that political and economic actors operating at national and international levels have not given effective and consistent leadership to the search for more sustainable development. The 2002 Johannesburg Summit drew renewed attention to disagreements between developed and developing countries over the meaning of sustainable development, which have repeatedly frustrated efforts to translate the fine ideals contained in Agenda 21 and other international statements of intent into effective action (see Chapter 12). Even at a national level, most governments have shown themselves unwilling or unable to commit significant resources to promoting more sustainable development. A growing emphasis on local initiative has, therefore, arisen partly by default. It reflects the hope that communities themselves will be able to circumvent any larger failure by advancing change from the bottom up.

Yet individual local initiatives ultimately achieve little unless they are ubiquitous and complementary. Both these requirements are problematic. As Soussan (see

Chapter 4) and Waley and Purvis (see Chapter 9) note, pilot projects intended as models of more sustainable development are often so demanding of resources, whether material or human, that they are not easily replicated. At the same time, a more spontaneous flowering of initiative is difficult to envisage, given the current inadequacies of local governance in many communities, particularly – but not only – in the developing world. Still more questionable, in practice, is the implication that if each locality is free to define a development path intended to meet its own needs in a sustainable way, these individual priorities will collectively deliver sustainable development at a higher level. Thinking and acting locally – as we are so often urged to do – will not of itself necessarily deliver a global solution.

Individual local projects may deliver tangible benefits, but as Grainger (see Chapter 3) points out, there are inherent difficulties in pursuing the ideal of sustainable development at the lowest levels of the social and spatial hierarchy. Existing inequalities in the geographical distribution of Natural, Human and Man-Made Capital mean that any attempt to secure a balance between economic, social and environmental interests solely within the boundaries of an individual locality is likely to fail. Thinking in this way is also at odds with the reality of the world as an interconnected system, within which individual places and territories are bound together by ties that are simultaneously economic, social, political, cultural and environmental. Decisions and outcomes at any specific location will necessarily be affected by, and impact upon, other people and places. Even well-designed and well-executed participatory projects, which appear perfectly attuned to the needs of their home communities, may generate outcomes – in terms such as the export of pollution or the import of non-renewable natural capital – that are incompatible with sustainable development elsewhere. Invariably, any such unequal allocation of costs and benefits is not random, but a reflection of established inequalities in the distribution of economic and political power within national and global systems. Again, this suggests that participatory and grassroots initiatives may offer the illusion of equity and democracy, while doing little to challenge the fundamental realities of unsustainable development.

This larger perspective raises further questions about the limitations of the resources – material, financial, institutional and political – that most individual localities are able to command in support of moves towards greater sustainability. Hence, Soussan (see Chapter 4) argues that bottom-up initiative is often inadequate to secure the wider systemic changes that are the necessary precursors to any significant and lasting improvement in the conditions of specific communities. Instead, his case studies suggest that local action is most effective when it is supported by institutional and political reforms at a national level, which place new powers and resources in local hands. It follows that an emphasis on participation and local initiative without any such wider support may represent a deliberate ploy to block change, or to deflect attention away from the moral responsibility of powerful political and economic actors to address poverty, social injustice and environmental abuse.

Consensus and Contest

Any balanced assessment of current sustainability strategies must conclude that while progress is possible in specific contexts, it would be foolish to assert that any single approach holds the key to sustainable development. Indeed, we should not delude ourselves that human ingenuity can necessarily deliver a cure for every ill. The limitations of existing scientific understanding mean that many environmental problems continue to defy practical or cost-effective solution. Equally, the history of established systems of socio-economic planning is hardly one of unblemished success. Despite a significant investment of resources in efforts to reduce social and geographical differentials in levels of wealth, well-being and access to opportunities, the world is still scarred by profound inequalities. There are also plenty of precedents to show that efforts to counter specific social, economic and environmental ills may themselves create new problems.

The success claimed for individual sustainability strategies is often partial and too many initiatives give only the illusion of significant progress. Widespread discussion of sustainable development has not markedly changed the priorities of most individuals, businesses, communities and governments. Collectively, we may pay more attention than in the recent past to social and environmental goals. Yet they are still often seen as secondary to our continuing preoccupation with short-term economic growth, rather than as integral elements of efforts to secure future material prosperity and social and political stability. At the same time, appeals to the precautionary principle have done little to check humanity's manipulation of the environment, or to slow the growth of genetic engineering, which has become a new source of uncertainties and insecurities.

The superficiality of change in societal priorities is echoed in the tendency of many practical strategies to treat the symptoms of unsustainability, rather than address its root causes. Thus, we attempt to apply individual, essentially uncoordinated and often geographically localized initiatives to resolve problems which, in many instances, derive from the workings of the capitalist world economy, the political exclusion of many of the world's poorest peoples and the condition of the global environment. Limited measures may succeed in marginally reducing the disadvantage of the poor, or in marginally curbing environmental degradation. Too often, however, they also deflect attention away from more searching questions about the deeper causes of social and environmental exploitation, and the links between them. The ways in which many current sustainability strategies are framed suggests not simply a mismatch in scale between the task and the tools, but also a failure to confront the contest that must accompany any significant progress towards sustainable development.

In their different ways, both technical and participatory strategies promote the illusion that positive change is not only possible, but also relatively painless to secure. This is the message of win–win arguments directed at business: that environmental responsibility is consistent with established concerns for minimizing waste and costs, and increasing sales and profitability. Equally, the very basis of the participatory approach is shared gain. To secure broadly based participation within a community there must be a general expectation that everyone will benefit in some way from patient dialogue and an eventual agreement to a compromise solution. Hence, the emphasis on participation seems to imply that there is no need to take difficult decisions, or for anyone to lose anything in trying to achieve more sustainable development.

In practice, however, the relationship between pain and gain is invariably more complicated. For some, ethical arguments provide sufficient justification for attempts to combat social injustice and environmental degradation. But more self-interested reasoning also underpins claims that change in current practice is absolutely vital to prevent social dislocation and environmental damage that will obstruct future economic development. Viewed in this way, the overall gains expected will outweigh almost any associated pain, even if sustainable development ultimately demands radical measures to secure economic restructuring, the redistribution of political power and change in the basis of decision-making about resource allocation. However, it appears that in judging the outcome of strategies for sustainable development, most individuals and groups will continue to place their own short-term interests above any notion of the long-term common good. Hence, for a significant and influential minority, who are the chief beneficiaries of the present maldistribution of wealth, access to resources and political power, the consequences of any change appear predominantly negative. Established elites are unlikely to welcome any reduction – whether absolute or relative – in their fortune and status. Moreover, as elites they are also richly endowed with the means to resist such change. If we do not confront this reality, efforts to secure more sustainable development are doomed to perpetual frustration and failure.

The Challenge of Sustainable Development

So far we have evaluated existing strategies largely in their own terms. In doing so, however, we have highlighted practical limitations that reflect the partial understanding of the ideal of sustainable development evident in the thinking of many of their sponsors. We now turn to some reflections on the ways in which the arguments of previous chapters can help us to formulate a more realistic conception of the challenge of sustainable development. This is a vital step towards defining more sophisticated and successful strategies for promoting sustainability in practice.

Space and spatial scale

As might be expected in a collection of essays by geographers, assertions of the importance of place, space and spatial scale to a more effective understanding of sustainable development have emerged as a recurring theme in this book. An emphasis on place-based initiative – often with the aspiration to secure development that meets the needs of a particular locality – is already established orthodoxy in planning for development. But rather less attention has been paid in the existing literature to the other members of our geographical trio. It is important, therefore, that we revisit some key points about space and spatiality developed in this volume.

As several of our authors note, the potential of action to promote more sustainable development will be reduced if it is not constructed at an appropriate spatial level.

We must therefore add to the pursuit of balance between economic, social and environmental dimensions of development a search for another ideal of balance: between action at a level that is small enough to be sensitive to the needs, circumstances and aspirations of particular populations, yet large enough to command the necessary material, intellectual and institutional resources to secure effective change. One way of advancing this search for the most effective framework of action is – as noted by Soussan (see Chapter 4) – to think in terms of subsidiarity. This preserves, but tempers, the stress on the local arena discussed above. A policy of subsidiarity promotes devolution of resources and responsibility within any political and territorial hierarchy, but with the crucial caveat that any transfer of authority is to the lowest levels at which effective action can be taken. This is the philosophy that, at least in part, informs the political reorganization of Arctic regions discussed by Atkinson (see Chapter 10). Subsidiarity recognizes both the value of local autonomy and the reality that many aspects of contemporary life – including environmental problems, trade and capital flows, and aspirations for equitable resource allocation – require coordinated action and regulation at a national and, increasingly, an international level.

Effective planning for sustainable development requires more, however, than the appropriate hierarchical division of responsibilities. Greater account must also be taken of the interaction between places and levels, and the ways in which initiatives can be complemented or confounded by action – or inaction – elsewhere. As Grainger (see Chapter 3) highlights, trade in goods and resources also involves the transfer of sustainability between territories. This recognition reinforces existing concerns that the terms of trade are often weighted against the least powerful players. It has long been evident that exports of primary produce, and even manufactures, frequently result in only limited financial rewards for developing countries. But more than this, their attempts to define a course towards greater sustainability may be undermined by externally generated social and environmental costs, often deriving ultimately from the demands of consumers in the developed North. Arguably, therefore, trade reform and compensation for the inequitable transfer of such costs have key roles to play in fostering more sustainable development.

The importance of coordination between initiatives at different scales is a theme further developed by Mitchell and Unsworth (see Chapters 5 and 6) in relation to urban sustainability. The metabolic structure of urban centres renders the ideal of the sustainable city as an isolated entity both unattainable and illogical. The very concentration of population and human activity means that urban centres cannot survive without the consumption of imported resources and the export of waste and pollution. It follows, however, that positive changes in the form and function of urban areas may simultaneously improve the quality of life for local residents and make a significant contribution to the attainment of greater sustainability at higher levels, up to and including the global. Measures to reduce urban transport demand, for example, not only promise immediate improvements in air quality, health and safety, but also help to address the international challenge of climate change (see Chapter 11). However, policy at the urban level can only fulfil this larger potential if it is consciously located within a broader framework. Urban managers, decision-makers and residents must be made aware of the wider significance of their activities. Ideally, this will lead to a more integrated approach to sustainable development involving active cooperation between responsible agencies at different hierarchical levels. This should ensure that individual towns and cities have the resources they need for effective and sustainable urban management, and that their efforts contribute to, and are reinforced by, initiatives at a national and international level.

Restating the ideals of sustainable development

This volume also aims to provoke a re-examination of presuppositions about sustainable development as an ideal. There is an evident danger that through the constant repetition of only a few key phrases from the Brundtland Report, sustainable development comes to be understood largely in terms of the obligation which each generation has to preserve the inheritance of its successors. But such thinking, essentially an environmental discourse upon sustainability, does little to address the current inequalities that are so often evident in geographical comparisons of livelihood systems, life chances and environmental conditions. Greater effort and political will must also, therefore, be applied to the other major goal identified by the Brundtland Report: increasing intra-generational equity, marked by real improvements in the circumstances of poor and marginalized communities in today's world.

There is, in fact, a powerful argument that immediate attention to intra-generational equity is vital if sustainability is to be secured for the long term. Many of the most significant contemporary challenges to social stability and the health of the environment are, ultimately, a product of inequality. Deeply entrenched differentials in the distribution of economic and political power allow a minority to claim a disproportionate share of the world's resources. This not only condemns the majority to continuing poverty; it is also a recipe for the profligate use of human and natural capital. Secure in the belief that their ability to appropriate resources is virtually limitless, the rich feel few constraints upon their consumption. At the same time, the poor may be forced into the destructive over-exploitation of vital social and environmental resources simply to secure short-term survival.

Thinking in this way helps to reinforce the message that sustainable development has a third, social, dimension. This is not, however, simply to endorse existing developmentalist discourses. Many of those who promote them evidently continue to prioritize economic growth over social equity. The historical experience often dubbed development has, in fact, perpetuated inequality and injustice. What is needed, therefore, is not more of the same, but the reassertion of the progressive *ideal* of development: that economic growth brings greatest benefits when its rewards are distributed equitably, leading to a general increase in social welfare.

The need to recognize opposing interests

Exploration of the relationship between existing conceptions of development and the new agenda of sustainable development is also important if we are to understand why, far from being the consensual process often presented, progress towards greater sustainability is so evidently halting and contested. Arguments for a new accommodation between economic growth, social welfare and environmental protection of themselves do little to ease the tensions that have long existed between these dimensions of development. The nature and potency of such tensions become clearer if we adopt more conventional terminology, particularly with regard to the economic and social dimensions of sustainability, which may be equated with established conceptions of Capital and Labour.

Relations between Capital and Labour are complex; for while they are bound together by mutual dependency, they are also locked in perpetual struggle over the allocation of the economic rewards that they generate together. Each side habitually aims to maintain or increase its share of these rewards in the knowledge that gain for one means a denial of existing or additional benefits to the other. Apparent concessions by Capital to Labour – evident in rising levels of income and social welfare in most developed countries over the past two centuries – have done little to temper this essentially antagonistic relationship. Indeed, it is striking how few concessions Capital has ultimately made to Labour. Modest improvements in wages and living standards may, apparently, have been the result of coordinated protest and political organization on the part of the work force; but most of the additional rewards granted to Labour also serve the interests of Capital. Rising incomes help to establish workers as consumers, thus creating the expansion in demand that is essential to maintain the profitable growth of industrial mass production. Equally, the diversion of a fraction of the rewards of economic growth to investment in social welfare provision benefits not simply – or even chiefly – the direct recipients of welfare, but also the capitalist interest. As a result of this modest investment, capital is guaranteed continuing social stability and a work force that is more productive because it consists of healthier and better educated individuals.

There is nothing here that speaks of any real commitment to social justice. If Capital continues to believe that its best interests will be secured by limited, and often tokenistic, concessions to Labour, there is little hope that the moral argument of sustainable development can effect significant change. Moreover, in much of the world, Capital and its political allies continue to resist any form of significant organization by Labour that might lead to enforced change in the distribution of income and property rights. In an era of globalization, the existence of particular state territories in which the interests of Capital remain so dominant is also effective in disciplining Labour elsewhere. The prospect of transferring jobs and investment away from existing sites in the global North to low-wage, low-regulation economies in the developing world can be a powerful means of protecting Capital from labour protest and state regulation.

If Capital makes only limited and, ultimately, self-interested concessions to Labour, there is little reason to suppose that its attitude to the environment and, by extension, to future generations will be greatly different. Moreover, the environment and future generations both lack Labour's obvious capacity to represent itself and to fight to secure its own interests. Business can be expected to promote environmentally sound initiatives that are likely to repay immediate dividends, or which seem necessary to secure the short-term survival of established economic systems. But this can never be a sufficient foundation for the creation of truly sustainable development. Capital is unlikely to be convinced by arguments that nature itself has any moral claim to retain its own resources. Indeed, the pursuit of profit is currently leading powerful business interests to claim ownership over natural species and even individual genes, in a way that denies both the integrity of nature and the habitual rights and livelihoods of the human communities who live alongside them. Nor are notions of obligation to future generations likely to prompt a significant change in the stance of Capital. Many, doubtless, still hold to Keynes's (1923) maxim about the importance of the short term because 'in the long run we are all dead'. Others will argue, often with genuine conviction, that the future can take care of itself because it will have access to knowledge and technologies as yet unknown that will fully address current concerns about sustainability. The indifference, even outright hostility, of Capital to any significant reallocation of claims upon natural resources, and to substantial investment in promoting the health of the environment, will thus remain a major obstacle to political or popular initiatives which aim to promote more sustainable development.

The problematic definition of equity

It is also clear that the key ideals of sustainable development can themselves become disputed in ways that obstruct any real progress. This applies particularly to the central notion of equity. The goal of greater equity poses both practical and definitional problems. In part, these difficulties reflect the different dimensions upon which equity must be constructed in order to secure greater sustainability. Many accounts of sustainable development pay particular attention to equity over time; throughout this volume, we have also stressed the equally powerful argument for equity across space. Any claims to have created truly sustainable development cannot be substantiated if an apparent balance between the accumulation and degradation of Natural, Human and Man-Made Capital within a particular territory is achieved only by exporting costs without compensation to other territories. It is, of course, possible to argue that localized inequality can be justified for the sake of the greater good. The original aim of sustainable development was, after all, to achieve development while safeguarding the integrity of the *global* environment. But there are powerful arguments that it would be inequitable to attempt this by requiring states in the global South to surrender some of their potential development so that large areas of natural ecosystems can be conserved. Equivalent concerns can be identified at every spatial level. At a national level, for example, it is questionable whether it would be right for a country to rely on increased nuclear capacity in order to meet its targets for cuts in greenhouse gas emissions if this imposed particular social and environmental costs on the communities in which the new power stations were located. The classic divide in discussions of sustainable development between utilitarian thinking – that some may suffer for the greater good – and egalitarian thinking – that all must suffer and benefit alike – is clearly evident in spatial, as well as temporal, equity problems.

Moreover, the conception of equity is itself politicized. Definitions of equity are not absolute; rather, they are a product of the specific circumstances prevailing at particular times and in particular places. In practice, the interpretation of what is fair in the allocation of resources, rewards, rights and responsibilities is often disputed both within and between societies. Those interpretations that prevail frequently represent the values and self-interest of the strongest parties in any contest. Thus, the equity that applies at the global level at any particular time is merely the dominant discourse of the states – and other key actors, such as multinational businesses – that currently wield the greatest economic and political power. Equally, definitions of equity at smaller spatial scales will reflect the interplay between these extensive influences and the dominant discourse advanced by more localized elites.

As Purvis notes in Chapter 11, the parties to the Framework Convention on Climate Change (FCCC) have all declared themselves committed to achieving an equitable solution to the challenge of reducing atmospheric levels of greenhouse gases. In practice, however, their conceptions of what constitutes equity differ widely. For most developing countries, equity demands that the lead is taken by the global North in recognition of its historical responsibility for changes in the chemistry of the atmosphere. Yet many US commentators are equally emphatic that it would be inequitable to hold current generations responsible for past actions over which they could have had no control. In the face of this difference of interpretation, moral arguments lose their power and are frequently submerged amidst the pursuit of self-interest.

Sustainable Development and Societal Change

In the opening sections of this chapter we explored the potential of current sustainable development strategies, while making the implicit assumption that existing societal structures would remain unchanged. But the subsequent argument has led us to a more politicized reading of the search for balance between the exploitation and conservation of capital that lies at the heart of sustainable development. Established theoretical accounts of sustainable development often present economy, society and environment in a neutral fashion as the dimensions of development. Here we have argued that each should also be regarded as being related to, and represented by, an active interest group. Economy and society are thus linked to the well-established forces of Capital and Labour, respectively, and the 20th century saw the beginnings of important, if still limited, moves to politicize the cause of the environment. We have argued further that both the existing distribution of power between these interest groups and the often antagonistic nature of their relationships currently creates a formidable obstacle to more than tokenistic measures to promote sustainable development. Logically, therefore, genuine progress towards more environmentally sustainable and socially equitable development requires the redistribution of power between Capital, Labour and Environment, and the re-examination of the relationships that bind them together. It follows that sustainable development cannot be achieved without significant societal change.

Evolutionary or revolutionary change?

This recognition of the importance of societal change, in turn, raises further questions. How are we to conceive of societal change in this context? One approach is to regard change as evolutionary. There are, perhaps, parallels to be drawn with previous changes in the constitution of society, not least the creation of capitalism on a foundation of feudalism. Such an example indicates the potential for profound change in conceptions of the purpose of economic activity, in the distribution of power within society and in humanity's relations with the natural world. But it also has much to tell us about the experience of transformation. With hindsight, we see the coming of capitalism as a decisive turning point in human history; in practice, however, it was not a consciously planned and managed process. Change was gradual, uneven and erratic. This being so, we might expect that further progress will be achieved in a similar fashion.

This evolutionary perspective receives support from the Social Learning Model of policy formulation, which suggests that societal structures evolve over time through a process of internal conflict. Every society is composed of a wide range of interest groups, which form and reform coalitions in response to changing circumstances. Continual competition between the coalitions leads to an almost Darwinian struggle for dominance and the power to establish the structures within which the policies that determine social mechanisms are formulated (Sabatier and Jenkins-Smith, 1993). Thinking in this way offers the prospect of societal change. However, it is also realistic about the rate at which it can occur, given the likely resistance to significant shifts in the balance of power between the various interest groups.

It is, indeed, possible to identify positive change in the contemporary world, which suggests that evolutionary progress towards a more sustainable development path is not simply a pipe dream. The 20th century saw a growing recognition that social injustice and environmental degradation do not simply blight lives in the communities most immediately affected, but ultimately work to the detriment of all our futures. In this respect, the definition of the ideal of sustainable development as a condition to aspire to is, itself, an important mark of progress. Although this rising consciousness has not yet been translated into decisive action, recent decades have seen a growing – if grudging – recognition of the need to redefine relations between the major sectional interests of Capital, Labour and Environment if the whole edifice of development is to be preserved and extended.

We might question, however, whether reliance on a gradualist approach can be justified, given the scale and immediacy of the social and environmental problems that beset the contemporary world. Can we really afford to think in terms of evolutionary change when the next half century seems likely to be characterized by unprecedented social and environmental stresses? Certainly, it is possible to conceive of an alternative, revolutionary, route to the creation of an equitable and eco-centric post-capitalist society. In the past, the premise that acceptable levels of economic and social equity could not be achieved within prevailing societal structures led sections of the Labour interest to attempt to overthrow the power of Capital. Equivalent thinking in today's world might inspire a coalition of social and environmental interests to dramatic action to force the pace of evolutionary progress towards sustainable development. At the start of the 21st century, however, the precedent of socialist revolution seems flawed. Moreover, sustainable development does not currently appear to attract anything approaching the levels of popular and political support that were formerly enjoyed by socialism. Nowhere have there been massive demonstrations in support of sustainable development and no government has ever been elected on a manifesto in which sustainable development forms a leading part. On the face of it, political reality seems to militate against revolutionary change.

This simple presentation of alternatives, however, by no means exhausts the range of potential futures. Recent work in regulation theory, discussed by Purvis in Chapter 2, suggests that it may be possible to conceive of quite rapid and radical shifts towards sustainability within the framework of capitalist society. If, as regulation theorists claim, capitalism is characterized by repeated crises, there will be periods when, rather than resisting change, established interests may accept its necessity in order to restore stability to the system. If the initiative can be captured during these moments of change by the proponents of sustainable development, they may be able to construct alternative regimes of regulation that will foster a new balance between the economic, social and environmental dimensions of development. Regulation theory, therefore, appears to offer a mechanism for securing change, a feature that is lacking from some other readings of sustainable development as a process. But regulation theory, too, has its limitations. It cannot explain why future crisis resolution should result in more sustainable development when the tendency, in the past, has been for crises to be resolved in ways that increase, rather than decrease, social and environmental exploitation.

Promoting societal change

It is beyond the scope of the present volume to resolve the many questions that surround the future course of societal change. However, it is perhaps appropriate to reflect briefly upon the extent to which it is possible or desirable to take active measures to direct and accelerate societal change in ways that will make sustainable development more likely. Given that it is not our purpose here to advocate eco-revolution, a number of other possibilities suggest themselves.

Some of those who advocate the established sustainable development strategies outlined earlier in this chapter have always claimed that limited initial changes offered a means of building towards more profound societal transformation in the longer term. The devolution of responsibility for resource management from a national to a regional or local level, for example, may be intended to encourage more far-reaching changes in attitudes towards nature and the resourcing of consumption and production. As a result, a new awareness of the importance of balance between environment, economy and social welfare may help to erode long-standing societal and political barriers to more sustainable development. Equally, promoting a participatory approach to solving a specific problem is sometimes designed to create, within a community, the confidence and sense of empowerment that enables it to take on other challenges and even assert its rights to political representation and equitable access to resources.

In practice, however, it is very difficult to anticipate and plan any such process of cumulative change. As we have seen, many projects fall at the first hurdle, failing to secure even the limited change necessary to inspire further action. Others lead to outcomes that are very different from those intended by the actors involved as sponsors and participants. The apparent solution of an immediate problem may induce contentment and complacency, rather than a desire for further progress. Equally – and ironically – technical and participatory measures designed to promote the appearance of more sustainable development while reinforcing the societal status quo may take on a life of their own. Technological innovations often modify our lifestyles and attitudes in ways that cannot be predicted in advance. Even a tokenistic attempt at community consultation may begin to erode apathy and inspire the first glimmerings of political activism.

These uncertainties make it difficult for us to revise our previous conclusion that current strategies are, in the main, limited. If they succeed in securing any substantial measure of progress towards sustainable development, it is almost as likely to be in spite of, rather than because of, the original intentions of their promoters. But our reflections on these strategies suggest the value of focusing upon two more specific areas. One is education; only if there is a clearer and more widespread understanding of the nature and the scale of the threat presented by current unsustainability can we expect to see any significant shift in popular and political opinion in favour of genuinely sustainable development. In its own modest way, we hope that the present volume will contribute to this educational process. But if education is to be an effective agent for change, it cannot be confined to the school room or the lecture theatre. There must also be a wide range of other initiatives to raise public awareness of the full consequences of the everyday decisions that we all take as consumers and producers.

The second focus of change is political. A more effective and democratic framework for decision-making cannot guarantee more sustainable development; but there is a powerful argument that significant progress will prove impossible in the absence of greater democracy. Existing participatory prescriptions for change are thus sound in principle, if flawed in practice. They reflect a recognition that sustainable development requires dialogue between all sections of society, including those who claim to speak for the environment. But rather than stress this direct participation in decision-making – which is problematic even at the local level and impossible at higher levels of the spatial and political hierarchy – we urge the extension of democratic representation. This reform of decision-making can and must involve all levels of the national political hierarchy. It requires a democratic political framework at each level, including not only a representative democracy with free elections, but also a pluralist political milieu in which all groups, particularly those favouring social justice and environmental interests, are free to organize and campaign for their points of view.

As yet, however, few developing countries enjoy anything approaching representative democracy at any level of government. It is also the case that true pluralism is something of a rarity in many countries, whatever their level of development. So even if democratization and pluralization – rather than more extensive and ambitious changes in societal structure – are seen as fundamental conditions for sustainable development, past experience of the slow pace of political change seems to militate against any expectation of rapid improvements in the sustainability of national development.

Equivalent change is also needed at an international level; this too will be no easy task. Just as national political institutions must evolve in order to protect the weak against the strong and the poor against the wealthy, so too must our fledgling international institutions be enhanced so that they distribute economic, social and environmental welfare more equitably between the states of the world. This is not an argument for the imposition of uniform social and environmental conditions to world trade rules, as has already been debated by the International Labour Organization (ILO) and the World Trade Organization (WTO) (see Chapter 12). Too often, such moves appear to be motivated primarily by a desire to protect developed countries against competition from imported produce, the low price of which reflects a failure to pay the full social and environmental costs incurred at their point of origin. Treating all states uniformly, whatever their level of development, is also inconsistent with the principle of differentiated obligations, now routinely adopted in international environmental regimes. This holds that lesser obligations should be imposed upon developing countries, either because they are less culpable for past environmental damage, or less capable of paying the full costs of current initiatives. The international community faces a massive challenge in finding structures for new international institutions that will ensure that the global path towards more sustainable development is equitable in its effects on today's diverse communities, as well as in fulfilling its obligations to future generations.

A More Pragmatic Response

It seems appropriate, however, to offer some specific reflections on initiatives that can and should be taken more immediately as part of a wider exercise in rethinking the nature of sustainable development, both as practice and as theory. Hence, the following section begins by outlining a series of principles that, we suggest, would improve planning for sustainable development. At the same time, we recognize that, in practice, planning cannot be divorced from the broader political context. Planning for sustainable development will require choices to be made that seem likely to be more challenging, and perhaps more controversial, than those to which we are already accustomed.

Improving planning for sustainable development

A pragmatic response to the debate on the need for societal change is to assume that it is not an essential prerequisite for more sustainable development. This gives scope for offering advice on how present societies could improve their planning methods. In this section we do this by bringing together some of the key findings of this book, with the additional assumption that sustainable development involves optimizing the allocation of welfare between the economic, social and environmental dimensions of development in order to ensure inter-generational and intra-generational equity over a range of levels on the spatial scale.

Six conditions for planning
A society of whatever size can plan for sustainable development if it can fulfil six conditions. It should be able to:

1. Identify a comprehensive set of strategies covering the economic, social and environmental dimensions of its development at the full range of levels on the spatial scale.
2. Account for the economic, social and environmental consequences of all actions within its territory in an integrated way, rather than treating them separately. Isolated improvements in each of the three dimensions will not guarantee that development will become more sustainable.
3. Balance changes in these three dimensions of its development in line with a recognized condition for sustainable development, such as one of those listed in Chapter 1 (see Tables 1.1 and 1.2).

4. Account for the consequences that this balance has for other societies with which it interacts and make any necessary adjustments in the light of this. More sustainable development cannot be achieved by exporting waste to another territory, or importing goods whose production incurred environmental damage or social exploitation in another territory (see Chapter 3).
5. Plan future activities by taking account of the past economic, social and environmental trends which have determined its long-term development path and its impacts upon the welfare of future generations. Any further reduction in Natural Capital, for example, must be made in the context of historic reductions and the stock of Natural Capital that remains in the territory concerned.
6. Identify the policies and institutions needed to implement the plan and its strategies at appropriate levels on the spatial scale in order to maximize coherency, effectiveness and geographical suitability and to optimize the balance between inter-generational and intra-generational equity.

Political influences on planning

The above conditions are rational in approach and limited in scope to costs and benefits that could, in principle, be given economic values. In practice, political considerations will also be influential in the planning process. As Grainger showed in Chapter 12, few states are currently willing to integrate the economic, social and environmental dimensions of their own development, although they frequently advocate precisely this stance as the best policy for other states. There are good reasons for this. First, they do not want to reduce their rate of economic development merely to conserve their own environment or even the global environment. Second, developing countries, especially, are loath to pay any of the costs incurred by other states in the past, but not paid for at the time.

Exactly when states will break through the political 'sustainability threshold' and formally recognize the need consciously to integrate the three dimensions of their development is uncertain. It could happen when the scientific case for conserving the environment is so strong that action cannot be delayed any more. But this does not seem tenable: scientific concern was first expressed about global climate change, for example, in the early 1970s, yet governments only began to take the threat seriously during the late 1980s. Another possibility is that it depends on environmental NGOs becoming as powerful as the business and social lobbies, and environmental concerns being ranked as at least equivalent to everyday economic and social concerns. But this does not seem likely either. Perhaps nature will only be treated seriously when its situation is perceived to pose a direct threat to our economic and social welfare (Kasperson, 1969).

The politics of trade-offs

One of the major lessons emerging from this book is that even after these political prerequisites have been satisfied and the notion of integrating the three dimensions of development has become more deeply embedded in the political fabric, societies and the bodies that govern them will find it far more difficult to make trade-offs between competing development objectives than they do at present.

Hitherto, two-way trade-offs have been the norm, balancing economic against social interests. During the 1980s, for example, the UK government was faced with a major dilemma. It could choose to end state subsidies to unprofitable coal mines to secure the more productive use of capital, in the full knowledge that that this would lead to the closure of many mines, leave large numbers of miners unemployed and result in the disintegration of mining communities. Alternatively, it could provide continued support so that mines would remain open, sustaining miners' livelihoods and the social fabric of mining communities, but at the cost of denying the use of that capital to more economically and socially productive ends. The outcomes of such trade-offs have generated considerable controversy, encapsulated in a class-based politics that is dominated by the conflict between the sectional interests of Capital and Labour. This was particularly evident in the national strike of 1984 to 1985 by British coalminers, called to protest against pit closures. Such conflict is not likely to disappear: issues about taxation, profitability, jobs and social investment in education and healthcare will continue to dominate the political agenda. Even advanced societies still find it difficult to sustain levels of healthcare, pension provision and other services that are acceptable to all.

Such two-way trade-offs will be increasingly superseded by three-way trade-offs, between economic growth, social welfare and the health of the environment. These have been relatively rare until now because the state of the environment has been seen more as a check on the balance between the economic and social dimensions of development, rather than as integral to a wider balance. In the case of the above policy dilemma over pit closures, if the UK government had taken a sustainable development approach during the 1980s, it would have balanced the net economic and social benefits of closing mines against the net environmental benefits derived from alternative strategies to substitute for the cut in domestic coal supplies. These could have included: (a) allowing energy generators to shift to power stations fuelled by natural gas, which emits less carbon dioxide per unit of electricity generated and therefore helps to reduce the threat posed by global climate change; (b) allowing the import of coal from overseas that is not only cheaper but is lower in sulphur, so that power stations emit lower concentrations of acidic gases which degrade forests and lakes in continental Europe.

Three-way trade-offs will be more difficult to make than two-way trade-offs, not only because of the extra dimension involved, but also because of the need to make trade-offs within each dimension – for example, between different environmental options. Thus, advocates of nuclear power assert that climate change creates an environmental argument for investing in expanding nuclear capacity because nuclear power stations do not emit carbon dioxide. Such claims do little to alter the stance of anti-nuclear campaigners. They perceive the industry as a threat not only to international peace, but also to the environment and human health. This reflects concerns about radiation emitted from permitted waste and the risk of much greater exposure should accidents occur in nuclear power stations or reprocessing and storage facilities. Balancing these different environmental impacts represents a difficult problem for planners. An even more challenging problem would be to try to balance the net economic, social and environmental benefits of coal-fired and nuclear power stations against those of windfarms and other renewable energy sources, which emit neither radiation nor carbon dioxide but which also incur their own environmental costs.

Thus, in three-way trade-offs the need to balance net economic and social benefits will not disappear. Instead, it will be complicated by the need to consider multiple interpretations of environmental welfare, each promoted by different interest groups and with its own distinctive combination of economic and social costs and benefits. Maintaining and extending existing nuclear capacity would protect the employment and social welfare of the industry's workers and their dependants. But is it the best use of available capital? Does it provide the most economically efficient solution to a country's energy needs? Or could sufficient energy be generated from renewable sources to make a significant contribution to meeting current demand? If the result of relying on new forms of generation is to raise energy prices in the short term, what will be the impacts on economic growth and social welfare? However, as noted above, political reality often inhibits attempts to improve the sustainability of development. Most (democratic) governments will also ask how their own immediate short-term fortunes and, in particular, their chances of re-election will be affected by public reaction to specific policy initiatives.

Each alternative set of trade-offs will have different implications for both intra-generational and inter-generational equity. As the 1986 disaster at the Chernobyl nuclear power station in the Ukraine showed only too clearly, the decisions made by one government about nuclear policy may have considerable implications for its neighbours, including those who have opted for a nuclear-free energy policy. The legacy for future generations is also likely to be contentious. It is, of course, possible that new standards in energy management and energy production technologies will emerge to define a win–win solution. Just as likely, however, is a series of other futures, all of them flawed. Are we to leave to future generations a world where nuclear hazards are limited, but climate is unstable; or a cooler world that is riddled with nuclear waste dumps and prone to nuclear accidents; or a poorer world where the limitations of energy supply have curbed economic and social progress? It is not clear that the need for such choices and the trade-offs they entail is widely appreciated yet amongst the general public, politicians and business leaders. Nor do we have the planning tools available that are needed to enable a society to make decisions on such complex issues in a rational and transparent way.

Achieving a balance between devolution, spatial coherence and equity

An exceptionally high degree of coherence will be needed within a single country to achieve an optimum balance between changes in the economic, social and environmental dimensions of national development. Trade-offs will be very complex and have to take account of connections between different regions. A totally bottom-up approach to planning, in which everything is decided independently in individual regions or in a much larger number of localities would undermine national coherency, as various examples in Chapter 3 showed. So the many virtues of devolution (and decentralization) must be combined with the coherence which top-down national planning can provide. This is not impossible if the spatially appropriate approach to implementing strategies, suggested earlier in this chapter, is followed. Approaching planning from a multiple spatial-level perspective could also be the solution to the practical problems that the huge number of independent localities in each country would face in achieving an ideal balance between the three dimensions of their own development.

Efforts to maximize coherency and equity in this way might seem to point to an equally high degree of homogeneity and uniformity in the treatment of particular places and societies. But given that sustainable development is characterized by both intra-generational equity and inter-generational equity, does achieving it at the global level mean that, at any particular time, every human being in the world should have the same income and enjoy all of the other components of welfare to the same degree, and every square kilometre on the planet should have the same stock of Natural Capital? Clearly, this would be impossible in practice; but would it be desirable in principle? Again, the answer is no, for two reasons. First, Natural Capital is distributed unevenly over the planet, as is Human and Man-Made Capital, and hence, the level of development. Second, at any moment, every country is at a different phase of development relative to every other country. It was argued in Chapter 3 that the only equitable way to compare countries is by their characteristics at *similar* phases of their development.

So how should the nations of the world act to increase international intra-generational equity? One option would be to formulate and implement some great global master plan. However, the analysis in Chapter 3, and the general realization of the deficiencies of top-down planning, suggests that it would be more appropriate to focus on taking action at national level but within a supportive international framework. Each country should therefore aim for a development path which optimizes the rise in the economic and social dimensions of development while minimizing impacts on the environmental dimension. In addition, it should minimize the degree to which it imports development from other countries (by processing their raw materials), imports sustainable development (by importing goods produced with unpaid environmental costs) or exports unsustainable development (by emitting gases and other pollutants that exert environmental costs on other states). This need not, indeed should not, mean an end to trade in goods, raw materials and other valued commodities. However, to ensure intra-generational equity, states benefiting from such trade must offer full reimbursement to the states that they exploit. If all pairs of states could achieve such equitable relations, then the whole world would be developing as sustainably as it could. To achieve this a new international institution would be needed to serve as a clearing house for compensation payments between countries and to ensure a 'level playing field' so that all states could act equitably in a social and environmental sense without undermining their international economic competitiveness. Such a mathematically perfect scheme is unlikely to happen. This reflects both the difficulty of achieving acceptable monetary valuations of compensation and of ensuring that the latter are allocated in an appropriate way. But this does not detract from the need for every country to ensure that its own development is as sustainable as possible.

The Limitations of Current Theories

We began our analysis in this chapter by examining current strategies, and have gradually increased the sophistication of our assessment of the conceptual requirements of sustainable development and the feasibility of achieving it in present-day societies. It is now time to compare this more realistic picture of the potential for actually achieving more sustainable development with the scope of existing theories.

Explaining equity

Existing economic theories of sustainable development tend to focus on inter-generational equity. Readers will struggle to find any mention in these theories of intra-generational equity within a society, even though this is at the heart of the theoretical concept of economic development and central to economic policy-making. Intra-generational equity is ignored by the Strong Condition of ecological economics, which focuses upon the environment to the exclusion of everything else. The Very Weak Condition of environmental economics does take a wider, two-dimensional view of development; but in balancing changes in the environmental dimension of development against those in the economic and social dimensions combined, it ignores the balance between the two latter dimensions.

Current economic theories also ignore intra-generational equity between developed and developing countries. Yet this is central to political economy theories of development, and the theory of political ecology derived from it. So must these two distinct areas of theoretical discourse continue on separate tracks, with academics choosing only one of them with which to analyse sustainable development, or could discussions between their proponents lead to mutual adaptation and convergence? It is difficult to answer this question because current economic theories of sustainable development are quite specific but limited in scope, while political economy theories have a wider scope but tend to offer only generalized explanations.

Explaining the spatial dimension

Both environmental and ecological economics theories have been applied spatially, but only to a limited extent. Those working within an ecological economics discourse have tried to take account of the spatial dimension – for example, by linking ecological footprints to estimated carrying capacities (see Chapter 5). However, as Grainger shows in Chapter 3, these offer inadequate portraits of sustainable development as they ignore its economic and social dimensions. There is more scope to extend environmental economics theory to encompass the spatial dimension. The attraction for geographers of working with the Very Weak Condition is that, in principle, the spatial distributions of different types of capital can be mapped, and changes in Natural Capital overlaid with those in Human and Man-Made Capital. One way to tackle the intra-generational equity issue at the global scale, for example, would be to extend the Very Weak Condition of environmental economics theory to assess the equity of exchanges of Natural Capital and Human and Man-Made Capital between countries. But even then the Very Weak Condition would still be limited by its aggregation of Human and Man-Made Capital.

Another way forward would be to extend the scope of existing theories of development which already incorporate the spatial dimension, so that they can encompass the principles of sustainable development. Mitchell has argued the case for geographical theories in Chapter 5, and a case could also be made for political economy theories of the world economy, though they do portray the world using rather simple spatial structures.

Explaining the political dimension

Theoretical discourses are inevitably limited in scope in order to maintain self-consistency. Hence, economic theories, for instance, are generally limited to predicting normative solutions to problems and ignore how these solutions will, in practice, be conditioned by political and other non-market influences. The record of class-based conflict over the allocation of the economic and social costs and benefits of development is largely ignored in present economic theories of sustainable develop-ment. Moreover, proposals by ecological economists that societies should become more eco-centric, to ensure that their economies function in line with ecological principles, are unconvincing because their theories do not incorporate the political mechanisms needed to achieve this transition. The best available solution to this dilemma might well be to apply economic theories in tandem with political economy theories, which can explain deviations from normative patterns in terms of the exercise of power.

Relevance to practical planning applications

If sustainable development is to fulfil its potential as a new and comprehensive planning framework, then the environmental dimension must be fully integrated into planning techniques in order to support the strategies suggested in the previous section. Yet neither ecological economics theory nor environmental economics theory is currently expressed in a manner which allows this. Ecological economics theory is incompatible with the basic model used for economic planning as it does not incorporate the economic and social dimensions of development. Environmental economics theory is more compatible, but it is limited in its ability to balance all three dimensions of development in an integrated way. This also limits the potential to use this theory as the basis for a new operational planning tool. Planners need the latter to make trade-offs between the three dimensions of development, but the Very Weak Condition provides no basis for doing this.

The need for a new theory

The limitations of existing theories appear to be so great that a new theoretical model seems an inevitable requirement if trends in the three dimensions of development are to be described separately. This is essential if planners are to have tools at their disposal which can account for the trade-offs customary in everyday planning applications, allow for inter-generational equity and intra-generational equity, and encompass the spatial and political dimensions of sustainable development. The possibilities for a new theory were first alluded to in a graphical model devised by Campbell (1996), which recognized that the ideal for planners was to balance the three goals of economic growth, social justice, and environmental protection. One approach might be to return to the definition of sustainable development advanced by Pearce (1991) as '[Development which] leads to non-declining human welfare over time', and divide human welfare explicitly into its economic, social and environmental components.

It is in our call for a new theory that we differ from other studies. This is evident if we compare our stance with a recent report from the UK-based Sustainable Development Research Network (2002). The report goes significantly further than the conventional technocratic approach to research, which gives priority to the development of new technologies and techniques for facilitating the political process. Indeed, the Network shares our concerns for: (a) developing better spatial planning systems; (b) gaining a better understanding of spatial and temporal scaling issues, for example, by optimizing the balance between top-down and bottom-up strategies; and (c) reducing environmental injustice. However, their research agenda remains largely focused on empirical observation of the current political process of sustainable development, which tries to achieve its ends through pragmatic experimentation.

There is a wide range of different perspectives on sustainable development, some of which are displayed in this book. The most effective theory will surely be one that can encompass as many of these perspectives as possible, while remaining internally consistent and practically relevant. Human beings have a tremendous ability to imagine a better world, yet as a species we also suffer from an unfortunate tendency to fail to realize such goals as a result of our social imperfections. Such failings are, in part, redeemed by a capacity to learn from our mistakes. The feedback received from the mistakes made in pursuing economic development has been transformed by the power of imagination to create the far more sophisticated and challenging vision that is sustainable development. We could learn how to realize this vision through trial and error, as with economic development. Yet such is the complexity of sustainable development that the period of pragmatic experimentation would be prolonged, even with the help of new technologies and feedback from applied research. Complementing these with fundamental research could significantly shorten the learning period.

The success of this research will heavily depend upon close collaboration between scientists from a wide range of disciplines, as the Sustainable Development Research Network (2002) also recognizes. Such interdisciplinary research is still embryonic, having been discouraged until recently by the science policies of governments in most industrialized countries. It is ironic that even our ability to imagine a better world has been constrained by the same deficiencies in organization which have so far prevented us from developing sustainably. To realize this vision will demand a recognition by society that it needs more from scientists than simply technologies to generate more income and an easier lifestyle. For their part scientists must recognize that they should pay greater heed to their own mode of social organization if they are to meet the needs of society and the environment. Present relationships between humanity and the planet are as fractured as those between the various societies which cover the planet. Somehow we must blend our social and scientific skills to heal these divisions which prevent us from realizing our potential. That is the challenge of sustainable development.

References

Abel, C (1998a) 'Path is clear for GM crop expansion in UK', *Farmers' Weekly*, 129(23): 56.

Abel, C (1998b) 'US sees rapid rise in precision techniques', *Farmers' Weekly*, 129(24): 44.

Abel, C (1999) 'GM crops special', *Farmers' Weekly*, 131(23): 56–63.

Abramovitz, J N (2001) 'Averting unnatural disasters', in Worldwatch Institute (ed) *State of the World 2001*, Earthscan, London, pp123–42.

Adam, D (2001) 'Royal Society disputes value of carbon sinks', *Nature*, 412: 108.

Adams, W M (1997) 'Rationalization and conservation: ecology and the management of nature in the United Kingdom', *Transactions of the Institute of British Geographers*, 22(3): 277–91.

Adams, W M (2001) *Green Development: Environment and Sustainability in the Third World*, 2nd edition, Routledge, London.

Agarwal, A (2002) 'A Southern perspective on curbing global climate change', in Schneider, S H, Rosencranz, A and Niles, J O (eds) *Climate Change Policy: A Survey*, Island Press, Washington, DC, pp373–91.

Agnew, J and Corbridge, S (1995) *Mastering Space: Hegemony, Territory and International Political Economy*, Routledge, London.

Agnew, J and Duncan, J (eds) (1989) *The Power of Place*, Unwin Hyman, Boston, MA.

Alden, E (1998) 'MacMillan Bloedel bows to pressure from Greenpeace', *Financial Times*, 19 June.

Alders, C, Haverkort, B and van Veldhuizen, L (eds) (1993) *Linking with Farmers: Networking for Low-External-Input and Sustainable Agriculture*, Intermediate Technology Publications, London.

Alexander, G (1996) 'Overview: The context of renewable energy technologies', in Boyle, G (ed) *Renewable Energy. Power for a Sustainable Future*, Oxford University Press, Oxford, pp1–40.

Amano, R (2001) *Damu to Nihon (Dams and Japan)*, Iwanami Shoten, Tokyo, Japan.

Anas, A (1994) *NYSIM (The New York Area Simulation Model): A Model for Cost-Benefit Analysis of Transportation Projects*, Regional Plan Association, New York, NY.

Anderson, K (1995) 'The political economy of coal subsidies in Europe', *Energy Policy*, 23(6): 485–96.

Anzorena, J, Bolnick, J, Boonyabancha, S, Cabannes, Y, Hardoy, A, Hasan, A, Levy, C, Mitlin, D, Murphy, D, Patel, S, Saborido, M, Satterthwaite, D and Stein, A (1998) 'Reducing urban poverty: some lessons from experience', *Environment and Urbanization*, 10(1): 167–86.

Aricia, G, Merino, L, Mata, A and O'Hanlon, B (1991) *Modelo Interactivo de Poblacion y Medio Ambiente en Costa Rica – Análisis y Proyecciones para el Valle Central*, Asociación Demográfica Costarricense, San José, Costa Rica.

Arimah, B C and Ebohon, O J (2000) 'Energy transition and its implications for environmentally sustainable development in Africa', *International Journal of Sustainable Development and World Ecology*, 7(3): 201–16.

Armstrong, T E (1952) *The Northern Sea Route: Soviet Exploitation of the North East Passage*, Cambridge University Press, Cambridge.

Armstrong-Brown, S M, Cook, H F and Lee, H C (2000) 'Topsoil characteristics from a paired survey of organic versus conventional farming in southern England', *Biological Agriculture and Horticulture*, 18(1): 37–54.

Asahi Shinbun (1996) 'Konkriito gogan mō yamemasu: kensetsushō ga hōshin tenkan' (An end at last to concrete river banks: the Ministry of Construction in a change of policy), *Asahi Shinbun (Asahi Newspaper)*, 10 September.

Asian Coalition for Housing Rights (2001) 'Building an urban poor people's movement in Phnom Penh, Cambodia', *Environment and Urbanization*, 13(2): 61–72.

Asian Development Bank (ASD) (1997) *Annual Report*, ASD, Manila, Philippines.

Atkinson, K (1988) 'Arctic ecosystems: their nature and conservation', in Atkinson, K and McDonald, A T (eds) *Arctic Canada*, Centre for Canadian Studies, University of Leeds, Leeds, pp42–71.

Atkisson, A (1996) 'Developing indicators of sustainable community: examples from Sustainable Seattle', *Environmental Impact Assessment Review*, 16: 337–50.

Aubert, C (1985) *The Use of Manures and Mineral Fertilizers in Organic Agriculture*, Soil Association, Stowmarket.

Audit Commission (1997) *It's a Small World: Local Government as a Steward of the Environment*, HMSO, London.

Avery, D T (2000) 'Besieging Stossel to protect organic myths', *Priorities for Health*, 12(3) (www.acsh.org/publication/priorities/1203/coverstory.html).

Azeez, G (2000) *The Biodiversity Benefits of Organic Farming*, Soil Association, Bristol.

Azzone, G and Bertelè, U (1994) 'Exploiting green strategies for competitive advantage', *Long Range Planning*, 27(6): 69–81.

B&Q (1997) Advertisement, *The Times*, 20 November.

Baharoglu, D (1996) 'Becoming a citizen to be a partner in socially sustainable urban settlements', *Third World Planning Review*, 19(2): iii–viii.

Bairoch, P (1975) *Economic Development of the Third World Since 1900*, Methuen, London.

Bairoch, P (1982) 'International industrialisation levels from 1750 to 1980', *Journal of European Economic History*, 11: 269–333.

Baker, S, Kousis, M, Richardson, D and Young, S (1997) *The Politics of Sustainable Development*, Routledge, London.

Baldock, D (1990) *Agriculture and Habitat Loss in Europe*, World Wide Fund for Nature, Gland, Switzerland.

Baldwin, D A (1993) 'Neorealism, neoliberalism and world politics', in Baldwin, D A (ed) *Neorealism and Neoliberalism: The Contemporary Debate*, Columbia University Press, New York, NY, pp1–25.

Barbier, E (1994) 'Natural Capital and the economics of environment and development', in Jansson, A-M, Hammer, M, Folke, C and Costanza, R (eds) *Investing in*

Natural Capital: The Ecological Economics Approach to Sustainability, Island Press, Washington, DC, pp291–322.

Barker, A (1996) 'Multi-sectoral Dynamic Model 9.0', in Cambridge Econometrics, *Regional Economic Prospects*, Cambridge Econometrics, Cambridge.

Barnes, W (2000) 'Poor nations assert place in global trade', *Financial Times*, 21 February.

Barraclough, S and Ghimire, K (1990) 'The social dynamics of deforestation in developing countries', *Discussion Paper* 16, UNRISD, Geneva, Switzerland.

Barton, H, Davis, G and Guise, R (1995) *Sustainable Settlements: A Guide for Planners, Designers and Developers*, Local Government Management Board, Luton.

Barton, J H (1999) *Biotechnology for Developing-Country Agriculture: Problems and Opportunities – Intellectual Property Management*, International Food Policy Research Institute, Washington, DC.

Batty, M (1976) *Urban Modelling*, Cambridge University Press, Cambridge.

Batty, M (1994) 'A chronicle of scientific planning: the Anglo-American experience', *Journal of the American Planning Association*, 60(1): 7–16.

BBC (2000) Reith Lectures: 'Respect for the Earth' (news.bbc.co.uk/hi/english/static/events/reith_2000/).

BBC (2002) 'US to plant more GM crops', *BBC News*, 29 March (news.bbc.co.uk/hi/english/...ericas/newsid_1900000/1900073.stm).

Beauregard, R A (1995) 'Theorising the global–local connection', in Knox, P L and Taylor, P J (eds) *World Cities in a World System*, Cambridge University Press, Cambridge, pp232–48.

Beck, U (1992) 'From industrial society to the risk society: questions of survival, social structure and ecological enlightenment', *Theory, Culture and Society*, 9: 97–123.

Beder, S (2002) *Global Spin: The Corporate Assault on Environmentalism*, revised edition, Green Books, Totnes.

Belsky, J M (2002) 'Beyond the natural resource and environmental sociology divide: insights from a transdisciplinary perspective', *Society and Natural Resources*, 15(3): 269–80.

Berger, T R (1977) *Northern Frontier, Northern Homeland: The Report to the Mackenzie Valley Pipeline Inquiry, Volume 1*, Supply and Services Canada, Ottawa, Canada.

Berkes, F, George, P and Preston, R J (1991) 'Co-management: the evolution in theory and practice of the joint administration of living resources', *Alternatives*, 18: 12–18.

Bernau, S and Duckworth, M (1998) 'An evaluation of integrated climate protection policies for the US', *Energy Policy*, 26(5): 357–74.

Berry, B J L (1967) *Geography of Market Centres and Retail Distribution*, Prentice-Hall, Englewood Cliffs, NJ.

Berry, B J L (1990) 'Urbanisation', in Turner II, B L, Clark, W C, Kates, R W, Richards, J F, Mathews, J T and Meyer, W B (eds) *The Earth as Transformed by Human Action. Global and Regional Changes in the Biosphere over the Past 300 Years*, Cambridge University Press, Cambridge, pp103–20.

Berry, B J L and Horton, F E (1970) *Geographical Perspectives on Urban Systems*, Prentice-Hall, Englewood Cliffs, NJ.

Berry, B J L, Conkling, E C and Ray, D M (1999) *The Global Economy in Transition*, 2nd edition, Prentice-Hall, Upper Saddle River, NJ.

Berry, W (1999) 'The death of the rural community', *The Ecologist*, 29(3): 183–84.

Bhagwati, J (1999) *A Stream of Windows: Unsettling Reflections on Trade, Immigration and Democracy*, MIT Press, Cambridge, MA.

BirdLife International (2003) *Agriculture and Enlargement of the European Union* (www.birdlifecapcampaign.org/eunew/text5.htm).

Birmingham City Council (1998) *Sustainability Indicators for Birmingham: How Do We Measure Up?* Environmental Services Department, Birmingham City Council, Birmingham.

Blaikie, P (1985) *The Political Economy of Soil Erosion in Developing Countries*, Longman, London.

Blaikie, P and Brookfield, H (1987) *Land Degradation and Society*, Methuen, London.

Blair, M M (1998) 'For whom should corporations be run? An economic rationale for stakeholder management', *Long Range Planning*, 31(2): 195–200.

Blake, A (ed) (1998) 'Energy crops special', *Farmers' Weekly*, 129(18): 64–67.

Blake, F (1990) *Organic Farming and Growing*, Crowood Press, Swindon.

Blowers, A (ed) (1993) *Planning for a Sustainable Environment: A Report by the Town and Country Planning Association*, Earthscan, London.

Blum, E (1993) 'Making biodiversity conservation profitable: a case study of the Merck-InBIO agreement', *Environment*, 35(4): 16–20 and 38–45.

Bodansky, D (1994) 'Prologue to the Climate Change Convention', in Mintzer, I and Leonard, J A (eds) *Negotiating Climate Change. The Inside Story of the Rio Convention*, Cambridge University Press, Cambridge, pp45–76.

Body, R (1991) *Our Food, Our Land. Why Contemporary Farming Practices Must Change*, Rider, London.

Boehmer-Christiansen, S (1997) 'A winning coalition of advocacy: climate research, bureaucracy and "alternative" fuels', *Energy Policy*, 25(4): 439–44.

Bookchin, M (1980) *Towards an Ecological Society*, Black Rose Books, Montreal, Canada.

Borione, D and Ripert, J (1994) 'Exercising common but differentiated responsibility', in Mintzer, I and Leonard, J A (eds) *Negotiating Climate Change. The Inside Story of the Rio Convention*, Cambridge University Press, Cambridge, pp77–96.

Borja, J and Castells, M (1997) *Local and Global: Management of Cities in the Information Age*, Earthscan, London.

Bossier, F and Bréchet, T (1995) 'A fiscal reform for increasing employment and mitigating CO_2 emissions in Europe', *Energy Policy*, 23(9): 789–98.

Boulton, L (1997a) 'Clinton tries to calm storm over climate', *Financial Times*, 6 October.

Boulton, L (1997b) 'Big cuts in greenhouse gas emissions win support', *Financial Times*, 11 November.

Bowers, J (1997) *Sustainability and Environmental Economics: An Alternative Text*, Longman, Harlow.

Bowler, I R, Bryant, C R and Cocklin, C (eds) (2002) *The Sustainability of Rural Systems: Geographical Interpretations*, Kluwer, Dordrecht.

Bowring, F (1998) 'LETS: An eco-socialist initiative?' *New Left Review*, 232: 91–111.

Boyden, S, Millar, S, Newcombe, K and O'Neil, B (1981) *The Ecology of a City and its People: The Case of Hong Kong*, Australian National University Press, Canberra, Australia.

Boyle, G (1996) 'Solar photovoltaics', in Boyle, G (ed) *Renewable Energy: Power for a Sustainable Future*, Oxford University Press, Oxford, pp89–136.

BP (2002) *Renewables and Alternatives*, BP (www.bpenergy.com/products/alternatives.html).

Bradshaw, M (1995) 'The Russian North in transition: general introduction', *Post-Soviet Geography*, 36: 195–203.

Brandt Commission (1980) *North–South: A Programme for Survival*, Pan Books, London.

Branford, S (2002) 'Sow resistant', *Guardian*, 17 April.

Branney, P and Yadav, K P (1998) *Changes in Community Forest Condition and Management 1994–1998*, NUKCFP, Kathmandu, Nepal.

Breheny, M J (1992) 'Towards sustainable urban development', in Mannion, A N and Bowlby, S R (eds) *Environmental Issues in the 1990s*, Wiley, Chichester, pp227–90.

Breheny, M J (1995) 'Counter-urbanization and sustainable urban forms', in Brotchie, J, Batty, M, Blakely, E, Hall, P and Newton, P (eds) *Cities in Competition*, Longman, Melbourne, Australia, pp402–29.

Breheny, M J and Rookwood, R (1993) 'Planning the sustainable city region', in Blowers, A (ed) *Planning for a Sustainable Environment*, Earthscan, London, pp150–89.

Bridge, G and McManus, P (2000) 'Sticks and stones: environmental narratives and discursive regulation in the forestry and mining sectors', *Antipode*, 32(1): 10–47.

Brierley, D (1997) 'Emission fears spur a nuclear reaction', *Independent on Sunday*, 26 October.

Brimblecombe, P (1987) *The Big Smoke: A History of Air Pollution in London since Medieval Times*, Methuen, London.

Bristow, H (1997) 'The information superhighway – a route to a more sustainable future', *UKCEED Bulletin*, 50: 19–21.

Broadbent, J (1998) *Environmental Politics in Japan: Networks of Power and Protest*, Cambridge University Press, Cambridge.

Brockett, C D (1990) *Land, Power and Poverty, Agrarian Transformation and Political Conflict in Central America*, Unwin Hyman, Boston, MA.

Brody, H (1998) *Maps and Dreams: Indians and the British Columbia Frontier*, Waveland Press, Prospect Heights, IL.

Bromley, D (1991) *Environment and Economy: Property Rights and Public Policy*, Blackwell, Oxford.

Brookes, A and Shields, F (eds) (1996) *River Channel Restoration: Guiding Principles for Sustainable Projects*, Wiley, Chichester.

Brown, G (1996) 'Geothermal energy', in Boyle, G (ed) *Renewable Energy: Power for a Sustainable Future*, Oxford University Press, Oxford, pp353–92.

Brown, L (1996) 'The acceleration of history', in Worldwatch Institute (ed) *The State of the World 1996*, Norton, New York, NY, pp3–20.

Brown, L (1998) 'Struggling to raise cropland productivity', in Worldwatch Institute (ed) *The State of the World 1998*, Norton, New York, NY, pp79–95.

Brown, P (2001a) 'Fears of insurance no-go zones as global warming claims rise', *Guardian*, 3 February.

Brown, P (2001b) 'MoD tries to veto wind farm sites', *Guardian*, 31 May.

Brown, P (2002) 'Trade war fears as public resists GM food', *Guardian*, 7 May.

Brugmann, J (1997) 'Is there method in our measurement? The use of indicators in local sustainable development planning', *Local Environment*, 20: 59–72.

Bryant, R L (1992) 'Political ecology: an emerging research agenda in Third World Studies', *Political Geography*, 11(1): 12–36.

Bryant, R L (1998) 'Power, knowledge and political ecology in the third world: a review', *Progress in Physical Geography*, 22(1): 79–94.

BT Environment Unit (1997) *Telecommunications Technologies and Sustainable Development*, BT, London.

Buckingham, L (1999) 'Claims for natural disasters rise to catastrophic high', *Guardian*, 16 March.

Buckingham-Hatfield, S and Percy, S (eds) (1999) *Constructing Local Environmental Agendas: People, Places and Participation*, Routledge, London.

Buitenkamp, M, Venner, H and Wams, T (1992) *Action Plan Netherlands*, Netherlands Friends of the Earth, Amsterdam, The Netherlands.

Bunge, W (1971) *Fitzgerald: Geography of a Revolution*, Schlenkman, Cambridge, MA.

Burgess, J, Harrison, C M and Filius, P (1998) 'Environmental communication and the cultural politics of environmental citizenship', *Environment and Planning A*, 30: 1445–60.

Burns, J (2000) 'Ministers want quality schemes', *Financial Times*, 5 April.

Burns, J and Timmins, N (2000) 'Council housing "set to disappear within a decade"', *Financial Times*, 22 February.

Burt, S and Grady, K (1994) *The Illustrated History of Leeds*, Breedon, Derby.

Burton, E (2000) 'The compact city', *Urban Studies*, 37(11): 1969–2006.

Burton, I and Kates, R W (1965) *Readings in Resource Management and Conservation*, University of Chicago Press, Chicago, IL.

Bush, R (1996) 'The politics of food and starvation', *Review of African Political Economy*, 68: 169–95.

Butler, D and Reichhardt, A (1999a) 'Long-term effects of GM crops serve up food for thought', *Nature*, 398(6729): 651–53.

Butler, D and Reichhardt, A (1999b) 'Assessing the threat to biodiversity on the farm', *Nature*, 398(6729): 654–56.

Byrne, J, Shen, B and Wallace, W (1998) 'The economies of sustainable energy for rural development: a study of renewable energy in rural China', *Energy Policy*, 26(1): 45–54.

Caldwell, L K (1990) *International Environmental Policy*, Duke University Press, Durham, NC.

Campbell, D (2003) 'Bush plan to exploit Alaskan oil thwarted', *Guardian*, 21 March.

Campbell, S (1996) 'Planning: green cities, growing cities, just cities? Urban planning and the contradictions of sustainable development', *Journal of the American Planning Association*, 62(3): 296–312.

Canadian Environmental Assessment Agency (1996) *NWT Diamonds Project*, Supply and Services Canada, Ottawa, Canada.

Capello, R, Nijkamp, P and Pepping, G (1999) *Sustainable Cities and Energy Policies*, Springer, New York, NY.

Carley, M, Jenkins, P and Smith, H (2001) *Urban Development and Civil Society: The Role of Communities in Sustainable Cities*, Earthscan, London.

Carney, D (1998) 'Implementing the Sustainable Rural Livelihoods Approach', Paper presented at DFID Natural Resources Advisors Conference, Sparsholt, July 1998.

Carney, D (1999) 'Approaches to sustainable livelihoods for the rural poor', *ODI Poverty Briefing Paper* 2, Overseas Development Institute, London.

Carrell, S (2000) 'Global warming: UK must halve pollution "to avert catastrophe"', *Independent*, 17 June.

Carroll, R (2002) 'Zambians starve as food aid lies rejected', *Guardian*, 17 October.

Carter, H (1983) *The Study of Urban Geography*, 3rd edition, Arnold, London.

Castella, J C, Jourdain, D, Trébuil, G and Napompeth, B (1999) 'A systems approach to understanding obstacles to effective implementation of IPM in Thailand: key issues for the cotton industry', *Agriculture, Ecosystems and Environment*, 72(1): 17–34.

Castells, M (1996) *The Rise of the Network Society*, Blackwell, Oxford.

Chamberlain, D and Stewart, Jnr, C N (1999) 'Transgene escape and transplastomics', *Nature Biotechnology* 17(4): 330–31.

Chambers, R (1983) *Rural Development: Putting the Last First*, Longman, Harlow.

Chandler, K, Goyal, S, Nandal, D P and Kapoor, K K (1998) 'Soil organic matter, microbial biomass and enzyme activities in a tropical agroforestry system', *Biology and Fertility of Soils*, 27(2): 168–72.

Changnon, S A (2000) 'Impacts of El Niño's weather', in Changnon, S A (ed) *El Niño 1997–1998: The Climate Event of the Century*, Oxford University Press, New York, NY, pp136–71.

Chapman, G P and Thompson, M (1995) *Water and the Quest for Sustainable Development in the Ganges Valley*, Mansell, London.

Chapman, S D (1987) *The Cotton Industry in the Industrial Revolution*, 2nd edition, Macmillan, London.

Charles, D (2001) *Lords of the Harvest: Biotech, Big Money and the Future of Food*, Perseus Press, Cambridge, MA.

Charter, M and Tischner, U (eds) (2001) *Sustainable Solutions: Developing Products and Services for the Future*, Greenleaf, Sheffield.

Chisholm, M (1990) 'The increasing separation of production and consumption', in Turner II, B L, Clark, W C, Kates, R W, Richards, J F, Mathews, J T and Meyer W B (eds) *The Earth as Transformed by Human Action. Global and Regional Changes in the Biosphere over the Past 300 Years*, Cambridge University Press, Cambridge, pp87–102.

Chisholm, S (2000) 'Oceanography: Stirring times in the Southern Ocean', *Nature*, 407: 685–87.

Cifuentes, L, Borja-Aburto, V H, Gouveia, N, Thurston, G and Davis, D L (2001) 'Hidden health benefits of greenhouse gas mitigation', *Science*, 293(5533): 1257–59.

City of Seattle (1996) *City of Seattle Comprehensive Plan Monitoring Report – Biennial Update on Seattle's Comprehensive Plan*, Office of Management and Planning, City of Seattle, Seattle, WA.

Clark, B and Hutton, B (1997) 'US to delay treaty ratification', *Financial Times*, 12 December.

Clark, R L and Lee, R (1998) 'Development of topographic maps for precision farming with kinematic GPS', *Transactions of the ASAE*, 41(4): 909–16.

Clarke, G P, Kashti, A, McDonald, A and Williamson, P (1996) 'Estimating small area demand for water: a new methodology', *Journal of the Institute of Water and Environmental Management*, 11: 186–92.

Clarke, P (1998) 'Biotech or world famine', *Farmers' Weekly*, 129(18): 56.

Clarke, T (1998) 'The stakeholder corporation: a business philosophy for the information age', *Long Range Planning*, 31(2): 182–94.

Cloke, P, Crang, P and Goodwin, M (eds) (1999) *Introducing Human Geographies*, Arnold, London.

Cloke, P, Milbourne, P and Thomas, C (1996) 'From wasteland to wonderland: opencast mining, regeneration and the English National Forest', *Geoforum*, 27(2): 159–74.

Clover, C (1999) 'American firm laps up Rachel's Dairy. US buy-out to accelerate growth of organic market', *Daily Telegraph*, 9 April.

Cobb, D, Feber, R, Hopkins, A, Stockdale, L, O'Riordan, T, Clements, B, Firbank, L, Goulding, K, Jarvis, S and Macdonald, D (1999) 'Integrating the environmental and economic consequences of converting to organic agriculture: evidence from a case study', *Land Use Policy*, 16(4): 207–21.

Coffey, W J (1996) 'The "newer" international division of labour', in Daniels, P W and Lever, W F (eds) *The Global Economy in Transition*, Longman, Harlow, pp40–61.

Coghlan, A (1992) 'Biodiversity Convention a "lousy deal", says US', *New Scientist*, 4 July, p9.

Cohen, S, Demeritt, D, Robinson, J and Rothman, D (1998) 'Climate change and sustainable development: towards dialogue', *Global Environmental Change: Human and Policy Dimensions*, 8(4): 341–71.

Colby, M E (1990) 'Environmental management in development: the evolution of paradigms', *World Bank Discussion Papers* 80, World Bank, Washington, DC.

Cole, M A, Rayner, A J and Bates, J M (1997) 'The environmental Kuznets curve: an empirical analysis', *Environment and Development Economics*, 2: 401–16.

Confederation of British Industry (CBI) (2002) 'News release: "Flawed" energy tax is damaging manufacturers while failing to deliver on energy efficiency', Confederation of British Industry, 31 October.

Connolly, K (2001) 'Poland's organic revival', *Guardian*, 9 May.

Connor, S (1999) 'US butterflies killed by modified pollen', *Independent*, 20 May.

Connor, S (2001) 'Hard-won agreement that irked the American right', *Independent*, 30 March.

Conway, G R (1985) 'Agroecosystem analysis', *Agricultural Administration*, 20: 31–55.

Conway, G R (1997) *The Doubly Green Revolution. Food for All in the 21st Century*, Penguin, Harmondsworth.

Conway, G R (1999) 'GM foods can help the Third World', *Independent*, 2 July.

Conway, G R and Pretty, J N (1991) *Unwelcome Harvest: Agriculture and Pollution*, Earthscan, London.

Cooke, P (1996) 'Reinventing the region: firms, clusters and networks in economic development', in Daniels, P W and Lever, W F (eds) *The Global Economy in Transition*, Longman, Harlow, pp310–27.

Corzine, R (1997) 'Oil exporters resist calls for more curbs', *Financial Times*, 21 October.

Corzine, R (2000) 'Shell close to healing Nigerian rift', *Financial Times*, 17 January.

Costanza, R (1994) 'Three general policies to achieve sustainability', in Jansson, A-M, Hammer, M, Folke, C and Costanza, R (eds) *Investing in Natural Capital: The Ecological Economics Approach to Sustainability*, Island Press, Washington, DC, pp392–407.

Cowell, R (1997) 'Stretching the limits: environmental compensation, habitat creation and sustainable development', *Transactions of the Institute of British Geographers*, 22(3): 292–306.

Cowell, R and Owens, S (1998) 'Suitable locations: equity and sustainability in the minerals planning process', *Regional Studies*, 32(9): 797–811.

Cragg, A W (1998) 'Sustainable development and mining: opportunity or threat to the industry', *CIM Bulletin*, 91(1023): 45–50.

Craig, A (1998) 'More and more make the move', *Farmers' Weekly*, 129(24): 55–56.

Craig, W J, Harris, T M and Weiner, D (eds) (2002) *Community Participation and Geographic Information Systems*, Taylor and Francis, London.

Craighill, A L and Powell, J C (1996) 'Lifecycle assessment and economic evaluation of recycling: a case study', *Resources, Conservation and Recycling*, 17: 75–96.

Crawley, M J (1999) 'Bollworms, genes and ecologists', *Nature*, 400(6744): 501–02.

Crispin, S W (1998) 'Without a net', *Far Eastern Economic Review*, 9 July, p69.

Crone, P (1989) *Pre-Industrial Societies*, Blackwell, Oxford.

Crush, J (ed) (1995a) *Power of Development*, Routledge, London.

Crush, J (1995b) 'Imagining Development', in Crush, J (ed) *Power of Development*, Routledge, London, pp1–26.

Cummings, M B (2002) 'Fuel cells, carbon sequestration, infrastructure and the transition to a hydrogen economy', in Schneider, S H, Rosencranz, A and Niles, J O (eds) *Climate Change Policy: A Survey*, Island Press, Washington, DC, pp447–68.

Curwell, S, Hamilton, A and Cooper, I (1998) 'The BEQUEST network: towards sustainable urban development', *Building Research and Information Journal*, 26(1): 56–65.

Dalby, S (1996) 'Reading Rio, writing the world: the *New York Times* and the "Earth Summit"', *Political Geography*, 15: 593–613.

Dalton, R (1999) 'US warms to carbon sequestration research', *Nature*, 401: 315.

Daly, H E (1990) 'Toward some operational principles of sustainable development', *Ecological Economics*, 2(1): 1–6.

Daly, H E (1999) *Ecological Economics and the Ecology of Economics*, Edward Elgar, Cheltenham.

Daly, H E and Cobb, J B (1989) *For the Common Good: Redirecting the Economy Towards the Community, the Environment and a Sustainable Future*, Beacon Press, Boston, MA.

Daly, H E and Goodland, R (1994) *An Ecological-Economic Assessment of Deregulation of International Commerce Under GATT*, Environment Department, World Bank, Washington, DC.

Daniels, P, Bradshaw, M, Shaw, D and Sidaway, J (eds) (2001) *Human Geography: Issues for the 21st Century*, Pearson, Harlow.

Dasgupta, C (1994) 'The climate change negotiations', in Mintzer, I and Leonard, J A (eds) *Negotiating Climate Change. The Inside Story of the Rio Convention*, Cambridge University Press, Cambridge, pp129–48.

Dauvergne, P (1999) 'The environmental implications of Asia's 1997 financial crisis', *IDS Bulletin*, 30(3): 31–42.

Davies, S (1996) *Adaptable Livelihoods*, Macmillan, London.

Day, J (2001) 'Organic food market booming', *Guardian*, 11 May.

de David, L (1992) 'Brazil: agrarian reform in Brazil', in Dudley, N, Madeley, J and Stolton, S (eds) *Land is Life: Land Reform and Sustainable Agriculture*, Intermediate Technology Publications, London, pp59–69.

Deen, T (1998) 'Asia's cash crisis a setback for poverty reduction', *Inter Press Service World News* (www.oneworld.org/ips2/feb98/asia_poverty.html).

DeGregori, T R (1996) 'Can organic agriculture feed the world?' *Priorities for Health*, 8(4) (www.acsh.org/publications/priorities/0804/agriculture.html).

De Jonquières, G (2000) 'WTO urged to break barrier of mistrust', *Financial Times*, 28 March.

Delaney, D and Leitner, H (1997) 'The political construction of scale', *Political Geography*, 16: 93–97.

De Leo, G A, Rizzi, L, Caizzi, A and Gatto, M (2001) 'Carbon emissions: The economic benefits of the Kyoto Protocol', *Nature*, 413(6855): 478–79.

Denny, C (2001) 'New hope for poor as world trade talks are saved', *Guardian*, 15 November.

Department of the Environment (Canada) (1991) *The State of Canada's Environment*, Supply and Services Canada, Ottawa, Canada.

Department of the Environment (DoE) (UK) (undated) *Energy, Environment and Profits. Making a Corporate Commitment*, Department of the Environment, London.

Department of the Environment (DoE) (UK) (1994) *The European Regional Development Fund. An Introductory Guide*, HMSO, London.

Department of the Environment (DoE) (UK) (1995) *Household Growth: Where Shall We Live?* HMSO, London.

Department of the Environment (DoE) (UK) (1996a) *Indicators of Sustainable Development for the United Kingdom*, HMSO, London.

Department of the Environment (DoE) (UK) (1996b) *Energy efficiency in the printing industry, Energy Efficiency Best Practice Programme, Guide 203*, Department of the Environment, London.

Department of the Environment (DoE) and Department of Transport (DoT) (UK) (1995) *PPG13: A Guide to Better Practice: Reducing the Need to Travel Through Land Use and Transport Planning*, HMSO, London.

Department of the Environment, Food and Rural Affairs (DEFRA) (UK) (2002a) *Annual Report of the Government-Industry Forum on Non-Food Uses of Crops*, Department of the Environment, Food and Rural Affairs, London.

Department of the Environment, Food and Rural Affairs (DEFRA) (UK) (2002b) *Action Plan to Develop Organic Food and Farming in England*, Department of the Environment, Food and Rural Affairs, London.

Department of the Environment, Food and Rural Affairs (DEFRA) (UK) (2002c) *The Strategy for Sustainable Farming and Food: Facing the Future*, Department of the Environment, Food and Rural Affairs, London.

Department of the Environment, Food and Rural Affairs (DEFRA) (UK) (2004a) *Achieving a Better Quality of Life. Review of Progress Towards Sustainable Development: Government Annual Report 2003*, HMSO, London.

Department of the Environment, Food and Rural Affairs (DEFRA) (UK) (2004b) *Quality of Life Counts. Indicators for a Strategy for Sustainable Development for the United Kingdom: 2004 Update*, HMSO, London.

Department of the Environment, Transport and the Regions (DETR) (UK) (1998a) *Transport White Paper*, HMSO, London.

Department of the Environment, Transport and the Regions (DETR) (UK) (1998b) *Planning for Sustainable Development: Towards Better Practice*, HMSO, London.

Department of the Environment, Transport and the Regions (DETR) (UK) (1999a) *Indicators of Climate Change in the UK*, HMSO, London.

Department of the Environment, Transport and the Regions (DETR) (UK) (1999b) *Towards an Urban Renaissance*, HMSO, London.

Department of the Environment, Transport and the Regions (DETR) (UK) (1999c) *Planning Policy Guidance No. 3*, HMSO, London.

Department of the Environment, Transport and the Regions (DETR) (UK) (1999d) *Urban White Paper* (www.regeneration.detr.gov.uk/policies/ourtowns/cm4911/pdf/chap1.pdf).

Department of the Environment, Transport and the Regions (DETR) (UK) (1999e) *A Better Quality of Life: A Strategy for Sustainable Development for the UK*, HMSO, London.

Department of the Environment, Transport and the Regions (DETR) (UK) (1999f) *Quality of Life Counts. Indicators for a Strategy for Sustainable Development for the United Kingdom: A Baseline Assessment*, HMSO, London.

Department of Trade and Industry (DTI) (UK) (1998) *International Statistics on Reuse of Waste*, Department of Trade and Industry, London.

Department of Trade and Industry (DTI) (UK) (2000) *DTI Sustainable Development Strategy*, Department of Trade and Industry, London.

Devas, N and Rakodi, C (1993) *Managing Fast Growing Cities*, Longman, Harlow.

de Waal, L, Large, A and Max Wade, P (eds) (1998) *Rehabilitation of Rivers: Principles and Implementation*, Wiley, Chichester.

Di Castri, F, Baker, F W G and Hadley, M (eds) (1984) *Ecology in Practice, Volume 2: The Social Response*, Tycooly International, Dublin, Ireland.

Dicken, P (2003) *Global Shift: Reshaping the Global Economic Map in the 21st Century*, 4th edition, Sage, London.

Dickens, P (1996) *Reconstructing Nature: Alienation, Emancipation and the Division of Labour*, Routledge, London.

Dincer, I (2000) 'Renewable energy and sustainable development: a crucial review', *Renewable and Sustainable Energy Reviews*, 4(2): 157–75.

Diskin, M (1991) 'Lack of access to land and food in El Salvador', in Whiteford, S and Ferguson, A E (eds) *Harvest of Want: Hunger and Food Security in Central America and Mexico*, Westview, Boulder, CO, pp103–25.

Djoghlaf, A (1994) 'The beginnings of an international climate law', in Mintzer, I and Leonard, J A (eds) *Negotiating Climate Change. The Inside Story of the Rio Convention*, Cambridge University Press, Cambridge, pp97–112.

Doak, J, Stott, M and Therivel, R (1998) 'From SEA to sustainability: A critical review of the life and times of the SERPLAN sustainability panel', *Regional Studies*, 32(1): 73–77.

Dodds, F (ed) (1997) *The Way Forward: Beyond Agenda 21*, Earthscan, London.

Dong, F and Hong, L (2000) 'Clean development mechanism and nuclear energy in China', *Progress in Nuclear Energy*, 37(1–4): 107–11.

Dorling, D (1995) *A New Social Atlas of Britain*, Wiley, Chichester.

Dorling, D and Fairbairn, D (1997) *Mapping: Ways of Representing the World*, Longman, Harlow.

Douglas, I (1983) *The Urban Environment*, Edward Arnold, London.

Dowie, W A, McCartney, D M and Tamm, J A (1998) 'A case study of an institutional solid waste environmental management system', *Journal of Environmental Management*, 53(2): 137–46.

Doyle, T (1998) 'Sustainable development and Agenda 21: the secular bible of global free markets and pluralist democracy', *Third World Quarterly*, 19(4): 771–86.

Drake, F (2000) *Global Warming: The Science of Climate Change*, Arnold, London.

Dréze, J and Sen, A (eds) (1990) *The Political Economy of Hunger* (3 volumes), Clarendon Press, Oxford.

Drummond, I and Marsden, T (1999) *The Condition of Sustainability*, Routledge, London.

Duckers, L (1996) 'Wave energy', in Boyle, G (ed) *Renewable Energy: Power for a Sustainable Future*, Oxford University Press, Oxford, pp315–52.

Dudley, N, Madeley, J and Stolton, S (eds) (1992) *Land is Life: Land Reform and Sustainable Agriculture*, Intermediate Technology Publications, London.

Duerden, F (1992) 'A critical look at sustainable development in the Canadian North', *Arctic*, 45: 219–25.

Dunford, M (1997) 'Divergence, instability and exclusion: regional dynamics in Great Britain', in Lee, R and Wills, J (eds) *Geographies of Economies*, Arnold, London, pp259–77.

Dunne, N (1992) 'US greens lose faith in promises', *Financial Times*, 12 February.

Dunne, N (2002) 'Bush warned on global warming', *Financial Times*, 12 July.

Dunne, T (1997) 'Realism', in Baylis, J and Smith, S (eds) *The Globalization of World Politics*, Oxford University Press, Oxford, pp109–24.

Dutta, S S (2000) 'Partnerships in urban development: a review of Ahmedabad's experience', *Environment and Urbanization*, 12(1): 13–26.

Echenique, M H (1994) 'Urban and regional studies at the Martin Centre: its origins, its present, its future', *Environment and Planning B: Planning and Design*, 21: 517–33.

Eckerberg, K and Forsberg, B (1998) 'Implementing Agenda 21 in local government: the Swedish experience', *Local Environment*, 3(3): 333–47.

Eden, S (1994) 'Using sustainable development: The business case', *Global Environmental Change: Human and Policy Dimensions*, 4(2): 160–67.

Edmonds, J, Pitcher, H M, Barnes, D, Baron, R, and Wise, M A (1991) *Modelling Future Greenhouse Gas Emissions: The Second Generation Model Description*, United Nations University Press, Washington, DC.

Edwards, B (ed) (1998) *Green Buildings Pay*, Spon, London.

Edwards, M and Hulme, D (eds) (1992) *Making a Difference*, Earthscan, London.

Ehrenfeld, J and Gertler, N (1997) 'Industrial ecology in practice: the evolution of interdependence at Kalundborg', *Journal of Industrial Ecology*, 1(1): 83–95.

Eigen, J (1998) 'Sustainable cities and local governance: lessons from a global UN program', in Fernandes, E (ed) *Environmental Strategies for Sustainable Development in Urban Areas*, Ashgate, Aldershot, pp155–62.

Ekins, P (1993) 'Making development sustainable', in Sachs, W (ed) *Global Ecology: A New Arena of Political Conflict*, Zed Books, London, pp91–103.

Ekins, P and Newby, L (1998) 'Sustainable wealth creation at the local level in an age of globalization', *Regional Studies*, 32(9): 863–71.

El-Fadel, M, Findikakis, A N and Leckie, J O (1997) 'Environmental impacts of solid waste landfilling', *Journal of Environmental Management*, 50(1): 1–25.

Elkin, T, McLaren, D, and Hillman, M (1991) *Reviving the City: Towards Sustainable Urban Development*, Friends of the Earth/Policy Studies Institute, London.

Elkington, J (1994) 'Towards the sustainable corporation: win–win–win business strategies for sustainable development', *California Management Review*, 36(2): 90–100.

Elkington, J (1999) *Cannibals with Forks: The Triple Bottom Line of 21st-Century Business*, Capstone, Oxford.

Elliott, D (1996) 'Tidal power', in Boyle, G (ed) *Renewable Energy: Power for a Sustainable Future*, Oxford University Press, Oxford, pp227–66.

Elliott, D (2000) 'Renewable energy and sustainable futures', *Futures*, 32(3–4): 261–74.

Elliott, J A (1999) *An Introduction to Sustainable Development*, 2nd edition, Routledge, London.

ENDS (1999a) 'Applying a biodiversity brake to genetically modified crops', *ENDS Report*, 289: 21–27.

ENDS (1999b) 'Half of pesticides in water may come from "farmyard" sources', *ENDS Report*, 290: 9–10.

ENDS (1999c) 'Pesticide link to genital deformities', *ENDS Report*, 290: 10.

ENDS (1999d) 'Sainsbury's, M & S in "GM-free" retailer consortium,' *ENDS Report*, 290: 33–34.

ENDS (1999e) 'Measuring corporate progress towards sustainability', *ENDS Report*, 296: 21–23.

ENDS (2000a) 'Renewables industry braces itself for "lean and mean" future', *ENDS Report*, 301: 15–19.

ENDS (2000b) 'Labelling, subsidies insufficient to boost energy efficient appliances', *ENDS Report*, 304: 36–37.

ENDS (2000c) 'Building rules to cut home CO_2 emissions by a quarter', *ENDS Report*, 305: 44–45.

ENDS (2002a) 'The Energy Review – make or break time for sustainable energy', *ENDS Report*, 325: 19–23.

ENDS (2002b) 'Progress towards green energy targets stuck in neutral', *ENDS Report*, 331: 11–12.

ENDS (2002c) 'ARBRE biomass plant declared insolvent', *ENDS Report*, 331: 12.

ENDS (2002d) 'Aviation's climate impact soars as RCEP slams airport growth plans', *ENDS Report*, 335: 30–32.

Enmarch-Williams, H (1996) 'Environmental risks and rewards for business: new challenges for the twenty-first century', in Enmarch-Williams, H (ed) *Environmental Risks and Rewards for Business*, Wiley, Chichester, pp119–30.

Environment Agency (2001) *Pollution Incident Report 2000*, HMSO, London.

Espiritu, A (1997) 'Aboriginal nations: natives in northwest Siberia and northern Alberta', in Smith, E A and McCarter, J (eds) *Contested Arctic: Indigenous Peoples, Industrial States, and the Circumpolar Environment*, University of Washington Press, Seattle, WA, pp35–57.

ESRC Global Environmental Change Programme (1999) *The Politics of GM Food: Risk, Science and Public Trust*, Special Briefing No 5, ESRC Global Environmental Change Programme, University of Sussex, Brighton.

Esteva, G (1992) 'Development', in Sachs, W (ed) *The Development Dictionary*, Zed Books, London, pp6–25.

Esty, D C (1994) *Greening the GATT: Trade, Environment and the Future*, Institute for International Economics, Washington, DC.

European Commission (1990) *European Green Paper on the Urban Environment*, Office for Official Publications of the European Community, Luxembourg.

European Commission (1993) *Towards Sustainability: A European Community Programme of Policy and Action in Relation to the Environment and Sustainable Development*, Directorate General for Environment, Nuclear Safety and Civil Protection, Luxembourg.

European Commission (1994) *European Sustainable Cities. Draft Report of an EC Expert Group on the Urban Environment, Sustainable Cities Project*, European Commission, Brussels, Belgium.

European Commission (1997a) *Data Collection on Eco-Industries in the EU in 1994*, Final Report to DGXI and Eurostat, CoECs, Brussels, Belgium.

European Commission (1997b) *Agenda 2000: For a Stronger and Wider Union*, Office for Official Publications of the European Communities, Luxembourg.

European Commission (1998) *Agenda 2000: The Future for European Agriculture*, European Commission, Brussels, Belgium.

European Commission (2002) *Corporate Social Responsibility: A Business Contribution to Sustainable Development*, Office for Official Publications of the European Communities, Luxembourg.

European Conference on Sustainable Cities and Towns (1994) *Charter of European Cities and Towns Towards Sustainability: The Aalborg Charter*, European Commission, Brussels, Belgium.

European Environment Agency (EEA) (1998) *Europe's Environment: The Second Assessment – An Overview*, Office for Official Publications of the European Union, Luxembourg.

European Forum for Renewable Energy Sources (EUFORES) (2000) *The Impact of Renewables on Employment and Economic Growth*, EUFORES Secretariat, Madrid, Spain (www.eufores.org/).

European Union (EU) (1999a) *The Common Agricultural Policy: The Old CAP* (europa. eu.int/en/eupol/oldcapen.htm).

European Union (EU) (2003) *CAP Reform – A Long-Term Perspective for Sustainable Agriculture* (europa.eu.int/comm/agriculture/capreform/index_en.htm).

European Wind Energy Association (EWEA) (1997) *Wind Energy in Europe – The Facts*, European Wind Energy Association, Brussels, Belgium.

Eurostat (1995) *Income in the European Regions*, Office for Official Publications of the European Union, Luxembourg.

Everett, R (1996) 'Solar thermal energy', in Boyle, G (ed) *Renewable Energy: Power for a Sustainable Future*, Oxford University Press, Oxford, pp41–88.

Everett, R and Boyle, G (1996) 'Integration', in Boyle, G (ed) *Renewable Energy: Power for a Sustainable Future*, Oxford University Press, Oxford, pp393–434.

Expert Group on the Urban Environment (1996) *European Sustainable Cities*, Office of Official Publications of the European Communities, Luxembourg.

Farrow, P (2000) 'Merrill to launch £200m green energy fund', *Sunday Telegraph*, 27 August.

Feder, G, Onchan, T, Chalamnong, Y and Hongladarom, C (1988) *Land Policies and Farm Productivity in Thailand*, Johns Hopkins University Press, Baltimore, MD.

Fennell, R (1997) *The Common Agricultural Policy: Continuity and Change*, Clarendon Press, Oxford.

Fernandes, K (1994) 'Katchi abadis: living on the edge', *Environment and Urbanization*, 6(1): 50–58.

Ferris, J, Norman, C and Sempik, J (2001) 'People, land and sustainability: community gardens and the social dimension of sustainable development', *Social Policy and Administration*, 35(5): 559–68.

Fiksel, J (1996) *Design for Environment. Creating Eco-Efficient Products and Processes*, McGraw Hill, New York, NY.

Fine, B (1997) 'Entitlement failure?' *Development and Change*, 28(4): 617–47.

Firey, W (1966) *Man, Mind and the Land: A Theory of Resource Use*, Free Press, Glencoe, IL.

Flaherty, M (1996) 'Meeting the challenge head-on? The World Business Council for Sustainable Development', in Enmarch-Williams, H (ed) *Environmental Risks and Rewards for Business*, Wiley, Chichester, pp113–18.

Flood, J (1997) 'Urban and housing indicators', *Urban Studies*, 34(10): 1635–65.

Flora, C B (1990) 'Sustainability of agriculture and rural communities', in Francis, C A, Flora, C B and King, L D (eds) (1990) *Sustainable Agriculture in Temperate Zones*, Wiley, New York, NY, pp343–60.

Folke, C, Hammer, M, Costanza, R and Jansson, A-M (1994) 'Investing in Natural Capital – why, what and how?' in Jansson, A-M, Hammer, M, Folke, C and Costanza, R (eds) *Investing in Natural Capital: The Ecological Economics Approach to Sustainability*, Island Press, Washington, DC, pp1–21.

Fondahl, G A (1995) 'The status of indigenous peoples in the Russian North', *Post-Soviet Geography*, 36: 215–24.

Fondahl, G A (1998) *Gaining Ground? Evenkis Land and Reform in Southeastern Siberia*, Allyn and Bacon, Toronto, Canada.

Food and Agriculture Organization of the United Nations (FAO) (1997) *Report of the World Food Summit, November 1996*, Food and Agriculture Organization, Rome, Italy.

Food and Agriculture Organization of the United Nations (FAO) (1998a) 'Extensive post-harvest losses prompt a new network to share solutions', *FAO News & Highlights* (www.fao.org/NEWS/1998/980801-e.htm).

Food and Agriculture Organization of the United Nations (FAO) (1998b) *Sustainable Food Security: The Role of the FAO's Sustainable Development Department* (www.fao.org/WAICENT/FAOINF...DEV/FSdirect/FBdirect/FSintro.htm).

Food and Agriculture Organization of the United Nations (FAO) (2002) *Report of the World Food Summit: Five Years Later*, Food and Agriculture Organization, Rome, Italy.

Forsyth, T (1999) *International Investment and Climate Change: Energy Technology for Developing Countries*, Earthscan, London.

Foster, C and Lampkin, N (2000) *Organic and In-Conversion Land Area, Holdings, Livestock and Crop Production in Europe: Final Report*, Welsh Institute of Rural Studies, Aberystwyth.

Francis, C A, Flora, C B and King, L D (eds) (1990) *Sustainable Agriculture in Temperate Zones*, Wiley, New York, NY.

Frank, A G (1969) *Capitalism and Underdevelopment in Latin America: Historical Studies of Chile and Brazil*, Monthly Review Press, New York, NY.

Freeman, H (1999) 'Food for thought for retailers', *Guardian*, 15 May.

French, H F (1997) 'Learning from the ozone experience', in Worldwatch Institute (ed) *The State of the World 1997*, Norton, New York, NY, pp151–71.

French, H F (1998) 'Assessing private capital flows to developing countries', in Worldwatch Institute (ed) *The State of the World 1998*, Norton, New York, NY, pp149–67.

Friends of the Earth Europe (FoE) (1995) *Towards Sustainable Europe: The Study*, Friends of the Earth, Brussels, Belgium.

Friends of the Earth (FoE) (1999) 'Global free trade in forest products?' (www.foe.org/international/wto/forests.html).

Friends of the Earth (FoE) (2000) *Gathering Storm: The Human Costs of Climate Change*, Friends of the Earth, Amsterdam and London.

Fuchs, R J, Brenbma, E, Chamie, J, Lo, F, and Uitto, J (eds) (1994) *Mega-City Growth and the Future*, United Nations University Press, Tokyo, Japan.

Fullerton, D and Wu, W (1998) 'Polices for green design', *Journal of Environmental Economics and Management*, 36(2): 131–48.

Gallagher, E (1997) 'Remarks at BOC Foundation Seminar', Environment Agency, Bristol, February 1997.

Gardner, G (1996) 'Preserving agricultural resources', in Worldwatch Institute (ed) *The State of the World 1996*, Norton, New York, NY, pp78–94.

Gaye, M and Diallo, F (1997) 'Community participation in the management of the urban environment in Rufisque (Senegal)', *Environment and Urbanization*, 9(1): 9–31.

Gaye, M, Diouf, L and Keller, N (2001) 'Moving towards LA21 in Rufisque', *Environment and Urbanization*, 13(2): 201–14.

Geertman, S C M and Ritsema van Eck, J R (1995) 'GIS and models of accessibility potential: an application for planning', *International Journal of Geographical Information Systems*, 9(1): 67–80.

General Agreement on Tariffs and Trade (GATT) (1992) *Trade and Environment*, General Agreement on Tariffs and Trade, Geneva, Switzerland.

Ghai, D and Vivian, J M (eds) (1992) *Grassroots Environmental Action: People's Participation in Sustainable Development*, Routledge, London.

Giaoutzi, M, and Nijkamp, P (1993) *Decision Support Models for Regional Sustainable Development*, Avebury, Aldershot.

Gibbon, P, Havnevik, K J and Hermele, K (1993) *A Blighted Harvest: The World Bank and African Agriculture in the 1980s*, James Currey, London.

Gibbs, D (1994) 'Towards sustainable local development: the UK experience', *International Journal of Sustainable Development and World Ecology*, 1: 121–29.

Gibbs, D (1996) 'Integrating sustainable development and economic restructuring: a role for regulation theory?' *Geoforum*, 27(1): 1–10.

Gibbs, D (1998) 'Regional development agencies and sustainable development', *Regional Studies*, 32(4): 365–68.

Gibbs, D (2002) *Local Economic Development and the Environment*, Routledge, London.

Gibbs, D C, Longhurst, J and Braithwaite, C (1998) ' "Struggling with sustainability": weak and strong interpretations of sustainable development within local authority policy', *Environment and Planning A*, 30(8): 1351–65.

Gibson, C, Ostrom, E and Ahn, T-K (1998) 'Scaling Issues in the Social Sciences', *IHDP Working Paper* 1, International Human Dimensions Programme on Global Environmental Change, Bonn, Germany.

Gilbert, A J, and Braat, L C (eds) (1991) *Modelling for Population and Sustainable Development*, Routledge, London.

Gilbert, R, Stevenson, D, Girardet, H and Stren, R (1996) *Making Cities Work: The Role of Local Authorities in the Urban Environment*, Earthscan, London.

Giles, J (2001) ' "Political fix" saves Kyoto deal from collapse', *Nature*, 412: 365.

Gilpin, R (1987) *The Political Economy of International Relations*, Princeton University Press, Princeton, NJ.

Gippel, C and Fukutome, S (1998) 'Rehabilitation of Japan's waterways', in de Waal,

L, Large, A and Max Wade, P (eds) *Rehabilitation of Rivers: Principles and Implementation*, Wiley, Chichester, pp301–17.

Girardet, H (1992) *The Gaia Atlas of Cities: New Directions for Sustainable Urban Living*, Gaia Books, London.

Gladwin, T N, Kennelly, J J and Krause, T-S (1995) 'Shifting paradigms for sustainable development: implications for management theory and research', *Academy of Management Review*, 20(4): 874–907.

Glaeser, B (ed) (1987) *The Green Revolution Revisited: Critique and Alternatives*, Allen and Unwin, London.

Gold, J R and Burgess, J (eds) (1982) *Valued Environments*, Allen and Unwin, London.

Goldemberg, J (1994) 'The road to Rio', in Mintzer, I and Leonard, J A (eds) *Negotiating Climate Change. The Inside Story of the Rio Convention*, Cambridge University Press, Cambridge, pp175–86.

Goldsmith, E (1999) 'Increasing trade – increasing pollution', *The Ecologist*, 29(2): 176–79.

Goldsmith, Z (1999) 'The Monsanto test', *The Ecologist*, 29(1): 5–8.

Gonçalves, E (2000) 'Heatwave sets fire to Portugal', *Observer*, 26 March.

Goodall, B (1987) *Penguin Dictionary of Human Geography*, Penguin Books, Harmondsworth.

Goodman, D and Watts, M J (eds) (1997) *Globalising Food: Agrarian Questions and Global Restructuring*, Routledge, London.

Goodwin, P (1998) 'Hired hands or local voices: understandings and experience of local participation in conservation', *Transactions of the Institute of British Geographers*, 23(4): 481–99.

Gordon, P and Richardson, H W (1989) 'Gasoline consumption and cities – a reply', *Journal of the American Planning Association*, 55(3): 342–46.

Goss-Custard, J D, Rufino, R and Luis, A (eds) (1997) *Effects of Habitat Loss and Change on Waterbirds: Proceedings of the Tenth International Waterfowl Ecology Symposium*, HMSO, London.

Gottschalk, C M (ed) (1996) *Industrial Energy Conservation*, Wiley, Chichester.

Gove, W, Hughes, M and Galle, O (1979) 'Overcrowding in the home: an empirical investigation of its possible pathological consequences', *American Sociological Review*, 44: 59–80.

Gow, D (2003) 'Five years for green power to prove its worth', *Guardian*, 25 February.

Graham, S (1992) 'Electronic infrastructures and the city: some emerging municipal policy roles in the UK', *Urban Studies*, 29(5): 755–82.

Grainger, A (1993) *Controlling Tropical Deforestation*, Earthscan, London.

Grainger, A (1997) 'Compensating for opportunity costs in forest-based strategies to mitigate global climate change', *Critical Reviews in Environmental Science and Technology*, 27: S163–76.

Gray, W B and Shadbegian, R J (1995) 'Pollution abatement costs, regulation and plant level productivity', *NBER Working Paper* 4994, NBER, Washington, DC.

Green, K, Morton, B and New, S (1996) 'Purchasing and environmental management: interactions, policies and opportunities', *Business Strategy and the Environment*, 5: 188–97.

Greene, O (1997) 'Environmental issues', in Baylis, J and Smith, S (eds) *The Globalization of World Politics*, Oxford University Press, Oxford, pp313–38.

Grigg, D B (1992) *The Transformation of Agriculture in the West*, Blackwell, Oxford.

Grimwade, K, Reid, A and Thompson, L (2000) *Geography and the New Agenda: Citizenship, PSHE and Sustainable Development in the Secondary Curriculum*, Geographical Association, Sheffield.

Groom, B (1998) 'Ageing regional aid policy is feeling the strain', *Financial Times*, 19 October.

Groom, B (1999a) 'Plans for south-east attacked', *Financial Times*, 19 May.

Groom, B (1999b) 'South-west body unveils strategy', *Financial Times*, 22 October.

Groom, B (1999c) 'Regions present plans to unlock potential', *Financial Times*, 26 October.

Groom, B (1999d) 'Warning on flight of jobs from cities', *Financial Times*, 30 November.

Groom, B and Newman, C (2000) 'Prescott rejects regions' cash plea', *Financial Times*, 14 January.

Guardian (2001) 'Tesco sets £1bn target for organics', *Guardian*, 1 November.

Grubb, M, Vrolijk, C and Brack, D (1999) *The Kyoto Protocol: A Guide and Assessment*, Royal Institute of International Affairs and Earthscan, London.

Gugler, J (1988) *The Urbanization of the Third World*, Oxford University Press, Oxford.

Gugler, J (ed) (1996) *The Urban Transformation of the Developing World*, Oxford University Press, Oxford.

Gugler, J (ed) (1997) *Cities in the Developing World*, Oxford University Press, Oxford.

Guha, R (1989) *The Unquiet Woods*, Oxford University Press, Oxford.

Gumbel, A (2001) 'President George W Bush, polluter of the free world', *Independent*, 30 March.

Guy, S (1994) 'Green houses – multiple sites: energy and the cultural dynamics of housebuilding worlds', Paper presented at Conference on Ideal Homes? Towards a Sociology of Domestic Architecture and Interior Design, University of Teesside, September 1994.

Guy, S and Shove, E (2000) *A Sociology of Energy, Buildings and the Environment. Constructing Knowledge, Designing Practice*, Routledge, London.

Haggett, P (2001) *Geography: A Global Synthesis*, Prentice Hall, Harlow.

Haigh, N (1996) 'Climate change policies and politics in the European Community', in O'Riordan, T and Jäger, J (eds) *Politics of Climate Change: A European Perspective*, Routledge, London, pp 155–85.

Hajer, M A (1995) *The Politics of Environmental Discourse. Ecological Modernization and the Policy Process*, Clarendon Press, Oxford.

Hajer, M A (1996) 'Ecological modernisation as cultural politics', in Lash, S, Szerszynski, B and Wynne, B (eds) *Risk, Environment and Modernity: Towards a New Ecology*, Sage, London, pp246–68.

Halberg, N, Kristensen, E S, and Kristensen, I S (1994) *Expected Yield Loss when Converting to Organic Farming in Denmark*, NJF-Sem: Converting to organic agriculture, Finland, March, Special print.

Hall, P (1983) *Growth and Development. An Economic Analysis*, Martin Robertson, Oxford.

Hall, P (1995) 'Towards a general urban theory', in Brotchie, J, Batty, M, Blakely, E, Hall, P and Newton, P (eds) *Cities in Competition*, Longman, Melbourne, Australia, pp3–31.

Hall, P (1996) *Cities of Tomorrow. An Intellectual History of Urban Planning and Design in the Twentieth Century*, revised edition, Blackwell, Oxford.

Hamm, U, Gronefeld F and Halpin, D (2002) *Analysis of the European Market for Organic Food*, School of Management and Business, University of Aberystwyth, Aberystwyth.

Hammond, G P (2000) 'Energy, environment and sustainable development: a UK perspective', *Process Safety and Environmental Protection*, 78(B4): 304–23.

Hampson, F O (1989) 'Climate change: building international coalitions of the like-minded', *International Journal*, 45: 36–74.

Hardin, G (1968) 'The tragedy of the commons', *Science*, 162: 1243–48.

Hardoy, E, Mitlin, D and Satterthwaite, D (1992) 'The future city', in Holmberg, J (ed) *Making Development Sustainable*, Island Press, Washington, DC.

Harpham, T and Werna, E (1996) 'The idea of healthy cities and its application', in Pugh, C (ed) *Sustainability, the Environment and Urbanization*, Earthscan, London, pp63–81.

Harris, B (1968) 'Quantitative models of urban development: their role in metropolitan policy making', in Perloff, H S and Wingo, L (eds) *Issues in Urban Economics*, Johns Hopkins University Press, Baltimore, MD, pp363–412.

Harris, N (1992) *Cities in the 1990s: The Challenge for Developing Countries*, UCL Press, London.

Harrison, M (2001a) 'Climate Change Levy to cost business £100m, engineering industry claims', *Independent*, 15 January.

Harrison, M (2001b) 'Business presses government to scrap climate change tax', *Independent*, 2 April.

Harrison, M (2001c) 'British Energy and Amec plan giant windfarm in Hebrides', *Independent*, 14 December.

Hart, J F (1982) 'The highest form of the geographer's art', *Annals of the Association of American Geographers*, 72: 1–29.

Hart, S L (1995) 'A natural resource-based view of the firm', *Academy of Management Review*, 20(4): 986–1014.

Hartwick, J M (1990) 'National resources, national accounting and economic depreciation', *Journal of Public Economics*, 43: 291–304.

Harvey, D (1973) *Social Justice and the City*, Johns Hopkins University Press, Baltimore, MD.

Harvey, D (1975) 'The geography of capitalist accumulation: a reconstruction of the Marxian theory', *Antipode*, 7: 9–21.

Harvey, D (1982) *The Limits to Capital*, Blackwell, Oxford.

Harvey, D (1985) *The Urbanization of Capital*, Blackwell, Oxford.

Harvey, L D (2000) *Global Warming: The Hard Science*, Pearson, Harlow.

Hasan, A (1992) *Manual for Rehabilitation Programmes for Informal Settlements Based on the Orangi Pilot Project Model*, Orangi Pilot Project: Research and Training Institute, Karachi, Pakistan.

Hasan, A (2002) 'The changing nature of the informal sector in Karachi as a result of global restructuring and liberalization', *Environment and Urbanization*, 14(1): 69–78.

Haughton, G (1999) 'Environmental justice and the sustainable city', *Journal of Planning Education and Research*, 18(3): 233–43.

Haughton, G and Hunter, C (1994) *Sustainable Cities*, Regional Studies Association/Kingsley, London.

Haverkort, B, van der Kamp, J and Waters-Bayer, A (eds) (1991) *Joining Farmers' Experiments*, Intermediate Technology Publications, London.

Hayhoe, K, Jain, A, Pitcher, H, MacCracken, C, Gibbs, M, Wuebbles, D, Harvey, R and Kruger, D (1999) 'Costs of multigreenhouse gas reduction targets for the USA', *Science*, 286(5441): 405–06.

Hecht, S B (1989) 'Indigenous soil management in the Amazon Basin: some implications for development', in Browder, J O (ed) *Fragile Lands of Latin America: Strategies for Sustainable Development*, Westview, Boulder, CO, pp166–81.

Heiman, M K (ed) (1996) 'Special issue: race, waste and class: new perspectives on environmental justice', *Antipode*, 28(2): 111–203.

Hein, L (1993) 'Growth versus success: Japan's economic policy in historical perspective', in Gordon, A (ed) *Postwar Japan as History*, University of California Press, Berkeley, CA, pp99–122.

Held, D and McGrew, A (eds) (2000) *The Global Transformation Reader: An Introduction to the Globalization Debate*, Polity Press, Malden, MA.

Henley, J, Connolly, K and Hartz, M (2001) 'Europe rethinks policies: organic methods on increase', *Guardian*, 28 February.

Herbert, I (1999) 'Asda sets up monthly farm market', *Independent*, 24 May.

Herod, A (1998) 'Of blocs, flows and networks. The end of the Cold War, cyberspace and the geo-economics of organized labour at the *fin de millénaire*', in Herod, A, Tuathail, G and Roberts, S M (eds) *An Unruly World? Globalization, Governance and Geography*, Routledge, London, pp162–95.

Hiemstra, W, Reijntjes, C and der Werf, E (eds) (1992) *Let Farmers Judge*, Intermediate Technology Publications, London.

Hill, C (1992) *Dying of Thirst: A Response to the Problems of Our Vanishing Wetlands*, Royal Society for Nature Conservation, Lincoln.

Hill, J, Marshall, I and Priddey, C (1994) *Benefiting Business and the Environment. Case Studies of Cost Saving and New Opportunities from Environmental Initiatives*, Institute of Business Ethics, London.

Hill, K E (1997) 'Supply-chain dynamics, environmental issues, and manufacturing firms', *Environment and Planning A*, 29(7): 1257–74.

Hillary, R (ed) (1997) *Environmental Management Systems and Cleaner Production*, Wiley, Chichester.

Hillary, R (ed) (2000) *ISO 14001: Case Studies and Practical Experiences*, Stationery Office, Norwich.

Hinchcliffe, F, Thompson, J, Pretty, J, Gujit, I and Shah, P (eds) (1999) *Fertile Ground: The Impacts of Participatory Watershed Management*, Intermediate Technology Publications, London.

Hinchliffe, S (1996) 'Helping the earth begins at home: The social construction of socioeconomic responsibilities', *Global Environmental Change: Human and Policy Dimensions*, 6(1): 53–62.

Hinchliffe, S (1997) 'Locating risk: energy use, the "ideal" home and the non-ideal world', *Transactions of the Institute of British Geographers*, 22: 197–209.

Ho, M-W (1999) *Genetic Engineering: Dream or Nightmare?* 2nd edition, Gateway, Dublin, Ireland.

Hobley, M (1996) *Participatory Forestry: The Process of Change in India and Nepal*, ODI, London.

Holliday, C O, Schmidheiny, S and Watts, P (2002) *Walking the Talk: The Business Case for Sustainable Development*, Greenleaf, Sheffield.

Hollinger, P (1995) 'Councils' fear on opencast coal sites', *Financial Times*, 20 January.

Holmberg, J, Lundqvist, U, Robert, K and Wackernagel, M (1999) 'The ecological footprint from a systems perspective of sustainability', *International Journal of Sustainable Development and World Ecology*, 6: 17–33.

Holmberg, J and Sandbrook, R (1992) 'Sustainable development: what is to be done?' in Holmberg, J (ed) *Making Development Sustainable: Redefining Institutions, Policies and Economics*, Island Press, Washington, DC, pp19–38.

Hordijk, M (1999) 'A dream of green and water: community-based formulation of a Local Agenda 21 in peri-urban Lima', *Environment and Urbanization*, 11(2): 11–29.

Houghton, J T (1994) *Global Warming: The Complete Briefing*, Lion, Oxford.

Houghton, J T, Jenkins, G J and Ephrams J J (eds) (1990) *Climate Change: The IPCC Scientific Assessment*, Cambridge University Press, Cambridge.

Houghton, R A (1993) 'The role of forests in global warming', in Ramakrishna, K and Woodwell, G M (eds) *World Forests for the Future: Their Use and Conservation*, Yale University Press, New Haven, CT, pp21–58.

House of Commons (Canada) (1997) *Canada and the Circumpolar World, Report of the Parliamentary Standing Committee, Department of Foreign Affairs and International Trade*, Supply and Services Canada, Ottawa, Canada.

Howard, S (1998) 'The burning season', *The World Today*, July, pp172–75.

Howes, R, Skea, J and Whelan, B (1997) *Clean and Competitive? Motivating Environmental Performance in Industry*, Earthscan, London.

Huddle, N and Reich, M (1991) *Island of Dreams: Environmental Crisis in Japan*, Autumn Press, New York, NY.

Huggins, R (2000) 'An index of competitiveness in the UK: local, regional and global analysis', *ESRC Social Capital and Economic Performance Project Research Paper* 1, Centre for Advanced Urban Studies, University of Wales, Cardiff.

Humphrey, W S and Stanislaw, J (1979) 'Economic growth and energy consumption in the UK, 1700–1975', *Energy Policy*, 7: 29–42.

Huntington, H P (1992) *Wildlife Management and Subsistence Hunting in Alaska*, Belhaven Press, London.

Hussain, M N (1991) 'Food security and adjustment programmes: the conflict', in Maxwell, S (ed) *To Cure All Hunger. Food Policy and Food Security in Sudan*, Intermediate Technology Publications, London, pp85–113.

Hyder, T O (1994) 'Looking back to see forward', in Mintzer, I and Leonard, J A (eds) *Negotiating Climate Change. The Inside Story of the Rio Convention*, Cambridge University Press, Cambridge, pp201–28.

Ibery, B, Bowler, I, Clark, G, Crockett, A and Shaw, A (1998) 'Farm-based tourism as an alternative farm enterprise: a case study from the Northern Pennines, England', *Regional Studies*, 32(4): 355–64.

Ichikawa, M, Takayama, S, Horiuchi, S and Kayane, I (1980) 'Inland water and water resources in Japan', in Association of Japanese Geographers (ed) *Geography of Japan*, Teikoku Shoin, Tokyo, Japan, pp73–98.

Imhoff, D (1996) 'Community-supported agriculture: Farming with a face on it', in Mander, J and Goldsmith, E (eds) *The Case Against the Global Economy and For a Turn Toward the Local*, Sierra Club Books, San Francisco, CA, pp425–33.

Intergovernmental Panel on Climate Change (IPCC) (1997) *The Regional Impacts of*

Climate Change: An Assessment of Vulnerability, Cambridge University Press, Cambridge.

Intergovernmental Panel on Climate Change (IPCC) (2001a) *Summary for Policymakers: A Report of Working Group I of the Intergovernmental Panel on Climate Change*, Intergovernmental Panel on Climate Change, Geneva, Switzerland.

Intergovernmental Panel on Climate Change (IPCC) (2001b) *Summary for Policymakers: Climate Change 2001: Impacts, Adaptation and Vulnerability*, Intergovernmental Panel on Climate Change, Geneva, Switzerland.

International Council for Local Environmental Initiatives (ICLEI) (1993) *Report of Municipal Leaders Summit on Climate Change and the Urban Environment, New York*, International Council for Local Environmental Initiatives, Toronto, Canada.

International Council for Local Environmental Initiatives (ICLEI) (1995) *The Role of Local Authorities in Sustainable Development: Fourteen Case Studies on the Local Agenda 21 Process*, United Nations Centre for Human Settlements, Nairobi, Kenya.

International Council for Local Environmental Initiatives (ICLEI) (2001) *Local Authorities' Self-Assessment of Local Agenda 21 (LASALA): Accelerating Local Sustainability – Evaluating European Local Agenda 21 Processes*, International Council for Local Environmental Initiatives, Freiburg, Germany.

International Council for Local Environmental Initiatives (ICLEI) (2002*) About the CCP* (www.iclei.org/co2/background.htm).

International Energy Agency (IEA) (2000) *World Energy Outlook 2000*, International Energy Agency, Paris, France.

International Energy Agency (IEA) (2002a) *Dealing with Climate Change. Policies and Measures in IEA Member Countries*, International Energy Agency, Paris, France.

International Energy Agency (IEA) (2002b) *World Energy Outlook 2002*, International Energy Agency, Paris, France.

International Federation of Red Cross and Red Crescent Societies (IFRC) (1999) *World Disasters Report*, International Federation of Red Cross and Red Crescent Societies, Geneva, Switzerland.

International Federation of Red Cross and Red Crescent Societies (IFRC) (2001) 'Post flood recovery in Viet Nam', in International Federation of Red Cross and Red Crescent Societies, *World Disasters Report: Focus on Recovery*, International Federation of Red Cross and Red Crescent Societies, Geneva, Switzerland, pp102–23.

International Union for the Conservation of Nature (IUCN) (1980) *World Conservation Strategy*, International Union for the Conservation of Nature (World Conservation Union), Gland, Switzerland.

International Union for the Conservation of Nature and Natural Resources (IUCN), United Nations Environment Programme (UNEP) and World Wide Fund for Nature (WWF) (1991) *Caring for the Earth: A Strategy for Sustainable Living*, International Union for Conservation of Nature and Natural Resources, Gland, Switzerland.

Ishikawa, T (1999) *Rupo: Nihon no Kawa (Reportage: Rivers of Japan)*, Ryokufū Shuppan, Tokyo, Japan.

Ives, J and Messerli, B (1989) *The Himalayan Dilemma*, United Nations University, London.

Jackson, T and Marks, N (1994) *Measuring Sustainable Economic Welfare: A Pilot Index 1950–1990*, New Economics Foundation, London.

Jackson, T, Begg, K and Parkinson, S (2001) *Flexibility in Climate Policy: Making the Kyoto Mechanisms Work*, Earthscan, London.

Jacobs, M and Stott, M (1992) 'Sustainable development and the local economy', *Local Economy*, 7(3): 261–72.

Jacobsen, B (ed) (2001) *Mapping Health Inequalities Across London*, London Health Observatory, Kings Fund, London.

Jayaraman, K S (1999) 'India intends to reap the full commercial benefits', *Nature*, 420(6760): 342–43.

Jeffery, S (2001) 'Renewable energy', *Guardian*, 14 December.

Johnson, A (1991) *Factory Farming*, Blackwell, Oxford.

Johnston, R J, Taylor, P J and Watts, M J (eds) (2002) *Geographies of Global Change: Remapping the World*, 2nd edition, Blackwell, Oxford.

Jopling, J and Girardet, H (1996) *Creating a Sustainable London*, Sustainable London Trust, London.

Jordan, A and O'Riordan, T (2000) 'Environmental politics and policy processes', in O'Riordan, T (ed) *Environmental Science for Environmental Management*, 2nd edition, Prentice Hall, Harlow, pp63–92.

Jordan, G (2002) 'GIS for community forestry user groups in Nepal: putting people before the technology', in Craig, W J, Harris, T M and Weiner, D (eds) *Community Participation and Geographic Information Systems*, Taylor and Francis, London, pp232–45.

Jowit, J (2004) 'Congestion charging sweeps the world', *Observer*, 15 February.

Jowsey, E and Kellet, J (1996) 'Sustainability and methodologies of environmental assessment for cities', in Pugh, C (ed) *Sustainability, the Environment and Urbanisation*, Earthscan, London.

Jury, L (1998) 'Anger at Monsanto's claim to "Feed the World" ', *Independent*, 25 July.

Jussila, H, Majoral, R and Cullen, B (eds) (2001) *Sustainable Development and Geographical Space: Issues of Population, Environment, Globalization and Education in Marginal Regions*, Ashgate, Aldershot.

Kamal, S (1993) *Situation Analysis of Children and Women in Sindh*, Government of Sindh and UNICEF, Karachi, Pakistan.

Kankyōchō (Environment Agency, Japan) (1996) *Kankyō Hakusho: Megumi Yutaka na Kankyō o Mirai ni Tsunagu Paatonaashippu (Environment White Paper: Partnership Connecting a Beneficent and Bounteous Environment to the Future)*, Government of Japan, Tokyo, Japan.

Kasemir, B, Dahinden, U, Swartling, A G, Schule, R, Tabara, D and Jaeger, C C (2000) 'Citizens' perspectives on climate change and energy use', *Global Environmental Change: Human and Policy Dimensions*, 10(3): 169–84.

Kasperson, R E (1969) 'Environmental stress and the municipal political system', in Kasperson, R E and Minghi, J V (eds) *The Structure of Political Geography*, Aldine, Chicago, IL, pp481–96.

Kassi, N (1987) 'This land has sustained us', *Alternatives*, 14: 20–21.

Kates, R W (1987) 'The human environment: the road not taken, the road still beckoning', *Annals of the Association of American Geographers*, 77(4): 525–34.

Kemp, D and Downer, A (2002) 'Global greenhouse challenge: The way ahead for Australia', Joint Media Release, 15 August, Department of the Environment and Heritage/Department of Foreign Affairs, Canberra, Australia.

Keohane, R (1984) *After Hegemony: Co-operation and Discord in the World Political Economy*, Princeton University Press, Princeton, NJ.

Keohane, R and Nye, J (1977) *Power and Interdependence: World Politics in Transition*, Little Brown, Boston, MA.

Kettle, M (2001) 'Bush wins vote on drilling in Alaska', *Guardian*, 3 August.

Keynes, J M (1923) *A Tract on Monetary Reform*, Macmillan, London.

Kimbrell, A (1998) 'Why biotechnology and high-tech agriculture cannot feed the world', *The Ecologist*, 28(5): 294–98.

King, L D (1990) 'Sustainable soil fertility practices', in Francis, C A, Flora, C B and King, L D (eds) *Sustainable Agriculture in Temperate Zones*, Wiley, New York, NY, pp144–77.

Kingsnorth, P (1999) 'India cheers while Monsanto burns', *Ecologist*, 29(1): 9–10.

Kinnon, F (1997) 'Agricultural co-operatives and sustainable agricultural development', *The World of Co-operative Enterprise 1997*, Plunkett Foundation, Oxford, pp107–20.

Kinsey, B H, (1999) 'Land reform, growth and equity: emerging evidence from Zimbabwe's resettlement programme', *Journal of Southern African Studies*, 25(2): 173–96.

Kiya, F, Nakamura, Y and Ishikawa, T (1992) *Toshi o Meguru Mizu no Hanashi (Talking About Water as it Relates to Cities)*, Inoue Shoin, Tokyo, Japan.

Klass, D L (1998) *Biomass for Renewable Energy, Fuels and Chemicals*, Academic, London.

Klein, N (2000) *No Logo*, Flamingo, London.

Klosterman, R E (1994a) 'Large-scale urban models: retrospect and prospect', *Journal of the American Planning Association*, 60(1): 3–6.

Klosterman, R E (1994b) 'An introduction to the literature on large-scale urban models', *Journal of the American Planning Association*, 60(1): 17–29.

Knight, J (1998) 'Tourist forests in Japan or re-commoditizing the Japanese forest', Paper presented at International Convention of Asian Scholars Conference, Noordwijkerhout, The Netherlands, 25–28 June.

Knox, P L and Agnew, J (1998) *The Geography of the World Economy: An Introduction to Economic Geography*, 3rd edition, Arnold, London.

Knox, P L and Pinch, S (2000) *Urban Social Geography: An Introduction*, 4th edition, Prentice Hall, Harlow.

Korn, M (1996) 'The dike-pond concept: sustainable agriculture and nutrient recycling in China', *Ambio*, 25(1): 6–13.

Kovats, R S, Menne, B, McMichael, A J, Corvalan, C and Bertollini, R (2000) *Climate Change and Human Health: Impact and Adaptation*, World Health Organization, Geneva, Switzerland.

Kraak, M J and Ormeling, F J (1996) *Cartography: Visualization of Spatial Data*, Longman, Harlow.

Krebs, J R, Wilson, J D, Bradbury, R B and Siriwardene, G M (1999) 'The second silent spring?' *Nature*, 400(6745): 611–12.

Krishna, A, Uphoff, N and Esman, M (eds) (1997) *Reasons for Hope: Instructive Experiences in Rural Development*, Kumarian Press, West Hartford, CT.

Lacey, R (1998) *Poison on a Plate: The Dangers in the Food We Eat – And How to Avoid Them*, Metro, London.

LaDeau, S L and Clark, J S (2001) 'Rising carbon dioxide levels and the fecundity of forest trees', *Science*, 292(5514): 95–98.

Lam, P (1999) *Green Politics in Japan*, Routledge, London.

Lamb, C (1992) 'Forest set fire to world passions', *Financial Times*, 15 June.

Lampkin, N (1992) *Organic Farming*, Farming Press, Ipswich.

Landes, D S (1969) *The Unbound Prometheus: Technological Change and Industrial Development in Western Europe from 1750 to the Present*, Cambridge University Press, Cambridge.

Lappé, M and Bailey, B (1998) *Against the Grain. Biotechnology and the Corporate Takeover of Your Food*, Common Courage Press, Monroe, ME.

Lari, Y (1996) *Karachi Handbook*, Heritage Foundation, Karachi, Pakistan.

Larsen, P (1996) 'Restoration of river corridors: The German experience', in Petts, G and Calow, P (eds) *River Restoration*, Blackwell, Oxford, pp124–37.

Lascelles, D (1995) 'Swamped by a sea of public anger', *Financial Times*, 22 June.

Lascelles, D and Lamb, C (1992a) 'Protection of biodiversity sparks Rio controversy', *Financial Times*, 8 June.

Lascelles, D and Lamb, C (1992b) 'A game of missed opportunities', *Financial Times*, 15 June.

LaTouche, S (1993) *In the Wake of the Affluent Society: An Exploration of Post-Development*, Zed Books, London.

Leach, M and Mearns, R (eds) (1996) *The Lie of the Land*, Heinemann and James Currey, London.

Lee, D B (1973) 'Requiem for large-scale urban models', *Journal of the American Institute of Planners*, 39(3): 163–78.

Lee, D B (1994) 'Retrospective on large-scale urban models', *Journal of the American Planning Association*, 60(1): 35–40.

Lee, R (1996) 'Moral money? LETS and the social construction of local economic geographies in Southeast England', *Environment and Planning A*, 28(8): 1377–94.

Leeds City Council (2000) *Leeds Local Agenda 21: Draft Strategy Statement and Action Plan*, Leeds City Council, Leeds.

Left, S (2002) 'Organic farming', *Guardian*, 30 July.

Lenssen, N and Roodman, D M (1995) 'Making better buildings', in Worldwatch Institute (ed) *State of the World 1995*, Norton, New York, NY, pp95–112.

Levermore, G J (1992) *Building Energy Management Systems: An Application to Heating and Control*, Spon, London.

Levett, R (1998) 'Rediscovering the public realm', *Town and Country Planning*, 67(1): 11–14.

Likeman, M J, Field, S R, Stevens, I M and Fleming, S E (1995) 'Applications of resource technology in Yorkshire', in Black, A R and Johnson, R C (eds) *Proceedings of the 5th National Hydrology Symposium*, Institute of Hydrology, Wallingford.

Lindzen, R S (1997) 'Can increasing carbon dioxide cause climate change?' *Proceedings of the National Academy of Sciences of the United States of America*, 94: 8335–42

Linhoff, B, Townsend, D W, Boland, D, Hewitt, G F, Thomas, B E A, Guy, A R and Marsland, R H (1994) *A User Guide on Process Integration for the Efficient Use of Energy*, revised edition, Institute of Chemical Engineers, Rugby.

Lipton, M (1989) *New Seeds and Poor People*, Unwin Hyman, London.

Liverman, D M (1999) 'Geography and the global environment', *Annals of the Association of American Geographers*, 89(1): 107–20.

Lytton-Hitchens, J A, Koppi, A J and McBratney, A B (1994) 'The soil condition of adjacent bio-dynamic and conventionally managed dairy pastures in Victoria, Australia', *Soil Use and Management*, 10: 79–87.

Local Government Management Board (LGMB) (1994a) *Sustainability Indicators Research Project. Report of Phase One*, Local Government Management Board, Luton.

Local Government Management Board (LGMB) (1994b) *Local Agenda 21 Principles and Process. A Step by Step Guide*, Local Government Management Board, Luton.

Local Government Management Board (LGMB) (1995) *Sustainability Indicators Research Project: Consultants' Report of the Pilot Phase*, Local Government Management Board, Luton.

Lock, D (1999) 'Not an election winner', *Town and Country Planning*, 68(8/9): 258–60.

Lockeretz, W, Shearer, G, Kohl, D H and Klepper, G (1984) 'Comparison of organic and conventional farming in the corn belt', *American Society of Agronomy Special Publication*, 46: 37–49.

Lopez Follegatti, J L (1999) 'Ilo: a city in transformation', *Environment and Urbanization*, 11(2): 181–202.

Low, N, Gleeson, B, Elander, I and Lidskog, R (2000) *Consuming Cities: The Urban Environment in the Global Economy after the Rio Declaration*, Routledge, London.

Lowry, I S (1964) *A Model of Metropolis, RM-4035-RC*, Rand Corporation, Santa Monica, CA.

LT Consultants (1999) *SPARTACUS: System for Planning and Research in Towns and Cities for Urban Sustainability – Summary of Final Report to CEC DGXII*, LT Consultants, Helsinki, Finland.

Lu, Y C, Daughtry, C, Hart, G and Watkins, B (1997) 'The current state of precision farming', *Food Reviews International*, 13(2): 141–62.

Lutz, W (ed) (1994) *Population, Development, Environment: Understanding their Interactions in Mauritius*, Springer-Verlag, Berlin, Germany.

Macalister, T (2001a) 'Clean energy rush: Money to be made looking after the environment?' *Guardian*, 13 June.

Macalister, T (2001b) 'New economy: Shell's $1bn green energy plan pleases campaigners', *Guardian*, 15 June.

MacDonald, R (2001) 'Climate change will affect UK health', *British Medical Journal*, 322(7283): 386.

Macilwain, C (1999) 'Access issues may determine whether agri-biotech will help the world's poor', *Nature*, 420(6760): 341–45.

Macnaghten, P and Jacobs, M (1997) 'Public identification with sustainable development: investigating cultural barriers to participation', *Global Environmental Change: Human and Policy Dimensions*, 7(1): 5–24.

Macrae, J and Zwi, J (eds) (1994) *War and Hunger: Rethinking International Responses to Complex Emergencies*, Zed Books, London.

Madden, J P (1990) 'The economics of sustainable low-input farming systems', in Francis, C A, Flora, C B and King, L D (eds) *Sustainable Agriculture in Temperate Zones*, Wiley, New York, NY, pp 315–42.

Mallet, V (1992) 'South prepares common stance for Rio Summit', *Financial Times*, 30 April.

Maltby, E (1986) *Waterlogged Wealth. Why Waste the World's Wet Places?* Earthscan, London.

Maltby, E, Immirzi, C P and McLaren, D P (1992) *Do Not Disturb! Peatbogs and the Greenhouse Effect: A Synthesis of the Case and Recommendations for Action*, Friends of the Earth, London.

Mander, J and Goldsmith, E (eds) (2001) *The Case Against the Global Economy and For a Turn Toward Localization*, 2nd edition, Earthscan, London.

March, P A and Fisher, R K (1999) 'It's not easy being green: environmental technologies enhance conventional hydropower's role in sustainable development', *Annual Review of Energy and the Environment*, 24: 173–88.

Marcil, A G (1992) 'Environmentally friendly development: Can the private sector succeed where others have failed?' *Columbia Journal of World Business*, 27(3/4): 194–200.

Markandya, A and Halsnaes, K (eds) (2002) *Climate Change and Sustainable Development. Prospects for Developing Countries*, Earthscan, London.

Markusen, A (1996) 'Sticky places in slippery space: A typology of industrial districts', *Economic Geography*, 72: 293–313.

Marsh, J S (1998) *A Review of the Role of Agriculture, Horticulture and Forestry in the UK Economy*, Department of Trade and Industry Foresight Publications (www.foresight.gov.uk/documents/fsza00003/fsza000032.html#toc_1).

Martens, P, Kovats, R S, Nijhof, S, de Vries, P, Livermore, M T J, Bradley, D J, Cox, J and McMichael, A J (1999) 'Climate change and future populations at risk of malaria', *Global Environmental Change: Human and Policy Dimensions*, 9 (Supplement): S89–107.

Martens, W J M and Martens, P (1998) *Health and Climate Change: Modelling the Impacts of Global Warming and Ozone Depletion*, Earthscan, London.

Martens, W J M, Slooff, R and Jackson, E K (1997) 'Climate change, human health and sustainable development', *Bulletin of the World Health Organization* 75(6): 583–88.

Martin, C (1978) *Keepers of the Game*, University of California Press, Berkeley, CA.

Martin, R (1994) 'Stateless monies, global financial integration and national economic autonomy: the end of geography?' in Corbridge, S, Martin, R and Thrift, N (eds) *Money, Power and Space*, Blackwell, Oxford, pp253–78.

Masood, E (1999) 'Collapse of talks on safety of GMO trade', *Nature*, 398(6722): 6.

Massey, D (2001) 'Geography on the agenda', *Progress in Human Geography*, 25(1): 5–17.

May, A D, Mitchell, G and Kupiszewska, D (1996) *The Quantifiable City: The Development of a Modelling Framework for Urban Sustainability Research*, European Union Council on Science and Technology Urban Civil Engineering C4 Workshop, Information Systems and Processes for Civil Engineering Applications, Rome, Italy.

Mayr, E (1982) *The Growth of Biological Thought: Diversity, Evolution and Inheritance*, Belknap Press, Cambridge, MA.

McAfee, K (1999) 'Selling nature to save it? Biodiversity and green developmentalism', *Environment and Planning D: Society and Space*, 17(2): 133–54.

McAuslan, P (1985) *Urban Land and Shelter for the Poor*, Earthscan, London.

McCarthy, M (2000) 'Treaty will give nations the right to block GM foods', *Independent*, 29 January.

McCarthy, O, Briscoe, R and Ward, M (2001) 'Mutuality through credit unions: a cross-national approach', in Birchall, J (ed) *The New Mutualism in Public Policy*, Routledge, London, pp41–59.

McComas, C (1995) 'Controlling purchasing and inventory to reduce waste', *Pollution Prevention Review*, 5: 27–38.

McCormack, G (1996) *The Emptiness of Japanese Affluence*, Sharpe, New York, NY.

McCormack, G (2001) 'Breaking the iron triangle', *New Left Review*, 13: 5–23.

McCormick, J (1997) *Acid Earth: The Politics of Acid Pollution*, 3rd edition, Earthscan, London.

McEvoy, D, Gibbs, D C and Longhurst, J W S (2000a) 'The employment implications of a low-carbon economy', *Sustainable Development*, 8(1): 27–38.

McEvoy, D, Gibbs, D C and Longhurst, J W S (2000b) 'City-regions and the development of sustainable energy supply systems', *International Journal of Energy Research*, 24(3): 215–37.

McGee, T G (1994) 'Labour force change and mobility in the extended metropolitan regions of Asia', in Fuchs, R J, Brenbma, E, Chamie, J, Lo, F, and Uitto, J (eds) *Mega-City Growth and the Future*, United Nations University Press, Tokyo, Japan, pp 62–102.

McGranahan, D (1993) 'Household environmental problems in low income cities: An overview of problems and prospects for improvement', *Habitat International*, 17: 105–121.

McGranahan, G, Songsore, J and Kjellen, M (1996) 'Sustainability, poverty and urban environmental transitions', in Pugh, C (ed) *Sustainability, the Environment and Urbanization*, Earthscan, London, pp 103–34.

McKean, M (1980) *Environmental Protest and Citizen Politics*, University of California Press, Berkeley, CA.

McManus, P (2000) 'Sustainable development', in Johnston, R J, Gregory, D, Pratt, G and Watts, M (eds) *The Dictionary of Human Geography*, 4th edition, Blackwell, Oxford, pp 812–16.

McMichael, A J (2001) 'Health consequences of global climate change', *Journal of the Royal Society of Medicine*, 94(3): 111–14.

McTaggart, W D (1993) 'Bio-regionalism and regional geography: place, people and networks', *Canadian Geographer*, 37: 307–19.

Meacher, M (2000) 'This is the world's chance to tackle global warming', *Sunday Times*, 3 September.

Meadows, D H, Meadows, D L, Randers, J, Behrens III, W W (1972) *The Limits to Growth: A Report for the Club of Rome's Project on the Predicament of Mankind*, Universe Books, New York, NY.

Meadows, D H, Meadows, D L, Randers, J (1992) *Beyond the Limits*, Earthscan, London.

Meckler, M (ed) (1994) *Retrofitting of Buildings for Energy Conservation*, Fairmont Ross, Englewood Cliffs, NJ.

Meeker-Lowry, S (1996) 'Community money. The potential of local currency', in Mander, J and Goldsmith, E (eds) *The Case Against the Global Economy and For a Turn Toward the Local*, Sierra Club Books, San Francisco, CA, pp446–59.

Meldrum, A (2002) 'The real victims of land seizures', *Guardian*, 18 September.

Menotti, V and Sobhani, L (1999) 'Globalisation and climate change', *The Ecologist*, 29(2): 178.

Merritt, J Q (1998) 'EMS into SME won't go? Attitudes, awareness and practices in the London Borough of Croydon', *Business Strategy and the Environment*, 7(2): 90–100.

Metz, B, Davidson, O, Swart, R and Pan, J (eds) (2001) *Climate Change 2001: Mitigation*, Cambridge University Press, Cambridge.

Michaels, P (1998) 'Long hot year: latest science debunks global warming hysteria', *Cato Policy Analysis Paper* 329, Cato Institute, Washington, DC.

Middleton, N, O'Keefe, P and Moyo, S (1993) *The Tears of the Crocodile: From Rio to Reality in the Developing World*, Pluto Press, London.

Middleton, N and Thomas, D (1997) *World Atlas of Desertification*, 2nd edition, Arnold, London.

Midmore, P and Lampkin, N H (1994) 'Modelling the impact of widespread conversion to organic farming: an overview', in Lampkin, N H and Padel, S (eds) *The Economics of Organic Farming: An International Perspective*, CAB International, Wallingford, pp371–80.

Mincer, J (1958) 'Investment in Human Capital and personal income distribution', *Journal of Political Economy*, 66: 281–302.

Ministry of Agriculture, Fisheries and Food (MAFF) (UK) (1998) *Alternative Crops Unit. United Kingdom Government Policy on Renewable Raw Materials for Industry and Energy* (www.maff.gov.uk/farm/acu/acu.htm).

Ministry of Agriculture, Fisheries and Food (MAFF) (UK) (2000) *England Rural Development Programme: Scheme Details* (www.maff.gov.uk/erdp/guidance/guidanceindex.htm).

Ministry of Environment, Urban Affairs, Forestry and Wildlife (Pakistan) (1996) *Pakistan National Report: Habitat II*, Ministry of Environment, Urban Affairs, Forestry and Wildlife, Islamabad, Pakistan.

Ministry of Indian Affairs and Northern Development and the Tungavik (Canada) (1993) *Nunavut Land Claims Agreement*, Ministry of Indian Affairs and Northern Development, Ottawa, Canada.

Mintzer, I and Leonard, J A (1994) 'Visions of a changing world', in Mintzer, I and Leonard, J A (eds) *Negotiating Climate Change: The Inside Story of the Rio Convention*, Cambridge University Press, Cambridge, pp3–44.

Mishan, E J (1967) *The Costs of Economic Growth*, Penguin, Harmondsworth.

Misra, R P (1972) 'Growth poles and growth centres in the context of India's urban and regional development', in Kuklinski, A (ed) *Growth Poles and Growth Centres in Regional Planning*, Mouton, The Hague, The Netherlands, pp141–68.

Mitchell, G (1996) 'Problems and fundamentals of sustainable development indicators', *Sustainable Development*, 4(1): 1–11.

Mitchell, G (1999a) 'Planning, environmental assessment, and catchment management: UK experiences in the sustainable development of land and water', *Urbanistica*, 112: 87–95.

Mitchell, G (1999b) 'Demand forecasting as a tool for the sustainable development of water resources', *International Journal of Sustainable Development and World Ecology*, 6: 231–41.

Mitchell, G (1999c) 'The long-term impact of waste minimisation', *The Demand Management Bulletin*, 37: 5.

Mitchell, G, May, A D and McDonald, A T (1995) 'PICABUE: a methodological framework for the development of indicators of sustainable development', *International Journal of Sustainable Development and World Ecology*, 2: 104–23.

Mitchell, G, Namdeo, A and Kay, D (2000) 'A new disease-burden method for estimating the impact of outdoor air quality on human health', *Science of the Total Environment*, 246(2–3): 153–63.

Mitchell, G and Vreeker, R (1999) *Decision Support for Sustainable Urban Development: A Proposed Framework for the BEQUEST Information System*, Unpublished report developed from the Built Environment Quality Evaluation for Sustainability through Time network meeting, Helsinki, Finland, September 1999.

Mitchell, J T, Thomas, D S K and Cutter, S L (1999) 'Dumping in Dixie revisited: the evolution of environmental injustices in South Carolina', *Social Science Quarterly*, 80(2): 229–43.

Miyamura, T (1989) *Kurashi ni Ikiru Kawa (Rivers in our Lives)*, Nōsangyoson Kyōkai, Tokyo, Japan.

Moctezuma, P (2001) 'Community-based organization and participatory planning in south-east Mexico City', *Environment and Urbanization*, 13(2): 117–33.

Moffatt, I (1996) 'An evaluation of Environmental Space as the basis for sustainable Europe', *International Journal of Sustainable Development and World Ecology*, 3: 49–69.

Moffatt, I (1997) *Sustainable Development: Principles, Analysis and Policies*, Parthenon, London.

Moffatt, I, Hanley, N and Gill, J P S (1994) 'Measuring and assessing indicators of sustainable development for Scotland', *International Journal of Sustainable Development and World Ecology*, 1: 170–77.

Moffatt, I and Wilson, M D (1994) 'An index of sustainable economic welfare for Scotland, 1980–1991', *International Journal of Sustainable Development and World Ecology*, 1(4): 264–91.

Mohan, G and Stokke, K (2000) 'Participatory democracy and empowerment: the dangers of localism', *Third World Quarterly*, 21(2): 247–68.

Monsanto (1998) *Biotech in the News* (www.monsanto.co.uk/).

Moock, J L and Rhoades, R E (eds) (1992) *Diversity, Farmer Knowledge and Sustainability*, Cornell University Press, Ithaca, NY.

Morgan, K (1997) 'The learning region: institutions, innovations and regional renewal', *Regional Studies*, 31(5): 491–503.

Mori, S (1995) 'Yokohama de no tonbo-ike-zukuri senryaku' (Strategies in Yokohama for making dragonfly ponds), *Konchū to Shizen (Insects and Nature)*, 30(8): 24–29.

Morris, J (ed) (1997) *Climate Change: Challenging the Conventional Wisdom*, Institute of Economic Affairs, London.

Mortished, C (1997) 'Beleaguered Shell takes on human rights', *The Times*, 17 March.

Moyo, S (2000) 'The political economy of land acquisition and redistribution in Zimbabwe, 1990–1999', *Journal of Southern African Studies*, 26(1): 5–28.

Mulvihill, P R and Jacobs, P (1991) 'Towards new south/north development strategies in Canada', *Alternatives*, 10: 34–39.

Murdoch, J (2000) 'Space against time: competing rationalities in planning for housing', *Transactions of the Institute of British Geographers*, 25(4): 503–19.

Murphy, J and Gouldson, A (2000) 'Environmental policy and industrial innovation: integrating environment and economy through ecological modernisation', *Geoforum*, 31: 33–44.

Murray, A (1999) 'US warns Europe of trade war over GM food', *The Times*, 12 August.

Myers, H (1996) 'Neither boom nor bust', *Alternatives*, 22: 18–23.

Myers, N (1997) 'Consumption: challenge to sustainable development', *Science*, 276(5309): 53–57.

Nagpaul, H (1988) 'India's giant cities', in Dogan, M and Kasarda, J D (eds) *The Metropolis Era. Volume 1: A World of Giant Cities*, Sage, Newbury Park, CA, pp252–90.

Namdeo, A K and Colls, J (1994) 'ROADFAC: A Computer Program to Calculate Automobile Emissions for UK Roads', Paper to the 3rd International Symposium on Transport and Air Pollution, Avignon, France, June 1994.

Namdeo, A K, Dixon, R K, Mitchell, G, May, A D and Kay, D (1999) 'Development and application of TEMMS: A suite of programs for modelling and mapping of urban traffic emissions', in *Proceedings of the Annual Conference of the Air and Waste Management Association*, St Louis, MO.

National Farmers' Union (NFU) (1995) *Organophosphate Sheep Dips and Human Health*, National Farmers' Union, London.

National Institute of Agricultural Botany (NIAB) (2002) *Monitoring Large-Scale Releases of Genetically Modified Crops*, Department of the Environment, Food and Rural Affairs, London.

Nature (1999) 'One third of population will go thirsty by 2025, says UN report', *Nature*, 398: 278.

Ndoine, E, De Leener, P, Ndiaya, M, Jacolin, P and Perier, J-P (1995) *The Future of Community Lands and Human Resources*, Intermediate Technology Publications, London.

Nelson, N and Wright, S (eds) (1995) *Power and Participatory Development*, Intermediate Technology Publications, London.

Neto, R B (1999a) '. . . as Brazilian scientists protest at GM ban', *Nature*, 400(6744): 495.

Neto, R B (1999b) 'Smugglers aim to circumvent GM court ban in Brazil', *Nature*, 420(6760): 344–45.

Neumann, R P (1995) 'Local challenges to global agendas: conservation, economic liberalization and the pastoralists' rights movement in Tanzania', *Antipode*, 27(4): 363–82.

New, S, Green, K and Morton, B (2000) 'Buying the environment: the multiple meanings of green supply', in Fineman, S (ed) *The Business of Greening*, Routledge, London, pp35–53.

New Agriculturalist (1998a) 'Water supply: the world's next challenge', *New Agriculturalist On-Line* 98-3 (www.new-agri.co.uk/98-3/debate.html).

New Agriculturalist (1998b) 'Focus on agroforestry', *New Agriculturalist On-Line* 98-3 (www.new-agri.co.uk/98-3/focuson.html).

New Agriculturalist (1998c) 'Perspective on Bangladesh', *New Agriculturalist On-Line* 98-5 (www.new-agri.co.uk/98-5/perspect.html).

New Scientist (1992a) 'Third World fends off controls on forests', *New Scientist*, 20 June, p5.

New Scientist (1992b) 'Oil producers campaign against carbon cuts', *New Scientist*, 20 June, p7.

Newson, M (1997) *Land, Water and Development: Sustainable Management of River Basin Systems*, Routledge, London.

Newton, T and Harte, G (1997) 'Green business: technicist kitsch?' *Journal of Management Studies*, 34(1): 75–98.

New Urban News (2002) *New Urban News* (www.newurbannews.com/whatsnew.html).

Nicholson, M (2000) 'Inverness takes the high-tech road', *Financial Times*, 7 March.

Nienhuis, P, Leuven, R and Ragas, A (eds) (1998) *New Concepts for Sustainable Management of River Basins*, Backhuys, Leiden, The Netherlands.

Niesewand, N (2000) 'Wind beneath the wings', *Independent*, 7 February.

Nihon Damu Kyōkai (undated) *Nihon Damu Kyōkai* (Japan Dam Foundation) (www.soc.nacsis.ac.jp/jdf).

Nijkamp, P and Perrels, A (1994) *Sustainable Cities in Europe: A Comparative Analysis of Urban-Energy Environmental Policies*, Earthscan, London.

Nitze, W A (1994) 'A failure of presidential leadership', in Mintzer, I and Leonard, J A (eds) *Negotiating Climate Change. The Inside Story of the Rio Convention*, Cambridge University Press, Cambridge, pp187–200.

Niu, W, Lu, J and Khan, A (1993) 'Spatial systems approach to sustainable development: a conceptual framework', *Environmental Management*, 17: 179–86.

Norberg-Hodge, H (1998) 'Think global – eat local! Delicious ways to counter globalization', *The Ecologist*, 28(4): 208–13.

Nordhaus, W D (2001) 'Climate change: Global warming economics', *Science*, 294(5545): 1283–84.

Norton, C (2000) 'Organic food "is a waste of money"', *Independent*, 2 September.

Nuffield Council on Bioethics (1999) *Genetically Modified Crops: The Ethical and Social Issues*, Nuffield Foundation, London.

Nuttall, N (1999a) 'Scientists give rice a vitamin supplement', *The Times*, 5 August.

Nuttall, N (1999b) 'Healthy growth for farm produce markets', *The Times*, 16 August.

Oakley, P (1991) *Projects with People: The Practice of Participation in Rural Development*, International Labour Organization, Geneva, Switzerland.

O'Connor, M (ed) (1994) *Is Capitalism Sustainable? Political Economy and the Politics of Ecology*, Guildford Press, New York, NY.

Ogley, R C (1994) 'International relations', in Outhwaite, W, Bottomore, T, Gellner, E, Nisbet, R and Touraine, N (eds) *The Blackwell Dictionary of Twentieth-Century Social Thought*, Blackwell, Oxford, pp295–97.

Ohlsson, L (ed) (1995) *Hydropolitics: Conflicts Over Water as a Development Constraint*, Earthscan, London.

Ohmae, K (1993) 'Rise of the region state', *Foreign Affairs*, 72(2): 78–87.

Ohmae, K (1995) *The End of the Nation State: The Rise of Regional Economies*, Free Press, New York, NY.

Okoji, M A and Moses, J (1998) 'Adoption of agroforestry for soil conservation in Akwa Iban State, Nigeria', *Journal of Sustainable Agriculture*, 13(1): 5–13.

Ōkuma, T (1988) *Kōzui to Chisui no Kawa Shi: Suigai no Seiatsu Kara Juyō e (A River History of Flooding and Water Control: From Suppression to Absorption of Flood Damage)*, Heibonsha, Tokyo, Japan.

O'Neill, B C, MacKellar, F L and Lutz, W (2001) *Population and Climate Change*, Cambridge University Press, New York, NY.

Ontario Institute for Studies in Education (2002) *IIGE Partnership: Brazil*, Ontario Institute for Studies in Education, University of Toronto (www.oise.utoronto.ca/iige/partnerships/brazil.htm).

Oregon Concerned Citizens for Safe Foods (2002) 'Give Oregon a Choice! Label Genetically Engineered Foods', Oregon Concerned Citizens for Safe Food (www.labelgefoods.org/).

Organic Centre Wales (2002) 'Certified and Policy-Supported Organic and In Conversion Land Area in Europe', Organic Centre Wales, University of Aberystwyth (www.organic.aber.ac.uk/statistics/euroarea.htm).

Organization for Economic Co-operation and Development (OECD) (1975) *The Polluter Pays Principle*, Organization for Economic Co-operation and Development, Paris, France.

Organization for Economic Co-operation and Development (OECD) (1977) *Environmental Policies in Japan*, OECD Publications, Paris, France.

Organization for Economic Co-operation and Development (OECD) (1994) *Environmental Performance Review: Japan*, OECD Publications, Paris, France.

O'Riordan, T, Cooper, C L, Jordan, A, Rayner, S, Richards, K R, Runci, P and Yoffe, S (1998) 'Institutional frameworks for political action', in Rayner, S and Malone, E L (eds) (1998) *Human Choice and Climate Change*, Battelle Press, Columbus, OH, pp345–439.

O'Riordan, T and Rowbotham, E J (1996) 'Struggling for credibility: the United Kingdom's response', in O'Riordan, T and Jäger, J (eds) *Politics of Climate Change: A European Perspective*, Routledge, London, pp228–67.

Ōsawa, K (1999) 'Tsurumigawa Ryūiki Nettowaakingu no Ryūiki Katsudō to Sono Shikumi' (Tsurumi River Basin Network Activities and Their Design), *Kasen (Rivers)*, May, pp 33–38.

Osborn, A (2002a) 'Tough European line on GM labelling', *Guardian*, 4 July.

Osborn, A (2002b) 'New EU rules to end ban on GM food', *Guardian*, 17 October.

Osborn, D and Bigg, T (1998) *Earth Summit II: Outcomes and Analysis*, Earthscan, London.

Ostrom, E (1990) *Governing the Commons: Evaluation of Institutions for Collective Action*, Cambridge University Press, Cambridge.

Owens, S (1986) *Energy, Planning and Urban Form*, Pion, London.

Owens, S and Cowell, R (2001) *Land and Limits. Interpreting Sustainability in the Planning Process*, Routledge, London.

Oxfam (1998) 'The real crisis in East Asia', *Oxfam International Press Briefing* (www.oxfam.org.uk/whatnew/features/equityapr98.htm).

Pacione, M (ed) (1999a) *Applied Geography: Principles and Practice. An Introduction to Useful Research in Physical, Environmental and Human Geography*, Routledge, London.

Pacione, M (1999b) 'The geography of poverty and deprivation', in Pacione, M (ed) *Applied Geography: Principles and Practice. An Introduction to Useful Research in Physical, Environmental and Human Geography*, Routledge, London, pp400–13.

Pacione, M (2001) *Urban Geography: A Global Perspective*, Routledge, London.

Padoch, C and de Jong, W (1989) 'Production and profit in agroforestry: an example from the Peruvian Amazon', in Browder, J O (ed) *Fragile Lands of Latin America: Strategies for Sustainable Development*, Westview, Boulder, CO, pp102–13.

Pain, D and Pienkowski, M W (eds) (1997) *Farming and Birds in Europe: The Common Agricultural Policy and its Implications for Bird Conservation*, Academic Press, London.

Parker, C and Pascual, A (2002) 'A voice that could not be ignored: community GIS and gentrification battles in San Francisco', in Craig, W J, Harris, T M and Weiner, D (eds) *Community Participation and Geographic Information Systems*, Taylor and Francis, London, pp55–64.

Parry, M, Arnell, N, Hulme, M, Nicholls, R and Livermore, M (1998) 'Buenos Aires and Kyoto targets do little to reduce climate change impacts', *Global Environmental Change: Human and Policy Dimensions*, 8(4): 285–89.

Patnaik, U (1995) 'Economic and political consequences of the green revolution in India', in Kirkby, J, O'Keefe, P and Timberlake, L (eds) *The Earthscan Reader in Sustainable Development*, Earthscan, London, pp146–50.

Paton Walsh, N (2004) 'Putin throws lifeline to Kyoto as EU backs Russia joining WTO', *Guardian*, 22 May.

Pattanayak, S and Mercer, D E (1998) 'Valuing soil conservation benefits of agroforestry: contour hedgerows in the Eastern Visayas, Philippines', *Agricultural Economics*, 18(1): 31–46.

Paxton, A (1994) *The Food Miles Report: The Dangers of Long Distance Food Transport*, Sustainable Agriculture, Food and Environment Alliance, London.

Pearce, D W (ed) (1991) *Blueprint 2: Greening the World Economy*, Earthscan, London.

Pearce, D W (1995) 'Climate change', in Pearce, D W (ed) *Blueprint 4: Capturing Global Environmental Value*, Earthscan, London, pp12–27.

Pearce, D W and Atkinson, G D (1993) 'Capital theory and the measurement of sustainable development: an indicator of "Weak" Sustainability', *Ecological Economics*, 8: 103–8.

Pearce, D W and Barbier, E B (2000) *Blueprint for a Sustainable Economy*, Earthscan, London.

Pearce, D W, Markandya, A and Barbier, E B (1989) *Blueprint for a Green Economy*, Earthscan, London.

Pearce, D W and Warford, J J (1993) *World Without End: Economics, Environment and Sustainable Development*, Oxford University Press, New York, NY.

Pearce, F (1992a) 'Draft treaty fails to put limits on emissions', *New Scientist*, 16 May, p5.

Pearce, F (1992b) 'How green was our summit?' *New Scientist*, 27 July, pp12–13.

Pearce, F (1995) 'Mediterranean Action Plan', *New Scientist*, 4 February, pp26–31.

Pearce, F (1997a) 'Rich nations squabble in the greenhouse', *New Scientist*, 15 March, p10.

Pearce, F (1997b) 'Dishonest brokers', *New Scientist*, 6 December, p4.

Pearce, F (1998) 'The fog descends', *New Scientist*, 7 November, p14.

Pearse, A (1980) *Seeds of Plenty, Seeds of Want: Social and Economic Implications of the Green Revolution*, Clarendon Press, Oxford.

Peet, R (ed) (1977) *Radical Geography: Alternative Viewpoints on Contemporary Social Issues*, Maaroufa Press, Chicago, IL.

Peet, R and Watts, M (eds) (1996) *Liberation Ecologies: Nature, Development and Social Movements*, Routledge, London.

Pell, D and Wismer, B (1987) 'The role and limitations of community based economic development in Canada', *Alternatives*, 14: 31–34.

Percy, S (1998) 'Real progress or optimistic hype?' *Town and Country Planning*, 67(1): 19–20.

Perrings, C (1994) 'Biotic diversity, sustainable development and Natural Capital', in Jansson, A-M, Hammer, M, Folke, C and Costanza, R (eds) *Investing in Natural Capital: The Ecological Economics Approach to Sustainability*, Island Press, Washington, DC, pp92–112.

Persley, G J and Doyle, J J (1999) *Biotechnology for Developing-Country Agriculture: Problems and Opportunities – Overview*, International Food Policy Research Institute, Washington, DC.

Petchey, O L, McPhearson, P T, Casey, T M and Morin, P J (1999) 'Environmental warming alters food-web structure and ecosystem function', *Nature*, 402(6757): 69–72.

Petek, J and Glavić, P (1996) 'An integral approach to waste minimization in process industries', *Resources, Conservation and Recycling*, 17(3): 169–88.

Peterson, D J (1993) *Troubled Lands*, Westview Press, San Francisco, CA.

Pezzey, J C V (1997) 'Sustainability constraints versus optimality versus intertemporal concern, and axioms versus data', *Land Economics*, 73: 448–466.

Philander, S G (1998) *Is the Temperature Rising? The Uncertain Science of Global Warming*, Princeton University Press, Princeton, NJ.

Phillips, R A and Reichart, J (2000) 'The environment as stakeholder? A fairness-based approach', *Journal of Business Ethics*, 23(2): 185–97.

Pierson, C (1996) *The Modern State*, Routledge, London.

Pinstrup-Andersen, P, Pandya-Lorch, R and Rosegrant, M W (1999) *World Food Prospects: Critical Issues for the Early Twenty-First Century*, International Food Policy Research Institute, Washington, DC.

Piore, M J and Sabel, C F (1984) *The Second Industrial Divide: Possibilities for Prosperity*, Basic Books, New York, NY.

PlanetYork (2002) *York: A Model for Tackling Climate Change*, PlanetYork (www.planetyork.co.uk/background.cfm).

Poduska, R A, Forbes, R H and Bober, M A (1992) 'The challenge of sustainable development. Kodak's response', *Columbia Journal of World Business*, 27(3/4): 286–91.

Pollan, M (2001) 'Going organinc.', *Observer*, 12 August.

Porter, M E (1990) *The Comparative Advantage of Nations*, Free Press, New York, NY.

Porter, M E (1991) 'America's green strategy', *Scientific American*, 264(4): 96.

Potter, C (1998) *Against the Grain: Agri-Environmental Reform in the United States and the European Union*, CAB International, Wallingford.

Potter, R, Binns, T, Elliott, J A and Smith, D (eds) (1999) *Geographies of Development*, Longman, London.

Potts Carr, A J (1998) 'Choctaw Eco-Industrial Park: an ecological approach to industrial land-use planning and design', *Landscape and Urban Planning*, 42: 239–57.

Power, J F (1990) 'Legumes and crop rotations', in Francis, C A, Flora, C B and King, L D (eds) *Sustainable Agriculture in Temperate Zones*, Wiley, New York, NY, pp178–204.

Power, M (2003) *Rethinking Development Geographies*, Routledge, London.

Prakash, A and Hart, J A (eds) (2000) *Globalization and Governance*, Routledge, London.

Pretty, J (1995) *Regenerating Agriculture*, Earthscan, London.

Pretty, J (1998) *The Living Land. Agriculture, Food and Community Regeneration in Rural Europe*, Earthscan, London.

Proops, J L R, Atkinson, G D, von Schlotheim, B F and Simon, S (1999) 'International trade and its sustainability footprint: a practical criterion for its assessment', *Ecological Economics*, 28(1): 75–98.

Pugh, C (1997) 'Habitat II: Editor's introduction', *Urban Studies*, 34(10): 1541–46.

Pugh, C (ed) (2000) *Sustainable Cities in Developing Countries*, Earthscan, London.

Punter, J and Carmona, M (1997) 'Design policies in local plans: recommendations for good practice', *Town Planning Review*, 68(2): 165–93.

Purvis, M, Drake, F, Hunt, J and Millard, D (1998) *Global Environmental Change and European Business: Global Atmospheric Change, Reactions and Responsibilities*, School of Geography, University of Leeds.

Purvis, M, Drake, F, Hunt, J and Millard, D (2000) 'The manager, the business and the big wide world', in Fineman, S (ed) *The Business of Greening*, Routledge, London, pp13–34.

Purvis, M, Hunt, J and Drake, F (2001) 'Global atmospheric change and the UK refrigeration industry: redefining problems and contesting solutions', *Geoforum*, 32(2): 143–56.

Putzel, J (1992) *A Captive Land: The Politics of Agrarian Reform in the Philippines*, Catholic Institute for International Relations, London.

Rabinovitch, J and Leitman, J (1996) 'Urban planning in Curitiba', *Scientific American*, 274(3), 26–33.

Radice, H (1984) 'The national economy: A Keynesian myth?' *Capital and Class*, 22: 111–40.

Rahman, A and Roncerel, A (1994) 'A view from the ground up', in Mintzer, I and Leonard, J A (eds) *Negotiating Climate Change. The Inside Story of the Rio Convention*. Cambridge University Press, Cambridge, pp239–76.

Ramage, J (1996) 'Hydroelectricity', in Boyle, G (ed) *Renewable Energy: Power for a Sustainable Future*, Oxford University Press, Oxford, pp183–226.

Ramage, J and Scurlock, J (1996) 'Biomass', in Boyle, G (ed) *Renewable Energy: Power for a Sustainable Future*, Oxford University Press, Oxford, pp137–82.

Rao, P K (2000) *Sustainable Development: Economics and Policy*, Blackwell, Oxford.

Raskin, P D (1992) 'PoleStar: Introduction, current status, future directions', *Working Paper*, Stockholm Environmental Institute, Stockholm, Sweden.

Ravetz, J (2000) *City Region 2020: Integrated Planning for a Sustainable Environment*, Earthscan, London.

Raynolds, L (1997) 'Restructuring national agriculture, agro-food trade, and agrarian livelihoods in the Caribbean', in Goodman, D and Watts, M J (eds) *Globalising Food: Agrarian Questions and Global Restructuring*, Routledge, London, pp119–32.

Redclift, M (1987) *Sustainable Development: Exploring the Contradictions*, Methuen, London.

Redclift, M (1992a) 'The meaning of sustainable development', *Geoforum*, 23: 395–403.

Redclift, M (1992b) 'Sustainable development and global environmental change: implications of a changing agenda', *Global Environmental Change: Human and Policy Dimensions*, 2(1): 32–42.

Redclift, M (1998) 'Dances with wolves? Interdisciplinary research on the global environment', *Global Environmental Change: Human and Policy Dimensions*, 8(3): 177–82.

Rees, J (1990) *Natural Resources. Allocation, Economics and Policy*, 2nd edition, Methuen, London.

Rees, J (1993) *Water for Life: Strategies for Sustainable Water Resources Management*, Council for the Protection of Rural England, London.

Rees, W E (1992) 'Ecological footprints and appropriated carrying capacity: what urban economics leaves out', *Environment and Urbanisation*, 4(2): 121–30.

Rees, W E (1995) 'Achieving sustainability: reform or transformation?' *Journal of Planning Literature*, 9: 343–61.

Rees, W E and Roseland, M (1998) 'Sustainable communities: planning for the 21st century', in Hamm, B and Muttagi, P K (eds) *Sustainable Development and the Future of Cities*, Intermediate Technology Publications, London, pp 203–21.

Reganold, J P, Palmer, A S, Lockhart, J C and MacGregor, A N (1993) 'Soil quality and financial performance of biodynamic and conventional farms in New Zealand', *Science*, 260(5106): 344–49.

Register, R (1987) *Ecocity Berkeley: Building Cities for a Healthy Future*, North Atlantic Books, Berkeley, CA.

Reid, D (1995) *Sustainable Development: an Introductory Guide*, Earthscan, London.

Reijntjes, C, Haverkort, B and Waters-Bayer, A (1992) *Farming for the Future: An Introduction to Low-External-Input and Sustainable Agriculture*, Macmillan, London.

Renner, M (2001) *Working for the Environment: A Growing Source of Jobs*, World Watch Institute, Washington, DC.

Repetto, R (1995) *Jobs, Competitiveness and Environmental Regulation: What Are the Real Issues?*, World Resources Institute, Washington, DC.

Repetto, R, McGrath, W, Wells, M, Beer, C and Rossini, F (1989) *Wasting Assets: Natural Resources in the National Income Accounts*, World Resources Institute, Washington, DC.

Ribāfuronto Seibi Sentā (Riverfront Preparation Centre) (ed) (1996) *Tashizen-gata Kawa-zukuri no Torikumi to Pointo: Machi to Mizube ni Yutaka na Shizen o III (Processes and Points for Multi-Nature-Style River Planning: An Abundant Nature in Towns and Along Rivers III)*, Sankaidō, Tokyo, Japan.

Richardson, H W (1993) 'Efficiency and welfare in LDC mega-cities', in Kasarda, J D and Parnell, A M (eds) *Third World Cities: Problems, Policies and Prospects*, Sage, Newbury Park, CA, pp32–57.

Riley, J (1998) 'Retailers split over future', *Farmers' Weekly*, 129(23): 57.

Ritzer, G (1993) *The McDonaldization of Society: An Investigation into the Changing Character of Contemporary Social Life*, Pine Forge Press, London.

Roberts, B (1995) *The Making of Citizens*, Arnold, London.

Robertson, G P, Paul, E A and Harwood, R R (2000) 'Greenhouse gases in intensive agriculture: contributions of individual gases to the radiative forcing of the atmosphere', *Science*, 289: 1922–25.

Robertson, J (1991) *Native and Newcomer: Making and Remaking a Japanese City*, University of California Press, Berkeley, CA.

Robertson, M M (2000) 'No net loss: wetland restoration and the incomplete capitalization of nature', *Antipode*, 32(4): 463–93.

Robins, N and Trisoglio, A (1995) 'Restructuring industry for sustainable development', in Kirkby, J, O'Keefe, P and Timberlake, L (eds) *The Earthscan Reader in Sustainable Development*, Earthscan, London, pp161–73.

Robinson, M and Pretes, M (1988) 'Beyond boom-and-bust: a strategy for sustainable development in the North', *Polar Record*, 25: 115–20.

Rogers, D J and Randolph, S E (2000) 'The global spread of malaria in a future, warmer world', *Science*, 289(5485): 1763–66.

Rogers, R (1997) *Cities for a Small Planet*, Faber and Faber, London.

Romer, P (1990) 'Endogenous technological change', *Journal of Political Economy*, 98: S71–102.

Rompel, D (1996) 'Opportunities for business in the greening of central and eastern Europe', in Enmarch-Williams, H (ed) *Environmental Risks and Rewards for Business*, Wiley, Chichester, pp93–98.

Roome, N (1992) 'Developing environmental management strategies', *Business Strategy and the Environment*, 1(1): 11–24.

Roseland, M (1998) *Towards Sustainable Communities: Resources for Citizens and their Governments*, New Society, Gabriola Island, Canada.

Rosenzweig, C and Hillel, D (1998) *Climate Change and the Global Harvest: Potential Impacts of the Greenhouse Effect on Agriculture*, Oxford University Press, New York, NY.

Ross, D (1995) *Power from the Waves*, Oxford University Press, Oxford.

Royal College of Physicians and Royal College of Psychiatrists (RCP) (1998) *Organophosphate Sheep Dip: Clinical Aspects of Long-Term Low-Dose Exposure*, Royal College of Physicians and Royal College of Psychiatrists, London.

Royal Society and Royal Society of Engineering (RS/RSE) (1999) *Nuclear Energy: The Future Climate*, Royal Society, London.

Royal Society for the Protection of Birds (RSPB) (2004) *Dire Warning for Europe's Farmland Birds* (www.rspb.org.uk/countryside/farming/policy/CAP/warning.asp).

Ruddle, K (1987) 'The impact of wetland reclamation', in Wolman, M G and Fournier, F G A (eds) *Land Transformation in Agriculture*, Wiley, Chichester, pp171–201.

Ruddle, K and Zhong, G (1988) *Integrated Agriculture-Aquaculture in South China; the Dike-Pond System of the Zhujiang Delta*, Cambridge University Press, Cambridge.

Russell, B (2001) 'Environment: "Nimby" mentality is holding up plans for greener energy', *Independent*, 23 March.

Ruttan, V W (1991) 'Constraints on sustainable growth in agricultural production: Into the 21st century', *Outlook on Agriculture*, 20(4): 225–34.

Sabatier, P and Jenkins-Smith, H C (1993) *Policy Change and Learning: An Advocacy Coalition Framework*, Westview Press, Boulder, CO.

Sachs, W, Loske, R and Linz, M (1998) *Greening the North: A Post-Industrial Blueprint for Ecology and Equity*, Zed, London.

Sagers, M J (1994) 'Oil spill in Russian Arctic', *Polar Geography and Geology*, 18: 95–102.

Sailor, W C, Bodansky, D, Braun, C, Fetter, S and van der Zwaan, R (2000) 'A nuclear solution to climate change?' *Science*, 288(5469): 1177–78.

Sala, O E, Chapin, F S, Armesto, J J, Berlow, E, Bloomfield, J, Dirzo, R, Huber-Sanwald, E, Huenneke, L F, Jackson, R B, Kinzig, A, Leemaas, R, Lodge, D M, Mooney, H A, Oesterheld, M, Poff, N L, Sykes, M T, Walker, B H, Walker, M and Wall, D H (2000) 'Global biodiversity scenarios for the year 2100', *Science*, 287(5459): 1770–74.

Sale, K (1985) *Dwellers in the Land: The Bioregional Vision*, Sierra Club Books, San Francisco, CA.

Sale, K (1996) 'Principles of bioregionalism', in Mander, J and Goldsmith, E (eds) *The Case Against the Global Economy and For a Turn Toward the Local*, Sierra Club Books, San Francisco, CA, pp471–84.

Salman, S (2001) 'Switched on', *Guardian*, 24 October.

Sandalow, D B and Bowles, I A (2001) 'Fundamentals of treaty-making on climate change', *Science*, 292(5523): 1839–40.

Sanderson, W C (1994) 'Simulation models of demographic, economic and environmental interactions', in Lutz, W (ed) *Population, Development, Environment: Understanding their Interactions in Mauritius*, Springer-Verlag, Berlin, Germany, pp33–71.

Satterthwaite, D (1997) 'Sustainable cities or cities that will contribute towards sustainable development?' *Urban Studies*, 34(10): 1667–91.

Saunders, J (1997) 'Local challenges for the 21st century: citizen science', Presentation to British Association Annual Festival of Science, University of Leeds, Leeds, September 1997.

Saunders, J (2001) *Gathering Resources for a Journey of Hope: A Future for Local Futures in England into the 21st Century – Can the Modernization of Local Government Lay the Foundations for Greater Coherence and Vision about the Journey towards a Sustainable Future?* MA thesis, Leeds Metropolitan University, Leeds.

Saywell, T (1998) 'Food for thought', *Far Eastern Economic Review*, 7 May, p50.

Schaberg, M (1999) *Globalization and the Erosion of National Financial Systems: Is Declining Autonomy Inevitable?*, Edward Elgar, Northampton, MA.

Schiermeier, Q (2001a) 'Accord in Morocco breathes new life into Kyoto Protocol', *Nature*, 414(6861): 238.

Schiermeier, Q (2001b) 'Cycle studies see carbon sinks rise to prominence', *Nature*, 414(6862): 385.

Schmidheiny, S (1992) *Changing Course: A Global Business Perspective on Development and the Environment*, MIT Press, Cambridge, MA.

Schmidt-Bleek, F (1992) 'Eco-restructuring economies: operationalising the sustainability concept', *Fresenius Environmental Bulletin*, 1: 46–51.

Schnapp, N and Schiermeier, Q (2001) 'Critics claim "sight-saving" rice is over-rated', *Nature*, 410(6828): 503.

Scholes, H (1998) 'Can energy crops become a realistic CO_2 mitigation option in South West England?' *Biomass and Bioenergy*, 15(4–5): 333–44.

Schoon, N (1997) 'I'll get you on the bus, says Prescott', *Independent*, 6 June.

Schultz, T W (1961) 'Investment in Human Capital', *American Economic Review*, 51: 1–17.

Scoones, I (1996) *Hazards and Opportunities*, Zed Press, London.

Scoones, I (1998) 'Sustainable rural livelihoods: a framework for analysis', *IDS Working Paper 72*, Institute of Development Studies, University of Sussex, Brighton.

Scott, J (1988) 'Deconstructing equality-versus-difference: or the uses of poststructuralist theory for feminism', *Feminist Studies*, 14: 33–50.

Scrivener, D (1999) 'Arctic environmental cooperation in transition', *Polar Record*, 35: 51–58.

Sebenius, J K (1994) 'Towards a winning climate coalition', in Mintzer, I and Leonard, J A (eds) *Negotiating Climate Change. The Inside Story of the Rio Convention*, Cambridge University Press, Cambridge, pp277–320.

Seki, M (1994) *Daichi no Kawa: Yomigaere, Nihon no Furusato no Kawa (Rivers of the Earth: Revive, Rivers of Japan's Countryside)*, Sōshisha, Tokyo, Japan.

Selman, P (1996) *Local Sustainability*, Paul Chapman, London.

Selman, P (1998) 'A real local agenda for the 21st century?' *Town and Country Planning*, 67(1): 15–17.

Sen, A K (1981) *Poverty and Famines: An Essay on Entitlement and Deprivation*, Clarendon Press, Oxford.

Shaw, N and Hanson, A J (1996) 'Linking trade and environment to promote sustainable development', in Sander, H and Inotai, A (eds) *World Trade After the Uruguay Round. Prospects and Policy Options for the Twenty-First Century*, Routledge, London, pp134–54.

Sheail, J (2002) *An Environmental History of Twentieth-Century Britain*, Palgrave, Basingstoke.

Shell (2000) 'Shell International Renewables' (www.shell.com/about/directory/1,1372,1369,00.html).

Shiva, V (1999) *Biopiracy*, Earthscan, London.

Short, J R and Kim, Y-H (1999) *Globalization and the City*, Longman, Harlow.

Shove, E (2000) 'Questions of comfort: challenging research and practice in the built environment', Department of Sociology, University of Lancaster (www.comp.lanc.ac.uk/sociology/soc093es.html).

Shrivastava, P (1995) 'The role of corporations in achieving ecological sustainability', *Academy of Management Review*, 20(4): 936–60.

Shrybman, S (1999) 'The World Trade Organization: the new world constitution laid bare', *The Ecologist*, 29(4): 270–75.

Simmons, I G (1996) *Changing the Face of the Earth: Culture, Environment, History*, 2nd edition, Blackwell, Oxford.

Simms, A (1999a) *Selling Suicide: Farming, False Promises and Genetic Engineering in Developing Countries*, Christian Aid, London.

Simms, A (1999b) 'Redefine environmental debts in atmosphere of equality', *Financial Times*, 3 November.

Simon, D, van Spengen, W, Dixon, C and Närman, A (1995) *Structurally Adjusted Africa: Poverty, Debt and Basic Needs*, Pluto Press, London.

Simon, J L (1981) *The Ultimate Resource*, Martin Robertson, Oxford.

Simonis, U (1989) 'Ecological modernisation of industrial society: three strategic elements', *International Social Science Journal*, 121: 347–61.

Simpson, E S (1987) *The Developing World: An Introduction*, Longman, London.

Skinner, R and Rodell, M (eds) (1983) *People, Poverty and Shelter*, Routledge, London.

Smallman-Raynor, M and Phillips, D (1999) 'Socio-spatial variations in health', in Pacione, M (ed) *Applied Geography: Principles and Practice. An Introduction to Useful Research in Physical, Environmental and Human Geography*, Routledge, London, pp425–37.

Smith, A (1776, reprinted 1961) *An Inquiry into the Nature and Causes of the Wealth of Nations*, Methuen, London.

Smith, D M (1977) *Human Geography: A Welfare Approach*, Arnold, London.

Smith, D M (1994) *Geography and Social Justice*, Blackwell, Oxford.

Smith, M, Whitelegg, J and Williams, N (1997) 'Life cycle analysis of housing', *Housing Studies*, 12(2): 215–29.

Smith, N (1990) *Uneven Development. Nature, Capital and the Production of Space*, 2nd edition, Blackwell, Oxford.

Smith, R T (2001) *Organic Farming, Sustaining Earth and People*, 2nd edition, Isura Sanwardana Kendraya, Colombo, Sri Lanka.

Smith, S (1997) 'New approaches to international theory', in Baylis, J and Smith, S (eds) *The Globalization of World Politics*, Oxford University Press, Oxford, pp165–92.

Sneddon, C S (2000) ' "Sustainability" in ecological economics, ecology and livelihoods: a review', *Progress in Human Geography*, 24(4): 521–49.

Soil Association (2002) *Seeds of Doubt*, Soil Association, Bristol.

Soil Association (2003) *Food and Farming Report 2003*, Soil Association, Bristol.

Solman, P (2000) 'Organic crop prices race ahead', *Financial Times*, 23 March.

Solow, R (1986) 'On the inter-generational allocation of natural resources', *Scandinavian Journal of Economics*, 88: 141–49.

Soussan, J (1990) *Alternative Energy Sources for Urban Areas in Somalia*, Report prepared for the Overseas Development Administration of the British Government. School of Geography, University of Leeds.

Soussan, J (1992) *Housing Conditions in the Plantations Sector*, Report prepared for the Governments of Sri Lanka, The Netherlands and Norway, School of Geography, University of Leeds.

Soussan, J and Datta, A (1998) *Final Evaluation Study of the Systems Rehabilitation Project*, University Press, Dhaka, Bangladesh.

Soussan, J, Emmel, N and Horworth, C (1999) 'Freshwater ecosystems management and social security', Paper prepared for IUCN Conference on Water and Nature, Harare, Zimbabwe.

Soussan, J, Shrestha, B K and Upretty, L P (1995) *The Social Dynamics of Deforestation: A Case Study From Nepal*, Parthenon Press, London.

Soussan, J, Turton, C, Dev, O P, Yadav, N P and Baumann, P (1998) *Community Forestry in Nepal: Comparing Policies and Practice*, Report to UK Government Department for International Development, School of Geography, University of Leeds.

Spaargaren, G and Mol, A (1991) *Sociology, Environment and Modernity: Ecological Modernisation as a Theory of Social Change*, LUW, Wageningen, The Netherlands.

Spangenberg, J H (1994) *Towards Sustainable Europe: The Study*, Wuppertal Institute for Climate, Environment and Energy/Friends of the Earth, Europe, Wuppertal, Germany.

Spengler, J J (1967) 'Africa and the theory of optimum city size', in Miner, H (ed) *The City in Modern Africa*, Pall Mall Press, London, pp55–89.

Stabler, J C (1987) 'Fiscal viability and the constitutional development of Canada's northern territories', *Polar Record*, 23: 551–68.

Stamp, L D (1963) *Applied Geography*, Penguin, Harmondsworth.

Stanhill, G (1990) 'The comparative productivity of organic agriculture', *Agriculture, Ecosystems and Environment*, 30: 1–26.

Stanners, D and Bordeau, P (eds) (1995) *Europe's Environment: The Dobříš Assessment*, European Environment Agency, Copenhagen, Denmark.

Starik, M (1995) 'Should trees have managerial standing? Toward stakeholder status for non-human nature', *Journal of Business Ethics*, 14: 207–17.

Steenblick, R P and Coroyannakis, P (1995) 'Reform of coal policies in Western and Central Europe: Implications for the environment', *Energy Policy*, 23(6): 537–54.

Stephens, C (2000) 'Inequalities in urban environments, health and power: reflections on theory and practice', in Pugh, C (ed) *Sustainable Cities in Developing Countries*, Earthscan, London, pp91–114.

Stern, P C, Dietz, T, Ruttan, V W, Socolow, R H and Sweeney, J L (eds) (1997) *Environmentally Significant Consumption. Research Directions*, National Academy Press, Washington, DC.

Stewart, J M (1995) 'The Khanty: oil, gas and the environment', *Sibirica*, 1: 25–34.

Still, B and Simmonds, B (1998) *DELTA/START: Adding Land Use Analysis to Integrated Transport Models*, Paper to the Eighth World Conference on Transport Research, Antwerp, Belgium, 12–17 July.

Stoddart, D (1987) 'To claim the high ground: geography for the end of the century', *Transactions of the Institute of British Geographers*, 12(3): 327–36.

Storper, M (1997) *The Regional World: Territorial Development in a Global Economy*, Guildford Press, New York, NY.

Strange, S (1998) *The Retreat of the State: The Diffusion of Power in the World Economy*, Cambridge University Press, Cambridge.

Straussfogel, D (1997) 'Redefining development as humane and sustainable', *Annals of the Association of American Geographers*, 87(2): 280–305.

Stuart, M D and Costa, P M (1998) *Climate Change Mitigation by Forestry: A Review of International Initiatives*, International Institute for Environment and Development, London.

Susskind, L E (1992) 'New corporate roles in global environmental treaty-making', *Columbia Journal of World Business*, 27(3/4): 62–73.

Sustainable Development Research Network (2002) *A New Agenda for UK Sustainable Development Research*, Policy Studies Institute, London.

Sustainable Seattle (1993) *1993 Indicators of a Sustainable Community*, Sustainable Seattle Network and Civic Forum, Seattle, WA.

Sutcliffe, A (1993) *Paris: An Architectural History*, Yale University Press, New Haven, CT.

Swyngedouw, E (1996) 'Producing futures: Global finance as a geographical project', in Daniels, P W and Lever, W F (eds) *The Global Economy in Transition*, Longman, Harlow, pp135–63.

Takahashi, Y (1995) 'Ryūiki kara mita kawa to shakai' (Rivers and society seen from river basins), in Ōuchi, T, Takahashi, Y and Shinmura, J (eds) *Ryūiki no Jidai Mori to Kawa no Fukken o Mezashite* (*The Era of River Basins: Aiming for a Rehabilitation of Forests and Rivers*), Gyōsei, Tokyo, Japan.

Takeuchi, K (1996) 'Official and popular approaches to water resources in Japan: The failures of an applied geography', in Berdoulay, V and van Ginkel, J A (eds) *Geography and Professional Practice*, Universiteit Utrecht, Utrecht, The Netherlands, pp219–26.

Taylor, A and Parker, G (1998) 'Prescott's urban renaissance plan attracts critics', *Financial Times*, 24 February.

Taylor, D (1996) Wind energy, in Boyle, G (ed) *Renewable Energy. Power for a Sustainable Future*, Oxford University Press, Oxford, pp267–314.

Taylor, R (1997a) 'ILO chief in appeal for "social labelling" ', *Financial Times*, 23 April.

Taylor, R (1997b) 'ILO chief comes under fire', *Financial Times*, 12 June.

Tellam, I (ed) (2000) *Fuel for Change. World Bank Energy Policy: Rhetoric and Reality*, Zed, London.

The Campaign (2003) 'The Campaign to Label Genetically Engineered Foods' (www.thecampaign.org/).

Thiesenhusen, W C (1995) *Broken Promises. Agrarian Reform and the Latin American Campesino*, Westview Press, Boulder, CO.

Thomas, D C and Schaefer, J (1991) 'Wildlife co-management defined: the Beverly and Kaminuriak Caribou Management Board', *Rangifer* 7: 73–89.

Thomas, D W, Blondel, J, Perret, P, Lambrechts, M M, Speakman, J R (2001) 'Energetic and fitness costs of mismatching resource supply and demand in seasonally breeding birds', *Science*, 291(5513): 2598–2600.

Thomas, W (ed) (1956) *Man's Role in Changing the Face of the Earth*, University of Chicago Press, Chicago, IL.

Thompson, M and Rayner, S (1998) 'Cultural discourses', in Rayner, S and Malone, E L (eds) *Human Choice and Climate Change. Volume 1: The Societal Framework*, Battelle Press, Columbus, OH, pp265–343.

Thrupp, L A, Bergeron, G and Waters, W F (1995) *Bittersweet Harvests for Global Supermarkets: Challenges in Latin America's Agricultural Export Boom*, World Resources Institute, Washington, DC.

Tilman, D, Fargione, J, Wolff, B, D'Antonio, C, Dobson, A, Howarth, R, Schindler, D, Schlesinger, W H, Simberloff, D and Swackhamer, D (2001) 'Forecasting agriculturally-driven global environmental change', *Science*, 292(5515): 281–84.

The Times (1992) 'Growth and greenery', *The Times*, 15 June.

Tjallingi, S P (1995) *Ecopolis: Strategies for Ecologically Sound Urban Development*, Backhuys, Leiden, The Netherlands.

Tóth, F L (ed) (1999) *Fair Weather? Equity Concerns in Climate Change*, Earthscan, London.

Townsend, P and Gordon, D (1999) 'Poverty, social exclusion and social polarisation: applying the 1995 UN Programme of Action on Absolute and Overall Poverty to all countries', Paper to Seminar on Poverty and Social Exclusion, 25–26 November 1999, Centro de Estudos Para a Intervencao Social, Lisbon, Portugal.

Travers, T (1997) 'A convergence of rich and poor', *Financial Times*, 22 December.

Trenbath, B R (1976) 'Plant interactions in mixed crop communities', in Papendick, R I, Sanchez, P A and Triplett, G B (eds) *Multiple Cropping*, American Society of Agronomy, Madison, WI, pp129–70.

Tuan, Y-F (1990) *Topophilia: A Study of Environmental Perception, Attitudes and Values*, Columbia University Press, New York, NY.

Tucker, E (1997) 'EU to reconsider regional aid', *Financial Times*, 19 December.

Tuluca, A (1997) *Energy Efficient Design and Construction for Commercial Buildings*, McGraw Hill, New York, NY.

Turner II, B L, Clark, W C, Kates, R W, Richards, J F, Mathews, J T and Meyer W B (eds) (1990) *The Earth as Transformed by Human Action. Global and Regional Changes in the Biosphere over the Past 300 Years*, Cambridge University Press, Cambridge.

Turner, J (1976) *Housing by People*, Marion Boyars, London.

Turner, R K (ed) (1993) *Sustainable Environmental Economics and Management: Principles and Practice*, Belhaven, London.

Turner, R K, Salmons, R, Powell, J and Craighill, A (1998) 'Green taxes, waste management and political economy', *Journal of Environmental Management*, 53(2): 121–36.

Tuxworth, B (1996) 'From environment to sustainability: survey and analysis of Local Agenda 21 process development in UK local authorities', *Local Environments*, 1(3): 277–97.

Uchida, K (1994) *Kindai Nihon no Suigai Chiiki Shakai Shi (A Social History of the Flood-Prone Areas of Modern Japan)*, Kokon Shoin, Tokyo, Japan.

Ui, J (1992) *Industrial Pollution in Japan*, United Nations University, Tokyo, Japan.

United Nations (UN) (1991) *World Urbanisation Prospects 1990: Estimates and Projections of Urban and Rural Populations and of Urban Agglomerations*, United Nations, New York, NY.

United Nations (UN) (1992) *Framework Convention on Climate Change*, United Nations, New York, NY.

United Nations (UN) (1993) *Agenda 21*, United Nations, New York, NY.

United Nations (UN) (1995) *World Urbanization Prospects: The 1994 Revision*, United Nations, New York, NY.

United Nations (UN) (2002) *Report of the World Summit on Sustainable Development, Johannesburg, South Africa, 26 August–4 September 2002*, A/CONF.199/20, United Nations, New York, NY.

United Nations (UN) (2003) *United Nations Framework Convention on Climate Change: Status of Ratification*, United Nations (unfccc.int/resource/kpstats.pdf).

United Nations Centre for Human Settlements (UNCHS) (1996) *An Urbanizing World: Global Report on Human Settlements 1996*, Oxford University Press, Oxford.

United Nations Centre for Human Settlements (UNCHS) (2001) *Cities in a Globalizing World: Global Report on Human Settlements*, Earthscan, London.

United Nations Conference on Environment and Development (UNCED) (1992a) *Earth Summit '92 (Agenda 21)*, Regency Press Corporation, London.

United Nations Conference on Environment and Development (UNCED) (1992b) *Agenda 21: An Action Plan for the Next Century*, United Nations Association, Rio de Janeiro, Brazil.

United Nations Development Programme (UNDP) (1991) *Human Development Report*, Oxford University Press, New York, NY.

United Nations Development Programme (UNDP) (1998) *Human Development Report*, Oxford University Press, New York, NY.

United Nations Development Programme (UNDP) (1999) *Human Development Report*, Oxford University Press, New York, NY.

United Nations Environmental Assessment Programme (UNEAP) (1995) *Earth Views*, 2(1) United Nations Environment Programme, Nairobi, Kenya.

University of Manchester (2002) *Sustainable City-Regions: Future Studies*, Centre for Urban and Regional Ecology (CURE), University of Manchester (www.art.man.ac.uk/planning/cure).

Unwin, R (ed) (1990) *Crop Protection in Organic and Low Input Agriculture. Options for Reducing Agrochemical Usage*, British Crop Protection Council, Farnham.

Usher, P W (1987) 'Indigenous management systems and the conservation of wildlife in the Canadian North', *Alternatives*, 14: 3–9.

Vale, B and Vale, R (1993) 'Building the sustainable environment', in Blowers, A (ed) *Planning for a Sustainable Environment*, Earthscan, London, pp93–110.

Vallance, E (1993) 'What is business for? Ethics and the aim of business', *Business Strategy Review*, 4(1): 45–52.

van den Berg, L and van Winden, W (2002) *Information and Communications Technology as Potential Catalyst for Sustainable Development: Experiences from Eindhoven, Helsinki, Manchester, Marseilles and The Hague*, Ashgate, Aldershot.

Van den Bergh, J C J M (1996) *Ecological Economics and Sustainable Development*, Edward Elgar, Cheltenham.

van Emden, H F and Peakall, D B (1996) *Beyond Silent Spring: Integrated Pest Management and Chemical Safety*, Chapman and Hall, London.

Van Vliet, D (1982) 'SATURN: A modern assignment model', *Traffic Engineering and Control*, 23(12): 578–81.

Vargas, C M (2000) 'Community development and micro-enterprises: fostering sustainable development', *Sustainable Development*, 8(1): 11–26.

Vatikiotis, M (1992) 'Priming for Rio', *Far Eastern Economic Review*, 14 May, p 22.

Velásquez, L S (1999) 'The local environment action plan for Olivares commune in Manizales, Colombia', *Environment and Urbanization*, 11(2): 41–50.

Venendaal, R, Jorgensen, U and Foster, C A (1997) 'European energy crops: a synthesis', *Biomass and Bioenergy*, 13(3): 147–85.

Vidal, J (2001a) 'GM trials face delay as crops destroyed', *Guardian*, 9 June.

Vidal, J (2001b) 'Global GM market starts to wilt', *Guardian*, 28 August.

Vidal, J (2004) 'Firm drops plan to grow GM maize', *Guardian*, 1 April.

Vincent, J R and Panayotou, T (1997) 'Consumption: challenge to sustainable development . . . or distraction?' *Science*, 276(5309): 53–57.

Vitebski, P (1990) 'Gas, environmentalism and native anxieties in the Soviet Arctic: the case of Yamal peninsula', *Polar Record*, 26: 19–26.

Vitousek, P M, Ehrlich, P R, Ehrlich, A H and Matson, P A (1986) 'Human appropriation of the products of photosynthesis', *Bioscience*, 36: 369–73.

von Weizsäcker, E, Lovins, A B and Lovins, L H (1997) *Factor Four: Doubling Wealth – Halving Resource Use*, Earthscan, London.

Vörösmarty, C J, Green, P, Salisbury, J and Lammers, R B (2001) 'Global water resources: vulnerability from climate change and population growth', *Science*, 289(5477): 284–88.

Wackernagel, M and Rees, W E (1996) *Our Ecological Footprint: Reducing Human Impact on the Earth*, New Society, Gabriola Island, Canada.

Wade, R (1998) 'The Asian debt and development crisis of 1997–?: Causes and consequences', *World Development*, 26(8): 1535–53.

Wagland, K (1997) 'Local challenges for the 21st century: citizen science', Presentation to British Association Annual Festival of Science, University of Leeds, Leeds, September 1997.

Waley, P (2000a) 'What's a river without fish? Symbol, space and ecosystem in the waterways of Japan', in Philo, C and Wilbert, C (eds) *Animal Places, Beastly Spaces: New Geographies of Human-Animal Relations*, Routledge, London, pp159–81.

Waley, P (2000b) 'Following the flow of Japan's river culture', *Japan Forum*, 12(2): 199–217.

Walker, J and Reuter, D J (1996) *Indicators of Catchment Health: A Technical Perspective*, CSIRO, Canberra, Australia.

Walker, R B J (1993) *Inside/Outside: International Relations as Political Theory*, Cambridge University Press, Cambridge.

Wallerstein, I (1974) *The Modern World System*, Academic Press, New York, NY.

Walley, N and Whitehead, B (1994) 'It's not easy being green', *Harvard Business Review*, 72(3): 46–52.

Wallis, W (1999) 'Nigeria set to tackle causes of oil region crisis', *Financial Times*, 24 November.

Wallner, H P, Narodoslawsky, M and Moser, F (1996) 'Islands of sustainability: a bottom-up approach to sustainable development', *Environment and Planning A*, 28(10): 1763–78.

Wall Street Journal (1995) 'How Greenpeace sank Shell's plan to dump big oil rig', *Wall Street Journal*, 7–8 July.

Wambugu, F (1999) 'Why Africa needs agricultural biotech', *Nature*, 400(6739): 15–16.

Warf, B (1999) 'The hypermobility of capital and the collapse of the Keynesian state', in Martin, R (ed) *Money and the Space Economy*, Wiley, Chichester, pp227–40.

Watkins, K (2003) 'Cancun was where the WTO found glasnost – and a chance for renewal', *Guardian*, 22 September.

Weeden, R B (1985) 'Northern people, northern resources, and the dynamics of carrying capacity', *Arctic*, 38: 116–20.

Wegener, M (1994) 'Operational urban models: state of the art', *Journal of the American Planning Association*, 60(1): 17–29.

Weiss, M D (1996) 'Precision farming and spatial economic analysis: research challenges and opportunities', *American Journal of Agricultural Economics*, 78(5): 1275–80.

Welch, H E, Bergmann, M A, Siferd, T D, Martin, K A, Curtis, M F, Crawford, R E, Conover, R J and Hop, H (1992) 'Energy flow through the marine ecosystem of the Lancaster Sound Region, Arctic Canada', *Arctic*, 45: 343–57.

Welford, R (1995) *Environmental Strategy and Sustainable Development: The Corporate Challenge for the Twenty-First Century*, Routledge, London.

Wenzel, G (1991) *Animal Rights-Human Rights: Ecology, Economy and Ideology in the Canadian Arctic*, University of Toronto Press, Toronto, Canada.

Wessex Water (2002) *Striking the Balance 2002*, Wessex Water, Bath.

Weybourne Atmospheric Observatory (1994) *Annual Report*, Weybourne Atmospheric Observatory, University of East Anglia, Norwich.

Wheale, P and McNally, R (eds) (1990) *The Bio-Revolution: Cornucopia or Pandora's Box?* Pluto, London.

Wheeler, D and Sillanpää, M (1997) *The Stakeholder Corporation: A Blueprint for Maximising Stakeholder Value*, Pitman, London.

White, A (1998) 'Children, pesticides and cancer', *The Ecologist*, 28(2): 100–05.

Whitelaw, B (1999) 'Towards designer milk', *Nature Biotechnology*, 17(2): 135–36.

Whiteside, M (1999) *Living Farms: Encouraging Sustainable Smallholders in Southern Africa*, Earthscan, London.

Whitworth, D (1999) 'US to check "food chain" drugs', *The Times*, 9 March.

Whyte, I D (1995) *Climatic Change and Human Society*, Arnold, London.

Wilbanks, T J (1994) ' "Sustainable development" in geographic perspective', *Annals of the Association of American Geographers*, 84(4): 541–56.

Williams, A M (1987) *The Western European Economy: A Geography of Post-War Development*, Hutchinson, London.

Williams, C C (1996) 'Local exchange and trading systems: a new source of work and credit for the poor and unemployed', *Environment and Planning A*, 28(8): 1395–1415.

Williams, F (1993) 'Green group calls for limits on world trade', *Financial Times*, 1 June.

Williams, F (1994) 'GATT shuts door on environmentalists', *Financial Times*, 21 July.

Williams, F (1995) 'Labour rights plea to WTO', *Financial Times*, 12 June.

Williams, F (1999a) 'Cuts urged in fishing and farm aid', *Financial Times*, 16 March.

Williams, F (1999b) 'WTO urged to make environment checks', *Financial Times*, 17 March.

Williams, K (1999) 'The wrong starting point', *Town and Country Planning*, 68(8/9): 263.

Williams, M (1990a) 'Forests', in Turner II, B L, Clark, W C, Kates, R W, Richards, J F, Mathews, J T and Meyer W B (eds) *The Earth as Transformed by Human Action. Global and Regional Changes in the Biosphere over the Past 300 Years*, Cambridge University Press, Cambridge, pp179–202.

Williams, M (1990b) *Wetlands: A Threatened Landscape*, Blackwell, Oxford.

Williams, P J (1989) *Pipelines and Permafrost: Science in a Cold Climate*, 2nd edition, Oxford University Press, Oxford.

Williamson, P (1998) 'Estimating and Projecting Private Household Water Demand for Small Areas', Paper at Workshop on Microsimulation in the New Millennium: Challenges and Innovations, Cambridge, August 1998.

Wilson, A G (1974) *Urban and Regional Models in Geography and Planning*, Wiley, Chichester.

Wilson, A G (1984) 'Making urban models more realistic: some strategies for future research', *Environment and Planning A*, 16: 1419–32.

Wing, S, Grant, G, Green, M and Stewart, C (1996) 'Community based collaboration for environmental justice: south-east Halifax environmental reawakening', *Environment and Urbanization*, 8(2): 129–40.

Winter, J (2000) 'Up for grabs', *BBC Focus on Africa*, 11(3): 18–19.

Wintour, P (2001a) 'Hill farmers "need to be land stewards"', *Guardian*, 20 April.

Wintour, P (2001b) 'Renewable energy targets to double', *Guardian*, 4 December.

Wohlgemuth, N and Missfeldt, F (2000) 'The Kyoto mechanisms and the prospects for renewable energy technologies', *Solar Energy*, 69(4): 305–14.

Wolf, S A and Buttel, F H (1996) 'The political economy of precision farming', *American Journal of Agricultural Economics*, 78(5): 1269–74.

Wolman, A (1965) 'The metabolism of cities', *Scientific American*, 213: 179–88.

Wood, C M and McDonald, D G (eds) (1997) *Global Warming: Implications for Freshwater and Marine Fish*, Cambridge University Press, New York, NY.

Wood, D (1993) *The Power of Maps*, Routledge, London.

Wood, W B (1999) 'Geo-analysis for the next century: new data and tools for sustainable development', in Demko, G J and Wood, W B (eds) *Reordering the World: Geographical Perspectives on the Twenty-First Century*, Westview, Boulder, CO, pp192–205.

Woodall, B (1996) *Japan Under Construction: Corruption, Politics and Public Works*, University of California Press, Berkeley, CA.

Woodward, L (1998) 'Organic farming is all very well, but can it feed the world?' *New Farmer and Grower*, 58: 19–21.

World Bank (1991) *Urban Policy and Economic Development: An Agenda for the 1990s*, World Bank, Washington, DC.

World Bank (1992) *World Development Report 1992: Development and the Environment*, Oxford University Press, New York, NY.

World Bank (1996) *Rural Energy and Development: Improving Energy Supplies for Two Billion People*, World Bank, Washington, DC.

World Bank (1999) *Papua New Guinea Mining Sector Institutional Strengthening Technical Assistance Project (P060330)*, Project Information Document, 26 October 1999, World Bank, Washington, DC.

World Bank (2000) *Energy and Development Report 2000. Energy Services for the World's Poor*, World Bank, Washington, DC.

World Bank (2002) *African Development Indicators*, World Bank, Washington, DC.

World Business Council for Sustainable Development (WBCSD) (2003) 'Case studies' (www.wbcsd.ch/templates/TemplateWBCSD1/layout.asp).

World Commission on Dams (WCD) (2000) *Dams and Development: A New Framework for Decision-Making*, Earthscan, London.

World Commission on Environment and Development (WCED) (1987) *Our Common Future*, Oxford University Press, Oxford.

World Resources Institute (1996) *World Resources: A Guide to the Global Environment – The Urban Environment*, Oxford University Press, New York, NY.

Worsley, P (1988) 'Permafrost and land-use problems – two case studies from the Northwest Territories of Canada', in Atkinson, K and McDonald, A T (eds) *Arctic Canada*, Centre for Canadian Studies, University of Leeds, Leeds, pp23–41.

Wrigley, E A (1988) *Continuity, Chance and Change: The Character of the Industrial Revolution in England*, Cambridge University Press, Cambridge.

Wuethrich, B (2000) 'How climate change alters rhythms of the wild', *Science*, 287(5454): 793–95.

Wyn Williams, S (1997) 'The "Brown Agenda": urban environmental problems and policies in the developing world', *Geography*, 82(1): 17–26.

Yamamoto, T (ed) (1999) *Deciding the Public Good: Governance and Civil Society in Japan*, Japan Centre for International Exchange, Tokyo, Japan and New York, NY.

Yapa, L S (1996) 'What causes poverty? A postmodern view', *Annals of the Association of American Geographers*, 86(4): 707–28.

Yeung, Y (1989) 'Bursting at the seams: strategies for controlling metropolitan growth in Asia', in Costa, F J, Dutt, A K, Ma, L J C and Noble, A G (eds) *Urbanization in Asia*, University of Hawaii Press, Honolulu, HI, pp311–32.

Yoshida, S (1999) 'Rethinking the public interest in Japan: civil society in the making', in Yamamoto, T (ed) *Deciding the Public Good: Governance and Civil Society in Japan*, Japan Centre for International Exchange, Tokyo, Japan and New York, NY, pp13–50.

Young, M D (1990) 'Natural resource accounting', in Common, M and Dovers, S (eds) *Moving Towards Global Sustainability: Policies and Implications for Australia*, Australian National University Press, Canberra, Australia, pp13–28.

Young, O (1996) *The Arctic Council: Marking a New Era in International Relations*, University Press of New England, Hanover, NH.

Young, R (1999) 'Health risk as farms overuse antibiotics', *The Times*, 19 August.

Index